**5.3 Complex Perceptual and Attentional Processes**
Attention

**Attention plays an important role in children's perception of social situations, which is explained in Module 12.4.**

**6.4 Beyond Piaget's Theory**
Vygotsky's Theory of Cognitive Development

**Parents often scaffold their preschool children's peer interactions, which is discussed in Module 15.1.**

**7.2 Memory**
Knowledge and Memory

**Infantile amnesia may be linked to a child's emerging sense of self, which is described in Module 11.1.**

**8.1 What Is Intelligence?**
Sternberg's Triarchic Theory

**The different contexts that influence children's development are described in Chapter 15.**

# Children

## and Their

# Development

Robert V. Kail
Purdue University

# Children
## and Their
# Development

second edition

Prentice
Hall

Upper Saddle River, NJ 07458

Library of Congress Cataloging in Publication Data

Kail, Robert V.
    Children and their development / Robert V. Kail.—2nd ed.
        p. cm
    Includes bibliographical references and index.
    ISBN 0-13-086765-9
      1. Child development.    2. Child psychology.    3. Memory in children.    4. Cognition in
    children.    I. Title
    HQ772.K216  2001
    305.231—dc21                                                    00-029348


*VP/Editorial Director:* Laura Pearson
*Senior Acquisitions Editor:* Jennifer Gilliland
*AVP/Director of Production and Manufacturing:* Barbara Kittle
*Managing Editor:* Mary Rottino
*Director of Development:* Susanna Lesan
*Development Editor:* Harriett Prentiss
*Editorial/Production Supervision:* Julie Sullivan
*Manufacturing Manager:* Nick Sklitsis
*Prepress and Manufacturing Buyer:* Tricia Kenny
*Creative Design Director:* Leslie Osher

*Assistant Creative Director:* Carole Anson
*Interior and Cover Design:* Anne Demarinis
*Electronic Illustrations:* Joseph Rattan Design;
  Dartmouth Publishing; Mirella Signoretto
*Production Manager, Formatting and Art:* Guy Ruggiero
*Director, Image Resource Center:* Melinda Reo
*Photo Research Supervisor:* Beth Boyd
*Image Permission Supervisor:* Kay Dellosa
*Photo Researcher:* Kathy Ringrose
*Cover Photos:* nonstøck; DigitalVision

Acknowledgments for copyrighted material may
be found beginning on p. 487, which constitutes
an extension of this copyright page.

This book was set in 10.5/13 Minion and Gill Sans Bold by TSI Graphics
and was printed and bound by Courier Company–Kendallville.
The cover was printed by Phoenix.

 © 2001, 1998 by Prentice-Hall, Inc.
A Division of Pearson Education
Upper Saddle River, NJ 07458

Printed in the United States of America
10  9  8  7  6  5  4  3

ISBN 0-13-086765-9

Prentice-Hall International (UK) Limited, *London*
Prentice-Hall of Australia Pty. Limited, *Sydney*
Prentice-Hall Canada Inc., *Toronto*
Prentice-Hall Hispanoamericana, S.A., *Mexico*
Prentice-Hall of India Private Limited, *New Delhi*
Prentice-Hall of Japan, Inc., *Tokyo*
Pearson Education Asia Pte. Ltd., *Singapore*
Editora Prentice-Hall do Brasil, Ltda., *Rio de Janeiro*

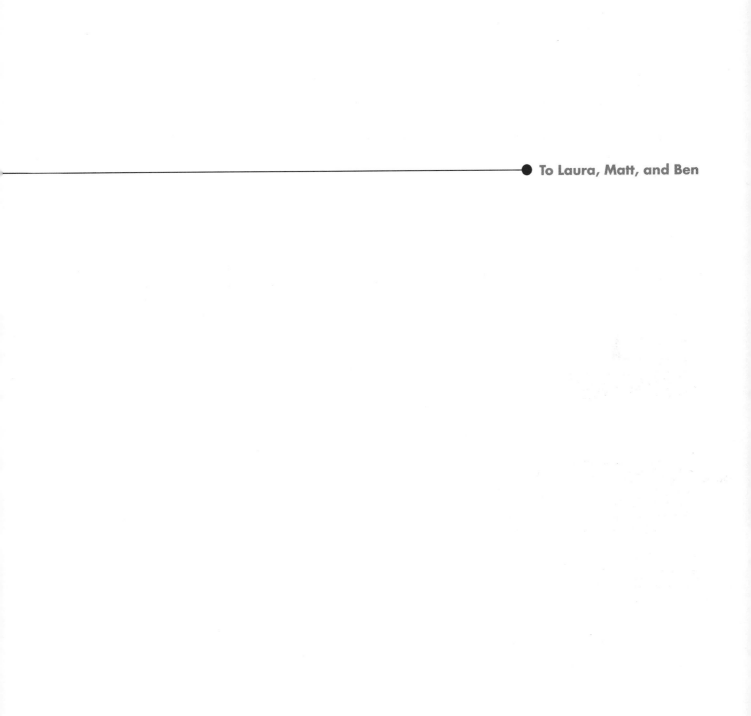

To Laura, Matt, and Ben

BRIEF CONTENTS

# FOCUS ON RESEARCH

# MAKING CHILDREN'S LIVES BETTER

# CULTURAL INFLUENCES

# REAL CHILDREN

When I first taught child development in 1975, I used a brand new textbook written by Mavis Hetherington and Ross Parke. Their book was among the first of the "modern" topically organized child development texts and provided students with an excellent overview of research in child development. In the twenty-five years since, researchers have made incredible progress in understanding children's development (and I'm proud to have been among those contributing). Unfortunately, authors have been overly enthusiastic about the emerging knowledge and textbooks have grown ever larger as more and more complex findings are added. As texts grew, my students complained to me that, with so much information in the book, they had difficulty separating the wheat from the chaff (an appropriate metaphor since I was teaching in the Midwestern United States).

Greater length and complexity was only part of the problem. Most textbook authors avoided effective pedagogy like the plague. They (along with many instructors) seemed to believe that students should be able to learn on their own, without relying on learning aids in the text. As a consequence, although child development texts still presented a valuable overview of the field, they were often ineffective tools for student learning.

In 1993, it seemed to me that a new book was needed—one that would meet instructors' needs for a solid, research-oriented overview of the field but would also emphasize effective pedagogy designed to enhance students' learning. *Children and Their Development*, first published in 1998, is my effort to meet these goals. This book is traditional in its focus on research. The organization, too, is familiar: I begin with theories and methods, move to biological bases of child development, then describe cognitive development and, later, social-emotional development. Where this book begins to differ from the competition is length: it has about 100 fewer pages than most competing texts. To make the truly important child development work stand out for students, I have deliberately omitted some topics and described others relatively briefly.

But the focus on a student-friendly book is really evident in the way I've structured the chapters to help students learn about child development. I describe my approach in detail in Module 1.1, so I'll simply sketch it here. Each chapter consists of three or four modules that provide a clear and well-defined organization to the chapter. Each module begins with a set of learning objectives and a vignette that introduces the topic to be covered. Within each module, all figures, tables, and photos are fully integrated, eliminating the need for students to search for a graphic. Similarly, boxlike feature material that is set off in other textbooks is fully integrated with the main text and identified by a distinctive icon. Each module ends with several questions designed to help students check their understanding of the major ideas in the module.

The end of each chapter includes several additional study aids. "In Perspective" recaps each module, then links the ideas in the chapter to a major developmental theme. "See for Yourself" suggests activities that allow students to observe topics in child development firsthand. "Resources" includes books and Web sites where students can learn more about child development. "Key Terms" is a list of all of the important terms that appeared in the chapter. The "Summary" is organized by module and the primary headings within each module; it reviews the entire chapter.

Each module includes at least one feature where selected issues are highlighted. The four different kinds of features are "Focus on Research," "Making Children's Lives Better," "Cultural Influences," and "Real Children." The features are described in Module 1.1, but "Focus on Research" warrants extra attention here. Most textbooks describe research methods early on, then ignore them for the rest of the book. *Children and Their Development* takes a different and unique approach. In Module 1.3, I portray child development research as a dynamic process in which scientists make a series of decisions as they plan their work. In the process, they create a study that has both strengths and weaknesses. Each of the remaining chapters of the book contains a "Focus on Research" feature that illustrates this process by showing—in a question-and-answer format—the different decisions that investigators made in designing a particular study. I trace each of the steps and explain the decisions that were made. Then the results are shown—usually with an annotated figure so that students can learn how to interpret graphs—and the investigators' conclusions are described. Thus, the research methods that are introduced in Chapter 1 reappear in every chapter, in a setting that makes research come alive as a set of decisions that often involve compromises. (In my classes, I encourage students to think how the "Focus on Research" studies could be improved with different methods. At the same time, I ask them why the investigators might have resorted to the methods they did.)

The "Focus on Research" and other pedagogical elements *are* effective; students using the first edition commented that the book is easy to read and presents complex topics in an understandable way. Reading *Children and Their Development,* students come to appreciate both what we know about children's development *and* the research process that produced this knowledge.

## Changes to the Second Edition

In writing the second edition, I have included hundreds of new citations to research published in the past few years. I have also made significant additions to every chapter. Of particular note is the following new material:

Chapter 1 includes information on how to study and explains the rationale for the book's organization.

Chapter 2 has material on methods from molecular genetics and two new major sections: one on pathways from genes to behavior and another on nonshared environmental influences.

Chapter 3 contains a new section on postpartum depression and information about the national "Back to Sleep" campaign to combat SIDS.

Chapter 4 now has information on sexual orientation, bulimia, and brain plasticity.

Chapter 5 includes new material on object perception and the development of attention.

Chapter 6 is reorganized to include two new modules, one that evaluates Piaget's theory and another that describes new approaches that complement Piaget's work. The latter module has a new section on "the child as a theorist."

Chapter 7 now describes inhibitory processes, autobiographical memory, infantile amnesia, and writing.

Chapter 8 contains new material on social intelligence and dynamic approaches to intelligence testing.

Chapter 9 now begins with a new section defining different aspects of language and has an expanded section on fast mapping of meaning to words.

Chapter 10 describes research on emotion regulation and work on adults' representations of their attachments with their own parents.

Chapter 11 has a new "Focus on Research" feature on identity in children of transracial adoptions and a new section on the consequences of low self-esteem.

Chapter 12 includes material that relates temperament to self-control, information on Kohlberg's Just Communities, and a new section dealing with victims of aggression.

Chapter 13 describes social class and race differences in gender stereotypes and also includes information on gender differences in physical and relational aggression.

Chapter 14 begins with a new section devoted to a systems approach to the study of the family and contains an expanded section on parental behaviors (with new material on direct instruction and coaching).

Chapter 15 has much expanded coverage of peer relations, material on cross-sex friendships and factors that contribute to long-lasting friendships, a new section about TV as a medium (in addition to material about TV content), a largely new section on schools (organized around factors that make schools effective), and brand new material about adolescents' part-time employment.

## Support Materials

*Children and Their Development* is accompanied by a superb set of materials. They include the following:

## For Instructors

**Instructor's Resource Manual,** prepared by Dale Grubb of Baldwin Wallace College. This IRM contains a wealth of material for new and experienced instructors alike. Each chapter includes chapter organizers, learning objectives, a detailed lecture outline with suggestions, classroom demonstrations and learning activities, critical thinking questions and exercises, assignment ideas, journal exercises, suggested films and videos, and classroom handouts.

**Test Item File,** prepared by Terri T. Combs of Indiana University-Purdue University. This test bank contains over 3,000 multiple choice, true/false, short-answer and essay questions that test factual, applied, and conceptual knowledge.

**Prentice Hall Test Manager.** One of the best-selling test-generating software programs on the market, Test Manager is available in Windows and Macintosh formats and contains a Gradebook, Online Network Testing, and many tools to help you edit and create tests. The program comes with full Technical Support and telephone "Request a Test" service.

**Prentice Hall's Color Transparencies for Developmental Psychology.** Designed in large-type format for lecture settings, these full color overhead transparencies add visual appeal to your lectures by augmenting the visuals in the text with a variety of new illustrations.

**PowerPoint Slides and Online Graphics Archive.** Available in the Faculty Module of the Companion Website at **www.prenhall.com/kail,** each chapter's art has been digitized and is available for download into any presentation software. PowerPoint lectures for each chapter are also available for download.

**Prentice Hall Video Libraries.** Prentice Hall has assembled a superior collection of video materials which range from short lecture launchers to full-length detailed features for use in the Developmental Psychology course. The videos below are available to qualified adopters.

**NEWS
ABCNEWS**

- **Films for the Humanities and Sciences.** A wealth of videos from the extensive library of Films for the Humanities and Sciences, on a variety of topics in developmental psychology, are available to qualified adopters. Contact your local Prentice Hall representative for a list of videos.
- **ABC News Videos for Developmental Psychology.** These videos consist of segments from ABC Nightly News with Peter Jennings, Nightline, 20/20, Prime Time Live, and The Health Show.

**Media Support for *Children and Their Development,* Second Edition.** Both instructors and students will find many useful resources in the media program to accompany this text.

**www.prenhall.com/kail Companion Website.** Prepared by Larry Jenkins of Tidewater Community College, this *free* online Study Guide allows students to review each chapter's material, take practice tests, research topics for course projects, and more. Professors should visit the Faculty Module of the site to download electronic versions of the Instructor's Resource Manual, Powerpoint Slides for each chapter, and an Online Graphics Archive.

**On-Line Course Management.** For professors interested in using the Internet and on-line course management in their courses, Prentice Hall offers fully customizable on-line courses in WebCT, BlackBoard, and eCollege to accompany this textbook. Contact your local Prentice Hall representative or visit **www.prenhall.com/demo** for more information.

## For Students

**Study Guide,** written by Dea DeWolff. This attractive, highly visual Study Guide reinforces the key pedagogical features of the textbook. The author incorporates both illustrations and design elements from the text. Each of the fifteen chapters follows the same modular organization as the text. Each of the modules in every chapter includes learning objectives, matching exercises to review key theories, definitions, terms and concepts, practice true/false questions, cumulative fill-in-the-blank chapter summaries, multiple choice questions, and essay questions.

**Psychology on the Internet.** This "hands-on" Internet tutorial features Web sites related to psychology and general information about using the Internet for research. This supplement is available *free* when packaged with the text and helps students capitalize on all the resources that the World Wide Web has to offer.

## Acknowledgments

Textbook authors do not produce books on their own. I want to thank the many reviewers who generously gave their time and effort to help sharpen my thinking about child development and shape the development of this text. I am especially grateful to the following people who reviewed various aspects of the manuscript: Jack Meacham,

University of Buffalo; Lesa Rae Vartanian, Purdue University; Adam Winsler, George Mason University; Tony Simon, Furman University; K. Robert Bridges, Pennsylvania State University; Frank Manis, University of Southern California; Marianne Taylor, University of Puget Sound; Karen Rudolph, University of Illinois; Cynthia Stifter, Pennsylvania State University; James Black, University of Illinois; Laura Hess, Purdue University; Lisa Oakes, University of Iowa; Jacquelyn Mice, Auburn University; Amy Weiss, University of Iowa; Brad Pillow, Northern Illinois University; Janet DiPietro, Johns Hopkins University; Lee Ann Thompson, Case Western Reserve University; Gary Ladd, University of Illinois. Thank you, as well, to those who reviewed the first edition of the manuscript: Susan McClure, Westmoreland County Community College; Rebecca Bigler, University of Texas-Austin; Kathleen Fox, Salisbury State University; Rick Medlin, Stetson University; Joan Cook, County College of Morris; Elizabeth Lemerise, Western Kentucky University; Jim Dannemiller, University of Wisconsin-Madison; Mark B. Alcorn, University of Northern Colorado; Vernon C. Hall, Syracuse University; and May X. Wang, Metropolitan State College of Denver. Without their thoughtful comments, this book would be less complete, less accurate, and less interesting.

I also owe a debt of thanks to many people who helped take this project from a first draft to a bound book. Jennifer Gilliland has supported this book enthusiastically and served as a savvy guide to its revision. As she did for the first edition, Harriett Prentiss labored long to make my writing clear and inviting. Laura Curry helped to compile the many new references that were added to this edition. Anne Demarinis, under the direction of Carole Anson, designed a book that is both beautiful and functional. Julie Sullivan skillfully orchestrated the many activities that were involved in actually producing the book. Kathy Ringrose found the marvelous photographs that appear throughout the book. To all these people, many, many thanks.

—*Robert V. Kail*

**Robert V. Kail** is Professor of Psychological Sciences at Purdue University. His undergraduate degree is from Ohio Wesleyan University, and he received his Ph. D. from the University of Michigan. Kail is currently Associate Editor of the *Journal of Experimental Child Psychology* and coeditor of *Advances in Child Development and Behavior.* He received the McCandless Young Scientist Award from the American Psychological Association, was named the Distinguished Sesquicentennial Alumnus in Psychology by Ohio Wesleyan University, and is a fellow in the American Psychological Society. His research interests are in the area of cognitive development and focus on the causes and consequences of developmental change in the speed of information processing. Kail has also written *The Development of Memory in Children* and, with John C. Cavanaugh, *Human Development: A Lifespan View.* Away from the office, he enjoys flying, working out, playing soccer with his daughter, and watching his young adult sons on stage.

# Children
### and Their
# Development

**1.1**

eginning as a microscopic cell, every person takes a fascinating journey designed to lead to adulthood. Like any journey worth taking, the journey to adulthood is filled with remarkable events that make the trip both interesting and challenging. In this book, we'll trace this journey as we learn about the science of child development, a multidisciplinary study of all aspects of growth from conception to adulthood. As an

adult, you've lived the years that are the heart of this book. I hope you enjoy reviewing your developmental journey from the perspective of child development research. I expect that this perspective will lead you to new insights into the developmental forces that made you the person you are today.

Chapter 1 sets the stage for our study of child development. I begin, in Module 1.1, by giving you some tips on how to use this book. In Module 1.2, I describe the themes and theories that are central to child development research. In Module 1.3, I explain the techniques that researchers use to study children and their development.

# The Science of Child Development

# 1.1

- **The Modular Format**
- **Terminology**
- **Organization**

## Using This Book

In most textbooks, the material on the next few pages appears in a preface entitled "To the Student." But I'm afraid that most students never read this material, so I'm including it here at the beginning of Chapter 1. Please don't skip it now; read on to learn how to use this book. It will save you time in the long run.

I want to begin by explaining the book's modular format, which should help you learn the science of child development.

### The Modular Format

Each of the 15 chapters in the book includes three or four modules that are listed on the first page of the chapter. As you can see in the inset page below, each module begins with a set of learning objectives phrased as questions. Next is a brief vignette that introduces the topic to be covered in the module by describing an issue or problem faced by real people. In the margin is a mini-outline listing the major subheadings of the module—a kind of roadmap for reading. The learning objectives, vignette, and mini-outline tell you what to expect in the module.

---

## 2.1

- **The Biology of Heredity**
- **Single Gene Inheritance**
- **Behavioral Genetics**

## Mechanisms of Heredity

**Learning Objectives**

- What are chromosomes and genes?
- What are dominant and recessive traits? How are they inherited?
- How does heredity influence behavioral and psychological development?

*Leslie and Glenn have decided to try to have a baby. They are thrilled at the thought of starting their own family but also worried because Leslie's grandfather had sickle cell disease and died when he was just 20 years old. Leslie is terrified that their baby could inherit the disease that killed her grandfather. Leslie and Glenn wish someone could reassure them that their baby will be okay.*

How could we reassure Leslie and Glenn? For starters, we need to know more about sickle cell disease. Red blood cells like the ones in the left photo carry oxygen and

---

Each module typically examines three to four major topics that are listed in the mini-outline. In addition, each module in Chapters 2–15 includes a special feature that expands or highlights a topic. There are four different kinds of features; you can recognize each one by its distinctive icon:

*Focus on Research* provides details on the design and methods used in a particular research study. Closely examining specific studies demystifies research and shows that scientific work is a series of logical steps conducted by real people.

*Making Children's Lives Better* shows how research and theory can be applied to improve children's development. These practical solutions to everyday problems show the relevance of research and theory to real life.

🌐 *Cultural Influences* shows how culture influences children and illustrates that developmental journeys are diverse. All children share the biological aspects of development, but their cultural contexts differ. This feature celebrates the developmental experiences of children from different backgrounds.

👥 *Real Children* provides a case study that illustrates an issue in child development in the life of a real child. These authentic accounts make the study of child development come alive.

The inset below shows another important element of each module: All illustrations and tables are integrated with the text. You won't need to turn pages searching for a picture or table that is described in the text; instead, pictures, tables, and words are linked to tell a unified story.

---

risk. Plomin and Rowe obtained permission from the mothers for the twins to participate.

*What were the results?* The primary results were expressed as correlations, which are shown in the graph. Each bar shows the size of the correlation for either identical or fraternal twins on one measure. For example, the first bar shows that the correlation for talking to the stranger was nearly .6 for identical twins. This means that if one identical twin talked often to the stranger, the other usually did, too; if one identical twin was quiet, the other usually was also. The important pattern in the graph is that, for each measure, the correlation is greater for identical twins than for fraternal twins. That is, as I described on page 44, the greater similarity among identical twins than fraternal twins is evidence that a behavior is inherited.

*What did the investigators conclude?* Sociability, at least as reflected in the measures that Plomin and Rowe devised, is influenced by heredity. ●

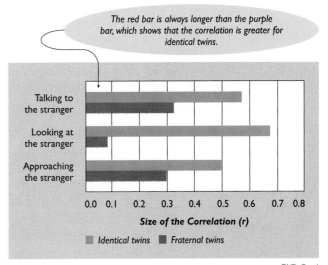

The red bar is always longer than the purple bar, which shows that the correlation is greater for identical twins.

*Size of the Correlation (r)*

■ Identical twins    ■ Fraternal twins

FIG 2–4

We will look at personality in greater detail later. For now, keep in mind two conclusions from twin studies like Plomin and Rowe's and from adoption studies. On the one hand, the impact of heredity on behavioral development is substantial and widespread. Research shows that heredity has a sizable influence on such different aspects of

---

Two other elements are designed to help you focus on the main points of the text. First, whenever a key term is introduced in the text, it appears in ***boldfaced italics like these*** and the definition appears in **boldface type**. This format should make key terms easier for you to find and learn. Second, about half the pages in the book include a sentence in large type that extends into the margin. This sentence summarizes a key point that is made in the surrounding text. When you see one of these sentences, take a moment to think about it because it is an important idea; reviewing these sentences later will help you prepare for exams.

Each module concludes with "Check Your Learning" questions to help you review the major ideas in the module. As you can see

A sentence in the margin like this summarizes the surrounding text. Use these sentences to help preview the text before you read.

in the inset, there are two kinds of questions: fill-in-the-blank and critical thinking. If you can answer the questions, you are on your way to mastering the material in the module. However, do not rely exclusively on "Check Your Learning" as you study for exams. The questions are designed to give you a quick spot check of your understanding, not a comprehensive assessment of your knowledge.

---

### Check Your Learning

1. In _____, an egg is fertilized by a sperm in a laboratory dish, then placed in the uterus.

2. The first 22 pairs of chromosomes are called _____.

3. A person is _____ when the alleles in a pair of chromosomes differ.

4. _____ reflects the combined activity of a number of distinct genes.

5. Traditionally, behavioral geneticists relied on twin and _____ studies.

6. Intelligence, _____, and personality are the psychological traits most strongly influenced by heredity.

A problem in twin studies is that identical twins may be treated more similarly than fraternal twins. A problem in adoption studies is that selective placement may cause biological parents to resemble a child's adoptive parents. How could an investigator determine if these problems were present in his or her research?

**Answers:** (1) in vitro fertilization, (2) autosomes, (3) heterozygous, (4) Polygenic inheritance, (5) adoption, (6) psychological disorders

---

At the very end of each chapter are additional study aids. "In Perspective" highlights the main idea in each module and then shows how these ideas relate to a major developmental theme. "See for Yourself" suggests some simple activities for exploring issues in child development on your own. "Resources" includes books and internet sites where you can learn more about children and their development. "Key Terms" lists all the important terms that appear in the chapter and the page where each term is defined. Finally, drawing the chapter to a close is a "Summary," organized by module and the primary headings within the module. I strongly encourage you to take advantage of these learning and study aids as you read the book.

Your instructor will probably assign about one chapter per week. Don't try to read an entire chapter in one sitting. Instead, on the first day, preview the chapter. Read the introduction and notice how the chapter fits into the whole book. Then page through the chapter, reading the learning objectives, vignettes, minioutlines, and major headings. Also read the large sentences in the margins and the bold-faced sentences. Your goal is to get a general overview of the entire chapter—a sense of what it's all about.

Now you're ready to begin reading. Go to the first module and preview it again, reminding yourself of the topics covered. Then start to read. As you do, think about what you're reading. Every few paragraphs, stop briefly. Try to summarize, in your own words, the main ideas; ask yourself if the ideas describe your own childhood or others that you know; or tell a roommate about something interesting in the material. In other words, read *actively*—get *involved* in what you're reading. Don't just stare glassy-eyed at the page!

Continue this pattern—reading, summarizing, thinking—until you finish the module. Then answer the questions in "Check Your Learning" to determine how well you've learned what you've read. If you followed the read-summarize-think cycle as you worked your way through the module, you should be able to answer most of the questions. The next time you sit down to read—preferably the next day—start by reviewing the second module and then tackle it with the read-summarize-think cycle. Repeat this procedure for all the modules.

After you've finished the last module, wait a day or two and then review each module, paying careful attention to the sentences in the margins, the bold-faced terms, and the "Check Your Learning" questions. Also, use the study aids at the end of the chapter to help you integrate the ideas in the chapter.

With this approach, it should take several 30- to 45-minute study sessions to complete each chapter. Don't be tempted to blast through an entire chapter in a single session. Research consistently shows that you learn more effectively by having daily (or nearly daily) study sessions devoted both to reviewing familiar material *and* taking on a relatively small amount of new material.

## Terminology

Every field has its own terminology, and child development is no exception. I will be using several terms to refer to different periods of infancy, childhood, and adolescence. Although these terms are familiar, when I use them, each will refer to a specific range of ages:

| | |
|---|---|
| Newborn | Birth to 1 month |
| Infant | 1 month to 1 year |
| Toddler | 1 to 2 years |
| Preschooler | 2 to 6 years |
| School-age child | 6 to 12 years |
| Adolescent | 12 to 18 years |
| Adult | 18 years and older |

Sometimes for the sake of variety I will use other terms that are less tied to specific ages, such as *babies, youngsters,* and *elementary-school children.* When I do, you will be able to tell from the context what groups are being described.

I will also use very specific terminology in describing research findings from different cultural and ethnic groups. The appropriate terms to describe different cultural, racial, and ethnic groups change over time. For example, the terms *colored people, Negroes, Black Americans,* and *African Americans* have all been used to describe Americans who trace their ancestry to the races that originated in Africa. In this book, I will use the term *African American* because it emphasizes the unique cultural heritage of this group of people. Following this same line of reasoning, I will use the terms *European American* (instead of *Caucasian* or *white*), *Native American* (instead of *Indian* or *American Indian*), *Asian American,* and *Hispanic American.*

These labels are not perfect. Sometimes they blur distinctions within ethnic groups. For example, the term *European American* ignores differences between individuals of northern or southern European ancestry; the term *Asian American* blurs variations among people whose heritage is Japanese, Chinese, or Korean. Whenever researchers have identified the subgroups in their research sample, I will use the more specific terms in describing results. When you see the more general terms, remember that conclusions may not apply to all subgroups within the group.

### Organization

In this book, we'll trace children's development from conception through childhood, adolescence, and young adulthood. Given this goal, you might think you would find chapters devoted to early childhood, middle childhood, and the like. In reality, if you look at the table of contents, you'll see that this book is organized differently, around topics. Chapters 2–5 are devoted to the genetic and biological bases of human development and the growth of perceptual and motor skills. Chapters 6–9 cover intellectual development—how children learn, think, reason, and solve problems. Chapters 10–15 concern social and emotional development— how children acquire customs of their society and learn to play the social roles expected of them.

This organization reflects the fact that, when scientists conduct research on children's development, they usually study how some specific aspect of a child develops. A researcher might, for example, study how memory changes as children grow or how friendship differs in children and adolescents. Thus the organization of the book reflects the way researchers actually study child development.

The many topics described in Chapters 2–15 all draw upon the same developmental theories and the same scientific methods. The next module describes the theories that are essential to developmental research. The last module in this chapter covers research methods.

# 1.2

— **Themes in Child Development Research**

— **Theories of Child Development**

## Themes and Theories

### Learning Objectives

● **What are some general themes in development that all child development scientists support?**

● **What are the major theories of child development? How do they account for change across infancy, childhood, and adolescence?**

> *Marcus has just graduated from high school, first in his class. For his proud mother, Betty, this is a time to reflect on Marcus's past and ponder his future. Marcus has always been a happy, easygoing child—a joy to rear. And he's always been interested in learning. Betty wonders why he is so perpetually good-natured and so curious. If she knew the secret, she laughed, she could write a best-selling book and be a guest on Oprah!*

Betty is not the first person to ask these questions about children. In fact, such questions have occupied some of the greatest philosophers in history. Nearly four hundred years ago, the English philosopher John Locke (1632–1704) claimed that the human infant is a *tabula rasa,* or "blank slate." Experience then molds the infant, child, adolescent, and adult into a unique individual. Locke's view was challenged by the French philosopher Jean Jacques Rousseau (1712–1778), who believed that newborns are endowed with an innate sense of justice and morality that unfolds naturally as children grow.

By the middle of the 19th century, progress in science had merged with growing concerns about children's welfare to bring about a new approach to understanding childhood (Sears, 1975). Speculation about the child's "nature" was replaced by efforts to record and study actual behavior and development. This was the dawn of the modern science of child development. To introduce you to this field, let's look at some of the major ideas or *themes* that guide modern thinking about child development.

## Themes in Child Development Research

If you asked 100 child development experts from around the world to describe general themes of development, several would appear on nearly everyone's list. I like to think of these themes as a foundation you can use to organize the many specific facts about child development that fill the rest of this book. These themes will help you unify your own understanding of child development. In fact, to help you do this, every chapter (except this one) ends with "In Perspective," where one of the themes is illustrated in detail with research from the chapter.

Here are the four unifying themes.

## Early Development Is Related to Later Development but Not Perfectly.

This theme has to do with the "predictability" of development. Do you believe that happy, cheerful 5-year-olds remain outgoing and friendly throughout their lives? If you do, this shows that you believe development is a continuous process: According to this view, once a child begins down a particular developmental pathway, he or she stays on that path throughout life. In other words, friendly and smart 5-year-olds become friendly and smart 15- and 25-year-olds. The other view, that development is not continuous, is shown in the cartoon. Sweet and cooperative Trixie has become a demanding, assertive child. According to this view, friendly and smart 5-year-olds may be obnoxious and foolish as 15-year-olds and quiet but wise as 25-year-olds. **Thus the *continuity-versus-discontinuity issue* is really about the "connectedness" of development: Are early aspects of development consistently related to later aspects?**

Hi and Lois © 1993. Reprinted with special permission of King Features Syndicate.

In reality, neither of these views is accurate. Development is not perfectly predictable. A friendly, smart 5-year-old does not guarantee a friendly, smart 15- or 25-year-old, but the chances of a friendly, smart adult are greater than if the child were obnoxious and foolish. There are many ways to become a friendly and smart 15-year-old; being a friendly and smart 5-year-old is not a required step, but it is probably the most direct route!

## Development Is Always Jointly Influenced by Heredity and Environment.

Let me introduce this theme with a story about my sons. Ben, my first son, was a delightful baby and toddler. He awoke each morning with a smile on his face, eager to start another fun-filled day. When Ben was upset, which occurred infrequently, he was quickly consoled by being held or rocked. I presumed that his cheerful disposition must reflect fabulous parenting. Consequently, I was stunned when my second son, Matt, spent much of the first year of his life being fussy and cranky. He was easily irritated and hard to soothe. Why wasn't the all-star parenting that had been so effective with Ben working with Matt? The answer, of course, is that Ben's parenting wasn't the sole cause of his happiness. I thought environmental influences accounted for his amiable disposition, but in fact biological influences also played an important role.

> Virtually all aspects of development are determined by the combined forces of heredity and environment.

**This anecdote illustrates the *nature-nurture issue:* What roles do biology (nature) and environment (nurture) play in child development?** Are children like Ben outgoing because of their heredity or because of their experiences? Scientists once hoped to answer questions like this by identifying either heredity or environment as the cause. Their goal was to be able to say, for example, that intelligence was due to heredity or that personality was due to experience. Today, we know that virtually no aspects of child development are due exclusively to either heredity or environment. Instead, development is always shaped by both—nature and nurture interact. In fact, a major aim of child development research is to understand how heredity and environment jointly determine children's development. Biology will be more influential in some areas and environment in others.

### Children Help Determine Their Own Development.

Whenever I teach child development, I ask students their plans for when they have children. How will they rear them? What do they want them to grow up to be? It's interesting to hear students' responses. Many have big plans for their future children. It's just as interesting, though, to watch students who already have children roll their eyes in a "You don't have a clue" way at what the others say. The parent-students in class admit that they, too, once had grand designs about child rearing. What they quickly learned, however, was that their children shaped the way in which they parented.

**These two points of view illustrate the *active-passive child issue:* Are children simply at the mercy of the environment (passive child) or do children actively influence their own development through their own unique individual characteristics (active child)?** The passive view corresponds to Locke's description of the child as a blank slate on which experience writes, whereas the active view corresponds to Rousseau's view of development as a natural unfolding that takes place within the child. Today, we know that experiences are indeed crucial but not always in the way Locke (and the early learning theorists) envisioned. Also, a child's unique characteristics may cause him or her to have some experiences but not others. Often, it's a child's interpretation of experiences that shapes his or her development. From birth, children are trying to make sense of their world, and in the process they help shape their own destinies.

### Development in Different Domains Is Connected.

As I explained on page 8, the chapters in this book are organized around different topics of development because of the way child development research is conducted. Researchers examine different domains or areas of development, like physical growth, cognition, language, personality, and social relationships. Describing this research is much more straightforward when the book is organized around the topics that child developmentalists actually explore. However, this topical organization does not mean that you should think of each aspect of development as an independent entity completely separate from the others. On the contrary, our 100 child development experts would definitely agree that development in different domains is always intertwined. Cognitive and social development are not independent; advances in one area affect advances in the other. The same could be said for the many other topics throughout the book.

Having introduced the themes, let me present them together one time before we move on.

- Early development is related to later development but not perfectly.
- Development is always jointly influenced by heredity and environment.
- Children help determine their own development.
- Development in different domains is connected.

Most experts would agree that these are important general themes in children's development. However, just as lumber, bricks, pipe, and wiring can be used to assemble an incredible assortment of homes, these themes show up in different ways in the major theories of child development, our next topic.

## Theories of Child Development

For many people, the word *theory* means "boring." Boring professors make up boring theories that have nothing to do with the real world. But that's not true. If you want to understand children's development, theories are essential because they provide the *whys* of development. What is a theory? **In child development, a *theory* is an organized set of ideas that is designed to explain development.** For example, suppose friends of yours have a baby who cries often. You could imagine several explanations for her crying. Maybe the baby cries because she's hungry; maybe she cries to get her parents to hold her; maybe she cries because she's simply a cranky, unhappy baby. Each of these explanations is a very simple theory: It tries to explain why the baby cries so much. Of course, real developmental theories are much more complicated, but the purpose is the same—to explain behavior and development.

Theories lead to predictions that we can test in research; in the process, the theory is supported or not. Think about the different explanations for the crying baby. Each one leads to unique predictions. If, for example, the baby is crying because she's hungry, we predict that feeding her more often should stop the crying. When results of research match the predictions, the theory gains support. When results differ from the predictions, the theory is incorrect and is revised.

Perhaps now you see why theories are essential for child development research: They are the source of predictions for research, which often lead to changes in the theories. These revised theories then provide the basis for new predictions, which lead to new research, and the cycle continues.

Many theories guide research and thinking about children's development. Some of these theories share ideas and assumptions about children and their development but differ in their details. **Similar theories are often grouped together to form a *theoretical perspective*.** In the next few pages, I briefly sketch five major theoretical perspectives in child development research: the biological, psychodynamic, learning, cognitive-developmental, and contextual. As you read about each perspective, think about how it differs from the others in its view of development.

## The Biological Perspective.

According to the biological perspective, intellectual and personality development, as well as physical and motor development, proceed according to a biological plan. One of the first biological theories, maturational theory, was proposed by Arnold Gesell (1880–1961), shown in the photo. **According to *maturational theory*, child development reflects a specific and prearranged scheme or plan within the body.** In Gesell's view, development is simply a natural unfolding of a biological plan; experience matters little. Like Jean Jacques Rousseau 200 years before him, Gesell encouraged parents to let their children develop naturally. Without interference from adults, Gesell claimed, behaviors like speech, play, and reasoning would emerge spontaneously according to a predetermined developmental timetable.

Other biological theories give greater weight to experience. *Ethological theory* **views development from an evolutionary perspective.** In this theory, many behaviors are adaptive—they have survival value. For example, clinging, grasping, and crying are adaptive for infants because they elicit caregiving from adults. Ethological theorists assume that people inherit many of these adaptive behaviors.

So far, ethological theory seems like maturational theory, with a dash of evolution for taste. How does experience fit in? Ethologists believe that all animals are biologically programmed so that some kinds of learning occur only at certain ages. **A *critical period* is the time in development when a specific type of learning can take place; before or after the critical period, the same learning is difficult or even impossible.**

One of the best-known examples of a critical period comes from the work of Konrad Lorenz (1903–1989), a Nobel-prize-winning Austrian zoologist. Lorenz noticed that newly hatched chicks follow their mother about. He theorized that chicks are biologically programmed to follow the first moving object that they see after hatching. **Usually this was the mother, so following her was the first step in *imprinting*, creating an emotional bond with the mother.** Lorenz tested his theory by showing that if he removed the mother immediately after the chicks hatched and replaced it with another moving object, the chicks would follow that object and treat it as "mother." As the photo shows, this included Lorenz himself!

Lorenz also discovered that the chick had to see the moving object within about a day of hatching. Otherwise, the chick would not imprint on the moving object. In other words, there is a critical period for imprinting that lasts about a day; when chicks experience the moving object outside of the critical period, imprinting does not take place. Even though the underlying mechanism is biological, experience is essential for triggering programmed, adaptive behaviors.

Ethological theory and maturational theory both highlight the biological bases of child development. Biological theorists remind us that children's genes, which are the product of a long evolutionary history, influence virtually every aspect of children's development. Consequently, a biological theorist would tell Betty, the mother of the high-school graduate in the module-opening vignette, that her son's good nature and his outstanding academic record are both largely products of heredity.

### The Psychodynamic Perspective.
This is the oldest scientific perspective on child development, tracing its roots to Sigmund Freud's (1856–1939) work in the late 19th and early 20th centuries. Freud, shown in the photo, was a physician who specialized in diseases of the nervous system. Many of his patients were adults who suffered from ailments that seemed to have no obvious biological cause. As Freud listened to his patients describe their problems and their lives, he became convinced that early experiences establish patterns that endure throughout a person's life. **Using his patients' case histories, Freud created the first *psychodynamic theory*, which holds that development is largely determined by how well people resolve conflicts they face at different ages.**

Two aspects of Freud's theorizing have influenced child development research. The first is his theory of personality. Freud proposed that personality includes three primary components that emerge at distinct ages. **The *id* is a reservoir of primitive instincts and drives.** Present at birth, the id presses for immediate gratification of bodily needs and wants. A hungry baby crying illustrates the id in action. **The *ego* is the practical, rational component of personality.** The ego begins to emerge during the first year of life, as infants learn that they cannot always have what they want. The ego tries to resolve conflicts that occur when the instinctive desires of the id encounter the obstacles of the real world. The ego often tries to channel the id's impulsive demands into more socially acceptable channels. **The third component of personality, the *superego*, emerges during the preschool years as children begin to internalize adult standards of right and wrong.** The superego is the "moral agent" in the child's personality.

A second influential aspect of Freud's work was his account of psychosexual development. He believed that humans want to experience physical pleasure from birth. As children grow, the focus of the pleasure shifts to different parts of the body. The result is a sequence of developmental stages, with each stage characterized by sensitivity in a particular part of the body or erogenous zone. For example, from birth to the first birthday, infants are in the oral stage. As the name suggests, they seek pleasure orally, usually by sucking.

Freud believed that development proceeds best when children's needs at each stage are met but not exceeded. If children's needs are not met adequately, they are frustrated and reluctant to move to other, more mature forms of stimulation. For example, a baby whose needs for oral stimulation were not met may try to satisfy these needs as an adolescent or adult by smoking. If, instead, children find one source of stimulation too satisfying, they see little need to progress to more advanced stages. In Freud's view, parents have the difficult task of satisfying children's needs without indulging them.

Freud's student, Erik Erikson (1902–1994), shown in the photo, believed that psychological and social aspects of development were more important than the biological and physical aspects that Freud emphasized. **In Erikson's *psychosocial theory*, development consists of a sequence of**

**stages, each defined by a unique crisis or challenge.** The complete theory includes the eight stages shown in the table. The name of each stage reflects the challenge that people face at a particular age. For example, the challenge for young adults is to become involved in a loving relationship. Adults who establish this relationship experience intimacy; those who don't experience isolation.

## The Eight Stages of Psychosocial Development in Erikson's Theory

| Psychosocial Stage | Age | Challenge |
| --- | --- | --- |
| Basic trust versus mistrust | Birth to 1 year | To develop a sense that the world is safe, a "good place" |
| Autonomy versus shame and doubt | 1 to 3 years | To realize that one is an independent person who can make decisions |
| Initiative versus guilt | 3–6 years | To develop a willingness to try new things and to handle failure |
| Industry versus inferiority | 6 years–adolescence | To learn basic skills and to work with others |
| Identity versus identity confusion | Adolescence | To develop a lasting, integrated sense of self |
| Intimacy versus isolation | Young adulthood | To commit to another in a loving relationship |
| Generativity versus stagnation | Middle adulthood | To contribute to younger people, through child rearing, child care, or other productive work |
| Integrity versus despair | Late life | To view one's life as satisfactory and worth living |

TABLE 1–1

Erikson also argued that the earlier stages of psychosocial development provide the foundation for the later stages. For example, adolescents who do not meet the challenge of developing an identity will not establish truly intimate relationships; instead, they will become overly dependent on their partners as a source of identity.

Whether we call them conflicts, challenges, or crises, the psychodynamic perspective emphasizes that the trek to adulthood is difficult because the path is strewn with obstacles. Outcomes of development reflect the manner and ease with which children surmount life's barriers. When children overcome early obstacles easily, they are better able to handle the later ones. A psychodynamic theorist would tell Betty that her son's cheerful disposition and his academic record suggest that he handled life's early obstacles well, which is a good sign for his future development.

*Psychodynamic theories emphasize that development is a product of the child's responses to life's challenges.*

**The Learning Perspective.** Learning theorists endorse John Locke's view that the infant's mind is a blank slate on which experience writes. John Watson (1878–1958) was the first theorist to apply this approach to child development. Watson argued that learning determines what children will be. He assumed that with the correct techniques anything could be learned by almost anyone. In other words, experience was just about all that mattered in determining the course of development.

Watson did little research to support his claims, but B. F. Skinner (1904–1990), shown in the photo, filled this gap. **Skinner studied *operant conditioning,* in which the consequences of a behavior determine whether a behavior is repeated in the future.** Skinner showed that two kinds of consequences were especially influential. **A *reinforcement* is a consequence that increases the future likelihood of the behavior that it follows.** Positive reinforcement consists of giving a reward like chocolate, gold stars, or paychecks to increase the likelihood of repeating a previous behavior. The parents of the child whose room is shown in the photograph could use positive reinforcement to encourage her to clean her room. Every time she cleaned her room, they could reinforce her with praise, food, or money. Negative reinforcement consists of rewarding people by taking away unpleasant things. The same parents could use negative reinforcement by saying that whenever she cleaned her room she wouldn't have to wash the dishes or fold laundry.

**A *punishment* is a consequence that decreases the future likelihood of the behavior that it follows.** Punishment suppresses a behavior by either adding something aversive or by withholding a pleasant event. When the child failed to clean her room, the parents could punish her by making her do extra chores (adding something aversive) or by not allowing her to watch television (withholding a pleasant event).

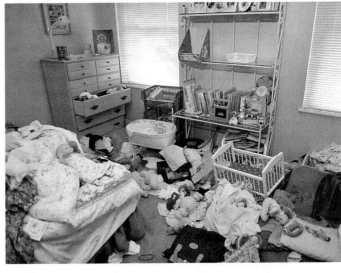

Skinner's research was done primarily with animals, but child development researchers soon showed that the principles of operant conditioning could be extended readily to children's behavior (Baer & Wolf, 1968). Applied properly, reinforcement and punishment are indeed powerful influences on children. However, researchers discovered that children sometimes learn without reinforcement or punishment. **Children learn a great deal simply by watching those around them, which is known as *imitation* or *observational learning.*** Imitation is occurring when one toddler throws a toy after seeing a peer do so or when a school-age child offers to help an older adult carry groceries because she's seen her parents do the same.

Perhaps imitation makes you think of "monkey-see, monkey-do," which is simple mimicking. Early investigators had this view, too, but research quickly showed that this was wrong. Children do not always imitate what they see around them. Children are more likely to imitate if the person they see is popular, smart, or talented. They're also more likely to imitate when the behavior they see is rewarded than when it is punished. Findings like these imply that imitation is more complex than sheer mimicry. Children do not mechanically copy what they see and hear; instead, they look to others for information about appropriate behavior. When popular, smart peers are reinforced for behaving in a particular way, it makes sense to imitate them.

**Albert Bandura (1925–  ) based his *social cognitive theory* on this more complex view of reward, punishment, and imitation.** Bandura, who is shown in the top photo, calls his theory "cognitive" because he believes that children are actively trying to understand what goes on in their world; the theory is "social" because, along with reinforcement and punishment, what other people do is an important source of information about the world.

**Bandura also argues that experience gives children a sense of *self-efficacy,* which refers to children's beliefs about their own abilities and talents.** Self-efficacy beliefs help determine when children will imitate others. A child who sees herself as athletically untalented, for example, will not try to imitate Michael Jordan dunking a basketball, despite the fact that he is obviously talented and popular. Thus whether children imitate others depends on who the other person is, on whether that person's behavior is rewarded, and on the children's beliefs about their own talents.

Bandura's social cognitive theory is a far cry from Skinner's operant conditioning. The operant conditioning child who responds mechanically to reinforcement and punishment has been replaced by the social cognitive child who actively interprets events. Nevertheless, Skinner, Bandura, and all learning theorists share the view that experience propels children along their developmental journeys. They would tell Betty that she can thank experience for making Marcus both happy and successful academically.

**The Cognitive-Developmental Perspective.** The cognitive-developmental perspective focuses on how children think and how their thinking changes over time. Jean Piaget (1896–1980), shown in the bottom photo, proposed the best known of these theories. Piaget believed that children naturally try to make sense of their world. Throughout infancy, childhood, and adolescence, youngsters want to understand the workings of both the physical and the social world. For example, infants want to know about objects: "What happens when I push this toy off the table?" And they want to know about people: "Who is this person who feeds and cares for me?"

Piaget argued that in their efforts to comprehend their world children act like scientists in creating theories about the physical and social worlds. They try to weave all that they know about objects and people into a complete theory. Children's theories are tested daily by experience because their theories lead them to expect certain things to happen. As with real scientific theories, when the predicted events do occur, a child's belief in her theory grows stronger. When the predicted events do not occur, the child must revise her theory. For example, an infant's theory of objects might include the idea that "toys pushed off the table fall to the floor." If the infant pushes some other object—a plate or an article of clothing—she will find that it, too, falls to the floor and can make the theory more general: "Objects pushed off the table fall to the floor."

Piaget also believed that at a few critical points in development children realize their theories have basic flaws. When this happens, they revise their theories radically. These changes are so fundamental that the revised theory is, in many respects, a brand new theory. Piaget claimed that radical revisions occurred three times in development: once at about age 2, a second time at about age 7, and a third time just before adolescence. These radical changes mean that children go through four distinct stages in cognitive development. Each stage represents a fundamental change in how children understand and organize their environment, and each stage is characterized by more sophisticated types of reasoning. For example, the sensorimotor stage begins at birth and lasts until about age 2. As the name implies, sensorimotor thinking is closely linked to the infant's sensory and motor skills. This stage and the three later stages are shown in the table.

## Piaget's Four Stages of Cognitive Development

| Stage | Approximate Age | Characteristics |
|---|---|---|
| Sensorimotor | Birth to 2 years | Infant's knowledge of the world is based on senses and motor skills. By the end of the period, infant uses mental representations. |
| Preoperational thought | 2 to 6 years | Child learns how to use symbols such as words and numbers to represent aspects of the world, but relates to the world only through his or her perspective. |
| Concrete operational thought | 7 to 11 years | Child understands and applies logical operations to experiences, provided they are focused on the here and now. |
| Formal operational thought | Adolescence and beyond | Adolescent or adult thinks abstractly, speculates on hypothetical situations, and reasons deductively about what may be possible. |

TABLE 1–2

Not all cognitive-developmental theorists view development as a sequence of stages. Information-processing theorists, for example, draw heavily on how computers work to explain thinking and how it develops through childhood and adolescence. **Just as computers consist of both hardware (disk drives, random-access memory, and a central processing unit) and software (the programs we use),** *information-processing theory* **proposes that human cognition consists of mental hardware and mental software.** Mental hardware refers to cognitive structures, including different memories where information is stored. Mental software includes organized sets of cognitive processes that allow children to complete specific tasks, such as reading a sentence, playing a video game, or hitting a baseball.

How do information-processing psychologists explain developmental change in thinking? To answer this question, think about improvements in personal computers. Today's personal computers can accomplish much more than a computer that was built just a few years ago. Why? Because today's computer has better hardware (for example, more memory and a faster central processing unit) and because it has more sophisticated software that takes advantage of the better hardware. Like modern computers, older children and adolescents have better hardware and better software than younger children, who are more like last year's out-of-date model. For example, older children typically can solve math word problems better than younger children because they have greater memory capacity to store the facts in the problem and because their methods for performing arithmetic operations are more efficient.

For both Piaget and information-processing theorists, children's thinking becomes more sophisticated as children develop. Piaget explains this change in terms of more sophisticated theories that children create; information-processing psychologists

> In the information-processing approach, cognitive development reflects change in mental hardware and mental software.

attribute it to more sophisticated mental hardware and mental software. Neither would have much to say to Betty about Marcus's good nature. As for his academic success, Piaget would explain that all children naturally want to understand their worlds; Marcus is simply unusually skilled in this regard. An information-processing psychologist would point to superior hardware and software as the keys to his academic success.

### The Contextual Perspective.

Most developmentalists agree that the environment is an important force in development. Traditionally, however, most theories of child development have emphasized environmental forces that affect children directly. Examples of direct environmental influences would be a parent praising a child, an older sibling teasing a younger one, and a nursery-school teacher discouraging girls from playing with trucks. These direct influences *are* important in children's lives, but in the contextual perspective they are one part of a much larger system, and no element of the system can act without influencing all other elements. This larger system includes one's parents and siblings as well as important individuals outside the family, such as extended family, friends, and teachers. The system also includes institutions that influence development, such as schools, television, the workplace, and a church or temple.

**All these people and institutions fit together to form a person's *culture*—the knowledge, attitudes, and behavior associated with a group of people.** Culture can refer to a particular country or people (e.g., French culture), to a specific point in time (e.g., popular culture of the 1990s), or to groups of individuals who maintain specific, identifiable cultural traditions (e.g., African Americans). A culture provides the context in which a child develops and thus is a source of many important influences on development throughout childhood and adolescence.

One of the first theorists to emphasize cultural context in children's development was Lev Vygotsky (1896–1934), shown in the top photo. A Russian psychologist, Vygotsky focused on ways that adults convey to children the beliefs, customs, and skills of their culture. Vygotsky believed that, because a fundamental aim of all societies is for children to acquire essential cultural values and skills, every aspect of a child's development must be considered against this backdrop.

Vygotsky was the first proponent of the contextual view, but Urie Bronfenbrenner (1917– ), shown in the bottom photo, is its best proponent today. Bronfenbrenner sees the developing child as embedded in a series of complex and interactive systems. As the diagram at the top of page 19 shows, Bronfenbrenner (1979; 1995; 1999) divides the environment into four levels: the microsystem, the mesosystem, the exosystem, and the macrosystem. **At any point in life, the *microsystem* consists of the people and objects in an individual's immediate environment.** These are the people closest to a child, such as parents or siblings. Some children have more than one microsystem; for example, a young child might have the microsystems of the family and of the day-care setting. As you can imagine, microsystems strongly influence development.

**Microsystems are connected to create the *mesosystem*.** The mesosystem represents the fact that what happens in one microsystem is likely to influence others. Perhaps you've found that if you have a stressful day at work or school you're grouchy at home. This indicates that your mesosystem is alive and well; your microsystems of home and work are emotionally interconnected for you.

The *exosystem* **refers to social settings that a person may not experience firsthand but that still influence development.** For example, a mother may pay more attention to her child when her work is going well and less attention when she's under a great deal of work-related stress. Although the influence of the exosystem is at least secondhand, its effects on the developing child can be quite strong.

The broadest environmental context is the *macrosystem*, **the subcultures and cultures in which the microsystem, mesosystem, and exosystem are embedded.** A mother, her workplace, her child, and the child's school are part of a larger cultural setting, such as Asian Americans living in southern California or Italian Americans living in large cities on the East Coast. Members of these cultural groups share a common identity, a common heritage, and common values. The macrosystem evolves over time; what is true about a particular culture today may or may not have been true in the past and may or may not be true in the future. Thus, each successive generation of children develops in a unique macrosystem.

FIG 1–1

Bronfenbrenner and other contextual theorists would agree with learning theorists in telling Betty that the environment has been pivotal in her son's amiable disposition and his academic achievements. However, the contextual theorist would insist that *environment* means much more than the reinforcements, punishments, and observations that are central to learning theory. The contextual theorist would emphasize the different levels of environmental influence on Marcus. Betty's ability to balance home and work so skillfully (which means that she is usually in a good mood herself) has contributed positively to Marcus's development, as has Betty's membership in a cultural group that values doing well in school.

In Bronfenbrenner's theory, the microsystem, the mesosystem, and the exosystem are different environmental systems embedded in the macrosystem.

## The Big Picture.
Comparing five major perspectives in eight pages is like trying to see all of the major sights of a large city in a day: It can be done, but it's demanding, and after a while everything blurs together. Relax. The table on page 20 gives a capsule account of all five perspectives and their important theories.

One way to highlight some similarities and differences in the perspectives is to relate them to the basic themes I described earlier. Let's think, for example, about the nature-nurture issue. Of the five perspectives, the biological is at one extreme in emphasizing the impact of nature; at the other extreme are the learning and contextual perspectives, which emphasize nurture.

The perspectives also see different degrees of "connectedness" across different domains of development. Piaget's cognitive-developmental theory takes the hardest line: Because children strive to have a single integrated theory to explain the world, cognitive and social growth are closely interconnected. That is, because children interpret all aspects of their lives with the same unified view of the world, everything is linked. The learning perspective, in contrast, holds that degree of connectedness

## Characteristics of Developmental Perspectives

| Perspective | Key Assumptions | Specific Theories |
|---|---|---|
| Biological | Development is determined primarily by biological forces. | *Maturational theory:* emphasizes development as a natural unfolding of a biological plan |
|  |  | *Ethological theory:* emphasizes the adaptive nature of behavior and the importance of experience during critical periods of development |
| Psychodynamic | Development is determined primarily by how a child resolves conflicts at different ages. | *Freud's theory:* emphasizes the conflict between primitive biological forces and societal standards for right and wrong |
|  |  | *Erikson's theory:* emphasizes the challenges posed by the formation of trust, autonomy, initiative, industry, and identity |
| Learning | Development is determined primarily by a child's environment. | *Skinner's operant conditioning:* emphasizes the role of reinforcement and punishment |
|  |  | *Bandura's social cognitive theory:* emphasizes children's efforts to understand their world, using reinforcement, punishment, and others' behavior |
| Cognitive-Developmental | Development reflects children's efforts to understand the world. | *Piaget's theory:* emphasizes the different stages of thinking that result from children's changing theories of the world |
|  |  | *Information-processing theory:* emphasizes changes in thinking that reflect changes in mental hardware and mental software |
| Contextual | Development is influenced by immediate and more distant environments, which typically influence each other. | *Vygotsky's theory:* emphasizes the role of parents (and other adults) in conveying culture to the next generation |
|  |  | *Bronfenbrenner's theory:* emphasizes the influences of the microsystem, mesosystem, exosystem, and macrosystem |

TABLE 1–3

depends entirely on the nature of environmental influences. Similar environmental influences in different domains of children's lives produce many connections; dissimilar environmental influences produce few connections.

We'll be referring to all these perspectives because no single perspective provides a truly complete explanation of all aspects of children's development. The cognitive-developmental perspective is useful for understanding how children's thinking changes as children grow older. The contextual and learning perspectives are particularly valuable in explaining how children's development is influenced by environmental forces such as parents, peers, schools, and culture. By drawing upon all the perspectives, we'll be better able to understand the different forces that contribute to children's development. Just as you can better appreciate a beautiful painting by examining it from different viewpoints, child development researchers often rely upon multiple perspectives to understand why children develop as they do.

The themes and the five theoretical perspectives will serve you well as we explore the field of child development. However, you need one more essential tool: You need to learn about the methods developmentalists use to conduct research. This is the topic of Module 1.3.

## Check Your Learning

**1.** The _____ issue concerns how early development relates to later development.

**2.** The extent to which children help to shape their own development is central to the _____ issue.

**3.** Ethological theorists claim that _____ is a time when a specific type of learning can take place.

**4.** The _____ perspective emphasizes the role of conflict in child development.

**5.** According to _____, development is linked to changes in mental hardware and mental software.

**6.** Vygotsky believed that a fundamental task for all cultures is _____.

> Of the five perspectives on development, which are most alike on the continuity-discontinuity issue? What about active-passive views of the child?

**Answers:** (1) continuity-discontinuity, (2) active-passive child, (3) a critical period, (4) psychodynamic, (5) the information-processing approach, (6) pass along beliefs, customs, and skills to children

# Doing Developmental Research

## Learning Objectives

**1.3**

Measurement in Child Development Research

General Designs for Research

Designs for Studying Development

Ethical Responsibilities

Communicating Research Results

● **How do scientists measure topics of interest in children's development?**

● **What general research designs are used in child development research? What designs are unique to child development research?**

● **What ethical procedures must researchers follow?**

● **How do researchers communicate results to other scientists?**

> *Leah and Joan are both mothers of 10-year-old boys. Their sons have many friends, but the bases for the friendships are not obvious to the mothers. Leah believes that "opposites attract"—children form friendships with peers who have complementary interests and abilities. Joan doubts this; her son seems to seek out other boys who are near clones of himself in their interests and abilities.*

Suppose that Leah and Joan know you're taking a course in child development, so they ask you to settle their argument. You know, from Module 1.2, that Leah and Joan each have simple theories about children's friendships. Leah's theory is that complementary children are more often friends, whereas Joan's theory is that similar children are more often friends. And you know that these theories should be tested with research. But how? In fact, child development researchers must make several important decisions as they prepare to study a topic. They need to decide how to measure the topic of interest; they must design their study; they must be sure their proposed research respects the rights of the individuals participating; and, once the study is complete, they must communicate their results to other researchers.

Child development researchers do not always stick to this sequence of steps. For example, often researchers consider the rights of research participants as they make each of the other decisions, perhaps rejecting a procedure because it violates the rights of research participants. Nevertheless, for simplicity, I will use this sequence as I describe the steps in doing developmental research.

## Measurement in Child Development Research

Research usually begins by deciding how to measure the topic or behavior of interest. For example, the first step toward answering Leah and Joan's question about friendships would be to decide how to measure friendships. Child development researchers typically use one of three approaches: observing systematically, using tasks to sample behavior, and asking children for self reports.

### Systematic Observation.

As the name implies, *systematic observation* involves watching children and carefully recording what they do or say. Two forms of systematic observation are common. In *naturalistic observation,* children are observed as they behave spontaneously in some real-life situation. Of course, researchers can't keep track of everything that a child does, so beforehand they must decide which variables—factors subject to change—to record. Researchers studying friendship might, for example, decide to observe children in a school lunchroom like the one in the photo. They would record where each child sits and who talks to whom. Further, they might decide to observe children at the start of the first year in a middle school because many children make new friends at this time.

In *structured observation,* the researcher creates a setting that is likely to elicit the behavior of interest. Structured observations are particularly useful for studying behaviors that are difficult to observe naturally. Some phenomena occur rarely, such as emergencies. An investigator using natural observations to study children's responses to emergencies wouldn't make much progress because, by definition, emergencies don't occur at predetermined times and locations. However, using structured observation, an investigator might stage an emergency, perhaps by having a nearby adult cry for help and observing children's response.

Other behaviors are difficult for researchers to observe because they occur in private settings, not public ones. For example, much interaction between friends takes place at home, where it would be difficult for investigators to observe unobtrusively. However, children who are friends could be asked to come to the researcher's laboratory, which might be furnished with comfortable chairs and tables. They would be asked to perform some activity typical of friends, such as playing a game or deciding what movie to see. By observing friends' interactions in a setting like the one in the photo at the top of page 23 (perhaps through a one-way mirror), researchers could learn more about how friends interact.

Though structured observations allow researchers to observe behavior(s) that would otherwise be difficult to study, investigators must be careful that the settings they create do not disturb the behavior of interest. For instance, observing friends as they play a game in a mock family room has many artificial aspects to it: The friends are not in their own homes, they were told (in general terms) what to do, and they know they're being observed. Any or all of these factors may cause children to behave differently than they would in the real world. Researchers must be careful that their method does not distort the behavior they are observing.

## Sampling Behavior with Tasks.

When investigators can't observe a behavior directly, an alternative is to create tasks that are thought to sample the behavior of interest. To measure memory, investigators sometimes use a digit span task: Children listen as a sequence of numbers is presented aloud. After the last digit is presented, children try to repeat the digits in order. To measure children's ability to recognize different emotions, investigators sometimes use the task shown in the diagram. The child has been asked to look at the photographs and point to the person who is happy.

Sampling behavior with tasks is popular with child development researchers because it is so convenient. A major problem with this approach, however, is whether the task really samples the behavior of interest. For example, asking children to judge emotions from photographs may not be valid because it underestimates what children do in real life. Can you think of reasons why this might be the case? I mention several reasons on page 31, just before "Check Your Learning."

FIG 1–2

## Self Reports.

The last approach to measurement, self reports, is actually a special case of using tasks to measure children's behavior. **Self reports are simply children's answers to questions about the topic of interest.** When questions are posed in written form, the report is a questionnaire; when questions are posed orally, the report is an interview. In either format, questions are created that probe different aspects of the topic of interest. For example, if you believe that children more often become friends when they have interests in common, then research participants might be told the following:

> *Tom and Dave just met each other at school. Tom likes to read, plays the clarinet in the school orchestra, and is not interested in sports; Dave likes to watch videos on MTV, tinkers with his car, and is a star on the football team. Do you think Tom and Dave will become friends?*

Children would decide, perhaps using a rating scale, whether the boys are likely to become friends.

Self reports are useful because they can lead directly to information on the topic of interest. They are also relatively convenient (particularly when they can be administered to groups of children). However, self reports are not always valid measures of children's behavior because children's answers may be inaccurate. Why? When asked about past events, children may not remember them accurately. For example, an adolescent asked about childhood friends may not remember those friendships well. Also, children sometimes answer incorrectly because of response bias; that is, some responses may be more socially acceptable than others, and children are more likely to select those responses than socially unacceptable answers. For example, many children would be reluctant to admit that they have no friends at all. But, as long as investigators keep these weaknesses in mind, self report is a valuable tool for child development research.

The three approaches to measurement are summarized in the table.

## Ways of Measuring Behavior in Child Development Research

| Method | Strength | Weakness |
|---|---|---|
| *Systematic observation* | | |
| Naturalistic observation | Captures children's behavior in its natural setting | Difficult to use with behaviors that are rare or that typically occur in private settings |
| Structured observation | Can be used to study behaviors that are rare or that typically occur in private settings | May be invalid if the structured setting distorts the behavior |
| *Sampling behavior with tasks* | Convenient—can be used to study most behaviors | May be invalid if the task does not sample behavior as it occurs naturally |
| *Self reports (questionnaires and interviews)* | Convenient—can be used to study most behaviors | May be invalid because children answer incorrectly because of forgetting or response bias |

TABLE 1–4

After researchers choose a method of measurement, they must show that it is both reliable and valid. **A measure is *reliable* if the results are consistent over time.** A measure of friendship, for example, would be reliable to the extent that it yields the same results about friendship each time it is administered. All measures used in child development research must be shown to be reliable or they cannot be used. **A measure is *valid* if it really measures what researchers think it measures.** For example, a measure of friendship is only valid if it can be shown to actually measure friendship (and not, for example, popularity).

Validity is often established by showing that the measure in question is closely related to another measure known to be valid. We could show the validity of a questionnaire that claims to measure friendship by showing that scores on the questionnaire are related to peers' and parents' measures of friendship. Because it is possible to have a measure that is reliable but not valid (e.g., a ruler reliably measures length but is not a valid measure of friendship), researchers must ensure that their measures are *both* reliable and valid.

Throughout this book, you'll come across many studies using these different methods. You'll also see that studies of the same topic or behavior often use different methods. That is because many topics can be studied in different ways. This is very desirable: Because the approaches to measurement have different strengths and weaknesses, finding the same results regardless of the approach leads to particularly strong conclusions. For example, if a researcher using self reports claimed that girls who are friends argue less than boys who are friends, it would be reassuring to know that other investigators have found the same result from systematic observation and sampling behavior with tasks.

### Representative Sampling.
Valid measures depend not only upon the method of measurement but also upon the children who are tested. **Researchers are usually interested in broad groups of children called *populations.*** Examples of populations would be all American 7-year-olds or all African American adolescents. **Virtually all studies include only a *sample* of children, which is a subset of the population.** Researchers must take care that their sample really is representative of the population of interest. An unrepresentative sample can lead to invalid research. For example, what would you think of a study of children's friendship if you learned that the sample consisted entirely of 8-year-olds who had no friends? You would, quite correctly, decide that this sample is not representative of the population of 8-year-olds and question its results.

> Researchers study samples of children to reach conclusions about larger populations.

As you read on, you'll discover that much of the research I describe was conducted with samples of middle-class European American youngsters. Are these samples representative of all children in the United States? Of all children in the world? Sometimes, but not always. Be careful not to assume that findings from this group necessarily apply to people in other groups.

## General Designs for Research

Having selected a way to measure the topic or behavior of interest, researchers must then put this measure into a research design. Child development researchers usually use one of two designs: correlational or experimental studies.

### Correlational Studies.
**In a *correlational study,* investigators look at relations between variables as they exist naturally in the world.** In the simplest possible correlational study, a researcher measures two variables, then sees how they are related. Imagine a researcher who wants to test the idea that smarter children have more friends. To test this claim, the researcher would measure two variables for each child in the sample. One would be the number of friends that the child has; the other would be the child's intelligence.

**The results of a correlational study are usually expressed as a *correlation coefficient,* abbreviated $r$, which stands for the strength and direction of a relation between two variables.** Correlations can range from $-1.0$ to $0$ to $+1.0$:

- When $r = 0$, two variables are completely unrelated: Children's intelligence is unrelated to the number of friends they have.
- When $r$ is greater than $0$, scores are related positively: Children who are smart tend to have more friends than children who are not as smart. That is, more intelligence is associated with having more friends.
- When $r$ is less than $0$, scores are related, but inversely: Children who are smart tend to have fewer friends than children who are not as smart. That is, more intelligence is associated with having fewer friends.

The results of a correlational study tell whether variables are related, but this design doesn't address the question of cause and effect between the variables. In other words, suppose a researcher finds that the correlation between intelligence and number of friends is .7. This means that children who are smarter have more friends than those who are not as smart. How would you interpret this correlation? The diagram shows that three interpretations are possible. Maybe being smart causes children to have more friends. Another interpretation is that having more friends causes children to be smarter. A third interpretation is that neither variable causes the other; instead, intelligence and number of friends are caused by a third variable that was not measured in the study. Perhaps parents who are warm and supportive tend to have children who are smarter and also have many friends. Any of these interpretations could be true. Cause and effect cannot be distinguished in a correlational study. When investigators want to track down causes, they must use a different design, an experimental study.

### Three Interpretations of a Correlation Coefficient

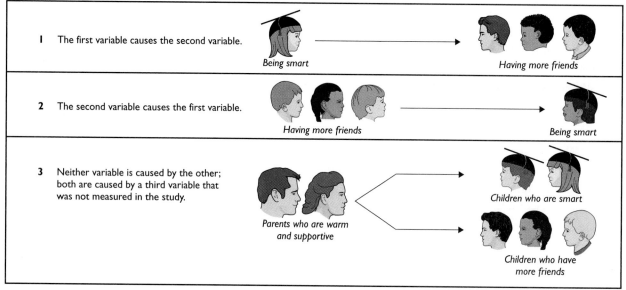

1. The first variable causes the second variable.

*Being smart* → *Having more friends*

2. The second variable causes the first variable.

*Having more friends* → *Being smart*

3. Neither variable is caused by the other; both are caused by a third variable that was not measured in the study.

*Parents who are warm and supportive* → *Children who are smart* / *Children who have more friends*

FIG 1–3

### Experimental Studies.

An *experiment* is a systematic way of manipulating the key factor(s) that an investigator thinks causes a particular behavior. The factor that is manipulated is called the *independent variable;* the behavior that is measured is called the *dependent variable.* In an experiment, the investigator begins with one or more treatments, circumstances, or events (independent variables) that are thought to affect a particular behavior. Children are then assigned randomly to different groups. Next, the dependent variable is measured in all groups. Because each child has an equal chance of being assigned to any group (the definition of random assignment), the groups should be the same except in the treatment they receive. Any differences between the groups can then be attributed to the differential treatment the children received in the experiment, rather than to other factors.

Suppose, for example, an investigator believes that children share more with friends than with children they do not know. The diagram on page 27 shows how the investigator might test this hypothesis. Based on random assignment, some fifth-grade children would be asked to come to the investigator's laboratory with a good friend. Other fifth-graders would come to the laboratory site without a friend and be paired with a child unknown to them. The laboratory itself would be decorated to look like a family room in a house. The investigator would create a task in which one child is given an interesting toy to play with but the other child receives nothing. The experimenter then claims that she needs to leaves the room briefly. Actually, the experimenter goes to a room with a one-way mirror and observes whether the child with the toy offers to share it with the other child.

This same scenario would be used with all pairs of children: The room and toy would be the same and the experimenter would always be away for the same amount of time. The circumstances would be held as constant as possible for all children except that some children participate with friends whereas others do not. If children who participated with friends give the toy more quickly or more readily to the other child, the investigator could say with confidence that children are more likely to share with their friends than with children they don't know. Conclusions about cause and effect are possible because there was a direct manipulation of an independent variable (participating with a friend or with an unknown child) under controlled conditions.

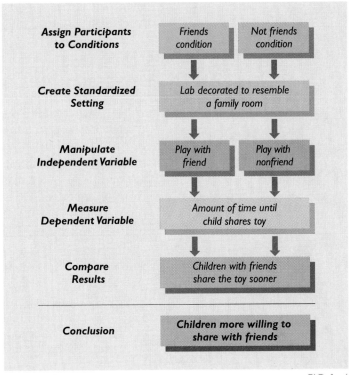

FIG 1–4

Child development researchers usually conduct their experiments in laboratory-like settings to control all the variables that might influence the outcome of the research. A shortcoming of laboratory work is that the behavior of interest is not studied in its natural setting. Consequently, there is always the potential problem that the results may be invalid because they are artificial—specific to the laboratory setting and not representative of the behavior in the "real world."

Both research designs used by developmentalists—correlational and experimental—have strengths and weaknesses. There is no one best method. Consequently, no single investigation can definitely answer a question, and researchers rarely rely on one study or even one method to reach conclusions. Instead, they prefer to find converging evidence from as many different kinds of studies as possible. Suppose, for example, our hypothetical experiment showed that children did, indeed, share more readily with their friends. One way to be more confident of this conclusion would be to do correlational research, perhaps by observing children during lunch and measuring how often they share food with different people.

> Unlike correlational studies, experimental studies allow conclusions about cause and effect.

## Designs for Studying Development

Sometimes child development research is directed at a single age group, such as fifth-grade children in the experiment on sharing between friends and non-friends. Or researchers might study mother-infant relationships in 1-year-olds or memory in preschool-age children. When this is the case, after deciding how to measure the behavior of interest and whether the study will be correlational or experimental, the investigator can skip directly to the last step and determine if the study is ethical. However, much research in child development concerns changes that occur as children develop over a period of time. In these cases, investigators must make one further decision: Will they do a longitudinal study or a cross-sectional study?

Longitudinal Studies. **In a *longitudinal study,* the same individuals are observed or tested repeatedly at different points in their lives.** As the name implies, the longitudinal approach takes a lengthwise view of development and is the most direct way to watch growth occur. In a longitudinal study children might be tested first at age 5 and then again at 7 and 9 years. The longitudinal approach is well suited to studying almost any aspect of development. More important, it is the only way to answer certain questions about the continuity or discontinuity of behavior: Will characteristics such as aggression, dependency, or mistrust observed in infancy or early childhood persist into adulthood? Will a traumatic event such as being abandoned by one's parents influence later social and intellectual development? How long will the beneficial effects of special academic training in the preschool years last? Such questions can be explored only by testing children early in development and then retesting them later in their development.

The longitudinal approach, however, has disadvantages that frequently offset its strengths. An obvious one is cost: The expense of merely keeping up with a large sample of individuals can be staggering. A related problem is the constancy of the sample over the course of research. It is difficult to maintain contact with children over several years in a highly mobile society. And even among those who do not move away, some lose interest and choose not to continue. These "dropouts" are often significantly different from their more research-minded peers, and this fact alone may distort the outcome. For example, a group of children may seem to show intellectual growth between ages 4 and 7. What has actually happened, however, is that those who found earlier testing most difficult are the very ones who have quit the study, thereby raising the group average on the next round.

> Only longitudinal studies can answer questions about the continuity of behavior over development.

Even when the sample remains constant, the fact that children are given the same test many times may make them "test-wise." Improvement over time that is attributed to development may actually stem from practice with a particular test. Changing the test from year to year solves the practice problem but raises the question of how to compare responses to different tests. Because of these and other problems with the longitudinal method, child development researchers often use cross-sectional studies instead.

Cross-sectional Studies. **In a *cross-sectional study,* developmental changes are identified by testing children of different ages at one point in their development.** In other words, a researcher might chart the differences in some attribute between, say, 5-, 7-, and 9-year-olds. The cross-sectional approach avoids almost all the problems associated with repeated testing, including costly record keeping and sample loss. But cross-sectional research has its own weaknesses. Because children are tested at only one point in their development, we learn nothing about the continuity of development. Consequently, we cannot tell if an aggressive 4-year-old remains aggressive at age 10 because a child would be tested at age 4 or age 10, but not at both ages.

**Cross-sectional studies are also affected by *cohort effects,* meaning that differences between age groups (cohorts) may result as much from environmental events as from developmental processes.** In a simple cross-sectional study, we compare children from two age groups. If we find differences, we attribute them to the difference in age, but this needn't be the case. Why? The cross-sectional study assumes that when the older children were younger, they were like children in the younger age group. This isn't always true. Suppose, for example, that a researcher measures creativity in 8- and 14-year-olds. If the 8-year-olds are found to be more imaginative than the 14-year-olds, should we conclude that imagination declines between these ages? Not necessarily. Perhaps a new curriculum to nourish creativity was introduced in kindergarten and first grade, before the 8-year-olds entered these grades but after the older children had completed them. Because only the younger children experienced the curriculum, the difference between them is difficult to interpret.

Each of the two general research designs can be used with either of the two designs that are unique to studying development. When combined, four prototypic designs result: cross-sectional correlational studies, cross-sectional experimental studies, longitudinal correlational studies, and longitudinal experimental studies.

The different designs are summarized in the table. In this book, you'll read about studies using these various designs, although the two cross-sectional designs will show up more frequently than the two longitudinal designs. Why? For most developmentalists, the ease of cross-sectional studies compared to longitudinal studies more than compensates for the limitations of cross-sectional studies.

## Summary of Designs Used in Child Development Research

| Type of Design | Definition | Strengths | Weaknesses |
|---|---|---|---|
| **General Designs** | | | |
| Correlational | Observe variables as they exist in the world and determine their relations | Behavior is measured as it occurs naturally | Cannot determine cause and effect |
| Experimental | Manipulate independent and dependent variables | Control of variables allows conclusions about cause and effect | Work is often laboratory-based, which can be artificial |
| **Developmental Designs** | | | |
| Longitudinal | One group of children is tested repeatedly as they develop | Only way to chart an individual's development and look at the continuity of behavior over time | Expensive, participants drop out, and repeated testing can distort performance |
| Cross-sectional | Children of different ages are tested at the same time | Convenient—solves all problems associated with longitudinal studies | Cannot study continuity of behavior; cohort effects complicate interpretation of differences between groups |

TABLE 1–5

## Ethical Responsibilities

Having selected a way of measuring the behavior of interest and chosen appropriate general and developmental designs, one very important step remains. Researchers must determine whether their research is ethical, that it does not violate the rights of the children who participate. Professional organizations and government agencies have codes of conduct that specify the rights of research participants and procedures to protect those participants. The following guidelines are included in all those codes:

- *Minimize risks to research participants:* Use methods that have the least potential for harm or stress for research participants. During the research, monitor the procedures to be sure to avoid any unforeseen stress or harm.

- *Describe the research to potential participants so they can determine if they wish to participate:* Prospective research participants should be told all details of the research so they can make an informed decision about participating. Children are minors and are not legally capable of giving consent; consequently, as shown in the photograph, researchers must describe the study to parents and ask them for permission for their children to participate.

- *Avoid deception; if participants must be deceived, provide a thorough explanation of the true nature of the research as soon as possible:* Providing complete information about a study in advance can sometimes bias or distort participants' responses. Consequently, investigators sometimes provide only partial information or even mislead participants about the true purpose of the study. As soon as it is feasible—typically just after the experiment—any false information must be corrected and the reasons for the deception must be provided.

- *Keep results anonymous or confidential:* Research results should be anonymous, which means that participants' data cannot be linked to their name. When anonymity is not possible, research results should be confidential, which means that the identities of the individuals are known only to the investigator conducting the study.

Ethical research minimizes risk and deception, allows individuals to decide if they want to participate, and keeps results confidential.

Researchers must convince review boards consisting of scientists from many disciplines that they have carefully addressed each of these ethical points. Only then can they begin their study. If the review board objects to some aspects of the proposed study, the researcher must revise those aspects and present them anew for the review board's approval.

### Communicating Research Results

When the study is complete and the data analyzed, researchers write a report of their work. This report describes, in great detail, what the researchers did and why, their results, and the meaning(s) behind their results. The researchers submit the report to one of several scientific journals that specialize in child development research, such as *Child Development, Developmental Psychology,* and *Journal of Experimental Child Psychology.* If the editor of the journal accepts the report, it appears in the journal where other child development researchers can learn of the results.

These reports of research are the basis for virtually all the information I present in this book. As you read, you'll see names in parentheses, followed by a date, like this:

(Levine, 1983).

This indicates the person who did the research and the year it was published. By looking in the References, which begin on page 461 and are organized alphabetically, you can find the title of the article and the journal where it was published.

Maybe all these different steps in research seem tedious and involved to you. For a child development researcher, however, much of the fun of doing research is planning a novel study that will provide useful information to other specialists. This is one of the most creative and challenging parts of child development research.

The "Focus on Research" features that appear in each chapter of this book are designed to convey both the creativity and the challenge of doing child development research. Each feature focuses on a specific study. Some are studies that have just recently been published; others are classics that defined a new area of investigation or provided definitive results in some area. In each "Focus" feature, I trace the decisions that researchers made as they planned their study. In the process, you'll see the ingenuity of researchers as they pursue questions of child development. You'll also see that any individual study has limitations. Only when all the converging evidence from many studies—each using a unique combination of measurement methods and designs—points to the same conclusion can we feel confident about research results.

*Responses to question on p. 23 about using photographs to measure children's understanding of emotions:* Children's understanding of emotions depicted in photographs may be less accurate than in real life because (1) in real life, facial features are usually moving—not still as in the photographs—and movement may be one of the clues that children naturally use to judge emotions; (2) in real life, facial expressions are often accompanied by sounds, and children use both sight and sound to understand emotion; and (3) in real life, children most often judge facial expressions of people they know (parents, siblings, peers, teachers), and knowing the "usual" appearance of a face may help children determine emotions accurately.

## Check Your Learning

1. In _____, children are observed as they behave spontaneously in a real-life setting.

2. A problem with _____ is that children may give distorted answers because of response bias.

3. A _____ is a group of individuals considered representative of some larger population.

4. In a _____, investigators look at relations between variables as they exist naturally.

5. The _____ variable is measured in an experiment in order to evaluate the impact of the variable that was manipulated.

6. Researchers must submit their plans for research to a review board that determines if the research _____.

Suppose that you wanted to determine the impact of divorce on children's academic achievement. What would be the merits of correlational versus experimental research on this topic? How would a longitudinal study differ from a cross-sectional study?

**Answers:** (1) naturalistic observation, (2) self report, (3) sample, (4) correlational study, (5) dependent, (6) preserves the rights of research participants

## See for Yourself

A good first step toward learning about child development research is to read the reports of research that scientists publish in journals. Visit your library and locate some of the child development journals that I mentioned on page 30. Look at the contents of an issue to get an idea of the many different topics that child development researchers study. When you find an article on a topic that interests you, skim the contents and try to determine what design the investigator(s) used. See for yourself!

## Resources

*For more information about . . .*

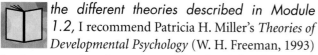 the different theories described in Module *1.2*, I recommend Patricia H. Miller's *Theories of Developmental Psychology* (W. H. Freeman, 1993) for its comprehensive account of each of the theoretical perspectives.

 research in child development, visit the Web site of the Society for Research in Child Development (SRCD)
**http://www.srcd.org**

## Key Terms

active-passive child issue 10
cohort effects 28
continuity-discontinuity issue 9
correlation coefficient 25
correlational study 25
critical period 12
cross-sectional study 28
culture 18
dependent variable 26
ego 13
ethological theory 12
exosystem 19
experiment 26
id 13

imitation (observational learning) 15
imprinting 12
independent variable 26
information-processing theory 17
longitudinal study 28
macrosystem 19
maturational theory 12
mesosystem 18
microsystem 18
naturalistic observation 22
nature-nurture issue 10
operant conditioning 15
population 25
psychodynamic theory 13

psychosocial theory 13
punishment 15
reinforcement 15
reliability 24
sample 25
self-efficacy 16
self reports 23
social cognitive theory 15
structured observation 22
superego 13
systematic observation 22
theoretical perspective 11
theory 11
validity 24

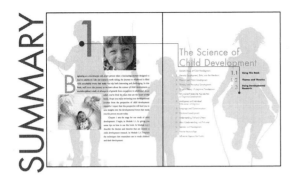

# SUMMARY

## 1.1 Using This Book

### The Modular Format
Each chapter includes three or four modules that begin with learning objectives, a vignette, and a mini-outline. In the text, key terms and their definitions appear in boldface type. Each module includes a special feature that examines a specific topic in depth. The module ends with questions that allow you to check your learning. Each chapter ends with several elements that should encourage you to think about the information in the chapter as well as a summary like the one you're reading now.

### Terminology
I use specific terms to refer to people of different ages: *newborn, infant, toddler, preschooler, school-age child, adolescent,* and *adult.* Also, when describing different ethnic groups, I use terms that identify the unique cultural heritage of each: *African American, Asian American, European American, Hispanic American,* and *Native American.*

### Organization
The book is organized around the topics that child development researchers investigate in their studies. Chapters 2–5 address biological, perceptual, and motor development. Chapters 6–9 cover intellectual development. Chapters 10–15 concern social and emotional development.

## 1.2 Themes and Theories

### Themes in Child Development Research
Four themes help unify the findings from child development research that are presented throughout this book: 1. Early development is related to later development but not perfectly. 2. Development is always jointly influenced by heredity and environment. 3. Children help determine their own development. 4. Development in different domains is connected.

### Theories of Child Development
Theories are important because they provide the explanations for development. Traditionally, five broad theoretical perspectives have guided researchers. According to the biological perspective, development is determined primarily by biological forces. According to the psychodynamic perspective, development is shaped by conflicts that arise at different ages. The learning perspective emphasizes the role of reward and punishment as well as the role of observing and inter-

preting others' behavior. The cognitive-developmental perspective emphasizes how thinking changes as children grow. According to contextual theories, development is influenced by cultural contexts, which include both immediate and more distant environments. No single perspective is entirely correct; instead, each explains some aspects of development well. We will draw upon each perspective throughout the book.

## 1.3 Doing Developmental Research

### Measurement in Child Development Research
Research typically begins by determining how to measure the topic of interest. Systematic observation involves recording children's behavior as it takes place, either in a natural environment (naturalistic observation) or in a structured setting (structured observation). Researchers sometimes create tasks to obtain samples of children's behavior. In self reports, children answer questions posed by the experimenter. Researchers must also obtain a sample that is representative of some larger population.

### General Designs for Research
In correlational studies, investigators examine relations between variables as they occur naturally. This relation is measured by a correlation coefficient, $r$, which can vary from −1 (strong negative relation) to 0 (no relation) to +1 (strong positive relation). Correlational studies cannot determine cause and effect, so researchers do experimental studies in which they manipulate an independent variable to determine the impact on a dependent variable. Experimental studies allow conclusions about cause and effect, but the strict control of all possible variables often makes the situation artificial. The best approach is to use both experimental and correlational studies to provide converging evidence.

### Designs for Studying Development
To study development, some researchers use a longitudinal design in which the same children are observed repeatedly as they grow. This approach provides evidence of actual patterns of individual growth but has several shortcomings: It is time-consuming and expensive, some children drop out of the project, and repeated testing can affect performance. The cross-sectional design involves testing children in different age groups. This design avoids the problems of the longitudinal design but provides no information about individual growth. Also, what appear to be differences due to age may be cohort effects. Because neither design is problem-free, the best approach is to use both to provide converging evidence.

### Ethical Responsibilities
Planning research also involves selecting methods that preserve the rights of research participants. Experimenters must minimize the risks to potential research participants, describe the research so that potential participants can decide if they want to participate, avoid deception, and keep results anonymous or confidential.

### Communicating Research Results
Once research data are collected and analyzed, investigators publish the results in scientific journals where they can be read and criticized by others. Such results form the foundation of scientific knowledge about child development.

**2.1**

I wish I had a dollar for every time my parents or in-laws said about one of my children, "He (or she) comes by that naturally." The usual prompt for their comment is that the child has just done something exactly as I or my wife did at the same age. By their remarks, grand-parents are reminding us that some behavioral characteristics are inherited from parents just as physical characteristics like height and hair color are inherited.

In this chapter, we'll see how heredity influences children and their development. We'll start, in Module 2.1, by examining the basic mechanisms of heredity. In Module 2.2, we'll focus on disorders that some children inherit. Finally, in Module 2.3, we'll see how the environment is crucial in determining how heredity influences development.

# Genetic Bases of Child Development

# 2.1

**The Biology of Heredity**

**Single Gene Inheritance**

**Behavioral Genetics**

## Mechanisms of Heredity

### Learning Objectives

● **What are chromosomes and genes?**

● **What are dominant and recessive traits? How are they inherited?**

● **How does heredity influence behavioral and psychological development?**

*Leslie and Glenn have decided to try to have a baby. They are thrilled at the thought of starting their own family but also worried because Leslie's grandfather had sickle cell disease and died when he was just 20 years old. Leslie is terrified that their baby could inherit the disease that killed her grandfather. Leslie and Glenn wish someone could reassure them that their baby will be okay.*

How could we reassure Leslie and Glenn? For starters, we need to know more about sickle cell disease. Red blood cells like the ones in the left photo carry oxygen and carbon dioxide to and from the body. When a person has sickle cell disease, the

red blood cells look like those in the right photo—long and curved like a sickle: These stiff, misshapen cells can't pass through small capillaries, so oxygen can't reach all parts of the body. The trapped sickle cells also block the way of white blood cells that are the body's natural defense against bacteria. As a result, people with sickle cell disease—including Leslie's grandfather and many other African Americans, who are more prone to this painful disease than other groups—often die from infections before age 20.

Sickle cell disease is inherited. Because Leslie's grandfather had the disorder, it apparently runs in her family. Would Leslie's baby inherit the disease? To answer this question, we need to examine the mechanisms of heredity.

### The Biology of Heredity

The teaspoon of semen released into the vagina during an ejaculation contains from 200 million to 500 million sperm. Only a few hundred of these actually complete the 6- or 7-inch journey to the fallopian tubes. If an egg is present, many sperm simultaneously begin to burrow their way through the cluster of nurturing cells that surround the egg. When a sperm like the one in the photo penetrates the cellular wall of the egg, chemical changes that occur immediately block out all other sperm. **Each egg and sperm cell contains 23 *chromosomes*, tiny structures in the nucleus that contain genetic material.** When a sperm penetrates an egg, their chromosomes combine to produce 23 pairs of chromosomes. The development of a new human being is under way.

For most of history, the merging of sperm and egg took place only after sexual intercourse. No longer. In 1978, Louise Brown captured the world's attention as the first test-tube baby conceived in a laboratory dish instead of in her mother's body. Today, this reproductive technology is no longer experimental; it is a multibillion-dollar business in the United States (Beck, 1994). Many new techniques are available to couples who cannot conceive a child through sexual intercourse. **The best known, *in vitro fertilization,* involves mixing sperm and egg together in a laboratory dish and then placing several fertilized eggs in the mother's uterus.** The photo shows this laboratory version of conception, with the sperm in the dropper being placed in the dish containing the eggs. If the eggs are fertilized, in about 24 hours they are placed in the mother's uterus, with the hope that they will become implanted in the wall of her uterus.

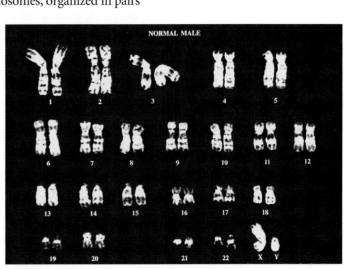

The sperm and egg usually come from the prospective parents, but sometimes they are provided by donors. Occasionally the fertilized egg is placed in the uterus of a surrogate mother who carries the baby throughout pregnancy. Thus, a baby could have as many as five "parents": the man and woman who provide the sperm and egg, the surrogate mother who carries the baby, and the mother and father who rear the child.

New reproductive techniques offer hope for couples who have long wanted a child, but there are difficulties. Only about 20 percent of attempts at in vitro fertilization succeed. Moreover, when a woman becomes pregnant, she is more likely to have twins or triplets because multiple eggs are transferred to increase the odds that at least one fertilized egg will implant in the mother's uterus. These problems emphasize that, although technology has increased the alternatives for infertile couples, pregnancy on demand is still in the realm of science fiction.

Whatever the source of the egg and sperm, and wherever they meet, their merger is a momentous event: The resulting 23 pairs of chromosomes define a child's heredity—what he or she "will do naturally." For Leslie and Glenn, this moment also determines whether or not their child inherits sickle cell disease.

To understand how heredity influences child development, let's begin by taking a closer look at chromosomes. The photo shows all 46 chromosomes, organized in pairs ranging from the largest to the smallest. **The first 22 pairs of chromosomes are called *autosomes;* the chromosomes in each pair are about the same size.** In the 23rd pair, however, the chromosome labeled X is much larger than the chromosome labeled Y. **The 23rd pair determines the sex of the child; hence, these two are known as the *sex chromosomes.*** An egg always contains an X 23rd chromosome, but a sperm contains either an X or a Y. When an X-carrying sperm fertilizes the egg, the 23rd pair is XX and the result is a girl. When a Y-carrying sperm fertilizes the egg, the 23rd pair is XY and the result is a boy.

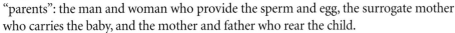

**Each chromosome actually consists of one molecule of *deoxyribonucleic acid*—DNA for short.** The DNA molecule resembles a spiral staircase. As you can

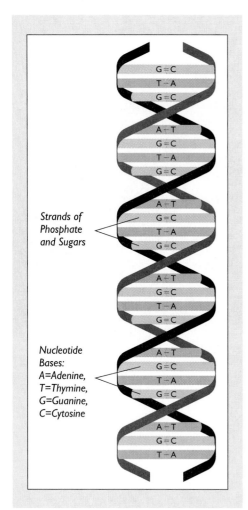

Strands of Phosphate and Sugars

Nucleotide Bases:
A=Adenine,
T=Thymine,
G=Guanine,
C=Cytosine

FIG 2–1

see in the diagram, the rungs of the staircase carry the genetic code, which consists of pairs of nucleotide bases: Adenine is paired with thymine, and guanine is paired with cytosine. The order of the nucleotide pairs is the code that causes the cell to create specific amino acids, proteins, and enzymes—important biological building blocks. **Each group of nucleotide bases that provides a specific set of biochemical instructions is a** *gene.* For example, three consecutive thymine nucleotides is the instruction to create the amino acid phenylalanine.

Altogether, a child's 46 chromosomes include roughly 100,000 genes. Through biochemical instructions that are coded in DNA, genes regulate the development of all human characteristics and abilities. **The complete set of genes makes up a person's heredity and is known as the person's** *genotype.* Genetic instructions, in conjunction with environmental influences, produce a *phenotype,* an individual's physical, behavioral, and psychological features.

In the rest of this module, we'll see the different ways that instructions contained in genes produce different phenotypes.

## Single Gene Inheritance

How do genetic instructions produce the misshapen red blood cells of sickle cell disease? **Genes come in different forms that are known as** *alleles.* In the case of red blood cells, for example, two alleles can be present on chromosome 11. One allele has instructions for normal red blood cells; another allele has instructions for sickle-shaped red blood cells. **The alleles in the pair of chromosomes are sometimes the same, which makes them** *homozygous.* **The alleles sometimes differ, which makes them** *heterozygous.* In Leslie's case, her baby could be homozygous, in which case it would have two alleles for normal cells or two alleles for sickle-shaped cells. Leslie's baby might also be heterozygous, which means that it would have one allele for normal cells and one for sickle-shaped cells.

How does a genotype produce a phenotype? The answer is simple if a person is homozygous. When both alleles are the same and therefore have chemical instructions for the same phenotype, that phenotype results. If Leslie's baby had alleles for normal red blood cells on both of the chromosomes in its 11th pair, the baby would be almost guaranteed to have normal cells. If, instead, the baby had two alleles for sickle-shaped cells, her baby would almost certainly suffer from the disease.

When a person is heterozygous, the process is more complex. **Often one allele is** *dominant,* **which means that its chemical instructions are followed whereas instructions of the other, the** *recessive* **allele, are ignored.** In the case of sickle cell disease, the allele for normal cells is dominant and the allele for sickle-shaped cells is recessive. This is good news for Leslie: As long as either she or Glenn contribute the allele for normal red blood cells, her baby will not develop sickle cell disease.

The diagram at the top of page 39 summarizes what we've learned about sickle cell disease. The letter *A* denotes the allele for normal blood cells, and *a* denotes the allele for sickle-shaped cells. In the diagram, Glenn's genotype is homozygous dominant because he's positive that no one in his family has had sickle cell disease. From Leslie's family history, she could be homozygous dominant or

*Genotype refers to a child's hereditary makeup. Phenotype refers to the physical, behavioral, and psychological characteristics that result when a genotype is exposed to a specific environment.*

heterozygous; in the diagram, I've assumed the latter. You can see that Leslie and Glenn cannot have a baby with sickle cell disease. However, their baby might be affected in another way. **Sometimes one allele does not dominate another completely, a situation known as** *incomplete dominance.* In incomplete dominance, the phenotype that results often falls between the phenotype associated with either allele. This is the case for the genes that control red blood cells. **Individuals with one dominant and one recessive allele have** *sickle cell trait:* **In most situations they have no problems, but when they are seriously short of oxygen they suffer a temporary, relatively mild form of the disease.** Thus, sickle cell trait is likely to appear when the person exercises vigorously or is at high altitudes (Sullivan, 1987). Leslie and Glenn's baby would have sickle cell trait if it inherited a recessive gene from Leslie and a dominant gene from Glenn.

One aspect of sickle cell disease that we haven't considered so far is why this disorder primarily affects African American children. The "Cultural Influences" feature addresses this point and, in the process, tells more about how heredity operates.

FIG 2–2

### Why Do African Americans Inherit Sickle Cell Disease?

Sickle cell disease affects about 1 in 400 African American children. In contrast, virtually no European American children have the disorder. Why? Surprisingly, because the sickle cell allele has a benefit: Individuals with this allele are more resistant to malaria, an infectious disease that is one of the leading causes of childhood death worldwide. Malaria is transmitted by mosquitos, so it is most common in warm climates, including many parts of Africa. Compared to Africans who have alleles for normal blood cells, Africans with the sickle cell allele are less likely to die from malaria, which means that the sickle cell allele is passed along to the next generation.

This explanation of sickle cell disease has two implications. First, sickle cell disease should be found in any group of people living where malaria is common. In fact, sickle cell disease affects Hispanic Americans who trace their roots to malaria-prone regions of the Caribbean, Central America, and South America. Second, malaria is rare in the United States, which means that the sickle cell allele has no survival value to African Americans. Accordingly, the sickle cell allele should become less common in successive generations of African Americans, and research indicates that this is happening.

There is an important general lesson here. The impact of heredity depends on the environment. An allele may have survival value in one environment but not in others. ●

The simple genetic mechanism responsible for sickle cell disease, involving a single gene pair with one dominant allele and one recessive allele, is also responsible for many other common traits, as shown in the table on page 40. In each case, individuals with the recessive phenotype have two recessive alleles, one from each parent. Individuals with the dominant phenotype have at least one dominant allele.

You'll notice that the table includes many biological and medical phenotypes but lacks behavioral and psychological phenotypes. Behavioral and psychological characteristics can be inherited, but the genetic mechanism is more elaborate, as we'll see in the next section.

| Some Common Phenotypes Associated with Single Pairs of Genes | |
| --- | --- |
| **Dominant Phenotype** | **Recessive Phenotype** |
| Curly hair | Straight hair |
| Normal hair | Pattern baldness (men) |
| Dark hair | Blond hair |
| Thick lips | Thin lips |
| Cheek dimples | No dimples |
| Normal hearing | Some types of deafness |
| Normal vision | Nearsightedness |
| Farsightedness | Normal vision |
| Normal color vision | Red-green color blindness |
| Type A blood | Type O blood |
| Type B blood | Type O blood |
| Rh-positive blood | Rh-negative blood |

Source: McKusick, 1995.

TABLE 2–1

## Behavioral Genetics

*behavioral genetics* **is the branch of genetics that deals with inheritance of behavioral and psychological traits.** Behavioral genetics is complex, in part because behavioral and psychological phenotypes are complex. The traits controlled by single genes usually represent "either-or" phenotypes. That is, the genotypes are usually associated with two (or sometimes three) well-defined phenotypes. For example, a person either has normal color vision or has red-green color blindness; a person has blood that clots normally, has sickle cell trait, or has sickle cell disease.

Most important behavioral and psychological characteristics are not either-or cases but represent an entire range of different outcomes. Take extroversion as an example. You probably know a few extremely outgoing individuals and a few intensely shy persons, but most of your friends and acquaintances are somewhere in between. Classifying your friends would produce a distribution of individuals across a continuum, from extreme extroversion at one end to extreme introversion at the other.

Many behavioral and psychological characteristics are distributed in this fashion, including intelligence and many aspects of personality. **When phenotypes reflect the combined activity of many separate genes, the pattern is known as** *polygenic inheritance.* Because so many genes are involved in polygenic inheritance, we usually cannot trace the effects of each gene. But we can use a hypothetical example to show how many genes work together to produce a behavioral phenotype that spans a continuum. Let's suppose that four pairs of genes contribute to extroversion, that the allele for extroversion is dominant, and that the total amount of extroversion is simply the sum of the dominant alleles. If we continue to use upper-case letters to represent dominant alleles and lower-case letters to represent the recessive allele, the four gene pairs would be *Aa, Bb, Cc,* and *Dd.*

> Many behavioral and psychological characteristics reflect polygenic inheritance in which the phenotype depends on the combined action of many separate genes.

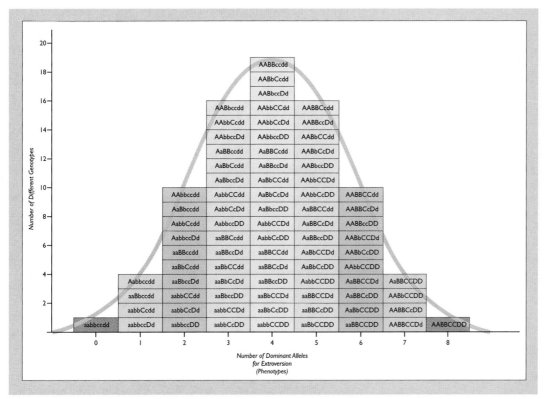

FIG 2–3

These four pairs of genes produce 81 different genotypes and 9 distinct phenotypes. For example, a person with the genotype *AABBCCDD* has 8 alleles for extroversion (a party animal). A person with the genotype *aabbccdd* has no alleles for extroversion (a wallflower). All other genotypes involve some combinations of dominant and recessive alleles, so these are associated with phenotypes representing intermediate levels of extroversion. In fact, the diagram shows that the most common outcome is for people to inherit exactly 4 dominant and 4 recessive alleles: 19 of the 81 genotypes produce this pattern (e.g., *AABbccDd, aaBbcCDd*). A few extreme cases (very outgoing or very shy), when coupled with many intermediate cases, produce the familiar bell-shaped distribution that characterizes many behavioral and psychological traits.

Remember, this example is completely hypothetical. Extroversion is not based on the combined influence of eight pairs of genes. I merely want to show how several genes working together could produce a continuum of phenotypes. Something like our example is probably involved in the inheritance of numerous human behavioral traits, except that many more pairs of genes are involved and the environment also influences the phenotype (Plomin et al., 1997).

**Methods of Behavioral Genetics.**   If many behavioral phenotypes involve countless genes, how can we hope to unravel the influence of heredity? Twins provide some important clues. **Identical twins are called *monozygotic twins* because they come from a single fertilized egg that splits in two.** Because identical twins come from the same fertilized egg, they have the same genes that control body structure, height, and facial features, which explains why identical twins like those in the photo look alike. **In contrast, fraternal or *dizygotic twins***

**come from two separate eggs fertilized by two separate sperm.** Genetically, fraternal twins are just like any other siblings; on average, about half their genes are the same. In twin studies, scientists compare identical and fraternal twins to measure the influence of heredity. If identical twins are more alike than fraternal twins, this implicates heredity.

An example will help illustrate the logic underlying comparisons of identical and fraternal twins. Suppose we want to determine whether extroversion is inherited. We would first measure extroversion in a large number of identical and fraternal twins. We might use a questionnaire with scores ranging from 0 to 100 (100 indicating maximal extroversion). Some of the results are shown in the table.

## Twins' Scores on a Measure of Extroversion

| Fraternal Twins | | | Identical Twins | | |
|---|---|---|---|---|---|
| Family | One Twin | Other Twin | Family | One Twin | Other Twin |
| Aikman | 80 | 95 | Bettis | 100 | 95 |
| Fernandez | 70 | 50 | Harbaugh | 32 | 30 |
| Herrod | 10 | 35 | Park | 18 | 15 |
| Stewart | 25 | 5 | Ramirez | 55 | 60 |
| Tomczak | 40 | 65 | Robinson | 70 | 62 |

TABLE 2–2

Look first at the results for the fraternal twins. Most have similar scores: The Aikman twins both have high scores but the Herrod twins have low scores. Looking at the identical twins, their scores are even more alike, typically differing by no more than five points. This greater similarity among identical twins than among fraternal twins would be evidence that extroversion is inherited, just as the fact that identical twins look more alike than fraternal twins is evidence that facial appearance is inherited.

Adopted children are another important source of information about heredity. In this case, adopted children are compared with their biological parents and their adoptive parents. The idea is that biological parents provide the child's genes but adoptive parents provide the child's environment. Consequently, if a behavior has genetic roots, then adopted children should resemble their biological parents even though they have never met them. But if the adopted children resemble their adoptive parents, we know that family environment affects behavior.

If we wanted to use an adoption study to determine whether extroversion is inherited, we would measure extroversion in a large sample of adopted children, their biological mothers, and their adoptive mothers. (Why just mothers? Obtaining data from biological fathers of adopted children is often difficult.) The results of this hypothetical study are shown in the table on page 43.

First, compare children's scores with their biological mothers' scores. Overall, they are related: Extroverted children like Michael tend to have extroverted biological mothers. Introverted children like Troy tend to have introverted biological mothers. In contrast, children's scores don't show any clear relation to their adoptive mothers' scores. For example, although Michael has the highest score and Troy has the lowest, their adoptive mothers have very similar scores. Children's

### Scores from an Adoption Study on a Measure of Extroversion

| Child's Name | Child's Score | Biological Mother's Score | Adoptive Mother's Score |
|---|---|---|---|
| Anita | 60 | 70 | 35 |
| Jerome | 45 | 50 | 25 |
| Kerri | 40 | 30 | 80 |
| Michael | 90 | 80 | 50 |
| Troy | 25 | 5 | 55 |

TABLE 2–3

greater similarity to biological than to adoptive parents would be evidence that extroversion is inherited.

Twin studies and adoption studies are not foolproof, however. Maybe you thought of a potential flaw in twin studies: Parents and other people may treat identical twins more similarly than they treat fraternal twins. This would make identical twins more similar than fraternal twins in their experiences as well as in their genes. Adoption studies have their own Achilles heel. Adoption agencies sometimes try to place youngsters in homes like those of their biological parents. For example, if an agency believes that the biological parents are bright, the agency may try harder to have the child adopted by parents that the agency believes are bright. This can bias adoption studies because biological and adoptive parents end up being similar.

The problems associated with twin and adoption studies are not insurmountable. Because twin and adoption studies have different faults, if the two kinds of studies produce similar results on the influence of heredity, we can be confident of those results. In addition, behavioral geneticists are moving beyond traditional methods such as twin and adoption studies (Plomin et al., 1997; Plomin & Rutter, 1998). Today, it is possible to isolate particular segments of DNA in human chromosomes. These segments then serve as markers for identifying specific alleles. The procedure is complicated, but the basic approach often begins by identifying people who differ in the behavior or psychological trait of interest. For example, researchers might identify children who are outgoing and children who are shy. Or they might identify children who read well and children who read poorly. The children rub the inside of their mouth with a cotton swab, which yields cheek cells that contain DNA. The cells are analyzed in a lab and the DNA markers for the two groups are compared. If the markers differ consistently, then the alleles near the marker probably contribute to the differences between the groups.

Techniques like these have the potential to identify the many different genes that contribute to complex behavioral and psychological traits. Of course, these new methods have limits. Some require very large samples of children, which can be hard to obtain with rare disorders. Also, some require that an investigator have an idea, before even beginning the study, about which chromosomes to search and where. These can be major hurdles. But, when used with traditional methods of behavioral genetics (e.g., adoption studies), the new methods promise much greater understanding of how genes influence behavior and development.

> Heredity is implicated when identical twins are more alike than fraternal twins and when adopted children resemble their biological parents more than their adoptive parents.

## Which Psychological Characteristics Are Affected by Heredity?

Research indicates that genetic influence is strongest in three psychological areas: intelligence, psychological disorders, and personality. In the case of intelligence, identical twins' scores on IQ tests are consistently more alike than fraternal twins' scores (Plomin et al., 1997). Research also shows that heredity is an important component of two major psychological disorders. **In *depression*, individuals have pervasive feelings of sadness, are irritable, and have low self-esteem. In *schizophrenia*, individuals hallucinate, have confused language and thought, and often behave bizarrely.** In twin studies, identical twins show remarkable similarity for these disorders. In depression, for example, if one identical twin is depressed, the other twin has roughly a 70 percent chance of being depressed. For fraternal twins, the odds are much lower—only 25 percent (Gottesman, 1993; Rowe, 1994).

Research that demonstrates the influence of heredity on personality is the topic of the "Focus on Research" feature.

> Intelligence, psychological disorders, and personality are all strongly influenced by heredity.

**FOCUS ON RESEARCH**

### Hereditary and Environmental Roots of Infants' Social Behavior

*Who were the investigators and what was the aim of the study?* Toddlers differ in the ways they interact with others, especially people they don't know well. Some toddlers interact easily and with little hesitation. Other toddlers are reluctant to interact and seem wary of people. This dimension of personality is known as sociability. Robert Plomin and David Rowe (1979) wanted to find out whether a toddler's sociability is determined, in part, by heredity.

*How did the investigators measure the topic of interest?* Plomin and Rowe decided to study sociability in identical and fraternal twins using structured observation. In the twins' home, an adult not known to the twins spent 5 minutes talking with the mother while the twins were nearby. Then the adult approached the twins and offered them a toy. During this time, two observers recorded the twins' behavior. Each observer was assigned one twin, so that the twins' behavior was assessed independently. The observers recorded many behaviors, but for simplicity, I'll focus on three:

1. the number of times the child spoke positively to the stranger (for example, describing himself or herself),
2. the amount of time spent looking at the stranger, and
3. how quickly the child approached the stranger when he offered the toy.

*Who were the children in the study?* The researchers obtained measures for 21 pairs of identical twins and 25 pairs of same-sex fraternal twins. Their average age was 22 months.

*What was the design of the study?* This study was correlational: Plomin and Rowe measured many variables, such as time looking at the stranger, and compared twins' similarity on these measures. The study focused on a single age group, so it was neither longitudinal nor cross-sectional.

*Were there ethical concerns with the study?* No. The situations that Plomin and Rowe created were routine in the toddlers' real life, so the children were not at risk. Plomin and Rowe obtained permission from the mothers for the twins to participate.

*What were the results?* The primary results were expressed as correlations, which are shown in the graph. Each bar shows the size of the correlation for either identical or fraternal twins on one measure. For example, the first bar shows that the correlation for talking to the stranger was nearly .6 for identical twins. This means that if one identical twin talked often to the stranger, the other usually did, too; if one identical twin was quiet, the other usually was also. The important pattern in the graph is that, for each measure, the correlation is greater for identical twins than for fraternal twins. That is, as I described on page 42, the greater similarity among identical twins than fraternal twins is evidence that a behavior is inherited.

*What did the investigators conclude?* Sociability, at least as reflected in the measures that Plomin and Rowe devised, is influenced by heredity. ●

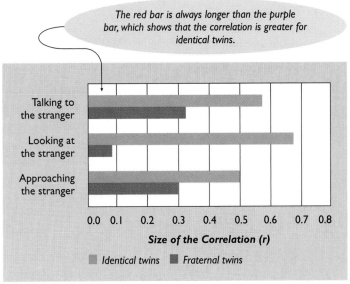

The red bar is always longer than the purple bar, which shows that the correlation is greater for identical twins.

FIG 2–4

We will look at personality in greater detail later. For now, keep in mind two conclusions from twin studies like Plomin and Rowe's and from adoption studies. On the one hand, the impact of heredity on behavioral development is substantial and widespread. Research shows that heredity has a sizable influence on such different aspects of development as intelligence and personality. In understanding children and their development, we must always think about how heredity may contribute. On the other hand, heredity is never the sole determinant of behavioral development. For example, 50 percent of the differences among children's scores on intelligence tests is due to heredity. But the remaining 50 percent is due to environment. Throughout this book, we'll see that the course of development is controlled by both heredity and environment.

## Check Your Learning

1. In _____, an egg is fertilized by a sperm in a laboratory dish, then placed in the uterus.

2. The first 22 pairs of chromosomes are called _____.

3. A person is _____ when the alleles in a pair of chromosomes differ.

4. _____ reflects the combined activity of a number of distinct genes.

5. Traditionally, behavioral geneticists relied on twin and _____ studies.

6. Intelligence, _____, and personality are the psychological traits most strongly influenced by heredity.

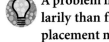 **A problem in twin studies is that identical twins may be treated more similarly than fraternal twins. A problem in adoption studies is that selective placement may cause biological parents to resemble a child's adoptive parents. How could an investigator determine if these problems were present in his or her research?**

**Answers:** (1) in vitro fertilization, (2) autosomes, (3) heterozygous, (4) Polygenic inheritance, (5) adoption, (6) psychological disorders

# 2.2

- **Inherited Disorders**
- **Abnormal Chromosomes**

## Genetic Disorders

### Learning Objectives

- **What disorders are inherited?**

- **What disorders are caused by too many or too few chromosomes?**

> *Carolyn and Doug, both 46, hadn't planned to have a baby, but Carolyn soon discovered that her lingering case of the flu was actually morning sickness. She and Doug both knew that with Carolyn's age they risked having a baby with Down syndrome, but they decided not to worry about this. When Carolyn gave birth to a baby boy, they learned that he did have Down syndrome. Carolyn and Doug were startled by the news, but it didn't change their joy at being parents. They did want to know more about the special challenges their son would face.*

Like Carolyn and Doug's baby, some children are affected by heredity in a special way: They have genetic disorders that disrupt the usual pattern of development. Genetics can derail development in two ways. First, some disorders are inherited. Sickle cell disease is one example of an inherited disorder. Second, sometimes eggs or sperm have more or fewer than the usual 23 chromosomes. In this module, we'll see how inherited disorders and abnormal numbers of chromosomes can alter a child's development. **We'll also learn more about *Down syndrome,* a genetic disorder caused by an extra 21st chromosome that results in mental retardation.**

### Inherited Disorders

n Module 2.1, we saw that sickle cell disease is a disorder that affects people who inherit two recessive alleles. In fact, sickle cell disease is one of many disorders that are homozygous recessive—triggered when a child inherits recessive alleles from both parents. The table lists four of the more common disorders that are inherited in this manner.

## Common Disorders Associated with Recessive Alleles

| Disorder | Frequency | Characteristics |
|---|---|---|
| Albinism | 1 in 10,000 to 1 in 20,000 births | Skin lacks melanin, which causes visual problems and extreme sensitivity to light. |
| Cystic fibrosis | 1 in 2,500 births among European Americans; less common in African and Asian Americans | Excess mucus clogs digestive and respiratory tracts. Lung infections common. |
| Phenylketonuria (PKU) | 1 in 10,000 births | Phenylalanine, an amino acid, accumulates in the body and damages the nervous system, causing mental retardation. |
| Tay-sachs disease | 1 in 3,000 births among Jews of European descent | The nervous system degenerates in infancy, causing deafness, blindness, mental retardation, and death. |

Based on Committee on Genetics, 1996; McKusick, 1995.

TABLE 2–4

Relatively few serious disorders are caused by dominant alleles. Why? If the allele for the disorder is dominant, every person with at least one of these alleles will have the disorder. But individuals affected with these disorders typically do not live long enough to reproduce, so dominant alleles that produce fatal disorders soon vanish from the species. **An exception is *Huntington's disease,* a fatal disease characterized by progressive degeneration of the nervous system.** Huntington's disease is caused by a dominant allele found on chromosome 4. Individuals who inherit this disorder develop normally through childhood, adolescence, and young adulthood. However, during middle age, nerve cells begin to deteriorate, causing muscle spasms, depression, and significant changes in personality (Shiwach, 1994). By the time symptoms of Huntington's disease appear, adults who are affected may already have produced children, many of whom go on to develop the disease themselves.

Fortunately, most inherited disorders are rare. PKU, for example, occurs once in every 10,000 births, and Huntington's disease occurs even less frequently. Nevertheless, adults who believe that these disorders run in their family want to know if their children are likely to inherit the disorder. The "Making Children's Lives Better" feature shows how these couples can get help in deciding whether to have children.

Inherited disorders that affect development are usually carried by recessive alleles, not dominant alleles.

### Genetic Counseling

Family planning is not easy for couples who fear that children they have may inherit serious or even fatal diseases. The best advice, though, is to seek the help of a genetic counselor before the woman becomes pregnant. With the couple's help, a genetic counselor constructs a detailed family history that can be used to decide whether it's likely that either the man or the woman has the allele for the disorder that concerns them.

A family tree for Leslie and Glenn, the couple from Module 2.1, would confirm that Leslie is likely to carry the recessive allele for sickle cell disease. The genetic counselor would then take the next step, obtaining a sample of Leslie's cells (probably from a blood test). The cells would be analyzed to determine if the 11th chromosome carries the recessive allele for sickle cell disease. If Leslie learns she has the dominant allele for healthy blood cells, then she and Glenn can be assured their children will not have sickle cell disease. If Leslie learns that she has the recessive allele, then she and Glenn will know they have a 50 percent risk of having a baby with sickle cell trait. Tests can also be administered after a woman is pregnant to determine whether the child she is carrying has an inherited disorder. We'll learn about these tests in Chapter 3. ●

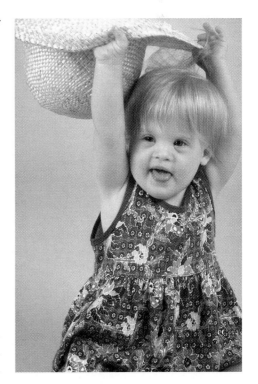

More common than inherited diseases are disorders caused by the wrong number of chromosomes, as we'll see in the next section.

## Abnormal Chromosomes

Sometimes individuals do not receive the normal complement of 46 chromosomes. If they are born with extra, missing, or damaged chromosomes, development is always disturbed. The best example is Down syndrome, the disorder that affects Carolyn and Doug's son. Like the child in the photo, persons with Down syndrome have almond-shaped eyes and a fold over the eyelid. Their head, neck, and nose are usually smaller than normal. During the first several months, babies with Down syndrome seem to develop normally. Thereafter, though, their mental and behavioral development begins to lag behind the average child's. For example, a child with Down syndrome might not sit up without help until about 1 year, not walk until 2, or not talk until 3, months or even years behind children without Down syndrome. By childhood, mental retardation is apparent.

Carolyn and Doug are right in believing that rearing a child with Down syndrome presents special challenges. During the preschool years, children with Down syndrome need special programs to prepare them for school. Educational achievements of children with Down syndrome are likely to be limited. Nevertheless, as we'll see in Chapter 8, many persons with Down syndrome lead fulfilling lives.

What causes Down syndrome? Individuals with Down syndrome typically have an extra 21st chromosome that is usually provided by the egg (Antonarakis & the Down Syndrome Collaborative Group, 1991). Why the mother provides two 21st chromosomes is unknown. However, the odds that a woman will bear a child with Down syndrome increase markedly as she gets older. For a woman in her late 20s, the risk of giving birth to a baby with Down syndrome is about 1 in 1,000; for a woman in her early 40s, the risk is about 1 in 50. The increased risk may be because a woman's eggs have been in her ovaries since her own prenatal development. Eggs may deteriorate over time as part of aging or because an older woman has a longer history of exposure to hazards in the environment, such as X-rays, that may damage her eggs.

An extra autosome (as in Down syndrome), a missing autosome, or a damaged autosome always has far-reaching consequences for development because the autosomes contain huge amounts of genetic material. In fact, nearly half of all fertilized eggs abort spontaneously within 2 weeks, primarily because of abnormal autosomes. Thus, most eggs that could not develop normally are removed naturally (Moore & Persaud, 1993).

Abnormal sex chromosomes can also disrupt development. The table lists four of the more frequent disorders associated with atypical numbers of X and Y chromosomes. Keep in mind that *frequent* is a relative term; although these disorders are more frequent than PKU or Huntington's disease, the table shows that most are rare.

## Common Disorders Associated with the Sex Chromosomes

| Disorder | Sex Chromosomes | Frequency | Characteristics |
|---|---|---|---|
| Klinefelter's syndrome | XXY | 1 in 500 male births | Tall, small testicles, sterile, below-normal intelligence, passive |
| XYY complement | XYY | 1 in 1,000 male births | Tall, some cases apparently have below-normal intelligence |
| Turner's syndrome | X | 1 in 2,500–5,000 female births | Short, limited development of secondary sex characteristics, problems perceiving spatial relations |
| XXX syndrome | XXX | 1 in 500–1,200 female births | Normal stature but delayed motor and language development |

Based on Bancroft et al., 1982; Downey et al., 1991; Linden et al., 1988; Plomin et al., 1990.

TABLE 2–5

Notice that no disorders consist solely of Y chromosomes. The presence of an X chromosome appears to be necessary for life.

These genetic disorders demonstrate the remarkable power of heredity. Nevertheless, to fully understand how heredity influences development, we need to consider the environment, which we'll do in Module 2.3.

## Check Your Learning

1. _____ is an inherited disorder caused by the accumulation of a particular amino acid, resulting in mental retardation.

2. Genetic disorders involving dominant alleles are rare because _____.

3. Down syndrome usually is caused by _____.

4. Many fertilized eggs are aborted spontaneously, primarily because of _____.

 As scientists learn more about heredity, we can tell people more about their own, unique genotype. What are some of the benefits of this knowledge? Can you think of any harmful consequences?

**Answers:** (1) PKU, (2) individuals with these disorders often do not live long enough to have children, (3) an extra 21st chromosome, (4) abnormal autosomes

# Heredity Is Not Destiny

**2.3**

Paths from Genes to Behavior

Reaction Range

Changing Relations Between Nature and Nurture

The Nature of Nurture

## Learning Objectives

● How do genes affect behavior?

● Does a genotype always lead to the same phenotype?

● How does the relation between heredity and environment change as children develop?

● How do family environments influence children's development?

> Sadie and Molly are fraternal twins. As babies, Sadie was calm and easily comforted, but Molly was fussy and hard to soothe. Their parents wondered if they'd always differ or if they'd become more alike as they grew older.

Many people mistakenly view heredity as a set of phenotypes that unfold automatically from the genotypes that are set at conception. Nothing could be further from the truth. Although genotypes are fixed when the sperm fertilizes the egg, phenotypes are not fixed. Instead, heredity and environment combine to direct a child's behavioral and psychological development. In this module, we'll look at links between heredity and environment. In the process, we'll learn if Sadie and Molly became more alike as they grew.

## Paths from Genes to Behavior

You know, from Module 2.1, that there is no single intelligence gene and no one shyness gene; instead, many genes work togther to influence these and other aspects of behavioral development. But how do genes work together to make some children brighter than others and some children more outgoing than others?

> The influence of genes on behavior is always indirect and depends upon the environment in which the genetic instructions are carried out.

That is, how does the information in strands of DNA influence a child's behavioral and psychological development?

The specific paths from genes to behavior are largely uncharted, but some of their general properties are known. The most important is that genes never cause behavior directly; instead, they influence behavior indirectly, by making behaviors more or less likely. For example, there is no gene for dunking a basketball, but genes do regulate bone length. Consequently, some people grow taller than others and they are therefore more capable of dunking. Similarly, there is no gene for alcoholism, but genes do regulate how the body breaks down alcohol that is consumed. Consequently, some people become nauseated because their bodies cannot break down alcohol and they are therefore less likely to become alcoholics. These examples show that genes for height and breaking down alcohol affect behavior indirectly, by changing the odds that a person can dunk a basketball or become an alcoholic.

Another important property of gene-behavior paths is that the behavioral consequences of genetic instructions depend on environments. In a basketball-less world, the gene for height would still produce taller people, but they would no longer be more likely to dunk. In other words, to understand how heredity affects behavior, we must consider the environment in which genetic instructions are carried out.

In the remaining sections of this module, we'll look at other aspects of links between heredity and environment.

## Reaction Range

f you read the fine print on a can of diet soda (and some other food products), you'll see the following warning:

> *"Phenylketonurics: contains phenylalanine."*

Children with phenylketonuria (PKU) are missing an enzyme that breaks down phenylalanine. When phenylalanine accumulates, it damages the nervous system. Today, most American hospitals check for PKU at birth with a blood or urine test. Newborns who have the disease are immediately placed on a diet that limits intake of phenylalanine, and mental retardation is avoided. Thus, an individual who has the genotype for PKU but is not exposed to phenylalanine has normal intelligence. PKU illustrates that development depends upon heredity and environmental factors—in this case, diet.

In general, heredity and environment jointly determine the direction of development. Therefore, a genotype can lead to a range of phenotypes. **Reaction range refers to this fact that a genotype is manifested in reaction to the environment where development takes place.** The graph illustrates this fact by showing how phenotypic

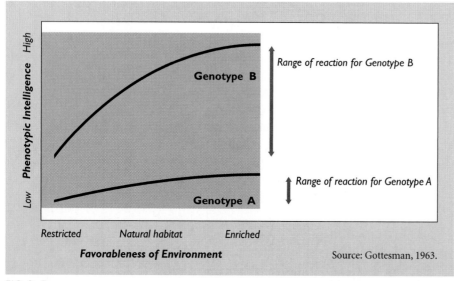

FIG 2–5

Source: Gottesman, 1963.

intelligence might vary, depending on the environment. Look first at genotypic intelligence *A,* which has a small reaction range. This genotype leads to much the same phenotypic intelligence, no matter whether development takes place in an enriched environment filled with stimulation from parents, siblings, and books or in an impoverished environment that lacks all such stimulation. In contrast, genotype *B* has a larger reaction range: The enriched environment leads to a much greater phenotypic intelligence than the impoverished environment. Thus a single genotype can lead to a range of phenotypes, depending on the quality of the rearing environment.

The conclusion to be drawn from the example is obvious: A genotype can lead to quite different phenotypes, all depending upon the level of intellectual stimulation in the environment. Of course, what makes a "good" or "rich" environment is not the same for all facets of behavioral or psychological development. Throughout this book, you will see how specific kinds of environments influence very particular aspects of development (Wachs, 1983).

## Changing Relations Between Nature and Nurture

How nature (genetics) and nurture (environment) work together partly depends on a child's age. Sandra Scarr (1992; Scarr & McCartney, 1983) describes three types of relations between heredity and environment. **In the first, a *passive gene-environment relation,* parents pass on genotypes to their children and provide much of the early environment for their young children.** For example, bright parents are likely to transmit genes that make for bright children. Bright parents are also likely to provide books, museum visits, and discussions that are intellectually stimulating. In this case, heredity and environment are positively related: Both foster brighter children. In both respects, children are passive recipients of heredity and environment. This passive type of relation is most common with infants and young children.

**In the second type of relation, *an evocative gene-environment relation,* different genotypes evoke different responses from the environment.** For example, children who are bright (due in part to their genes) may pay greater attention to their teachers and ask more questions and, in turn, receive greater positive attention in school than children who are not as bright. Or, children who are friendly and outgoing (again, due in part to their genes) may elicit more interactions with others (and, in particular, more satisfying interactions) than children who are not as friendly and outgoing. In the evocative relation, which is common in young children, a child's genotype evokes or prompts people to respond differently to the child.

**In the third type of relation, *an active gene-environment relation,* individuals actively seek environments related to their genetic makeup.** Children who are bright (due in part to heredity) may actively seek peers, adults, and activities that strengthen their intellectual development. Similarly, children like the one in the photo, who are outgoing (due in part to heredity), seek the company of other people, particularly extroverts like themselves. **This process of deliberately seeking environments that fit one's heredity is called *niche-picking.*** Niche-picking is first seen in childhood and becomes more common as children get older and can control their environments. The "Real Children" feature shows niche-picking in action.

### Sadie and Molly Pick Their Niches

Did Sadie and Molly, the twins in the module-opening vignette, become more alike as they grew? No. Even as a young baby, Sadie was always a "people person." She relished contact with other people and preferred play that involved others. Molly was more withdrawn and was quite happy to play alone. When they entered school, Sadie enjoyed making friends while Molly looked forward to the new activities and barely noticed the new faces. These differences reveal heredity in action because sociability is known to have important genetic components (Braungart et al., 1992).

As adolescents, Sadie and Molly continued to seek environments that fit their differing needs for social stimulation. Sadie was in school plays and sang in the school choir. Molly developed a serious interest in crafts, which she pursued by herself. Sadie was always doing something with friends. Molly enjoyed the company of some long-time friends, but she was just as happy to be working alone on some new craft project. Sadie and Molly chose distinctive and very different niches, choices that were influenced by the genes that regulate sociability. ●

The description of Sadie and Molly illustrates that genes and environment rarely influence development alone. Instead, nature and nurture interact. Experiences determine which phenotypes emerge, and genotypes influence the nature of children's experiences. The story of Sadie and Molly also makes it clear that, to understand how genes influence development, we need to look carefully at how environments work, our next topic.

## The Nature of Nurture

Traditionally, psychologists have considered some environments beneficial for children and others detrimental. This view has been especially strong in regard to family enviroments. Some parenting practices are thought to be more effective than others, and parents who use these effective practices are believed to have children who are, on average, better off than children of parents who don't use these practices. This view leads to a simple prediction: Children within a family should be similar because they all receive the same type of effective (or ineffective) parenting. However, dozens of behavioral genetic studies show that, in reality, siblings are not very much alike in their cognitive and social development (Dunn & Plomin, 1990).

Does this mean that family environment is not important? No. **These findings point to the importance of *nonshared environmental influences*, the forces within a family that make children different from one another.** Although the family environment is important, it usually affects each child in a unique way, which makes siblings differ. For example, parents may be more affectionate with one child than another, they may use more physical punishment with one child than another, or they may have higher expectations for school achievement for one child than another. All these contrasting parental influences tend to make siblings different, not alike. Family environments are important, but, as I describe their influence throughout this book, you should remember that families really create multiple unique environments, one for each child.

Much of what I have said about genes, environment, and development is summarized in the diagram on page 53. Parents are the source of children's genes and, at least for young children, the primary

For each of their children, parents provide a unique set of genes and a unique environment.

source of children's experiences. Children's genes also influence the experiences that they have and the impact of those experiences on them. However, to capture the idea of nonshared environmental influences, we would need a separate diagram for each child, reflecting the fact that parents provide unique genes and a unique family environment for each of their offspring.

Most of this book is devoted to explaining the links between nature, nurture, and development. We can first see the interaction of nature and nurture during prenatal development, which is the topic of Chapter 3.

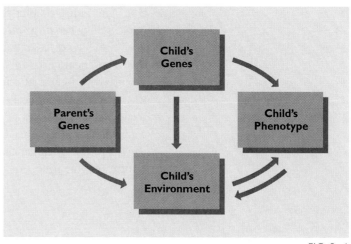

FIG 2–6

## Check Your Learning

**1.** The path from genes to environment is always _____ .

**2.** _____ refers to the fact that the same genotype can be associated with many different phenotypes.

**3.** In _____ gene-environment relations, children's genotypes cause others to respond differently to them.

**4.** Nonshared environmental influences tend to make siblings _____ .

 Leslie and Glenn, the couple from Module 2.1 who were concerned that their baby could have sickle cell disease, are already charting their baby's life course. Leslie, who has always loved to sing, is confident that her baby will be a fantastic musician and easily imagines a regular routine of music lessons, rehearsals, and concerts. Glenn, a pilot, is just as confident that his child will share his love of flying; he is already planning trips the two of them can take together. What advice might you give to Leslie and Glenn about factors they are ignoring?

**Answers:** (1) indirect, by making some behaviors more or less likely, (2) Reaction range, (3) evocative, (4) different rather than similar

# Genetic Bases of Child Development

IN PERSPECTIVE

The 46 chromosomes of a fertilized egg are like a roadmap, guiding development along its path to adulthood. In Module 2.1, we reviewed the mechanisms that regulate genetic functioning. Behavioral development usually follows a pattern of polygenic inheritance, in which behavioral traits reflect the combined effects of many pairs of genes and the environment. In Module 2.2, we saw how heredity can disrupt development. Some children inherit diseases such as sickle cell disease or PKU. Other children have the wrong number of chromosomes, which can produce disorders like Down syndrome. In Module 2.3, we examined the complexities of the relation between heredity and environment. A single genotype can lead to many phenotypes, and genes can influence a child's experiences.

This entire chapter is devoted to a single theme: *Development is always jointly influenced by heredity and environment.* We saw, again and again, how heredity and environment are essential ingredients in all developmental recipes, though not always in equal parts. In sickle cell disease, an allele has survival value in malaria-prone environments but not in environments where malaria has been eradicated. In PKU, persons who inherit the disorder become retarded when their dietary environment includes foods with phenylalanine but not when they avoid phenylalanine. And children with genes for normal intelligence develop below-average, average, or above-average intelligence, depending upon the environment in which they grow. Nature and nurture . . . development always depends on both.

## See for Yourself

The Human Genome Project, launched in the late 1980s by U.S. scientists, aims to identify the exact location of all 100,000 human genes. It is a vast undertaking that first requires determining the sequence of roughly 3 billion pairs of nucleotides like those shown in the diagram on page 38. The project has produced maps of each chromosome showing the location of known genes. You can see these maps at a Web site maintained by the Human Genome Project. The address is: http://www.ncbi.nlm.nih.gov/genemap99. At this site, you can select a "favorite" chromosome and see which genes have been located on it. See for yourself!

## Resources

*For more information about . . .*

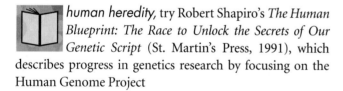 *human heredity,* try Robert Shapiro's *The Human Blueprint: The Race to Unlock the Secrets of Our Genetic Script* (St. Martin's Press, 1991), which describes progress in genetics research by focusing on the Human Genome Project

 *children with Down syndrome,* visit the Down syndrome Web site:
**http://www.nas.com/downsyn**

## Key Terms

active gene-environment relation 51
alleles 38
autosomes 37
behavioral genetics 40
chromosomes 36
deoxyribonucleic acid (DNA) 37
depression 44
dizygotic (fraternal) twins 41
dominant 38
Down syndrome 46

evocative gene-environment relation 51
gene 38
genotype 38
heterozygous 38
homozygous 38
Huntington's disease 47
in vitro fertilization 37
incomplete dominance 39
monozygotic (identical) twins 41
niche-picking 51

nonshared environmental influences 52
passive gene-environment relation 51
phenotype 38
polygenic inheritance 40
reaction range 50
recessive 38
schizophrenia 44
sex chromosomes 37
sickle cell trait 39

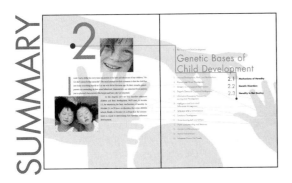

# SUMMARY

## 2.1 Mechanisms of Heredity

### The Biology of Heredity
At conception, the 23 chromosomes in the sperm merge with the 23 chromosomes in the egg. The 46 chromosomes that result include 22 pairs of autosomes plus 2 sex chromosomes. Each chromosome is one molecule of DNA, which consists of nucleotides organized in a structure that resembles a spiral staircase. A section of DNA that provides specific biochemical instructions is called a gene. All of a person's genes make up a genotype; phenotype refers to the physical, behavioral, and psychological characteristics that develop when the genotype is exposed to a specific environment.

### Single Gene Inheritance
Different forms of the same gene are called alleles. A person who inherits the same allele on a pair of chromosomes is homozygous; in this case, the biochemical instructions on the allele are followed. A person who inherits different alleles is heterozygous; in this case, the instructions of the dominant allele are followed whereas those of the recessive allele are ignored. In incomplete dominance, the person is heterozygous but the phenotype is midway between the dominant and recessive phenotypes.

### Behavioral Genetics
Behavioral and psychological phenotypes that reflect an underlying continuum (such as intelligence) often involve polygenic inheritance. In polygenic inheritance, the phenotype reflects the combined activity of many distinct genes. Polygenic inheritance has been examined traditionally by studying twins and adopted children, and more recently, by identifying DNA markers. These studies indicate substantial influence of heredity in three areas: intelligence, psychological disorders, and personality.

## 2.2 Genetic Disorders

### Inherited Disorders
Most inherited disorders are carried by recessive alleles. Examples include sickle cell disease, albinism, cystic fibrosis, phenylketonuria, and Tay-sachs disease. Inherited disorders are rarely carried by dominant alleles because individuals with such a disorder usually don't live long enough to have children. An exception is Huntington's disease, which doesn't become symptomatic until middle age.

### Abnormal Chromosomes
Most fertilized eggs that do not have 46 chromosomes are aborted spontaneously soon after conception. One exception is Down syndrome, caused by an extra 21st chromosome. Down syndrome individuals have a distinctive appearance and are mentally retarded. Disorders of the sex chromosomes, which are more common because these chromosomes contain less genetic material than autosomes, include Klinefelter's syndrome, XYY complement, Turner's syndrome, and XXX syndrome.

## 2.3 Heredity Is Not Destiny

### Paths from Genes to Behavior
Genes never influence behavior directly. Instead, they affect behavior indirectly by increasing the odds that a child will behave in a particular way. Also, the impact of a gene on behavior depends on the environment in which the genetic instructions are carried out.

### Reaction Range
PKU does not lead to mental retardation when individuals with the disorder maintain a diet low in phenylalanine. This demonstrates the concept of reaction range—the same genotype can lead to different phenotypes. The outcome of heredity depends upon the environment in which development occurs.

### Changing Relations Between Nature and Nurture
In infants and young children, the gene-environment relation is passive: parents pass on genotypes to their children and provide much of the early environment for their young children. An evocative gene-environment relation increasingly occurs during development as the child's genotype evokes responses from the environment. In older children and adolescents, an active gene-environment relation is common: Individuals actively seek environments related to their genetic makeup.

### The Nature of Nurture
Family environments affect siblings differently, which is known as nonshared environmental influences. Parents provide a unique environment for each child in the family as well as providing a unique genotype for each child.

3

f you ask parents to name some of the most memorable experiences of their lives, many mention events associated with pregnancy and childbirth. From the exciting news that a woman is pregnant through birth 9 months later, the entire experience evokes awe and wonder. The events of pregnancy and birth provide the foundation upon which all child development is built. In Module 3.1, we'll trace the events of prenatal development that transform sperm and egg into a living, breathing human being. In Module 3.2, we'll learn about some developmental problems that can occur before birth. In Module 3.3, we'll turn to birth. We'll see what happens during labor and delivery and some problems that can arise. In Module 3.4, we'll discover what newborn babies are like.

# Prenatal Development, Birth, and the Newborn

3.1 **From Conception to Birth**

3.2 **Influences on Prenatal Development**

3.3 **Happy Birthday!**

3.4 **The Newborn**

# 3.1

- **Period of the Zygote**
- **Period of the Embryo**
- **Period of the Fetus**

## From Conception to Birth

### Learning Objectives

- What happens to a fertilized egg in the first 2 weeks after conception?
- When do body structures and internal organs emerge in prenatal development?
- When do body systems begin to function well enough to support life?

> *Eun Jung has just learned that she is pregnant with her first child. Like many other parents-to-be, she and her husband Kinam are ecstatic. But they also soon realize how little they know about "what happens when" during pregnancy. Eun Jung is eager to visit her obstetrician to learn more about the normal timetable of events during pregnancy.*

**The changes that transform a fertilized egg into a newborn human make up *prenatal development*.** Prenatal development takes an average of 38 weeks, which are divided into three stages: the period of the zygote, the period of the embryo, and the period of the fetus. Each period gets its name from the term used to describe the baby-to-be at that point in prenatal development.

In this module, I'll trace the major developments during each period. As we go, you'll learn the answer to the "what happens when" question that intrigues Eun Jung.

### Period of the Zygote (Weeks 1–2)

The diagram traces the major events of the the first period of prenatal development, which begins with fertilization and lasts about 2 weeks. **It ends when the fertilized egg, called a *zygote*, implants itself in the wall of the uterus.**

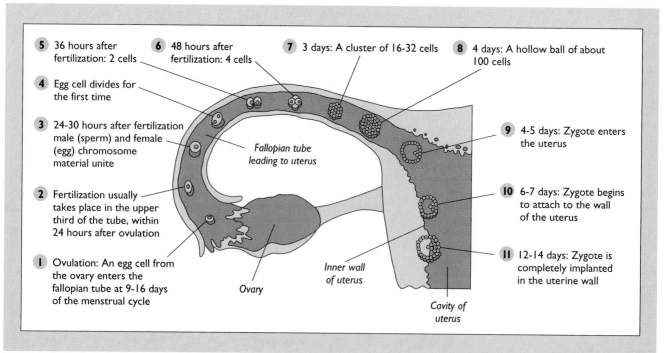

**5** 36 hours after fertilization: 2 cells

**6** 48 hours after fertilization: 4 cells

**7** 3 days: A cluster of 16-32 cells

**8** 4 days: A hollow ball of about 100 cells

**4** Egg cell divides for the first time

**3** 24-30 hours after fertilization male (sperm) and female (egg) chromosome material unite

*Fallopian tube leading to uterus*

**9** 4-5 days: Zygote enters the uterus

**2** Fertilization usually takes place in the upper third of the tube, within 24 hours after ovulation

**10** 6-7 days: Zygote begins to attach to the wall of the uterus

**1** Ovulation: An egg cell from the ovary enters the fallopian tube at 9-16 days of the menstrual cycle

*Inner wall of uterus*

*Ovary*

**11** 12-14 days: Zygote is completely implanted in the uterine wall

*Cavity of uterus*

FIG 3–1

During these 2 weeks, the zygote grows rapidly through cell division and travels down the fallopian tube toward the uterus. Within hours, the zygote divides for the first time; then division occurs every 12 hours. Occasionally, the zygote separates into two clusters that develop into identical twins. Fraternal twins, which are more common, are created when two eggs are released and each is fertilized by a different sperm cell. After about 4 days, the zygote consists of about 100 cells and resembles a hollow ball.

By the end of the first week, the zygote reaches the uterus. **The next step is *implantation*: The zygote burrows into the uterine wall and establishes connections with the mother's blood vessels.** Implantation takes about a week to complete and triggers hormonal changes that prevent menstruation, letting the woman know she has conceived.

The implanted zygote, shown in the photograph, is less than a millimeter in diameter. Yet its cells have already begun to differentiate. In the diagram, which shows a cross-section of the zygote and the wall of the uterus, you can see different layers of cells. **A small cluster of cells near the center of the zygote, the *germ disc*, eventually develops into the baby.** The other cells are destined to become structures that support, nourish, and protect the developing organism. **The layer of cells closest to the uterus becomes the *placenta*, a structure for exchanging nutrients and wastes between the mother and the developing organism.**

Implantation and differentiation of cells mark the end of the period of the zygote. Comfortably sheltered in the uterus, the zygote is well prepared for the remaining 36 weeks of the marvelous journey to birth.

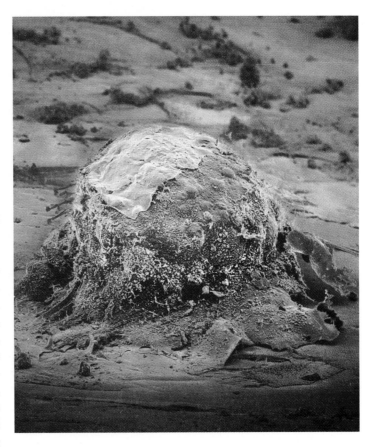

## Period of the Embryo (Weeks 3–8)

Once the zygote is completely embedded in the uterine wall, it is called an *embryo*. This new period typically begins the third week after conception and lasts until the end of the eighth week. During the period of the embryo, body structures and internal organs develop. At the beginning of the period, three layers form in the embryo. **The outer layer or *ectoderm* will become hair, the outer layer of skin, and the nervous system; the middle layer or *mesoderm* will form muscles, bones, and the circulatory system; the inner layer or *endoderm* will form the digestive system and the lungs.**

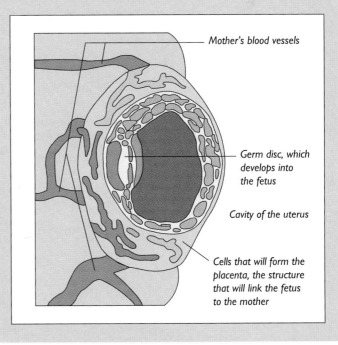

Mother's blood vessels

Germ disc, which develops into the fetus

Cavity of the uterus

Cells that will form the placenta, the structure that will link the fetus to the mother

FIG 3–2

One dramatic way to see the changes that occur during the embryonic period is to compare a 3-week-old embryo with an 8-week-old embryo. The 3-week-old embryo shown in the left photo is about 2 millimeters long. Cell specialization is under way, but the organism looks more like a salamander than a human being. But growth and specialization proceed so rapidly that an 8-week-old embryo—shown in the photo on the right—looks very different: You can see eyes, jaw, arms, and legs. The brain and the nervous system are also developing rapidly, and the heart has been

beating for nearly a month. Most of the organs found in a mature human are in place, in some form. (The sex organs are a notable exception). Yet, being only an inch long and weighing a fraction of an ounce, the embryo is much too small for the mother to feel its presence.

The embryo's environment is shown in the diagram on page 61. **The embryo rests in a sac called the *amnion*, which is filled with *amniotic fluid* that cushions the embryo and maintains a constant temperature.** The embryo is linked to the mother by two structures. **The *umbilical cord* houses blood vessels that join the embryo to the placenta.** In the placenta, the blood vessels from the umbilical cord run close to the mother's blood vessels but aren't actually connected to them. Instead, the blood flows through villi, finger-like projections from the umbilical blood vessels that are shown in the figure on page 61. As you can see, villi lie in close proximity to the mother's blood vessels and thus allow nutrients, oxygen, vitamins, and waste products to be exchanged between mother and embryo.

*Body parts and systems are formed in the period of the embryo and begin to work effectively in the period of the fetus.*

Growth in the period of the embryo follows two important principles: First, the head develops before the rest of the body. **Such growth from the head to the base of the spine illustrates the *cephalocaudal principle.*** Second, arms and legs develop before hands and feet. **Growth of parts near the center of the body before those that are more distant illustrates the *proximodistal principle.*** Growth after birth also follows these principles.

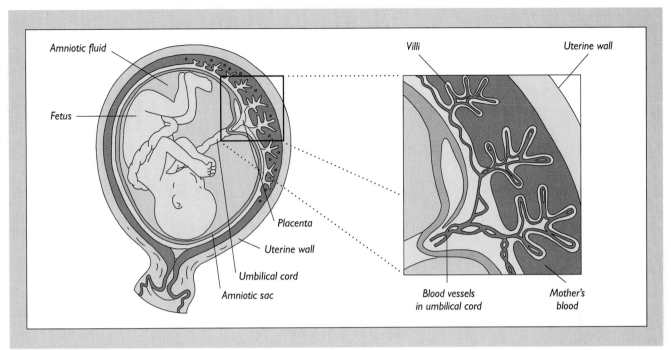

Amniotic fluid

Fetus

Villi

Uterine wall

Placenta

Uterine wall

Umbilical cord

Amniotic sac

Blood vessels
in umbilical cord

Mother's
blood

FIG 3–3

With body structures and internal organs in place, another major milestone passes in prenatal development. What's left is for these structures and organs to begin working properly. This is accomplished in the final period of prenatal development, as we'll see in the next section.

## Period of the Fetus (Weeks 9–38)

The final and longest phase of prenatal development, the *period of the fetus,* **extends from the ninth week after conception until birth.** During this period, the baby-to-be becomes much larger and its bodily systems begin to work. The increase in size is remarkable. At the beginning of this period, the fetus weighs less than an ounce. At about 4 months, the fetus weighs roughly 4 to 8 ounces, enough for the mother to feel its movements. In the last 5 months of pregnancy, the fetus gains an additional 7 or 8 pounds before birth. The chart on page 62, which depicts the fetus at one-eighth of its actual size, shows these incredible increases in size.

During the fetal period, the finishing touches are put on the body systems that are essential to human life, such as the nervous system, respiration, and digestion. Some highlights of this period include the following:

- In the fifth and sixth months after conception, eyebrows, eyelashes, and scalp hair emerge. **The skin thickens and is covered with a thick greasy substance, *vernix,* that protects the fetus during its long bath in amniotic fluid.**

- Near the end of the embryonic period, male embryos develop testes and female embryos develop ovaries. In the third month, the testes in a male fetus secrete a hormone that causes a set of cells to become a penis and scrotum; in a female fetus, this hormone is absent, so the same cells become a vagina and labia.

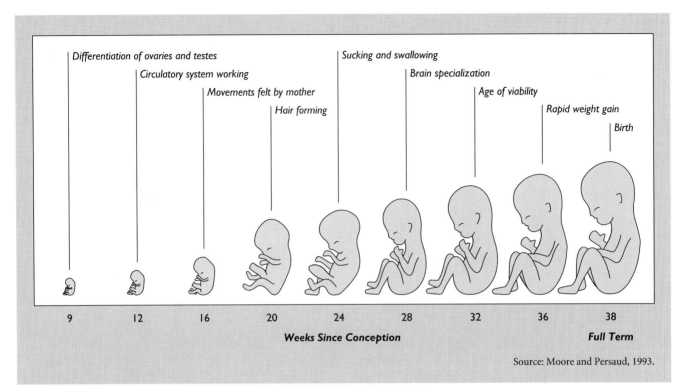

*Differentiation of ovaries and testes*

*Circulatory system working*

*Movements felt by mother*

*Hair forming*

*Sucking and swallowing*

*Brain specialization*

*Age of viability*

*Rapid weight gain*

*Birth*

| 9 | 12 | 16 | 20 | 24 | 28 | 32 | 36 | 38 |

**Weeks Since Conception**                                                    **Full Term**

Source: Moore and Persaud, 1993.

FIG 3–4

- At four weeks after conception, a flat set of cells curls to form a tube. One end of the tube swells to form the brain; the rest forms the spinal cord. By the start of the fetal period, the brain has distinct structures and has begun to regulate body functions. **During the period of the fetus, all regions of the brain grow, particularly the *cerebral cortex*, the wrinkled surface of the brain that regulates many important human behaviors.**

**With these and other rapid changes, by 22 to 28 weeks most systems function well enough that a fetus born at this time has a chance to survive, which is why this age range is called the *age of viability*.** By this age, the fetus has a distinctly baby-like look, as you can see in the photo. However, babies born this early have trouble breathing because their lungs are not yet mature. Also they cannot regulate their body temperature very well because they lack the insulating layer of fat that appears in the eighth month after conception. With modern neonatal intensive care, infants born this early can survive, but they face other challenges, as I'll describe in Module 3.3.

The changes of the fetal period also mean that the fetus actually starts to behave! The fetus develops regular periods of activity: Most mothers report times when the fetus is moving and other times when the fetus is still (DiPietro et al., 1996). The eyes and ears also respond to stimulation: The fetal heart beats more rapidly after a loud noise, and the eyes blink in response to light (Birnholz & Benacerraf, 1983; Kisilevsky & Low, 1998).

Remarkably, newborns apparently can recognize some of the sounds they hear during prenatal development. DeCasper and Spence (1986) had pregnant women read aloud the famous Dr. Seuss story *The Cat in the Hat* twice a day for the last 1½ months of pregnancy. As newborns, then, these babies had heard *The Cat in the Hat* for more than 3 hours. The newborns were then allowed to suck on a mechanical nipple connected to a tape recorder so that the baby's sucking could turn the tape on or off. The investigators discovered that babies would suck to hear a tape of their mother reading The *Cat in the Hat* but not to hear her reading other stories. Evidently, newborns recognized the familiar, rhythmic quality of *The Cat in the Hat* from their prenatal story times.

Findings like these tell us that the last few months of prenatal development prepare the fetus remarkably well for independent living as a newborn baby. But these astonishing prenatal changes can only take place when a woman provides a healthy environment for her baby-to-be. The "Making Children's Lives Better" feature describes what pregnant women should do to provide the best foundation for prenatal development.

> By the end of the fetal period, the fetus has regular periods of activity and the eyes and ears respond to stimulation.

## MAKING CHILDREN'S LIVES BETTER

### Five Steps Toward a Healthy Baby

1. Visit a health care provider for regular prenatal checkups. You should have monthly visits until you get close to your due date, when you will have a checkup every other week or maybe even weekly.

2. Eat healthy foods. Be sure your diet includes foods from each of the five major food groups (cereals, fruits, vegetables, dairy products, and meats and beans). Your health care provider may recommend that you supplement your diet with vitamins, minerals, and iron to be sure you are providing your baby with all the nutrients it needs.

3. Stop drinking alcohol and caffeinated beverages. Stop smoking. Consult your health care provider before taking any over-the-counter medications or prescription drugs.

4. Exercise throughout pregnancy. If you are physically fit, your body is better equipped to handle the needs of the baby.

5. Get enough rest, especially during the last 2 months of pregnancy. Also, attend childbirth education classes so that you'll be prepared for labor, delivery, and your new baby. ●

As critically important as these steps are, they unfortunately do not guarantee a healthy baby. In Module 3.2, we'll see how prenatal development can sometimes go awry.

## Check Your Learning

**1.** Fraternal twins develop when _____.

**2.** The period of the zygote ends _____.

**3.** Body structures and internal organs form during the period of the _____.

**4.** The embryo rests in a fluid-filled sac called the _____.

**5.** _____ is called the age of viability because at this time most body systems function well enough to support life.

Health professionals often divide the 9 months of pregnancy into three 3-month trimesters. Describe the highlights of prenatal development during each trimester.

**Answers:** (1) two eggs are fertilized by two sperm, (2) at 2 weeks after conception (when the zygote is completely implanted in the wall of the uterus), (3) embryo, (4) amnion, (5) Between 22 and 28 weeks

# 3.2

- **General Risk Factors**
- **Teratogens: Diseases, Drugs, and Environmental Hazards**
- **How Teratogens Influence Prenatal Development**
- **Prenatal Diagnosis and Treatment**

# Influences on Prenatal Development

## Learning Objectives

- How is prenatal development influenced by a pregnant woman's nutrition, the stress she experiences while pregnant, and her age?

- What is a teratogen, and what specific diseases, drugs, and environmental hazards can be teratogens?

- How exactly do teratogens affect prenatal development?

- How can prenatal development be monitored? Can abnormal prenatal development be corrected?

*Chloe was barely 2 months pregnant at her first prenatal checkup. As she waited for her appointment, she looked at the list of questions that she wanted to ask her obstetrician. "I spend much of my workday at a computer. Is radiation from the monitor harmful to my baby?" "When my husband and I get home from work, we'll have a glass of wine to help unwind from the stress of the day. Is moderate drinking like this okay?" "I'm 38. I know older women more often give birth to mentally retarded babies. Is there any way I can know if my baby will be mentally retarded?*

All of Chloe's questions concern potential harm to her baby-to-be. She worries about the safety of her computer monitor, about her nightly glass of wine, and about her age. Chloe's concerns are well founded. Beginning with conception, environmental factors influence the course of prenatal development, and they are the focus of this module. If you're sure you can answer all of Chloe's questions, skip this module and go directly to Module 3.3 on page 75. Otherwise, read on to learn about problems that sometimes arise in pregnancy.

## General Risk Factors

As the name implies, general risk factors can have widespread effects on prenatal development. Scientists have identified three general risk factors: nutrition, stress, and a mother's age.

Nutrition. The mother is the developing child's sole source of nutrition, so a balanced diet that includes foods from each of the five major food groups is vital. Most pregnant women need to increase their intake of calories by about 10 to 20 percent to meet the needs of prenatal development. A woman should expect to gain between 25 and 35 pounds during pregnancy, assuming that her weight was normal before pregnancy. A woman who was underweight before becoming pregnant may gain as much as 40 pounds; a woman who was overweight should gain at least 15 pounds (Institute of Medicine, 1990). Of this gain, about one-third reflects the weight of the baby, the placenta, and the fluid in the amniotic sac; another third comes from increases in a woman's fat stores; yet another third comes from the increased volume of blood and increases in the size of her breasts and uterus (Whitney & Hamilton, 1987).

Problems during pregnancy are more common when a woman's nutrition is inadequate and when she is under chronic stress.

Sheer amount of food is only part of the equation for a healthy pregnancy. What a pregnant woman eats is also very important. Proteins, vitamins, and minerals are essential for normal prenatal development. For example, folic acid, one of the B vitamins, is important for the nervous system to develop properly (Shaw et al., 1995). **When mothers do not consume adequate amounts of folic acid, their babies are at risk for *spina bifida*, a disorder in which the embryo's neural tube does not close properly during the first month of pregnancy.** Since the neural tube develops into the brain and spinal cord, when it does not close properly, the result is permanent damage to the spinal cord and the nervous system. Many children with spina bifida need crutches, braces, or wheelchairs. Other prenatal problems have also been traced to inadequate proteins, vitamins, or minerals, so health care providers typically recommend that pregnant women supplement their diet with additional proteins, vitamins, and minerals.

When a pregnant woman does not provide adequate nourishment, the infant is likely to be born prematurely and to be underweight. Inadequate nourishment during the last few months of pregnancy can particularly affect the nervous system, because this is a time of rapid brain growth. Finally, babies who do not receive adequate nourishment are vulnerable to illness (Guttmacher & Kaiser, 1986).

**Stress.**  Does a pregnant woman's mood affect the zygote, embryo, or fetus in her uterus? Is a woman who is happy during pregnancy more likely to give birth to a happy baby? Is a pregnant woman like the harried office worker in the photo more likely to give birth to an irritable baby? **These questions address the impact on prenatal development of chronic *stress*, which refers to a person's physical and psychological responses to threatening or challenging situations.** We can answer these questions with some certainty for nonhumans. When pregnant female animals experience constant stress—such as repeated electric shock or intense overcrowding—their offspring are often smaller than average and prone to other physical and behavioral problems (Schneider, 1992).

Determining the impact of stress on human pregnancy is more difficult because we must rely solely on correlational studies. (It would be unethical to do an experiment that assigned some pregnant women to a condition of extreme stress.) Studies typically show that women who report greater anxiety during pregnancy more often give birth early or have babies who weigh less than average (Copper et al., 1996; Paarlberg et al., 1995).

Increased stress can harm prenatal development in several ways. First, when a pregnant woman experiences stress, her body secretes hormones that reduce the flow of oxygen to the fetus while increasing its heart rate and activity level. Second, stress can weaken a pregnant woman's immune system, making her more susceptible to illness (Cohen & Williamson, 1991), which can, in turn, damage fetal development. Third, pregnant women under stress are more likely to smoke or drink alcohol and less likely to rest, exercise, and eat properly. All these behaviors endanger prenatal development.

I want to emphasize that the results described here apply to women who experience prolonged, extreme stress. Virtually all women sometimes become anxious or upset while pregnant. But occasional, relatively mild anxiety is not thought to have any harmful consequences for prenatal development.

### Mother's Age.

Traditionally, the 20s were thought to be the prime childbearing years. Teenage women as well as women who were 30 or older were considered less fit for the rigors of pregnancy. Is being a 20-something really important for a successful pregnancy? Let's answer this question separately for teenage and older women. Compared to women in their 20s, teenage women are more likely to have problems during pregnancy, labor, and delivery. This is largely because pregnant teenagers do not get good prenatal care, usually because they are unaware of the need and do not seek it out. For example, research done on African American adolescents suggests that when differences in prenatal care are taken into account, teenagers are just as likely as women in their 20s to have problem-free pregnancies and give birth to healthy babies (Goldenberg & Klerman, 1995).

Nevertheless, even when a teenager receives adequate prenatal care and gives birth to a healthy baby, all is not rosy. Children of teenage mothers generally do less well in school and more often have behavioral problems (Dryfoos, 1990). The

problems of teenage motherhood—incomplete education, poverty, and marital difficulties—affect the child's later development (Furstenberg, Brooks-Gunn, & Morgan, 1987).

Of course, not all teenage mothers and their infants follow this dismal life course. Some teenage mothers finish school, find good jobs, and have happy marriages; their children do well in school, academically and socially. However, teenage pregnancies with "happy endings" are definitely the exception; for most teenage mothers and their children, life is a struggle. Educating teenagers about the true consequences of teen pregnancy is crucial.

Are older women better suited for pregnancy? This is an important question because today's American woman is waiting longer than ever to have her first child. Completing an education and beginning a career often delay childbearing. In fact, the birthrate in the 1990s among 30- to 34-year-olds was nearly triple what it was in the early 1970s (U.S. Department of Health and Human Services, 1995).

Traditionally, older women like the one in the photo were thought to have more difficult pregnancies and more complicated labor and deliveries. Today, we know that women in their 30s who are in good health are no more risk-prone during pregnancy, labor, and delivery than women in their 20s (Ales, Druzin, & Santini, 1990). Women in their 40s, however, are more liable to give birth to babies with Down syndrome.

In general, then, prenatal development is most likely to proceed normally when women are healthy and eat right, get good health care, and lead lives that are free of chronic stress. But even in these optimal cases, prenatal development can be disrupted, as we'll see in the next section.

## Teratogens: Diseases, Drugs, and Environmental Hazards

In the late 1950s, many pregnant women in Germany took thalidomide, a drug to help them sleep. Soon, however, came reports that many of these women were giving birth to babies with deformed arms, legs, hands, or fingers (Jensen, Benson, & Bobak, 1981). **Thalidomide was a powerful *teratogen*, an agent that causes abnormal prenatal development.** Ultimately, more than 7,000 babies worldwide were harmed before thalidomide was withdrawn from the market (Moore & Persaud, 1993).

Prompted by the thalidomide disaster, scientists began to study teratogens extensively. Today, we know a great deal about the three primary types of teratogens: diseases, drugs, and environmental hazards. Let's look at each.

Diseases.   Sometimes women become ill while pregnant. Most diseases, such as colds and many strains of flu, do not affect the developing organism. However, several bacterial and viral infections can be very harmful and, in some cases, fatal to the embryo or fetus; five of the most common are listed in the chart.

### Teratogenic Diseases and Their Consequences

| Disease | Potential Consequences |
| --- | --- |
| AIDS | Frequent infections, neurological disorders, death |
| Cytomegalovirus | Deafness, blindness, abnormally small head, mental retardation |
| Genital herpes | Encephalitis, enlarged spleen, improper blood clotting |
| Rubella (German measles) | Mental retardation; damage to eyes, ears, and heart |
| Syphilis | Damage to the central nervous system, teeth, and bones |

TABLE 3–1

Some of these diseases pass from the mother through the placenta to attack the embryo or fetus directly. They include cytomegalovirus (a type of herpes), rubella, and syphilis. Other diseases attack at birth: The virus is present in the lining of the birth canal, and the baby is infected as it passes through to be born. Genital herpes is transmitted this way. AIDS is transmitted both ways—through the placenta and during passage through the birth canal.

The only way to guarantee that these diseases do not harm prenatal development is for a woman to not contract the disease before or during her pregnancy. Medication may help the woman, but does not prevent the disease from damaging the developing baby.

Drugs.   Thalidomide illustrates the harm that drugs can cause during prenatal development. The chart on page 68 lists other drugs that are known teratogens.

| Teratogenic Drugs and Their Consequences | |
| --- | --- |
| **Drug** | **Potential Consequences** |
| Alcohol | Fetal alcohol syndrome, cognitive deficits, heart damage, retarded growth |
| Aspirin | Deficits in intelligence, attention, and motor skill |
| Caffeine | Lower birth weight, decreased muscle tone |
| Cocaine and heroin | Retarded growth, irritability in newborns |
| Marijuana | Lower birth weight, less motor control |
| Nicotine | Retarded growth, possible cognitive impairments |

TABLE 3–2

Notice that most of the drugs in the list are substances that you may use routinely—alcohol, aspirin, caffeine, and nicotine. Nevertheless, when consumed by pregnant women, they present special dangers (Behnke & Eyler, 1993).

Cigarette smoking is typical of the potential harm from teratogenic drugs (Cornelius et al., 1995; Fried, O'Connell, & Watkinson, 1992). The nicotine in cigarette smoke constricts blood vessels and thus reduces the oxygen and nutrients that can reach the fetus over the placenta. Therefore, pregnant women who smoke are more likely to miscarry (abort the fetus spontaneously) and to bear children who are smaller than average at birth. Birth complications are also more frequent. And, as children develop, they are more likely to show signs of impaired attention, language, and cognitive skills. Finally, even second-hand smoke harms the fetus: When pregnant women don't smoke but fathers do, babies tend to be smaller at birth (Friedman & Polifka, 1996). The message is clear and simple: Pregnant women shouldn't smoke and they should avoid others who do.

Alcohol also carries serious risk. **Pregnant women who consume large quantities of alcoholic beverages often give birth to babies with** *fetal alcohol syndrome (FAS).* Children with FAS usually grow more slowly than normal and have heart problems and misshapen faces. Like the child in the photo, youngsters with FAS often have a small head, a thin upper lip, a short nose, and widely spaced eyes. They are often mentally retarded and may have limited motor skills (Niebyl, 1991).

Fetal alcohol syndrome is most likely when pregnant women drink 3 or more ounces of alcohol daily. Does this mean that moderate drinking is safe? No. When women drink moderately throughout pregnancy, their children often have lower scores on tests of attention, memory, and intelligence (Streissguth et al., 1994).

Is there any amount of drinking that's safe during pregnancy? Maybe, but that amount is yet to be determined. Gathering definitive data is complicated by two factors: First, researchers usually determine the amount a woman drinks by her own responses to interviews or questionnaires. If for some reason she does not accurately report her consumption, it is impossible to accurately estimate the amount of harm associated with drinking. Second, any safe level of consumption is probably not the same for all women. Based on their health and heredity, some women may be able to consume more alcohol more safely than others.

These factors make it impossible to guarantee safe levels of alcohol or any of the other drugs listed in the table at the top of this page. The best policy, therefore, is for a woman to avoid all drugs throughout pregnancy.

Environmental Hazards.   As a byproduct of life in an industrialized world, people are often exposed to toxins in food they eat, fluids they drink, and air they breathe. Chemicals associated with industrial waste are the most common environmental teratogens, and the quantities involved are usually minute. However, as was true for drugs, amounts that go unnoticed by an adult can cause serious damage to prenatal development. Several environmental hazards that are known teratogens are listed in the table.

## Environmental Teratogens and Their Consequences

| Hazard | Potential Consequences |
|---|---|
| Lead | Mental retardation |
| Mercury | Retarded growth, mental retardation, cerebral palsy |
| PCBs | Impaired memory and verbal skill |
| X-rays | Retarded growth, leukemia, mental retardation |

TABLE 3–3

You'll notice that although X-rays are included in this table, radiation associated with computer monitors and video display terminals (VDTs) is not. Several major studies have examined the impact of exposure to the electromagnetic fields that are generated by VDTs, and they have found no negative results. For example, Schnorr and her colleagues (1991) compared the pregnancies in telephone operators who worked at VDTs at least 25 hours weekly with operators who never used VDTs. For both groups of women, about 15 percent of the pregnancies ended in miscarriage. Other studies have not found a connection between exposure to VDTs and birth defects (Parazzini et al., 1993). Evidently, VDTs can be used safely by pregnant women.

In the "Focus on Research" feature, we look at one of the environmental teratogens in detail.

FOCUS ON RESEARCH

### Impact of Prenatal Exposure to PCBs on Cognitive Functioning

*Who were the investigators, and what was the aim of the study?* For many years, polychlorinated biphenyls (PCBs) were used in electrical transformers and paints, but the U.S. government banned them in the 1970s. Like many industrial byproducts, they seeped into the waterways, where they contaminated fish and wildlife. The amount of PCBs in a typical contaminated fish does not affect adults, but Joseph Jacobson, Sandra Jacobson, and Harold Humphrey (1990) wanted to determine if this level of exposure was harmful to prenatal development. In particular, they knew from earlier work that substantial prenatal exposure to PCBs affected infants' cognitive skills; they hoped to determine if prenatal exposure similarly affected preschoolers' cognitive skills.

*How did the investigators measure the topic of interest?* Jacobson and his colleagues needed to measure prenatal exposure to PCBs and cognitive skill. To measure prenatal exposure, they measured concentrations of PCBs in (a) blood obtained from the umbilical cord and (b) breast milk of mothers who were breast-feeding. To measure cognitive skill, they used a standardized test, the McCarthy Scales for Children's Abilities. The McCarthy Scales measure children's abilities in five areas: verbal, perceptual, quantitative, memory, and motor abilities.

*Who were the children in the study?* The sample included 236 children who were born in western Michigan in 1980–1981. This region was chosen because, at the time, Lake Michigan contained many contaminated salmon and lake trout.

*What was the design of the study?* The study was correlational because Jacobson and his colleagues were interested in the relation that existed naturally between two variables: exposure to PCBs and cognitive skill. The study was longitudinal because children were tested twice: Their exposure to PCBs was measured immediately after birth, and their cognitive skill was measured at age 4 years.

*Were there ethical concerns with the study?* No. The children had been exposed to PCBs naturally, prior to the start of the study. (Obviously, it would not have been ethical for researchers to do an experiment that involved asking pregnant women to eat contaminated fish.) The investigators obtained permission from the parents for the children to participate.

*What were the results?* PCB exposure was unrelated to performance on the perceptual, quantitative, and motor scales of the McCarthy tests. That is, children with high levels of PCB exposure were just as likely to get high scores on these tests as children with low levels of PCB exposure. However, PCB exposure did affect scores on the verbal and memory scales. Looking at the graphs, you can see that verbal and memory

*The purple bars are always longest and the green bars the shortest, which shows that children with the least PCB exposure had the highest scores and those with the greatest exposure had the lowest scores.*

FIG 3–5

scores were highest in children who had the least prenatal exposure to PCBs and lowest for the 4-year-olds who had the greatest prenatal exposure. In other words, as prenatal exposure to PCBs increased, verbal and memory skills decreased.

*What did the investigators conclude?* Prenatal exposure to PCBs affects at least two aspects of cognitive development—memory and verbal skill. Though children's scores were in the normal range, their reduced memory and verbal skills will probably cause some trouble in school, such as in learning to read. ●

Environmental teratogens are treacherous because people are unaware of their presence in the environment. The women in the Jacobson, Jacobson, and Humphrey (1990) study, for example, did not realize that they were eating PCB-laden fish. This invisibility makes it more difficult for a pregnant woman to protect herself from environmental teratogens. Pregnant women need to be particularly careful of the foods they eat and the air they breathe. Be sure all foods are cleaned thoroughly to rid them of insecticides. Avoid convenience foods, which often contain many chemical additives. Stay away from air that's been contaminated by household products such as cleansers, paint strippers, and fertilizers. Women in jobs that require contact with potential teratogens (e.g., housecleaners, hairdressers) should switch to less potent chemicals. For example, they should use baking soda instead of more chemically laden cleansers. And they should wear protective gloves, aprons, and masks to reduce their contact with potential teratogens. Finally, because environmental teratogens continue to increase, check with a health care provider to learn if other materials should be avoided.

## How Teratogens Influence Prenatal Development

By assembling all the evidence of harm caused by diseases, drugs, and environmental hazards, scientists have identified four important general principles about how teratogens usually work (Hogge, 1990; Vorhees & Mollnow, 1987).

1. *The impact of a teratogen depends upon the genotype of the organism.* A substance may be harmful to one species but not to another. To determine its safety, thalidomide had been tested on pregnant rats and rabbits, and their offspring had had normal limbs. Yet, when pregnant women took the same drug in comparable doses, many had children with deformed limbs. Thalidomide was harmless to rats and rabbits but not to people. Moreover, some women who took thalidomide gave birth to babies with normal limbs, yet others who took comparable doses at the same time in their pregnancies gave birth to babies with deformities. Apparently, heredity makes some individuals more susceptible than others to a teratogen.

2. *The impact of teratogens changes over the course of prenatal development.* The timing of exposure to a teratogen is very important. The chart shows how the

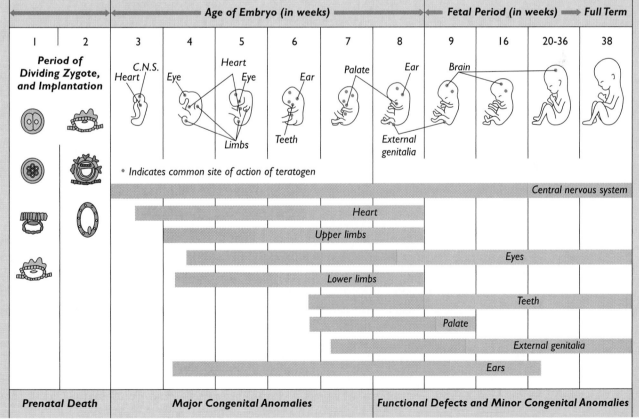

FIG 3–6

consequences of teratogens differ for the periods of the zygote, embryo, and fetus. During the period of the zygote, exposure to teratogens usually results in spontaneous abortion of the fertilized egg. During the embryonic period, exposure produces major defects in body structure. For example, women who took thalidomide during the embryonic period had babies with ill-formed or missing limbs. Women who contract rubella during the embryonic period have babies with heart defects. During the fetal period, exposure to teratogens produces either minor defects in body structure or causes body systems to function improperly. For example, when women drink large quantities of alcohol during the fetal period, the fetus develops fewer brain cells.

Even within the different periods of prenatal development, developing body parts and systems are more vulnerable at some times than others. The purple shading in the chart on page 72 indicates a time of maximum vulnerability; orange shading indicates a time when the developing organism is less vulnerable. The heart, for example, is most sensitive to teratogens during the first two-thirds of the embryonic period. Exposure to teratogens before this time rarely produces heart damage; exposure after this time results in milder damage.

3. *Each teratogen affects a specific aspect (or aspects) of prenatal development.* Said another way, teratogens do not harm all body systems; instead, damage is selective. If a woman contracts rubella, the baby may have problems with eyes, ears, and heart, but limbs will be normal. If a mother consumes PCB-contaminated fish, the baby typically has normal body parts and normal motor skills but below-average memory and verbal skills.

4. *Damage from teratogens is not always evident at birth but may appear later in life.* In the case of malformed limbs or babies born addicted to cocaine, the effects of a teratogen are obvious immediately. A cocaine baby goes through withdrawal—shaking, crying, and being unable to sleep. Sometimes, however, the damage from a teratogen becomes evident only as the child develops. For example, between 1947 and 1971 many pregnant women in North America and Europe took the drug diethylstilbestrol (DES) to prevent miscarriages. The babies appeared normal at birth, but, as adults, they are more likely to have a rare cancer of the vagina and to have difficulty becoming pregnant themselves (Friedman & Polifka, 1996). Sons of women who took DES may be less fertile and at risk for cancer of the testes (Sharpe & Skakkebaek, 1993). Here is a case in which the impact of the teratogen is not evident until decades after birth.

### The Real World of Prenatal Risk.

I have discussed risk factors individually, as if each were the only potential threat to prenatal development. In reality, many infants are exposed to multiple general risks and multiple teratogens (Giberson & Weinberg, 1992; Richardson, 1998). Pregnant women who drink alcohol often smoke and drink coffee. Pregnant women who are under stress often drink alcohol, and may self-medicate with aspirin or other over-the-counter drugs. Many of these same women live in poverty, which means they may have inadequate nutrition and receive minimal medical care during pregnancy. When all the risks are combined, prenatal development is rarely optimal.

From what I've said so far in this module, you may think that the developing child has little chance of escaping harm. But most babies are born in good health. Of course, a good policy for pregnant women is to avoid diseases, drugs, and environmental hazards that are known teratogens. This, coupled with thorough prenatal medical care and adequate nutrition, is the best recipe for normal prenatal development.

## Prenatal Diagnosis and Treatment

" I really don't care whether I have a boy or girl, just as long as it's healthy." Legions of parents worldwide have felt this way, but until recently all they could do was hope for the best. Today, however, advances in technology give parents a much better idea whether their baby is developing normally.

Even before a woman becomes pregnant, a couple may go for genetic counseling, which I described in Module 2.2. A counselor constructs a family tree for each prospective parent to check for heritable disorders. If it turns out that one (or both) carries a disorder, further tests can determine the person's genotype. With this more detailed information, a genetic counselor can discuss choices with the prospective parents. They may choose to go ahead and conceive "naturally," taking their chances that the child will be healthy. Or they could decide to use sperm or eggs from other people. Yet another choice would be to adopt a child.

After a woman is pregnant, how can we know if prenatal development is progressing normally? Traditionally, obstetricians gauged development by feeling the size and position of the fetus through a woman's abdomen. This technique was not very precise and, of course, couldn't be done at all until the fetus was large enough to feel. Today, however, new techniques have revolutionized our ability to monitor prenatal growth and development. **A standard part of prenatal care in North America is *ultrasound*, a procedure using sound waves to generate a picture of the fetus.** As the photo shows, an instrument about the size of a hair dryer is rubbed over the woman's abdomen; the image is shown on a nearby TV monitor. The pictures that are generated are hardly portrait quality; they are grainy and it takes an expert's eye to distinguish what's what. Nevertheless, the procedure is painless and parents are thrilled to be able to see their baby and watch it move.

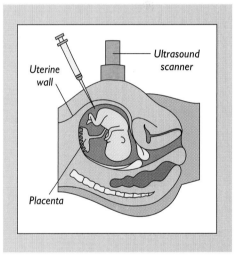

FIG 3–7

Ultrasound can be used as early as 4 or 5 weeks after conception; before this time the fetus is not large enough to generate an interpretable image. Ultrasound pictures are useful for determining the position of the fetus in the uterus and, at 16 to 20 weeks after conception, its sex. Ultrasound can also help in detecting twins or other multiple pregnancies. Finally, ultrasound can be used to identify gross physical deformities, such as abnormal growth of the head.

When a genetic disorder is suspected, two other techniques are particularly valuable because they provide a sample of fetal cells that can be analyzed. **In *amniocentesis*, a needle is inserted through the mother's abdomen to obtain a sample of the amniotic fluid that surrounds the fetus.** Amniocentesis is typically performed at approximately 16 weeks after conception. As you can see in the top diagram, ultrasound is used to guide the needle into the uterus. The fluid contains skin cells that can be grown in a laboratory dish and then analyzed to determine the genotype of the fetus.

**In *chorionic villus sampling (CVS)*, a sample of tissue is obtained from the chorion, part of the placenta, and analyzed.** The bottom diagram shows that a small tube, inserted through the vagina and into the uterus, is used to

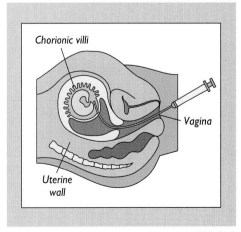

FIG 3–8

collect a small plug of cells from the placenta. CVS is often preferred over amniocentesis because it can be done about 8 weeks after conception, nearly 2 months earlier than amniocentesis. In both cases, results are returned from the lab within several days.

With samples obtained from either amniocentesis or CVS, about 200 different genetic disorders can be detected. These procedures are virtually error-free, but they have a price: Miscarriages are slightly more likely—1 or 2 percent—after amniocentesis or CVS (Cunningham, MacDonald, & Gant, 1989). A woman must decide if the information gained from amniocentesis or CVS justifies the slight risk of a miscarriage.

Ultrasound, amniocentesis, and chorionic villus sampling have made it much easier to determine if prenatal development is progressing normally. But what happens when it is not? Until recently a woman's options were limited: She could continue the pregnancy or end it. But options are expanding. **A whole new field called *fetal medicine* is concerned with treating prenatal problems before birth.** One approach in fetal medicine is to treat disorders medically, by administering drugs or hormones to the fetus. In one case, when ultrasound pictures showed a fetus with an enlarged thyroid gland that would have made delivery difficult, a hormone was injected into the amniotic fluid to shrink the thyroid gland and allow normal delivery (Davidson et al., 1991). In another case, amniocentesis revealed that a fetus had inherited an immune system disorder that would leave the baby highly vulnerable to infections, so healthy immune cells were injected into the umbilical cord (Elmer-DeWitt, 1994).

Another way to correct prenatal problems is fetal surgery. Doctors partially remove the fetus from the uterus, perform corrective surgery, then return the fetus to the uterus. Some cases of spina bifida have been corrected with fetal surgery in the seventh or eighth month of pregnancy. Surgeons cut through the mother's abdominal wall to expose the fetus, then cut through the fetal abdominal wall; the spinal cord is repaired, and the fetus is returned to the uterus (Grovak, 1999).

*The emerging field of fetal medicine treats prenatal problems medically, with surgery or with genetic engineering.*

Fetal surgery has also been used to correct some heart defects and urinary tract blockages (Ohlendorf-Moffat, 1991). Fetal surgery holds great promise, but it is still highly experimental and therefore considered as a last resort.

Yet another approach to treating prenatal problems is genetic engineering—replacing defective genes with synthetic normal genes. Take PKU as an example. Remember, from Module 2.2, that if a baby inherits the recessive allele for PKU from both parents, toxins accumulate that cause mental retardation. In theory, it should be possible to take a sample of cells from the fetus, remove the recessive genes from the 12th pair of chromosomes, and replace them with the dominant genes. These "repaired" cells could then be injected into the fetus, where they would multiply and cause enough enzyme to be produced to break down phenylalanine, thereby avoiding PKU (Verma, 1990).

As with fetal surgery, however, translating idea into practice has been difficult, and there are many problems yet to be solved (Marshall, 1995). Nevertheless, gene therapy has been successful in a few cases.

Fetal medicine may sound like science fiction, but these techniques have been used with humans. Granted, they are highly experimental and failures occur, but just as the end of the 20th century has seen huge progress in prenatal diagnosis, so the turn of the century should make prenatal treatment more common.

*Answers to Chloe's questions:* Return to Chloe's questions in the module-opening vignette (page 64) and answer them for her. If you're not certain, I'll help by giving you the pages in this module where the answers appear:

- Question about her computer monitor—page 69
- Question about her nightly glass of wine—page 68
- Question about giving birth to a baby with mental retardation—page 66

## Check Your Learning

**1.** Important general risk factors in pregnancy include a woman's nutrition, _____, and her age.

**2.** Adolescent girls can have problem-free pregnancies and give birth to healthy babies if _____.

**3.** When it comes to drugs, the best advice for a pregnant woman is _____.

**4.** Some of the most dangerous teratogens are _____ because a pregnant woman is often unaware of their presence.

**5.** During the period of the zygote, exposure to a teratogen typically _____.

**6.** Two techniques used to determine if a fetus has a hereditary disorder are amnio-centesis and _____.

> **Imagine that you are 42 years old and pregnant. Would you want to have amniocentesis or CVS to determine the genotype of your fetus? Why or why not?**

**Answers:** (1) prolonged stress, (2) they receive adequate prenatal care, (3) to avoid all drugs, including aspirin, caffeine, and nicotine, (4) environmental hazards, (5) results in miscarriage (spontaneous abortion of the fertilized egg), (6) chorionic villus sampling (CVS)

# Happy Birthday!

## Learning Objectives

- **What are the stages in labor and delivery?**
- **What are "natural" ways of coping with the pain of childbirth? Is childbirth at home safe?**
- **What are the effects of postpartum depression?**
- **What are some complications that can occur during birth?**

## 3.3

Labor and Delivery

Approaches to Childbirth

Postpartum Depression

Birth Complications

*Marlena is about to begin classes to prepare for her baby's birth. She is relieved that the classes are finally starting because this means the end of pregnancy is in sight. But all the talk she has heard about "breathing exercises" and "coaching" sounds pretty silly to her. Marlena would prefer to get knocked out for the delivery and wake up when everything is over.*

As women like Marlena near the end of pregnancy, they find that sleeping and breathing become more difficult, they tire more rapidly, they become constipated, and their legs and feet swell. Women look forward to birth, both to relieve their discomfort and, of course, to see their baby. In this module, we'll see the different stages involved in birth, review various approaches to childbirth, and look at problems that can arise. We'll also look at childbirth classes like the one Marlena is taking.

## Labor and Delivery

In a typical pregnancy, a woman goes into labor about 38 weeks after conception. Scientists don't know all the events that initiate labor, but one key element seems to be a "ready" signal from an area of the fetal brain that tracks the progress of developing body organs and systems (Palca, 1991).

*Labor* is named appropriately, for it is the most intense, prolonged physical effort that humans experience. Labor is usually divided into the three stages shown in the diagram. The first stage begins when the muscles of the uterus start to contract. These contractions force amniotic fluid up against the cervix, the opening at the bottom of the uterus that is the entryway to the birth canal. The wavelike motion of the amniotic fluid with each contraction causes the cervix to enlarge gradually.

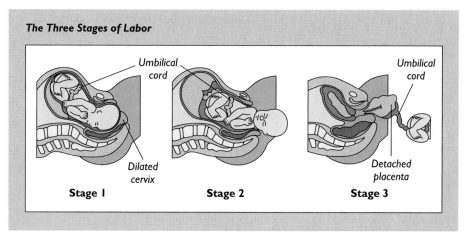

*The Three Stages of Labor*

Umbilical cord

Dilated cervix

**Stage 1**

Umbilical cord

**Stage 2**

Umbilical cord

Detached placenta

**Stage 3**

FIG 3–9

In the early phase of Stage 1, the contractions are weak and spaced irregularly. By the end of the early phase, the cervix is about 5 centimeters (2 inches) in diameter. In the late phase of Stage 1, contractions are stronger and occur at regular intervals. By the end of the late phase, the cervix is about 7 to 8 centimeters (3 inches) in diameter. In the transition phase of Stage 1, contractions are intense and sometimes occur without interruption. Women report that the transition phase is the most painful part of labor. At the end of transition, the cervix is about 10 centimeters (4 inches) in diameter.

Stage 1 lasts from 12 to 24 hours for the birth of a first child, and most of the time is spent in the relative tranquility of the early phase. Stage 1 is usually shorter for subsequent births, with 3 to 8 hours being common. However, as the wide ranges suggest, these times are only rough approximations; the actual times vary greatly among women and are virtually impossible to predict.

> In the first stage of labor, contractions cause the cervix to expand; in the second, the baby is born; and in the third, the placenta is expelled.

When the cervix is fully enlarged, the second stage of labor begins. Most women feel a strong urge to push the baby out, using their abdominal muscles. This pushing, along with uterine contractions, propels the baby down the birth canal. **Soon the top of the baby's head appears, an event known as** *crowning.* In about an hour for first births and less for later births, the baby passes through the birth canal and emerges from the mother's body. **Most babies arrive head first, but a small percentage come out feet or bottom first, which is known as a** *breech presentation.* (I was one of these rare bottom-first babies and have been the butt of bad jokes ever since.) The baby's birth marks the end of the second stage of labor.

With the baby born, you might think that labor is over, but it's not. There is a third stage, in which the placenta (also called, appropriately, the *afterbirth*) is expelled from the uterus. The placenta becomes detached from the wall of the uterus and contractions force it out through the birth canal. This stage is quite brief, typically lasting 10 to 15 minutes.

## Approaches to Childbirth

When my mother went into labor (with me), she was admitted to a nearby hospital, where she soon was administered a general anesthetic. My father went to a waiting room, where he and other fathers-to-be anxiously awaited news of their babies. Some time later my mother recovered from anesthesia and learned that she had given birth to a healthy baby boy. My father, who had grown tired of waiting, had gone back to work, so he got the good news in a phone call.

These were standard hospital procedures in 1950, and virtually all American babies were born this way. No longer. Since the 1960s, many women have used more "natural" or prepared approaches to childbirth, viewing labor and delivery as life events to be celebrated, not medical procedures to be endured. One of the fundamental beliefs of all prepared approaches is that birth is more likely to be problem-free and rewarding when mothers and fathers understand what's happening during pregnancy, labor, and delivery. Consequently, prepared childbirth means going to classes to learn basic facts about pregnancy and childbirth (not unlike the material presented in this chapter).

Childbirth classes also spend considerable time showing women how to handle the pain of childbirth. Natural methods of dealing with pain are emphasized over medication. Why? When a woman is anesthetized—either with general anesthesia or local anesthesia (only the lower body is numbed)—she can't use her abdominal muscles to help push the baby through the birth canal. Without this pushing, the obstetrician may have to use mechanical devices to pull the baby through the birth canal, which involves some risk to the baby (Johanson et al., 1993). Also, drugs that reduce the pain of childbirth cross the placenta and can affect the baby. Consequently, when a woman receives large doses of pain-relieving medication, her baby is often withdrawn or irritable for days or even weeks (Brazelton, Nugent, & Lester, 1987). These effects are temporary, but they may give the new mother the impression that she has a difficult baby. It is best, therefore, to minimize the use of pain-relieving drugs during birth.

Childbirth classes emphasize three strategies to counter birth pain without drugs. First, because pain often feels greater when a person is tense, pregnant women learn ways to relax during labor. One technique is deep breathing. Second, women are taught visual imagery, picturing in detail a reassuring, pleasant scene or experience. Whenever they begin to experience pain during labor, they focus intensely on this image instead of the pain. A third strategy is to involve a supportive "coach." The father-to-be, a relative, or close friend attends childbirth classes with the mother-to-be. The coach learns the techniques for coping with pain and, like the man in the photo, practices them with the pregnant woman. During labor and delivery, the coach is present to help the woman use the techniques she has learned and to offer support and encouragement.

Although Marlena, the pregnant woman in the vignette at the beginning of the module, may have her doubts about childbirth classes, research shows that they are useful (Hetherington, 1990). Although most mothers who attend childbirth classes use some medication to reduce the pain of labor, they typically use less than mothers who do not attend childbirth classes. Also, mothers and fathers who attend childbirth classes feel more positive about labor and birth compared to mothers and fathers who do not attend classes.

Another basic premise of the trend toward natural childbirth is that birth need not always take place in a hospital. Virtually all babies in the United States are born in hospitals—only 1 percent are born at home. However, home birth is a common practice in Europe. In the Netherlands, for example, about one-third of all births take place at home. Advocates note that home delivery is less expensive and that most women are more relaxed during labor in their homes. Many women also enjoy the greater control they have over labor and birth in a home delivery. A health care professional is present for home labor and delivery. Sometimes this is a doctor, but more often it is a trained nurse-midwife like the one in the photo.

For Americans accustomed to hospital delivery, home delivery can seem like a risky proposition. Is it safe? Yes, but with a very important catch. Birth problems are no more common in babies delivered at home than in babies delivered in a hospital *if* the woman is healthy, her pregnancy has been problem-free, the labor and delivery are expected to be problem-free, and a trained health care professional is there to assist (Rooks et al., 1989). If there is any reason to believe that problems requiring medical assistance might occur, labor and delivery should take place in the hospital, not at home.

Another alternative to home or hospital birth is the freestanding birth center. Birthing centers are typi-

Home delivery is safe when a woman's pregnancy has been problem-free, birth is expected to be trouble-free, and a health care professional is present.

cally small, independent clinics. A woman, her coach, and other family members and friends are assigned a birthing room that is often decorated to look homelike rather than institutional. A doctor or nurse-midwife assists in labor and delivery, which takes place entirely in the birthing room, where it can be observed by all. Like home deliveries, birthing centers are best for deliveries that are expected to be trouble-free.

## Postpartum Depression

For parents, the time immediately after a trouble-free birth is full of excitement, pride, and joy—the much anticipated baby is finally here! Yet roughly half of all new mothers find that their initial excitement gives way to irritation, resentment, and crying spells. These feelings usually last a week or two and probably reflect both the stress of caring for a new baby and the physiological changes that take place as a woman's body returns to a nonpregnant state (Brockington, 1996).

**For 10 to 15 percent of new mothers, however, irritability continues for months and is often accompanied by feelings of low self-worth, disturbed sleep,**

**poor appetite, and apathy—a condition known as** *postpartum depression.* Postpartum depression does not strike randomly. Biology contributes: Particularly high levels of hormones during the later phases of pregnancy place women at risk for postpartum depression (Harris et al., 1994). Experience also contributes: Women are more likely to experience postpartum depression when they were depressed before pregnancy, are coping with other life stresses (e.g., death of a loved one, moving), did not plan to become pregnant, and lack other adults (e.g., the father) to support their adjustment to motherhood (Brockington, 1996; Campbell et al., 1992).

Women who are lethargic and emotionless do not mother warmly and enthusiastically. They don't touch and cuddle their new babies much or talk to them. If the depression lasts only a few weeks, babies are unaffected. However, if postpartum depression lasts for months and months, children of depressed mothers are more likely to become depressed themselves and are also at risk for other behavior problems (e.g., Murray, Fiori-Cowley, & Hooper, 1996).

All new mothers need support from family and friends, but if depression doesn't lift after a few weeks, the mother should see a mental health professional.

## Birth Complications

Women who are healthy when they become pregnant usually have a normal pregnancy, labor, and delivery. When women are not healthy or don't receive adequate prenatal care, problems can surface during labor and delivery. (Of course, even healthy women face these problems, but not as often.) In this section, we'll look at problems associated with lack of oxygen, being born too early, and being born underweight.

Lack of Oxygen.  Until birth, the fetus obtains oxygen from the mother's blood that flows through the placenta and umbilical cord. **If this flow of blood is disrupted, infants do not receive adequate oxygen, a condition known as** *anoxia.* Anoxia sometimes occurs during labor and delivery because the umbilical cord is pinched or squeezed shut, cutting off the flow of blood. **Anoxia may also reflect** *placental abruption,* **which occurs when the placenta becomes detached from the wall of the uterus, severing the connection to the mother's blood supply.** Anoxia is very serious because it can lead to mental retardation or death (Petrie, 1991).

To guard against anoxia, fetal heart rate is monitored during labor, either by ultrasound or with a tiny electrode that is passed through the vagina and attached to the scalp of the fetus. An abrupt change in heart rate can be a sign that the fetus is not receiving enough oxygen. If the heart rate does change suddenly, a health care professional will try to confirm that the fetus is in distress, perhaps by measuring fetal heart rate with a stethoscope on the mother's abdomen.

When a fetus is in distress, a doctor may decide to remove it from the mother's uterus surgically (Guillemin, 1993). **In a** *cesarean section* **(or** *C-section)* **an incision is made in the abdomen to remove the baby from the uterus.** A C-section poses little risk for babies, although they are often depressed from the anesthesia that the mother receives before the operation. However, for mothers, a C-section is riskier than a vaginal delivery because of increased bleeding and greater danger of infection.

In the United States, about 25 percent of babies are delivered by C-section, up from only 5 percent 30 years ago (Ventura et al., 1994). Many health care professionals believe C-sections are often performed unnecessarily. Because methods for monitoring fetal heart rate are not foolproof, many C-sections are performed when the fetus is not really in distress. C-sections are also frequently used to end a slow or difficult labor. The U.S. Public Health Service has urged doctors to reduce the number of C-sections, saving the procedure only for emergencies that demand immediate delivery (Ventura et al., 1994).

### Prematurity and Low Birth Weight.

Normally, gestation takes 38 weeks from conception to birth. *Premature infants* **are born less than 38 weeks after conception.** *Small-for-date infants* **are substantially smaller than would be expected based on the length of time since conception.** Sometimes these two complications coincide, but not necessarily. Some, but not all, small-for-date infants are premature. And some, but not all, premature infants are small-for-date. In other words, an infant can go the full 9-month term and be under the average 7- to 8-pound birth weight of newborns; the child is therefore small-for-date but not premature. Similarly, an infant born at 7 months that weighs 3 pounds (the average weight of a 7-month fetus) is only premature. But if the baby born after 7 months weighs less than the average, it is both premature and small-for-date.

Premature babies often develop normally, but small-for-date babies usually do not.

Of the two complications, prematurity is the less serious. In the first year or so, premature infants often lag behind full-term infants in many facets of development, but by age 2 or 3 years, differences vanish and most premature infants develop normally thereafter (Greenberg & Crnic, 1988).

Prospects are usually not so optimistic for small-for-date babies like the one shown in the photo. These infants are most often born to women who smoke or drink alcohol frequently during pregnancy or who do not eat enough nutritious food (Chomitz, Cheung, & Lieberman, 1995). Babies that weigh less than 1,500 grams (3.3 pounds) at birth often do not survive; when they do, they are usually delayed in their cognitive and motor development (Ventura et al., 1994).

Small-for-date babies who weigh more than 1,500 grams have better prospects, though some do not reach as high a developmental level as others. (This is also true but to a lesser extent for babies who weigh less than 1,500 grams.) Why? Environmental factors turn out to be critical. Development of small-for-date infants depends upon the quality of care they receive in the hospital and at home. These babies can thrive if they receive excellent medical care and if their home environment is supportive and stimulating. Unfortunately, not all at-risk babies have these optimal experiences. Many receive inadequate medical care because their families are living in poverty and can't afford it. Others experience stress or disorder in their family life. In these cases, development is usually delayed.

The importance of a supportive environment for at-risk babies was demonstrated dramatically in a longitudinal study of all children born in 1955 on the Hawaiian island of Kauai (Werner, 1995). At-risk newborns who grew up in stable homes were indistinguishable from children born without birth complications. ("Stable family environment" was defined as two supportive, mentally healthy parents present throughout childhood.) When at-risk newborns had an unstable family environment because of divorce, parental alcoholism, or mental illness, for example, they lagged behind their peers in intellectual and social development.

The Hawaiian study underscores a point I have made several times in this chapter: Development is best when pregnant women receive good prenatal care and children live in a supportive environment. The "Cultural Influences" feature makes the same point in a different way, by looking at infant mortality around the world.

### Infant Mortality

In many respects, medical facilities in the United States are the finest in the world. Why, then, do American babies fare so poorly compared to infants from other countries? *Infant mortality* **is the number of infants out of 1,000 births who die before their first birthday.** In the United States, about 9 babies out of 1,000—roughly 1 percent—live less than a year. This figure places the United States near the bottom of the industrialized countries of the world (Wegman, 1994).

One reason so many American babies die is low birth weight. The United States has more babies with low birth weight than virtually all other industrialized countries, and we've already seen that low birth weight places an infant at risk. Low birth weight can usually be prevented if a pregnant woman gets regular prenatal care, but many pregnant women in the United States receive inadequate or no prenatal care. Virtually all the countries that rank ahead of the United States provide complete prenatal care at little or no cost. Many of these countries also provide for paid leaves of absence for pregnant women (Kamerman, 1993).

Prenatal development is the foundation of all development, and only with regular prenatal checkups can we know if this foundation is being laid properly. Pregnant women and the children they carry need this care, and countries need to be sure that they receive it. ●

## Check Your Learning

1. The first (and longest) stage of labor includes early, late, and _____ phases.

2. The highlight of the third stage of labor is that _____.

3. Two problems with using anesthesia during labor are that a woman can't use her abdominal muscles to help push the baby down the birth canal and _____.

4. To help women cope with labor pain without drugs, childbirth classes emphasize the importance of relaxation, a soothing visual image, and _____.

5. After giving birth, women who suffer _____ often feel irritable, have poor appetite and disturbed sleep, and are apathetic.

6. High infant mortality rates in the United States reflect low birth weight, which has been linked to _____.

> Do studies on the long-term effects of prematurity and low birth weight provide evidence for continuity in development or discontinuity in development? Why?

**Answers:** (1) transition, (2) the placenta is expelled, (3) medication crosses the placenta and affects the baby, (4) a supportive coach, (5) postpartum depression, (6) inadequate prenatal care

# 3.4

# The Newborn

## Learning Objectives

● How do we determine if a baby is healthy and adjusting to life outside the uterus?

● How do reflexes help newborns interact with the world?

● What behavioral states are observable in newborns?

● How well do newborns experience the world? Can they learn from experience?

*Lisa and Steve, the proud but exhausted parents, were astonished at how their lives revolved around 10-day-old Dan's eating and sleeping. Lisa felt as if she were feeding Dan around the clock. When Dan napped, Lisa would think of many things she should do but usually napped herself because she was so tired. Steve wondered when Dan would start sleeping through the night so that he and Lisa could get a good night's sleep themselves.*

The newborn baby that thrills parents like Lisa and Steve is actually rather homely, as this photo of my son Ben shows. I took it when he was 20 seconds old. Like other newborns, Ben is covered with blood and vernix, the white-colored "grease" that protects the fetus's skin during the many months of prenatal development. His head is temporarily distorted from coming through the birth canal, he has a beer belly, and he is bow-legged. Still, to us he was beautiful, and we were glad he'd finally arrived.

What can newborns like Dan and Ben do? We'll answer that question in this module and, as we do, learn when Lisa and Steve can expect to resume a full night's sleep.

## Assessing the Newborn

Imagine that a mother has just asked you if her newborn baby is healthy. How would you decide? You would probably check to see if it seemed to be breathing and if its heart seemed to be beating. **In fact, breathing and heartbeat are two vital signs that are included in the** *Apgar score,* **a measure devised by Virginia Apgar to evaluate the newborn baby's condition.** The other vital signs are muscle tone, presence of reflexes such as coughing, and skin tone. Each of the five vital signs receives a score of 0, 1, or 2, with 2 being optimal. For example, a newborn whose muscles are completely limp receives a 0; a baby who shows strong movement of arms and legs receives a 2. The five scores are added together, with a score of 7 or more indicating a baby in good physical condition. A score of 4 to 6 means the newborn will need special attention and care. A score of 3 or less signals a life-threatening situation that requires emergency medical care (Apgar, 1953).

The Apgar score provides a quick, approximate assessment of the newborn's status by focusing on the body systems needed to sustain life. For a comprehensive evaluation of the newborn's well-being, pediatricians and child development specialists use the Neonatal Behavioral Assessment Scale, or NBAS (Brazelton, 1984). The NBAS evaluates a broad range of newborn abilities and behaviors that the infant needs to adjust to life outside the uterus. It measures reflexes, hearing, vision, alertness, irritability, and consolability (how easily the infant is soothed). The NBAS, along with a thorough physical examination, is particularly helpful in diagnosing disorders of the central nervous system (Brazelton et al., 1987).

## The Newborn's Reflexes

Most newborns are well prepared to begin interacting with their world. **The newborn is endowed with a rich set of *reflexes*, unlearned responses that are triggered by a specific form of stimulation.** The following chart shows the many reflexes commonly found in newborn babies.

### Some Major Reflexes Found in Newborns

| Name | Response | Significance |
|------|----------|--------------|
| Babinski | A baby's toes fan out when the sole of the foot is stroked from heel to toe | Unknown |
| Blink | A baby's eyes close in response to bright light or loud noise | Protects the eyes |
| Moro | A baby throws its arms out and then inward (as if embracing) in response to loud noise or when its head falls | May help a baby cling to its mother |
| Palmar | A baby grasps an object placed in the palm of its hand | Precursor to voluntary walking |
| Rooting | When a baby's cheek is stroked, it turns its head toward the stroking and opens its mouth | Helps a baby find the nipple |
| Stepping | A baby who is held upright by an adult and is then moved forward begins to step rhythmically | Precursor to voluntary walking |
| Sucking | A baby sucks when an object is placed in its mouth | Permits feeding |
| Withdrawal | A baby withdraws its foot when the sole is pricked with a pin | Protects a baby from unpleasant stimulation |

TABLE 3–4

Some reflexes pave the way for newborns to get the nutrients they need to grow: Rooting and sucking ensure that the newborn is well prepared to begin a new diet of life-sustaining milk. Other reflexes protect the newborn from danger in the environment. The blink and withdrawal reflexes, for example, help newborns avoid unpleasant stimulation.

Yet other reflexes serve as the foundation for larger, voluntary patterns of motor activity. For example, the stepping reflex looks like a precursor to walking. In fact, we'll see in Module 4.4 that babies who practice the stepping reflex learn to walk earlier (Zelazo, 1983).

Reflexes indicate whether or not the newborn's nervous system is working properly. For example, infants with damage to their sciatic nerve, which is found in the spinal cord, do not show the withdrawal reflex, and infants who have problems with the lower part of the spine do not show the Babinski reflex. If these or other reflexes are weak or missing altogether, a thorough physical and behavioral assessment is called for.

### Newborn States

ewborns spend most of their day alternating among four states (St James-Roberts & Plewis, 1996; Wolff, 1987):

- *Alert inactivity.* The baby is calm with eyes open and attentive; the baby looks as if he is deliberately inspecting his environment.
- *Waking activity.* The baby's eyes are open, but they seem unfocused; the baby moves her arms or legs in bursts of uncoordinated motion.
- *Crying.* The baby cries vigorously, usually accompanying this with agitated but uncoordinated motion.
- *Sleeping.* The baby's eyes are closed and the baby drifts back and forth from periods of regular breathing and stillness to periods of irregular breathing and gentle arm and leg motion.

Crying. Of these states, crying captures the attention of parents and researchers alike. Newborns spend 2 to 3 hours each day crying or on the verge of crying. If you've not spent much time around newborns, you might think that all crying is pretty much alike. In fact, scientists and parents can identify three distinctive types of cries (Snow, 1998). **A *basic cry* starts softly, then gradually becomes more intense and usually occurs when a baby is hungry or tired; a *mad cry* is a more intense version of a basic cry; and a *pain cry* begins with a sudden, long burst of crying, followed by a long pause and gasping.**

Crying is actually the newborn's first attempt to communicate with others. When a baby like the one in the photo cries, it's telling parents that it's hungry, tired, angry, or hurt. By responding, parents encourage their newborn's efforts to communicate.

Parents are naturally concerned when their baby cries, and if they can't quiet a crying baby, their concern mounts and can easily give way to frustration and annoyance. It's no surprise, then, that parents develop little tricks for soothing their babies. The "Real Children" feature shows what one mother did when her baby cried.

REAL CHILDREN

### Calming Jake

Whenever 4-week-old Jake cried, Peggy's first reaction was to try to figure out why he was crying. Was he hungry? Was his diaper wet? Simply addressing the needs that caused Jake to cry in the first place usually worked. If he continued to cry, she found that the best way to quiet Jake was to lift him to her shoulder and rock him or walk with him. The combination of being upright, restrained, in physical contact with her, and moving all helped to calm him. Sometimes Peggy would swaddle Jake—wrap him tightly in a blanket—and then rock him in a cradle or take him for a ride in a stroller. Another method Peggy used sometimes was to give Jake a pacifier to suck; sucking seemed to allow Jake to calm himself. Sometimes, as a last resort, she'd strap Jake in his car seat and go on a drive. The motion of the car seemed to soothe him.

Peggy's techniques weren't foolproof. Some would work one day but not another. Sometimes Peggy combined these techniques, for example, taking a swaddled Jake to her shoulder. Sometimes nothing seemed to work, so she'd just put Jake in his crib. And sometimes, as if he were teasing Peggy, Jake would stop crying spontaneously and go right to sleep! ●

## Sleeping.

Crying may get parents' attention, but sleep is what newborns do more than anything else. They sleep 16 to 18 hours daily. The problem for tired parents, like Lisa and Steve from the vignette, is that newborns sleep in naps taken round the clock. Newborns typically go through a cycle of wakefulness and sleep about every four hours. That is, they will be awake for about an hour, sleep for three hours, then start the cycle anew. During the hour when newborns are awake, they regularly move between the different waking states several times. Cycles of alert inactivity, waking activity, and crying are common.

As babies grow older, the sleep-wake cycle gradually begins to correspond to the day-night cycle (St James-Roberts & Plewis, 1996). Most babies begin sleeping through the night at about three or four months, a major milestone for bleary-eyed parents like Lisa and Steve.

**Roughly half of newborns' sleep is *irregular* or *rapid-eye-movement (REM) sleep*, a time when the body is quite active.** During REM sleep, newborns move their arms and legs, they may grimace, and their eyes may dart beneath their eyelids. Brain waves register fast activity, the heart beats more rapidly, and breathing is more rapid. **In *regular* or *nonREM sleep*, breathing, heart rate, and brain activity are steady and newborns lie quietly without the twitching associated with REM sleep.** REM sleep becomes less frequent as infants grow. By four months, only 40 percent of sleep is REM sleep. By the first birthday, REM sleep drops to 25 percent, not far from the adult average of 20 percent (Halpern, MacLean, & Baumeister, 1995).

The function of REM sleep is still debated. Older children and adults dream during REM sleep, and brain waves during REM sleep resemble those of an alert, awake person. Consequently, many scientists believe that REM sleep stimulates the brain in some way that helps foster growth in the nervous system (Halpern et al., 1995; Roffwarg, Muzio, & Dement, 1966).

## Sudden Infant Death Syndrome.

For many parents of young babies, sleep is sometimes a cause of concern. **In *sudden infant death syndrome (SIDS)*, a healthy baby dies suddenly, for no apparent reason.** Approximately 1 to 3 of every 1,000 American babies dies from SIDS. Most of them are between 2 and 4 months old.

Scientists don't know the exact causes of SIDS, but they do know several contributing factors. Babies are more vulnerable to SIDS if they were born prematurely or with low birth weight. They are also more vulnerable if their parents smoke. SIDS is more likely when a baby sleeps on its stomach (face down) than when it sleeps on its back (face up). Finally, SIDS is more likely during winter, when babies sometimes become overheated from too many blankets and too heavy sleepwear (Carroll & Loughlin, 1994). Evidently, SIDS infants, many of whom were born prematurely or with low birth weight, are less able to withstand physiological stresses and imbalances that are brought on by cigarette smoke, breathing that is temporarily interrupted, or overheating.

In 1992, based on mounting evidence that SIDS more often occurred when infants slept on their stomachs, the American Academy of Pediatrics (AAP) began advising parents to put babies to sleep on their backs or sides. In 1994, the AAP joined forces with the U. S. Public Health Service to launch a national program to educate parents about the dangers of SIDS and the importance of putting babies to sleep on their backs. The "Back to Sleep" campaign was widely publicized through brochures, posters like the one shown here, and videos. Since the "Back to Sleep" campaign began, research shows that far more infants are now sleeping on their backs and that the incidence of SIDS has dropped (NIH, 1998). The best advice for parents—particularly if their babies were premature or small-for-date—is to keep their babies away from smoke, to put them on their backs to sleep, and don't overdress them or wrap them too tightly in blankets (Willinger, 1995).

## Perception and Learning in the Newborn

Do you believe it is important to talk to newborns and give them fuzzy little toys? Should their rooms be bright and colorful? If you do, you really believe two things about newborns. First, you believe that newborns can perceive experiences—they can see, smell, hear, taste, and feel. Second, you believe that sensory experiences are somehow registered in the newborn—through learning and memory—because unless experiences are registered, they can't influence later behavior. You'll be happy to know that research confirms your beliefs. All the basic perceptual systems are operating at some level at birth. The world outside the uterus can be seen, smelled, heard, tasted, and felt (Aslin, 1987). Moreover, newborns show the capacity to learn and remember. They change their behavior based on their experiences (Rovee-Collier, 1987).

We'll discuss these perceptual changes in more detail in Chapter 5, and we'll discuss learning and memory in Chapter 7. For now, the important point is that newborns are remarkably prepared to interact with the world. Adaptive reflexes coupled with perceptual and learning skills provide a solid foundation for the rest of child development.

## Check Your Learning

1. The _____ is based on five vital functions and provides a quick indication of a newborn's physical health.

2. Some reflexes help infants get necessary nutrients; other reflexes protect infants from danger; and still other reflexes _____.

3. A baby lying calmly with its eyes open and focused is in a state of _____.

4. Common among infants are the basic cry, the mad cry, and the _____ cry.

5. The campaign to reduce SIDS emphasizes that infants should _____.

**Newborns are remarkably well prepared to interact with their environments. Which of the theories described in Module 1.2 predict such preparedness? Which do not?**

**Answers:** (1) Apgar score, (2) serve as the basis for later motor behavior, (3) alert inactivity, (4) pain, (5) sleep on their backs

# Prenatal Development, Birth, and the Newborn

# 3

## IN PERSPECTIVE

Prenatal development sets the stage for a child's life. In Module 3.1, we saw that prenatal development includes the period of the zygote, when the fertilized egg is implanted in the uterine wall; the period of the embryo, when major body parts are formed; and the period of the fetus, when body systems begin to function. In Module 3.2, we discovered that prenatal development can be disrupted by inadequate nutrition, stress, diseases, drugs, and environmental hazards. Advances in prenatal diagnosis make it easier to track prenatal development, and the new field of fetal medicine may one day make it possible to correct problems before birth. In Module 3.3, we traced the three stages of labor and delivery, learned about natural childbirth, and saw the complications associated with lack of oxygen, prematurity, and low birth weight. Finally, in Module 3.4, we found how newborns' health and behavioral development can be assessed, and we saw that newborns are born with many reflexes. We also learned about newborn states and discovered that newborns are quite able to perceive experiences and learn from them.

This chapter is a good opportunity to highlight the theme that *early development is related to later development but not perfectly*. Remember the Hawaiian study? This study showed that outcomes for at-risk infants are not uniform. When at-risk infants grow up in a stable, supportive environment, they become quite normal children. But when they grow up in stressful environments, they lag intellectually and socially. Similarly, SIDS is more likely to affect babies born prematurely and with low birth weight, yet not all of these babies die of SIDS. When premature and low-birth-weight babies sleep on their backs, are not overheated, and do not inhale smoke, they're unlikely to die from SIDS. Traumatic events early in development, such as being born early or underweight, do not predetermine the rest of a child's life, but they do make some developmental paths easier to follow than others.

## See for Yourself

Words can hardly capture the miracle of a newborn baby. If you have never seen a newborn, you need to see one, or even better, a roomful. Arrange to visit the maternity ward of a local hospital, which will include a nursery for newborns. Through a large viewing window, you will be able to observe a few or as many as 15 to 20 newborns. These babies will no longer be covered with blood or vernix, but you will be able to see how the newborn's head is often distorted by its journey from the birth canal.

As you watch the babies, look for reflexive behavior and changes in states. Watch while a baby sucks its fingers. Find a baby who seems to be awake and alert, then note how long the baby stays this way. When alertness wanes, watch for the behaviors that replace it. Finally, observe how different the newborns look and act from each other. The wonderful variety and diversity found among human beings is already evident in humans who are hours or days old. See for yourself!

## Resources

*For more information about . . .*

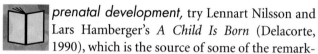 *prenatal development,* try Lennart Nilsson and Lars Hamberger's *A Child Is Born* (Delacorte, 1990), which is the source of some of the remarkable photographs of the zygote, embryo, and fetus that appear in this chapter

 *virtually any aspect of pregnancy,* visit the New York Online Access to Health (NOAH) Web site:

**http://www.noah.cuny.edu/pregnancy/pregnancy.html**

## Key Terms

**age of viability** 62
**amniocentesis** 73
**amnion** 60
**amniotic fluid** 60
**anoxia** 79
**Apgar score** 82
**basic cry** 84
**breech presentation** 76
**cephalocaudal principle** 60
**cerebral cortex** 62
**cesarean section (C-section)** 79
**chorionic villus sampling (CVS)** 73
**crowning** 76
**ectoderm** 59
**embryo** 59

**endoderm** 59
**fetal alcohol syndrome (FAS)** 68
**fetal medicine** 74
**germ disc** 59
**implantation** 59
**infant mortality** 81
**mad cry** 84
**mesoderm** 59
**non-REM (regular) sleep** 85
**pain cry** 84
**period of the fetus** 61
**placenta** 59
**placental abruption** 79
**postpartum depression** 79
**premature infants** 80

**prenatal development** 58
**proximodistal principle** 60
**rapid-eye-movement (REM) sleep (irregular sleep)** 85
**reflexes** 83
**small-for-date infants** 80
**spina bifida** 65
**stress** 65
**sudden infant death syndrome (SIDS)** 85
**teratogen** 67
**ultrasound** 73
**umbilical cord** 60
**vernix** 61
**zygote** 58

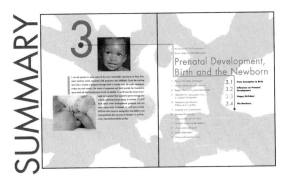

# 3.1 From Conception to Birth

## Period of the Zygote
The first period of prenatal development lasts 2 weeks. It begins when the egg is fertilized by the sperm and ends when the fertilized egg has implanted in the wall of the uterus.

## Period of the Embryo
The second period of prenatal development begins 2 weeks after conception and ends 8 weeks after. This is a period when most major body structures are formed. Growth in this period is cephalocaudal and proximodistal.

## Period of the Fetus
The third period of prenatal development begins 8 weeks after conception and lasts until birth. In this period, the fetus becomes much larger and body systems begin to function.

# 3.2 Influences on Prenatal Development

## General Risk Factors
Prenatal development can be harmed if a pregnant woman does not provide adequate nutrition for the developing organism or experiences considerable stress. Teenagers often have problem pregnancies because they rarely receive adequate prenatal care. Women in their 30s are likely to have problem-free pregnancies if they are in good health.

## Teratogens: Diseases, Drugs, and Environmental Hazards
Teratogens are agents that can cause abnormal prenatal development. Several diseases are teratogens. Only by avoiding these diseases entirely can a pregnant woman escape their harmful consequences. Many drugs that adults take are teratogens. Environmental teratogens are particularly dangerous because a pregnant woman may not know when these substances are present.

## How Teratogens Influence Prenatal Development
The effect of teratogens depends upon the genotype of the organism, when during prenatal development the organism is exposed to the teratogen, and the amount of exposure. The impact of a teratogen may not be evident until later in life.

## Prenatal Diagnosis and Treatment
Ultrasound uses sound waves to generate a picture of the fetus that reveals the position of the fetus, its sex, and any gross physical deformities. When genetic disorders are suspected, amniocentesis or chorionic villus sampling is used to determine the genotype of the fetus. Fetal medicine corrects problems of prenatal development medically, surgically, or through genetic engineering.

# 3.3 Happy Birthday!

## Labor and Delivery
Labor consists of three stages. In Stage 1, the muscles of the uterus contract, causing the cervix to enlarge. In Stage 2, the baby moves through the birth canal. In Stage 3, the placenta is delivered.

## Approaches to Childbirth
Prepared childbirth assumes that parents should understand what takes place during pregnancy and birth. In natural childbirth, women learn to cope with pain through relaxation, visual imagery, and the help of a supportive coach.

Although most American babies are born in hospitals, home birth is safe when the mother is healthy, the delivery is expected to be trouble-free, and a health care professional is present.

## Postpartum Depression
After giving birth, some women experience postpartum depression—they are irritable, have poor appetite and disturbed sleep, and are apathetic.

## Birth Complications
During labor and delivery, the flow of blood to the fetus can be disrupted, causing anoxia, a lack of oxygen to the fetus. If the fetus is endangered, the doctor may do a cesarean section, removing it from the uterus surgically.

Premature babies develop more slowly at first but catch up in a few years. Small-for-date babies often do not fare well, particularly if they weigh less than 1,500 grams at birth and if their environment is stressful.

Infant mortality is relatively high in the United States, primarily because of low birth weight and inadequate prenatal care.

# 3.4 The Newborn

## Assessing the Newborn
The Apgar score measures five vital signs to determine a newborn's physical well-being. The Neonatal Behavioral Assessment Scale provides a comprehensive evaluation of a baby's behavioral and physical status.

## The Newborn's Reflexes
Some reflexes help infants to adjust to life outside the uterus, some protect them, and some are the basis for later motor behavior.

## Newborn States
Newborns spend their day in one of four states: alert inactivity, waking activity, crying, and sleeping. A newborn's crying includes a basic cry, a mad cry, and a pain cry.

Newborns spend approximately two-thirds of every day asleep and go through a complete sleep-wake cycle once every 4 hours. Newborns spend about half their time in REM sleep, characterized by active brain waves and frequent movements of the eyes and limbs. REM sleep may stimulate nervous system growth.

Some healthy babies die from sudden infant death syndrome (SIDS). Babies are vulnerable to SIDS when they are premature, have low birth weight, sleep on their stomachs, are overheated, and are exposed to cigarette smoke. Encouraging parents to have babies sleep on their backs has reduced the number of SIDS cases.

## Perception and Learning in the Newborn
Newborns' perceptual and learning skills function reasonably well, which allows them to experience the world.

# 4

Humans take longer to become physically mature than any other animal. We spend about 20 percent of our lives—all of childhood and adolescence—growing physically. This slow journey to physical maturity is an interesting story in itself. But physical growth is just as important for its impact on other aspects of children's development, including cognition, social behavior, and personality. As children grow physically, they

become less dependent on others for care, they're treated differently by adults, and they come to view themselves as older and more mature. By knowing more about children's physical growth, you'll be better prepared to understand other aspects of development that we'll study in the rest of the book.

In this chapter, we'll learn how children grow physically. In Module 4.1, we'll look at different facets of physical growth and some of the reasons why people differ in their physical growth and stature. Then, in Module 4.2, we'll explore problems that can disrupt physical growth. In Module 4.3, we'll look at physical growth that's not so obvious—the development of the brain. Finally, in Module 4.4, we'll see how physical growth is accompanied by greater control of the body, which increases children's ability to explore, understand, and enjoy their world.

# Physical and Motor Development

# 4.1

## Physical Growth

### Learning Objectives

● What are the important features of physical growth during childhood? How do they vary from child to child?

● How do heredity, hormones, and nutrition contribute to physical growth?

● What are the physical changes associated with puberty, and what are their consequences?

● Why are some adolescents sexually active? Why do so few use contraceptives?

> *Pete has just had his 15th birthday, but, as far as he is concerned, there is no reason to celebrate. Although most of his friends have grown about 6 inches in the past year or so, have a much larger penis and larger testicles, and have mounds of pubic hair, Pete looks just as he did when he was 10 years old. He is embarrassed by his appearance, particularly in the locker room, where he looks like a little boy among men. "Won't I ever change?" he wonders.*

For parents and children alike, physical growth is a topic of great interest. Parents marvel at how quickly babies add pounds and inches; 2-year-olds proudly proclaim, "I bigger now!" Many adolescents take great satisfaction in finally becoming taller than a parent; others, like Pete, suffer through their teenage years as they wait for the physical signs of maturity.

In this module, we'll examine some of the basic features of physical growth and variations in growth patterns. We'll also consider the mechanisms responsible for growth. Finally, we'll end the module with puberty—a phase of physical growth that is so special it needs to be considered separately.

### Features of Human Growth

Probably the most obvious way to measure physical growth is in terms of sheer size—height and weight. The growth charts at the top of page 93 show the average changes in height and weight that take place as children grow from birth to age 20. Between birth and 2 years, for example, average height increases from 19 to 32 inches; average weight increases from 7 to 22 pounds. (An interesting rule of thumb is that boys achieve half their adult height by 2 years, and girls by 18 months.)

What is not so obvious in growth charts is that increases in height and weight are not steady. Looking at the average *increase* in weight and height annually—as opposed to the average total weight and height for each year—gives quite a different picture of the pattern of physical growth. The graphs at the bottom of page 93 show that growth is extraordinarily rapid during the first year, when the average baby gains about 10 inches and 15 pounds. Growth is fairly steady through the preschool and elementary-school years, about 3 inches and 7 to 8 pounds each year. In early adolescence, growth is rapid again. During this growth spurt, which corresponds to the peaks in the middle of the charts, teenagers typically grow 4 inches and 16 to 17 pounds each year. After this spurt, growth again slows as children reach adulthood.

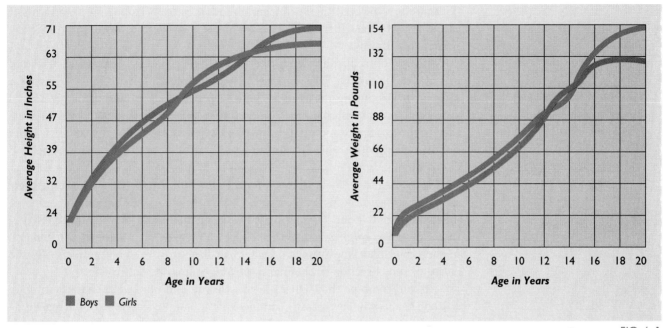

FIG 4–1

Another important feature of human growth is that it follows the cephalo-caudal principle that was introduced in Module 3.1 (p. 60). That is, the head and trunk develop first; infants and young children are not simply scaled-down versions of adults. Toddlers tend to have disproportionately large heads and trunks, making them look top-heavy compared to older boys. As growth of the hips, legs, and feet catches up later in childhood, bodies take on more adult proportions.

A third important feature of physical growth takes place inside the body, with the development of muscle, fat, and bones. Virtually all the body's muscle

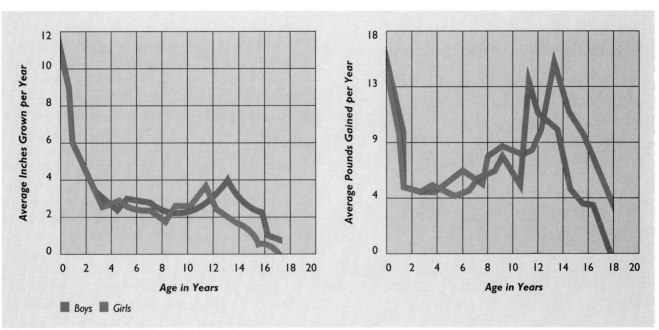

FIG 4–2

fibers are present at birth. During childhood, muscles become longer and thicker as individual fibers fuse together. This process accelerates during adolescence, particularly for boys.

A layer of fat first appears under the skin near the end of the fetal period of prenatal development. Fat continues to accumulate rapidly during the first year after birth, producing the familiar look we call baby fat. During the preschool years, children actually become leaner, but in the early elementary-school years they begin to acquire more fat again. This happens gradually at first, then more rapidly during adolescence. The increase in fat in adolescence is more pronounced in girls than in boys.

Bone begins to form during prenatal development. What will become bone starts as cartilage, a soft, flexible tissue. During the embryonic period, the center of the tissue turns to bone. **Then, shortly before birth, the ends of the cartilage structures, known as *epiphyses*, turn to bone.** Now the structure is hard at each end and in the center. Working from the center, cartilage turns to bone until finally the enlarging center section reaches the epiphyses, ending skeletal growth.

If you combine the changes in muscle, fat, and bone with changes in body size and shape, you have a fairly complete picture of physical growth during childhood. What's missing? The central nervous system, which we cover separately in Module 4.3.

Of course, the picture of children's physical growth that I have described in the last few pages is a typical profile; there are important variations on this prototype, as you'll see in the next section.

## Variations on the Average Profile

When the University of Oregon Ducks won the first NCAA basketball tournament in 1939, the average height of their starting lineup was 6 feet, 2 inches. When the Michigan State Spartans won the tournament in 2000, the average height of their starting lineup was 6 feet, 6 inches, a difference of 4 inches. Of course, the changing heights of basketball players simply correspond to changes in the U.S. population at large. Today, adults and children are taller and heavier than previous generations.

**Changes in physical development from one generation to the next are known as *secular growth trends.*** Secular trends have been quite large, as you can see in the graph. Swedish 12-year-olds in the 1960s were more than 5 inches taller than their counterparts in the 1880s. Put another way, each generation of Swedish 12-year-olds was just over 1 inch taller than its predecessor. (We are using statistics for Swedish children because equally comprehensive data for American children don't exist.)

Not only does "average" physical growth vary from one generation to the next, it varies from one country to another. The graph at the top of page 95 shows the average height of 8-year-old boys and girls in several countries around the world. Youngsters from

FIG 4-3

the United States, Western European countries, Japan, and China are about the same height, approximately 49 inches. Children in Africa and India are shorter, averaging just under 46 inches. And 8-year-olds in Polynesia are shorter still, averaging 43 inches.

We also need to remember that "average" and "normal" are not the same. Many children are much taller or shorter than average and perfectly normal, of course. For example, among American 8-year-old boys, normal weights range from approximately 44 pounds to 76 pounds. In other words, an extremely light but normal 8-year-old boy would weigh only slightly more than half as much as his extremely heavy but normal peer. What is "normal" can vary greatly, and this applies not only to height and other aspects of physical growth but to all aspects of development. Whenever a "typical" or "average" age is given for a developmental milestone, you should remember that the normal range for passing the milestone is much wider. Some children pass the milestone sooner than the stated age and some later, but all are normal.

We've seen that children's heights vary within a culture, across time, and between cultures. What accounts for these differences? To answer this question, we need to look at the mechanisms that are responsible for human growth.

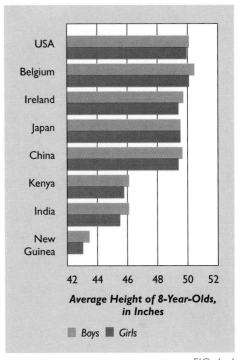

FIG 4–4

## Mechanisms of Physical Growth

It's easy to take physical growth for granted. Compared to other milestones of child development, such as learning to read, physical growth seems to come so easily. Children, like weeds, seem to sprout without any effort at all. In reality, of course, physical growth is complicated; to understand it, we need to consider three factors: heredity, hormones, and nutrition.

Heredity.   Twin studies show that heredity helps to determine children's height: The correlation between heights of identical twins is usually larger than .9, whereas the correlation for fraternal twins is approximately .5 (Wilson, 1986). Both parents contribute equally to their children's height. The correlation between the average of the two parents' height and their child's is about .7 (Plomin, 1990). Obviously, as a general rule, two tall parents will have tall children; two short parents will have short children; and one tall parent and one short parent will have average-height offspring.

Hormones.   How are genetic instructions translated into actual growth? **Part of the answer involves *hormones*, chemicals that are released by glands and that travel in the bloodstream to act on other body parts.** One of these glands, the pituitary, is located deep in the brain. A few times each day, the pituitary secretes growth hormone (GH). This usually happens during sleep but sometimes after exercise. From the pituitary, GH travels to the liver, where it triggers the release of another hormone, somatomedin, which causes muscles and bones to grow (Tanner, 1990).

Without adequate amounts of GH, a child develops into a dwarf. As adults, dwarfs have normal proportions but are quite short, measuring about 4 to 4½ feet tall. Dwarfism can be treated with injections of GH, which allow children to grow to normal height.

**Another hormone, *thyroxine*, released by the thyroid gland in the neck, is essential for the proper development of nerve cells.**

Heredity, hormones, and nutrition all play important roles in children's physical growth.

Without thyroxine, nerve cells do not develop properly and mental retardation is the result. Thyroxine also seems to be essential for most cells in the body to function properly, so deficiencies in thyroxine can retard physical growth by making the pituitary gland itself ineffective.

Nutrition.    The third factor affecting physical growth is nutrition. Nutrition is particularly important during infancy, when physical growth is so rapid. In a 2-month-old, roughly 40 percent of the body's energy is devoted to growth. Most of the remaining energy fuels basic bodily functions, such as digestion and respiration.

Because growth requires so much high energy, young babies must consume an enormous number of calories in relation to their body weight. While an adult needs to consume only 15 to 20 calories per pound, depending upon level of activity (National Research Council, 1989), a 12-pound 3-month-old should eat about 50 calories per pound of body weight, or 600 calories. What's the best way for babies to receive the calories they need? The "Making Children's Lives Better" feature has some answers.

MAKING CHILDREN'S LIVES BETTER

### What's the Best Food for Babies?

Breast-feeding is the best way to ensure that babies get the nourishment they need. Human milk contains the proper amounts of carbohydrates, fats, protein, vitamins, and minerals for babies. Breast-feeding also has several other advantages compared to bottle-feeding (Shelov, 1993; Sullivan & Birch, 1990). First, breast-fed babies are ill less often because breast milk contains the mother's antibodies. Second, breast-fed babies are less prone to diarrhea and constipation. Third, breast-fed babies typically make the transition to solid foods more easily, apparently because they are accustomed to changes in the taste of breast milk that reflect a mother's diet. Fourth, breast milk cannot be contaminated, which is a significant problem in developing countries when formula is used to bottle-feed babies.

The many benefits of breast-feeding do not mean that bottle-feeding is harmful. Formula, when prepared in sanitary conditions, provides generally the same nutrients as human milk, but infants are more prone to develop allergies from formula, and formula does not protect infants from disease. However, bottle-feeding has advantages of its own. A mother who cannot readily breast-feed can still enjoy the intimacy of feeding her baby, and other family members can participate in feeding. In fact, long-term longitudinal studies typically find that breast- and bottle-fed babies are similar in physical and psychological development (Fergusson, Horwood, & Shannon, 1987), so women in industrialized countries can choose either method and know that their babies' dietary needs will be met.

*When babies are breast-fed, they get proper nourishment, are ill less often, and adjust to solid food more readily.*

In the United States and Canada, newborns and very young babies are often breast-fed exclusively. Between 3 and 6 months of age, infants are weaned from the breast and given formula. At about the same time, solid foods are introduced into the baby's diet. For example, parents might introduce rice cereal at 4 months and strained vegetables at 6 months (Whitney, Cataldo, & Rolfes, 1987).

A good rule is to introduce only one food at a time. A 7-month-old having cheese for the first time, for instance, should have no other new foods for a few days. In this way, allergies that may develop—skin rash or diarrhea—can be linked to a particular food, making it easier to prevent reoccurrences. ●

By 2 years, growth slows, so children need less to eat. This is also a time when many children become picky eaters. Like the little girl in the photo, toddlers and preschool children find foods that they once ate willingly "yucky." As a toddler, my daughter loved green beans. When she reached 2, she decided that green beans were awful and adamantly refused to eat them. Though such finickiness can be annoying, it may actually be adaptive for increasingly independent preschoolers. Because preschoolers don't know what is safe to eat and what isn't, eating only familiar foods protects them from potential harm (Birch & Fisher, 1995).

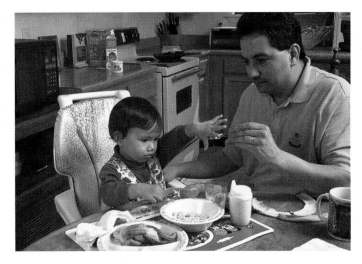

Adolescents need to eat more to provide the nutrition necessary for the adolescent growth spurt. Unfortunately, many adolescents have notoriously poor diets, eating far too many Big Macs and fries. Consequently, many teenagers do not get adequate nutrients, such as iron and calcium (Malina, 1990). Furthermore, their eating habits often lead to obesity, which I'll discuss in Module 4.2.

## The Adolescent Growth Spurt and Puberty

As the graphs on page 93 show, physical growth is slow during the elementary-school years: In an average year, a 6- to 10-year-old girl or boy gains about 5 to 7 pounds and grows 2 to 3 inches. But during the peak of the adolescent growth spurt, a girl may gain as much as 20 pounds in a year and a boy, 25 (Tanner, 1970). This growth spurt lasts a few years, so that girls typically achieve most of their mature stature by age 15 and boys by age 17.

**The adolescent growth spurt is one of several physical changes known collectively as _puberty._** In addition to the growth spurt, puberty also includes maturation of the reproductive system. The chart shows these reproductive changes and the ages when they typically occur for boys and girls. For girls, puberty begins with growth of the breasts and the growth spurt, followed by the appearance of pubic hair. _Menarche,_ **the onset of menstruation, typically occurs at about age 13.** Early menstrual cycles are usually irregular and without ovulation.

For boys, puberty usually commences with the growth of the testes and scrotum, followed by the appearance of pubic hair, the start of the growth spurt, and growth of the penis. At about age 13, most boys have their first spontaneous ejaculation, a discharge of fluid containing sperm. Initial ejaculations often contain relatively few sperm; only months or sometimes years later are there sufficient sperm to fertilize an egg (Chilman, 1983).

### Rate of Maturation.
Of course, puberty does not always begin at age 10 for girls and age 12 for boys. For many children, puberty begins months or even years before or after these norms. An early-maturing boy

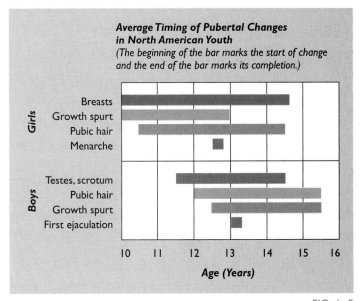

*Average Timing of Pubertal Changes in North American Youth*
*(The beginning of the bar marks the start of change and the end of the bar marks its completion.)*

FIG 4–5
Source: Tanner, 1978.

might begin puberty at age 11, whereas a late-maturing boy might start at 15 or 16. An early-maturing girl might start puberty at 9, and a late-maturing girl, at 14 or 15. For example, the girls shown in the photo are the same age, but only one has reached puberty.

The timing of maturity is regulated partly by genetics. For example, a mother's age at menarche is related to her daughter's age at menarche (Graber, Brooks-Gunn, & Warren, 1995). However, experience also influences the onset of puberty, at least for girls. Menarche occurs at younger ages in girls who experience much family conflict (Belsky, Steinberg, & Draper, 1991; Moffit et al., 1992). Furthermore, girls who are depressed begin to menstruate at a younger age than girls who are not depressed (Graber et al., 1995). Family conflict and depression may lead to early menarche by affecting the levels of hormones that trigger menstruation (Graber et al., 1995).

Maturing early or late has psychological consequences that differ for boys and girls. Several longitudinal studies show that early maturation benefits boys but most often not girls. Boys who mature early tend to be more independent and self-confident. They're also more popular with peers. In contrast, girls who mature early often lack self-confidence, are less popular, and are more likely to be depressed and have behavior problems (Ge, Conger, & Elder, 1996; Simmons & Blyth, 1987; Swarr & Richards, 1996).

Why does rate of maturation have these consequences? Early maturation may benefit boys because others perceive them as more mature and may be more willing to give them adultlike responsibilities. Late-maturing boys, like Pete in the vignette at the beginning of this section, are often frustrated because others treat them like little boys instead of like young men. Early maturation may hamper girls' development by leading them to associate with older adolescents, who apparently encourage them to engage in age-inappropriate activities, such as drinking, smoking, and sex, for which they are ill-prepared (Ge et al., 1996).

By young adulthood, many of the effects associated with rate of maturation vanish. When Pete, for example, finally matures, others will treat him like an adult

**Early maturation typically benefits boys (because others treat them as more mature) but not girls (because older teens encourage them to drink and have sex).**

and the few extra years of being treated like a child will not be harmful. But for some adolescents, particularly early-maturing girls, rate of maturation can have long-lasting effects. A girl who matures early, is pressured into sex, and becomes pregnant ends up with a different life course than a girl who matures later and is better prepared to resist pressures for sex. Thus, sometimes rate of maturation can lead to events that pick the path that development follows through the rest of life.

### Sexual Behavior.

At the beginning of this chapter, I emphasized that physical growth has important links to other aspects of children's behavior and development. Nowhere are these links more apparent than in adolescent sexuality. The obvious physical changes in adolescence make sexuality a central issue for teenagers. Teens are also preoccupied with sex because it is emphasized on television and in movies and because it is seen as a way to establish adult status.

By the end of adolescence, most American boys and girls have had intercourse at least once (Jakobsen, 1997; Miller et al., 1997; Rodgers & Rowe, 1993). Why are some adolescents sexually active? A number of factors are involved (Capaldi, Crosby, & Stoolmiller, 1996; Windle & Windle, 1996). Parents' and peers' attitudes towards sex play a key role. In one study of high-school students (Treboux & Busch-Rossnagel, 1990), positive attitudes toward sex by parents and friends were associated with students' positive attitudes, which, in turn, were associated with more frequent and more intense sexual behavior.

Adolescents' sexual behavior is a cause for concern because approximately 1 in 10 American adolescent girls becomes pregnant. About 60 percent of pregnant teenagers give birth; the remaining 40 percent abort the pregnancy (Henshaw, 1993). The result is that roughly 500,000 babies are born to American teenagers annually. African American and Hispanic American adolescents are the most likely to become teenage moms; Asian American adolescents are the least likely (Ventura et al., 1997).

As I described in Module 3.2, teenage mothers and their children usually face bleak futures. If this is the case, why do so many teens become pregnant? The answer is simple: Few sexually active teenagers use birth control. Those who do often use ineffective methods, such as withdrawal, or practice contraception inconsistently (Besharov & Gardiner, 1997; National Research Council, 1987).

Adolescents' infrequent use of contraceptives can be traced to several factors (Adler, 1994; Gordon, 1996):

- *Ignorance:* Many adolescents are seriously misinformed about the facts of conception. For example, many do not know when conception is most likely to occur during the menstrual cycle.
- *Illusion of invulnerability:* Too many adolescents deny reality. They believe they are invincible—"It couldn't happen to me"—and that only others become pregnant.
- *Lack of motivation:* For some adolescent girls, becoming pregnant is appealing. They think having a child is a way to break away from parents, gain status as an independent-living adult, and have "someone to love them."
- *Lack of access:* Some teenagers do not know where to obtain contraceptives, and others are embarrassed to buy them. Still others don't know how to use contraceptives.

The best way to deal with adolescent sexual behavior is to give adolescents the facts about sex, teenage pregnancy, and contraception (Boyer & Hein, 1991). Effective programs teach the biological aspects and emphasize responsible sexual behavior or abstaining from premarital sex altogether (Dryfoos, 1990). For example, in the program called "Postponing Sexual Involvement" (Howard & McCabe, 1990), trained, older adolescents lead student groups in discussions of the pressures to become involved sexually. They discuss common "lines" that teens use to induce others to have sex and strategies for responding to these lines. Students also practice refusal strategies in role-playing sessions. Youth who participate in programs like this one are less likely to have intercourse; when they do have intercourse, they are more likely to use contraceptives (Howard & McCabe, 1990).

> Adolescents are less likely to be sexually active when they know about the biology of sex, the need for responsible sexual behavior, and ways to respond to pressure to be sexually active.

### Sexual Orientation.

For most adolescents, sexual behavior involves members of the opposite sex. However, roughly 15 percent of adolescent boys and girls report emotional and sexual attractions to members of their own sex. For most adolescents, these experiences are simply a part of the larger process of role experimentation common to adolescence. However, like the teens in the photo, about 5 percent of teenage boys and girls identify their sexual orientation as gay (D'Augelli, 1996).

The roots of sexual orientation are poorly understood. Scientists have, however, discredited several theories of sexual orientation. Research (Bell, Weinberg, & Hammersmith, 1981; Golombok & Tasker, 1996; Patterson, 1992) shows that each of the following is *false:*

- Sons become gay when raised by a domineering mother and a weak father.
- Girls become lesbians when their father is their primary role model.
- Children raised by gay or lesbian parents usually adopt their parents' sexual orientation.
- Gay and lesbian adults were, as children, seduced by an older person of their sex.

If all these ideas are false, what determines a person's sexual orientation? The exact factors probably differ from one person to the next, but many scientists today believe that biology plays an important role. Some evidence suggests that heredity and hormones influence sexual orientation (Hamer et al., 1993; Meyer-Bahlberg et al., 1995). One intriguing idea (Bem, 1996) is that genes and hormones don't produce sexual orientation per se but lead to temperaments that affect children's preference for same- and opposite-sex activities. Children who do not enjoy gender-typical activities come to see themselves as different and thus ultimately acquire a different gender identity.

In concluding this module, it's important to recognize that sexual behavior and sexuality are enormously complicated and emotionally charged issues, even for adults. Adults who deal with adolescents need to recognize this complexity and help provide teenagers with skills for dealing with the issues involved in their emerging sexuality.

## Check Your Learning

1. Physical growth is most rapid during the first year and during _____.

2. Physical growth involves increases in height and weight, changes in _____, and changes in bone, muscle, and fat.

3. Changes in physical development from one generation to the next are called _____.

4. Normal physical growth depends upon heredity, hormones, and _____.

5. Compared to bottle-fed babies, breast-fed babies are ill less often, _____, and make the transition to solid foods more readily.

6. Early maturation often benefits boys because _____.

7. Sexually active adolescents usually don't use contraceptives because of ignorance, the illusion of invulnerability, lack of motivation, and _____.

8. Modern explanations of sexual orientation emphasize the role of _____.

 In Module 2.1, you learned that polygenic inheritance is often involved when phenotypes form a continuum. Height is such a phenotype. Propose a simple polygenic model to explain how height might be inherited.

**Answers:** (1) the adolescent growth spurt, (2) body proportions, (3) secular growth trends, (4) nutrition, (5) are less prone to diarrhea and constipation, (6) others are more likely to give them adult responsibilities, (7) lack of access to contraceptives, (8) biology

# Problems of Physical Growth

## Learning Objectives

● What is malnutrition? What are its consequences? What is the solution to malnutrition?

● How do nature and nurture lead some adolescent girls to diet excessively?

● Why do some children become obese? How can they lose weight permanently?

*Ricardo, 12, has been overweight for most of his life. He dislikes the playground games that entertain most of his classmates during recess, preferring to stay indoors. He has relatively few friends and is not particularly happy with his lot in life. Many times Ricardo has lost weight from dieting, but he's always regained it quickly. His parents know that being overweight is a health hazard, and they wonder if there is anything that will help their son.*

Two major problems of physical growth concern nutrition. Growth requires enormous reserves of energy, and many children do not eat enough food to provide this energy. Other children and adolescents eat too much. We'll look at these problems in this module, and as we do, we'll understand some of the reasons why Ricardo is overweight and what he can do about it.

## Malnutrition

An adequate diet is only a dream to many of the world's children. **Worldwide, about one in three children under age 5 is *malnourished*, as indicated by being small for his or her age** (World Health Organization, 1996). Many, like the little girl in the photo, are from third-world countries. But malnutrition is regrettably common in industrialized countries, too. Many American children growing up homeless and in poverty are malnourished. Approximately 20 percent of American children receive inadequate amounts of iron, and 10 percent go to bed hungry (Children's Defense Fund, 1996; Pollitt, 1994).

Malnourishment is especially damaging during infancy because growth is so rapid during these years. A longitudinal study conducted in Barbados in the West Indies (Galler & Ramsey, 1989; Galler, Ramsey, & Forde, 1986) followed a group of children who were severely malnourished as infants and a group from similar family environments who had adequate nutrition as infants. As older children, the two groups were indistinguishable physically: Children who were malnourished as infants were just as tall and weighed just as much as their peers. However, the children with a history of infant malnutrition had much lower scores on intelligence tests. They also had difficulty maintaining attention in school; they were easily distracted. Malnutrition during rapid periods of growth apparently damages the brain, affecting a child's intelligence and ability to pay attention (Morgane et al., 1993).

Malnutrition would seem to have a simple cure—an adequate diet. But the solution is more complex than that. Malnourished children are frequently listless and inactive (Ricciuti, 1993), behaviors that are useful because they conserve energy. At the same time, when children are routinely unresponsive and lethargic, parents may provide fewer and fewer experiences that foster their children's development. For example, parents who start out reading to their children at night may stop because their malnourished children seem uninterested and inattentive. The result is a self-perpetuating cycle in which malnourished children are forsaken by parents, who feel that nothing they do gets a response, so they quit trying. A biological influence—lethargy stemming from insufficient nourishment—causes a profound change in the experiences—parental teaching—that shape a child's development.

To break the vicious cycle, children need more than an improved diet. Their parents must also be taught how to foster their children's development. Programs that combine dietary supplements with parent training offer promise in treating malnutrition (Valenzuela, 1997). Children in these programs often catch up with their peers in physical and intellectual growth, showing that the best way to treat malnutrition is by addressing both biological and sociocultural factors (Super, Herrera, & Mora, 1990).

## Anorexia and Bulimia

Tracey Gold, an actress on the TV program *Growing Pains*, had to leave the show in the early 1990s. She had begun dieting compulsively, had withered away to a mere 90 pounds, and had to be hospitalized (Sporkin, Wagner, & Tomashoff, 1992). Tracey suffered from an eating disorder. ***Anorexia nervosa* is a disorder marked by a persistent refusal to eat and an irrational fear of being overweight.** Individuals with anorexia nervosa have a grossly distorted image of their own body. Like the girl in the photo, they claim to be overweight despite being painfully thin (Wilson, Heffernan, & Black, 1996).

Anorexia is a very serious disorder, often leading to heart damage. Without treatment, as many as 15 percent of adolescents with anorexia die (Wicks-Nelson & Israel, 1991). The "Real Children" feature describes a teenage girl with anorexia.

REAL CHILDREN

### Layla's Battle with Anorexia

Layla had always been a pleasant and obedient child. She was an above-average student in school, though she could never quite make the honor roll as her older brothers always did. At 15, Layla was 5 feet, 4½ inches tall and weighed 120 pounds. Her weight was perfectly normal for her height, but she decided she was fat and began to diet. Over the next year, Layla lost 35 pounds. She looked pale, tired, and wasted, and she no longer menstruated. Layla insisted she looked fine and that nothing was wrong with her, but her parents and family doctor were so concerned they insisted she be hospitalized. Forced to eat regular meals in the hospital, Layla gained some weight and was sent home. But this cycle was repeated several times over the next two years: Layla would diet to the point that she looked like a skeleton draped in skin, and then she would be hospitalized. In her generally weakened condition, Layla developed mononucleosis and hepatitis; ultimately her liver and kidneys failed. Three days before her 18th birthday, Layla had a heart attack and died. ●

A related eating disorder is bulimia nervosa. **Individuals with *bulimia nervosa* alternate between binge eating—periods when they eat uncontrollably—and purging through self-induced vomiting or with laxatives.** The frequency of binge eating varies remarkably among people with bulimia nervosa, from a few times a week to more than 30 times. What's common to all is the feeling that they cannot stop eating (Mizes et al., 1995).

Anorexia and bulimia are alike in many respects. Both disorders primarily affect females. Girls are 10 times more likely than boys to be affected (Wilson et al., 1996).

Also, both disorders emerge in adolescence and typically in girls who are well-behaved, conscientious, and good students (Attie, Brooks-Gunn, & Petersen, 1990).

Why do girls like Layla develop anorexia or bulimia? It probably won't surprise you that nature and nurture both play a role. Let's start with nurture and cultural ideals of the female body. In many industrialized cultures—and certainly in the United States—the ideal female body is tall and slender. As girls enter adolescence, these cultural norms becomes particularly influential. Also during adolescence, girls experience a "fat spurt," gaining about 25 pounds, most of it fat. Though this pattern of growth is normal, some girls unfortunately perceive themselves as overweight and begin to diet (Halpern et al., 1999). This is especially the case when the girl's mother is preoccupied with her own weight (Attie et al., 1990). Faced with a cultural value of being thin and a change in their bodies, adolescent girls believe they are fat and try to lose weight.

Family dynamics also contribute to anorexia. Adolescent girls are more prone to anorexia if their parents are autocratic and leave their adolescent daughters with little sense of self-control. Dieting allows the girls to assert their autonomy and achieve an individual identity (Graber et al., 1994; Swarr & Richards, 1996). Layla, for example, who was entering mid-adolescence and seeking greater personal autonomy, enjoyed the sense of control over her weight that dieting gave her.

Cultural emphases on thinness, combined with a regimented home life, can explain many cases of anorexia. Of course, most teenage girls growing up in regimented homes in the United States do *not* become anorexic, which raises the question of biological factors. Twin and family studies point to an inherited predisposition for anorexia and bulimia, perhaps in the form of personality that tends to be rigid and anxious (Strober, 1995). Thus, anorexia is most likely to develop in girls who inherit the predisposition, who internalize cultural ideals of thinness, and whose parents grant them little independence.

> Anorexia and bulimia, eating disorders that affect teenage girls, can be linked to family dynamics and to cultural ideals concerning the female body.

## Obesity

Ricardo, the boy in the module-opening vignette, is typical of the 5 to 10 percent of American children and adolescents who are obese, at least 20 percent over the ideal body weight for their age and height. Overweight youngsters like the boy in the photo are often unpopular and have low self-esteem (Braet, Mervielde, & Vandereycken, 1997). Furthermore, throughout life they are at risk for many medical problems, including high blood pressure and diabetes, because the vast majority of overweight children and adolescents become overweight adults (Serdula et al., 1993).

Heredity plays an important role in juvenile obesity. In adoption studies, children and adolescents' weight is related to the weight of their biological parents, not to the weight of their adoptive parents (Stunkard et al., 1986). Genes may influence obesity by influencing a person's activity level. In other words, being genetically more prone to inactivity makes it more difficult to burn off calories and easier to gain weight. **Heredity may also help set *basal metabolic rate*, the speed at which the body consumes calories.** Children and adolescents with a slower basal metabolic rate burn off calories less rapidly, making it easier for them to gain weight (Epstein & Cluss, 1986).

The environment is also influential. Television advertising, for example, encourages youth to eat tasty but fattening foods. Parents play a role, too. They may inadvertently encourage obesity by emphasizing external rather than internal eating signals. Infants eat primarily because of internal signals: They eat when they experience hunger and stop eating when they feel full. During the preschool years, this internal control of eating is often gradually replaced by external signals. Parents who urge their children to "clean their plates" even when they are no longer hungry are teaching their children to ignore internal cues to eating. Thus, obese children and adolescents may overeat because they rely on external cues and disregard internal cues to stop (Birch, 1991).

Obese youth *can* lose weight. The most effective programs have several features in common (Epstein et al., 1995; Foreyt & Goodrick, 1995; Israel et al., 1994):

- The focus of the program is to change obese children's eating habits, encourage them to become more active, and discourage sedentary behavior.

- As part of the treatment, children learn to monitor their eating, exercise, and sedentary behavior. Goals are established in each area, and rewards are earned when the goals are met.

- Parents are trained to help children set realistic goals and to use behavioral principles to help children meet these goals. Parents also monitor their own lifestyles to be sure they aren't accidentally fostering their child's obesity.

When programs incorporate these features, obese children do lose weight. However, even after losing weight, many of these children remain overweight. It is best to establish good eating and exercise habits to avoid obesity in the first place.

### Check Your Learning

**1.** Malnourishment is particularly damaging during infancy because _____.

**2.** Malnourished children need an adequate diet and _____.

**3.** Individuals with _____ alternate between binge eating and purging.

**4.** Parents may inadvertently contribute to their children's obesity by _____.

**5.** Effective programs for childhood obesity focus on changing eating habits, encouraging children to become more active, and discouraging _____.

 On *Larry King Live,* you hear a caller complain, "Experts always try to make everything so complicated. Fat people get that way 'cause they eat too much. 'Nough said." In your call to Larry, set the record straight.

**Answers:** (1) growth is so rapid during this period, (2) parents who foster their development, (3) bulimia nervosa, (4) encouraging them to ignore internal cues to eating, (5) sedentary behavior

# 4.3

- **Organization of the Mature Brain**

- **The Developing Brain**

## The Developing Nervous System

### Learning Objectives

● **What are the parts of a nerve cell? How is the brain organized?**

● **When is the brain formed in prenatal development? When do different regions of the brain begin to function?**

*While crossing the street, 10-year-old Martin was struck by a passing car. He was in a coma for a week, but then gradually became more alert, and now he seems to be aware of his surroundings. Needless to say, Martin's mother is grateful that he survived the accident, but she wonders what the future holds for her son.*

The physical changes that we see as children grow are impressive, but even more awe-inspiring are the changes we cannot see, those involving the brain and the nervous system. An infant's feelings of hunger, a child's laugh, and an adolescent's efforts to learn algebra all reflect the functioning brain and the rest of the nervous system. All the information that children learn—including language and other cognitive skills—are stored in the brain.

How does the brain accomplish these many tasks? How is the brain affected by an injury like the one that Martin suffered? To begin to answer these questions, let's look at how the brain is organized in adults.

## Organization of the Mature Brain

The basic unit of the brain and the rest of the nervous system is the *neuron*, a cell that specializes in receiving and transmitting information. Neurons come in many different shapes, as you can see in the different photos. The diagram below makes it easier to understand the basic parts found in all neurons. **The *cell body* at the center of the neuron contains the basic biological machinery that keeps the neuron alive. The receiving end of the neuron, the *dendrite*, looks like a tree with many branches.** The highly branched dendrite allows one neuron to receive input from many thousands of other neurons (Morgan & Gibson, 1991). **The tubelike structure at the other end of the cell body is the *axon*, which sends information to other neurons. The axon is wrapped in *myelin*, a fatty sheath that allows it to transmit information more rapidly.** The boost in neural speed from myelin is like the difference between driving and flying: from about 6 feet per second to 50 feet per second. **At the end of the axon are small knobs called *terminal buttons*, which release *neurotransmitters*,** chemicals that carry information to nearby neurons. Finally, you'll see that the terminal buttons of one axon don't actually touch the dendrites of other neurons. **The gap between one neuron and the next is a *synapse*.** Neurotransmitters cross synapses to carry information between neurons.

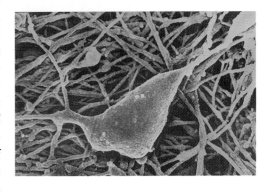

Take 50 to 100 billion neurons like these and you have the beginnings of a human brain. An adult's brain weighs a little less than 3 pounds, and it easily fits into your hands. **The wrinkled surface of the brain is the *cerebral cortex;* made up of about 10 billion neurons, the cortex regulates many of the functions that we think of as distinctly human. The cortex consists of left and right halves, called *hemispheres*, that are linked by millions of axons in a thick bundle called the *corpus callosum*.** The characteristics that you value most—your engaging personality, your "way with words," your uncanny knack for reading others—are all controlled by specific regions of the cortex, many of which are shown in the diagram at the top of page 106.

**Personality and your ability to make and carry out plans are largely functions of an area at the front of the cortex that is called, appropriately, the *frontal cortex*.** For most people, the ability to produce and

FIG 4–6

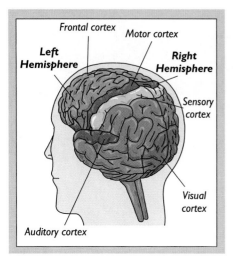

Frontal cortex    Motor cortex

**Left Hemisphere**    **Right Hemisphere**

Sensory cortex

Visual cortex

Auditory cortex

FIG 4–7

understand language, to reason, and to compute is largely due to neurons in the cortex of the left hemisphere. Also for most people, artistic and musical abilities, perception of spatial relationships, and the ability to recognize faces and emotions come from neurons in the right hemisphere.

Now that we know a bit of the organization of the mature brain, let's look at how the brain develops and begins to function.

### The Developing Brain

Scientists who study the brain's development are guided by several key questions: How and when do brain structures develop? When do different brain regions begin to function? Why do brain regions take on different functions? In this section, we'll see how research has answered each question.

Emerging Brain Structures.    We know from Module 3.1 that the beginnings of the brain can be traced to the period of the zygote. **At roughly 3 weeks after conception, a group of cells form a flat structure known as the** *neural plate.* At four weeks, the neural plate folds to form a tube that ultimately becomes the brain and spinal cord. When the ends of the tube fuse shut, neurons are produced in one small region of the neural tube. Production of neurons begins about 10 weeks after conception, and by 28 weeks the developing brain has virtually all the neurons it will ever have. During these weeks, neurons form at the incredible rate of more than 4,000 per second (Kolb, 1989).

From the neuron-manufacturing site in the neural tube, neurons migrate to their final positions in the brain. The brain is built in stages, beginning with the innermost layers. Neurons in the deepest layer are positioned first, followed by neurons in the second layer, and so on. This layering process continues until all six layers of the mature brain are in place, which occurs about 7 months after conception (Rakic, 1995).

In the fourth month of prenatal development, axons begin to acquire myelin—the fatty wrap that speeds neural transmission. This process continues through infancy and into childhood and adolescence (Casaer, 1993). Neurons that carry sensory information are the first to acquire myelin; neurons in the cortex are among the last. You can see the effect of more myelin in improved coordination and reaction times. The older the infant and, later, the child, the more rapid and coordinated are his or her reactions. (We'll talk more about this phenomenon when we discuss fine-motor skills in Module 4.4.)

*During infancy and childhood, some synapses are pruned; axons become wrapped in myelin, allowing them to transmit more rapidly.*

In the months after birth, the brain grows rapidly. Axons and dendrites grow longer, and, like a maturing tree, dendrites quickly sprout new limbs. As the number of dendrites increases, so does the number of synapses, reaching a peak at about the first birthday. **Soon after, synapses begin to disappear gradually, a phenomenon known as** *synaptic pruning.* Thus, beginning in infancy and continuing into early adolescence, the brain goes through its own version of "downsizing," weeding out unnecessary connections between neurons (Johnson, 1998).

Structure and Function.    Since the mature brain is specialized, with different psychological functions localized in particular regions, a natural question for developmental researchers is, "How early in development does brain functioning become localized?" To answer this question, scientists have used many different methods to map functions onto particular brain regions.

- *Studies of children with brain damage:* Children who suffer brain injuries provide valuable insights into brain structure and function. If a region of the brain regulates a particular function (e.g., understanding speech), then damage to that region should impair the function.

- *Studies of electrical activity:* **Metal electrodes placed on an infant's scalp, as shown in the photo, produce an** *electroencephalogram (EEG),* **a pattern of brain waves.** If a region of the brain regulates a function, then the region should show distinctive EEG patterns while a child is using that function.

- *Studies using imaging techniques:* **One method,** *functional magnetic resonance imaging (F-MRI),* **uses magnetic fields to track the flow of blood in the brain. Another method,** *positron emission tomography (PET-scan),* **traces use of glucose in the brain.** If a region of the brain helps to regulate a function, then blood flow and use of glucose (a sugar that is a source of energy) should be higher in that region when a child is performing that function.

None of these methods is perfect; each has drawbacks. When studying children with brain injuries, for example, multiple areas of the brain may be damaged, making it hard to link impaired functioning to a particular brain region. Most imaging techniques are used sparingly because of potential hazards. PET-scan, for example, requires injecting children with a radioactive form of glucose.

Despite these limitations, the combined outcome of research using these different approaches indicates that many areas of the cortex begin to function early in life. EEG studies, for example, show that a newborn infant's left hemisphere generates more electrical activity in response to speech than the right hemisphere (Molfese & Burger-Judisch, 1991). Thus, by birth, the cortex of the left hemisphere is already specialized for language processing. As we'll see in Chapter 9, this specialization allows for language to develop rapidly during infancy.

Is the right hemisphere equally well prepared to function at birth? This is a difficult question to answer, in part because the right hemisphere influences so many nonlinguistic functions. Music elicits greater electrical activity in the infant's right hemisphere than in the left. Furthermore, children who suffer brain damage to the right hemisphere often have difficulty integrating parts to form an integrated whole (Stiles et al., in press), implicating the right hemisphere in understanding spatial relations. Other functions, such as recognizing faces, come more gradually but are under the right hemisphere's control by the preschool years (Hahn, 1987).

The frontal cortex, too, begins to function early. The photo shows PET-scans for infants at several different ages. There is little activity in the frontal cortex of 5-day-old babies. Activity increases considerably by 11 weeks and approaches adult levels 7 or 8 months after birth (Chugani & Phelps, 1986). Obviously, 8-month-olds cannot plan and function as adults do, but their frontal cortex has become very active.

What is the frontal cortex regulating in PET-scans like the ones in the photo? Deliberate, goal-oriented behavior is a good bet. To understand research that leads to this conclusion, think back to a time when you had to change your regular routine. At the start of a new school year, perhaps you were assigned a new locker. For the first few days, you might have turned down the old hallway, reflecting last year's habit, instead of walking on to your new locker. To override your old response, maybe you deliberately reminded yourself to walk past the old hallway and turn at the new one.

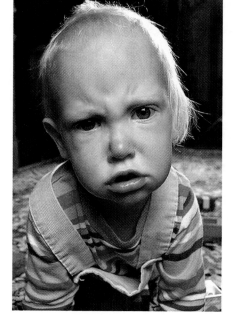

Overriding responses that become incorrect or inappropriate is an important part of deliberate, goal-directed behavior. Children and adults with damage to the frontal cortex often have difficulty inhibiting responses that are no longer appropriate (Diamond et al., 1997). The frontal cortex begins to regulate inappropriate responses at about 1 year and gradually achieves greater control throughout the preschool and school-age years (Welsh, Pennington, & Groisser, 1991). Thus, children gradually become better able to regulate their behavior to achieve cognitive and social goals.

Not only does the frontal cortex regulate responses, it also regulates feelings such as happiness, sadness, and fear. Nathan Fox (1991) believes that "emotional experience arises from two opposing innate action tendencies in the organism: approach and exploration of the novel versus freezing, fleeing, or withdrawal from harmful or dangerous stimuli" (p. 865). That is, emotions like happiness and curiosity stem from an organism's desire to approach a stimulus, and emotions like distress, disgust, or fear come from the desire to avoid a stimulus.

Fox and his co-investigators have shown that the left frontal cortex tends to regulate emotions stemming from the tendency to approach, and the right frontal cortex regulates emotions stemming from avoidance. For example, when babies display joy, the EEG reveals more activity in the left frontal area, and when babies like the one in the photo display stress or disgust, the right frontal area is more electrically active.

Babies also differ in their typical patterns of brain activity. These differences in brain activity are the subject of the "Focus on Research" feature.

FOCUS ON RESEARCH

### Frontal Cortex Activity and Reactivity to Novel Stimuli

*Who were the investigators, and what was the aim of the study?* Previous research had shown that in neutral situations—situations where no stimuli obviously elicit attraction or avoidance—some babies have more spontaneous activity in the left frontal areas, whereas other babies have greater right frontal activity. Infants with greater right frontal activity do not cope as well with stress. For example, they cry more when separated from their mothers than babies who have more spontaneous left frontal activity. Susan Calkins, Nathan Fox, and Timothy Marshall (1996) wanted to know if they could predict differences in brain activity from infants' behavior. Specifically, they wanted to know if there was a connection between infants' responses to novel stimuli at 4 months and their brain activity at 9 months. The investigators expected that infants who responded negatively to the mild stress of a novel stimulus at 4 months (by fussing and crying) would have more right frontal activity at 9 months; infants who responded positively to novelty at 4 months (by smiling and vocalizing) would have more left frontal activity at 9 months.

*How did the investigators measure the topic of interest?* Calkins and her colleagues needed to measure infants' response to novelty at 4 months. They did this by presenting novel sights (colored toys

The left frontal cortex regulates emotions like happiness and curiosity; the right frontal cortex regulates emotions like distress and fear.

presented about 12 inches from the infant's face), novel sounds (tape-recorded syllables and sentences presented at increasingly loud volume), and novel odors (different concentrations of diluted alcohol presented on a cotton swab ½ inch from the baby's nose). The infants were videotaped as the stimuli were presented. Later, the investigators determined the degree of positive and negative emotion that babies expressed. Positive emotion was defined as smiling and vocalizing; negative emotion was defined as fussing, fretting, and crying.

The next step was to measure brain activity at 9 months. Calkins and her colleagues attached electrodes to different sites on the infants' scalps, including over the frontal cortex. Then they recorded electrical activity at each site while the infant sat on the mother's lap watching different colored balls move in a container. (The moving balls were simply meant to capture the infants' attention and keep them still for the 2 minutes required to measure brain activity.)

*Who were the children in the study?* The researchers tested 207 4-month-olds. Of these, the 49 whose responses to novelty were particularly positive or negative were retested as 9-month-olds.

*What was the design of the study?* This study was correlational because Calkins and her colleagues were interested in the natural relationship between two variables: response to novelty and electrical activity in the frontal cortex. The study was longitudinal because children were tested twice at different ages: Their response to novelty was measured at 4 months, and their brain activity was measured at 9 months.

*Were there ethical concerns with the study?* No. The novel stimuli were mildly upsetting to some infants, but they were no more fear-provoking than other novel stimuli that young babies encounter in daily life. Measuring brain activity with EEGs is painless and safe. The investigators obtained permission from the parents for the children to participate.

*What were the results?* The infants were divided into two groups, based on their response to novelty as 4-month-olds: infants who responded positively and infants who responded negatively. Then Calkins and her colleagues looked at patterns of electrical activity in the left and right frontal cortex. They calculated the difference between activity in these two regions: A positive number meant relatively greater activation in the left frontal cortex, and a negative number meant relatively greater activation in the right frontal cortex. The graph shows that infants who responded negatively to novelty as 4-month-olds had relatively more right frontal activity as 9-month-olds. In contrast, infants who responded positively to novelty as 4-month-olds had relatively more left frontal activity as 9-month-olds.

*What did the investigators conclude?* Infants' response to novelty at 4 months predicts their brain activity at 9 months. Babies who respond to novelty by fussing and crying have a more active right frontal cortex, the region that regulates emotions linked to avoidance. Babies who respond to novelty by smiling have a more active left frontal cortex, the region that regulates emotions linked to approach. These differences provide further evidence that, in the first year, the left frontal cortex regulates infants' tendency to approach or explore stimuli and the right frontal cortex regulates infants' tendency to avoid or escape stimuli. ●

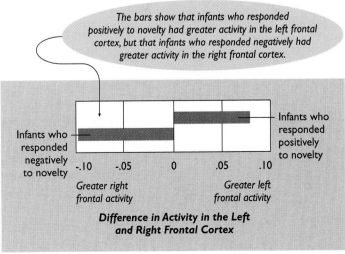

The bars show that infants who responded positively to novelty had greater activity in the left frontal cortex, but that infants who responded negatively had greater activity in the right frontal cortex.

Infants who responded negatively to novelty

Infants who responded positively to novelty

-.10    -.05    0    .05    .10

*Greater right frontal activity*    *Greater left frontal activity*

**Difference in Activity in the Left and Right Frontal Cortex**

FIG 4–8

The "Focus on Research" highlights an important point in this module: The brain begins to specialize early in life. Language processing is associated primarily with the left hemisphere; recognizing nonspeech sounds, emotions, and faces is associated with the right hemisphere; and regulating emotions and intentional behavior is a function of the frontal cortex. Of course, this early specialization does not mean that the brain is functionally mature. Over the remainder of childhood and into adulthood, these and other regions of the brain continue to become more specialized.

I have described the typical pattern of brain localization, but it is not the only pattern. In some left-handed individuals, for example, the assignment of function to left and right hemispheres is reversed from the usual pattern (Springer & Deutsch, 1998). And, when individuals suffer brain injury, some cognitive functions are usually impaired. But, over months and years, some functioning (less often, all functioning) is restored (Kolb & Whishaw, 1998). These examples raise the issue of how certain functions come to be localized in brain regions and how readily they are transferred to other regions. The next section will address these issues.

### Brain Plasticity. *Plasticity* **refers to the extent to which brain organization is flexible.** How plastic is the human brain? Answers to this question reflect the familiar views on the nature-nurture issue (Nelson, 1999; Stiles, 1998). Some theorists believe that organization of brain function is predetermined genetically; it's simply in most children's genes that, for example, the left hemisphere will specialize in language processing. In this view, the brain is like a house—a structure that's specialized from the very beginning, with some rooms designed for cooking, others for sleeping, others for bathing. Other theorists believe that few functions are rigidly assigned to specific brain sites at conception. Instead, experience helps determine the functional organization of the brain. In this view, the brain is more like an office building—an all-purpose structure with rooms designed to be used flexibly to meet the different business needs of the companies with offices in the building.

Research designed to test these views shows that the brain has some plasticity. Remember Martin, the child whose brain was damaged when he was struck by a car? His language skills were impaired after the accident. This was not surprising, because the left hemisphere of Martin's brain had absorbed most of the force of the collision. But, within several months, Martins had completely recovered his language skills. Apparently other neurons took over language-related processing from the damaged neurons. This recovery of function is not uncommon—particularly for young children—and shows that the brain is plastic (Witelson, 1987).

*When children suffer brain damage, cognitive processes are usually impaired; over time, these processes often recover, showing the brain's plasticity.*

However, the brain is not completely plastic—brains have a similar structure and similar mapping of functions on those structures. Visual cortex, for example, is almost always near the back of the brain. Sensory and motor cortex always run across the middle of the brain. But if a neuron's function is not specified at conception, how do different neurons take on different functions and in much the same pattern for most people? Researchers are trying to answer this question and many details still need to be worked out. The answer probably lies in complex biochemical processes (Barinaga, 1997; Kunzig, 1998). You can get an idea of what's involved by imagining people arriving for a football game at a stadium where there are no reserved seats. As fans enter the stadium, they see others wearing their own school colors and move in that direction. Of course, not everyone does this. Some fans sit with friends from the other team. Some pick seats based on other factors (e.g., to avoid looking into the sun, to be close to the concession stand). In general, though, by game time, most fans have taken seats on their respective sides of the field.

In much the same way, as neurons are created and begin migrating through the layers of cortex, cellular biochemistry makes some paths more attractive than others. Yet, just as each fan can potentially sit anywhere because there are no reserved seats, an individual neuron can end up in many different locations because genetic instructions do not assign specific brain regions. Thus, the human brain is plastic—it's organization and function can be affected by experience—but its development follows some general biochemical instructions that ensure most people end up with brains organized along similar lines.

## Check Your Learning

1. The _____ is the part of the neuron that contains the basic machinery that keeps the cell alive.

2. Terminal buttons release _____, chemicals that carry neural transmissions to nearby neurons.

3. The wrinkled surface of the brain is the _____.

4. During prenatal development, the brain forms from a flat group of cells called the _____.

5. During the first year, axons and dendrites grow and many synapses form; however, starting at about the first birthday, _____.

6. To study brain organization, researchers study children with brain damage, _____, and use imaging techniques.

7. Human speech elicits more electrical activity from the _____ of an infant's brain.

8. A good example of brain plasticity is the fact that, although children with brain damage often have impaired cognitive processes, _____.

 **How does the pattern of development of the brain compare to the general pattern of physical growth described in Module 4.1?**

**Answers:** (1) cell body, (2) neurotransmitters, (3) cerebral cortex, (4) neural plate, (5) unnecessary synapses disappear, a phenomenon known as synaptic pruning, (6) measure electrical activity in children's brains (EEGs), (7) left hemisphere, (8) over time, they often regain their earlier skills

# Motor Development

**4.4**

Locomotion

Fine-Motor Skills

Maturation, Experience, and Motor Skill

## Learning Objectives

● **What are the component skills involved in learning to walk, and at what age do infants typically master them?**

● **How do infants learn to coordinate the use of their hands? When and why do most children begin to prefer to use one hand?**

● **How do maturation and experience influence children's acquisition of motor skills?**

*Nancy is 14 months old and a world-class crawler. Using hands and knees, she gets nearly anywhere she wants to go. Nancy does not walk and seems to have no interest in learning how. Her dad wonders whether he should be doing something to help Nancy progress beyond crawling. And down deep, he worries that perhaps he should have provided more exercise or training for Nancy when she was younger.*

These photos have a common theme. **Each depicts an activity involving *motor skills*—coordinated movements of the muscles and limbs.** In each activity, success demands that each movement be done in a precise way and in a specific sequence. For example, to use a stick shift properly, you need to move the clutch pedal, gas pedal, and the stick shift in specific ways and in exactly the right sequence. If you don't give the car enough gas as you let out the clutch, you'll kill the engine. If you give it too much gas, the engine races and the car lurches forward.

If new activities are demanding for adults, think about the challenges infants face. **Infants must learn *locomotion*, that is, to move about in the world.** Newborns are relatively immobile, but infants soon learn to crawl, stand, and walk. Learning to move through the environment upright leaves the arms and hands free. Taking full advantage of this arrangement, the human hand has fully independent fingers (instead of a paw), with the thumb opposing the remaining four fingers. An opposable thumb makes it possible for humans to grasp and manipulate objects. **Infants must learn the *fine-motor skills* associated with grasping, holding, and manipulating objects.** In the case of feeding, for example, infants progress from being fed by others to holding a bottle, to feeding themselves with their fingers, to eating with a spoon. Each new skill requires incredibly complex physical movements.

Although demanding, locomotion and fine-motor skills are well worth mastering because of their benefits. Being able to locomote and to grasp gives children access to an enormous amount of information about their environment. They can explore objects that look interesting, and they can keep themselves close to parents. Improved motor skills promote children's cognitive and social development, not to mention make a child's life more interesting!

In this module, we'll see how children acquire locomotor and fine-motor skills. As we do, we'll find out if Nancy's dad should be worrying about her lack of interest in walking.

## Locomotion

In little more than a year, advances in posture and locomotion change the newborn from an almost motionless being into an upright, standing individual who walks through the environment. The chart on page 113 shows some of the important milestones in motor development and the age by which most infants achieve them. By about 4 months, most babies can sit upright with support. By 7 months, they can sit

| 0 month:<br>Fetal posture | 1 month:<br>Chin up | 2 months:<br>Chest up | 3 months:<br>Reach and miss |
| --- | --- | --- | --- |
| 4 months:<br>Sit with support | 5 months:<br>Sit on lap, grasp object | 6 months:<br>Sit on high chair, grasp dangling object | 7 months:<br>Sit alone |
| 8 months:<br>Stand with help | 9 months:<br>Stand holding furniture | 10 months:<br>Creep | 11 months:<br>Walk when led |
| 12 months:<br>Pull to stand by furniture | 13 months:<br>Climb stair steps | 14 months:<br>Stand alone | 15 months:<br>Walk alone |

FIG 4–9
Source: Based on Shirley, 1931 and Bayley, 1969.

without support, and by 9 months, can stand if they hold on to an object for support. A typical 14-month-old can stand alone briefly and walk with assistance. **Youngsters at this age are called *toddlers*, after the toddling manner of early walking.** Of course, not all children walk at exactly the same age. Some walk before their first birthday; others, like Nancy, the world-class crawler in the module-opening vignette, take their first steps as late as 17 or 18 months of age. By 24 months, most children can climb steps, walk backwards, and kick a ball.

Researchers once thought these developmental milestones reflected maturation (e.g., McGraw, 1935). Walking, for example, emerged naturally when the necessary muscles and neural circuits matured. Today, however, locomotion—and, in fact, all of motor development—is viewed from a new perspective. **According to *dynamic systems theory*, motor development involves many distinct skills that are organized and reorganized over time to meet the demands of specific tasks.** For example, walking includes maintaining balance, moving limbs, perceiving the environment, and having a reason to move. Only by understanding each of these skills and how they are combined to allow movement in a specific situation can we understand walking (Thelen & Smith, 1998).

In the remainder of this section, we'll see how learning to walk reflects the maturity and coalescence of many component skills.

### Posture and Balance.

The ability to maintain an upright posture is fundamental to walking. But upright posture is virtually impossible for newborns and young infants because of the shape of their body. Cephalocaudal growth means that an infant is top-heavy. Consequently, as soon as a young infant starts to lose her balance, she tumbles over. Only with growth of the legs and muscles can infants maintain an upright posture (Thelen, Ulrich, & Jensen, 1989).

Once infants can stand upright, they must continuously adjust their posture to avoid falling down. By a few months after birth, infants begin to use visual cues and an inner-ear mechanism to adjust their posture. To show the use of visual cues for balance, researchers had babies sit in a room with striped walls that moved. When adults sit in such a room, they perceive themselves as moving (not the walls) and adjust their posture accordingly; so do infants, which shows that they use vision to maintain upright posture (Bertenthal & Clifton, 1998). In addition, when 4-month-olds who are propped in a sitting position lose their balance, they try to keep their head upright. They do this even when blindfolded, which means they are using cues from their inner ear to maintain balance (Woollacott, Shumway-Cook, & Williams, 1989).

*To master walking, infants must acquire distinct skills of standing upright, maintaining balance, stepping alternately, and using perceptual information to evaluate surfaces.*

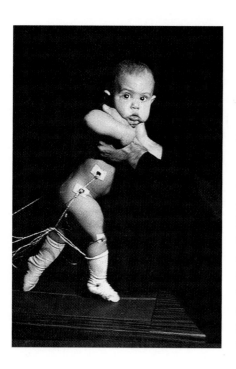

### Stepping.

Another essential element of walking is moving the legs alternately, repeatedly transferring the weight of the body from one foot to the other. Children don't step spontaneously until approximately 10 months because they must be able to stand to step.

Can younger children step if they are held upright? Thelen and Ulrich (1991) devised a clever procedure to answer this question. Infants were placed on a treadmill and held upright by an adult. When the belt on the treadmill started to move, infants could respond in one of several ways. They might simply let both legs be dragged rearward by the belt. Or they might let their legs be dragged briefly, then move them forward together in a hopping motion. Many 6- and 7-month-olds demonstrated the mature pattern of alternating steps on each leg that is shown in the photo. Even more amazing is that when the treadmill was equipped with separate belts for each leg that moved at different speeds, babies adjusted, stepping more rapidly on the faster belt. Apparently, the alternate stepping motion that is essential for walking is evident long before infants walk alone. Walking unassisted is not possible, though, until other component skills are mastered.

### Perceptual Factors.

Many infants learn to walk in the relative security of flat, uncluttered floors at home. But they soon discover that the environment offers a variety of surfaces, some more conducive to walking than others. Infants use perceptual information to judge whether a surface is suitable for walking. When placed on a surface that gives way underfoot (e.g., a waterbed), they quickly judge it unsuitable for walking and resort to crawling (Gibson et al., 1987). And when toddlers encounter a surface that slopes down steeply, few try to walk down (which would result in a fall). Instead, they slide or scoot backwards (Adolph, Eppler, & Gibson, 1993; Adolph, 1997). Results like these show that infants use perceptual cues to decide whether a surface is safe for walking.

### Coordinating Skills.

Dynamic systems theory emphasizes that learning to walk demands orchestration of many individual skills. Each component skill must first be mastered alone and then integrated with the other skills (Werner, 1948). **That is,** mastery of intricate motions requires both *differentiation*—mastery of component skills—and their *integration*—combining them in proper sequence into a coherent, working whole. In the case of walking, not until 12 to 15 months of age has the child mastered the component skills so that they can be coordinated to allow independent, unsupported walking.

### Beyond Walking.

If you can recall the feeling of freedom that accompanied your first driver's license, you can imagine how the world expands for infants and toddlers as they learn to move independently. The first tentative steps soon are followed by others that are more skilled. Most children learn to run a few months after they walk alone. Like walking, running requires moving the legs alternately. But running is more complicated because a runner actually becomes airborne briefly. To progress beyond walking to running, children must learn to propel themselves into the air and to maintain their balance while landing (Bertenthal & Clifton, 1998).

By age 7, most youngsters have mastered jumping, hopping, running, and skipping (Roberton & Halverson, 1988). And they take enormous pleasure in all these forms of locomotion, not only for their own sake but also because they are so useful (Bertenthal, Campos, & Kermoian, 1994). Now toddlers can get to desired objects like toys and food alone, without depending upon a parent. Of course, once the desired object is reached, fine-motor skills are called to action, which we discuss next.

> Motor development involves mastering individual skills and integrating them into a coherent, working whole.

### Fine-Motor Skills

A major accomplishment of infancy is skilled use of the hands (Bertenthal & Clifton, 1998). Newborns have little apparent control of their hands, but 1-year-olds are extraordinarily talented.

### Reaching and Grasping.

At about 4 months, infants can successfully reach for objects (Bertenthal & Clifton, 1998). These early reaches often look clumsy, and for a good reason. When infants reach, they don't move their arm and hand directly and smoothly to the desired object (as older children and adults do). Instead, the infant's hand moves like a ship under the direction of an unskilled navigator. It moves a short distance, slows, then moves again in a slightly different direction, a process that's repeated until the hand finally contacts the object (McCarty & Ashmead, 1999). As infants grow, their reaches have fewer movements, though they are still not as continuous and smooth as older children's and adults' reaches (Berthier, 1996).

Grasping, too, becomes more efficient during infancy. Most 4-month-olds just use their fingers to hold objects, gripping them tightly as if in a vise. Not until 7 or 8 months do most infants use their thumbs to hold objects (Siddiqui, 1995). At about this same age, infants begin to position their hands to make it easier to grasp an object. If trying to grasp a long thin rod, for example, infants place their fingers perpendicular to the rod, which is the best position for grasping (Bertenthal & Clifton, 1998).

Infants' growing control of each hand is accompanied by greater coordination of the two hands. Although 4-month-olds use both hands, their motions are not coordinated; rather, each hand seems to have a mind of its own. Infants may hold a toy motionless in one hand while shaking a rattle in the other. At roughly 5 to 6 months of age, infants can coordinate the motions of their hands so that each hand performs different actions that serve a common goal. So a child might, for example, hold a toy animal in one hand and pet it with the other (Karniol, 1989).

These many changes in reaching and grasping are well illustrated as infants learn to feed themselves. At about 6 months, they are often given "finger foods" such as sliced bananas and green beans. Infants can easily pick up such foods, but getting them into their mouths is another story. The hand grasping the food may be raised to the cheek, then moved to the edge of the lips, and finally shoved into the mouth. Mission accomplished, but only with many detours along the way! Eye-hand coordination improves rapidly, so before long foods that vary in size, shape, and texture reach the mouth directly.

At about the first birthday, youngsters are usually ready to try eating with a spoon. At first, they simply play with the spoon, dipping it in and out of a dish filled with food or sucking on an empty spoon. With a little help, they learn to fill the spoon with food and place it in their mouth, though the motion is awkward because they don't rotate their wrist. Instead, most 1-year-olds fill a spoon by placing it directly over a dish, and lowering it until the bowl of the spoon is full. Then, like the child in the photo, they raise the spoon to the mouth—all the while keeping the wrist rigid. In contrast, 2-year-olds rotate the hand at the wrist while scooping food from a dish and placing the spoon in the mouth—the same motion that adults use.

Fine-motor skills progress beyond infancy. Most 18-month-olds scribble with a crayon and build with blocks. As preschoolers, they typically learn to draw simple geometric figures and the human body (Frankenburg & Dobbs, 1969). Soon youngsters master using scissors, buttoning shirts and coats, and tying shoelaces.

In each of these actions, the same principles of dynamic systems theory apply as applied to locomotion. Complex acts involve many component movements. Each must be performed correctly and in the proper sequence. Development involves first mastering the separate elements and then assembling them to form a smoothly functioning whole. Eating finger food, for example, requires grasping food, moving the hand to the mouth, then releasing the food.

As the demands of tasks change and as children develop, the same skills are often reassembled to form a different sequence of movements.

## Handedness.

When young babies reach for objects, they don't seem to prefer one hand over the other; they use their left and right hands interchangeably. They may shake a rattle with their left hand and moments later pick up blocks with their right. In one study, infants and toddlers were videotaped as they played with toys that could be manipulated with two hands, such as a pinwheel (Cornwell, Harris, & Fitzgerald, 1991). The 9-month-olds used their left and right hands equally, but by 13 months most grasped the toy with their right hand. Then, like the toddler in the photo, they used their left hand to steady the toy while the right hand manipulated the object. This early preference for one hand becomes stronger and more consistent during the preschool years. By the time children are ready to enter kindergarten, handedness is well established and very difficult to reverse (McManus et al., 1988).

What determines whether children become left- or right-handed? Heredity plays a role (Corballis, 1997). Parents who are both right-handed tend to have right-handed children. Children who are left-handed generally have a parent or grandparent who was also left-handed. But experience also contributes to handedness. Modern industrial cultures favor right-handedness. School desks, scissors, and can openers, for example, are designed for right-handed people and can be used by left-handers only with difficulty.

Sometimes cultural values influence handedness. The Islam religion dictates that the left hand is unclean, and so forbids its use in eating and greeting others. Writing with the left hand is a cultural taboo in China, but when children of Chinese parents grow up elsewhere, about 10 percent of them write with their left hand, the typical figure worldwide (Harris, 1983). In the United States, elementary-school teachers used to urge left-handed children to use their right hands. As this practice has diminished in the last 50 years, the percentage of left-handed children has risen steadily (Levy, 1976). Thus, handedness seems to have both hereditary and environmental influences.

## Maturation, Experience, and Motor Skill

For locomotion and fine-motor skill, the big picture is much the same: Progress is rapid during the first year as fundamental skills are mastered and combined to generate even more complex behaviors. Is the progress that we observe due primarily to maturation? That is, do skills gradually unfold, regardless of the child's upbringing? Or do motor skills develop only with training, practice, and experience? As you might imagine, maturation and experience both contribute.

Let's begin with the impact of maturation on motor development, which is well documented. The sequence of motor development that we have described for locomotion and fine-motor skill holds for most cultures. That is, despite enormous variation across cultures in child-rearing practices, motor development proceeds in much the same way and at roughly the same rate worldwide. This general point is well illustrated in the "Cultural Influences" feature.

**CULTURAL INFLUENCES**

### Learning to Walk in a Native American Culture

Traditionally, infants in the Hopi culture are secured to cradle boards, like the one shown in the photo. Cradle boards prevent babies from moving hands or legs, rolling over, or raising their bodies. Infants feed and sleep while secured to the board; they are removed from the cradle board only for a change of clothes. This practice begins the day the infant is born and continues for the first 3 months. Thereafter, infants are allowed time off the boards so they can move around. Time off the cradle board increases gradually, but for most of the first year, infants sleep on the boards and spend some part of their waking time on them as well.

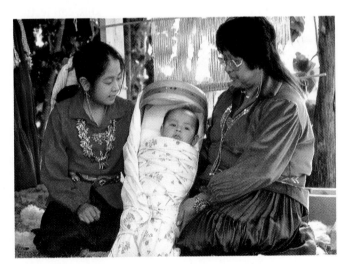

Obviously, the cradle board strictly limits the infant's ability to locomote during much of the first year, a time when most infants are learning to sit, creep, and crawl. Nevertheless, Dennis and Dennis (1940) discovered that infants reared with cradle boards learn to walk at approximately 15 months—about the same age as Hopi children reared by parents who had adopted Western practices and no longer used cradle boards.

Thus, a restrictive environment that massively reduces opportunities for practice has no apparent effect on the age of onset for walking. This suggests that the timing of an infant's first steps is determined more by an underlying genetic timetable than by specific experiences or practice. So the worried father of Nancy, our world-class crawler in the opening vignette, can be reassured that his daughter's motor development is perfectly normal. ●

When the Dennis and Dennis (1940) study was repeated more than 40 years later, the story remained the same. Chisholm (1983) studied Navajo infants who spent much of their infancy secured to cradle boards. They, too, began to walk at about the same age as infants whose parents did not use cradle boards, confirming the importance of maturation in learning to walk.

Of course, maturation and experience are not mutually exclusive. Just because maturation figures importantly in the development of one motor skill, walking, does not imply that experience plays no role. In fact, practice and training do affect children's mastery of many motor skills. Here, too, studies of other cultures are revealing. In some African countries, young infants are given daily practice walking under the tutelage of a parent or sibling. In addition, infants are commonly carried by their parents in the "piggyback" style shown in the photo, which helps develop muscles in the infants' trunk and legs. These infants walk months earlier than American infants (Super, 1981).

Experience can improve the rate of motor development, but the improvement is limited to the specific muscle groups that are involved. In other words, just as daily practice kicking a soccer ball won't improve your golf game, infants who receive much practice in one motor skill usually don't improve in others. For example, in a study by Zelazo and her colleagues (1993), parents had their 6-week-olds practice stepping. Other parents had their infants practice sitting. After 7 weeks of practice, the two groups of infants, as well as a control group of 6-week-olds who had had no practice of any kind, were tested in their ability to step and sit. For both stepping and sitting, infants improved the skill they had practiced. When infants were tested on the skill they had not practiced, they did no better than infants in the control group. Thus, the impact of practice is specific, not widespread.

Similarly, when infants practice crawling on their bellies, this helps them crawl on hands and feet because many of the motions are the same (Adolph, Vereijken, & Denny, 1998). But when infants practice crawling on steep slopes, there is no transfer to walking on steep slopes, because the motions differ (Adolph, 1997).

Experience becomes even more important in complex actions. Mastering discrete skills, connecting them in the correct sequence, and then timing them properly requires more than a few simple repetitions. Observing others, practicing repeatedly, and getting feedback on errors are required. Of course, learning a complex behavior must build upon maturational changes. But with biological readiness and practice, youngsters learn a gamut of complex motor behaviors—from hitting a tennis ball, to playing a violin, to signing to communicate with people who do not hear.

## Check Your Learning

1. Motor skills are coordinated movements of the muscles and _____.

2. According to _____, motor development involves many distinct skills that are organized and reorganized over time, depending on task demands.

3. Skills important in learning to walk include maintaining upright posture and balance, stepping, and _____.

**4.** Motor development involves differentiation of individual skills and their _____ into a cohesive whole.

**5.** Not until age _____ do children rotate their wrists while using a spoon.

**6.** Handedness is determined by heredity and _____.

**7.** Compared to infants reared in less restrictive environments, infants reared on cradle boards learn to walk _____.

**8.** When infants practice motor skills, the impact of this practice is _____.

 **Some children begin walking before their first birthday; others don't begin until a few months after. Describe some possible advantages of walking early. Can you think of possible disadvantages? (Hint—you might consider the advantages and disadvantages of reaching puberty early.)**

**Answers:** (1) limbs, (2) dynamic systems theory, (3) using perceptual information, (4) integration, (5) 2 years, (6) environmental influences, (7) at about the same time, (8) limited to the practiced skill; there is no widespread effect

# Physical and Motor Development
## IN PERSPECTIVE

Physical growth seems so simple—children just keep getting bigger and bigger. Yet we saw in this chapter that physical and motor development are, in reality, quite intricate. In Module 4.1, we saw that physical growth does not simply refer to height and weight; that physical growth varies considerably within the normal range; and that heredity, hormones, and nutrition are the keys to growth. We also saw that puberty has enormous impact on adolescents. In Module 4.2, we examined some problems of physical growth, including malnutrition, anorexia, bulimia, and obesity. In Module 4.3, we looked at a less obvious aspect of physical growth—development of the nervous system. We discovered the organization of the neuron and the brain, and saw that different regions of the brain have specialized functions very soon after birth. Finally, in Module 4.4, we saw that locomotion and fine-motor coordination involve differentiation and integration of component skills and that both nature and nurture play important roles in motor development.

This chapter is an excellent opportunity to highlight the theme that *development in different domains is connected*. Consider the impact of timing of puberty. Whether a child matures early or late affects social development (early-maturing boys date more often), self-esteem (early-maturing boys feel good about themselves but early-maturing girls don't), and academic performance (early-maturing girls often do poorly in school). Or consider the impact of malnutrition. Malnourished youngsters are often listless, which affects how their parents interact with them (they're less likely to provide stimulating experiences). Less stimulation, in turn, slows the children's intellectual development. Physical, cognitive, social, and personality development are linked: Change in one area almost always leads to change of some kind in the others.

## See for Yourself

How can we decide if a preschooler is left- or right-handed? Adults can simply tell us which hand they use in writing or throwing, but we need a more concrete approach with preschoolers, few of whom even know left from right.

1. Draw a face with a pen
2. Color a square
3. Throw a ball
4. Thread a bead onto a wire
5. Turn over cards placed on a table

You should see that younger preschoolers use their left hand on some tasks and their right on others. However, by the time children are 5 years old, most will do at least eight

With the permission of a local nursery school or day-care center, you could ask several preschoolers of different ages—say 2 to 5 years—to do the following tasks (from McManus et al., 1988):

6. Show how they use a spoon to eat
7. Brush their teeth with an imaginary toothbrush
8. Comb their hair with an imaginary comb
9. Blow their nose with a tissue
10. Pick a piece of candy from a bag

of these activities with one hand, showing that handedness is now well established. See for yourself!

## Resources

*For more information about . . .*

 *ways to help children and adolescents stay physically fit,* try Kenneth Cooper's *Kid Fitness* (Random House, 1992), which describes a program of diet and exercise developed by the originator of the concept of aerobic fitness

 *sexual and reproductive health, birth control, sexually transmitted diseases, and sexuality education,* visit the Planned Parenthood Federation of America Web site: **http://www.plannedparenthood.org**

## Key Terms

**anorexia nervosa** 102
**axon** 105
**basal metabolic rate** 103
**bulimia nervosa** 102
**cell body** 105
**cerebral cortex** 105
**corpus callosum** 105
**dendrite** 105
**differentiation** 115
**dynamic systems theory** 113
**electroencephalogram (EEG)** 107
**epiphyses** 94
**fine-motor skills** 112

**frontal cortex** 105
**functional magnetic resonance imaging (F-MRI)** 107
**hemispheres** 105
**hormones** 95
**integration** 115
**locomotion** 112
**malnourished** 101
**menarche** 97
**motor skills** 112
**myelin** 105
**neural plate** 106
**neuron** 105

**neurotransmitters** 105
**plasticity** 110
**positron emission tomography (PET-scan)** 107
**puberty** 97
**secular growth trends** 94
**synapse** 105
**synaptic pruning** 106
**terminal buttons** 105
**thyroxine** 95
**toddlers** 113

# SUMMARY

## 4.1 Physical Growth

### Features of Human Growth
Physical growth is particularly rapid during infancy, slows during the elementary school years, then accelerates again during adolescence. Growth follows the cephalocaudal principle, with the head and trunk developing before the limbs. Physical growth refers to not only height and weight but also to development of muscle, fat, and bones.

### Variations on the Average Profile
Children are taller today than in previous generations. Average heights vary around the world and, within any culture, there is considerable variation in the normal range of height.

### Mechanisms of Physical Growth
A person's height and weight as an adult are influenced by heredity. Hormones are also important for physical development: Growth hormone (GH) affects bone and muscle growth, and thyroxine affects nerve cells.

Nutrition is particularly important during periods of rapid growth, such as infancy and adolescence. Breast-feeding provides babies with all the nutrients they need and has other advantages. Many adolescents do not get adequate nutrients because of poor diets.

### The Adolescent Growth Spurt and Puberty
Puberty includes the adolescent growth spurt as well as sexual maturation. Early puberty tends to benefit boys but is often harmful for girls.

Sexual behavior begins in adolescence. Most U.S. teenagers are sexually active, particularly if their parents and peers view sex positively. Few teenagers use contraception because of ignorance, the illusion of invulnerability, lack of motivation, or lack of access.

A small percentage of adolescents are attracted to members of their own sex. Sexual orientation probably has its roots in biology.

## 4.2 Problems of Physical Growth

### Malnutrition
Malnutrition is a problem worldwide—including in the United States—that is particularly harmful during infancy, when growth is so rapid. Malnutrition can cause brain damage, affecting children's intelligence and ability to pay attention. Treating malnutrition requires improving children's diet and training their parents to provide stimulating environments.

### Anorexia and Bulimia
Anorexia and bulimia are eating disorders that typically affect adolescent girls. They are characterized by an irrational fear of being overweight. Several factors contribute to these disorders, including cultural standards of thinness, a need for independence within an autocratic family, and heredity.

### Obesity
Many obese children and adolescents are unpopular, have low self-esteem, and are at risk for medical disorders. Obesity reflects both heredity and acquired eating habits. In the most effective programs for treating obesity in youth, both children and their parents set eating and exercise goals and monitor their daily progress.

## 4.3 The Developing Nervous System

### Organization of the Mature Brain
Nerve cells, called neurons, are composed of a cell body, a dendrite, and an axon. The mature brain consists of billions of neurons organized into nearly identical left and right hemispheres connected by the corpus callosum. The frontal cortex is associated with personality and goal-directed behavior; the cortex in the left hemisphere, with language; and the cortex in the right hemisphere, with nonverbal processes.

### The Developing Brain
Brain structure begins in prenatal development, when neurons form at an incredible rate. After birth, neurons in the central nervous system become wrapped in myelin, allowing them to transmit information more rapidly. Throughout childhood, unused synapses disappear gradually through a process of pruning.

Methods used to investigate brain functioning in children include (a) studying children with brain damage, (b) recording electrical activity (the electroencephalogram or EEG), and (c) using imaging techniques. Research with these methods reveals that an infant's brain begins to function early in life. The cortex in the left hemisphere specializes in language processing at (or soon after) birth. The cortex in the right hemisphere controls some nonverbal functions, such as perception of music, very early in infancy; control of other right-hemisphere functions, such as understanding spatial relations, is achieved by the preschool years. The frontal cortex has begun to regulate goal-directed behavior and emotions by the first birthday.

## 4.4 Motor Development

### Locomotion
Infants progress through a sequence of motor milestones during the first year, culminating in walking a few months after the first birthday. Like most motor skills, learning to walk involves differentiation of individual skills, such as maintaining balance and stepping on alternate legs, and then integrating these skills into a coherent whole. This differentiation and integration of skills is central to the dynamic systems theory of motor development.

### Fine-Motor Skills
Infants first use only one hand at a time, then both hands independently, then both hands in common actions, and, finally, both hands in different actions with a common purpose.

Most people are right-handed, a preference that emerges after the first birthday and that becomes well established during the preschool years. Handedness is determined by heredity but can be influenced by experience and cultural values.

### Maturation, Experience, and Motor Skill
Biology and experience both shape the mastery of motor skills. The basic developmental timetable for motor milestones is similar worldwide, which indicates underlying biological causes. However, specific experience can accelerate motor development, particularly for complex motor skills.

# 5

hen my firstborn, Ben, was a preschooler, he loved to watch reruns of ChiPs. (Maybe you, too, remember Erik Estrada zooming along the L.A. freeways on his Kawasaki.) Ben was totally absorbed by the show and oblivious to everything else. The house could burn, the family room could flood with dollar bills, and Courtney Love could give a concert in the kitchen, but Ben wouldn't notice. Ben's behavior is a common but powerful example of perception in action. Our systems are assaulted with stimulation, but much of it is ignored. **Sensory and perceptual processes are the means by which the nervous system receives, selects, modifies, and organizes stimulation from the world.** Sensory and perceptual processes are the first step in the complex process of accumulating information that eventually results in "knowing."

We'll begin our study of sensory and perceptual processes in Module 5.1 by examining different theories of perceptual development. In Module 5.2, we'll look at the origins of sensory processes in infancy; and in Module 5.3 we'll see how more complex sensory and perceptual processes develop throughout childhood.

# Sensory and Perceptual Development

# 5.1

## Approaches to Perceptual Development

### Learning Objectives

● What are the essential elements of the empirical approach to perception?

● What is the cognitive approach to perception, and how does it differ from the empirical approach?

● What features of Gibson's theory distinguish it from the empirical and cognitive views?

> *Jeff is a frustrated stand-up comic who loves to tell funny stories and play practical jokes. Most people don't think he's very funny, but his 7-month-old daughter, Erin, loves it when Jeff puts on an old top hat and makes silly faces at her. Erin smiles, giggles, and waves her hands in excitement at Jeff's "top-hat routine." In his more serious moments, Jeff wonders why Erin finds him funny when no one else does!*

We can't help Jeff improve his humor, but we can learn how Erin recognizes her dad and his "top-hat routine." Sensory and perceptual skills hold the key. In this first module, you'll learn three general approaches to understanding sensory and perceptual skills like those that Erin uses to recognize her dad and his antics. We'll begin with the empirical approach, then consider the cognitive approach, and end with Eleanor Gibson's theory of perceptual development.

## The Empirical Approach

This approach traces its roots to the great Greek philosopher, Aristotle (384–322 B.C.), who was the first empiricist. Aristotle believed that experience is the source of all knowledge. **The *empirical approach* holds that sensory experience is the foundation of all perception and, ultimately, all knowledge.** You can think of a sensory experience as a snapshot of sensory input at a particular point in time. As infants have more and more experience in the world, they accumulate more and more of these snapshots. Gradually, they notice that some snapshots occur repeatedly, such as their mother's face during nursing. Infants also notice that other snapshots, though different, resemble each other, such as their mother's face while nursing and while playing with them.

The snapshot analogy is most appropriate for vision, but the same sort of phenomenon occurs with all senses. In hearing, for example, the "snapshot" might consist of segments of sounds. Babies gradually come to recognize the same sound snapshots, such as their mother calling them by name. And they recognize similarities in different sounds, such as a mother's voice. Over time, infants make connections between their speech snapshots and their visual snapshots. These snapshots then become associated with snapshots from other senses, until ultimately they assemble the concept "mother."

How does the empirical approach explain Erin's recognition of her dad? Erin's initial sensory experiences might be of individual elements of Jeff's face. She notices that many snapshots have white ellipses with a dark circle in the center. Eventually she notices there are two ellipses and they appear side by side. Gradually, other facial features are associated with the eyes, until Erin finally recognizes that this stable configuration of elements is Jeff's face. With even more experience, she recognizes the sound of Jeff's voice and comes to associate it with the configuration of features that makes up his face.

Erin's recognition of Jeff illustrates the fundamental assumptions of the empirical approach to perceptual development. First, experience provides the data necessary for infants (and children and adults) to observe how objects are alike and how they differ, which is the starting point for understanding the world. Erin needs to see and hear Jeff repeatedly to recognize him. Second, the simple sensory experience is the basic unit of perception; over time, sensory experiences are assembled to form perceptions. Each time Erin sees Jeff, she has a new, unique sensory snapshot that is connected with other similar snapshots. Third, the flow of perceptual processing is one way. Sensory experience influences perception and understanding but not the reverse. That is, even though Erin may have 10, 100, or 1,000 other snapshots of Jeff, every time she sees him the process is the same—another snapshot is created and linked to similar snapshots.

> The empirical and cognitive approaches both emphasize the role of experience in perception, but only the cognitive approach claims that knowledge can influence perception.

As you'll see in the next few pages, experience is also important in the cognitive approach and Gibson's theory. These other approaches, however, believe that perception involves more than just experience.

## The Cognitive Approach

If I were to create a list of my favorite 10 experiments, it would definitely include one by Ballin (cited by Solley, 1966). In the weeks leading up to Christmas, 5- to 7-year-olds were shown a picture of Santa Claus. They were asked to estimate Santa's size by selecting a disk that looked, to them, to be the same size as Santa. Children chose increasingly larger disks as Christmas drew near, but after Christmas had passed, they chose smaller disks. Even though Santa remained the same size, evidently he looked larger as Christmas approached. Apparently, children's emotions and values—in this case, their excitement over the upcoming holiday—can influence their perception.

The results of Ballin's study would trouble an empiricist because they suggest that understanding influences sensory and perceptual processing, counter to the one-way flow of information in the empirical approach. Ballin's experiment supports a second approach to perceptual development—the cognitive. **In the *cognitive approach,* not only does sensory experience influence perception and understanding, but understanding also influences sensory and perceptual processing.**

A variety of research shows that understanding influences perception. For example, cross-cultural studies have produced some fascinating demonstrations of perception based on understanding; we'll look at one example in the "Cultural Influences" feature.

**CULTURAL INFLUENCES**

### Culture Influences How We Perceive the World

Are the lines marked A and B the same length? Or is one line longer than the other? Most children and adults think line A is longer, but A and B are really the same length. **The tendency to see a line with inward-facing arrows as longer than the same line with outward-facing arrows** is the *Müller-Lyer illusion.*

Why are people fooled by the Müller-Lyer illusion? One explanation says it's because we mistakenly use our experience with corners of rooms and buildings. You can see in the drawing at the top of page 126 that corners near us seem to be outward-facing, and corners farther away seem to be inward-facing. Thus, our understanding of the normal appearance of corners leads us to interpret the inward-facing arrows on line A to mean it is farther away than line B, and that line A is therefore longer than line B.

FIG 5–1

FIG 5–2

If this explanation is accurate, what should happen if we test children and adults who grow up in environments that don't have the rectangular corners found in urban industrial countries? Someone who has had little or no experience with corners should not interpret the arrows as clues to the distance of the vertical line and should therefore say that lines A and B are the same length.

In fact, several studies show that individuals who grow up in nonindustrialized cultures are less susceptible to the Müller-Lyer illusion (Pederson & Wheeler, 1983; Segall et al., 1990). For example, the Navajo, Native Americans whose traditional homes are circular, are less prone to the Müller-Lyer illusion. So are people who grow up in parts of Africa, Asia, and Australia that don't have the straight-line and right-angle buildings that come with urbanization and economic development.

Cross-cultural studies of the Müller-Lyer illusion thus show that children and adults interpret sensory information in a particular way based on their experience. Because children growing up in different cultures have different experiences, they may interpret sensory information differently. ●

FIG 5–3

Laboratory studies also show that understanding influences perception. In one study, children were asked to identify ambiguous pictures like the one shown here. Identifying these pictures is very difficult for children unless they're given a clue (Potter, 1966). For example, if told that this figure depicts a large animal often found in zoos, children can "see" the picture almost instantly.

Another way to show the impact of context on children's ability to recognize words or pictures is through priming experiments, experiments that somehow prepare the participant to respond. As you can see in the bottom diagram, the task is simple: Children merely read words or name pictures as rapidly as they can. However, they perform much more rapidly when the target word or picture is related to the preceding phrase than when it is not (Morris, 1994; Potter et al., 1993). In this case (as with the ambiguous picture in the previous study), knowledge primes perception: Knowing what to see, children perceive stimuli more accurately and more rapidly.

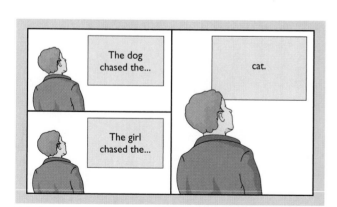

FIG 5–4

How does the cognitive approach explain Erin's behavior when Jeff tries to make her laugh? Part of the explanation follows the empirical approach: Erin gradually comes to associate the features—eyes, nose, mouth, and sounds—that go together, and this leads to the knowledge of what Jeff looks and sounds like. But the cognitive approach goes on to say that Erin's knowledge then influences her perception. If Jeff is out of sight but she hears his voice, this primes her to see his face. Similarly, seeing Jeff don his top hat primes Erin to expect his funny faces. The cognitive approach thus goes beyond the empirical approach by saying that Erin's growing understanding of her dad causes her to interpret sensory information in a particular way.

Cognitive theories of perception tend to be more about cognition than perception. (This shouldn't surprise you, knowing that this approach emphasizes the influence of knowledge and understanding on perception.) One of the most important cognitive theorists is Piaget, whose work was introduced in Module 1.2. Piaget emphasized that perception is regulated by cognition; he performed experiments showing that children are less influenced by perceptual illusions as they grow older because of their growing understanding of the world (Piaget & Albertini, 1950–1952). To use Piaget's own terminology, sensory experiences are assimilated into one's knowledge.

For Piaget and other cognitive theorists, perception and understanding are linked by a two-way street: Perception influences understanding and understanding influences perception.

> The empirical and cognitive approaches view perception as a gradual accumulation of sensory experiences, but Gibson's differentiation theory views perception as the extraction of complex information.

## Gibson's Differentiation Theory

The empirical and cognitive approaches are alike in claiming that, over time, sensory inputs are gradually associated and give rise to perception. An influential theory of perceptual development proposed by Eleanor Gibson, who is pictured here, takes a different tack. According to Gibson (1969), "the environment is rich in varied and complex potential stimulus information, capable of giving rise to diverse, meaningful, complex perceptions" (p. 75). But, Gibson contends, this complex information is not perceived piece by piece as the empirical and cognitive theorists would have us believe. Instead, complex stimuli are *extracted from* the flow of perceptual information; they are *not assembled* from elementary sensory experiences. In other words, complex patterns can be perceived directly, if you know what to look for. **According to Gibson's *differentiation theory*, perception reflects children's growing ability to identify the features that distinguish complex patterns.**

To understand the idea of differentiation that is central to Gibson's theory, consider the following:

- To the average adult, all red wines taste pretty much the same; however, a skilled wine taster can differentiate an incredible number of varieties.

- For most people, an X-ray is simply a meaningless mixture of shades of gray; however, a skilled radiologist sees a wealth of information.

- For very young children, the letters of the alphabet are simply a jumble of curved and straight lines; however, to older children and adults they are recognizable symbols that can be used to create words.

In each of these cases, a complex pattern of stimulation is present and potentially perceivable by all. However, only individuals with sufficient experience can identify the critical features that distinguish a burgundy from a Chianti, a healthy lung from one that is diseased, and the letter *b* from the letter *p*.

Applied to Erin's perception of Jeff's face, Gibson's theory holds that, as a newborn, Erin saw Jeff's face in much the same way that a novice sees an X-ray: as a complex but undifferentiated pattern. With repeated exposure to faces, Erin became able to extract some features, such as two eyes separated by a nose, that differentiate faces from other complex stimuli. Eventually Erin differentiated Jeff's features from features of other faces.

The process by which Erin came to recognize Jeff demonstrates the basic assumptions of Gibson's differentiation theory. First, infants (and children and adults) are not passive recipients of sensory experience. Instead, they actively try to make sense out of their sensory experiences. Erin did not simply passively register successive snapshots

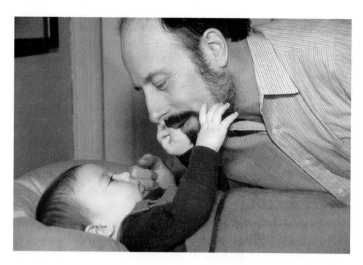

of Jeff. Instead, she actively abstracted the properties of his face that were constant against the backdrop of ever-changing sensory information. Like the baby in the photo, Erin noticed that regardless of Jeff's facial expression, his eyes were always next to each other and his nose was above his lips. Second, with greater and greater experience, infants make ever-sharper distinctions between features. Just as a radiologist differentiates more features in X-rays with greater experience, so Erin differentiated more of Jeff's facial expressions with greater experience.

Gibson's theory, the cognitive approach, and the empirical approach are the three major views of perceptual development. One way for you to see the similarities and differences in these views is to think about the role that nature and nurture plays in each. The empirical approach is the simplest to understand. Empiricists claim that heredity provides the sense organs that allow children to perceive. They also believe that perception requires experience; without experience, there is no sensory information to perceive.

The cognitive approach and Gibson's theory include these assumptions, too, but they cast a larger role for nature. Cognitive theorists believe we have a built-in ability to use knowledge to interpret sensory information. As soon as infants acquire knowledge, this knowledge influences their perception. Gibson believes that perception involves actively trying to interpret sensory experience by searching for constant perceptual features. From birth, infants don't simply see and hear; they look and listen, trying to make sense of their experiences (Gibson, 1969).

The three approaches to perception that we have discussed have stimulated a great deal of research into sensory and perceptual development. In the next two modules of this chapter, we'll look at some of this research. As we do, ask yourself whether the findings are most consistent with the empirical approach, the cognitive approach, or with Gibson's theory.

## Check Your Learning

1. _____ emphasizes sensory experiences as the basic building blocks from which perception is constructed.

2. According to _____, knowledge influences sensory and perceptual processing.

3. Differentiation of distinctive features is a central element of _____.

4. Of the three approaches to perception, only _____ views perception as a one-way street—sensory experiences lead to knowledge but knowledge does not influence perception.

5. One explanation of the Müller-Lyer illusion is based upon people growing up in cultures that _____.

 **Compare the three approaches to perceptual development in terms of the active-passive child issue described in Module 1.2.**

**Answers:** (1) The empirical approach, (2) the cognitive approach, (3) Gibson's differentiation theory, (4) the empirical approach, (5) have environments with many rectangular corners like those found in urban industrialized countries

# Basic Sensory and Perceptual Processes

## Learning Objectives

**5.2**

Smell, Taste, and Touch ─

Hearing ─

Seeing ─

Integrating Sensory
Information ─

● **Are newborn babies able to smell, taste, and respond to touch?**

● **How well do infants hear? How do they use sounds to understand their world?**

● **How accurate is infants' vision? Do infants perceive color?**

● **How do infants integrate information from different senses?**

> *Darla adores her 3-day-old daughter, Olivia. She loves holding her, talking to her,
> and simply watching her. Darla is certain that Olivia is already getting to know
> her, coming to recognize her face and the sound of her voice. Darla's husband,
> Steve, thinks she is crazy. He tells her, "Everyone knows that babies are born blind.
> And they probably can't hear much either." Darla doubts that Steve is right, but
> she wishes someone would tell her about babies' vision and hearing.*

Darla's questions are really about her newborn daughter's sensory and perceptual
skills. To help her, we need to remember that humans have different kinds of sense
organs, each receptive to a unique kind of physical energy. The retina at the back of
the eye, for example, is sensitive to some types of electromagnetic energy, and sight is
the result. The eardrum detects changes in air pressure, and hearing is the result.
Cells at the top of the nasal passage detect airborne molecules, and smell is the result.
In each case, the sense organ translates the physical stimulation into nerve impulses
that are sent to the brain.

The senses begin to function early in life, which is why this module is devoted
entirely to infancy. How can we know what an infant senses? Since infants can't tell us
what they smell, hear, or see, researchers have had to devise other ways to find out. In
many studies, an investigator presents two stimuli to a baby, such as a high-pitched
tone and a low-pitched tone or a sweet-tasting substance and a sour-tasting substance.
Then the investigator records the baby's responses, such as heart rate or facial expression or head movement. If the baby consistently responds differently to the two stimuli, the baby must be distinguishing between them.

Another approach is based on the fact that infants usually prefer novel stimuli
over familiar stimuli. **When a novel stimulus is presented, babies pay much attention, but they pay less attention as it becomes more familiar, a phenomenon
known as** *habituation.* Researchers use habituation to study perception by repeatedly presenting a stimulus such as a low-pitched tone
until an infant barely responds. Then they present a second stimulus,
such as a higher-pitched tone. If the infant responds strongly, then it
can distinguish the two stimuli.

In this module, you'll learn what researchers using these techniques have discovered about infants' perception. We begin with smell,
taste, and touch because these senses are particularly mature at birth.

Techniques used to study infants'
perception typically involve
presenting several distinct stimuli,
then determining if infants respond
the same to all or differently.

## Smell, Taste, and Touch

Newborns have a keen sense of smell. Infants respond positively to pleasant
smells and negatively to unpleasant smells (Mennella & Beauchamp, 1997).
They have a relaxed, contented-looking facial expression when they smell

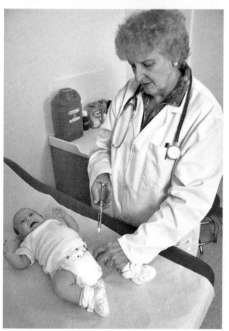

honey or chocolate but frown, grimace, or turn away when they smell rotten eggs or ammonia. Young babies can also recognize familiar odors. Newborns will look in the direction of a pad that is saturated with their own amniotic fluid (Schaal, Marlier, & Soussignan, 1998). They will also turn toward a pad saturated with the odor of their mother's breast or her perfume (Porter et al., 1991).

Newborns also have a highly developed sense of taste. They readily differentiate salty, sour, bitter, and sweet tastes (Rostenstein & Oster, 1997). Most infants seem to have a "sweet tooth." They react to sweet substances by smiling, sucking, and licking their lips. In contrast, you can probably guess what the infant in the photo has tasted! This grimace is typical when infants are fed bitter- or sour-tasting substances (Kaijura, Cowart, & Beauchamp, 1992). Infants are also sensitive to changes in the taste of breast milk that reflect a mother's diet. Infants will nurse more after their mother has consumed a sweet-tasting substance such as vanilla (Mennella & Beauchamp, 1996).

Newborns are sensitive to touch. As I described in Module 3.4, many areas of the newborn's body respond reflexively when touched. Touching an infant's cheek, mouth, hand, or foot produces reflexive movements, documenting that infants perceive touch.

If babies react to touch, does this mean they experience pain? This is difficult to answer because pain has such a subjective element to it. The same pain-eliciting stimulus that leads some adults to complain of mild discomfort causes others to report that they are in agony. Since infants cannot express their pain to us directly, we must use indirect evidence.

The infant's nervous system definitely is capable of transmitting pain: Receptors for pain in the skin are just as plentiful in infants as they are in adults (Anand & Hickey, 1987). Furthermore, babies' behavior in response to apparent pain-provoking stimuli also suggests that they experience pain (Buchholz et al., 1998). Look, for example, at the baby in the photo who is receiving an inoculation. She lowers her eyebrows, purses her lips, and, of course, opens her mouth to cry. Although we can't hear her, the sound of her cry is probably the unique pattern associated with pain. The pain cry begins suddenly, is high-pitched, and is not easily soothed. This baby is also agitated, moving her hands, arms, and legs (Craig et al., 1993). All together, these signs strongly suggest that babies experience pain.

Perceptual skills are extraordinarily useful to newborns and young babies. Smell and touch help them recognize their mothers. Smell and taste make it much easier for them to learn to eat. Early development of smell, taste, and touch prepares newborns and young babies to learn about the world.

## Hearing

Do you remember, from Module 3.1, the study with mothers in late pregnancy who read *The Cat in the Hat* aloud every day? This research showed that the fetus can hear at 7 or 8 months. As you would expect from these results, newborns typically respond to sounds in their surroundings. If a parent is quiet but then coughs, an infant may startle, blink his eyes, and move his arms or legs. These responses may seem natural, but they do indeed indicate that infants are sensitive to sound.

Not surprisingly, infants do not hear as well as adults. **Auditory threshold refers to the quietest sound that a person can hear.** An adult's auditory threshold is fairly easy to measure: A tone is presented, and the adult simply tells when he or she hears it. To test auditory thresholds in infants, who obviously cannot report what they hear, researchers have devised a number of clever techniques (Aslin, Jusczyk, & Pisoni, 1998). For example, in one simple method, the infant is seated on a parent's lap. Both parent and baby wear headphones, as does an observer seated in another room who watches the baby through an observation window. When the observer believes the baby is attentive, he signals the experimenter, who sometimes presents a tone over the baby's headphones and sometimes does nothing. Neither the observer nor the parent knows when tones are going to be presented, and they can't hear the tones through their headphones. On each trial, the observer simply judges if the baby responds in any fashion, such as by turning its head or changing its facial expression or activity level. Afterwards, the experimenter determines how well the observer's judgments match the trials: If a baby can hear the tone, the observer should have noted a response only when a tone was presented.

This type of testing reveals that, overall, adults can hear better than infants; adults can hear some very quiet sounds that infants can't (Aslin et al., 1998). More importantly, this testing shows that infants hear sounds best that have pitches in the range of human speech—neither very high- nor very low-pitched. Infants can differentiate vowels from consonant sounds, and by 4½ months they can recognize their own names (Jusczyk, 1995; Mandel, Jusczyk, & Pisoni, 1995).

Infants also use sound to locate objects, determining whether they are left or right and near or far. In one study (Clifton, Perris, & Bullinger, 1991), 7-month-olds were shown a rattle. Then the experimenters darkened the room and shook the rattle, either 6 inches away from the infant or about 2 feet away. Infants often reached for the rattle in the dark when it was 6 inches away but seldom when it was 2 feet away. These 7-month-olds were quite capable of using sound to estimate distance, in this case distinguishing a toy they could reach from one they could not.

Thus, by the middle of the first year, most infants respond to much of the information provided by sound. However, not all infants are able to do so, which is the topic of the "Making Children's Lives Better" feature.

> Infants can distinguish different sounds and they use sound to judge the distance and location of objects.

MAKING CHILDREN'S LIVES BETTER

### Hearing Impairment in Infancy

Some infants are born with limited hearing. Others are born deaf. (Exact figures are hard to come by because infants' hearing is rarely tested precisely.) African, Asian, European, and Hispanic American babies are equally susceptible. Heredity is the leading cause of hearing impairment in newborns. After birth, the leading cause is meningitis, an inflammation of the membranes surrounding the brain and spinal cord.

What are signs of hearing impairment that a parent should watch for? Obviously, parents should be concerned if a young baby never responds to sudden, loud sounds. They should also be concerned if their baby has repeated ear infections, if it does not turn its head in the direction of sounds by 4 or 5 months, does not respond to its own name by 8 or 9 months, and does not begin to imitate speech sounds and simple words by 12 months.

If parents see these problems, their baby should be examined by a physician, who will check for ear problems, and an audiologist, who will measure the infant's hearing. Parents should never delay checking for possible hearing impairment. The earlier the problem is detected, the more the baby can be helped (Smith et al., 1998).

If testing reveals that a baby has impaired hearing, several treatments are possible, depending upon the degree of hearing loss. Some children with partial hearing benefit from mechanical devices, such as hearing aids, and some benefit from training in lipreading. Children with profound hearing loss can learn to communicate with sign language. By mastering language (either oral language or sign language) and communicating effectively, a child's cognitive and social development will be normal. The key is to recognize impairment promptly. ●

## Seeing

If you've watched infants you've probably noticed that, while awake, they spend a lot of time looking around. Sometimes they seem to be scanning their environment broadly, and sometimes they seem to be focusing on nearby objects. But what do they actually see? Is their visual world a sea of gray blobs? Or do they see the world essentially as adults do? Actually, neither is the case, but, as you'll see, the second is closer to the truth.

From birth, babies respond to light and can track moving objects with their eyes. But what is the clarity of their vision, and how can we measure it? ***Visual acuity is defined as the smallest pattern that can be distinguished dependably.*** You've undoubtedly had your visual acuity measured by trying to read rows of progressively smaller letters or numbers from a chart. The same basic logic is used in tests of infants' acuity, which are based on two premises. First, most infants will look at patterned stimuli instead of plain, nonpatterned stimuli. For example, if we were to show the two stimuli in the top diagram to infants, most would look longer at the striped pattern than the gray pattern. Second, as we make the lines narrower (along with the spaces between them), there comes a point at which the black and white stripes become so fine that they simply blend together and appear gray, just like the all-gray pattern.

FIG 5–5

To estimate an infant's acuity, then, we pair the gray square with squares that differ in the width of their stripes, like those in the bottom diagram: When infants look at the two stimuli equally, it indicates that they are no longer able to distinguish the stripes of the patterned stimulus. By measuring the width of the stripes and their distance from an infant's eye, we can estimate acuity (detecting thinner stripes indicates better acuity).

Measurements of this sort indicate that newborns and 1-month-olds see at 20 feet what normal adults see at 200 to 400 feet. Infants' acuity improves rapidly and, by the first birthday, is essentially the same as a normal adult's (Kellman & Banks, 1998).

FIG 5–6

Not only do infants begin to see the world with greater acuity during the first year; they also begin to see it in color! How do we perceive color? The wavelength of light is the source of color perception. The diagram at the top of page 133 shows that lights we see as red have a relatively long wavelength, whereas violet, at the other end of the color spectrum, has a much shorter wavelength. **We detect wavelength—and therefore color— with specialized neurons called *cones* that are in the retina of the eye.** Some cones are particularly sensitive to short-wavelength light (blues and violets), others are sensitive to medium-wavelength light (greens and yellows), and still others to long-wavelength light (reds and oranges). These different kinds of cones are linked in

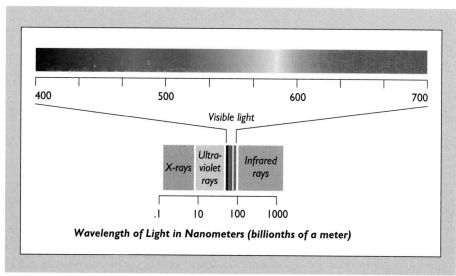

FIG 5–7

complex circuits of neurons in the eye and in the brain, and this neural circuitry allows us to see the world in color.

These circuits gradually begin to function in the first few months after birth. Newborns and young babies can perceive few colors, but by 3 months the three kinds of cones and their associated circuits are working and infants are able to see the full range of colors (Kellman & Banks, 1998).

In fact, by 3 to 4 months, infants' color perception seems similar to adults' (Adams & Courage, 1995). In particular, infants, like adults, tend to see categories of color. For example, if a yellow light's wavelength is gradually increased, the infant will suddenly perceive it as a shade of red rather than a shade of yellow.

To study infants' perception of color categories, researchers use the habituation technique described on page 129. First, infants are repeatedly shown the same colored light; it might be a light with a wavelength of 600 nanometers (billionths of a meter), which adults call yellow. Infants look intently initially, then habituate (look less). After infants have habituated, a new light is shown. The wavelength of the new light always differs from the original by the same amount—20 nanometers, for example. For some babies, the wavelength is *decreased* 20 nanometers; adults still consider this a yellow light. For other babies, the wavelength is *increased* 20 nanometers; adults judge this a green light. Infants look longer at a new light from a new color category than a new light from the same, familiar color category. This result indicates that infants view the stimuli as adults do—in categories of color (Dannemiller, 1998; Teller & Bornstein, 1987).

The ability to perceive color, along with rapidly improving visual acuity, gives infants great skill in making sense out of their visual experiences. What makes this growing visual skill even more powerful is that, as we'll see in the next section, infants are also starting to connect information obtained from different senses.

## Integrating Sensory Information

So far, we have discussed infants' sensory systems separately. In reality, of course, most infant experiences are better described as "multimedia events." A nursing mother provides visual and taste cues to her baby. A rattle stimulates vision, hearing, and touch. From experiences like these, infants learn to integrate information from different senses.

Infants readily integrate information from different senses, linking seeing to hearing and seeing to touch.

Research shows that by 1 month—and possibly at birth—infants can integrate sensory information. For example, 1-month-olds can recognize an object visually that they have only touched previously (Gibson & Walker, 1984). By 4 months, infants are quite skilled at integrating sights and sounds: They can connect the characteristic sounds of male and female voices with the characteristic appearances of male and female faces (Poulin-Dubois et al., 1994).

Another example of how infants integrate vision and hearing is the topic of the "Focus on Research" feature.

FOCUS ON RESEARCH

### Do Infants Integrate Sight and Sound When Others Speak?

*Who were the investigators, and what was the aim of the study?* Compared to adults, children have a distinctive facial appearance and a distinctive sound when speaking. Children's faces tend to be more rounded, their eyes look larger, and their skin is softer. Children's voices tend to be higher-pitched, more variable in loudness, and often not as well controlled. Thus, adults know that individuals with rounded, soft-skinned faces (children) tend to have quavering, high-pitched voices; individuals with more angular, rougher-skinned faces (adults) tend to have steady, lower-pitched voices. Can infants, too, make connections between faces and voices? Lorraine Bahrick, Dianelys Netto, and Maria Hernandez-Reif (1998) conducted a study to answer this question.

FIG 5–8

*How did the investigators measure the topic of interest?* Bahrick and her colleagues created the setup shown in the diagram. They presented pairs of 20-second videotapes on two video monitors placed side by side. One monitor showed a close-up of a boy's face; the other, a close-up of a man's face. Both the boy and the man appeared to be talking. When the videos started, a separate audiotape began with a boy or a man reciting one particular nursery rhyme. As the infants heard the audiotape, research assistants recorded which video the infant watched. Infants saw 12 pairs of videotapes.

What should infants do when they see these videos? If infants know the rules

*boyish face = boyish voice*

*man-like face = man-like voice*

then they should look at the video that matches the sound: They'll watch the video of the man when they hear the man's voice and the video of the boy when they hear the boy's voice.

*Who were the children in the study?* Bahrick and her colleagues tested sixteen 4-month-olds and sixteen 7-month-olds.

*What was the design of the study?* This study was experimental. One independent variable was the infant's age. Another was the grouping of the pairs of videos—the first 6 pairs of videos versus the last 6 pairs. The dependent variable was the amount of time the infants spent watching the video depicting a person who was the same age as the person speaking on the audiotape. The study included two age groups tested at the same point in time, so it was cross-sectional.

*Were there ethical concerns with the study?* No. Most infants seemed to enjoy watching the videos. All parents agreed to allow their infants to participate.

*What were the results?* If infants had no preference for the videotape that matched the audiotape, they should look at the two videos equally. That is, they would spend about 50 percent of the time looking at the video that matched the audio. The bars in the graph show the percentage of time that infants actually spent watching the video showing a person who was the same age as the person speaking. The 4-month-olds had no preference on the first 6 videos, but looked longer at the matching videos on the second 6 videos. For 7-month-olds, the pattern was reversed: They looked longer at the matching video during the first 6 videos, but not on the second 6.

*What did the investigators conclude?* Both 4- and 7-month-olds are able to integrate the typical appearances of face and the typical sounds of voices. That is, infants know that childish faces tend to have childish voices and adult-like faces tend to have adult-like voices. The fact that these outcomes were found in different sets of videos also shows the obstacles of doing experimentation with young infants: Apparently the 4-month-olds took longer to figure out what was involved in the study and the 7-month-olds lost interest more quickly. ●

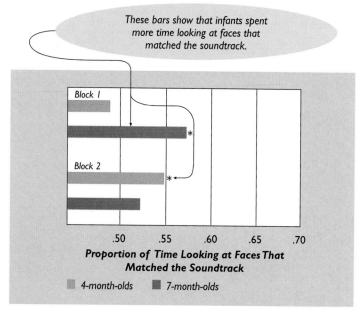

*These bars show that infants spent more time looking at faces that matched the soundtrack.*

**Proportion of Time Looking at Faces That Matched the Soundtrack**

■ 4-month-olds  ■ 7-month-olds

FIG 5–9

Integrating sight and sound is yet another variation on the theme that has dominated this module: Infants' sensory and perceptual skills are impressive. Darla's newborn daughter, from the opening vignette, can definitely smell, taste, and feel pain. She can distinguish sounds, and at about 7 months she will use sound to locate objects. Her vision is a little blurry now but will improve rapidly, and in a few months she'll see the full range of colors. Within only a month, she'll be making connections between sights and sounds and between other senses. In short, Darla's daughter, like most infants, is well prepared to make sense out of her environment.

## Check Your Learning

1. Babies react to sweet substances by smiling and sucking but grimace when fed substances with a _____ taste.

2. Babies probably experience pain because their nervous system is capable of transmitting pain and because _____.

3. Studies of auditory thresholds reveal that adults can hear better than infants, particularly _____.

4. Infants use sound to judge the distance and _____ of objects.

5. By age _____, infants have approximately the same visual acuity as adults.

6. At 3 months, infants see the full range of colors and, like adults, perceive colors as _____.

**7.** In the first few months of life, infants integrate what they see with what they _____ and what they see with what they hear.

 **How would a psychologist who takes the empirical approach (described in Module 5.1) explain the research findings on sensory integration described on pages 134–135? How would the explanations of psychologists from the cognitive and Gibsonian perspectives differ?**

**Answers:** (1) bitter or sour, (2) they respond to pain-provoking stimulation, (3) softer sounds, (4) location, (5) 1 year, (6) categories, (7) feel

# 5.3

— **Perceiving Objects**

— **Attention**

— **Attention Deficit Hyperactivity Disorder**

# Complex Perceptual and Attentional Processes

## Learning Objectives

● **How do infants perceive objects?**

● **How does attention improve as children grow older?**

● **What is attention deficit hyperactivity disorder?**

*Linda was only 36 hours old when John and Jean brought her home from the hospital. They quickly noticed that loud noises startled Linda, which worried them because their apartment was near an entrance ramp to a freeway. Trucks accelerating to enter the freeway made an incredible amount of noise that caused Linda to "jump" and sometimes cry. John and Jean wondered if Linda would get enough sleep. However, within days, the trucks no longer disturbed Linda; she slept blissfully. Why was a noise that had been so troubling no longer a problem?*

Where we draw the dividing line between "basic" and "complex" perceptual processes is quite arbitrary. As you'll see, Module 5.3 is a logical extension of the information presented in Module 5.2. We'll begin by looking at how we perceive objects. We'll also look at the processes of attention and some children who have attentional problems. By the end of the module, you'll know why Linda is no longer bothered by noises that once disturbed her.

## Perceiving Objects

When you look at this pattern, what do you see? You probably recognize it as part of a human eyeball, even though all that's physically present in the photograph are many different colored dots. In this case, perception actually creates an object from sensory stimulation.

How do perceptual processes define objects? Edges play an important role (Kellman & Banks, 1998). ***Edges* are lines that mark the boundaries of objects.** We use edges to distinguish an object from another and from background. In the photo of the eyeball, for example, two circles of blue dots define the inner and outer edges of the iris; these edges cause us to see all the other blue dots as part of the same "thing"—the iris.

Early in the first year, infants use edges to identify objects. Infants' perception of edges is shown in some fascinating research involving patterns like the one shown here. When you look at the pattern, what do you see? If you're like most people, it's almost impossible to not see a square. Of course, there's no actual physical stimulus that corresponds to the square. Instead, the cut-out portions of each circle are corners that define lines, creating an edge. It's this created edge that allows our perceptual system to "see" a square.

When infants view these circles, do they, too, "see" a square? The answer seems to be yes. In one study (Ghim, 1990), 3-month-olds were shown a simple square. After six presentations of the square, one of the four patterns in the diagram was shown. You can see that all consist of four circles, but only Pattern A creates the subjective experience of "seeing" a square. Having seen squares repeatedly, 3-month-olds looked much longer at Patterns B, C, and D than

FIG 5–10

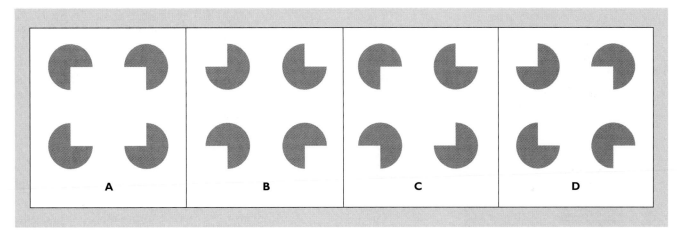

FIG 5–11
Source: Ghim, 1990.

at Pattern A. Evidently, Pattern A looked familiar, so they looked less. Of course, the only way that Pattern A could be familiar is if infants "saw" a square created by the four circles and interpreted this as yet another presentation of the actual square they had seen previously.

Edges are most useful in distinguishing stationary objects. When motion is present, we use it to help define objects by following a simple rule: Elements that move together are usually part of the same object (Kellman & Banks, 1998). For example, at the left of the diagram, a pencil appears to be moving back and forth behind a colored square. If the square were removed, you would be surprised to see a pair of pencil stubs, as shown on the right side of the diagram. The common movement of the pencil's eraser and point lead us to believe that they're part of the same pencil.

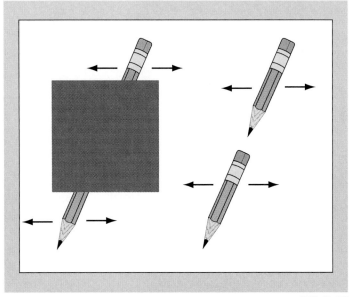

FIG 5–12

By 2 to 4 months of age, infants, too, are surprised by demonstrations like this. If they see a display like the moving pencils, they will then look very briefly at a whole pencil, apparently because they expected it. In contrast, if after seeing the moving pencil they're shown the two pencil stubs, they look much longer, as if trying to figure out what happened (Eizenman & Bertenthal, 1998; Johnson & Aslin, 1995). Evidently, even very young babies use common motion to create objects from different parts.

Distinguishing objects with edges and motion is an important first step in perceiving objects, but only the first. Perceptual constancies are important, too.

**Perceptual Constancies.** Any time a mother moves away from her baby, the image that she casts on the retinas of her baby's eyes gets smaller. Do babies have a nightmare that their mother's head is shrinking as she moves away? No. **Early on, infants master *size constancy,* the realization that an object's actual size remains the same despite changes in the size of its retinal image.**

How do we know that infants have a rudimentary sense of size constancy? Suppose we let an infant look at an unfamiliar teddy bear. Then we show the infant the same bear, at a different distance, paired with a larger replica of the bear. If infants lack size constancy, the two bears will be equally novel and babies should respond to each similarly. If, instead, babies have size constancy, they will recognize the first bear as familiar, the larger bear as novel, and be more likely to respond to the novel bear. In fact, by 4 or 5 months, babies treat the bear that they've seen twice at different distances—and, therefore, with different retinal images—as familiar (Granrud, 1986). This outcome is possible only if infants have size constancy. Thus, infants do not believe that mothers (and other people or objects) constantly change size as they move closer or farther away.

Size is just one of several perceptual constancies. Others are brightness and color constancy as well as shape constancy, shown in the diagram. All these constancies are achieved, at least in rudimentary form, by 4 months (Aslin, 1987; Dannemiller, 1998).

The message from the perceptual constancies is that "seeing is not always believing." A good part of perception, therefore, is knowing how to make sense out of what we see. Another important part of "making sense" out of what we see is deciding how near or far an object is.

*Shape Constancy: Even though the door appears to change shape as it opens, we know that it really remains a rectangle.*

FIG 5-13

**Depth.** People see objects as having three dimensions: height, width, and depth. The retina of the eye is flat, so height and width can be represented directly on its two-dimensional surface. But the third dimension, depth, cannot be represented directly on this surface, so how do we perceive depth? How do we decide if objects are nearby or far away? We use perceptual processing to infer depth.

Can infants perceive depth? Eleanor Gibson and Richard Walk (1960) addressed this question using a special apparatus. **The *visual cliff* is a glass-covered platform; on one side a pattern appears directly under the glass, but on the other it appears several feet below the glass.** Consequently, one side looks shallow but the other appears to have a steep drop-off, like a cliff.

As you can see in the photo, in the experiment the baby is placed on the platform and the mother coaxes her infant to come to her. Most babies willingly crawl to their mothers when she stands on the shallow side. But virtually all babies refuse to cross the deep side, even when the mother calls the infant by name and tries to lure him or her with an attractive toy. Clearly, infants can perceive depth by the time they are old enough to crawl.

What about babies who cannot yet crawl? When babies as young as 1½ months are simply placed on the deep side of the platform, their heartbeat slows down. Heart rate often decelerates when people notice something interesting, so this would suggest that 1½-month-olds notice that the deep side is different. At 7 months, infants' heart rate accelerates, a sign of fear. Thus, although young babies can detect a difference between the shallow and deep sides of the visual cliff, only older, crawling babies are actually afraid of the deep side (Campos et al., 1978).

How do infants infer depth, on the visual cliff or anywhere? They use several kinds of cues. **One, *retinal disparity*, is based on the fact that the left and right eyes often see slightly different versions of the same scene.** When objects are distant, the images appear in very similar positions on the retina; when objects are near, the images appear in much different positions. Thus, greater disparity in positions of the image on the retina signals that an object is close. By 4 to 6 months, infants use retinal disparity as a depth cue, correctly inferring that objects are nearby when disparity is great (Kellman & Banks, 1998; Yonas & Owsley, 1987).

By 7 months, infants use several cues for depth that depend on the arrangement of objects in the environment.

***Texture gradient:* The texture of objects changes from coarse but distinct for nearby objects to finer and less distinct for distant objects.** In the photo, we judge the distinct flowers to be close and the blurred ones, distant.

*Relative size:* **Nearby objects look substantially larger than objects in the distance.** Knowing that the runners are really about the same size, we judge the ones that look smaller to be farther away.

*Interposition:* **Nearby objects partially obscure more distant objects.** The glasses obscure the bottle, so we decide the glasses are closer (and use this same cue to decide the grapes are closer than the left glass).

So far in this module, we've seen that young babies use simple relations between stimuli to infer an object, recognize that objects are the same despite changes in appearance, and use many cues to infer depth. We can understand infants' perceptual skills from a different perspective by looking at their perception of faces.

**Perceiving Faces.** The human face is a particularly important object to infants. Young babies readily look at faces. From the diagram, which shows a pattern of eye fixations, you can see that 1-month-olds look mostly at the outer edges of the face. Three-month-olds, however, focus almost entirely on the interior of the face, particularly the eyes and lips.

Some scientists believe that general principles of perception explain how infants perceive faces (Aslin, 1987). They argue that infants are attracted to faces because faces have stimuli that move (the eyes and mouth) and stimuli with dark and light contrast (the eyes, lips, and teeth). Research by Dannemiller and Stephens (1988) supports this view. They found that when face and nonface stimuli are matched for a number of important variables (such as the amount of black/white contrast, the size and number of elements), 1½-month-olds typically look

**1-Month-Olds**

Finish

Start

**3-Month-Olds**

Start

Finish

FIG 5–14

at face and nonface stimuli equally. In other words, infants look at faces because of general perceptual principles (for example, babies prefer contrasting stimuli), not because faces are intrinsically attractive to infants.

Other theorists, however, argue that babies are innately attracted to stimuli that are facelike. The claim here is that some aspect of the face—perhaps two eyes and a mouth in the correct arrangement—constitutes a distinctive stimulus that is readily recognized, even by newborns. For example, look at the different facelike stimuli in the diagram. In one study (Morton & Johnson, 1991), newborns turned their eyes to follow a moving face (at the left of the diagram) more than they turned their eyes for stimuli that had either facial elements or a facial configuration but not both (the remaining three stimuli in the diagram). Infants preferred faces over facelike stimuli, which supports the view that infants are innately attracted to faces.

FIG 5–15
Source: Morton & Johnson, 1990.

More research is needed to decide whether face perception follows general perceptual principles or represents a special case. What is clear, though, is that by 3 or 4 months babies have the perceptual skills that allow them to begin to distinguish individual faces (Carey, 1992). This ability is essential, for it provides the basis for social relationships that infants form during the rest of the first year.

## Attention

Have you ever been in a class where you knew you should be listening and taking notes, but the lecture was just so boring that you started noticing other things—the construction going on outside or an attractive person seated nearby? After a while, maybe you reminded yourself to "pay attention!" We get distracted because our perceptual systems are marvelously powerful. They provide us with far more information at any time than we could possible interpret. **Attention is the process by which we select information that will be processed further.** In a class, for example, where the task is to direct your attention to the lecture, it is easy to ignore other stimuli if the lecture is interesting. But if the lecture is not interesting, other stimuli intrude and capture your attention.

The roots of attention can be seen in infancy. Remember Linda, the newborn in the vignette, who jumped when trucks accelerated past her home? Her response was normal not only for infants but also for children and adults. **When presented with a strong or unfamiliar stimulus, an *orienting response* usually occurs: A person startles, fixes the eyes on the stimulus, and shows changes in heart rate and brain wave patterns.** Collectively, these responses indicate that the infant is attending to this stimulus. Remember, too, that Linda soon began to ignore the sounds of trucks. After repeated presentations of a stimulus, people become accustomed to it, so their orienting response diminishes and eventually disappears, signs of habituation, which we discussed on page 129. Habituation indicates that attention is selective: A stimulus that once garnered attention no longer does.

The orienting response and habituation can both be demonstrated easily in the laboratory. For example, in one study (Zelazo et al., 1989) speech was played through one of two loudspeakers placed on either side of an infant. Most newborns, at first, turned their heads toward the source of the speech, but after several trials they no longer responded. Thus, newborns oriented to the novel sound but then gradually habituated to the sound as it became more familiar.

The orienting response and habituation are both useful to infants. On the one hand, orienting makes the infant aware of potentially important or dangerous

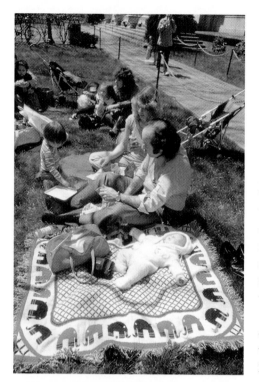

events in the environment. On the other hand, constantly responding to insignificant stimuli is wasteful, so habituation keeps infants like the one in the photo from wasting too much energy on biologically nonsignificant stimuli (Rovee-Collier, 1987). Given the biological significance of being able to habituate, it's not too surprising that infants who habituate more rapidly tend to grow up to be more intelligent children (Rose et al., 1997).

During the preschool years, children gradually become better able to regulate their attention. You can see these changes in the results of a study of 2½- to 4½-year-olds by Ruff, Capozzoli, and Weissberg (1998). These investigators observed preschoolers in several settings. In one, children sat at a table watching hand puppets and dolls enact brief skits. In another, children were told they could play with an assortment of toys on a table top. Ruff and her colleagues videotaped children in both settings, then analyzed the tapes for many different behaviors. Children who were actively engaged in the puppet show or free play—as inferred by their posture, facial expressions, spontaneous comments, and the like—exhibited *focused attention*. Children who left the table exhibited *active inattention*.

The results, shown in the graph, illustrate two important characteristics of attention during the preschool years. First, attention improved markedly in this period. In both settings, the 4½-year-olds spent much more time than the 2½-year-olds in focused attention and much less time in active inattention.

Second, the 4½-year-olds, though much more attentive than the younger children, still spent less than half the time in a state of focused attention. Maintaining focused attention is a demanding skill, one that emerges gradually beyond the preschool and school-age years (Enns, 1990).

Why does attention improve with age? For one thing, older children and adolescents are simply more likely to remind themselves that they need to pay attention. They are also more likely to have mastered some attentional "tricks of the trade." For example, if asked to determine if two objects are the same, older children and adolescents are more likely to compare them feature by feature until they find features that do not match or they run out of features to check (Vurpillot, 1968). By directing their attention in this manner, children are guaranteed that they will do the task accurately and in the least amount of time possible. Asked if the two houses in the diagram at the top of page 143 are the same, older children typically start by comparing the top windows and work down until they have compared all six pairs of windows. In contrast, younger children direct their attention haphazardly—not systematically checking corresponding windows—so they often don't find the differing windows.

Young children need help to pay attention better. One approach is to make relevant information more salient than irrelevant information. For example, closing a classroom door may not eliminate competing sounds and smells entirely, but it will make them less salient. Or, when preschoolers are working at a table or desk, we can remove all objects that are not necessary for the task. It's also very helpful, particularly for young children, to remind them periodically to pay attention only to relevant

FIG 5–16

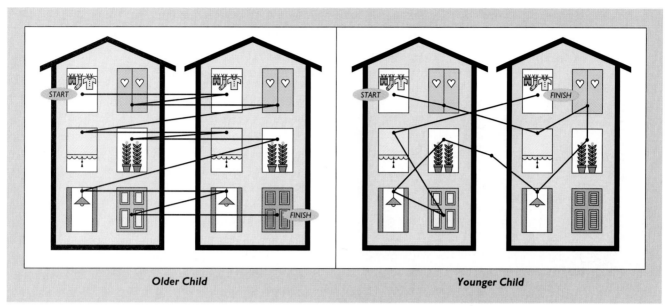

Older Child                                    Younger Child

FIG 5–17

information and ignore the rest. These techniques improve some but not all children's attention, as we'll see in the next section.

## Attention Deficit Hyperactivity Disorder

Children with attention deficit hyperactivity disorder—ADHD for short—have special problems when it comes to paying attention. Roughly 3 to 15 percent of all school-age children are diagnosed with ADHD; boys outnumber girls by a 3:1 ratio (Wicks-Nelson & Israel, 1991). The "Real Children" feature describes one boy with ADHD.

### Why Can't Stephen Pay Attention?

Soon after Stephen entered kindergarten, his teacher remarked that he sometimes seemed out of control. Stephen was easily distracted, often moving aimlessly from one activity to another. He also seemed to be impulsive, and compared to other youngsters his age, he had much more difficulty waiting his turn. At first, Stephen's parents just attributed his behavior to boyish energy. But when Stephen progressed to first and second grade, his pattern of behavior continued. He began to fall behind in reading and arithmetic. His classmates were annoyed by his behavior and began to avoid him. This just made Stephen mad, so he often got into fights with his classmates. Finally, Stephen's parents took him to a psychologist, who determined that Stephen had attention deficit hyperactivity disorder. ●

Stephen exhibits three symptoms at the heart of ADHD (American Psychiatric Association, 1987):

- *Overactivity:* Children with ADHD are unusually energetic, fidgety, and unable to keep still, especially in situations like school classrooms where they need to limit their activity.

- *Inattention:* Youngsters with ADHD skip from one task to another. They do not pay attention in class and seem unable to concentrate on schoolwork.
- *Impulsivity:* Children with ADHD often act before thinking; they may run into a street before looking for traffic or interrupt others who are speaking.

Not all children with ADHD show all these symptoms to the same degree. Some, like the boy in the photograph, may be primarily hyperactive. Others may be primarily impulsive and show no signs of hyperactivity; their disorder is often described simply as attention-deficit disorder (Barkley, 1990). Furthermore, symptoms often vary with the setting. Some youngsters who are unable to maintain attention in school may sit still for hours playing a video game at home (Barkley, 1996).

In light of these inconsistencies, it probably won't surprise you that researchers disagree about the number of different subtypes of ADHD and the factors that give rise to it (Barkley, 1996; Panksepp, 1998). However, it *is* clear that children with ADHD often have problems with conduct and academic performance. Like Stephen, many hyperactive children are aggressive and therefore are not liked by their peers (Barkley, 1990; McGee, Williams, & Feehan, 1992). Although youngsters with ADHD usually have normal intelligence, their scores on reading, spelling, and arithmetic achievement tests are often below average (Pennington, Groisser, & Welsh, 1993).

One myth about ADHD is that most children "grow out of it" in adolescence or young adulthood. More than half the children who are diagnosed with ADHD will have problems related to overactivity, inattention, and impulsivity as adolescents and young adults. Few of these young adults complete college, and some will have work- and family-related problems (Fischer et al., 1993; Rapport, 1995).

Why are some children afflicted with ADHD? Does too much sugar cause children to become "hyper"? Are food additives the culprit? In fact, except for a few children who are overly sensitive to sugar or allergic to food dyes, research shows no connection between children's diet and ADHD (McGee, Stanton, & Sears, 1993; Wolraich et al., 1994).

The primary causes of ADHD lie elsewhere. Heredity contributes: Identical twins more often both have ADHD than fraternal twins (Edelbrock et al., 1995). A stressful home environment also contributes: Youngsters with ADHD often come from families with parents in conflict or under great stress themselves (Bernier & Siegel, 1994). Some children evidently inherit a predisposition for the disorder, which can be triggered by stress at home.

ADHD is often treated with stimulant drugs, such as Ritalin. It may seem odd that stimulants are given to children who are already overactive, but these drugs stimulate the parts of the brain that normally inhibit hyperactive and impulsive behavior. Thus, stimulants actually have a calming influence for many youngsters with ADHD, allowing them to focus their attention (Aman, Roberts, & Pennington, 1998).

By itself, though, medication does not improve children's performance in school because it ignores psychological and social

*Children with ADHD are overactive, inattentive, and impulsive; as a consequence, they often do poorly in school and are disliked by peers.*

influences on ADHD. Children with ADHD need to learn to regulate their behavior and attention. For example, children can be taught to remind themselves to read instructions before starting assignments. And they need reinforcement from others for inhibiting impulsive and hyperactive behavior (Barkley, 1994).

Parents can also encourage attention and goal-oriented behavior at home. Anastopoulos and his colleagues (1993) arranged for parents of children with ADHD to attend nine training sessions on using positive reinforcement to foster attention and compliance. Parents also learned effective ways to punish children for being inattentive. Following training, children had fewer symptoms of ADHD. Equally important, the parents felt that the training made them feel more competent in parenting. They also reported feeling significantly less parental stress.

The best approach for children with ADHD involves all of these techniques—medication, instruction, and parent training. Comprehensive treatment helps a child with ADHD become more attentive, less disruptive, and stronger academically (Carlson et al., 1992).

## Check Your Learning

1. Like adults, infants use _____ and motion to help distinguish objects.

2. An infant understands _____ if she knows that her father does not really become larger as he moves closer to her.

3. On the visual cliff, infants who can crawl _____, which shows that they can perceive depth.

4. Some theorists explain infants' perception of faces in terms of general principles of perception, but others _____.

5. Older children and adolescents have better attentional skills because they remind themselves to pay attention more often and because _____.

6. The three primary symptoms of ADHD are overactivity, inattention, and _____.

 **Psychologists often refer to "perceptual-motor skills," which implies that the skills described in this module are related to the motor skills discussed in Module 4.4. How might motor skills influence perception? How could perception influence motor skills?**

**Answers:** (1) edges, (2) size constancy, (3) avoid the "deep side," (4) believe that babies are innately attracted to facelike stimuli, (5) they have mastered more attentional "tricks of the trade," (6) impulsivity

# Sensory and Perceptual Development
## IN PERSPECTIVE

5

Knowledge and understanding begin with sensory and perceptual processes. In Module 5.1, we saw that the empirical approach, the cognitive approach, and Gibson's differentiation theory provide three explanations of the way perceptual processes operate. In Module 5.2, we discovered that young babies are perceptually quite skilled—they can smell, taste, touch, hear, and see. In Module 5.3, we learned that infants are masterful in perceiving objects, that selective attention improves gradually as children develop, and why children with ADHD have difficulty paying attention.

Each module in this chapter touched on the theme that *development is always jointly influenced by heredity and environment.* In Gibson's theory, for example, infants are endowed with the basic perceptual abilities that allow them to differentiate their environments. However, the specific stimuli that they differentiate depends on the experiences that they have. We also saw that heredity is the most common reason why children are born with hearing impairment. At the same time, experience is critical in shaping the lives of children with hearing impairment. If their impairment is recognized early, they can learn to communicate very well. Finally, ADHD has its roots in both nature and nurture: Heredity makes some children prone to the disorder, but environmental stress may actually trigger it. Heredity and environment are like the Democrats and Republicans of development—sometimes antagonistic, sometimes cooperative, always influential.

## See for Yourself

To see the origins of attention, you need a baby and a small bell. A 1- to 5-month-old is probably best because babies at this age can't locomote, so they won't wander away. While the infant is awake, place it on its back. Then move behind the baby's head (out of sight) and ring the bell a few times. You don't need to ring the bell loudly—an "average" volume will do. You should see the orienting response described on page 141: The baby will open its eyes wide and perhaps try to turn in the direction of the sound. Every 2 or 3 minutes, ring the bell again. You should see the baby respond less intensely each time until, finally, it ignores the bell completely. Attention in action! See for yourself!

## Resources

*For more information about . . .*

 *infant development in general,* including perceptual development, try Charles W. Snow's *Infant Development* (2nd edition) (Prentice-Hall, 1998)

 *ADHD,* visit this Web site maintained by the U.S. National Institute of Mental Health:

**http://www.nimh.nih.gov/publicat/adhdmenu.cfm**

## Key Terms

**attention** 141
**auditory threshold** 130
**cognitive approach** 125
**cones** 132
**differentiation theory** 127
**edges** 136

**empirical approach** 124
**habituation** 129
**interposition** 140
**Müller-Lyer illusion** 125
**orienting response** 141
**relative size** 140

**retinal disparity** 139
**sensory and perceptual processes** 122
**size constancy** 138
**texture gradient** 139
**visual acuity** 132
**visual cliff** 139

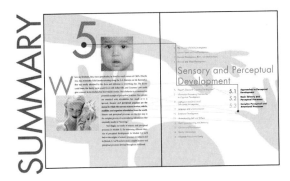

# SUMMARY

## 5.1 Approaches to Perceptual Development

### The Empirical Approach

According to the empirical tradition, perception and, ultimately, knowledge are based upon sensory experience. Over time, sensory experiences accumulate and are assembled into perceptions and knowledge. This tradition emphasizes experience and a one-way flow of sensory and perceptual processing.

### The Cognitive Approach

This approach shares the basic assumptions of the empirical tradition, but goes beyond it to say that knowledge influences perception. In other words, sensory and perceptual processing flows in two directions. Piaget's theory is a cognitive approach to sensory and perceptual processing.

### Gibson's Differentiation Theory

According to Eleanor Gibson, perception is not a process of gradual accumulation and integration of basic sensory experiences. Instead, complex stimuli are actively extracted from the flow of perceptual information and can be perceived directly if the child recognizes the features of complex patterns.

## 5.2 Basic Sensory and Perceptual Processes

### Smell, Taste, and Touch

Newborns are able to smell and can recognize their mother's odor; they also taste, preferring sweet substances and responding negatively to bitter and sour tastes. Infants respond to touch. Judging from their responses to painful stimuli, which are similar to older children's, we can say they experience pain.

### Hearing

Babies can hear, although they are less sensitive to higher- and lower-pitched sounds than adults. Babies can distinguish different sounds and use sound to locate objects in space.

### Seeing

A newborn's visual acuity is relatively poor, but 1-year-olds can see as well as adults with normal vision. Color vision develops as different sets of cones begin to function; by 3 or 4 months, children can see color as well as adults.

### Integrating Sensory Information

Soon after birth, infants begin to coordinate information from different senses. They can recognize by sight an object that they've felt previously. And infants can integrate what they see with what they hear.

## 5.3 Complex Perceptual and Attentional Processes

### Perceiving Objects

Infants, like adults, use edges and motion to distinguish objects. By about 4 months, infants have begun to master size, brightness, shape, and color constancy. Infants perceive depth by means of retinal disparity and other cues such as texture gradient, relative size, and interposition.

Infants perceive faces early in the first year. However, it is not clear whether perception of faces involves specific perceptual mechanisms or whether it is based on the same processes used to perceive other objects.

### Attention

Attention helps select information for further processing. Infants orient to a novel stimulus, but as it becomes more familiar, they habituate, meaning that they respond less.

Compared to older children, preschoolers are less able to pay attention to a task. Older children are better able to pay attention because they have developed strategies for maintaining attention. Younger children's attention can be improved by getting rid of irrelevant stimuli.

### Attention Deficit Hyperactivity Disorder

Children with ADHD are typically overactive, inattentive, and impulsive. They sometimes have conduct problems and do poorly in school. ADHD is due to heredity and to environmental factors, particularly a stressful home environment. A comprehensive approach to treatment—involving medication, instruction, and parent training—produces best results.

**6**

n the movie *Look Who's Talking,* we are privy to an infant's thoughts on everything from his birth and diaper changes to his mother's boyfriends. The humor, of course, turns on the idea that babies are capable of sophisticated thinking—they just can't express it. But what thoughts *do* lurk in the mind of an infant who is not yet speaking? And how do an infant's fledgling thoughts blossom into the powerful reasoning skills that older children, adolescents, and adults use daily? In other words, how does thinking change as children develop, and why do these changes take place?

For many years, the best answers to these questions came from the theory proposed by Jean Piaget that is the focus of this chapter. We begin, in Module 6.1, with some background on Piaget's theory. In Module 6.2, we look at the four stages of cognitive development that are the hallmark of Piaget's theory. In Module 6.3, we examine some criticisms of the theory, and in Module 6.4 we look at alternate theories.

# Piaget's Theory of Cognitive Development

# 6.1

- Schemes
- Assimilation and Accommodation
- Equilibration and Stages of Cognitive Development

# General Principles of Piaget's Theory

## Learning Objectives

- What are schemes?
- How do assimilation and accommodation help children understand experience?
- What is equilibration, and how does it explain changes in how children think?

> When John, an energetic 2½-year-old, saw a monarch butterfly for the first time, his mother, Patrice, told him, "Butterfly, butterfly; that's a butterfly, John." A few minutes later, a zebra swallowtail landed on a nearby bush and John shouted in excitement, "Butterfly, Mama, butterfly!" A bit later, a moth flew out of another bush; with even greater excitement in his voice, John shouted, "Butterfly, Mama, more butterfly!" As Patrice was telling John, "No, honey, that's a moth, not a butterfly," she marveled at how rapidly John seemed to grasp new concepts with so little direction from her. How was this possible?

For many years, our best answer to Patrice's question came from Jean Piaget, who began work on his theory of mental development in the 1920s. Piaget was trained as a biologist, but he developed a keen interest in the branch of philosophy dealing with the nature and origins of knowledge. He decided to investigate the origins of knowledge not as philosophers had—through discussion and debate—but by doing experiments with children.

We'll begin our study of Piaget's work by looking at some key principles of his theory and, as we do, discover why John understands as quickly as he does.

## Schemes

Piaget believed that children are naturally curious. They constantly want to make sense out of their experience and, in the process, construct their understanding of the world. For Piaget, children at all ages are like scientists in that they create theories about how the world works. Of course, children's theories are often incomplete. Nevertheless, their theories are valuable because they make the world seem more predictable.

**According to Piaget, children come to understand the world by using** *schemes,* **psychological structures that organize experience.** That is, schemes are mental categories of related events, objects, and knowledge. During infancy, most schemes are based on actions. Infants group objects based on the actions they can perform on them. For example, infants suck and grasp, and they use these actions to create categories of objects that can be sucked and objects that can be grasped.

Schemes are just as important after infancy, but then they are based primarily on functional or conceptual relationships, not actions. For example, preschoolers learn that forks, knives, and spoons form a functional category of "things I use to eat." Or they learn that dogs, cats, and goldfish form a conceptual category of "pets."

Like preschoolers, older children and adolescents use schemes based on functional and conceptual schemes, but they also have schemes that are based on increasingly abstract properties. For example, an adolescent might put fascism, racism, and sexism in a category of "ideologies that I despise."

Schemes are mental categories that organize experience, based on actions in infancy and progressing to abstract properties in adolescence.

Thus, children use schemes of related objects, events, and ideas throughout development. But as children develop, their basis for creating schemes shifts from physical activity to functional, conceptual, and later abstract properties of objects, events, and ideas.

## Assimilation and Accommodation

Schemes change constantly, adapting to children's experiences. In fact, intellectual adaptation involves two processes working together: assimilation and accommodation. *Assimilation* **occurs when new experiences are readily incorporated into existing schemes.** Imagine a baby who is familiar with the grasping scheme. Like the baby in the photograph, she will soon discover that the grasping scheme works not only on toys, but also on blocks, balls, and other small objects. Extending the existing grasping scheme to new objects illustrates assimilation. *Accommodation* **occurs when schemes are modified based on experience.** Soon the infant learns that some objects can only be lifted with two hands and that some can't be lifted at all. Changing the scheme so that it works for new objects (for example, using two hands to grasp a big stuffed animal) illustrates accommodation.

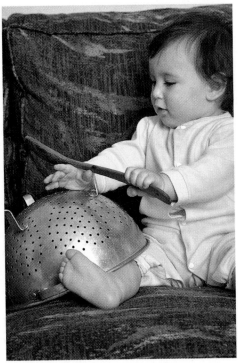

Assimilation and accommodation are easy to understand if you remember Piaget's belief that infants, children, and adolescents create theories to understand the world around them. The infant whose theory is that objects can be lifted with one hand finds that her theory is confirmed when she tries to pick up small objects, but she's in for a surprise when she tries to pick up a big stuffed animal. The unexpected result forces the infant, like a good scientist, to revise her theory to include this new finding.

Assimilation and accommodation are illustrated in the vignette at the beginning of the module. Piaget would say that when Patrice named the monarch butterfly for John, he formed a scheme something like "butterflies are bugs with big wings." The second butterfly differed in color but was still a bug with big wings, so it was readily *assimilated* into John's new scheme for butterflies. However, when John referred to the moth as a butterfly, Patrice corrected him. Presumably, John was then forced to *accommodate* to this new experience. The result was that he changed his scheme for butterflies to make it more precise; the new scheme might be something like "butterflies are bugs with thin bodies and big, colorful wings." He also created a new scheme, something like "a moth is a bug with a bigger body and plain wings."

## Equilibration and Stages of Cognitive Development

Assimilation and accommodation are usually in balance, or equilibrium. That is, children find they can readily assimilate most experiences into their existing schemes, but occasionally they need to accommodate their schemes to adjust to new experiences. This balance between assimilation and accommodation is illustrated both by the baby grasping larger objects and John's understanding of butterflies.

Periodically, however, the balance is upset and a state of disequilibrium results. Children discover that their current schemes are not adequate because they are spending much more time accommodating than assimilating. **When disequilibrium occurs, children reorganize their schemes to return to a state of equilibrium, a process that Piaget called** *equilibration.* To restore the balance, current but now-outmoded ways of thinking are replaced by a qualitatively different, more advanced set of schemes.

One way to understand equilibration is to return to the metaphor of the child as a scientist. As discussed in Module 1.2, good scientific theories readily explain some phenomena but usually must be revised to explain others. Children's theories allow them to understand many experiences by predicting, for example, what will happen ("It's morning, so it's time for breakfast") or who will do what ("Mom's gone to work, so Dad will take me to school"), but they too must be modified when predictions go awry ("Dad thinks I'm old enough to walk to school, so he won't take me").

Sometimes scientists find that their theories contain critical flaws, so they can't simply revise; they must create a new theory that draws upon the older theory but is fundamentally different. For example, when Copernicus realized that the earth-centered theory of the solar system was wrong, he retained the concept of a central object but proposed that it was the sun, a fundamental change in the theory. In much the same way, children periodically reach a point when their current theories seem to be wrong much of the time, so they abandon these theories in favor of more advanced ways of thinking about their physical and social worlds.

According to Piaget, these revolutionary changes in thought occur three times over the life span, at approximately 2, 7, and 11 years of age. This divides cognitive development into the following four stages:

| Stage of Development | Age Range |
| --- | --- |
| Sensorimotor stage | Infancy (0 to 2 years) |
| Preoperational stage | Preschool and early elementary-school years (2 to 6 years) |
| Concrete operational stage | Middle and late elementary-school years (7 to 11 years) |
| Formal operational stage | Adolescence and adulthood (11 years and older) |

Each of these stages is marked by a distinctive way of thinking about and understanding the world. The ages listed are only approximate: Some youngsters move through the stages more rapidly than others, depending on their ability and their experience. However, Piaget held that all children go through all four stages and in exactly this sequence. Sensorimotor thinking always gives rise to preoperational thinking; a child cannot "skip" preoperational thinking and move directly from sensorimotor to concrete operational thought.

In the next module, we will look at each of the four stages of cognitive development in detail.

> All children pass through all four of Piaget's stages in the same order, but some do so more rapidly than others.

## Check Your Learning

**1.** In Piaget's theory, a _____ is a mental structure that is used to organize information.

**2.** Schemes are based primarily on _____ in infancy and progress to abstract properties in adolescence.

**3.** _____ takes place when a scheme is modified based on experience.

**4.** A toddler who has a scheme for flowers sees a tulip for the first time and says, "flower!" This demonstrates _____.

**5.** Piaget believed that when _____ occurs, children reorganize their schemes so that assimilation and accommodation are again in balance.

 **Based on what you've learned so far, what would Piaget's position have been on the continuity-discontinuity and active-passive child issues discussed in Module 1.2?**

**Answers:** (1) scheme, (2) actions, (3) Accommodation, (4) assimilation, (5) disequilibrium

# Piaget's Four Stages of Cognitive Development

## Learning Objectives

- How do schemes become more advanced as infants progress through the six substages of the sensorimotor stage?

- What are the distinguishing features of the preoperational stage?

- What are the strengths and weaknesses of concrete operational thinking?

- What kinds of reasoning skills define formal operational thinking?

**6.2**

The Sensorimotor Stage

The Preoperational Stage

The Concrete Operational Stage

The Formal Operational Stage

*Three-year-old Jamila loves talking to Grandma Powell on the telephone, but sometimes these conversations get derailed: When Grandma Powell asks a question, Jamila often replies by nodding her head. Jamila's dad has explained that Grandma Powell (and others on the phone) can't see her nodding, that she needs to say "yes" or "no." But, no luck. Jamila invariably returns to head-nodding. Her dad can't understand why such a bright and talkative child doesn't realize that nodding is meaningless over the phone.*

If Piaget were here, he would reassure Jamila's dad that her behavior is perfectly normal—children between the ages of 2 and 7 generally believe that others see the world as they do. Piaget would also emphasize the extraordinary amount of cognitive development that has taken place in Jamila's 3 years, development that begins with the sensorimotor period, the first topic in this module.

## The Sensorimotor Stage

Before we begin our discussion of Piaget's first stage of cognitive development, let's review some of the facts of infancy that we've already learned.

- Infants' locomotor skills improve rapidly during the first year, culminating in walking at 14 or 15 months of age (Module 4.4).
- Fine-motor skills develop rapidly during this same period, so that by the middle of the first year infants coordinate both hands to grasp and manipulate objects (Module 4.4).
- Perceptual skills function early in infancy and improve quickly throughout the first year (Modules 5.2 and 5.3).

Piaget proposed that rapidly changing perceptual and motor skills in the first 2 years of life form a distinct phase in human development: **The *sensorimotor stage,* which spans birth to 2 years, consists of six substages during which the infant progresses from simple reflex actions to symbolic processing.** All infants move through the six substages in the same order. However, they progress at different rates, so the ages listed here are only approximations.

*Substage 1: Exercising reflexes (roughly birth to 1 month).* You know from Module 3.4 that newborns respond reflexively to many stimuli. As infants use their reflexes during the first month, they become more coordinated. Just as major-league players swing a bat with greater power and strength than Little Leaguers, 1-month-olds suck more vigorously and steadily than newborns.

*Substage 2: Learning to adapt (roughly 1 to 4 months).* During these months, reflexes become modified by experience. **The chief mechanism for change is the *primary circular reaction,* which occurs when an infant accidentally produces some pleasing event and then tries to recreate the event.** For example, an infant may inadvertently touch her lips with her thumb, thereby initiating sucking and the pleasing sensations associated with sucking. Later, the infant tries to recreate these

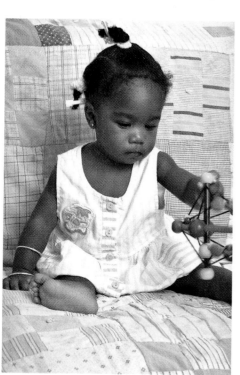

sensations by guiding her thumb to her mouth. Sucking no longer occurs only reflexively when a mother places a nipple at the infant's mouth; instead, the infant has found a way to initiate sucking herself.

*Substage 3: Making interesting events (roughly 4 to 8 months).* Primary circular reactions are centered on the infant's own body, typically involving reflexes like sucking or grasping. However, beginning in Substage 3, the infant shows greater interest in the world; now objects are more often the focus of circular reactions. For example, the infant shown in the photo accidentally shook a new rattle. Hearing the interesting noise, the infant grasped the rattle again, tried to shake it, and expressed great pleasure at the noise. This sequence was repeated several times.

**Novel actions that are repeated with objects are called *secondary circular reactions.*** Secondary circular reactions are significant because they represent infants' first efforts to learn about the objects in their environment, to explore their properties and their actions. No longer are infants grasping objects "mindlessly," simply because something is in contact with their hands. Instead, they are learning about the sights and sounds associated with objects.

*Substage 4: Using means to achieve ends (roughly 8 to 12 months).* This substage marks the onset of deliberate, intentional behavior. Why? For the first time, the "means" and "end" of activities are distinct. If, for example, a father places his hand in front of a toy, an infant will move his hand to be able to play with the toy. "The moving the hand" scheme is the means to achieve the goal of "grasping the toy." Using one action as a means to achieve another end is the first indication of purposeful, goal-directed behavior during infancy.

*Substage 5: Experimenting (roughly 12 to 18 months).* The infant at this stage is an active experimentalist. **An infant will repeat old schemes with novel objects, in what Piaget called a *tertiary circular reaction,* as if she is trying to understand why different objects yield different outcomes.** An infant in Substage 5 may deliberately shake a number of different objects trying to discover which produce sounds and which do not. Or an infant may decide to drop different objects to see what happens. An infant in a crib will discover that stuffed animals land quietly whereas bigger toys often make a more satisfying "clunk" when they hit the ground.

Tertiary circular reactions represent a significant extension of the intentional behavior that emerged in Substage 4. Now babies repeat actions with different objects solely for the purpose of seeing what will happen.

*Substage 6: Using symbols (roughly 18 to 24 months).* By 18 months, most infants have begun to talk and gesture, evidence of the emerging capacity to use symbols. Words and gestures are symbols that stand for something else. When the baby in the photo waves, it is just as effective and symbolic as saying "goodbye" to bid farewell. Children also begin to engage in pretend play, another use of symbols. A 20-month-old may move her hand back and forth in front of her mouth, pretending to brush her teeth.

Once infants can use symbols, they can begin to anticipate the consequences of actions mentally instead of having to perform them. Imagine that an infant and parent construct a tower of blocks next to an open door. Leaving the room, a baby in Substage 5 might close the door, knocking over the tower, because he cannot foresee the outcome of closing the door. But a baby in Substage 6 can anticipate the consequence of closing the door and move the tower beforehand.

Using symbols is the crowning achievement of the sensorimotor period. In just 2 years, the infant progresses from reflexive responding to symbolic processing. A summary of these changes looks like this:

## Six Substages of Sensorimotor Development

| Substage | Age (months) | Accomplishment | Example |
|---|---|---|---|
| 1 | 0-1 | Reflexes become coordinated. | Sucking a nipple |
| 2 | 1-4 | Primary circular reactions appear—an infant's first learned adaptations to the world. | Thumb sucking |
| 3 | 4-8 | Secondary circular reactions emerge, allowing infants to learn about objects. | Shaking a toy to hear it rattle |
| 4 | 8-12 | Means-end sequencing develops, marking the onset of intentional behavior. | Moving an obstacle to reach a toy |
| 5 | 12-18 | Tertiary circular reactions appear, allowing children to experiment. | Shaking different toys to hear the sounds they make |
| 6 | 18-24 | Symbolic processing is revealed in language, gestures, and pretend play. | Eating pretend food with a pretend fork |

TABLE 6–1

The ability to use mental symbols marks the end of sensorimotor thinking and the beginning of preoperational thinking, which we'll examine next.

### The Preoperational Stage

With the magic power of symbols, the child crosses the hurdle into preoperational thinking. **The *preoperational stage*, which spans ages 2 to 7, is marked by the child's use of symbols to represent objects and events.** Throughout this period, preschool children gradually become proficient at using

Sensorimotor thinking begins with reflexive responding and ends with symbolic processing, which improves gradually during the preoperational period.

common symbols, such as words, gestures, graphs, maps, and models. For example, the ability to use scale models develops early in the preoperational period. If young children watch an adult hide a toy in a full-size room, then try to find the toy in a scale model of the room that contains all the principal features of the full-scale room (e.g., carpet, window, furniture), 3-year-olds find the hidden toy readily but 2½-year-olds do not (DeLoache, 1995).

Why is this task so easy for 3-year-olds and so difficult for 2½-year-olds? Do the younger children simply forget the location of the toy by the time they look at the scale model of the room? No. If returned to the full-size room, they easily find the hidden toy. Judy DeLoache believes that 2½-year-olds' "attention to a scale model as an interesting and attractive object makes it difficult for them to simultaneously think about its relation to something else" (DeLoache, Miller, & Rosengren, 1997, p. 308). In other words, young children are drawn to the model as a real object and therefore find it hard to think about the model as a symbol of the full-size room.

If this argument is correct, 2½-year-olds should be more successful using the model if they don't have to think of it as a symbol for the full-size room. DeLoache tested this hypothesis in the study described in the "Focus on Research" feature. (This study is another of my 10 favorite studies, for reasons that will soon be obvious.)

### Finding Toys in a Shrunken Room

*Who were the investigators, and what was the aim of the study?* Judy DeLoache, Kevin Miller, and Karl Rosengren (1997) believed that 2½-year-olds could not find the toy in the model because it was difficult for them to think of the model as an object *and* as a symbol of the full-size room. To test this argument, they created a condition designed to eliminate the need for children to think of the model as an object and as a symbol. Children were told that a machine could shrink the full-size room. In this case, the model is no longer a symbol of the full-size room; it *is* the room, just shrunken. Consequently, DeLoache and her colleagues expected 2½-year-olds to find the hidden toy because they believed the model was the full-size room shrunken to miniature size.

*How did the investigators measure the topic of interest?* Some children were tested with the usual procedures: hiding the toy in the full-size room and asking children to find it in the scale model. Other children were tested in the new condition designed to help them find the toy. Children saw the oscilloscope shown in the photograph, which was described as a shrinking machine. They saw a toy doll—"Terry the Troll"—placed in front of the oscilloscope; then the experimenter and child left the room briefly while a tape recorder played sounds that were described as sounds "the machine makes when it's shrinking something." When experimenter and child returned, Terry had shrunk from 8 inches to 2 inches. Next, Terry was hidden in the full-size room, the experimenter aimed the "shrinking machine" at the full-size room, then experimenter and child left the room. While the tape recorder played shrinking sounds, research assistants quickly removed everything from the full-size room and substituted the model. Experimenter and child returned and the child was asked to find Terry. This procedure was repeated so that children searched for Terry on four separate trials.

*Who were the children in the study?* DeLoache and her colleagues tested 32 children whose average age was 2½ years.

*What was the design of the study?* The study was experimental. The independent variable was the presence or absence of the shrinking machine. The dependent variable was the percentage of trials on which the children found Terry.

*Were there ethical concerns with the study?* For children tested with the "shrinking machine," the study involved deception. Parents were fully informed about the shrinking machine before they gave consent, and parents were present throughout the experiment. Immediately after the experiment, children were told that the machine could not really shrink objects. They were shown the model, the full-size room, and both small and large versions of Terry. The deception seemed warranted, and no children seemed upset when they were told what really happened.

*What were the results?* The top part of the graph shows the percentage of trials in which children found the toy. Children rarely found the toy in the standard condition, but they frequently found it in the "shrinking machine" condition. The bottom part of the graph shows the percentage of children who found Terry on at least three of the four trials. No children in the standard condition were this accurate, but most children in the "shrinking machine" condition were.

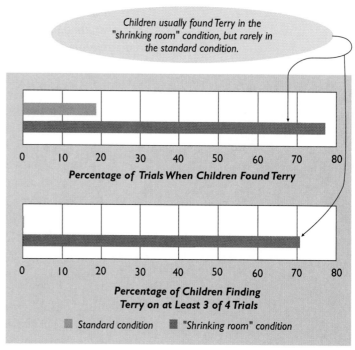

Children usually found Terry in the "shrinking room" condition, but rarely in the standard condition.

*Percentage of Trials When Children Found Terry*

*Percentage of Children Finding Terry on at Least 3 of 4 Trials*

▨ *Standard condition*     ▪ *"Shrinking room" condition*

FIG 6–1

*What did the investigators conclude?* When 2½-year-olds must think of the model as an object and as a symbol, they find this very difficult and, consequently, cannot find the hidden toy, even though the model is an exact replica of the full-size room. When children can think of the model *as* the room, but much smaller, they readily find the toy. Young children's symbol skills are just emerging, yet within a few months they improve rapidly. ●

Why are young children's symbol skills so fragile at first? To answer this question, we need to look at some important characteristics of thought during the preoperational stage.

Egocentrism.   Preoperational children typically believe that others see the world—both literally and figuratively—exactly as they do. **Egocentrism refers to young children's difficulty in seeing the world from another's viewpoint.** When youngsters stubbornly cling to their own way, they are not simply being contrary. Instead, preoperational children do not comprehend that other people have different ideas and feelings.

Suppose, for example, you ask the preschooler in the drawing to select the photograph that shows how the objects on the table look to you. Most will select photo 1, which shows how the objects look to the child, not photo 2, the correct choice. Preoperational youngsters evidently suppose that the mountains are seen the same way by all; they presume that theirs is the only view, not one of many conceivable views (Piaget & Inhelder, 1956).

Egocentrism also explains why Jamila, the 3-year-old in the vignette, nods her head when talking on the phone. Jamila assumes that because she is aware that her head is moving up and down (or side to side!), her grandmother must be aware of it, too.

FIG 6–2

Their egocentrism sometimes leads preoperational youngsters to attribute their own thoughts and feelings to others. **Preoperational children sometimes credit inanimate objects with life and lifelike properties, a phenomenon known as** *animism* **(Piaget, 1929).** A 3½-year-old I know, Christine, illustrated preoperational animism in a conversation we had on a rainy day:

RK:         Is the sun happy today?
CHRISTINE: No. It's sad today.
RK:         Why?
CHRISTINE: Because it's cloudy. He can't shine. And he can't see me!
RK:         What about your trike? Is it happy?
CHRISTINE: No, he's very sad, too.
RK:         Why is that?
CHRISTINE: Because I can't ride him. And because he's all alone in the garage.

Caught up in her egocentrism, Christine believes that objects like the sun and her tricycle think and feel as she does.

Centration. Children in the preoperational stage also have the psychological equivalent of tunnel vision: They often concentrate on one aspect of a problem but totally ignore other equally relevant aspects. *Centration* **is Piaget's term for this narrowly focused thought that characterizes preoperational youngsters.**

Piaget demonstrated centration in his experiments involving conservation. In the conservation experiments, Piaget wanted to determine when children realize that important characteristics of objects (or sets of objects) stay the same despite changes in their physical appearance. Some tasks that Piaget used to study conservation are shown in the diagram on page 159. Each begins with identical objects (or sets of objects). Then one of the objects (or sets) is transformed and children are asked if the objects are the same in terms of some important feature.

A typical conservation problem, involving conservation of liquid quantity, is shown in the photo. Children are shown identical beakers filled with the same amount of juice. After children agree that the the two beakers have the same amount, juice is poured from one beaker into a taller, thinner beaker. The juice looks different in the tall, thin beaker—it rises higher—but of course the amount is unchanged. Nevertheless, preoperational children claim that the tall, thin beaker has more juice than the original beaker. (And, if the juice is poured into a wider beaker, they believe it has less.)

Preoperational children often overlook others' perspectives, focus on one aspect of a problem, and confuse appearance with reality.

What is happening here? According to Piaget, preoperational children center on the level of the juice in the beaker. If the juice is higher after it is poured, preoperational children believe that there must be more juice now than before. Because preoperational thinking is centered, these youngsters ignore the fact that the change in the level of the juice is always accompanied by a change in the diameter of the beaker.

In other conservation problems, preoperational children also tend to focus on only one aspect of the problem. In conservation of number, for example, preoperational children concentrate on the fact that, after the transformation, one row of objects is now longer than the other. In conservation of length, preoperational children concentrate on the fact that, after the transformation, the end of one stick is farther to the right than the end of the other. Preoperational children's centered thinking means that they overlook other parts of the problem that would tell them the quantity is unchanged.

| Type of Conservation | Starting Configuration | Transformation | Final Configuration |
|---|---|---|---|
| Liquid quantity | Is there the same amount of water in each glass? | Pour water from one glass into a shorter, wider glass. | Now is there the same amount of water in each glass, or does one have more? |
| Number | Are there the same number of pennies in each row? | Stretch out the top row of pennies, push together the bottom row. | Now are there the same number of pennies in each row, or does one row have more? |
| Length | Are these sticks the same length? | Move one stick to the left and the other to the right. | Now are the sticks the same length, or is one longer? |
| Mass | Does each ball have the same amount of clay? | Roll one ball so that it looks like a sausage. | Now does each piece have the same amount of clay, or does one have more? |
| Area | Does each cow have the same amount of grass to eat? | Spread out the squares in one field. | Now does each cow have the same amount to eat, or does one cow have more? |

FIG 6–3

## Appearance as Reality.

Preschool children believe an object's appearance tells what the object is really like. For instance, many a 3-year-old has watched with quiet fascination as an older brother or sister put on a ghoulish costume only to erupt in frightened tears when their siblings put on scary makeup. For the youngster in the photo, the scary made-up face is reality, not just something that looks frightening but really isn't.

Confusion between appearance and reality is not limited to costumes and masks. It is a general characteristic of preoperational thinking. Consider the following cases where appearances and reality conflict:

- A boy is angry because a friend is being mean but smiles because he's afraid the friend will leave if he reveals his anger.

- A glass of milk looks brown when seen through sunglasses.
- A piece of hard rubber looks like food (for example, like a piece of pizza).

Older children and adults know that the boy looks happy, the milk looks brown, and the object looks like food but that the boy is really angry, the milk is really white, and the object is really rubber. Preoperational children, however, confuse appearance and reality, thinking the boy is happy, the milk is brown, and the piece of rubber is edible.

Preoperational children's confusion of appearance and reality was demonstrated in a study by Friend and Davis (1993). Stories were presented to 4- and 7-year-olds about a person whose outward appearance conflicted with his or her underlying feelings. For example, children were told about Sally, a school-age child who was sad because her uncle gave her a baby rattle for her birthday. Sally didn't want to hurt her uncle's feelings, so she smiled as she took the gift out of the box. A photograph showed Sally smiling at her uncle. Children in the study were asked if Sally looks happy or sad and if she really is happy or sad.

FIG 6-4

The graph shows how accurately children answered the questions. Questions about Sally's appearance were easy for all children; 4- and 7-year-olds readily judged that Sally looked happy. Questions about her real feelings were much more difficult: Most 4-year-olds and even some 7-year-olds answered the questions incorrectly. Thus, when presented with stories about people who feel sad but look happy, preoperational youngsters cannot distinguish between appearance and reality and so think that if people look happy, they are really and truly happy! In contrast, 7-year-olds, who are more likely to have progressed to concrete operational thinking, respond much more accurately.

Are you skeptical that young children can be this confused? Many researchers shared your skepticism when these findings were first reported, and they went to great lengths to show that young children were somehow being misled by some minor aspects of the experiment. But most of the follow-up experiments failed; rewording the instructions, using different materials, or even training children all had relatively little effect (Siegler, 1998). Confusion about appearance and reality is a deep-seated characteristic of preoperational thinking (especially in the early years of this stage), as are egocentrism and centration.

## The Concrete Operational Stage

During the early elementary-school years, children enter a new stage of cognitive development that is distinctly more adultlike and much less childlike. **In the concrete operational stage, which spans ages 7 to 11, children first use mental operations to solve problems and to reason.** What are the mental operations that are so essential to concrete operational thinking? *Mental operations are strategies and rules that make thinking more systematic and more powerful.* Some mental operations apply to numbers. For example, addition, subtraction, multiplication, and division are familiar arithmetic operations that concrete operational children use. Other mental operations apply to categories of objects. For example, classes can be added (mothers + fathers = parents) and subtracted (parents − mothers = fathers). Still other mental operations apply to spatial relations among objects. For example, if point A is near points B and C, then points B and C must be close to each other.

Mental operations give concrete operational thinking a rule-oriented, logical flavor that is missing in preoperational thought. Applied properly, mental operations yield consistent results. Taking the familiar case of arithmetic operations, 4 + 2 is always 6, not just usually or only on weekends.

Another important property of mental operations is that they can be reversed. Each operation has an inverse that can "undo" or reverse the effect of an operation. If you start with 5 and add 3, you get 8; by subtracting 3 from 8, you reverse your steps and return to 5. For Piaget, reversibility of this sort applied to all mental operations. Concrete operational children are able to reverse their thinking in a way that preoperational youngsters cannot. In fact, reversible mental operations is part of why concrete operational children pass the conservation tasks described on page 159: Concrete operational thinkers understand that if the transformation were reversed (for example, the juice was poured back into the original container), the objects would be identical.

> Concrete operational thinking is based on mental operations that yield consistent results and that can be reversed.

Concrete operational thinking is much more powerful than preoperational thinking. Remember that preoperational children are egocentric (believing that others see the world as they do), are centered in their thinking, and confuse appearances with reality. None of these limitations applies to children in the concrete operational stage.

Egocentrism wanes as youngsters have more experiences with friends and siblings who assert their own perspectives on the world (LeMare & Rubin, 1987). Learning that events can be interpreted in different ways helps children realize that many problems have different facets (thereby avoiding centration) and that appearances can be deceiving.

Concrete operational thinking is a major cognitive advance, but it has its own limits. As the name implies, concrete operational thinking is limited to the tangible and real, to the here and now. The concrete operational youngster takes "an earthbound, concrete, practical-minded sort of problem-solving approach, one that persistently fixates on the perceptible and inferable reality right there in front of him" (Flavell, 1985, p. 98). That is, thinking abstractly and hypothetically is beyond the ability of concrete operational thinkers.

## The Formal Operational Stage

In the *formal operational stage,* which extends from roughly age 11 into adulthood, children and adolescents apply mental operations to abstract entities; they think hypothetically and reason deductively. Freed from the concrete and the real, adolescents explore the possible—what might be and what could be.

Unlike reality-oriented concrete operational children, formal operational thinkers understand that reality is not the only possibility. They can envision alternative realities and examine their consequences. For example, ask a concrete operational child, "What would happen if gravity meant that objects floated up?" or "What would happen if men gave birth?" and you're likely to get a confused or even irritated look and comments like "It doesn't—they fall" or "They don't—women have babies." Reality is the foundation of concrete operational thinking. In contrast, formal operational adolescents use hypothetical reasoning to probe the implications of fundamental change in physical or biological laws.

Formal operations also allow adolescents to take a different, more sophisticated approach to problem solving. Formal operational thinkers can solve problems by creating hypotheses (sets of possibilities) and testing them. Piaget (Inhelder & Piaget, 1958) showed this aspect of adolescent thinking by presenting children and adolescents with several flasks, each containing what appeared to be the same clear liquid. They were told that one combination of the clear liquids would produce a blue liquid and were asked to determine the necessary combination.

A typical concrete operational youngster, like the ones in the photograph, plunges right in, mixing liquids from different flasks in a haphazard way. But formal operational adolescents understand that setting up the problem in abstract, hypothethical terms is the key. The problem is not really about pouring liquids but about forming hypotheses about different combinations of liquids and testing them systematically.

A teenager might mix liquid from the first flask with liquids from each of the other flasks. If none of those combinations produces a blue liquid, the adolescent would conclude that the liquid in the first flask is not an essential part of the mixture. Next, he or she would mix the liquid in the second flask with each of the remaining liquids. A formal operational thinker would continue in this manner until he or she found the critical pair that produced the blue liquid. For adolescents, the problem is not one of concrete acts of pouring and mixing; rather, they understand that the problem consists of identifying possible hypotheses (in this case, combinations of liquids) and then evaluating each one. The adolescent's approach to problem solving is also illustrated in the "Real Children" feature.

### Hypothetical Reasoning Goes to the Races

REAL CHILDREN

As a 15-year-old, I delivered the Indianapolis *Star*. In the spring of 1966, the newspaper announced a contest for all newspaper carriers. The person who created the most words from the letters contained in the words "SAFE RACE" would win two tickets to the Indianapolis 500 auto race.

I realized that this was a problem in hypothetical reasoning. All I needed to do was create all possible combinations of letters, then look them up. Following this procedure I had to win (or, at worst, tie). So, I created endless lists of possible words, beginning with each of the letters individually, then all possible combinations of two letters, and worked my way up to possible combinations of all eight letters (e.g., SCAREEFA, SCAREEAF). This was monotonous enough, but no more than looking up all these possible words in a dictionary. (Remember, this was in the days before computerized spell checkers.) Weeks later, I had generated a list of 126 words. A few months later, I learned that I had won the contest. Hypothetical reasoning has its payoffs! ●

Because adolescents' thinking is not concerned solely with reality, they are also better able to reason logically from premises and draw appropriate conclusions. **The ability to draw appropriate conclusions from facts is known as *deductive reasoning*.** Suppose we tell a person the following two facts:

1. If you hit a glass with a hammer, the glass will break.

2. Don hit a glass with a hammer.

The correct conclusion, of course, is that "the glass broke," a conclusion that formal operational adolescents will reach. Concrete operational youngsters, too, will sometimes reach this conclusion, but based on their experience and not because the conclusion is logically necessary. To see the difference, imagine that the two facts are now:

1. If you hit a glass with a feather, the glass will break.

2. Don hit a glass with a feather.

The conclusion "the glass broke" follows from these two statements just as logically as it did from the first pair. In this instance, however, the conclusion is counterfactual—it goes against what experience tells us is really true. Concrete operational 10-year-olds resist reaching conclusions that are counter to known facts; they reach conclusions based on their knowledge of the world. In contrast, formal operational 15-year-olds often reach counterfactual conclusions (Markovits & Vachon, 1989). They understand that these problems are about abstract entities that need not correspond to real-world relations.

*Formal operational adolescents can think hypothetically and reason deductively.*

Hypothetical reasoning and deductive reasoning are powerful tools for formal operational thinkers. In fact, we can characterize this power by paraphrasing the quotation about concrete operational thinking that appears on page 161: "Formal operational youth take an abstract, hypothetical approach to problem solving; they are not constrained by the reality that is staring them in the face but are open to different possibilities and alternatives." The ability to ponder different alternatives makes possible the experimentation with lifestyles and values that occurs in adolescence, topics we'll encounter on several occasions later in this book.

With the achievement of formal operations, cognitive development is over in Piaget's theory. Of course, adolescents and adults acquire more knowledge as they grow older, but their fundamental way of thinking remains unchanged, in Piaget's view. The table, which you first saw in Module 1.2, summarizes the cognitive changes between birth and adulthood that Piaget described.

## Piaget's Four Stages of Cognitive Development

| Stage | Approximate Age | Characteristics |
|---|---|---|
| Sensorimotor thought | Birth to 2 years | Infant's knowledge of the world is based on senses and motor skills. By the end of the period, infant uses mental representations. |
| Preoperational thought | 2 to 6 years | Child learns how to use symbols such as words and numbers to represent aspects of the world, but relates to the world only through his or her perspective. |
| Concrete operational thought | 7 to 11 years | Child understands and applies logical operations to experiences, provided they are focused on the here and now. |
| Formal operational thought | Adolescence and beyond | Adolescent or adult thinks abstractly, speculates on hypothetical situations, and reasons deductively about what may be possible. |

TABLE 6–2

## Check Your Learning

**1.** Sensorimotor thought begins with reflexive responding and ends with _____.

**2.** In a _____, an infant accidentally produces something pleasant, then tries to recreate that pleasing event.

**3.** An important characteristic of preoperational thought is _____, which refers to children's inability to see the world as others do.

**4.** Because of their egocentrism, preoperational children sometimes attribute life-like properties to inanimate objects, a phenomenon known as _____.

**5.** Unlike preoperational children, concrete operational children are capable of _____, which are actions that can be performed on objects or ideas.

**6.** During the concrete operational stage, children cannot reason _____.

**7.** The formal operational period marks the onset of _____ reasoning and deductive reasoning.

 **How might nature and nurture be involved in an infant's progression through the stages of sensorimotor development?**

**Answers:** (1) symbolic processing, (2) primary circular reaction, (3) egocentrism, (4) animism, (5) mental operations, (6) abstractly and hypothetically, (7) hypothetical

---

# 6.3

- **Applying Piaget's Theory**
- **Criticisms of the Theory**

# Evaluating Piaget's Theory

## Learning Objectives

- How have parents and teachers applied Piaget's theory?

- What are some criticisms of Piaget's theory?

*Chris, a 14-year-old boy, was an enigma to his mother, Terri. On the one hand, Chris's growing reasoning skills impressed and sometimes even surprised her. He not only readily grasped technical discussions of her medical work, but he was becoming adept at finding loopholes in her explanations of why he wasn't allowed to do some things with his friends. On the other hand, sometimes Chris was a real teenage "space cadet." Simple problem solving stumped him, or he made silly mistakes and got the wrong answer. Chris didn't correspond to Terri's image of the formal operational thinker that she remembered from her college child development class.*

Like Terri, child development researchers have observed that adolescents' thinking is not always as sophisticated as Piaget's theory predicts. This is one of several criticisms of Piaget's work that we'll examine in the second part of this module. But first, let's look at some of the ways parents and teachers have used Piaget's theory to improve children's learning.

## Applying Piaget's Theory

Because Piaget's theory is so comprehensive, it has stimulated a great deal of research. Much of this work supports Piaget's view that children actively try to understand the world around them and organize their knowledge, and that cognitive development includes major qualitative changes (Brainerd, 1996; Flavell, 1996).

Many teachers and parents also have found Piaget's theory a rich source of ideas for fostering children's development (Siegler, 1998). Some of these ideas are described in the "Making Children's Lives Better" feature.

## MAKING CHILDREN'S LIVES BETTER

### Fostering Cognitive Growth

Piaget's view of cognitive development has some straightforward implications for teaching practices that promote cognitive growth:

1. Cognitive growth occurs as children construct their *own* understanding of the world, so the teacher's role is to create environments where children can discover *for themselves* how the world works. A teacher shouldn't simply try to tell children how addition and subtraction are complementary but instead should provide children with materials that allow them to discover the complementarity themselves.

2. Children profit from experience only when they can interpret this experience with their current cognitive structures. It follows, then, that the best teaching experiences are slightly ahead of the children's current level of thinking. As a youngster begins to master basic addition, don't jump right to subtraction but go to slightly more difficult addition problems.

3. Cognitive growth can be particularly rapid when children discover inconsistencies and errors in their own thinking. Teachers should therefore encourage children to look at the consistency of their thinking but then let children take the lead in sorting out the inconsistencies. If a child is making mistakes in borrowing on subtraction problems, a teacher shouldn't correct the error directly but should encourage the child to look at a large number of these errors to discover what he or she is doing wrong. ●

## Criticisms of the Theory

Despite the success of many aspects of Piaget's theory in fostering children's development, some elements of his theory have held up better than others. Let's look at some of the problems critics have identified.

**Alternative Explanations of Performance.**  Piaget explained cognitive development with constructs like accommodation, assimilation, and equilibration. Subsequent researchers, however, have found other ways to explain age differences in children's performance on Piaget's tasks.

For example, preoperational children's performance on the conservation task appears to reflect, at least in part, their growing sensitivity to language, not purely their centration. In fact, it is the questions concerning the amount of water that are critical (Winer, Craig, & Weinbaum, 1992). Remember that in this procedure youngsters are twice asked if the amount of juice in the two beakers is the same—once before the juice is poured and once after. In everyday conversation, a question is usually repeated like this because the answer was wrong the first time. Or it may be repeated because the answer was correct at first but something has changed so that it is now wrong. Both of these rules about questions would lead young children who had answered "yes" to the first question to wonder if they were wrong or if a different answer is expected and perhaps say "no" the second time. In fact, when the procedure is changed (for example, by asking the question only once), preschoolers are more likely to conserve. Thus, children's performance on conservation problems is based partly on language development, not just the processes that Piaget described.

Researchers have also reexamined infants' understanding that objects exist independently of oneself and one's actions. Piaget claimed that 1- to 4-month-olds

> A criticism of Piaget's theory is that researchers have discovered better ways to explain children's performance on Piaget's tasks.

believe that objects no longer exist when they disappear from view—out of sight means out of mind. If you take a favorite toy from a 3-month-old and hide it under a cloth directly in front of her, she will not look for it even though the shape of the toy is clearly visible under the cloth and within reach!

At 8 months, infants search for objects, but their understanding of object permanence remains incomplete. If 8- to 10-month-olds see an object hidden under one container, then see it repeatedly hidden under a second container, they will routinely look for the toy under the first container. Piaget claimed that this behavior shows only a fragmentary understanding of objects because infants do not distinguish the object from the actions they use to locate it, such as lifting a particular container. Not until approximately 18 months do infants apparently have full understanding of object permanence.

Investigators have since questioned Piaget's conclusions (Smith et al., 1999). Some fairly minor changes in procedures can affect 8- to 10-month-olds' success on the hidden object task. An infant is more likely to look under the correct container if, for example, the interval between hiding and looking is brief and if the containers are easily distinguished from each other. Therefore, infants who are unsuccessful at this task may be showing poor memory rather than inadequate understanding of the nature of objects (Wellman, Cross, & Bartsch, 1986).

In addition, by devising some clever procedures, other investigators have shown that babies understand objects much earlier than Piaget claimed. Renée Baillargeon (1987, 1994), for example, assessed object permanence using a procedure in which infants first saw a silver screen that appeared to be rotating back and forth. When they were familiar with this display, one of two new displays was shown. In the *possible event*, an orange box appeared in a position behind the screen, making it impossible for the screen to rotate as far back as it had previously. Instead, the screen rotated until it made contact with the box, then rotated forward. In the *impossible event*, shown in the diagram, the orange box appeared, but the screen continued to rotate

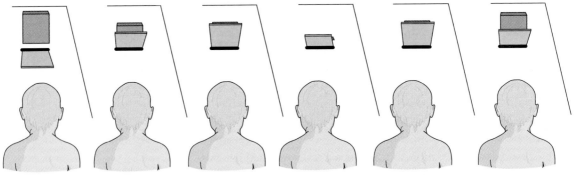

FIG 6–5

as before. The screen rotated back until it was flat, then rotated forward, again revealing the orange box. The illusion was possible because the box was mounted on a movable platform that allowed it to drop out of the way of the moving screen. However, from the infant's perspective, it appeared as if the box vanished behind the screen, only to reappear.

The disappearance and reappearance of the box violates the idea that objects exist permanently. Consequently, an infant who understands the permanence of objects should find the impossible event a truly novel stimulus and look at it longer than the possible event. Baillargeon found that 4½-month-olds consistently looked longer at the impossible event than the possible event. Infants apparently thought that the impossible event was novel, just as we are surprised when an object vanishes from a magician's scarf. Evidently, then, infants have some understanding of object permanence early in the first year of life.

Alternative explanations for children's performance on object permanence and conservation tasks do not mean that Piaget's theory is fundamentally wrong. They merely mean that the theory needs some revision to include important constructs that Piaget overlooked.

### Consistency in Performance.

In Piaget's view, each stage of intellectual development has unique characteristics that leave their mark on everything a child does. Just as you can recognize McDonald's by its golden arches, you can recognize preoperational thinking by its egocentrism and formal operational thinking by its abstractness. Consequently, children's performance on different tasks should be very consistent. On the conservation and the three-mountains tasks, for instance, a 4-year-old should always respond in a preoperational way: He should say the water is not the same after pouring, and the other person sees the mountains the same way he does.

What does research tell us about the consistency of children's performance on different tasks? There is some consistency, but exceptions are common, too. A good illustration comes from Siegler (1981), who tested children on three different Piagetian tasks. Only one-third of the children performed at the same level on all three tasks. The remainder were inconsistent, sometimes differing considerably from one task to the next. For example, all 11 children who performed at the formal operational level on the balance scale only performed at the concrete operational level on the shadows task. This inconsistent performance on different tasks does not support Piaget's view that children's thinking should always reflect the distinctive imprint of their current stage of cognitive development.

> Contrary to Piaget's theory, children's performance often varies across tasks that have the same logical structure.

### Training Piagetian Concepts.

According to Piaget, children master different concepts as they move from one stage to the next. Children master conservation as they move from preoperational to concrete operational thinking, and they master hypothetical reasoning as they move from concrete to formal operational thinking. Consequently, it should not be possible to teach children concepts at an earlier stage: Preoperational children should not be able to learn conservation, for instance. However, many investigators have shown that children can be taught Piagetian concepts ahead of schedule.

In an early study, Gelman (1969) argued that a preschool child's attention is drawn to many cues in the conservation task, such as the size, height, and diameter of the beakers and the level of the liquid. Most of these cues change as the liquid is poured from one beaker to another, which may lead youngsters to believe that the amount of liquid has changed. Gelman wondered if, by teaching children that quantities are the same despite looking different, they could learn to conserve. Consequently, she presented many problems in which two quantities were the same but a third differed; the task was to select the two quantities that were the same. For example, in the problem in the figure, the child chose the two rows that had the same number of dots. To answer correctly, children had to pay attention only to the number of dots and ignore other distracting cues, such as the length of the rows. After training, 5-year-olds

FIG 6-6

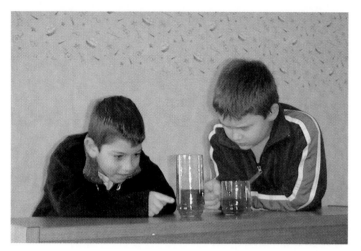

were quite successful on a variety of conservation tasks. Thus, when trained to focus strictly on one cue and when given many examples, children ignored misleading cues and recognized that quantity does not change in the conservation task.

Training procedures like Gelman's, although successful, may seem artificial because children don't ordinarily experience such a structured set of problems. However, children can learn to conserve another way—through discussion with peers. When, as shown in the photo, nonconservers and nonconservers solve conservation problems together, their joint answer is likely to be a conservation response. More importantly, when nonconservers are later tested alone, they conserve. These children are not simply parroting the conservers' answers; they explain the conservation response correctly, and the training generalizes to new conservation tasks (Ames & Murray, 1982; Miller & Brownell, 1975).

### A Theory of Actual Thinking or Possible Thinking?

Simply because children and adolescents attain a particular level of reasoning in Piaget's theory does not mean that they always reason at that level. Children who are in the concrete operational period often revert to preoperational thinking. Adolescents often fail to reason logically, even when they are capable and when it would be beneficial. For example, adolescents typically show more sophisticated reasoning when the problems are relevant to them personally than when they are not (Ward & Overton, 1990). Also, when the product of reasoning is consistent with adolescents' own beliefs, they are less likely to find flaws in the reasoning (Klaczynski & Narasimham, 1998): Hearing a flawed argument, for example, that Baptists make better parents, Baptist adolescents are more likely to overlook the errors in the argument.

Thus, Terri, the mother in the opening vignette, should not be so perplexed by her son's seemingly erratic thinking: Adolescents (and adults, for that matter) simply do not always use the most powerful levels of thinking that they possess. Piaget's account of intellectual development is really a description of how children and adolescents *can* think, not how they always or even usually think.

Because of the criticisms of Piaget's theory, many researchers have taken several different paths in studying cognitive development. In the next module, we'll look at three different approaches that are linked to Piaget's work. In Chapter 7, we'll look at a very different view of cognitive development, the information-processing approach.

### Check Your Learning

**1.** According to Piaget's theory, the best teaching experiences are _____.

**2.** Cognitive growth can be very rapid when children discover _____.

**3.** One criticism of Piaget's theory is that children's performance on tasks like conservation and object permanence is _____.

**4.** When tested on many different Piagetian tasks, children's level of performance typically _____.

**5.** Researchers have found that they can teach children Piagetian concepts and, more importantly, that such teaching _____.

**6.** Compared to what would be expected from Piaget's theory, adolescents' thinking is often _____.

 **Suppose that you wanted to teach a kindergarten child to add. Use the guidelines in the "Making Children's Lives Better" feature to suggest how you might try to accomplish this goal.**

**Answers:** (1) slightly ahead of the child's level of thinking, (2) inconsistencies and errors in their own thinking, (3) better explained by ideas that are not part of Piaget's theory, (4) varies from one task to the next, (5) generalizes to other, new tasks, (6) less sophisticated

## Beyond Piaget's Theory

### Learning Objectives

● **How do neo-Piagetian theories differ from Piaget's original theory?**

● **What naive theories do children hold about physics, psychology, and biology?**

● **Why did Vygotsky view development as an apprenticeship?**

> *Victoria, a 4-year-old, enjoys solving jigsaw puzzles, coloring, and building towers with blocks. While doing these activities, she often talks to herself. For example, once while coloring a picture, she said, "Where's the red crayon? Stay inside the lines. Color the blocks blue." These remarks were not directed at anyone else; after all, Victoria was alone. Why did she say these things? What purpose did they serve?*

Many theories have been proposed to complement Piaget's view of cognitive development. In this last module, we'll look at three. As we do, you'll learn why Victoria often talks to herself.

### Neo-Piagetian Approaches to Cognitive Development

Beginning in the 1970s, several researchers (e.g., Case, 1998; Fischer & Granott, 1995; Halford, 1993; Pascuale-Leone, 1970) proposed theories that elaborated and updated Piaget's theory. **As a group, these are called** *neo-Piagetian theories* **because they are modern theories rooted in Piaget's basic assumptions about cognitive development.** The neo-Piagetian theorists generally retain Piaget's belief that important qualitative changes occur in thinking as children develop, but their theories reflect the new research findings we have just been discussing and thus allow for much greater variation in performance from task to task.

Three basic ideas are at the heart of most neo-Piagetian theories:

• Between infancy and adulthood there are three or four qualitatively different levels of cognitive functioning, with each successive level building on elements of the previous level.

• Children develop many distinct conceptual structures (e.g., understanding numbers, understanding spatial relations) that reflect a child's own experiences and culture, and that consequently are quite variable from one child to the next.

- The capacity and efficiency of working memory—a structure that includes ongoing cognitive processes and the information required for those processes—improves with age, making it possible for children's thinking to become more complex.

*Neo-Piagetian theories include qualitatively different stages of thought, but also include the idea that children develop many distinct conceptual structures.*

The first idea comes directly from Piaget's theory and is largely why these theories are called neo-Piagetian. The second idea is quite different from Piaget's idea that the mind is homogeneous at each developmental stage. Neo-Piagetian theories believe that cognitive development in different areas may progress at different rates, which fits with research showing that children are often more advanced in some areas than others. Of course, this same research shows that there is *some* consistency in children's performance on different tasks (but not the near-perfect consistency expected by Piaget's theory). Working memory helps explain this consistency by showing that, at any age, there is a limit to the cognitive complexity that children can handle.

Thus, in Piaget's view, children's thinking changes quantitatively as they develop, at a fairly common pace in all domains. Developmental change reflects the equilibration process described on page 151. In contrast, in neo-Piagetian views, children's thinking changes quantitatively as they develop, at different rates in different domains, depending on children's experiences. Developmental change reflects greater capacity and efficiency of working memory.

Phrased somewhat differently, neo-Piagetian theories share Piaget's effort to provide a general account of cognitive development, one that has at its core the idea that thinking changes qualitatively with development. However, neo-Piagetian theories also incorporate a mechanism to explain why a child's thinking may mature more rapidly in some areas than others.

In the next section, you'll see that some researchers take the second neo-Piagetian idea—that children develop distinct conceptual structures in different areas—as their starting point for explaining cognitive development.

## The Child as Theorist

Piaget believed that children, like scientists, formulate theories about how the world works. Children's theories are usually called "naive theories" because, unlike real scientific theories, they are not created by specialists and they are rarely evaluated by formal experimentation. Naive theories are nevertheless valuable because they allow children (and adults) to understand new experiences and predict future events.

In Piaget's view, children formulate a grand, comprehensive theory that attempts to explain an enormous variety of phenomena—including reasoning about objects, people, and morals, for example—within a common framework. More recent views cling to the idea of children as theorists, but propose that children, like real scientists, develop specialized theories about much narrower areas. Some of the theories that young children first develop concern physics, psychology, and biology. That is, based on their experiences, young children rapidly develop theories that organize their knowledge about properties of objects, people, and living things (Wellman & Gelman, 1998). Let's look at children's naive theories in each of these areas.

Naive Physics.  We know from Module 5.3 that young babies are able to distinguish objects. From their perceptions, what do infants learn about the properties of objects? A lot! Child development researchers have discovered that, by 3 or 4 months, infants have already mastered some important basic facts about objects. They know, for instance, that objects move along connected, continuous paths and that objects cannot move "through" other objects (Spelke, 1994; von Hofsten et al., 1998). Infants look longer at moving objects that violate these properties (e.g., a ball that somehow rolls "through" a solid wall) than moving objects that are consistent with them, suggesting that infants are surprised when objects move in ways not predicted by their naive theory of physics. By the middle of the first year, babies also understand that one object striking a second object will cause the latter to move (Kotovsky & Baillargeon, 1998; Spelke, 1994).

Later in the first year, infants come to understand the importance of gravity. At this time, but not before, infants will look intently at an object that appears to float in midair with no obvious means of support, because it violates their understanding of gravity (Baillargeon, 1998).

These amazing demonstrations attest to the fact that the infant is indeed an accomplished naive physicist. Of course, the infant's theories are far from complete; naive understanding of physics takes place throughout the preschool years and later (e.g., Au, 1994). However, the important point is that infants rapidly create a reasonably accurate theory of some basic properties of objects, a theory that helps them understand why objects such as toys act as they do.

Naive Psychology.  Think back to the last time you wanted to figure out why someone—a friend, lover, coworker, sibling, or parent—acted as he or she did. Why did your friend go to a movie with someone else instead of going to a concert with you? Why did your brother say nothing about your brand new coat? In common situations like this, adults are often naive psychologists—we try to explain why people act as they do and usually our explanations emphasize that desires or goals cause people's behavior. Your friend went to the concert because she was mad at you for not loaning her your car; your brother didn't comment on your coat because he was preoccupied with something else. Just as naive physics allows us to predict how objects act, naive psychology allows us to predict how people act (Lillard, 1999).

**Collectively, a person's ideas about connections between thoughts, beliefs, and behavior form a *theory of mind,* a naive understanding of the relations between mind and behavior.** One of the leading researchers on theory of mind, Henry Wellman (1992; 1993), believes that children's theory of mind moves through three phases during the preschool years. In the earliest phase, common in 2-year-olds, children are aware of desires, and they often speak of their wants and likes, as in "Lemme see" or "I wanna sit." Also, they often link their desires to their behavior, as in "I happy there's more cookies" (Wellman, 1990). Thus, by age 2, children understand that they and other people have desires and that desires can cause behavior.

By about age 3, an important change takes place. Now children clearly distinguish the mental world from the physical world. For example, if told about one girl who has a cookie and another girl who is thinking about a cookie, 3-year-olds know that only the first girl's cookie can be seen, touched, and eaten (Harris et al., 1991). And, most 3-year-olds use "mental verbs" like *think, believe, remember,* and *forget,* which suggests that they have a beginning understanding of different mental states (Bartsch & Wellman, 1995). Although 3-year-olds

During the preschool years, children form a theory of mind— a naive understanding of connections between thoughts, beliefs, and behavior.

This is Sally. Sally has a basket.

This is Anne. Anne has a box.

Sally has a marble.

She puts the marble into her basket.

Sally goes out for a walk.

Anne takes the marble out of the basket and puts it into the box.

Now Sally comes back. She wants to play with her marble. Where will she look for her marble?

FIG 6–7

talk about thoughts and beliefs, they nevertheless emphasize desires when trying to explain why people act as they do.

Not until age 4 years do mental states really take center stage in children's understanding of their own and other people's actions. That is, by age 4, children understand that their own and other people's behavior is based on their beliefs about events and situations, even when those beliefs are wrong.

This developmental transformation is particularly evident when children are tested on false belief tasks like the one shown in the figure. In all false belief tasks, a situation is set up so that the child being tested has accurate information, but someone else does not. For example, in the story in the figure, the child being tested knows that the marble is really in the box, but Sally, the girl in the story, believes that the marble is still in the basket. Remarkably, although 4-year-olds correctly say that Sally will look for the marble in the basket (acting on her false belief), most 3-year-olds say she will look in the box. The 4-year-olds understand that Sally's behavior is based on her beliefs, despite the fact that her beliefs are incorrect (Frye, 1993). As Bartsch and Wellman (1995) phrase it, 4-year-olds "realize that people not only have thoughts and beliefs, but also that thoughts and beliefs are crucial to explaining why people do things; that is, actors' pursuits of their desires are inevitably shaped by their beliefs about the world" (p. 144).

After the preschool years, children's naive psychology moves beyond theory of mind and embraces an ever-expanding range of psychological phenomena. We'll see in Module 10.1, for example, that school-age children understand that emotions can cause people to behave differently. And, in Module 11.3, we'll discover that, as children develop, their descriptions of other people become more abstract and more psychological. For now, though, the important point is that children's naive psychology flourishes in the preschool years. Armed with this theory, children see that other people's behavior is not unpredictable but follows regular patterns.

**Naive Biology.**   When your computer crashes, do you think to yourself, "Oh, it must be feeling ill"? When you accidentally break your coffee mug, do you say, "Gosh, its parents will be terribly upset"? Of course not. Computers and coffee cups are inanimate, but illness and parenthood are properties of animate objects. In fact, the difference between animate and inanimate objects is so fundamental that when we know an object is animate, our naive theory of biology allows us to infer many properties of the object.

Even toddlers apparently have some basic understanding of different properties of animate and inanimate objects. This conclusion is based on studies in which an adult demonstrates an object drinking, then encourages the child to imitate the drinking using toys that include animate and inanimate objects. Typically, 14-month-olds demonstrate drinking with animate objects (a toy lamb), not inanimate objects (a toy car). However, if prompted to imitate using a key, 14-month-olds select inanimate objects more often than animate objects (Mandler & McDonough, 1998). Evidently, the distinction between animate and inanimate objects is established fairly early.

During the preschool years, children's naive theories of biology come to include many of the specific properties associated with animate objects (Wellman & Gelman, 1998). Many 4-year-olds' theories of biology include the following elements:

- *Movement:* Children understand that animals can move themselves but inanimate objects can only be moved by other objects or by people. Shown an animal and a toy hopping across a table in exactly the same manner, preschoolers claim that only the the animal can move itself (Gelman & Gottfried, 1996).

- *Growth:* Children understand that, from their first appearance, animals get bigger and physically more complex but that inanimate objects do not change in this way. They believe, for example, that sea otters and termites become larger as time goes by but that tea kettles and teddy bears do not (Rosengren et al., 1991).

- *Internal parts:* Children know that the insides of animate objects contain different materials than the insides of inanimate objects. Preschool children judge that blood and bones are more likely to be inside an animate object but that cotton and metal are more likely to be inside an inanimate object (Simons & Keil, 1995).

- *Inheritance:* Children realize that only living things have offspring that resemble their parents. Asked to explain why a dog is pink, preschoolers believe that some biological characteristic of the parents probably made the dog pink; asked to explain why a can is pink, preschoolers rely on mechanical causes (e.g., a worker used a machine), not biological ones (Springer & Keil, 1991; Weissman & Kalish, 1999).

- *Healing:* Children understand that, when injured, animate things heal by regrowth whereas inanimate things must be fixed by humans. Preschoolers know that hair will grow back when cut from a child's head but must be repaired by a person when cut from a doll's head (Backscheider, Shatz, & Gelman, 1993).

Findings like these make it clear that preschoolers' naive theories of biology are complex. Of course, their theories aren't complete; they don't know, for instance, that genes are the biological basis for inheritance (Springer & Keil, 1991). And preschoolers' theories include some misconceptions; they believe, for example, that adopted children will physically resemble their adoptive parents (Solomon et al., 1996). Nevertheless, children's naive theories of biology, when joined with their naive theories of physics and psychology, provide powerful tools for making sense of their world and for understanding new experiences.

## Vygotsky's Theory of Cognitive Development

Like many authors, I often refer to child development as a journey that can proceed along many different paths. For Piaget and neo-Piagetian theorists, children make the journey alone. Other people (and culture in general) certainly influence the direction that children take, but the child is seen as a solitary adventurer-explorer boldly forging ahead.

Lev Vygotsky (1896–1934), a Russian psychologist, proposed a very different account. Vygotsky saw development as an apprenticeship in which children advance when they collaborate with others who are more skilled. According to Vygotsky (1978), children rarely make much headway on the developmental path when they walk alone; they progress when they walk hand in hand with an expert partner.

Vygotsky died of tuberculosis when he was only 37 years old, so he never had the opportunity to formulate a complete theory of cognitive development as Piaget did. Nevertheless, his ideas are influential because they fill some gaps in the Piagetian and neo-Piagetian accounts. Three of Vygotsky's most important contributions are the zone of proximal development, scaffolding, and private speech.

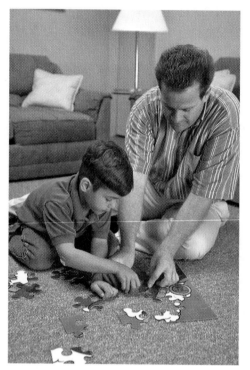

### The Zone of Proximal Development.

Four-year-old Ian and his dad often work on puzzles together. Ian does most of the work; like the father in the photo, his dad sometimes finds a piece that Ian needs or correctly orients a piece. When Ian tries to do the same puzzles himself, he rarely can complete them. **The difference between what Ian can do with assistance and what he can do alone defines the *zone of proximal development.*** That is, the zone refers to the difference between the level of performance a child can achieve when working independently and the higher level of performance that is possible when working under the guidance of more skilled adults or peers (Wertsch & Tulviste, 1992).

Think, for example, about a preschooler who is asked to clean her bedroom. She doesn't know where to begin. By structuring the task for the child—"start by putting away your books, then your toys, then your dirty clothes"—an adult can help the child accomplish what she cannot do by herself. Just as training wheels help children learn to ride a bike by allowing them to concentrate on other aspects of bicycling, collaborators help children perform effectively by providing structure, hints, and reminders.

The idea of a zone of proximal development follows naturally from Vygotsky's basic premise that cognition develops first in a social setting and only gradually comes under the child's independent control. Understanding how the shift from social to individual learning occurs brings us to the second of Vygotsky's key contributions.

### Scaffolding.

Have you ever had the good fortune to work with a master teacher, one who seemed to know exactly when to say something to help you over an obstacle but otherwise let you work uninterrupted? *Scaffolding* **refers to a teaching style that matches the amount of assistance to the learner's needs.** Early in learning a new task, when a child knows little, the teacher provides a lot of direct instruction. But, as the child begins to catch on to the task, the teacher provides less instruction and only occasional reminders (McNaughton & Leyland, 1990).

> Vygotsky viewed cognitive development as a colloboration between a novice child and more skilled teachers who scaffold children's learning.

We saw earlier how a parent helping a preschooler clean her room must provide detailed structure. But, as the child does the task more often, the parent needs to provide less structure. Similarly, when high school students first try to do proofs in geometry, the teacher must lead them through each step; as the students begin to understand how proofs are done and can do more on their own, the teacher gradually provides less help.

Do parents worldwide scaffold their children's learning? If so, do they use similar methods? The "Cultural Influences" feature answers these questions.

### How Do Parents in Different Cultures Scaffold Their Children's Learning?

Cross-cultural research by Barbara Rogoff and her colleagues (1993) suggests that parents and other adults in many cultures scaffold learning, but they do it in different ways. These researchers studied parents and 1- to 2-year-olds in four different settings: a medium-sized U.S. city, a small tribal village in India, a large city in Turkey, and a town in the highlands of Guatemala. In one part of the study, parents tried to get their toddlers to operate a novel toy (for example, a wooden doll that danced when a string was pulled). No ground rules or guidelines concerning teaching were given; parents were free to be as direct or uninvolved as they cared.

What did parents do? In all four cultural settings, the vast majority attempted to scaffold their children's learning, either by dividing a difficult task into easier subtasks or by doing parts of the task themselves, particularly the more complicated parts. However, as the graphs show, parents in different cultures scaffold in different ways.

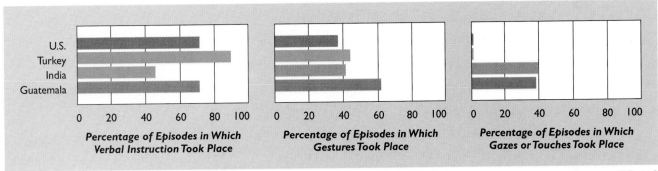

FIG 6–8

Turkish parents give the most verbal instruction and use some gestures (pointing, nodding, shrugging). U.S. parents also use these methods but to slightly lesser degrees. Turkish and U.S. parents almost never touch (such as nudging a child's elbow) or gaze (use eye contact, such as winking or staring). Indian parents seem to use roughly equal amounts of speech, gesture, and touch or gaze to scaffold. Guatemalan parents also use all three techniques, and, overall, Guatemalan parents give the most scaffolding of the four cultures. Evidently, parents worldwide try to simplify learning tasks for their children, but the methods that they use to scaffold learning vary across cultures. ●

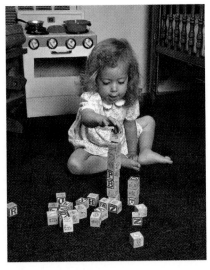

The defining characteristic of scaffolding—giving help but not more than is needed—clearly promotes learning (Plumert & Nichols-Whitehead, 1996). Youngsters do not learn readily when they are constantly told what to do or when they are simply left to struggle through a problem unaided. However, when teachers collaborate with them—allowing children to take on more and more of a task as they master its different elements—they learn more effectively (Pacifici & Bearison, 1991). Scaffolding is an important technique for transferring cognitive skills from others to the child.

**Private Speech.** Like Victoria from the vignette, the little girl in the photo is talking to herself as she is playing. **This behavior demonstrates** *private speech,*

**comments not directed to others but intended to help children regulate their own behavior.** Vygotsky (1934/1986) viewed private speech as an intermediate step toward self-regulation of cognitive skills. At first, children's behavior is regulated by speech from other people that is directed toward them. When youngsters first try to control their own behavior and thoughts without others present, they instruct themselves by speaking aloud. **Finally, as children gain ever greater skill, private speech becomes *inner speech,* Vygotsky's term for thought.**

If children use private speech to help control their behavior, then we should see children using it more often on difficult tasks than on easy tasks, and more often after a mistake than after a correct response. These predictions are generally supported in research (Berk, 1992), which documents the power of language in helping children learn to control their own behavior and thinking.

Vygotsky's view of cognitive development as an apprenticeship, a collaboration between expert and novice, complements the other views of cognitive development described in this module. Each perspective—the neo-Piagetian approaches, the child as theorist, and Vygotsky's work—provides a unique lens for viewing cognitive development. The chief characteristics of each perspective are described in the table.

### Characteristics of Some Alternatives to Piaget's Theory

| Approach | Characteristics |
|---|---|
| Neo-Piagetian theory | The closest of the alternatives to Piaget's original theory; includes qualitatively different stages of thinking, distinct conceptual structures, and increasing capacity of working memory as a growth mechanism. |
| The child as theorist | Key element is the idea that children form extensive naive theories in specialized areas, including physics, psychology, and biology; though incomplete and sometimes wrong, children's naive theories help them to understand their world. |
| Vygotsky's theory | Views cognitive development as a social enterprise; experts use scaffolding to help a novice acquire knowledge; children use private speech to help regulate their own thinking. |

TABLE 6–3

Contributing further to our understanding of cognitive development is information processing, the topic of Chapter 7.

## Check Your Learning

**1.** Neo-Piagetian theories typically retain Piaget's belief that _____.

**2.** By 3 or 4 months, infants know that objects move _____.

**3.** According to Wellman, the basic element of 2-year-olds' theory of mind is that _____.

**4.** Most 4-year-olds know that living things move, _____, have internal parts, resemble their parents, and heal when injured.

**5.** The _____ refers to the difference between what children can do alone and what they can do with skilled help.

**6.** Children use private speech more on difficult tasks than on easy tasks and more often after _____.

**Compare the role of cultural influences in Piaget's theory, neo-Piagetian theory, and Vygotsky's theory.**

**Answers:** (1) cognitive development includes qualitatively different stages of thinking, (2) along connected, continuous paths, (3) people have desires that cause behavior, (4) grow, (5) zone of proximal development, (6) they've made a mistake

# Piaget's Theory of Cognitive Development
## IN PERSPECTIVE

We know, of course, that infants do not have mature thoughts like the infant in *Look Who's Talking*. Instead, adultlike cognition is achieved gradually during infancy and childhood. In Module 6.1, we saw that Piaget's account of cognitive development is based on the idea that children actively try to understand their worlds. In Module 6.2, we discovered that children's search for understanding takes them through four distinct stages of thinking, beginning with sensorimotor thinking in infancy and ending with formal operational thinking in adolescence. In Module 6.3, we looked at strengths and weakness of Piaget's theory. In Module 6.4, we learned about three complementary views of cognitive development, the neo-Piagetian approach, the child as theorist, and Vygotsky's theory.

This chapter emphasizes that *children help determine their own development*. This idea is the cornerstone of Piaget's theory. Beginning in infancy and continuing through childhood and adolescence, children are constantly trying to make sense out of what goes on around them. Their understanding—and the shortcomings therein—is what propels cognitive development to more sophisticated levels. Experiences provide intellectual food for children to digest. Parents, teachers, and peers are important in cognitive development, not so much for what they teach directly as for the guidance and challenges they provide. Thus, as children take their developmental journeys, Piaget's child is a busy navigator, trying to understand the routes available and trying to decide among them.

## See for Yourself

The best way to see some of the developmental changes that Piaget described is to test some children with the same tasks that Piaget used. The conservation tasks shown on page 159 are good because they're simple to set up and children usually enjoy them. For each task, ask a 3- or 4-year-old and a 7- or 8-year-old to confirm that the two amounts are the same. Then transform one quantity as illustrated in the diagram on page 159 and ask children if the quantities are still the same. Ask them to explain their answers. The differences between 3- and 7-year-olds' answers are truly remarkable. See for yourself!

## Resources

*For more information about . . .*

activities for babies that promote cognitive development, read S. H. Jacobs's *Your Baby's Mind* (Bob Adams, 1992), which describes learning games and exercises for babies that are derived from Piaget's view of sensorimotor intelligence.

 Piaget's life, his theory, and his research (as well as related research on cognitive development), visit the Web site of the Jean Piaget Society: **http://www.piaget.org**

## Key Terms

accommodation 151
animism 158
assimilation 151
centration 158
concrete operational stage 160
deductive reasoning 162
egocentrism 157
equilibration 151

formal operational stage 161
inner speech 176
mental operations 160
neo-Piagetian theories 169
preoperational stage 155
primary circular reaction 154
private speech 175
scaffolding 174

scheme 150
secondary circular reaction 154
sensorimotor stage 153
tertiary circular reaction 154
theory of mind 171
zone of proximal development 174

SUMMARY

6

Piaget's Theory of
Cognitive Development

6.1  General Principles
     of Piaget's Theory
6.2  Piaget's Four Stages of
     Cognitive Development
6.3  Evaluating Piaget's Theory
6.4  Beyond Piaget's Theory

## 6.1 General Principles of Piaget's Theory

### Schemes

In Piaget's view, children construct their understanding of the world by creating schemes—mental categories of related events, objects, and knowledge. Infants' schemes are based on actions, but older children's and adolescents' schemes are based on functional, conceptual, and abstract properties.

### Assimilation and Accommodation

Schemes change constantly. In assimilation, experiences are readily incorporated into existing schemes. In accommodation, experiences cause schemes to be modified.

### Equilibration and Stages of Cognitive Development

When accommodation becomes much more frequent than assimilation, it is a sign that children's schemes are inadequate, so children reorganize them. This reorganization produces four different stages of mental development from infancy through adulthood. All individuals go through all four phases, but not necessarily at the same rate.

## 6.2 Piaget's Four Stages of Cognitive Development

### The Sensorimotor Stage

The first 2 years of life constitute Piaget's sensorimotor stage, which is divided into six substages. As infants progress through the substages, schemes become more sophisticated. By 8 to 12 months, one scheme is used in the service of another; by 12 to 18 months, infants experiment with schemes; and by 18 to 24 months, infants begin to engage in symbolic processing.

### The Preoperational Stage

From ages 2 to 7 years, children are in Piaget's preoperational stage. Although now capable of using symbols, their thinking is limited by egocentrism, the inability to see the world from another's point of view. Preoperational children also are centered in their thinking and sometimes confuse appearance with reality.

### The Concrete Operational Stage

Between ages 7 and 11 children begin to use and can reverse mental operations to solve perspective-taking and conservation problems. The main limit to thinking at this stage is that it is focused on the concrete and real.

### The Formal Operational Stage

With the onset of formal operational thinking, adolescents can think hypothetically and reason abstractly. In deductive reasoning, they understand that conclusions are based on logic, not experience.

## 6.3 Evaluating Piaget's Theory

### Applying Piaget's Theory

Teachers and parents have used Piaget's theory to foster children's development. The theory emphasizes the roles of discovery in learning, of providing experiences slightly ahead of the child's level, and of learning from inconsistencies and errors.

### Criticisms of the Theory

Piaget's theory has been faulted because children's performance on tasks is sometimes better explained by ideas that are not part of his theory. A second shortcoming is that children's performance from one task to the next is not as consistent as the theory predicts. A third is that, with training, children can readily grasp ideas that should be too advanced for them based on their Piagetian stage. A fourth shortcoming is that children and adolescents often use simpler forms of reasoning than they should for their Piagetian stage.

## 6.4 Beyond Piaget's Theory

### Neo-Piagetian Approaches to Cognitive Development

Neo-Piagetian theorists adhere to the basic premise of Piaget's theory that thought progresses through qualitatively different stages. However, neo-Piagetian theories propose that children develop distinct conceptual structures in different domains. In these theories, development to more advanced cognitive structures is thought to reflect, in part, increases in the capacity of working memory.

### The Child as Theorist

Another approach to cognitive development is rooted in Piaget's metaphor of the child as scientist. However, in contrast to Piaget's idea that children create a comprehensive theory that integrates all their knowledge, the modern view is that children are specialists, generating naive theories in particular domains, including physics, psychology, and biology.

### Vygotsky's Theory of Cognitive Development

Vygotsky believed that cognition develops first in a social setting and only gradually comes under the child's independent control. The difference between what children can do with assistance and what they can do alone defines the zone of proximal development.

Control of cognitive skills is most readily transferred from others to the child through scaffolding, a teaching style that allows children to take on more and more of a task as they master its different components.

Children often talk to themselves, particularly when the task is difficult or after they have made a mistake. Such private speech is one way that children regulate their behavior, and it represents an intermediate step in the self-regulation of cognitive skills.

**7**

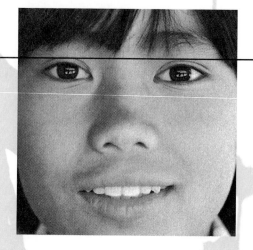

Perhaps you've seen the classic science fiction film *2001: A Space Odyssey.* The plot involves a computer—HAL*—who becomes upset and then diabolical when he learns that he is to be disconnected in order to solve a problem on board his spaceship. When Arthur Clarke wrote *2001* in 1968, "living, feeling computers" must have seemed like wild stuff. Even today, the question of whether computers can think (or feel) stimulates

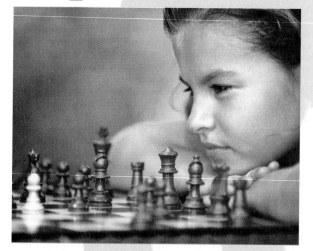

heated debate. What is not arguable, however, is that many psychologists have borrowed heavily from computer science to formulate their ideas about human thinking and how it develops. Their approach, called information processing, is the focus of this chapter. We'll begin, in Module 7.1, by talking about some general characteristics of the information-processing approach. In Module 7.2, we look at children's memory, an aspect of development that information processing has illuminated well. In Module 7.3, we'll consider information-processing research on academic skills like reading, writing, and arithmetic.

---

*Part of the trivia associated with *2001* is that Clarke created the name HAL by moving backward in the alphabet from each of the letters in IBM.

# Information-Processing Approaches to Cognitive Development

# 7.1

- **Basic Features of the Information-Processing Approach**
- **How Information Processing Changes with Development**
- **Comparing Information Processing and Piaget's Theory**

## An Introduction to Information Processing

### Learning Objectives

- What are the basic characteristics of the information-processing approach?
- According to information-processing psychologists, how does children's thinking change as they develop?
- How does information processing differ from Piaget's theory?

> *Phung, a 15-year-old girl, has just completed driver's ed and loves getting behind the wheel. Most of the time, her parents are okay when she drives; they don't scream or get hysterical if she goes a little fast or hits the brakes too hard. But every time Phung asks to turn on the radio, they go ballistic. "No, no, no, you need to pay attention to your driving, not listen to music," they say. Phung thinks this is stupid. What does listening to music have to do with how well she drives?*

Phung's question is a good one, and later in this module we'll see that information-processing researchers have an answer for her. But first, let's learn more about information processing as a theoretical approach.

### Basic Features of the Information-Processing Approach

A few weeks ago, a friend of mine, Jim, bought a new computer for his office. Jim was eager to use the new machine to handle his correspondence, prepare graphs for sales meetings, and when his boss wasn't looking, surf the Web. But enthusiasm soon turned to disappointment: Although Jim's computer could do all these things, it was incredibly slow and time-consuming. The word-processing software seemed to take forever to load, and it seemed to Jim that he'd spent hours staring at the Windows 98© hourglass while waiting for Web pages to appear. After some oaths not fit to print in a G-rated textbook, it gradually dawned on Jim that saving a few hundred dollars by getting a slower processor and less memory was probably a mistake. His computer simply lacked the hardware necessary to make the software run efficiently.

**This simple distinction between computer hardware and computer software is the basis of an approach to human thinking known as *information processing.*** The information-processing approach arose in the 1960s and is now one of the principal approaches to cognitive development (Kail & Bisanz, 1992; Klahr & MacWhinney, 1998). You remember, from Module 1.2, that information-processing theorists believe human thinking is based on both mental hardware and mental software. Mental hardware refers to mental and neural structures that are built in and that allow the mind to operate. If the hardware in a personal computer refers to random-access memory, the central processor, and the like, what does mental hardware refer to? Information-processing theorists generally agree that mental hardware has three components: sensory memory, working memory, and long-term memory. The diagram shows how they are related.

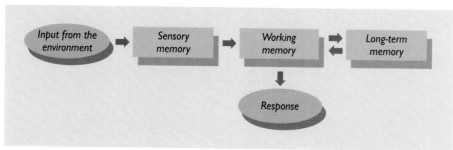

FIG 7–1

*Sensory memory* **is where information is held in raw, unanalyzed form very briefly (no longer than a few seconds).** For example, look at your hand as you clench your fist, then rapidly open your hand (so that your fingers are extended) and then rapidly reclench your fist. If you watch your fingers, you'll see an image of your fingers that lasts momentarily after you reclench your hand. What you're seeing is an image stored in sensory memory.

*Working memory* **is the site of ongoing cognitive activity.** Some theorists liken working memory to a carpenter's workbench, which includes space for storing the materials for a current project as well as space for the carpenter to do the sawing, nailing, and painting involved in the project (Klatzky, 1980). In much the same way, working memory includes both ongoing cognitive processes and the information that they require (Baddeley, 1996). For example, as you read these sentences, part of working memory is allocated to the cognitive processes responsible for determining the meanings of individual words; working memory also stores the results of these analyses briefly while they are used by other cognitive processes to give meaning to sequences of words.

This description of working memory probably has a familiar ring to it. That's because working memory is a common element in neo-Piagetian approaches to cognitive development, described in Module 6.4. And, if you're familiar with personal computers, you'll recognize that working memory resembles random-access memory because that's where we load programs we want to run and temporarily store the data those programs are using.

In the information-processing view, mental hardware includes sensory, working, and long-term memories.

*Long-term memory* **is a limitless, permanent storehouse of knowledge of the world.** Long-term memory is like a computer's hard drive, a fairly permanent storehouse of programs and data. It includes facts (e.g., Charles Lindberg flew the Atlantic in the "Spirit of St. Louis"), personal events (e.g., "I moved to Maryland in July 1999"), and skills (e.g., how to swim the butterfly).

Information rarely is forgotten from long-term memory, though it is sometimes hard to access. For example, do you remember the name of the African American agricultural chemist who pioneered crop rotation methods and invented peanut butter? If his name doesn't come to mind, look at this list:

*Marconi   Carver   Fulton   Luther*

Now do you know the answer? (If not, it appears before "Check Your Learning," on page 187.) Just as books are sometimes misplaced in a library, you sometimes cannot find a fact in long-term memory. Given a list of names, though, you can go directly to the location in long-term memory associated with each name and determine which is the famed chemist.

Mental hardware allows us to "run" mental software, so the next question is, what is mental software? To answer this question, think about personal computer software you've used, such as programs for word processing, spreadsheets, or graphing. In each case, the software was designed to accomplish a specific function. In much the same way, mental software refers to mental programs that are the basis for performing particular tasks. According to information-processing psychologists, children have special mental software that allows them to accomplish particular tasks, such as reading, doing arithmetic, or finding their way to and from school.

Let's look at a simple example to see how information-processing psychologists analyze cognitive processes. Suppose a mother asks her son to make his bed, brush his teeth, and take out the trash. A bit later, the mother wonders if she asked

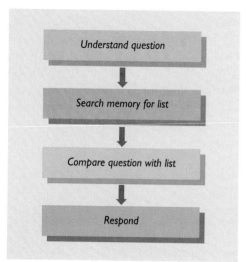

FIG 7–2

her son about the trash, so she says, "Did I ask you to take out the trash?" Almost immediately, he says, "Yes." Despite the speed of the boy's reply, information-processing theorists believe that his mental software has gone through four general steps to answer the question, as shown in the diagram. First, the mental software must understand the mother's question. That is, the software must decode the sounds of the mother's speech and give them meaning. Next, the software searches working memory and long-term memory for the mother's earlier requests. When that list is located and retrieved, the software compares "take out the trash" with each of the items on the list. Finding a match, the software selects "yes" as the appropriate answer to the question. Thus, the processes of understanding, searching, comparing, and responding create a mental program that allows the boy to answer his mother.

In the next section, we'll see how child development researchers use these ideas to understand how children's thinking changes as they grow older.

## How Information Processing Changes with Development

All theories of cognitive development try to explain how experiences and mental structures interact to produce cognitive growth. You may recall from Module 6.1 that Piaget's explanation of cognitive development emphasized equilibration—the process by which mental structures are massively reorganized so that schemes can assimilate information more readily. Information-processing theorists believe that developmental change comes in several important forms, rather than through a single mechanism like equilibration (Kail & Bisanz, 1992; Siegler, 1989). Let's look at five of them.

### More Efficient Strategies.
Older children rely upon more efficient strategies to solve problems (Shrager & Siegler, 1998; Schneider & Bjorklund, 1998). That is, as children develop they use strategies that are faster, more accurate, and easier. Having lost a hat on the way to school, a younger child might search the entire route; an older child might recall taking off the hat midway to school and so only search the last half of the route (Sophian & Wellman, 1987). Both children will probably find the missing hat, but the older child's approach is more efficient.

*As children develop, they use more efficient strategies, have more working memory, have better inhibitory processes, more automatic processes, and more rapid processing.*

How do children learn more effective strategies? Of course, parents and teachers often show youngsters more effective strategies. However, youngsters also learn new strategies by watching more skilled children (Crowley & Siegler, 1999). For example, children and adolescents at an arcade watch others play in order to learn good game strategies. Children also discover new strategies on their own (Siegler & Jenkins, 1989). For example, when my daughter was 5, I watched her match words with their antonyms in a language workbook. The pages always had an equal number of words and antonyms, so she quickly learned to connect the last word with the one remaining antonym, without thinking about the meaning of either.

Thus, with input from parents, teachers, peers, and their own observations, children's mental software becomes more powerful and more efficient. Sometimes these changes occur abruptly—when children immediately see the benefits of a better way of solving a problem—but more often they occur gradually (Alibali, 1999).

### Increased Capacity of Working Memory.

Remember that working memory is the part of mental hardware responsible for ongoing mental activity. What would happen if this work space became larger as children grew? To answer this question, think about technological change in personal computers: Today's personal computers run much more impressive software, in part, because they have much more random-access memory available than their counterparts from the 1980s and 1990s. If you apply this technological change to children's development, the implication is clear. The diagram shows that, compared to younger children, older children have more working memory to allocate to mental software and to storing information (Case, 1992; Kail, 1995). Consequently, older children usually outperform younger children on tasks where working memory is important for performance, such as reading or solving complicated problems.

FIG 7–3

### More Effective Inhibitory Processes.

Yesterday I was listening to the radio and heard that classic oldie "The Lion Sleeps Tonight." Unfortunately, I spent the rest of the afternoon hearing "aweem away, aweem away" over and over in my mind. Undoubtedly, you, too, have had this experience—a thought gets into your head and you can't get rid of it. Returning to the workbench metaphor of working memory, interfering ideas are tools or materials left from previous projects that are not needed for a current project but nevertheless take up precious space on the workbench.

Fortunately, most of the time irrelevant and unwanted ideas do not intrude on our thinking. Why not? **Inhibitory processes prevent task-irrelevant information from entering working memory.** These processes, which rely upon the attentional processes described in Module 5.3, improve steadily during childhood (Dempster, 1995). Consequently, older children and adolescents' thinking is more sophisticated because better inhibition means fewer disruptions from irrelevant stimulation and therefore more efficient working memory. When an older child is deciding the best way to a new friend's house, the sound of popcorn popping or thoughts of an upcoming swim meet are less likely to intrude on working memory and disrupt his planning (Casey et al., 1997; Harnishfeger, 1995).

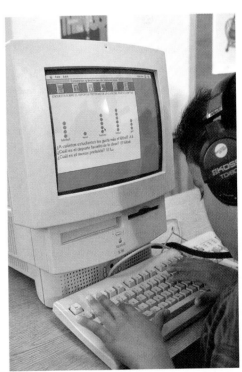

### Increased Automatic Processing.

Think back to the days when you were learning a brand new skill, like how to type. In the beginning, you had to think about every single step in the process. If, as a novice typist, you were asked to type "child," you probably started like the child in the photograph, by trying to remember the location of "c" on the keyboard and then deciding which finger to use to reach that key. You had to repeat this process for each of the remaining four letters. But as your skill grew, each step became easier until you could type "child" without even thinking about it; your fingers seem to move automatically to the right keys, in the right sequence. **Cognitive activities that require virtually no effort are known as *automatic processes.***

To understand how automatic processes affect developmental change, we need to return to working memory. In the early phases of learning a skill, each individual step (such as finding a "c" on the keyboard) must be stored in working memory. Because there are so many steps, an unmastered skill can easily occupy much of the capacity of working memory. In contrast, when a skill has been mastered, individual steps are no longer stored in working memory, which means that more capacity is available for other activities. Thus, beginning drivers like Phung are told to keep the music turned off because listening would consume capacity of working memory that is needed for driving. However, with more experience behind the wheel, many driving skills become automatic, freeing capacity that can be used to listen to the radio. (Patience, Phung, your time will come!)

Compared to adolescents and adults, children have limited experience in most tasks, so they perform few processes automatically. Instead, like Phung, their processing requires substantial working memory capacity. As children gain experience, however, some processes become automatic, freeing working memory capacity for other processes (Kail & Park, 1990). Thus, when faced with complex tasks involving many processes, older children are more likely to succeed because they can perform some of the processes automatically. In contrast, younger children must think about all or most of the processes, taxing or even exceeding the capacity of their working memory.

### Increased Speed of Processing.

As children develop, they complete most mental processes at an ever-faster rate (Cerella & Hale, 1994). Improved speed is obvious when we measure how fast children of different ages respond on tasks. Across a wide range of cognitive tasks such as deciding which of two numbers is greater, naming a pictured object, and searching memory, 4- and 5-year-olds are generally one-third as fast as adults, whereas 8- and 9-year-olds are one-half as fast as adults (Kail, 2000).

Age differences in processing speed are critical when a specified number of actions must be completed in a fixed period of time. For example, perhaps you've had the unfortunate experience of trying to understand a professor who lectures at warp speed. The instructor's speech was so rapid that your cognitive processes couldn't keep up, which meant that you didn't get much out of the lecture. The problem is even more serious for children, who process information much more slowly than adults.

The five types of developmental change—more efficient strategies, more working memory, better inhibitory processes, more automatic processing, and more rapid processing—occur throughout infancy, childhood, adolescence, and adulthood. Furthermore, sometimes the different types of change interact with each other. To understand this interaction, think back to the analogy of working memory as a workbench. A carpenter who quickly finds the tools she needs can complete the project on her workbench promptly and move on to other projects. A carpenter who must search endlessly for tools will complete the project much more slowly. In much the same way, as children process information more rapidly, they use working memory more efficiently. With the five types of change interacting in this fashion (and functioning independently), information processing provides a very detailed account of cognitive development.

## Comparing Information Processing and Piaget's Theory

Piaget's theory is so influential that it has long been the standard by which other approaches to cognitive development are measured. By comparing information processing with Piaget's theory, you can see some of the strengths and weaknesses of each (Kail & Bisanz, 1992).

One important difference is that Piaget's work is a single comprehensive theory, whereas information processing represents a general approach encompassing many different theories to describe specific components of cognitive development. Thus, the advantage of Piaget's work is that it is comprehensive—all the links between different facets of cognitive development are included in his theory. But the advantage of the information-processing approach is that specific components of cognition are described with incredible precision. In essence, Piaget emphasized the "whole" of cognitive development, whereas information processing emphasizes the "parts." Both the whole and the parts are important for complete understanding of cognitive development, so Piaget's theory and information processing complement each other.

A second difference is that Piaget emphasized periodic, qualitative change in cognition: Children's thinking remains at one stage for years, then changes abruptly as equilibration propels thinking into the next, qualitatively different stage. In contrast, when the five types of change in information processing are combined, the result is a steady age-related increase in cognitive skill. Unlike Piaget's account, there are no abrupt or qualitative changes that create distinct cognitive stages. Instead, as you can see in the diagram, cognitive change is constant and gradual. Since both types of change play a role in development, here, too, Piaget's theory and information processing complement each other.

Keep these differences in mind as you read about the development of memory (Module 7.2) and academic skills (Module 7.3). Think about the need to balance the "whole" with the "parts," and think about the role of abrupt change versus gradual change in cognitive development.

*Piaget emphasized the "whole" of cognitive growth and abrupt change; information processing emphasizes the "parts" of cognitive growth and gradual change.*

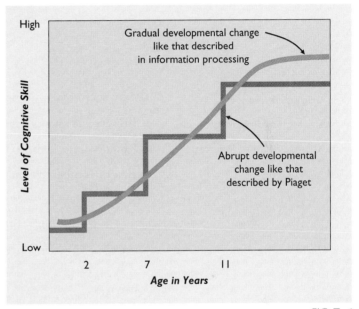

FIG 7–4

*Response to question on page 183:* The agricultural chemist who pioneered crop rotation while on the faculty of Tuskegee Institute of Technology is George Washington Carver.

## Check Your Learning

**1.** Information-processing psychologists believe that mental hardware includes sensory memory, working memory, and _____.

**2.** Random-access memory in a personal computer is analogous to _____, according to the information-processing view.

**3.** _____ refers to specialized processes that allow children to complete particular tasks, such as reading or arithmetic.

**4.** According to the information-processing view, the older child's greater cognitive skill can be traced to more efficient strategies, _____, more effective inhibition, increased automatic processing, and more rapid speed of processing.

**5.** Piaget's theory provides a comprehensive account of cognitive development, whereas information processing provides _____.

**6.** Piaget emphasizes distinct stages in cognitive development, whereas information processing emphasizes _____.

 In Module 3.3, you learned that infants with low birth weight often lag behind their peers. Use the information-processing approach to propose some specific ways that these children's cognitive development might be delayed.

**Answers:** (1) long-term memory, (2) working memory, (3) Mental software, (4) increased working memory capacity, (5) very detailed explanations of specific aspects of cognitive growth, (6) steady, gradual change

# 7.2

- **Origins of Memory**
- **Strategies for Remembering**
- **Knowledge and Memory**

## Memory

### Learning Objectives

● **How well do infants remember?**

● **How do strategies help children to remember?**

● **How does children's knowledge influence what they remember?**

*One afternoon 4-year-old Cheryl came home sobbing and reported that Mr. Johnson, a neighbor and longtime family friend, had taken down her pants and touched her "private parts." Her mother was shocked. Mr. Johnson had always seemed an honest, decent man, which made her wonder if Cheryl's imagination had simply run wild. Yet, at times, he did seem a bit peculiar, so her daughter's claim had a ring of truth.*

Regrettably, episodes like this are all too common in America today. When child abuse is suspected, and the child is the sole eyewitness, the child must testify to prosecute the alleged abuser. But can preschool children like Cheryl be trusted to recall events accurately on the witness stand? To answer this question, we need to understand more about how memory develops. We'll start by examining the origins of memory in infancy, then see what factors contribute to the development of memory in childhood and adolescence.

### Origins of Memory

Roots of memory are laid down in the first few months after birth. Young babies remember events for days or even weeks at a time. Some of the studies that opened our eyes to the infant's ability to remember were conducted by Carolyn Rovee-Collier (1997; 1999). The method used in her studies is shown in the photo. A ribbon from a mobile is attached to a 2- or 3-month old's leg; within a few minutes, the babies learn to kick to make the mobile move. When Rovee-Collier brought the mobile to the infants' homes several days or a few weeks later, babies would still kick to make the mobile move. If Rovee-Collier waited several weeks to return, most babies forgot that kicking moved the mobile. When that happened, she gave them a reminder—she moved the mobile herself without attaching the ribbon to their foot. Then she would return the next day, hook up the apparatus, and the babies would kick to move the mobile.

Rovee-Collier's experiments show that three important features of memory exist as early as 2 and 3 months of age: (1) an event from the past is remembered, (2) over time, the event can no longer be recalled, and (3) a cue can serve to dredge up a memory that seems to have been forgotten.

Once youngsters begin to talk, we can study their memory skills using most of the same methods we use with older children and adults. Research using these methods has linked age-related improvement in memory to two factors (Kail, 1990; Schneider & Bjorklund, 1998). First, as children grow, they use more effective strategies for remembering. Second, children's growing factual knowledge of the world allows them to organize information more completely and therefore to remember better. We'll look at each of these factors in the next few pages.

## Strategies for Remembering

Last week, I wrote four pages for this book that would have made Tom Clancy green with envy, when the unthinkable happened—a power failure knocked out my computer and all those wonderful words were lost. If I had only saved the text to the hard drive . . . but I hadn't.

This tale of woe sets the stage for understanding how strategies aid memory. Recall that working memory is used for briefly storing a small amount of information, such as the words in these sentences. However, as you read additional sentences, they displace words read earlier from working memory. For you to learn this information, it must be transferred to long-term memory. Anything not transferred from working memory to long-term memory is lost, just as my words vanished from the computer's memory with the power failure.

***Memory strategies* are activities that improve remembering.** Some strategies help maintain information in working memory. Others help transfer information to long-term memory. Still others help retrieve information from long-term memory. Obviously, there are many memory strategies.

> As children develop, they begin to use different strategies to improve memory.

Children begin to use memory strategies early. Preschool children look at or touch objects that they've been told to remember (DeLoache, 1984). Looking and touching aren't very effective, but they tell us that preschoolers understand that they should be doing something to try to remember; remembering doesn't happen automatically!

During the elementary-school years, children begin to use more powerful strategies. For example, 7- and 8-year-olds use rehearsal, a strategy of repetitively naming information that is to be remembered. As children get older, they learn other memory strategies and they learn when it is best to use them. That is, children and adolescents begin to identify different kinds of memory problems and which memory strategies are most appropriate. For example, when reading a textbook or watching a television newscast, the aim is to remember the main points, not the individual words or sentences. Rehearsal is ineffective for this task, but outlining or writing a summary are good strategies because they identify the main points and organize them (Kail, 1990). Older children and adolescents often use outlines to help them remember information in textbooks. Also, as children grow, they are more likely to write down information on calendars so that, like the boy in the photo, they won't forget future events.

Thus, successful learning and remembering involve identifying the goals of memory problems and choosing suitable strategies (Schneider & Bjorklund, 1998). As you might expect, younger children sometimes misjudge the objectives of a memory task and then choose an inappropriate strategy. For example, young children may believe that they are supposed to remember a textbook passage verbatim whereas they really only need to remember its gist. Or, they may understand the memory task, but not pick the best strategy. For example, to remember the gist of a textbook paragraph, a younger child might rehearse it (a bad choice) whereas an older child would outline it (a good choice). Children gradually become more skilled at identifying task goals and selecting appropriate strategies, but even high-school students do not always use effective learning strategies when they should (Lovett & Pillow, 1996; Slate, Jones, & Dawson, 1993).

After children choose a memory strategy, they need to monitor its effectiveness. That is, they need to decide if the strategy is working. If it's not, they need to begin anew, reanalyzing the memory task to select a better approach. If the strategy is working, they should determine the portion of the material they have not yet mastered and concentrate their efforts there.

Monitoring improves gradually with age. For example, elementary-school children can accurately identify which material they have not yet learned, but they do not consistently focus their study efforts on this material (Kail, 1990).

The diagram summarizes the sequence of steps in monitoring. Perhaps this diagram looks familiar? It should. Analyzing, strategizing, and monitoring are the key elements of productive studying. Study goals may change when you move from this book to your math text to a novel that you are reading for English, but the basic sequence still holds. Studying should always begin with a clear understanding of what goal you are trying to achieve, because this sets the stage for all the events that follow. Too often, students just read a text, without any clear idea of what they should be getting out of the material. Always plan a study session with a well-defined goal, such as "Become familiar with the basic contents of Module 7.2 in my child development book." With this goal, you would start by carefully reading the outline, learning objectives, and vignette that begin the module. Then skim the module, paying close attention to headings, sentences in the margins, boxes, and topic sentences of paragraphs. Now—before even reading the module—write an outline of its main topics. If you can't, then you need to skim again and try again—you don't yet understand the overall structure of the module. If you can write an outline, then you know you are familiar with the basic contents of the chapter, and you're ready to go on to reading the module carefully to master its details.

Skilled use of strategies is one aspect of effective remembering; as you'll see in the next few pages, knowledge is also an aid to memory.

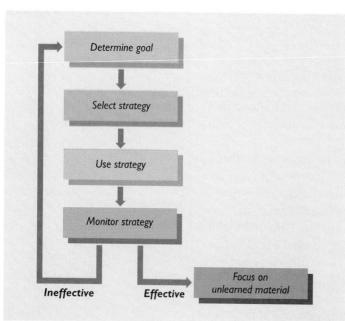

FIG 7–5

## Knowledge and Memory

Let's start our examination of how knowledge influences memory by looking at a study by Michelene Chi (1978). She asked 10-year-olds and adults to remember sequences of numbers. In the graph, you can see that adults remembered more numbers than children. Next she asked participants to remember the positions of objects in a matrix. This time 10-year-olds' recall was much better than adults'.

What was responsible for this unusual reversal of the expected age difference? Actually, the objects were chess pieces on a chessboard, and the children were skilled chess players but the adults were novices. The positions of the pieces were taken from actual games, so they were familiar configurations for the child chess players. For the adults, who lacked knowledge of chess, the patterns seemed arbitrary. But the children had the knowledge to organize and give meaning to the patterns, so they could recognize and then recall the whole configuration instead of many isolated pieces. It was as if the adults were seeing this meaningless pattern:

*n n c c b a s b c c b n*

whereas the children were seeing this:

*n b c   c b s   a b c   c n n.*

The link between knowledge and memory is also illustrated in the "Real Children" feature.

FIG 7–6

### Keith Visits the Air Force Museum

A few years ago, I went with a troop of Boy Scouts to visit the U.S. Air Force Museum in Dayton, Ohio. On the drive home, I asked James, a 12-year-old who likes computers and basketball but not airplanes, what he had seen in the museum. "Uh, lotsa planes. Some jets and prop jobs. Oh, and some rockets, too," was his reply. I posed the same question to Keith, another 12-year-old, whose father is a pilot and aeronautical engineer and who lives and breathes airplanes. Keith began, "This was so incredibly cool. I started in the Air Power Gallery and saw a Lightning, a Mustang, a Thunderbolt, a Mitchell, a Liberator, a Flying Fortress, and a Super Fort. Then we went to the Modern Flight hangar. They had a Stratojet, a Stratofort, and a Hustler. There was a Sabre and a Super Sabre there, too." Keith went on like this for another 5 minutes. When he was done, I estimated that Keith had remembered the names of 40 to 50 airplanes.

Amused, I asked Keith to try to remember the following words: *table, green, rain, bus, spoon, dad, coal, doll, salt, doctor, hill, tennis, shirt, piano, nickel, robin.* He paused for a moment, then began to remember words. He finished with 6 words from the list of 16. How could Keith recall so few words from my list when he had remembered 7 or 8 times that many planes? The key is Keith's extensive aeronautical knowledge, which allowed him to organize his recall of planes. He began by recalling World War II fighters (Lightning, Mustang, Thunderbolt), then World War II bombers (Mitchell, Liberator, Flying Fortress, Super Fortress). He continued this way, organizing his recall by category. However, when asked to recall my 16 words, where his knowledge of airplanes was useless, Keith had just an average 12-year-old's memory. For Keith, as for Chi's chess experts, knowledge is memory power. ●

FIG 7–7

Source: Kail, 1990.

Usually, of course, the knowledge that allows a child to organize information and give it meaning increases gradually with age (Schneider & Bjorklund, 1998). Researchers often depict knowledge as a network like this one, which shows part of a 13-year-old's knowledge of animals. The entries in the network are linked by different types of associations. Some of the links denote membership in categories (dalmatian is a dog), and others denote properties (elephant has a trunk). **Still others denote a** *script,* **a memory structure used to describe the sequence in which events occur.** The list of events in walking the dog is a script.

A network diagram like this for a younger child would have fewer entries and fewer and weaker connecting links. Consequently, the youngster cannot organize information as extensively, which makes remembering more difficult than for an older child.

Nevertheless, the knowledge that young children have is organized, and this turns out to be a powerful asset. In the case of events that fit scripts, for example, they needn't try to remember each individual activity; instead, they simply remember the script. When the preschooler in the photo wants to tell his dad about baking cookies, he can simply retrieve the "baking cookies" script and use it to organize his recall of the different events.

Though knowledge can improve memory, it can also distort memory. If a specific experience does not correspond to children's knowledge, the experience is likely to be forgotten or distorted so that it conforms to the child's knowledge. For example, told a story about a female helicopter pilot, many youngsters will remember the pilot as a man because their network specifies that pilots are men (Levy & Boston, 1994).

Scripts, too, can distort memory because children cannot distinguish what they experienced from what is specified in the script. For example, the boy baking cookies may remember greasing the cookie sheet simply because this is part of the baking cookie script, not because he actually did the greasing (Hudson, 1988).

Thus, although children's growing knowledge usually helps them to remember, sometimes it can interfere with accurate memory. In the next section, we'll look at another link between knowledge and memory—children's memory of their own lives.

## Autobiographical Memory.   Start by answering these questions:

*Who was your teacher in fourth grade?*

*Where (and with whom) was your first kiss?*

*Was your high-school graduation indoors or outdoors?*

In answering these questions, you searched memory, just as you would search memory to answer questions such as "What is the capitol of Ohio?" and "Who invented the sewing machine?" However, answers to questions about Ohio and sewing machines are based on general knowledge that you have not experienced personally; answers to questions about *your* fourth-grade teacher, *your* first kiss, and *your* high-school graduation are based on knowledge unique to your own life. **Autobiographical memory refers to people's memory of the significant events and experiences of their own lives.** Autobiographical memory is important because it helps people construct a personal life history. In addition, autobiographical memory allows people to relate their experiences to others, creating socially shared memories (Nelson, 1993).

Autobiographical memory originates in the preschool years, when parents encourage children to think about the past by asking them to recall recent events. Picking up a 3-year-old from preschool, a parent may ask, "Who did you play with?" "What did you have for snack?" In questions like these, parents usually focus on *who, what, where, when,* and *why.* In this way, they teach their children the aspects of events that are important. Their questions also emphasize the importance of temporal and causal order in organizing the past (Schneider & Bjorklund, 1998).

Although autobiographical memory begins in the preschool years, older children, adolescents, and adults remember little from these years (Kail, 1990). **Infantile amnesia refers to the inability to remember events from one's early life.** Adults recall nothing from infancy, but they remember an ever-increasing number of events from about age 3 or 4 years (Eacott, 1999; Schneider & Bjorklund, 1998). For example, when the 2-year-old in the photo is older, he won't remember his brother's birth (Peterson & Rideout, 1998; Quas et al., 1999).* But there's a good chance the 2-year-old will remember his brother's second—or certainly his third—birthday.

Infantile amnesia has several possible explanations. One emphasizes language, the topic of Chapter 9. Once children learn to talk (at about age 2 years), they tend to rely on language to represent their past (Nelson, 1993). Consequently, their earlier, prelingual experiences may be difficult to retrieve from memory, just as after you re-organize your bedroom you may have trouble finding things.

Another explanation for infantile amnesia is based on a child's sense of self. I describe this in detail in Module 11.1, but the key idea is that 1- and 2-year-olds rapidly acquire a sense that they exist independently. Some theorists (Howe & Courage, 1997) argue that a child's sense of self provides an organizing framework for autobiographical memory. Infants and toddlers lack a sense of self, so their experiences are not represented in autobiographical memory, which is why they can't be recalled later in life.

Infantile amnesia, in which people can't recall events from early in life, may be due to limits in infants' and toddlers' language and their sense of self.

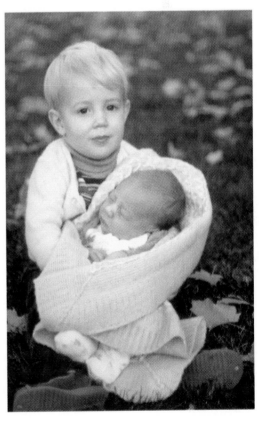

---

*Perhaps you're not convinced, because you can vividly recall significant events that occurred when you were 2, such as the birth of a sibling, a move to a different home, or the death of a close friend or relative. In reality, you are probably *not* remembering the actual event. Instead, I can almost guarantee that you're remembering others' retelling of these events and your role in them, not the events themselves. Events like these are often socially shared memories and that's what you're remembering.

Thus, personal experiences from our earliest years usually can't be recalled because of inadequate language or inadequate sense of self. Beginning in the preschool years, however, autobiographical memory provides a cohesive framework for remembering life's significant events. Unfortunately, some children's autobiographical memories include memories of abuse. Can these memories be trusted? We'll see in the next section.

## Eyewitness Testimony.

Remember Cheryl, the 4-year-old in the module-opening vignette who claimed that a neighbor had touched her "private parts"? If Cheryl's comments lead to a police investigation, Cheryl's testimony will be critical. But can her recall of events be trusted? This question is difficult to answer. In legal proceedings, children are often interviewed repeatedly, sometimes as many as 10 to 15 times. Over the course of repeated questioning, they may confuse what actually happened with what others suggest may have happened. When, as in the situation in the photo, the questioner is an adult in a position of authority, children often believe that what is suggested by the adult actually happened (Lampinen & Smith, 1995). As you'll see in the "Focus on Research" feature, preschoolers are particularly prone to confusion of this sort (Ceci & Bruck, 1995; 1998).

FOCUS ON RESEARCH

### Do Stereotypes and Suggestions Influence Preschoolers' Reports?

*Who were the investigators and what was the aim of the study?* During legal proceedings, children are often interviewed repeatedly. In the process, interviewers sometimes suggest that certain events took place. Cheryl might be asked, "When Mr. Johnson touched your private parts, was anyone else around?" a question implying that Mr. Johnson definitely touched Cheryl. Furthermore, interviewers may suggest to children that the accused is a "bad person," which may make suggestions of abuse more plausible to children. Michelle D. Leichtman and Stephen J. Ceci (1995) wanted to know if repeated questioning and hints about an adult's "nature" would influence preschool children's recall of events.

*How did the investigators measure the topic of interest?* Leichtman and Ceci had a man named Sam Stone briefly visit classes of 3- and 4-year-olds and 5- and 6-year-olds at a day-care center. During his visit, Sam greeted the teacher, who introduced him to the class. Sam mentioned that the story being read by the teacher was one of his favorites; then he waved goodbye and left the room.

Leichtman and Ceci created four different conditions, shown in the diagram at the top of page 195, that differed in what children were told before and after Sam's visit. Children in the *control* condition were interviewed after the visit, every week for 4 weeks. In these interviews, youngsters were simply asked to describe Sam's visit.

The *stereotype* condition differed from the control condition in one way: Three times prior to Sam's visit, teachers described Sam as a nice but clumsy man, thereby implying that children should expect Sam to be clumsy. The *suggestions* condition also differed from the control condition: During each of the four weekly interviews that followed Sam's visit, the interviewer made misleading suggestions that Sam had ripped a book and soiled a teddy bear, such as "Remember when Sam Stone ripped the book? Did he rip it on purpose or by accident?" (p. 577). Of course, he had done neither. In the fourth condition, *stereotypes plus suggestions,* teachers told

| Condition | Phase 1 | Phase 2 | Phase 3 | Phase 4 |
|---|---|---|---|---|
| Control | | | 4 neutral interviews | |
| Stereotypes | Sam is nice but clumsy | Sam visits the day-care center briefly | 4 neutral interviews | Neutral interview with specific questions about Sam's actions |
| Suggestions | | | 4 suggestive interviews | |
| Stereotypes plus Suggestions | Sam is nice but clumsy | | 4 suggestive interviews | |

FIG 7–8

children about Sam's clumsiness before the visit and interviewers made misleading suggestions afterward.

Finally, 10 weeks after Sam had visited the classroom, a different interviewer, one not present during Sam's visit or the previous interviews, asked children several questions about what had happened when Sam visited, including whether Sam had ripped a book or soiled a teddy bear.

*Who were the children in the study?* A total of 176 preschool children participated. Half were 3- and 4-year-olds and half were 5- and 6-year-olds.

*What was the design of the study?* This study was experimental. There were three independent variables: (a) the age of the child, (b) whether the child was told before Sam's visit that he was clumsy, and (c) whether the child received misleading suggestions after Sam's visit. The dependent variable was the child's answer to the interviewers' misleading questions. That is, Leichtman and Ceci counted the percentage of time that children said they had actually seen Sam rip a book or soil the teddy bear, events that never happened. The study was also cross-sectional because it included a group of younger children (3- and 4-year-olds) and a group of older children (5- and 6-year-olds).

*Were there ethical concerns with the study?* No. Sam's visit, the teachers' comments about Sam beforehand, and the interviews afterward posed no special risks to children.

*What were the results?* Children's answers to the misleading questions are shown in the graph. For simplicity, I've shown only the data for 3- and 4-year-olds. The data for 5- and 6-year-olds were similar but the effects were smaller. (That is, the older children were less suggestible than the younger children.) Almost no children in the control condition claimed to have seen Sam rip a book or soil a bear. However, some children in the stereotyped condition claimed to have seen Sam rip a book or soil a bear, and more than one-third of the children in the suggestions condition claimed he did one or the other. When stereotypes and suggestions were combined, almost half the

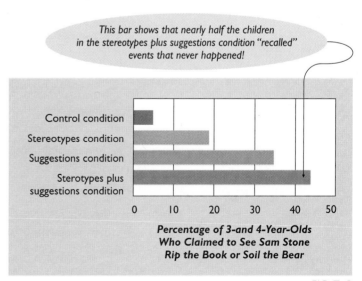

This bar shows that nearly half the children in the stereotypes plus suggestions condition "recalled" events that never happened!

*Percentage of 3-and 4-Year-Olds Who Claimed to See Sam Stone Rip the Book or Soil the Bear*

FIG 7–9

children said they had seen events that never took place. Although the 5- and 6-year-olds described events much more accurately, even 15 percent of these youngsters claimed to have seen Sam rip a book or soil a bear.

*What did the investigators conclude?* Leichtman and Ceci believe that whether preschoolers are suggestible depends entirely upon how their memory for events is probed. The results from their control condition suggest that, without stereotypes and suggestions, preschoolers are unlikely to report events that never happened. However, when adults suggest that a person is likely to behave in a particular way and later imply that some events actually did happen, many preschoolers will go along. From their results, since Cheryl's report was spontaneous, not elicited by repeated questions, it is probably trustworthy. ●

> Unless misled by others, preschoolers rarely "recall" events that didn't happen.

Perhaps you're skeptical. Surely it must be possible to tell when a young child is describing events that never happened. In fact, law enforcement officials and child protection workers believe they can usually tell if children are telling the truth (Brigham & Spier, 1992). But research points to a different conclusion. Later in their study, Leichtman and Ceci (1995) asked experts to watch videotapes of preschoolers who were telling the truth as well as other preschoolers who were describing events that had not happened, such as Sam's ripping the book. Law enforcement officials, case workers, and developmental psychologists could not distinguish the truthful children from the fabricators.

So what conclusions can we finally draw about preschoolers on the witness stand? If Cheryl's parents press charges against Mr. Johnson, can Cheryl's testimony be trusted? Preschoolers can provide reliable testimony, but many commonly used legal procedures can undermine their credibility. Here are guidelines for improving the reliability of child witnesses (Ceci & Bruck, 1995; 1998):

- Warn children that interviewers may sometimes try to trick them or suggest things that didn't happen.

- Interviewers' questions should evaluate alternative explanations of what happened and who was involved.

- Children should not be questioned repeatedly on a single issue.

Following these guidelines will foster the conditions under which preschoolers (and older children, too) are likely to recall the past more accurately and thereby be better witnesses.

## Check Your Learning

1. Four-month-old Tanya has forgotten that kicking moves a mobile. To remind her of the link between kicking and the mobile's movement, we could _____.

2. Children and adolescents often select a memory strategy after they _____.

3. The term _____ refers to periodically evaluating a strategy to determine whether it is effective.

4. The knowledge that children acquire can distort their recall, either by causing them to forget information that does not conform to their knowledge or by _____.

5. A _____ is a memory structure that describes the sequence in which events occur.

**6.** Infantile amnesia, the inability to remember events from early in life, may be due to infants' and toddlers' limited language skills or to their lack of a _____.

**7.** Preschoolers' testimony is more likely to be reliable if interviewers test alternate hypotheses and avoid repeated questioning, and if we warn children that _____.

 **An "expert" on a talk radio show says, "It's a waste of time to have pre-school children testify in court. They can never be trusted because once the seed of abuse is planted, their imaginations run wild." Defend or refute this claim.**

**Answers:** (1) show her a moving mobile, (2) determine the goal of a memory task, (3) monitoring, (4) causing them to recall events that are part of a script but that did not actually take place, (5) script, (6) sense of self, (7) interviewers may try to trick them

## Academic Skills

### Learning Objectives

- **What are the components of skilled reading?**

- **As children develop, how does their writing improve?**

- **When do children understand and use quantitative skills?**

# 7.3

Reading

Writing

Knowing and Using
Numbers

> *When Harriett, a bubbly 3-year-old, is asked how old she'll be on her next birthday, she proudly says, "Four!" while holding up five fingers. Asked to count four objects, whether they're candies, toys, or socks, Harriett almost always says, "1, 2, 6, 7 . . . SEVEN!" Harriett's older brothers find all this very funny, but her mother thinks that, the obvious mistakes notwithstanding, Harriett's behavior shows that she knows a lot about numbers and counting. But what, exactly, does Harriett understand? That question has her mother stumped!*

According to information-processing psychologists, cognitive development consists of acquiring mental software for specific domains. Some of the mental software that children must acquire for success in school is in the domains of reading, writing, and quantitative skill. Information-processing psychologists have studied these domains extensively, as you'll see in this module, which examines the traditional 3 Rs: reading, 'riting, and 'rithmetic. We'll start with reading, then examine writing, and end with numbers, where you'll learn why Harriett counts as she does.

## Reading

Try reading the following sentence:

> *Sumisu-san wa nawa o naifu de kirimashita.*

You probably didn't make much headway, did you? (Unless you know Japanese.) Now try this one:

> *Snore secretary green plastic sleep trucks.*

These are English words and you probably read them quite easily, but did you get anything more out of this sentence than the one in Japanese? These examples show two important processes involved in skilled reading. **Word recognition is the process of identifying a unique pattern of letters.** Unless you know Japanese, your word recognition was not successful in the first sentence. You did not know that *nawa* means *rope* or that *kirimashita* is the past tense of the English verb *cut*. Furthermore, because you could not recognize individual words, you had no idea of the meaning of this sentence. **Comprehension is the process of extracting meaning from a sequence of words.** In the second sentence, your word recognition was perfect, but comprehension was still impossible because the words were presented in a random sequence. These examples remind us just how difficult learning to read can be.

In the next few pages, we'll look at some of the skills that children must acquire if they are to learn to read and to read well. We'll start with prereading skills, then move to word recognition and comprehension.

Prereading Skills. English words are made up of individual letters, so children need to know their letters before they can learn to read. Consequently, it's not surprising that kindergarten children who know most of their letters learn to read more easily than their peers who don't know their letters (Stevenson et al., 1976).

> Prereading skills include knowing the letters of the alphabet and the sounds they make.

**The ability to hear the distinctive sounds of letters is a skill known as *phonological awareness.*** Children who can readily distinguish these sounds learn to read more readily than children who do not. For example, Wagner, Torgesen, and Rashotte (1994) measured kindergarten children's phonological awareness in a number of ways. In one task, the experimenter presented four words—*fun, pin, bun, gun*—and asked the child to pick the word that didn't rhyme with the others. In another task, children were asked to say the first, last, or middle sound of a word: "What's the first sound in *cat*?"

After these children entered first grade, the experimenters measured their ability to read individual words. The investigators found that the correlation between children's performance on phonological awareness tasks in kindergarten and their reading score in first grade was .82. That is, kindergarten children who were aware of letter sounds tended to be skilled readers in first grade whereas kindergarten children who were unaware of letter sounds tended to be unskilled readers in first grade. As the children in this longitudinal study get older, phonological skills continue to be the best predictor of their reading ability (Wagner et al., 1999).

Much other research confirms the idea that sensitivity to the sounds of language is an essential step in learning to read (e.g., Hatcher & Hulme, 1999). Furthermore, phonological skills are not only important in learning to read in alphabet-based languages such as English; they are also important in learning to read in non-alphabet-based languages such as Chinese (Ho & Bryant, 1997).

If phonological skills are so essential, how can we help children master them? The "Making Children's Lives Better" feature describes one easy way.

### Rhyme Is Sublime Because Sounds Abounds

*The Cat in the Hat* and *Green Eggs and Ham* are two books in the famous Dr. Seuss series. You probably know these stories for their zany plots and extensive use of rhyme. When parents frequently read rhymes—not just Dr. Seuss, but also Mother Goose and other nursery rhymes—their children become more aware of word sounds. Passages like this draw children's attention to the different sounds that make up words:

> *I do not like them in a house. I do not like them with a mouse. I do not like them here or there. I do not like them anywhere. I do not like green eggs and ham. I do not like them, Sam-I-am (Geisel, 1960, p. 20).*

The more parents read rhymes to their children, the greater their children's phonological awareness, which makes learning to read much easier (Bradley & Bryant, 1983; Goswami & Bryant, 1990).

So the message is clear. Read to children—the more, the better. As the photo shows, children love it when adults read to them, and learning more about word sounds is icing on the cake! ●

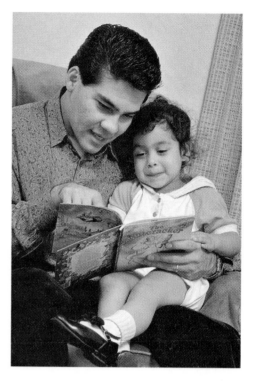

**Recognizing Words.** The first step in actual reading is identifying individual words. One way to do this is to say the sounds associated with each letter and then blend the sounds to produce a recognizable word. Such "sounding out" is a common technique among beginning readers. Older children sometimes sound out words, but only when they are unfamiliar, which points to another common way of recognizing words (Coltheart et al., 1993). Words are recognized through direct retrieval from long-term memory: As the individual letters in a word are identified, long-term memory is searched to see if there is a matching sequence of letters. After the child knows that the letters are, in sequence, *c-a-t*, long-term memory is searched for a match and the child recognizes the word as *cat.*

So far, word recognition may seem like a one-way street where readers first recognize letters and then recognize words. In reality, we know that information flows both ways, as described in the cognitive approach to perception (Module 5.1). Readers constantly use context to help them recognize letters and words. For example, readers typically recognize *t* faster in *cast* than in *asct*. That is, readers recognize letters faster when they appear in words than in nonwords. How do the nearby letters in *cast* help readers to recognize the *t*? As children recognize the first letters in the word as *c, a,* and *s,* the possibilities for the last letter become more limited. Because English only includes four 4-letter words that start with *cas* (well, five if you include *Cass*), the last letter can only be *e, h, k,* or *t.* In contrast, there are no four-letter words (in English) that begin with *acs,* so all 26 letters must be checked, which takes more time than just checking four letters. In this way, a reader's knowledge of words simplifies the task of recognizing letters, which in turn makes it easier to recognize words (Seidenberg & McClelland, 1989).

Readers also use the sentence context to speed word recognition. Read these two sentences:

> *The last word in this sentence is cat.*
> *The little girl's pet dog chased the cat.*

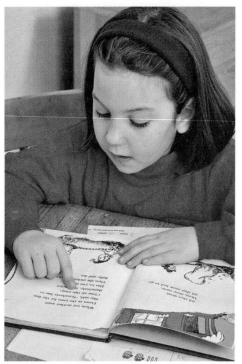

Most readers recognize *cat* more rapidly in the second sentence. The reason is that the first seven words put severe limits on the last word: It must be something "chaseable," and because the "chaser" is a *dog*, *cat* is a very likely candidate. In contrast, the first seven words in the first sentence put no limits on the last word; virtually any word could end the sentence. Beginning and skilled readers both use sentence context like this to help them recognize words (Kim & Goetz, 1994).

As you can imagine, most beginning readers, like the child in the photo, rely more heavily on "sounding out" because they know fewer words. As they gain more reading experience, they are more likely to be able to retrieve a word directly from long-term memory. You might be tempted to summarize this as "Beginning readers sound out and more advanced readers retrieve directly." Don't! From their very first efforts to read, most children use direct retrieval for a few words. From that point on, the general strategy is to try retrieval first and, if that fails, to sound out the word or ask a more skilled reader for help (Siegler, 1986). For example, when my daughter Laura was just beginning to read, she knew *the*, *Laura*, and several one-syllable words that ended in *at*, such as *bat*, *cat*, and *fat*. Shown a sentence like

*Laura saw the fat cat run,*

she would say, "Laura s-s-s . . . ah-h . . . wuh . . . saw the fat cat er-r-r . . . uh-h-h . . . n-n-n . . . run." Familiar words were retrieved rapidly, but the unfamiliar ones were slowly sounded out. With more experience, fewer words are sounded out and more are retrieved (Siegler, 1986), but even skilled readers sometimes fall back on sounding out when they confront unfamiliar words. Try reading

*The rock star rode to the concert in a palanquin.*

You may well need to do some sounding out, then consult a dictionary (or look in the answers prior to "Check Your Learning") for the correct meaning.

**Comprehension.**  Once individual words are recognized, reading begins to have a lot in common with understanding speech. That is, the means by which people understand a sequence of words is much the same whether the source of words is printed text or speech or, for that matter, Braille or sign language (Crowder & Wagner, 1992). **In all these cases, children derive meaning by combining words to form** *propositions* **or ideas and then combining propositions.** For example, as you read

*The tall boy rode his bike,*

you spontaneously derive a number of propositions, including "There is a boy," "The boy is tall," and "The boy was riding." If this sentence were part of a larger body of text, you would derive propositions for each sentence, then link the propositions together to derive meaning for the passage as a whole (Perfetti & Curtis, 1986).

As children gain more reading experience, they better comprehend what they read. Several factors contribute to this improved comprehension (Siegler, 1998):

- *Working memory capacity increases, which means that older and better readers can store more of a sentence in memory as they try to identify the propositions it contains* (Nation et al., 1999; Siegel, 1994): This extra capacity is handy when readers move from sentences like "Kevin hit the ball" to "In the bottom of the ninth, with the bases loaded and the Cardinals down 7-4, Kevin put a line drive into the left-field bleachers, his fourth home run of the Series."

- *Children acquire more general knowledge of their physical, social, and psychological worlds, which allows them to understand more of what they read* (Bisanz et al., 1992; Graesser, Singer, & Trabasso, 1994): For example, even if a 6-year-old could recognize all of the words in the longer sentence about Kevin's home run, the child would not fully comprehend the meaning of the passage because he or she lacks the necessary knowledge of baseball.

- *With experience, children better monitor their comprehension:* When readers don't grasp the meaning of a passage because it is difficult or confusing, they read it again (Baker, 1994). Try this sentence (adapted from Carpenter & Daneman, 1981): "The Midwest State Fishing Contest would draw fishermen from all around the region, including some of the best bass guitarists in Michigan." When you first encountered "bass guitarists" you probably interpreted "bass" as a fish. This didn't make much sense, so you reread the phrase to determine that "bass" refers to a type of guitar. Older readers are better able to realize that their understanding is not complete and take corrective action.

- *With experience, children use more appropriate reading strategies:* The goal of reading and the nature of the text dictate how you read. When reading a novel, for example, do you often skip sentences (or perhaps paragraphs or entire pages) to get to "the good parts"? This approach makes sense for pleasure reading but not for reading textbooks or recipes or how-to manuals. Reading a textbook requires attention to both the overall organization and the relationship of details to that organization. Older, more experienced readers are better able to select a reading strategy that suits the material being read (Brown et al., 1996).

> Older children comprehend more of what they read because of their greater working memory capacity, greater world knowledge, better monitoring skill, and appropriate reading strategies.

Greater working memory capacity, greater world knowledge, greater monitoring skill, and use of more appropriate reading strategies are all part of the information-processing explanation of how older and more experienced readers get more meaning from what they read. In the next part of this module, you'll see how information-processing psychologists use similar ideas to explain children's developing ability to write.

## Writing

Though few of us end up being a Maya Angelou, a Sandra Cisneros, or a John Grisham, most adults do write, both at home and at work. The basics of good writing are remarkably straightforward (Williams, 1997), but writing skill develops very gradually during childhood, adolescence, and young adulthood. Research indicates a number of factors that contribute to improved writing as children develop (Adams, Treiman, & Pressley, 1998; Siegler, 1998).

### Greater Knowledge and Access to Knowledge About Topics.

Writing is about telling "something" to others. With age, children have more to tell as they gain more knowledge about the world and incorporate this knowledge into their writing (Benton et al., 1995). For example, asked to write about a mayoral election, children are apt to describe it as much like a popularity contest; adolescents more often describe it in terms of political issues that are both subtle and complex. Of course, students are sometimes asked to write about topics quite unfamiliar to them. In this case, older children's and adolescents' writing is usually better because they are more adept at finding useful reference material and incorporating it into their writing.

### Greater Understanding of How to Organize Writing.

One difficult aspect of writing is organization, arranging all the necessary information in a manner that readers find clear and interesting. In fact, children and young adolescents organize their writing differently than older adolescents and adults (Bereiter & Scardamalia, 1987). **Young writers often use a *knowledge-telling strategy*, writing down information on the topic as they retrieve it from memory.** For example, asked to write about the day's events at school, a second grader wrote:

> *It is a rainy day. We hope the sun will shine. We got new spelling books. We had our pictures taken. We sang Happy Birthday to Barbara. (Waters, 1980, p. 155)*

The story has no obvious structure. The first two sentences are about the weather, but the last three deal with completely independent topics. Apparently, the writer simply described each event as it came to mind.

**During adolescence, writers begin to use a *knowledge-transforming strategy*, deciding what information to include and how best to organize it for the point they wish to convey to their reader.** This approach involves considering the purpose of writing (e.g., to inform, to persuade, to entertain) and the information needed to achieve this purpose. It also involves considering the needs, interests, and knowledge of the anticipated audience.

Asked to described the day's events, older adolescents' writing can take many forms, depending on the purpose and audience. An essay written to entertain peers about humorous events at school would differ from one written to convince parents about problems in schoolwork. And both of these essays would differ from one written to inform an exchange student about a typical day in a U.S. high school. In other words, although children's knowledge-telling strategy gets words on paper, the more mature knowledge-transforming strategy produces a more cohesive text for the reader.

### Greater Ease in Dealing with the Mechanical Requirements of Writing.

Soon after I earned my pilot's license, I took my son Matt for a flight. A few days later, he wrote the following story for his second-grade weekly writing assignment:

> *This weekend I got to ride in a one propellered plane. But this time my dad was alone. He has his license now. It was a long ride. But I fell asleep after five minutes. But when we landed I woke up. My dad said, "You missed a good ride." My dad said, "You even missed the jets!" But I had fun.*

Matt spent more than an hour writing this story, and the original (hanging in my office) is filled with erasures where he corrected misspelled words, ill-formed letters, and incorrect punctuation. Had Matt simply *described* our flight aloud (instead of writing it), his task would have been much easier. In oral language, he could ignore capitalization, punctuation, spelling, and printing of individual letters. These many mechanical aspects of writing can be a burden for all writers, but particularly for young writers.

In fact, research shows that when youngsters like the one in the photo at the top of page 203 are absorbed by the task of printing letters correctly, the quality of their writing usually suffers (Jones & Christensen, 1999). As children master printed and cursive letters, they can pay more attention to other aspects of writing. Similarly, correct spelling and good sentence structure are particularly hard for younger writers;

as they learn to spell and to generate clear sentences, they write more easily and more effectively (Graham et al., 1997; McCutchen et al., 1994).

### Greater Skill in Revising.

Few authors get it down right the first time. Instead, they revise and revise, then revise some more. In the words of one expert, "Experienced writers get something down on paper as fast as they can, just so they can revise it into something clearer" (Williams, 1997, p. 11).

Unfortunately, young writers often don't revise at all—the first draft is usually the final draft. To make matters worse, when young writers revise, the changes do not necessarily improve their writing (Fitzgerald, 1987). Effective revising requires being able to detect problems and knowing how to correct them (Baker & Brown, 1984; Beal, 1996). As children develop, they're better able to find problems and to know how to correct them. Children and adolescents are more likely to find flaws in others' writing than in their own (Cameron et al., 1997). And they are more likely to revise successfully when the topic is familiar to them (McCutchen, Francis, & Kerr, 1997).

If you look over these past few paragraphs, it's quite clear why good writing is so long in developing. Many different skills are involved and each is complicated in its own right. Mastering them collectively is a huge challenge, one that spans all of childhood, adolescence, and adulthood. Much the same could be said for mastering quantitative skills, as we'll see in the next section.

## Knowing and Using Numbers

Basic number skills originate in infancy, long before babies learn names of numbers. Many babies experience daily variation in quantity. They play with two blocks and see that another baby has three; they watch as a father sorts laundry and finds two black socks but only one blue sock, and they eat one hot dog for lunch while an older brother eats three.

From these experiences, babies apparently come to appreciate that quantity or amount is one of the ways in which objects in the world can differ. This conclusion is based on research in which babies are shown pictures like these. The actual objects in

FIG 7–10

the pictures differ, as do their size, color, and position in the picture. The only common element is that each picture always depicts two of something.

When the first of these pictures is shown, an infant will look at it for several seconds. After several have been shown, an infant habituates (Module 5.3); he or she will glance at the picture briefly, then look away, as if saying, "Enough of these pictures of two things; let's move on to something else." And, in fact, if a picture of a single object or of three objects is then shown, infants will again look for several seconds, their interest apparently renewed. Because the only systematic change is the number of objects depicted in the picture, we know that babies can distinguish stimuli on the basis of number. Typically, 5-month-olds can distinguish two objects from three and, less often, three objects from four (Canfield & Smith, 1996; Wynn, 1996).

How do infants distinguish differences in quantity? Older children might count, but, of course, infants have not yet learned names of numbers. Instead, the process is probably more perceptual in nature. As we saw in Module 5.2, the infant's perceptual system is sensitive to characteristics such as shape and color (Bornstein, 1981). Quantity may well be another characteristic of stimuli to which infants are sensitive. That is, just as colors (reds, blues) and shapes (triangles, squares) are basic perceptual properties, small quantities ("twoness" and "threeness") may be perceptually obvious (Strauss & Curtis, 1984).

Names of numbers are not among most babies' first words, but by 2 years, youngsters know some number words and have begun to count. Usually, their counting is full of mistakes. In Harriett's counting sequence that was described in the vignette—"1, 2, 6, 7"—she skips 3, 4, and 5. But if we ignore her mistakes momentarily, the counting sequence reveals that she does understand a great deal.

Gelman and Meck (1986) charted preschoolers' understanding of counting. They simply placed several objects in front of a child and asked, "How many?" By analyzing children's answers to many of these questions, Gelman and Meck discovered that by age 3 most children have mastered three basic principles of counting, at least when it comes to counting up to five objects.

- *One-to-one principle:* **There must be one and only one number name for each object that is counted.** A child who counts three objects as "1, 2, a" understands this principle because the number of number words matches the number of objects to be counted.

- *Stable-order principle:* **Number names must be counted in the same order.** A child who counts in the same sequence—for example, consistently counting four objects as "1, 2, 4, 5"—shows understanding of this principle.

- *Cardinality principle:* **The last number name differs from the previous ones in a counting sequence by denoting the number of objects.** Typically, 3-year-olds reveal their understanding of this principle by repeating the last number name, often with emphasis: "1, 2, 4, 8 . . . EIGHT!"

During the preschool years, children master these basic principles and apply them to ever larger sets of objects. By age 5, most youngsters apply these counting principles to as many as nine objects. Of course, children's understanding of these principles does not mean that they always count accurately. To the contrary, children can apply all these principles consistently while counting incorrectly. They must master the conventional sequence of the number names and the counting principles to learn to count accurately. (To see if you understand the counting principles, go back to Harriett's counting in the vignette and decide which principles she has mastered; my answer is given before "Check Your Learning" on page 208.)

Learning the number names beyond 9 is easier because the counting words can be generated based on rules for combining decade number names (20, 30, 40) with unit names (1, 2, 3, 4). Later, similar rules are used for hundreds, thousands, and so on. By age 4, most youngsters know the numbers to 20, and some can count to 99. Usually, they stop counting at a number ending in 9 (29, 59), apparently because they don't know the next decade name (Siegler & Robinson, 1982).

Learning to count beyond 10 is more complicated in English than in other languages. For example, *eleven* and *twelve* are completely irregular names, following no rules. Also, the remaining "teen" number names differ from the 20s, 30s, and the rest in that the decade number name comes after the unit (thir-*teen*, four-*teen*) rather than before (*twenty*-three, *thirty*-four). Also, some decade names only loosely correspond to the unit names on which they are based: *twenty*, *thirty*, and *fifty* resemble *two*, *three*, and *five* but are not the same.

In contrast, the Chinese, Japanese, and Korean number systems are almost perfectly regular. *Eleven* and *twelve* are expressed as *ten-one* and *ten-two*. There are no special names for the decades: *Two-ten* and *two-ten-one* are names for 20 and 21. These simplified number names help explain why youngsters growing up in Asian countries count more accurately than U.S. preschool children of the same age (Miller et al., 1995). Furthermore, the direct correspondence between the number names and the base-ten system makes it easier for Asian youngsters to learn base-ten concepts (Miura et al., 1988).

### Adding and Subtracting.

Counting is the starting point for children as they learn to add. For instance, suppose you ask a preschooler to solve the following problem: "John had four oranges. Then Mary gave him two more oranges. How many oranges does John have now?" Like the child in the photo, many 6-year-old children solve the problem by counting. They first count out four fingers on one hand, then count out two more on the other. Finally, they count all six fingers on both hands. To subtract, they do the same procedure in reverse (Siegler & Jenkins, 1989; Siegler & Shrager, 1984).

Youngsters soon abandon this approach for a slightly more efficient method. Instead of counting the fingers on the first hand, they simultaneously extend the number of fingers on the first hand corresponding to the larger of the two numbers to be added. Next, they count out the smaller number with fingers on the second hand. Finally, they count all of the fingers to determine the sum (Groen & Resnick, 1977).

After children begin to receive formal arithmetic instruction in first grade, addition problems are less often solved by counting aloud or by counting fingers. Instead, children add and subtract by counting mentally. That is, children act as if they are counting silently, beginning with the larger number, and adding on. By age 8 or 9, children have learned the addition tables so well that sums of the single-digit integers (from 0 to 9) are facts that are simply retrieved from memory (Ashcraft, 1982).

These counting strategies do not occur in a rigid developmental sequence. Individual children use many or all of these strategies,

Children use many strategies to add, including counting on fingers, counting aloud, and retrieving answers directly from memory.

depending upon the problem. Children usually begin by trying to retrieve an answer from memory. If they are not reasonably confident that the retrieved answer is correct, then they resort to counting aloud or on fingers (Siegler, 1988). Retrieval is most likely for problems with small addends (e.g., 1 + 2, 2 + 4) because these problems are presented frequently in textbooks and by teachers. Consequently, the sum is highly associated with the problem, which makes the child confident that the retrieved answer is correct. In contrast, problems with larger addends, such as 9 + 8, are presented less often. The result is a weaker link between the addends and the sum and, consequently, a greater chance that children will need to determine an answer by counting.

Of course, arithmetic skills continue to improve as children move through elementary school. They become more proficient in addition and subtraction, learn multiplication and division, and move on to the more sophisticated mathematical concepts involved in algebra, geometry, trigonometry, and calculus.

### Comparing U.S. Students with Students in Other Countries.

Let's return to the issue of cultural differences in mathematical competence. When compared to students worldwide in terms of math skills, U.S. students don't fare well. For example, the graph shows the results of the Third International Math and Science

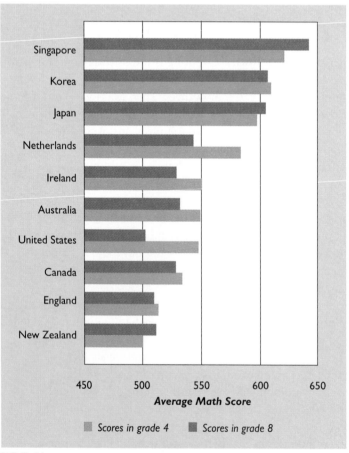

FIG 7–11

Study (1997), which compares math and science achievement of students in 41 different countries. U.S. fourth and eighth graders have substantially lower scores than students in the leading nations. Phrased another way, the very best U.S. students only perform at the level of average students in Asian countries like Singapore and Korea. Furthermore, the cultural differences in math achievement hold for both math operations and math problem solving (Stevenson & Lee, 1990).

Why do American students rate so poorly? The "Cultural Influences" feature gives some answers.

### Fifth Grade in Taiwan

Shin-ying is an 11-year-old attending school in Taipei, the largest city in Taiwan. Like most fifth graders, Shin-ying is in school from 8 a.m. until 4 p.m. daily. Most evenings, she spends 2 to 3 hours doing homework. This academic routine is grueling by U.S. standards, where fifth graders typically spend 6 to 7 hours in school each day and less than an hour doing homework. I asked Shin-ying what she thought of school and schoolwork. Her answers surprised me.

RK:         Why do you go to school?

SHIN-YING: I like what we study.

RK:         Any other reasons?

SHIN-YING: The things that I learn in school are useful.

RK:         What about homework? Why do you do it?

SHIN-YING: My teacher and my parents think it's important. And I like doing it.

RK:         Do you think that you would do nearly as well in school if you didn't work so hard?

SHIN-YING: Oh no. The best students are always the ones who work the hardest.

Schoolwork is the focal point of Shin-ying's life. Although many American schoolchildren are unhappy when schoolwork intrudes on time for play and television, Shin-ying is enthusiastic about school and school-related activities.

Shin-ying is not unusual among Chinese elementary-school students. Many of her comments exemplify Stevenson and Lee's findings (1990) in a study comparing students in Japan, Taiwan, and the United States:

- *Time in school and how it is used.* By fifth grade, students in Japan and Taiwan spend 50 percent more time than American students in school, and more of this time is devoted to academic activities than in the U.S.

- *Time spent in homework and attitudes toward it.* Students in Taiwan and Japan spend more time on homework and value homework more than American students.

- *Parents' attitudes.* American parents are more often satisfied with their children's performance in school; in contrast, Japanese and Taiwanese parents set much higher standards for their children.

- *Parents' beliefs about effort and ability.* Japanese and Taiwanese parents believe more strongly than American parents that effort, not native ability, is the key factor in school success.

Thus, students in Japan and Taiwan excel because they spend more time both in and out of school on academic tasks. Furthermore, their parents (and teachers) set loftier scholastic goals and believe that students can attain these goals with hard work. Japanese classrooms even post a motto describing ideal students—*gambaru kodomo*—those who strive the hardest.

Parents underscore the importance of schoolwork in many ways to their children. For example, even though homes and apartments in Japan and China are very small by U.S. standards, Asian youngsters, like the child in the photo, typically have a desk in a quiet area where they can study undisturbed (Stevenson & Lee, 1990). For Japanese and Taiwanese teachers and parents, academic excellence is paramount, and it shows in their children's success. ●

What can Americans learn from Japanese and Taiwanese educational systems? From their experiences with Asian students, teachers, and schools, Stevenson and Stigler (1992) suggest several ways American schools could be improved:

- Give teachers more free time to prepare lessons and correct students' work.
- Improve teachers' training by allowing them to work closely with older, more experienced teachers.
- Organize instruction around sound principles of learning such as providing multiple examples of concepts and giving students adequate opportunities to practice newly acquired skills.
- Set higher standards for children, who need to spend more time and effort in school-related activities in order to achieve those standards.

> American schools could be improved by giving teachers better training and more time to prepare lessons, basing teaching on principles of learning, and setting higher standards.

Changing teaching practices and attitudes toward achievement would begin to reduce the gap between American students and students in other industrialized countries, particularly Asian countries. Ignoring the problem will mean an increasingly undereducated work force and citizenry in a more complex world—an alarming prospect for the 21st century.

*Definition on page 200:* A palanquin is a covered couch resting on two horizontal poles that are carried by four people, one at each end of the poles.

*Response to question about Harriett's counting on page 205:* Since Harriett uses four number names to count four objects ("1, 2, 6, 7 . . . SEVEN!"), she understands the one-to-one principle. The four number names are always used in the same order, so she grasps the stable-order principle. And, finally, she repeats the last number name with emphasis, so she understands the cardinality principle.

### Check Your Learning

**1.** Important prereading skills include knowing letters and _____.

**2.** Beginning readers typically recognize words by sounding them out; with greater experience, readers are more likely able to _____.

**3.** Older and more experienced readers understand more of what they read because the capacity of working memory increases, they have more general knowledge of the world, _____, and they are more likely to use appropriate reading strategies.

**4.** Children typically use a _____ to organize their writing.

**5.** Children revise best when revising other children's writing and when _____.

**6.** By age 3 years, most children have mastered the _____, stable-order, and cardinality principles of counting.

**7.** The simplest way of solving addition problems is to _____; the most advanced way is to retrieve sums from long-term memory.

**8.** Compared to students in U.S. elementary schools, students in Japan and Taiwan spend more time in school, and a greater proportion of that time is _____.

 **A perennial debate in education is whether children should be taught to read with phonics (sounding out words) or with whole-word methods (recognizing entire words). Does the research described in Module 7.3 provide evidence that either method is more effective?**

**Answers:** (1) sounds associated with each letter, (2) retrieve words from long-term memory, (3) they monitor their comprehension more effectively, (4) knowledge-telling strategy, (5) the topic is familiar to them, (6) one-to-one, (7) count on one's fingers, (8) devoted to academic activities

# Information-Processing Approaches to Cognitive Development

## IN PERSPECTIVE

The information-processing approach to cognitive development is derived from computer science. We saw, in Module 7.1, that information processing distinguishes mental hardware from mental software. Furthermore, information-processing psychologists propose that cognitive development can be linked to changes in strategies, working memory, inhibitory processes, automatic processing, and processing speed. In Module 7.2, we looked at the development of memory. Memory is evident in infancy and improves rapidly as children learn to use memory strategies and acquire more knowledge of the world. In Module 7.3, we examined information-processing accounts of how and why reading and writing improve with children's age. We also saw that developmental change in quantitative skill begins with infants' awareness of number and rapidly leads to counting and arithmetic operations.

This chapter highlights the theme that *children help determine their own development:* Japanese and Chinese elementary-school children typically like studying (an attitude fostered by their parents), and this makes them quite willing to do homework for 2 or 3 hours nightly. This, in turn, contributes to their high levels of scholastic achievement. American schoolchildren usually abhor homework and do as little of it as possible, which contributes to their relatively lower level of scholastic achievement. Thus, children's attitudes help to determine how they behave, which determines how much they will achieve over the course of childhood and adolescence.

## See for Yourself

Create several small sets of objects that vary in number. You might have two pennies, three candies, four buttons, five pencils, six erasers, seven paper clips, and so on. Place each set of objects on a paper plate. Then find some preschool children—4- and 5-year-olds would be ideal. Put a plate in front of each child and ask, "How many?" Then watch to see what the child does. If possible, tape-record the children's counting so that you can analyze it later. If this is impossible, try to write down exactly what each child says as he or she counts. Later, go back through your notes and determine if the children follow the counting principles described on page 204. You should see that children, particularly younger ones, more often follow the principles while counting small sets of objects than larger sets. See for yourself!

## Resources

*For more information about . . .*

 *cultural differences in scholastic achievement,* try Harold W. Stevenson and James W. Stigler's *The Learning Gap* (Summit Books, 1992), which describes research comparing schooling in the United States and in Asia.

 *tips and exercises to help develop better study skills for college,* visit the Web site of the University Counseling Center of the Virginia Polytechnic Institute and State University, **http://www.ucc.vt.edu/stdysk/stdyhlp.html**

## Key Terms

**autobiographical memory** 193
**automatic processes** 185
**cardinality principle** 204
**comprehension** 198
**infantile amnesia** 193
**information processing** 182
**inhibitory processes** 185

**knowledge-telling strategy** 202
**knowledge-transforming strategy** 202
**long-term memory** 183
**memory strategies** 189
**one-to-one principle** 204
**phonological awareness** 198

**propositions** 200
**script** 192
**sensory memory** 183
**stable-order principle** 204
**word recognition** 198
**working memory** 183

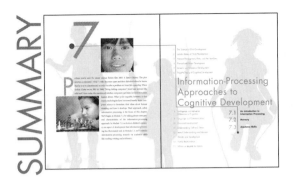

# SUMMARY

## Information-Processing Approaches to Cognitive Development

7.1 An Introduction to Information Processing
7.2 Memory
7.3 Academic Skills

## 7.1 An Introduction to Information Processing

### Basic Features of the Information-Processing Approach

According to the information-processing approach, cognitive development involves changes in mental hardware and mental software. Mental hardware refers to mental processes that are built-in and allow the mind to function, including sensory, working, and long-term memories. Mental software refers to mental programs that allow people to perform specific tasks.

### How Information Processing Changes with Development

Information-processing psychologists believe that cognitive development reflects more effective strategies, increased capacity of working memory, more effective inhibitory processes, increased automatic processing, and increased speed of processing.

### Comparing Information Processing and Piaget's Theory

Piaget's theory is a single, comprehensive theory, whereas information processing is a general approach encompassing many specific theories. In addition, Piaget's theory emphasizes qualitative change in development, whereas information processing emphasizes quantitative change.

## 7.2 Memory

### Origins of Memory

Rovee-Collier's studies of kicking show that infants can remember, forget, and be reminded of events that occurred in the past.

### Strategies for Remembering

Beginning in the preschool years, children use strategies to help them remember. With age, children use more powerful strategies, such as rehearsal and outlining. Using memory strategies successfully depends, first, upon analyzing the goal of a memory task and, second, upon monitoring the effectiveness of the chosen strategy. Both skills improve gradually during childhood and adolescence.

### Knowledge and Memory

A child's knowledge of the world can be used to organize information that is to be remembered. When several events occur in a specific order, they are remembered as a single script. Knowledge improves memory for children and adolescents, although older individuals often reap more benefit because they have more knowledge. Knowledge can also distort memory by causing children and adolescents to forget information that does not conform to their knowledge or to remember events that are part of their knowledge but that did not actually take place.

Autobiographical memory refers to a person's memory about his or her own life. Autobiograpical memory emerges in the early preschool years, often prompted by parents' asking children about past events. Infantile amnesia, children's and adults' inability to remember events from early in life, may reflect the acquisition of language or a sense of self.

Young children's memory in court cases is often inaccurate because children are questioned repeatedly, which makes it hard for them to distinguish what actually occurred from what adults suggest may have occurred. Children's testimony would be more reliable if interviewers tested alternate hypotheses during their questioning, avoided repeated questioning, and warned children that they may try to trick them.

## 7.3 Academic Skills

### Reading

Information-processing psychologists divide reading into a number of component skills. Prereading skills include knowing letters and the sounds associated with them. Word recognition is the process of identifying a word. Beginning readers more often accomplish this by sounding out words; advanced readers more often retrieve a word from long-term memory. Comprehension, the act of extracting meaning from text, improves with age because of several factors: working memory capacity increases, readers gain more world knowledge, and readers are better able to monitor what they read and to match their reading strategies to the goals of the reading task.

### Writing

As children develop, their writing improves, reflecting several factors: They know more about the world and so they have more to say; they use more effective ways of organizing their writing; they master the mechanics (e.g., handwriting, spelling) of writing; and they become more skilled at revising their writing.

### Knowing and Using Numbers

Infants can distinguish quantities, probably by means of basic perceptual processes. Children begin to count by about age 2, and by 3 years most children have mastered the one-to-one, stable-order, and cardinality principles, at least when counting small sets of objects. Counting is how children first add, but it is replaced by more effective strategies such as retrieving sums directly from memory.

In mathematics, American students lag behind students in most other industrialized nations, chiefly because of cultural differences in the time spent on schoolwork and homework and in parents' attitudes towards school, effort, and ability.

**8**

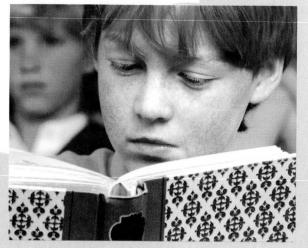

Have you ever stopped to think how many standardized tests you've taken in your student career? You probably took either the SAT or the ACT to enter college. Before that you took countless achievement and aptitude tests during elementary school and high school. Psychological testing is an integral part of American education and has been for most of the 20th century.

Of all standardized tests, none attracts more attention and generates more controversy than tests designed to measure intelligence. Intelligence tests have been hailed by some as one of psychology's greatest contributions to society and cursed by others. Intelligence tests and what they measure are the focus of Chapter 8. We'll start, in Module 8.1, by looking at different definitions of intelligence. In Module 8.2, we'll see how intelligence tests work and examine some factors that influence test scores. Finally, in Module 8.3, we'll look at special children—youngsters whose intelligence sets them apart from their peers.

# Intelligence and Individual Differences in Cognition

8.1 **What Is Intelligence?**

8.2 **Measuring Intelligence**

8.3 **Special Children, Special Needs**

# 8.1

# What Is Intelligence?

## Learning Objectives

● What is the psychometric view of the nature of intelligence?

● How does Gardner's theory of multiple intelligences differ from the psychometric approach?

● What are the three components of Sternberg's triarchic theory of intelligence?

*Max is 22 years old and is moderately mentally retarded. That is, he performs most tasks at the level of a nonretarded 5- or 6-year-old. For example, he can't do many of Piaget's conservation tasks and he reads very slowly and with much effort. Nevertheless, if Max hears a song on the radio, he can immediately sit down at the piano and play the melody flawlessly, despite having had no musical training. Everyone who sees Max do this is astonished. How can a person who is otherwise so limited intellectually perform such an amazing feat?*

Before you read further, how would you answer the question that is the title of this module? What is your definition of intelligence? If you're typical of most Americans, your definition probably includes the ability to reason logically, connect ideas, and solve real problems. You might mention verbal ability, meaning the ability to speak clearly and articulately. You might also mention social competence, referring, for example, to an interest in the world at large and an ability to admit when you make a mistake (Sternberg & Kaufman, 1998).

As you'll see in this module, many of these ideas about intelligence are included in psychological theories of intelligence. We'll begin by considering the oldest theories of intelligence, those associated with the psychometric tradition. Then we'll look at two newer approaches and, along the way, get some insights into Max's uncanny musical skill.

## Psychometric Theories

**P**sychometricians **are psychologists who specialize in measuring psychological characteristics such as intelligence and personality.** When psychometricians want to research a particular question, they usually begin by administering a large number of tests to many individuals. Then they look for patterns in performance across the different tests. The basic logic underlying this technique is similar to the logic a jungle hunter uses to decide whether some dark blobs in a river are three separate rotting logs or a single alligator (Cattell, 1965). If the blobs move together, the hunter decides they are part of the same structure, an alligator. If they do not move together, they are three different structures, three logs. Similarly, if changes in performance on one test are accompanied by changes in performance on a second test—that is, they move together—one could assume that the tests are measuring the same attribute or factor.

When psychometricians have examined patterns of performance on intelligence tests, they have found evidence for general intelligence as well as for specific abilities.

Suppose, for example, that you believe there is such a thing as general intelligence. That is, you believe that some people are smart regardless of the situation, task, or problem, whereas others are not so smart. According to this view, children's performance should be very consistent across tasks. Smart children should always receive high scores, and the less smart youngsters should always get lower scores.

As early as 1904, Charles Spearman reported findings supporting the idea that a general factor for intelligence, or *g*, is responsible for performance on all mental tests.

Other researchers, however, have found that intelligence consists of distinct abilities. For example, Thurstone and Thurstone (1941) analyzed performance on a wide range of tasks and identified seven distinct patterns, each reflecting a unique ability: perceptual speed, word comprehension, word fluency, space, number, memory, and induction. Thurstone and Thurstone also acknowledged a general factor that operated in all tasks, but they emphasized that the specific factors were more useful in assessing and understanding intellectual ability.

These conflicting findings have led many psychometric theorists to propose hierarchical theories of intelligence that include both general and specific components. John Carroll (1993), for example, proposed the hierarchical theory with three levels that's shown in the diagram. At the top of the hierarchy is *g*, general intelligence.

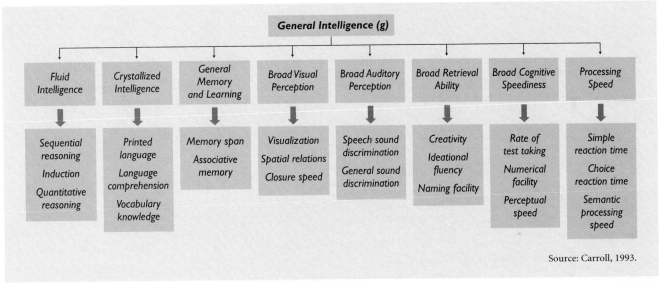

Source: Carroll, 1993.

FIG 8–1

In the level underneath *g* are eight broad categories of intellectual skill, ranging from fluid intelligence to processing speed. Each of the abilities in the second level is further divided into the skills listed in the third and most specific level. Crystallized intelligence, for example, includes understanding printed language, comprehending language, and knowing vocabulary.

Carroll's hierarchical theory is, in essence, a compromise between the two views of intelligence—general versus distinct abilities. But some critics still find it unsatisfactory because it ignores the research and theory on cognitive development described in Chapters 6 and 7. They believe we need to look beyond the psychometric approach to understand intelligence. In the remainder of this module, then, we'll look at two newer theories that have gained a following.

## Gardner's Theory of Multiple Intelligences

Only recently have developmental psychologists viewed intelligence from the perspective of Piaget's theory and information-processing psychology. These new theories present a much broader theory of intelligence and how it develops. Among the most ambitious is Howard Gardner's (1983; 1993) theory of multiple intelligences. Rather than using test scores as the basis for his theory, Gardner draws on research in child development, studies of brain-damaged persons, and studies of exceptionally talented people. He proposes seven distinct intelligences that are shown in the table. The first three intelligences in this list—

## Seven Intelligences in Gardner's Theory of Multiple Intelligences

| Type of Intelligence | Definition |
| --- | --- |
| Linguistic | Knowing the meaning of words, having the ability to use words to understand new ideas, and using language to convey ideas to others |
| Logical-mathematical | Understanding relations that can exist among objects, actions, and ideas, as well as the logical or mathematical operations that can be performed on them |
| Spatial | Perceiving objects accurately and imagining in the "mind's eye" the appearance of an object before and after it has been transformed |
| Musical | Comprehending and producing sounds varying in pitch, rhythm, and emotional tone |
| Bodily-kinesthetic | Using one's body in highly differentiated ways, as dancers, craftspeople, and athletes do |
| Interpersonal | Identifying different feelings, moods, motivations, and intentions in others |
| Intrapersonal | Understanding one's emotions and knowing one's strengths and weaknesses |

Source: Gardner, 1983; 1993

TABLE 8–1

linguistic intelligence, logical-mathematical intelligence, and spatial intelligence—are included in psychometric theories of intelligence. The last four intelligences are not: Musical, bodily-kinesthetic, interpersonal, and intrapersonal intelligences are unique to Gardner's theory. According to Gardner, a gifted athlete, a talented dancer, and a sensitive, caring child are showing intelligence as is the child who writes well or is skilled at math.

How did Gardner arrive at these seven distinct intelligences? First, each has a unique developmental history. Linguistic intelligence, for example, develops much earlier than the other six. Second, each intelligence is regulated by distinct regions of the brain, as shown in studies of brain-damaged persons. Spatial intelligence, for example, is regulated by particular regions in the brain's right hemisphere. Third, each has special cases of talented individuals. **Musical intelligence is often shown by *savants,* individuals with mental retardation who are extremely talented in one domain.** Max, the 22-year-old in the module-opening vignette, is a savant whose special talent is music. Like Max, Eddie B., the 10-year-old savant in the photo, can play a tune correctly after a single hearing and without ever having had formal musical training (Shuter-Dyson, 1982).

Prompted by Gardner's theory, researchers have begun to look at nontraditional aspects of intelligence. **For example, one aspect of interpersonal intelligence is** *social-cognitive flexibility,* **which refers to a person's skill in solving social problems with relevant social knowledge.** Jones and Day (1997) studied social-cognitive flexibility by presenting different social scenarios to adolescents. In one scenario, a man and a woman walk past each other; the woman says "hello" but the man ignores her. Following each scenario, adolescents were asked a series of questions about what happened in the scenario. Some adolescents were much better at understanding that each scenario might have many different interpretations (e.g., "The man ignored the woman because he's very shy," "The man was lost in thought and didn't see her") and that a person's interpretation of the scenario would cause him or her to act differently.

Adolescents who understood the different interpretations of the scenarios were not more skilled in solving verbal or logical reasoning problems, but they were more competent socially (e.g., could deal more effectively with peers) and were less likely to have social problems (e.g., be shy or anxious). Thus, as Gardner's theory predicts, acting skillfully in social situations is an element of intelligence that is distinct from the linguistic and logical-mathematical intelligences of psychometric theories.

The theory of multiple intelligence has important implications for education. Gardner (1993; 1995) believes that schools should foster all intelligences, not just the traditional linguistic and logical-mathematical intelligences. Teachers should capitalize on the strongest intelligences of individual children. Some students may best understand unfamiliar cultures, for example, by studying their dance, while other students may understand these cultures by studying their music.

Some American schools have enthusiastically embraced Gardner's ideas (Gardner, 1993). Are these schools better? We don't really know because school performance is usually evaluated with tests, and there aren't acceptable tests to evaluate progress in all the areas covered by Gardner's theory. At this point, researchers are still evaluating the theory and the educational reforms it has inspired. However, there is no doubt that Gardner's work has helped liberate researchers from narrow psychometric-based views of intelligence. A comparably broad but different view of intelligence comes from another new theory that we'll look at in the next section.

## Sternberg's Triarchic Theory

Robert Sternberg's (1977) early work included a theory of how adults solve problems on intelligence tests. **He later elaborated this theory into what he called the** *triarchic theory* **because it includes three parts or subtheories** **(Sternberg, 1985).**

**According to the** *contextual subtheory,* **intelligent behavior involves skillfully adapting to an environment.** That is, intelligence is always partly defined by the demands of an environment or cultural context. What is intelligent for children growing up in cities in North America may not be intelligent for children growing up in the Sahara desert, in the Australian outback, or on a remote island in the Pacific Ocean. Moreover, what is intelligent at home may not be intelligent in the neighborhood. The "Cultural Influences" feature illustrates how intelligent behavior is always defined by the context.

### How Culture Defines What Is Intelligent

In Brazil, many elementary-school-age boys like the two in the top photo sell candy and fruit to bus passengers and pedestrians. These children often cannot identify the numbers on paper money, yet they know how to purchase their goods from wholesale stores, make change for customers, and keep track of their sales (Saxe, 1988).

Adolescents who live on Pacific Ocean islands near New Guinea learn to sail boats like the one in the bottom photo hundreds of miles across open seas to get from one small island to the next. They have no formal training in mathematics, yet they are able to use a complex navigational system based on the positions of stars and estimates of the boat's speed (Hutchins, 1983).

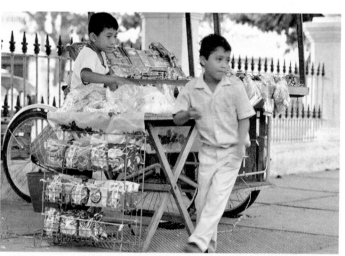

If either the Brazilian vendors or the island navigators were given the tests that measure intelligence in American students, they would fare poorly. Does this mean they are less intelligent than American children? Of course not. The skills that are important to American conceptions of intelligence and that are assessed on our intelligence tests are less valued in these other cultures and so are not cultivated in the young. Each culture defines what it means to be intelligent, and the specialized computing skills of vendors and navigators are just as intelligent in their cultural settings as verbal skills are in American culture (Sternberg & Kaufman, 1998). ●

The triarchic theory includes two other subtheories. **According to the *experiential subtheory,* intelligence is revealed in both novel and familiar tasks.** For novel tasks, intelligence is associated with the ability to apply existing knowledge to a new situation. At the start of a new school year, for example, readily adjusting to new tasks is a sign of intelligence. Bright children learning multiplication readily draw upon relevant math knowledge to grasp what's involved in multiplication.

For familiar tasks, intelligence is associated with the automatic processing that was described in Module 7.1. Completing a task automatically means using few mental resources. At the end of a school year, performing now-familiar school tasks automatically rather than with effort is a sign of intelligence. Bright children now solve multiplication problems automatically, without thinking about the intermediate steps.

**According to the *componential subtheory,* intelligence depends on basic cognitive processes called *components.*** A component is simply Sternberg's term for the different information-processing skills described in Chapter 7, such as monitoring and retrieval. Whether the task is solving an item on an intelligence test, reading a newspaper,

In the triarchic theory, intelligence reflects strategies children use to complete tasks plus the familiarity and relevance of those tasks.

or understanding a conversation, components must be selected and organized in the proper sequence to complete the task successfully. In this subtheory, intelligence reflects more efficient organization and use of components.

In contrast to the psychometric approach and to Gardner's theory, the triarchic theory does not identify specific contents of intelligence. Instead, Sternberg defines intelligence in terms of processes: the strategies people use to complete tasks (componential subtheory), the familiarity of those tasks (experiential subtheory), and the relevance of the tasks to personal and cultural goals (contextual subtheory).

Sternberg's theory also underscores the dangers of comparing test scores of different cultural, ethnic, or racial groups. Comparisons are usually invalid because the test items are not equally relevant in different cultures. In addition, most test items are not equally novel in different cultures. A vocabulary test, for example, is useful in assessing intelligence in cultures where formal education is essential to skilled adaptations (because skilled use of language is important for success in schools). In cultures where schooling is not a key to success, a vocabulary test would not provide useful information because it would be irrelevant to cultural goals and much too novel.

As with Gardner's theory, researchers are still evaluating Sternberg's theory. And, as you can see in the table that summarizes the different approaches, theorists are still debating the question of what intelligence is. But, however it is defined, the fact is that individuals differ substantially in intellectual ability, and numerous tests have been devised to measure these differences. The construction, properties, and limitations of these tests are the focus of the next module.

## Features of Major Perspectives on Intelligence

| Approach to Intelligence | Distinguishing Features |
| --- | --- |
| Psychometric | Intelligence as a hierarchy of general and specific skills |
| Gardner's theory of multiple intelligences | Seven distinct intelligences—linguistic, logical-mathematical, spatial, musical, bodily-kinesthetic, interpersonal, and intrapersonal intelligences |
| Sternberg's triarchic theory | Intelligence is defined by context, experience, and information-processing components |

TABLE 8–2

## Check Your Learning

1. If some children consistently have high scores on different intelligence tests while other children consistently have lower scores on the same tests, this would support the view that intelligence _____.

2. According to _____ theories, intelligence includes both general intelligence as well as more specific abilities, such as verbal and spatial skill.

3. Gardner's theory of multiple intelligences includes linguistic, logical-mathematical, and spatial intelligences, which are included in psychometric theories, as well as musical, _____, interpersonal, and intrapersonal intelligences, which are ignored in psychometric theories.

**4.** Based on Gardner's view of intelligence, teachers should _____.

**5.** According to Sternberg's _____ subtheory, intelligence refers to adapting to an environment to achieve goals.

**6.** Sternberg's theory emphasizes that comparing test scores of children from cultural groups is dangerous because _____.

 **If Jean Piaget were asked to define intelligence, how might his definition differ from a psychometrician's? How might it differ from Gardner's and Sternberg's definitions of intelligence?**

**Answers:** (1) consists of a general factor, g (2) hierarchical, (3) bodily-kinesthetic, (4) adjust their teaching to capitalize on a child's strongest intelligences, (5) contextual, (6) test items are neither equally relevant nor equally novel for children from different groups

# 8.2

- **Binet and the Development of Intelligence Testing**
- **Do Tests Work?**
- **Hereditary and Environmental Factors**
- **Impact of Ethnicity and Social Class**

# Measuring Intelligence

## Learning Objectives

● Why were intelligence tests devised initially? What are modern tests like?

● How well do modern intelligence tests work?

● What are the roles of heredity and environment in determining intelligence?

● How do ethnicity and social class influence intelligence test scores?

> *Charlene, an African American third grader, received a score of 75 on an intelligence test administered by a school psychologist. Based on the test score, the psychologist believes that Charlene is mildly mentally retarded and should receive special education. Charlene's parents are indignant; they believe that the tests are biased against African Americans and that the score is meaningless.*

American schools faced a crisis at the beginning of the 20th century. Between 1890 and 1915, school enrollment nearly doubled nationally as great numbers of immigrants arrived and as reforms restricted child labor and emphasized education (Chapman, 1988). Increased enrollment meant that teachers now had larger numbers of students who did not learn as readily as the "select few" who had populated their classes previously. How to deal with these less capable children was one of the pressing issues of the day. In this module, you'll see how intelligence tests were devised initially to address a changed school population. Then we'll look at a simple question: "How well do modern tests work?" Finally, we'll examine how race, ethnicity, social class, environment, and heredity influence intelligence, and we'll learn how to interpret Charlene's test score.

## Binet and the Development of Intelligence Testing

The problems facing educators at the beginning of the 20th century were not unique to the United States. In 1904, the minister of public instruction in France asked two noted psychologists, Alfred Binet and Theophile Simon, to formulate a way to recognize children who needed special instruction in school. Binet and Simon's approach was to select simple tasks that French children of different ages ought to be able to do, such as naming colors, counting backwards, and remembering numbers in order. Based on preliminary testing, Binet and Simon determined problems that normal 3-year-olds could solve, that normal 4-year-olds could solve, and so on. **Children's *mental age* or *MA* referred to the difficulty of the problems that they could solve correctly.** A child who solved problems that the average 7-year-old could pass would have an MA of 7.

Binet and Simon used mental age to distinguish "bright" from "dull" children. A "bright" child would have the MA of an older child; for example, a 6-year-old with an MA of 9 was considered bright. A "dull" child would have the MA of a younger child, for example, a 6-year-old with an MA of 4. Binet and Simon confirmed that "bright" children did better in school than "dull" children. Voilá—the first objective measure of intelligence!

Binet and Simon created the first intelligence test by using simple tasks to distinguish children who would do well in school from children who wouldn't.

### The Stanford-Binet.

Lewis Terman, of Stanford University, revised Binet and Simon's test and published a version known as the Stanford-Binet in 1916. **Terman described performance as an *intelligence quotient*, or *IQ*, which was simply the ratio of mental age to chronological age, multiplied by 100:**

$$IQ = MA/CA \times 100$$

At any age, children who are perfectly average will have an IQ of 100 because their mental age equals their chronological age. The figure shows the typical distribution of test scores in the population. You can see that roughly two-thirds of children taking a test will have IQ scores between 85 and 115 and that 95 percent will have scores between 70 and 130.

The IQ score can also be used to compare intelligence in children of different ages. A 4-year-old with an MA of 5 has an IQ of 125 (5/4 × 100), the same as an 8-year-old with an MA of 10 (10/8 × 100).

IQ scores are no longer computed in this manner. Instead, children's IQ scores are determined by comparing their test performance to that of others their age.

FIG 8–2

When children perform at the average for their age, their IQ is 100. Children who perform above the average have IQs greater than 100; children who perform below the average have IQs less than 100. Nevertheless, the concept of IQ as the ratio of MA to CA helped popularize the Stanford-Binet test.

By the 1920s, the Stanford-Binet had been joined by many other intelligence tests. Educators enthusiastically embraced the tests as an efficient and objective way to assess a student's chances of succeeding in school (Chapman, 1988).

Today, more than 75 years later, the Stanford-Binet remains a popular test. It was last revised in 1986. Like the earlier versions, today's Stanford-Binet consists of various cognitive and motor tasks, ranging from the extremely easy to the extremely difficult. The test may be administered to individuals ranging in age from approximately 2 years to adulthood, but not every individual is given every question. For example, preschool children may be asked to name pictures of familiar objects, string beads, answer questions about everyday life, or fold paper into shapes. Older individuals may be asked to define vocabulary words, solve an abstract problem,

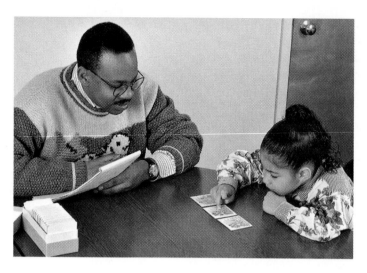

or decipher an unfamiliar code. The examiner determines, according to specific guidelines, the appropriate starting place on the test and administers progressively more difficult questions until the child fails all the questions at a particular level. An IQ score is assigned on the basis of how many questions the child passed compared with the average number passed by children of the same age.

The Stanford-Binet is administered to one person at a time, rather than to a group. Group tests of intelligence have the advantage of providing information about many individuals quickly and inexpensively, often without the need of highly trained psychologists. But individual testing like that shown in the photo optimizes the motivation and attention of the examinee and provides an opportunity for a sensitive examiner to assess factors that may influence test performance. The examiner may notice that the examinee is relaxed and that test performance is therefore a reasonable sample of the individual's talents. Or the examiner may observe that intense anxiety is interfering with performance. Such determinations are not possible with group tests. Consequently, most psychologists prefer individualized tests of intelligence over group tests.

Let's look briefly at two other types of individualized tests, the Wechsler Intelligence Scale for Children—III (WISC-III) and the Kaufman Assessment Battery for Children (K-ABC).

### The Wechsler Scales.

A set of intelligence scales widely used in assessment and research with children is based on the work of David Wechsler. The original Wechsler scale, the Wechsler-Bellevue, was published in 1939 and was designed specifically to measure adult intelligence for clinical (medical, not school) use. Later revisions produced tests for adults (Wechsler Adult Intelligence Scale, or WAIS), for schoolchildren (Wechsler Intelligence Scale for Children—III), and for children 4 to 6 years of age (Wechsler Preschool and Primary Scale of Intelligence—Revised, or WPPSI-R). All these tests follow a similar format.

The WISC-III, unlike the Stanford-Binet, includes subtests for verbal and performance skills, some of which are shown in the figure at the top of page 223. Children thus are assessed on verbal IQ, performance IQ, and a combination of the two, the full-scale IQ. A second major difference between the WISC-III and the Stanford-Binet is that each child receives the same subtests, with some adjustment for either age level or competence or both.

### The Kaufman Assessment Battery for Children.

Alan Kaufman directed the 1974 revision of the WISC and wrote a well-known book on the proper use of the WISC (Kaufman, 1979). From these experiences, he and Nadeen Kaufman developed a new test of intelligence for 2- through 12-year-olds, the Kaufman Assessment Battery for Children, or K-ABC (Kaufman & Kaufman, 1983a; 1983b). **One scale of the K-ABC measures *simultaneous processing,* how well a child integrates different information at the same time.** We use such "mental synthesis" to understand pictures in which many elements must be integrated to form a cohesive whole. **Another scale assesses *sequential processing,* how well a child integrates information over time.** We integrate in sequence to comprehend language, where

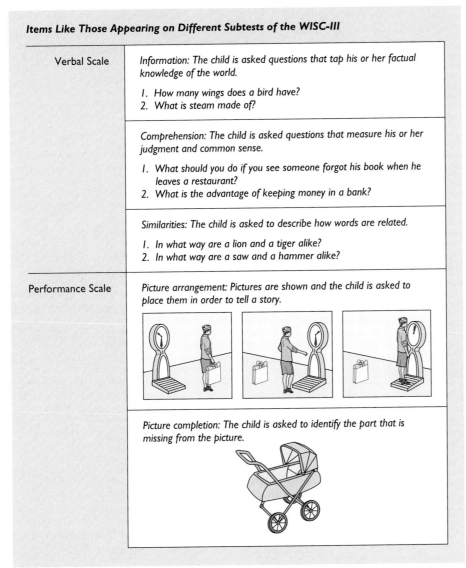

*Items Like Those Appearing on Different Subtests of the WISC-III*

| Verbal Scale | *Information: The child is asked questions that tap his or her factual knowledge of the world.* |
| | 1. *How many wings does a bird have?* |
| | 2. *What is steam made of?* |
| | *Comprehension: The child is asked questions that measure his or her judgment and common sense.* |
| | 1. *What should you do if you see someone forgot his book when he leaves a restaurant?* |
| | 2. *What is the advantage of keeping money in a bank?* |
| | *Similarities: The child is asked to describe how words are related.* |
| | 1. *In what way are a lion and a tiger alike?* |
| | 2. *In what way are a saw and a hammer alike?* |
| Performance Scale | *Picture arrangement: Pictures are shown and the child is asked to place them in order to tell a story.* |
| | *Picture completion: The child is asked to identify the part that is missing from the picture.* |

FIG 8–3

Source: Simulated items similar to those in the Wechsler Intelligence Scales for Adult and Children. Copyright 1949, 1955, 1974, 1981, and 1990 by the Psychological Corporation. Reproduced by permission    ights reserved.

meaning hinges on the particular order of words. A third scale measures academic achievement.

The Stanford-Binet, WISC-III, and K-ABC are the most widely used individualized tests of children's intelligence. The basic approach of each is similar—asking children to solve simple tasks, some of which are novel and some of which are relatively familiar—but they provide different results. The Stanford-Binet reports a single IQ score; the WISC-III provides verbal, performance, and overall IQ scores; and the K-ABC provides simultaneous and sequential processing scores along with academic achievement.

**Infant Tests.**   The Stanford-Binet, WISC-III, and K-ABC cannot be used to test intelligence in infants. For this purpose, many psychologists use the Bayley Scales of Infant Development (Bayley, 1970).

The Stanford-Binet measures overall IQ; the WISC-III measures verbal and performance IQ; and the K-ABC measures simultaneous and sequential processing and academic achievement.

Designed for 2- to 30-month-olds, the Bayley Scales consist of mental and motor scales. The mental scale assesses adaptive behavior, such as attending to visual and auditory stimuli, following directions, looking for a fallen toy, and imitating. The motor scale assesses an infant's control of its body, its coordination, and its ability to manipulate objects. For example, 6-month-olds should turn their head toward an object that the examiner drops on the floor, 12-month-olds should imitate the examiner's actions, and 16-month-olds should build a tower from three blocks.

The Bayley Scales were revised recently (Bayley, 1993). They can now be used with children as old as 42 months, and they assess additional abilities, including habituation, memory, and problem solving.

## Do Tests Work?

To determine whether intelligence tests work, we need to consider two separate issues, reliability and validity. As I described in Module 1.2, a test is reliable if it yields scores that are consistent. Reliability is often measured by administering similar forms of a test on two occasions. If the test is reliable, a child will have similar scores both times. Today's intelligence tests are very reliable. If a child takes an intelligence test and then retakes it days or a few weeks later, the two scores are usually quite similar (Wechsler, 1991).

Reliability over the long term is more complex. In general, scores from infant intelligence tests are not related to IQ scores obtained later in childhood, adolescence, or adulthood (McCall, 1989). Apparently, children must be at least 18 to 24 months old before their Bayley scores, or scores from similar scales, can predict later IQ scores on the Wechsler or Stanford-Binet scales (Kopp & McCall, 1982).

Why don't scores on infant intelligence tests predict childhood or adult IQ more accurately? One reason is that infant tests measure different abilities than tests administered to children and adolescents: Infant tests place more emphasis on sensorimotor skills and less on tasks involving cognitive processes such as language, thinking, and problem solving.

According to this reasoning, a measure of infant cognitive processing might yield more accurate predictions of later IQ. In fact, habituation, a measure of information processing described in Module 5.2, does predict later IQ more effectively than scores from the Bayley. The average correlation between habituation and later IQ is approximately .5 (Bornstein, 1997). That is, 1- to 6-month-olds who habituate to visual stimuli more rapidly tend to have higher IQs as children. Apparently, infants who rapidly make sense of their world—in this case, thinking "I've seen this picture before, so let's see something new!"—are smarter during the elementary-school years.

If scores on the Bayley Scales do not predict later IQs, why are these tests used at all? The answer is that they are important diagnostic tools: They can be used to determine if development is progressing normally. For example, the Bayley mental scale can detect the impact of prenatal exposure to teratogens (Bellinger et al., 1987). It can also assess whether the infant's home environment provides sufficient stimulation for mental development (Bradley et al., 1987).

Although infant test scores don't reliably predict IQ later in life, scores obtained in childhood do. The graph at the top of page 225 shows the results from several longitudinal studies that correlated IQ scores obtained at different points in childhood or adolescence and at maturity. (Each line in the graph represents a different study.) You can see that the correlation between IQ at 5 years and maturity is approximately .5 and that the correlations get steadily larger as children get older.

These correlations appear to support the idea that intelligence is relatively stable from early childhood on. However, when individual performance over time is examined, stability is not a hard-and-fast rule. McCall, Appelbaum, and Hogarty (1973) conducted a longitudinal study in which 80 individuals had their intelligence tested roughly 14 times between ages 2 and 17. They discovered several different developmental patterns. The most common pattern—found in nearly 50 percent of the participants—was for little change in IQ from 2 to 17 years of age. However, for about 15 percent of the participants, IQ scores first increased, then decreased with age. For another 15 percent, the pattern was just the opposite: IQ scores first decreased, then increased with age.

McCall and his colleagues (1973) also found that children were most likely to have increasing IQ scores when their parents deliberately trained their intellectual and motor skills. When parents did not train their youngsters' intellectual and motor development (or, in some cases, actively discouraged it), IQ scores were likely to decline as children got older. Thus, although IQ is often relatively stable throughout childhood and adolescence, this is definitely not the only pattern. For many children, IQ will change both up and down as they develop.

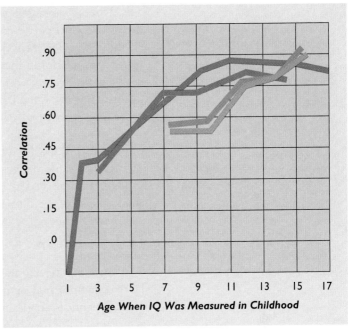

FIG 8–4
Source: Bloom, 1964.

### Are Tests Valid?

Reliability of tests, whether short- or long-term, is not the only criterion for evaluating a test. What do test scores mean? Are they really measuring intelligence? These questions raise the issue of validity, which refers to the extent that a test really measures what it claims to measure. Validity is usually measured by determining the relation between test scores and other independent measures of what the test is thought to measure. For example, to measure the validity of a test of extroversion, we would have children take the test, then observe them in a social setting, such as a school recess, and record who is outgoing and who is shy. The test would be valid if scores correlated highly with our independent observations of extroverted behavior.

How would we extend this approach to intelligence tests? Ideally, we would administer the intelligence tests and then correlate the scores with other independent estimates of intelligence. Therein lies the problem. There are no other independent ways to estimate intelligence; the only way to measure intelligence is with tests. Consequently, many follow Binet's lead and obtain measures of performance in school, such as grades or teachers' ratings of their students. Correlations between these measures and scores on intelligence tests typically fall somewhere between .4 and .6 (Neisser et al., 1996). For example, the correlation between scores on the WISC-III and grade point average is .47 (Wechsler, 1991). This correlation is positive but far from a correlation of 1. Obviously, some youngsters with high test scores do not excel in school, whereas others with low scores get good grades. In general, however, tests do a reasonable job of predicting school success.

*Most test developers argue that their tests are valid—actually measure intelligence—by showing that test scores are related to children's performance in school.*

Not only are intelligence tests reasonable predictors of performance in school, they also predict performance in the workplace, particularly for more complex jobs (Gottfredson, 1997; Schmidt & Hunter, 1998). Workers with higher IQ scores tend to be more successful in their on-the-job training and, following training, more successful in their actual work performance. If, for example, two teenagers have summer jobs running tests in a biology lab, the smarter of the two will probably learn the procedures more rapidly and, once learned, conduct them more accurately.

### Increasing Validity with Dynamic Testing.

Traditional tests of intelligence such as the Stanford-Binet and the WISC-III measure knowledge and skills that a child has accumulated up to the time of testing. These tests do *not* directly measure a child's potential for future learning; instead, the usual assumption is that children who have learned more in the past will probably learn more in the future. Critics argue that tests would be more valid if they directly assessed a child's potential for future learning.

*Dynamic testing* **measures a child's learning potential by having the child learn something new in the presence of the examiner and with the examiner's help.** Thus, dynamic testing is interactive and measures new achievement rather than past achievement. It is based on Vygotsky's ideas of the zone of proximal development and scaffolding (pages 174–175). Learning potential can be estimated by the amount of material the child learns during interaction with the examiner and from the amount of help the child needs to learn the new material (Grigorenko & Sternberg, 1998).

To understand the difference between traditional, static methods of intelligence testing and new, dynamic approaches, imagine a group of children attending a week-long soccer camp. On the first day, all children are tested on a range of soccer skills and receive a score that indicates their overall level of soccer skill. If this score were shown to predict later success in soccer, such as number of goals scored in a season, this would be a valid static measure of soccer skill. To make this a dynamic measure of soccer skill, children would spend all week at camp being instructed in new skills. At the end of the week, the test of soccer skills would be readministered. The amount of the child's improvement over the week would measure learning potential, with greater improvement indicating greater learning potential.

Together, static and dynamic testing provide a comprehensive view of a child's talents.

Dynamic testing is a recent innovation and is still being evaluated. Preliminary research does indicate, however, that static and dynamic testing both provide useful and independent information. If the aim is to predict future levels of a child's skill, it is valuable to know a child's current level of skill (static testing) as well as the child's potential to acquire greater skill (dynamic testing). By combining both forms of testing, we achieve a more comprehensive view of a child's talents than by relying on either method alone (Day et al., 1997).

### Hereditary and Environmental Factors

oanna, a 5-year-old girl, was administered the WISC-III and obtained a score of 112. Ted, a 5-year-old boy, took the same test and received a score of 92. What accounts for the 20-point difference in these youngsters' scores? Heredity and experience both matter.

Some of the evidence for hereditary factors is shown in the graph at the top of page 227. If genes influence intelligence, then siblings' test scores should become more alike as siblings become more similar genetically (Plomin & Petrill, 1997). In other words, since identical twins are identical genetically, they typically have

FIG 8–5

virtually identical test scores, which would be a correlation of 1. Fraternal twins have about 50 percent of their genes in common, just like nontwins of the same biological parents. Consequently, their test scores should be (a) less similar than scores for identical twins, (b) as similar as other siblings who have the same biological parents, and (c) more similar than scores of children and their adopted siblings. You can see in the graph that each of these predictions is supported.

Heredity also influences developmental profiles for IQ scores (Wilson, 1983). Developmental profiles for IQ are more alike for identical twins than for fraternal twins. If one identical twin gets higher IQ scores with age, the other twin almost certainly will, too. In contrast, if one fraternal twin gets higher scores with age, the other twin may not necessarily show the same pattern. Thus, identical twins are not only more alike in overall IQ, but in developmental change in IQ as well.

Studies of adopted children suggest that the impact of heredity increases during childhood and adolescence: If heredity helps determine IQ, then children's IQs should be more like their biological parents' IQs than their adoptive parents' IQs. In fact, these correlations were computed in the Colorado Adoption Project (Plomin et al., 1997), which included adopted children as well as their biological and adoptive parents. Biological parents' IQ was measured before the child was born; adoptive parents' IQ was measured before the child's first birthday; children's IQs were tested repeatedly in childhood and adolescence. The results, shown in the graph, are clear. At every age, the correlation between children's IQ and their biological parents' IQ (shown by the blue line) is greater than the correlation between children's IQ and their adoptive parents' IQ (shown by the red line). In fact, children's IQ scores are essentially unrelated to their adoptive parents' IQs.

Notice, too, that the relation between children's IQ and their biological parents' IQ actually gets *stronger* as children get older. In other words, as adopted children get older, their test scores increasingly resemble their biological parents' scores. These results are evidence for the greater impact of heredity on IQ as a child grows.

Do these results mean that heredity is the sole determiner of intelligence? No. Two areas of research show the importance of environment on intelligence. The first is research on characteristics of families and homes. The second is research on the impact of preschool intervention or enrichment programs.

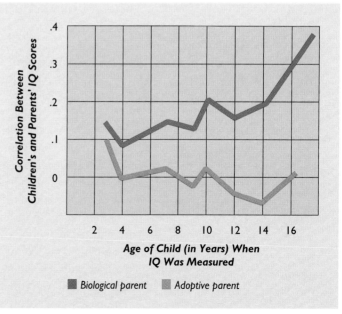

FIG 8–6

If intelligence were solely due to heredity, environment should have little or no impact on children's intelligence. But we know that many characteristics of parents' behavior and home environments are related to children's intelligence. Bettye Caldwell and Robert Bradley (1994) developed the Home Observation for Measurement of the Environment (HOME), an inventory for assessing parents' behavior as well as the quality and organization of the child's home environment.

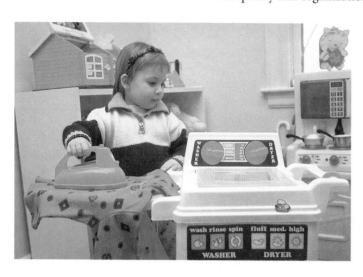

HOME testing indicates that children with high test scores typically have parents who are stimulating, responsive, and involved (Bradley, Caldwell, & Rock, 1988). In addition, among European American children, an environment like the one in the photo that includes plenty of variety and appropriate play materials is linked to high test scores. For African American children, a well-organized home environment is associated with higher scores (Bradley et al., 1989).

The importance of a stimulating environment for intelligence is also demonstrated by intervention programs that prepare economically disadvantaged children for school. When children grow up in never-ending poverty, the cycle is predictable and tragic: Youngsters have few of the intellectual skills to succeed in school, so they fail; lacking an education, they find minimal jobs (if they can work at all), guaranteeing that their children, too, are destined to grow up in poverty.

Since Project Head Start was begun in 1965, massive educational intervention has been an important tool in the effort to break this repeated cycle of poverty. Head Start and other intervention programs teach preschool youngsters basic school readiness skills and social skills and offer guidance to parents (Ramey & Ramey, 1990). When children participate in these enrichment programs, their test scores go up and school achievement improves, particularly when intervention programs are extended beyond preschool into the elementary-school years (Reynolds & Temple, 1998). In the "Focus on Research" feature, we look at one of these success stories in detail.

FOCUS ON RESEARCH

### The Carolina Abecedarian Project

*Who were the investigators, and what was the aim of the study?* Since the 1960s, many intervention programs have demonstrated that young children's intelligence test scores can be raised with enrichment, but the improvement is often short-lived. That is, within a few years after completing the intervention program, test scores are at the same level as before the program. Frances Campbell and Craig Ramey (1994; Ramey & Campbell, 1991) designed the Carolina Abecedarian Project to see if massive and sustained intervention could produce more long-lasting changes.

*How did the investigators measure the topic of interest?* Some children did not participate in any intervention program. Other children attended a special day-care facility daily from 4 months until 5 years. The curriculum emphasized mental, linguistic, and social development for infants, and prereading skills for preschoolers. Some children went on to participate in another intervention program during their first 3 years of elementary school. During this phase, a teacher visited the home a few times each month, bringing materials for improving reading and math. The teachers taught parents how to use the materials with their child and acted as facilitators between home and school. Campbell and Ramey measured the impact of intervention in several ways, including scores on intelligence tests, scores on achievement tests, and children's need for special services in school.

*Who were the children in the study?* At the start, the project included 111 children; most were born to African American mothers who had less than a high-school education, an average IQ score of 85, and typically no income. Over the course of the study, 21 children dropped out of the project, leaving 90 children at the end.

*What was the design of the study?* This study was experimental because children were randomly assigned to an intervention condition (preschool intervention, elementary-school intervention, both, or no intervention). The independent variable was the intervention condition. The dependent variables included performance on intelligence and achievement tests. The study was longitudinal because children were tested repeatedly over an 8-year period.

*Were there ethical concerns with the study?* No. The nature of the study was explained fully to parents, including how their child was assigned to a particular intervention condition.

*What were the results?* The graph shows children's performance on three achievement tests that they took as 12-year-olds, 4 years after the elementary-school intervention had ended. In all three areas that were tested—written language, math, and reading—performance clearly reflects the amount of intervention. Youngsters who had a full 8 years of intervention generally have the highest scores; children with no intervention have the lowest scores.

*What did the investigators conclude?* Massive, continued intervention works. An improvement of 7 to 10 points may not strike you as very much, but it is a substantial improvement from a practical standpoint. For example, the written language scores of the youngsters with 8 years of intervention place them near the 50th percentile, meaning that their scores are greater than about half of the children taking the test. In contrast, children with no intervention have scores at the 20th percentile, making their scores greater than only 20 percent of the children taking the test. Thus, after intervention, children moved from being substantially below average to average, quite an accomplishment.

Of course, massive intervention over 8 years is expensive. But so are the economic consequences of poverty, unemployment, and their byproducts. Programs like the Abecedarian Project show that the repetitive cycle of school failure and education can be broken. In the process, they show that intelligence is fostered by a stimulating and responsive environment. ●

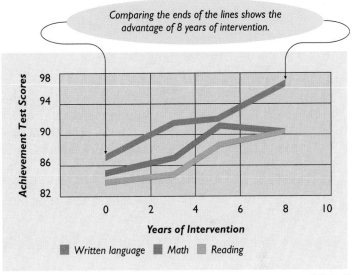

FIG 8–7

Massive, long-term intervention increases children's intelligence and achievement.

## Impact of Ethnicity and Social Class

The results in the graph at the top of page 230 have been the source of controversy for decades. They show that on many intelligence tests African Americans score about 15 points lower than European Americans (Brody, 1992). What accounts for this difference? Some of the difference is due to social class. Typically, children from

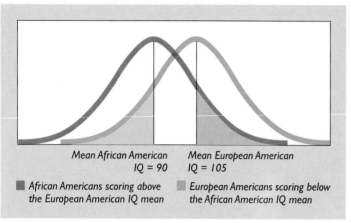

*Mean African American*
*IQ = 90*

*Mean European American*
*IQ = 105*

■ *African Americans scoring above*
*the European American IQ mean*

■ *European Americans scoring below*
*the African American IQ mean*

FIG 8–8

lower social classes have lower scores on intelligence tests, and African American children are more likely than European American children to live in lower-socioeconomic-class homes. When European American and African American children of comparable social class are compared, the difference in IQ test scores is reduced but not eliminated (Brooks-Gunn, Klebanov, & Duncan, 1996). So social class explains some but not all of the difference between European American and African American children's IQ scores.

Some critics contend that the difference in test scores reflects bias in the tests themselves. They argue that test items reflect the cultural heritage of the test creators, most of whom are middle-class European Americans, and so tests are biased against lower-class and African American children. They point to test items like this one:

*A conductor is to an orchestra as a teacher is to what?*

*book    school    class    eraser*

Children whose background includes exposure to orchestras are more likely to answer this question correctly than children who lack this exposure.

**The problem of bias has led to the development of** *culture-fair intelligence tests,* **which include test items based on experiences common to many cultures.** An example is Raven's Progressive Matrices, which consists solely of items like the one shown here. Examinees are asked to select the piece that would complete the design correctly (6, in this case).

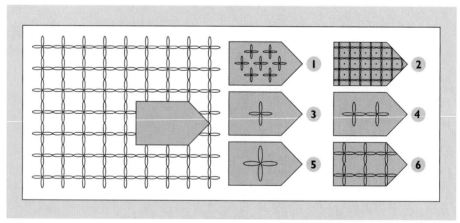

FIG 8–9

Culture-fair tests predict achievement in school, but do not eliminate group differences in test scores: European and African Americans still differ (Anastasi, 1988; Herrnstein & Murray, 1994). Why? Culture can influence a child's familiarity with the entire testing situation, not simply familiarity with particular items. A culture-fair test will underestimate a child's intelligence if, for example, the child's culture encourages children to solve problems in collaboration with others and discourages them from excelling as individuals.

Moreover, because they are wary of questions posed by unfamiliar adults, many African American and other economically disadvantaged children often answer test questions by saying, "I don't know." Obviously, this strategy guarantees an artificially low test score. When these children are given extra time to feel at ease with the examiner, they respond less often with "I don't know" and their test scores improve considerably (Zigler & Finn-Stevenson, 1992).

If all tests reflect cultural influences, at least to some degree, how should we interpret test scores? Remember that tests assess successful adaptation to a particular cultural context. Most intelligence tests predict success in a school environment, which usually espouses middle-class values. Regardless of ethnic group—African American, Hispanic American, or European American—a child with a high test score has the intellectual skills needed for academic work based on middle-class values. A child with a low test score, like Charlene in the module-opening vignette, apparently lacks those skills. Does a low score mean Charlene is destined to fail in school? No. It simply means that, based on her current skills, she's unlikely to do well. As we saw in the "Focus on Research" feature on the Abecedarian Project, improving Charlene's skills will improve her school performance.

By focusing on groups of people, it's easy to lose sight of the fact that individuals within these groups differ in intelligence. Look again at the graph on page 230; you'll see that the average difference in IQ scores between European Americans and African Americans is very small compared to the entire range of scores for these groups. Many African Americans achieve higher IQ scores than the average European American; many European Americans achieve lower IQ scores than the average African American.

> A low score on an intelligence test means that a child currently lacks skills needed to succeed in school, not that the child will forever fail in school.

## Check Your Learning

**1.** The Stanford-Binet introduced the idea of the intelligence quotient, which was _____, multiplied by 100.

**2.** The WISC-III provides a verbal IQ score and a _____.

**3.** Infant intelligence tests, such as the Bayley scales, do not predict childhood IQ scores but are useful for _____.

**4.** Modern intelligence tests are typically validated by _____.

**5.** As identical twins develop, their IQ scores _____.

**6.** As adopted children get older, their IQ scores increasingly resemble the IQ scores of their _____ parents.

**7.** Evidence for the impact of environment on intelligence comes from studies of families and homes as well as from _____.

**8.** The problem of cultural bias on intelligence tests led to the development of _____.

 **IQ scores from the Stanford-Binet, WISC-III, and K-ABC tests tend to be highly related. A child who has a high score on the Stanford-Binet usually has a high score on the WISC-III and the K-ABC. What does this tell us about the tests and the nature of intelligence? What does this say about the general and specific factors in intelligence described in Module 8.1?**

**Answers:** (1) MA/CA, (2) performance IQ score, (3) determining whether development is progressing normally, (4) showing that test scores correlate with measures of performance in school, (5) follow the same developmental profile, (6) biological, (7) studies on the impact of intervention and enrichment programs, (8) culture-fair intelligence tests, which have test items common to many cultures

# 8.3

## Special Children, Special Needs

### Learning Objectives

● **What are the characteristics of gifted and creative children?**

● **What are the different forms of mental retardation?**

● **What are learning disabilities?**

*Sanjit, a second grader, has taken two separate intelligence tests, and both times he had above-average scores. Nevertheless, Sanjit absolutely cannot read. Letters and words are as mysterious to him as Metallica's music would be to Mozart. His parents took him to an ophthalmologist, who determined that Sanjit's vision was 20-20; nothing is wrong with his eyes. What is wrong?*

Throughout history, societies have recognized children with limited mental abilities as well as those with extraordinary talents. Today, we know much about the extremes of human talents. We'll begin this module with a look at gifted and creative children. Then we'll look at children with mental retardation and learning disabilities and discover why Sanjit can't read.

### Gifted and Creative Children

In many respects the boy in the photo, Bernie, is an ordinary middle-class 12-year-old: He is the goalie on his soccer team, takes piano lessons on Saturday mornings, sings in his church youth choir, and likes to go roller blading. However, when it comes to intelligence and academic prowess, Bernie leaves the ranks of the ordinary. He received a score of 175 on an intelligence test and is taking a college calculus course. **Bernie is *gifted,* which traditionally has referred to individuals with scores of 130 or greater on intelligence tests** (Horowitz & O'Brien, 1986).

Bernie doesn't fit the stereotype of gifted children, who are often thought to be emotionally troubled and unable to get along with their peers (Halpern & Luria, 1989). In fact, research shows that gifted youngsters tend to be more mature than their peers and have fewer emotional problems (Luthar, Zigler, & Goldstein, 1992). Gifted children's thinking seems to develop in the same sequence as nongifted children's thinking, just more rapidly. Gifted children simply think like older nongifted children (Jackson & Butterfield, 1986).

Because giftedness has traditionally been defined in terms of IQ scores, exceptional ability has been associated exclusively with scholastic skill. But modern definitions of giftedness are broader and include exceptional talent in an assortment of areas, including art, music, creative writing, and dance (Robinson & Clinkenbeard, 1998).

Whether the field is music or math, though, exceptional talent seems to have several prerequisites (Feldman & Goldsmith, 1991; Rathunde & Csikszentmihalyi, 1993):

- The child loves the subject and has an almost overwhelming desire to master it.

- Instruction to develop the child's special talent usually begins at an early age with inspiring and talented teachers.

- Parents are committed to promoting their child's talent.

The message here is that exceptional talent must be nurtured. Without encouragement and support from parents and stimulating and challenging mentors, a youngster's talents will wither. Talented children need a curriculum that is challenging and complex; they need teachers who know how to foster talent; and they need like-minded peers who stimulate their interests (Feldhusen, 1996).

**Creativity.**    If you've seen the movie *Amadeus,* you know the difference between being talented and being creative. Mozart and Salieri were rival composers in Europe during the 18th century. Both were talented, ambitious musicians. Yet, more than 200 years later, Mozart is revered and Salieri is all but forgotten. Why? Then and now, Mozart was considered creative but Salieri was not. What is creativity, and how does it differ from intelligence?

**Intelligence is associated with *convergent thinking,* using information that is provided to determine a standard, correct answer. In contrast, creativity is associated with *divergent thinking,* where the aim is not a single correct answer (often there isn't one) but novel and unusual lines of thought** (Guilford, 1967).

Divergent thinking is often measured by asking children to produce many ideas in response to some specific stimulus (Kogan, 1983). For example, children might be asked to name different uses for a common object, such as a coat hanger. Or they might be shown a page filled with circles and asked to draw as many different pictures as they can, as shown in the figure. Both the number of responses and the originality of the responses are used to measure creativity.

Creativity, like giftedness, must be cultivated. The "Making Children's Lives Better" feature gives some guidelines for fostering children's creativity.

FIG 8–10

**Fostering Creativity**

Here are some guidelines for helping children be more creative.

1. Encourage children to take risks. Not all novel ideas bear fruit; some won't work and some are silly. But only by repeatedly thinking in novel and unusual ways are children likely to produce something truly original.

2. Encourage children to think of alternatives to conventional wisdom. Have them think what would happen if accepted practices were changed. For example, "What would life be like without cars?" or "Why not eat breakfast in the evening and dinner in the morning?"

3. Praise children for working hard. As the saying goes, creativity is one part inspiration and nine parts perspiration. The raw creative insight must be polished to achieve the luster of a finished product.

4. Help children get over the "I'm not creative" hurdle. Too often they believe that only others are creative. Assure children that anyone who follows these guidelines will become more creative. ●

Gifted and creative children represent one extreme of human ability. At the other extreme are youngsters with mental retardation, the topic of the next section.

## Children with Mental Retardation

"ittle David" was the oldest of four children. He learned to sit only days before his first birthday, he began to walk at 2, and he said his first words as a 3-year-old. By age 5, David was far behind his agemates developmentally. David had Down syndrome, described in Module 2.2. An extra 21st chromosome caused David's retarded mental development.

> Mental retardation is defined not just by below-average scores on intelligence tests but by problems adapting to the environment.

*Mental retardation* **refers to substantially below-average intelligence and problems adapting to an environment that emerge before the age of 18.** Below-average intelligence is defined as a score of 70 or less on an intelligence test such as the Stanford-Binet. Adaptive behavior is usually evaluated from interviews with a parent or other caregiver and refers to the daily living skills needed to live, work, and play in the community—skills for caring for oneself and social skills. Only individuals who are under 18, have problems in these areas, and IQ scores of 70 or less are considered mentally retarded (Baumeister & Baumeister, 1995).

### Types of Mental Retardation.

Your image of a mentally retarded child may be someone with Down syndrome, like the child shown on page 47. In reality, mentally retarded individuals are just as varied as nonretarded people. How, then, can we describe this variety? One approach is to distinguish the causes of mental retardation. **Some cases of mental retardation—no more than 25 percent—can be traced to a specific biological or physical problem and are known as** *organic mental retardation.* Down syndrome is the most common organic form of mental retardation. Other types of mental retardation apparently do not involve biological damage. *Familial mental retardation* **simply represents the lower end of the normal distribution of intelligence.**

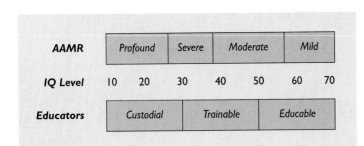

FIG 8–11

Organic mental retardation is usually substantial, and familial mental retardation is usually less pronounced. The American Association on Mental Retardation identifies four levels of retardation. The levels, along with the range of IQ scores associated with each level, are shown in the chart. Also shown are the three levels of retardation typically used by educators in the United States (Cipani, 1991).

Fortunately, the most severe forms of mental retardation are relatively uncommon. Profound, severe, and moderate retardation together make up only 10 percent of all cases. Profoundly and severely retarded individuals usually have so few skills that they must be supervised constantly. Consequently, they usually live in institutions for retarded persons, where they can sometimes be taught self-help skills such as dressing, feeding, and toileting (Reid, Wilson, & Faw, 1991).

Moderately retarded persons may develop the intellectual skills of a nonretarded 7- or 8-year-old. With this level of functioning, they can sometimes support themselves, typically at a sheltered workshop, where they perform simple tasks under close supervision.

The remaining 90 percent of individuals with mental retardation are classified as mildly or educable mentally retarded. These individuals go to school and can master many academic skills, but at an older age than a nonretarded child. Individuals with mild mental retardation can lead independent lives. Like the man in the photograph, many mildly retarded people work. Some marry. Comprehensive training programs that focus on vocational and social skills help individuals with mild mental retardation be productive citizens and satisfied human beings (Ellis & Rusch, 1991), as you can see by learning more about "little David" in the "Real Children" feature.

REAL CHILDREN

### Little David, the Rest of the Story

"Little David," so named because his father was also named David, was the oldest of four children; none of his siblings was mentally retarded. As the children grew up, they interacted the way most siblings do—laughing and playing together and some-times fighting and arguing. Beginning as a teenager and continu-ing into adulthood, each day David took a city bus from home to his job at a sheltered workshop. He worked 6 hours at such tasks as making bows for packages and stuffing envelopes. He saved his earnings to buy what became his prized posses-sions—a camera, a color TV, and a VCR. As David's siblings entered adulthood, they began their own families. David relished his new role as "Uncle David" and looked forward to visits from his nieces and nephews. As David entered his 40s, he began to suffer memory loss and was often confused. When he died, at age 47, family and friends grieved over their loss. Yet they all marveled at the richness of David's life. By any standards, David had led a full and satisfying life. ●

Little David's mental retardation represents one end of the intelligence spec-trum; Bernie's precocity represents the other. Falling between these two extremes are other special children, those with learning disabilities.

## Children with Learning Disabilities

For some children with normal intelligence, learning is a struggle. **These young-sters have a *learning disability:* they (a) have difficulty mastering an academic subject, (b) have normal intelligence, and (c) are not suffering from other con-ditions that could explain poor performance, such as sensory impairment or inadequate instruction (Hammill, 1990).**

In the United States, about 5 percent of school-age children are classified as learning disabled, which translates into roughly 2 million youngsters (Moats & Lyon, 1993). The number of distinct disabilities and the degree of overlap among them are still debated (Stanovich, 1993). However, one common classification scheme distin-guishes disability in language (including listening, speaking, and writing), in read-ing, and in arithmetic (Dockrell & McShane, 1993).

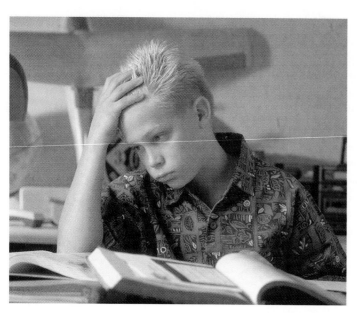

The variety of learning disabilities complicates the task for teachers and researchers because it suggests that each type of learning disability may have its own cause and treatment (Lyon, 1996). Take reading, the most common area of learning disability, as an example. Many children with a reading disability have problems in phonological awareness (described in Module 7.3), which refers to understanding and using the sounds in written and oral language. For a reading-disabled child like Sanjit (in the vignette) or the boy in the photograph, all vowels sound alike. Thus *pin* sounds like *pen,* which sounds like *pan.* These youngsters benefit from explicit, extensive instruction on the connections between letters and their sounds (Lyon, 1996; Wise, Ring, & Olson, 1999).

In the case of arithmetic disability, children often have difficulty recognizing what operations are needed and how to perform them. Here, instruction emphasizes determining the goal of arithmetic problems, using goals to select correct arithmetic operations, and using operations accurately (Goldman, 1989).

The key to helping these children is to move beyond the generic label *learning disability* to pinpoint specific cognitive and academic deficits that hamper an individual child's performance in school. Then instruction can be specifically tailored to improve the child's skills (Moats & Lyon, 1993).

Planning effective instruction for children with learning disabilities is much easier said than done, however, because diagnosing learning disability is very difficult. Some children have both reading and language disabilities; other children have reading and arithmetic disabilities. Despite these difficulties, with ingenuity, hard work, and care, children with learning disabilities—and all exceptional children, for that matter—can develop their full intellectual potential.

## Check Your Learning

1. Traditionally, giftedness was defined solely in terms of _____.

2. Creativity is associated with _____ thinking, in which the goal is to think in novel and unusual directions.

3. Cases of _____ mental retardation are due to specific biological or physical problems.

4. Most individuals with mental retardation are classified as _____.

5. Children with a learning disability are unable to master an academic subject, have _____, and have no other condition, such as sensory impairment, that could explain their poor performance.

6. Children with reading disability often benefit from instruction on _____.

> How might our definitions of giftedness and mental retardation change if they were based on Robert Sternberg's triarchic theory? On Jean Piaget's cognitive-developmental theory?

# Intelligence and Individual Differences in Cognition

**8**

## IN PERSPECTIVE

Navigating to a distant island, running a business selling candy, and speaking fluently—these are just a few manifestations of the marvelous thing called human intelligence. In Module 8.1, we found that human intelligence does indeed come in many varieties but that researchers have yet to agree on how many and what they are. In Module 8.2, we saw that several tests can be used to assess children's intelligence reliably and validly, but that most of these tests focus on those aspects of intelligence involved in school success. In Module 8.3, we saw that the extremes of intelligence include gifted and creative children as well as children with mental retardation and learning disabilities.

In this chapter, I want to underscore the theme that *development is always jointly influenced by heredity and environment.* In no other area of child development is this theme as important, because the implications for social policy are so profound. If intelligence were completely determined by heredity, for example, intervention programs would be a waste of time and tax dollars because no amount of experience would change nature's prescription for intelligence. But we've seen several times in this chapter that neither heredity nor environment is all-powerful when it comes to intelligence. Studies of twins, for example, remind us that heredity clearly has substantial impact on IQ scores. Identical twins' IQs are consistently more alike than fraternal twins', a result that documents heredity's influence on intelligence. Yet, at the same time, intervention studies like the Carolina Abecedarian Project show that intelligence is malleable. Children's intelligence can be enhanced by intensely stimulating environments.

Thus, heredity imposes some limits on how a child's intelligence will develop, but the limits are fairly modest. We can nurture all children's intelligence considerably if we are willing to invest the time and effort.

## See for Yourself

We've seen that the definition of intelligence differs across cultural settings. See how parents define intelligence by asking them to rate the importance of four common aspects of intelligence:

- Problem-solving skill (thinking before acting, seeing different sides to a problem)
- Verbal skill (speaking clearly, having a large vocabulary)
- Creative skill (asking many questions, trying new things)

- Social skill (playing and working well with other people, respecting and caring for others)

Ask parents to rate the importance of each element on a 6-point scale, where 1 means extremely unimportant to intelligence and 6 means extremely important. Try to ask parents from different ethnic groups; then compare your results with other students' results to see if parents' views of intelligence are similar or different and if cultural background affects parents' definitions. See for yourself!

## Resources

*For more information about . . .*

*the lives of brilliant and creative people,* read Howard Gardner's *Creating Minds* (Basic Books, 1993), which illustrates each different intelligence in Gardner's theory by tracing its development in the life of an extraordinary person, including Albert Einstein, Martha Graham, and Pablo Picasso.

 *different psychological tests, including tests that measure intelligence and creativity,* visit the Web site of the library of the Psychology Department, Macquarie University,
**http://www.bhs.mq.edu.au/lib/testref.html**

## Key Terms

componential subtheory 218
components 218
contextual subtheory 217
convergent thinking 233
culture-fair intelligence tests 230
divergent thinking 233
dynamic testing 226

experiential subtheory 218
familial mental retardation 234
gifted 232
intelligence quotient (IQ) 221
learning disability 235
mental age (MA) 221
mental retardation 234

organic mental retardation 234
psychometricians 214
savants 216
sequential processing 222
simultaneous processing 222
social-cognitive flexibility 217
triarchic theory 217

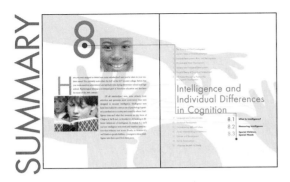

Intelligence and
Individual Differences
in Cognition

8.1  What Is Intelligence?
8.2  Measuring Intelligence
8.3  Special Children,
     Special Needs

# 8.1 What Is Intelligence?

### Psychometric Theories

Psychometric approaches to intelligence include theories that describe intelligence as a general factor as well as theories that include specific factors. Hierarchical theories include both general intelligence as well as various specific skills, such as verbal and spatial ability.

### Gardner's Theory of Multiple Intelligences

Gardner's theory of multiple intelligences proposes seven distinct intelligences. Three are found in psychometric theories (linguistic, logical-mathematical, and spatial intelligence), but four are new (musical, bodily-kinesthetic, interpersonal, and intrapersonal intelligence). Gardner's theory has stimulated research on nontraditional forms of intelligence, such as social-cognitive flexibility. The theory also has implications for education, suggesting, for example, that schools should adjust teaching to each child's unique intellectual strengths.

### Sternberg's Triarchic Theory

Robert Sternberg's triarchic theory includes (a) the contextual subtheory, which specifies that intelligent behavior must always be considered in relation to the individual's culture, (b) the experiential subtheory, which specifies that intelligence is associated with the familiarity of the task, and (c) the componential subtheory, which specifies that intelligent behavior involves organizing basic cognitive processes into an efficient strategy for completing a task.

# 8.2 Measuring Intelligence

### Binet and the Development of Intelligence Testing

Binet created the first intelligence test to identify students who would have difficulty in school. Using this work, Terman created the Stanford-Binet, which introduced the concept of the intelligence quotient (IQ). Other widely used tests are the WISC-III and K-ABC. These tests provide IQs based on subtests (e.g., the verbal subscale of the WISC-III). Infant tests, such as the Bayley Scales, typically assess mental and motor development.

### Do Tests Work?

In the short term, intelligence tests are reliable, which means that people usually get consistent scores on the tests. In the longer term, scores on infant intelligence tests do not predict adult IQ scores, but infant habituation predicts childhood IQs, and preschool IQ scores predict adult IQs. Intelligence tests are reasonably valid measures of achievement in school. They also predict people's performance in the workplace. Dynamic tests are designed to improve validity by measuring children's potential for future learning.

### Heredity and Environmental Factors

Evidence for the impact of heredity on IQ comes from the findings that (a) siblings' IQ scores become more alike as siblings become more similar genetically, and (b) adopted children's IQ scores are more like their biological parents' test scores than their adoptive parents' scores. Evidence for the impact of the environment comes from the finding that children who live in responsive, well-organized home environments tend to have higher IQ scores, as do children who participate in intervention programs.

### Impact of Ethnicity and Social Class

The average IQ score for African Americans is lower than the average score for European Americans, a difference attributed to the fact that more African American children live in poverty and that the test assesses knowledge based on middle-class experiences. IQ scores remain valid predictors of school success because middle-class experience is often a prerequisite for school success.

# 8.3 Special Children, Special Needs

### Gifted and Creative Children

Traditionally, gifted children have been those with high scores on IQ tests. Contrary to folklore, gifted children are socially mature and emotionally stable. Modern definitions of giftedness are broader and include exceptional talent in, for example, the arts.

Creativity is associated with divergent thinking, thinking in novel and unusual directions. Tests of divergent thinking can predict which children are most likely to be creative when they are older. Creativity can be fostered by experiences that encourage children to think flexibly and explore alternatives.

### Children with Mental Retardation

Individuals with mental retardation have IQ scores of 70 or lower and problems in adaptive behavior. Organic mental retardation is due to specific biological or physical causes; familial mental retardation reflects the lower end of the normal distribution of intelligence. Most retarded persons are classified as mildly or educably retarded; they attend school, work, and have families.

### Children with Learning Disabilities

Children with a learning disability have normal intelligence but have difficulty mastering specific academic subjects. The most common is reading disability, which often can be traced to inadequate understanding and use of language sounds.

**9**

my Tan, a contemporary American writer, once said, "I am fascinated by language in daily life . . . the way it can evoke an emotion, a visual image, a complex idea, or a simple truth." Language is a remarkable human tool. Language allows us to express thoughts and feelings to others and to preserve our ideas and learn from the past.

At first glance, acquiring language may seem like nothing more than learning

words. But this is far from accurate and underestimates the complexity of the task. In fact, children must master four different aspects of language, and each is the focus of a module in this chapter. For most children, distinguishing speech sounds is the essential first step in acquiring language. In Module 9.1, we'll see when infants can first hear and produce speech sounds. Module 9.2 concerns how children learn to speak and how they learn new words thereafter. Soon after children begin to speak, they start to form simple sentences. Even these earliest sentences follow simple rules; what these rules are and how children learn them is the focus of Module 9.3. Finally, in Module 9.4, we'll learn how children use language to communicate with others.

# Language and Communication

**9.1** The Road to Speech

**9.2** Learning the Meanings of Words

**9.3** Speaking in Sentences

**9.4** Using Language to Communicate

# 9.1

- **Elements of Language**
- **Perceiving Speech**
- **Public Speaking in a Few Easy Steps**

## The Road to Speech

### Learning Objectives

- What are phonemes, and how well can infants distinguish them?
- How does infant-directed speech help children learn about language?
- What is babbling, and how does it become more complex in older infants?

*When Kathy moved from Atlanta to Montreal, she enrolled her 8-month-old son, Richard, in a day-care center where everyone spoke French. Richard did not yet talk, but he did make many sounds that resembled words, like "gah-gah" and "beh-beh." What surprised Kathy was that, after just a few weeks in the day-care center, Richard's speech started to sound like French to her, even though he was still not talking. Was this possible, or was her imagination just getting the best of her?*

From birth, infants make sounds—they laugh, cry, and, like Kathy's son Richard, produce sounds that resemble speech. Yet, for most of their first year, infants do not talk. This contrast raises two important questions about infants as nonspeaking creatures. First, can babies who are unable to speak understand any of the speech that is directed to them? Second, how do infants progress from crying to more effective methods of oral communication, such as speech? We'll answer both questions in this module, but let's begin by considering exactly what we mean by language.

### Elements of Language

When you think of language, what comes to mind? English, perhaps? Or maybe German, Spanish, Korean, or Zulu? What about American Sign Language? Maybe BASIC or C++? *Language* **is a broad term referring to any rule-based system for expressing ideas.** Languages are expressed in many forms—through speech, writing, and gesture. Furthermore, languages consistent of different subsystems. Spoken languages usually involve four distinct but interrelated elements:

- *Phonology* **refers to the sounds of a language.** For example, all the different words in English are constructed from about 45 different sounds.
- *Semantics* **is the study of words and their meaning.** *Webster's Third New International Dictionary* has roughly a half million entries, and a typical college-educated English speaker has a vocabulary of about 150,000 words.
- *Grammar* **refers to the rules used to describe the structure of a language. The most important element of grammar is** *syntax,* **rules that specify how words are combined to form sentences.**
- *Pragmatics* **is the study of how people use language to communicate effectively.** Our communication must be appropriate, suited to the audience and occasion. We wouldn't, for example, using fancy vocabulary and long sentences with a 5-year-old.

*The elements of language include phonology, semantics, grammar, and pragmatics.*

Learning language involves mastering each of these elements. Children must learn to hear the differences in speech sounds and how to produce them; they must learn the meaning of words and rules for combining them in sentences; and they must learn appropriate and effective ways to talk with others. In the remainder of this module (and the three others in this chapter), we'll see how children come to understand language and speak it themselves.

## Perceiving Speech

We learned in Module 5.2 that even newborn infants hear remarkably well. But can babies distinguish speech sounds? To answer this question, we first need to know more about the elements of speech. **The basic building blocks of language are *phonemes,* unique sounds that can be joined to create words.** Phonemes include consonant sounds such as the sound of *t* in *toe* and *tap* along with vowel sounds such as the sound of *e* in *get* and *bed*. Infants can distinguish many of these sounds, some of them by as early as 1 month after birth (Aslin, Jusczyk, & Pisoni, 1998).

FIG 9–1

How do we know that infants can distinguish different vowels and consonants? Researchers have devised a number of clever techniques to determine if babies respond differently to distinct sounds. One approach is illustrated in the diagram. A rubber nipple is connected to a tape recorder so that sucking turns on the tape and sound comes out of a loudspeaker. In just a few minutes, 1-month-olds learn the relation between their sucking and the sound: They suck rapidly to hear a tape that consists of nothing more than the sound of *p* as in *pin, pet,* and *pat* (pronounced "puh").

After a few more minutes, infants seemingly tire of this repetitive sound and suck less often, which represents the habituation phenomenon described in Module 5.2. But, if the tape is changed to a different sound such as the sound of *b* in *bed, bat,* or *bird* (pronounced "buh") babies begin sucking rapidly again. Evidently, they recognize that the sound of *b* is different from *p* because they suck more often to hear the new sound (Jusczyk, 1995).

Infants can even discriminate speech sounds that they have never heard before. Not all languages use the same set of phonemes; a distinction that is important in one language may be ignored in another. For example, unlike English, French and Polish differentiate between nasal and nonnasal vowels. To hear the difference, say the word *rod*. Now repeat it, but holding your nose. The subtle difference between the two sounds illustrates a nonnasal vowel (the first version of *rod*) and a nasal one (the second).

Babies growing up in homes where English is spoken have no systematic experience with nasal versus nonnasal vowels, but they can still hear differences like this one. Interestingly, toward their first birthday, infants apparently lose this competence and no longer readily distinguish sounds that are not part of their own language environment. For example, Werker and Lalonde (1988) found that 6- to 8-month-old infants of English-speaking parents could distinguish speech sounds that are used in Hindi but not in English. By 11 to 13 months of age, the infants, like their parents, could no longer tell the difference.

Findings like these suggest that newborns are biologically capable of hearing the entire range of phonemes in all languages worldwide. But as babies grow and are more exposed to a particular language, they only notice the linguistic distinctions that are meaningful in that environment. For example, the Japanese youngster in the photo at the top of page 244 will learn language sounds used in Japanese but will have difficulty hearing sounds used in other languages, such as English. Specialization in one language apparently comes at a cost; the potential to hear other language sounds easily is lost (Best, 1995; Kuhl, 1993).

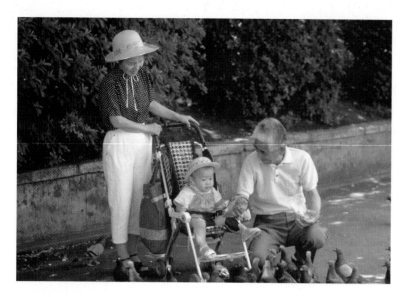

Of course, hearing individual phonemes is only the first step in perceiving speech. One of the biggest challenges for infants is identifying recurring patterns of sounds—words. Imagine, for example, an infant overhearing this conversation between a parent and an older sibling:

SIBLING: Jerry got a new *bike.*
PARENT: Was his old *bike* broken?
SIBLING: No. He'd saved his allowance to buy a new mountain *bike.*

An infant listening to this conversation hears *bike* three times. Can the infant learn from this experience? Yes. When 7- to 8-month-olds hear a word repeatedly in different sentences, they later pay more attention to this word than to words they haven't heard previously. Evidently, 7- and 8-month-olds can listen to sentences and recognize the sound patterns that they hear repeatedly (Juscyzk & Aslin, 1995; Saffran, Aslin, & Newport, 1996). And, by 6 months, infants look at the correct parent when they hear "mommy" or "daddy" (Tincoff & Jusczyk, 1999).

In normal conversation, there are no silent gaps between words, so how do infants pick out words? Stress is one important clue. English contains many one-syllable words that are stressed and many two-syllable words that have a stressed syllable followed by an unstressed syllable (e.g., *dough´-nut, tooth´-paste, bas´-ket*). Infants pay more attention to stressed syllables than unstressed syllables, which is a good strategy for identifying the beginnings of words (Aslin et al., 1998; Mattys et al., 1999).

Of course, stress is not a foolproof sign. Many two-syllable words have stress on the second syllable (e.g., *gui-tar´, sur-prise´*), so infants need other methods to identify words in speech. One method is statistical. Infants notice syllables that go together frequently. For example, in a study by Aslin, Saffran, and Newport (1998), 8-month-olds heard the following sounds, which consisted of 4 three-syllable artificial words, said over and over in a random order.

*pa bi ku  go la tu  da ro pi  ti bu do  da ro pi  go la tu  pa bi ku  da ro pi . . .*

I've underlined the words and inserted gaps between them so that you can see them more easily, but in the study there were no breaks at all—just a steady flow of syllables for 3 minutes. Later, infants listened to these words less than to new words that were novel combinations of the same syllables. They had detected *pa bi ku, go la tu, da ro pi,* and *ti bu do* as familiar patterns and listened to them less than to words like *tu da ro,* a new word made up from syllables they'd already heard.

Detecting stressed syllables and syllables that co-occur provides infants with two powerful tools for identifying words in speech. Of course, they don't yet understand the meanings of these words; they just recognize a word as a distinct configuration of sounds.

Parents (and other adults) often help infants master language sounds by talking in a distinctive style. **In *infant-directed speech,* adults speak slowly and with exaggerated changes in pitch and loudness.** If you could hear the mother in the photo talking to her baby, you would notice that she alternates between speaking softly and loudly and between high and low pitches. (Infant-directed speech was once known as *motherese* until it became clear that most caregivers, not just mothers, talk this way to infants.)

Infant-directed speech may attract infants' attention more than adult-directed speech (Kaplan et al., 1995) because its slower pace and accentuated changes provide infants with more—and more salient—language clues. Similarly, it's easier to understand people speaking a foreign language when they talk slowly and carefully.

Infant-directed speech, then, helps infants perceive the sounds that are fundamental to their language. But how do infants accomplish the next step, producing speech? We answer this question in the next section of this module.

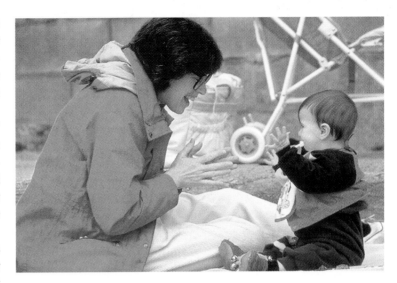

## Public Speaking in a Few Easy Steps

As any new parent can testify, newborns and young babies use sound to communicate—they cry to indicate discomfort or distress. At 2 months, though, babies begin to make sounds that are language-based. **They begin to produce vowel-like sounds, such as "ooooooo" or "ahhhhhh," a phenomenon known as** *cooing.* Sometimes infants become quite excited as they coo, perhaps reflecting the joy of simply playing with sounds.

**After cooing comes** *babbling,* **speechlike sound that has no meaning.** A typical 5- or 6-month-old might say "dah" or "bah," utterances that sound like a single syllable consisting of a consonant and a vowel. Over the next few months, babbling becomes more elaborate as babies apparently experiment with more complex speech sounds. Older infants sometimes repeat a sound as in "bahbahbah" and begin to combine different sounds, "dahmahbah" (Oller & Lynch, 1992).

**At roughly 7 months, infants' babbling includes** *intonation,* **a pattern of rising or falling pitch.** In English declarative sentences, for example, pitch first rises, then falls toward the end of the sentence. In questions, however, the pitch is level, then rises toward the end of the question. Older babies' babbling reflects these patterns: Babies who are brought up by English-speaking parents have both the declarative and question patterns of intonation in their babbling. Babies exposed to a language with different patterns of intonation, such as Japanese or French, reflect their language's intonation in their babbling (Levitt & Utman, 1992). Richard, the baby in the vignette who hears French at his day-care center, will definitely babble with French intonation!

The appearance of intonation in babbling indicates a strong link between perception and production of speech: Infants' babbling is influenced by the characteristics of the speech that they hear. If hearing is crucial for the development of babbling, then can deaf children babble? The "Real Children" feature has the answer.

> Babbling appears at 5 or 6 months with a single consonant and vowel, then combines different speech sounds, and, later, adds intonation.

REAL CHILDREN

### Lorraine Learns to Babble

Lorraine, now 22 months old, has been deaf since birth. She has worn a hearing aid since she was 7 months old and receives language therapy weekly from a speech-language therapist. At 11 months, Lorraine occasionally made simple sounds consisting of a consonant and a vowel, such as "bah." Her babbling remained very simple until about 15 months, when she began uttering longer, repetitive sequences of syllables. Thus, compared to children with normal hearing, Lorraine's babbling was delayed by several months.

In another respect, Lorraine's language skills developed right on schedule: As soon as Lorraine's parents learned of her deafness, they began using American Sign Language to communicate with her. They noticed that, at about 8 months, Lorraine began to imitate parts of the signs they used with her. At 13 months, she began to produce sequences of signs that were meaningless but matched the tempo and duration of real signing. In other words, Lorraine was going through different phases of babbling with her signing. ●

Lorraine is typical of deaf children: Compared to children with normal hearing, her babbling was much delayed as spoken language but right on schedule as sign language (Oller & Eilers, 1988; Pettito & Marentette, 1991). Evidently, in the middle of the first year, infants try to reproduce the sounds of language that others use in trying to communicate with them (or, in the case of deaf infants, the signs that others use). Hearing *dog,* an infant may first say "dod," then "gog" before finally saying "dog" correctly. In the same way that beginning typists gradually link movements of their fingers with particular keys, through babbling infants learn to use their lips, tongue, and teeth to produce specific sounds, gradually making sounds that approximate real words (Poulson et al., 1991). Fortunately, learning to produce language sounds is easier for most babies than the cartoon suggests!

**B.C.**                                                                                        **by johnny hart**

Reprinted by permission of Johnny Hart and Creators Syndicate, Inc.

The ability to produce sound, coupled with the 1-year-old's advanced ability to perceive speech sounds, sets the stage for the infant's first true words. In Module 9.2, we'll see how this happens.

### Check Your Learning

**1.** Phonology, semantics, _____, and pragmatics are the four principal elements of language.

2. _____ is the study of how people use language to communicate appropriately and effectively.

3. Young infants can distinguish many language sounds, but older infants are more likely to notice only _____.

4. Infants identify words in speech by detecting stressed syllables and _____.

5. Adults using infant-directed speech speak slowly and exaggerate the loudness and _____ of their speech.

6. At about 7 months, most infants' babbling includes phrases that sound like questions, which shows that infants are learning about patterns of _____.

7. Deaf children babble later than average in spoken language but _____ in sign language.

When adults sign to deaf infants, how might children identify the beginning of a sign?

**Answers:** (1) grammar, (2) Pragmatics, (3) sounds that they hear in their language environment, (4) syllables that occur together frequently, (5) pitch, (6) intonation, (7) right on schedule

## Learning the Meanings of Words

### Learning Objectives

● How do children make the transition from babbling to talking?

● What different styles of language learning do young children use?

● What rules do children follow to learn new words?

● What conditions foster children's learning of new words?

# 9.2

Understanding Words as Symbols

Styles of Learning Language

Fast Mapping Meanings to Words

Encouraging Word Learning

*Efrat is 20 months old and loves to talk. What amazes her parents is how quickly she adds words to her vocabulary. For example, the day her parents brought home a computer, Efrat watched as they set it up. The next day, she spontaneously pointed to the computer and said, "puter." This happens all the time—Efrat hears a word once or twice, then uses it correctly herself. Efrat's parents wonder how she does this, particularly because learning vocabulary in a foreign language is so difficult for them!*

At about their first birthday, most youngsters say their first words. Typically, these words are an extension of advanced babbling, consisting of a consonant-vowel pair that may be repeated. *Mama* and *dada* are probably the most common first words that stem from advanced babbling. Other early vocabulary words include animals, food, and toys (Nelson, 1973). Also common are words that denote actions (for example, *go*). By age 2, most youngsters have a vocabulary of a few hundred words, and by age 6, a typical child's vocabulary includes over 10,000 words (Anglin, 1993).

Like Efrat, most children learn new words with extraordinary ease and speed. How they do it? We'll answer that question in this module.

## Understanding Words as Symbols

When my daughter, Laura, was 9 months old, she sometimes babbled "bay-bay." A few months later, she still said "bay-bay" but with an important difference. As a 9-month-old, "bay-bay" was simply an interesting set of sounds that she made for no reason (at least, none that was obvious to us). As a 13-month-old, "bay-bay" was her way of saying "baby." What had happened between 9 and 13 months? Laura had begun to understand that speech is more than just entertaining sound. She realized that sounds form words that refer to objects, actions, and properties. Put another way, Laura recognized that words are symbols, entities that stand for other entities. She already had formed concepts such as "round, bouncy things" and "furry things that bark" and "little humans that adults carry" based on her own experiences. With the insight that speech sounds can denote these concepts, she began to match words and concepts (Reich, 1986).

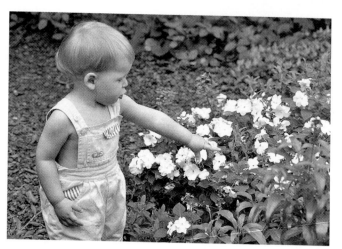

If this argument is correct, we should find that children use symbols in other areas, not just in language. They do. Gestures are symbols, and like the baby in the photo, infants begin to gesture shortly before their first birthday (Goodwyn & Acredolo, 1993). Young children may smack their lips to indicate hunger or wave "bye-bye" when leaving. In these cases, gestures and words convey a message equally well. Both reflect the child's developing ability to use symbols to represent actions and objects, which is one of the grand achievements of human development.

## Styles of Learning Language

As youngsters expand their vocabulary, they often adopt a distinctive style of learning language (Bates, Bretherton, & Snyder, 1988). **Some children have a** *referential style;* **their vocabularies mainly consist of words that name objects, persons, or actions. Other children have an** *expressive style;* **their vocabularies include some names but also many social phrases that are used like a single word, such as "go away," "what'd you want?" and "I want it."**

Katherine Nelson (1973) was the investigator who discovered these two basic styles of learning language. She studied 18 children for about a year, starting at approximately their first birthdays, a period during which the children's vocabularies increased from fewer than 10 words to nearly 200. She visited each child monthly for about an hour to tape-record samples of spontaneous speech and to test language development.

> Language is primarily an intellectual tool for referential children and primarily a social tool for expressive children.

By the time children had 50-word vocabularies—typically at about 1½ years—two distinct groups had emerged. Children in the referential group had vocabularies dominated by names of objects, persons, or actions, such as *milk, Jo-Jo,* and *up.* Other children, the expressive group, learned some names but knew a much higher percentage of words that were used in social interactions (*go away, I want it, lemme see*) and question words (*what, where*). For example, Rachel, a referential child, had 41 name words in her 50-word vocabulary but only 2 words for social interaction or questions. Elizabeth, an expressive child, had a more balanced vocabulary: 24 name words and 14 for social interactions and questions.

Children with the referential style primarily use language as an intellectual tool—a means of learning and talking about objects (Masur, 1995). In contrast, children with an expressive style use language as more of a social tool—a way of enhancing interactions with others. Of course, both of these functions—intellectual and social—are important functions of language, and, as you might expect, most children blend the referential and expressive styles of learning language.

## Fast Mapping Meanings to Words

Once children have the insight that a word can symbolize an object or action, their vocabularies grow slowly at first. A typical 15-month-old, for example, may learn 2 to 3 new words each week. **However, at about 18 months, many children experience a *naming explosion* during which they learn new words—particularly names of objects—much more rapidly than before.** Children now learn 10 or more new words each week (Fenson et al., 1994).

This rapid rate of word learning is astonishing when we realize that most words have many plausible but incorrect referents. To illustrate, imagine what's going through the mind of the child in the photo. The mother has just pointed to the flowers and said, "Flowers. These are flowers. See the flowers." To the mother (and you), this all seems crystal clear and incredibly straightforward. But what might a child learn from this episode? Perhaps the correct referent for "flowers." But a youngster could, just as reasonably, conclude that "flowers" refers to the petals, to the color of the flowers, or to the mother's actions in pointing to the flowers.

Surprisingly, though, most youngsters learn the proper meanings of simple words in just a few presentations. **Children's ability to connect new words to referents so rapidly that they cannot be considering all possible meanings for the new word is termed *fast mapping*.** Fast mapping meaning onto new words means that children must use rules to link words with their meanings (Carey, 1978). Researchers have found that young children use different fast-mapping strategies to help learn word meanings (Woodward & Markman, 1998).

Joint Attention.    Parents encourage word learning by carefully watching what interests their children. When toddlers touch or look at an object, parents often label it for them. When a youngster points to a banana, a parent may say, "Banana, that's a banana." Of course, to take advantage of this help, infants must be able to tell when parents are labeling instead of just conversing. In fact, when adults label an unfamiliar object, 18- to 20-month-olds assume that the label is the object's name *only* when adults show signs that they are referring to the object. For example, toddlers are more likely to learn an object's name when adults look at the object while saying its name than when adults look elsewhere while labeling (Baldwin et al., 1996; Moore, Angelopoulos, & Bennett, 1999). Thus, beginning in the toddler years, parents and children work together to create conditions that foster word learning: Parents label objects and youngsters rely on adults' behavior to interpret the words they hear.

**Constraints on Word Names.** Joint attention simplifies word learning for children, but the problem still remains: How does a toddler know that *banana* refers to the object that she's touching, as opposed to her activity (touching) or to the object's color? Many researchers believe that young children follow several simple rules that limit their conclusions about what labels mean.

A study by Au and Glusman (1990) identified one of the rules that young children use. Au and Glusman presented preschoolers with a stuffed animal with pink horns that otherwise resembled a monkey and called it a *mido*. *Mido* was then repeated several times, always referring to the monkeylike stuffed animal with pink horns. Later, these youngsters were asked to find a *theri* in a set of stuffed animals that included several *mido*. Never having heard of a *theri*, what did the children do? They never picked a *mido*; instead, they selected other stuffed animals. Knowing that *mido* referred to monkeylike animals with pink horns, evidently they decided that *theri* had to refer to one of the other stuffed animals.

Apparently children were following this simple but effective rule for learning new words:

- If an unfamiliar word is heard in the presence of objects that already have names and objects that don't, the word refers to one of the objects that doesn't have a name.

Researchers have discovered several other simple rules that help children match words with the correct referent (Hall & Graham, 1999; Waxman & Markow, 1995; Woodward & Markman, 1998):

- A name refers to a whole object, not its parts or its relation to other objects, and refers not just to this particular object but to all objects of the same type. For example, when a grandparent points to a stuffed animal on a shelf and says "dinosaur," children conclude that *dinosaur* refers to the entire dinosaur, not just its ears or nose, not to the fact that the dinosaur is on a shelf, and not to this specific dinosaur but to all dinosaur-like objects.

- If an object already has a name and another name is presented, the new name denotes a subcategory of the original name. If the child who knows the meaning of *dinosaur* sees a brother point to another dinosaur and hears the brother say "T-rex," the child will conclude that *T-rex* is a special type of dinosaur.

- Given many similar category members, a word applied consistently to only one of them is a proper noun. If a child who knows *dinosaur* sees that one of a group of dinosaurs is always called "Dino," the child will conclude that *Dino* is the name of that dinosaur.

Rules like these make it possible for children like Efrat, the child in the vignette, to learn words rapidly because they reduce the number of possible referents. The child in the photo on page 249 follows these rules to decide that *flower* refers to the entire object, not its parts or the action of pointing to it.

**Sentence Cues.** Children hear many unfamiliar words embedded in sentences containing words they already know. The other words and the overall sentence structure can be helpful clues to a word's meaning.

For example, when a parent describes an event using familiar words but an unfamiliar verb, children often infer that the verb refers to the action performed by the subject of the sentence (Fisher, 1996; Woodward & Markman, 1998). When the youngsters in the photograph hear, "The man is juggling," they will infer that *juggling* refers to the man's actions with the bowling pins, because they already know *man.*

As another example of how sentence context aids word learning, look at the blocks in the diagram and point to the "boz block." I imagine you pointed to the middle block. Why? In English, adjectives usually precede the nouns they modify, so you inferred that *boz* is an adjective describing *block.* Since *the* before *boz* implies that only one block is *boz,* you picked the middle one, having decided that *boz* means "winged." Preschool children, too, use sentence cues like these to judge word meanings (Gelman & Markman, 1985; Hall, Waxman, & Hurwitz, 1993).

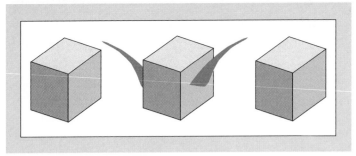

FIG 9–2

**Naming Errors.** Of course, these rules for learning new words are not perfect. **A common mistake is *underextension,* defining a word too narrowly.** Using *car* to refer only to the family car and *ball* to a favorite toy ball are examples of underextension. **Between 1 and 3 years, children sometimes make the opposite error, *overextension,* defining a word too broadly.** Children may use *car* to also refer to buses and trucks or use *doggie* to refer to all four-legged animals.

The overextension error occurs more frequently when children are producing words than when they are comprehending words. Two-year-old Jason may say "doggie" to refer to a goat but nevertheless correctly point to a picture of a goat when asked. Because overextension is more common in word production, it may actually reflect another fast-mapping rule that children follow: "If you can't remember the name for an object, say the name of a related object" (Naigles & Gelman, 1995).

Both underextension and overextension disappear gradually as youngsters refine meanings for words based on the feedback they receive from parents and others.

### Encouraging Word Learning

How can parents and other adults help children learn words? For children to expand their vocabularies, they need to hear others speak. Not surprisingly, then, children learn words more rapidly if their parents speak to them frequently (Roberts, Burchinal, & Durham, 1999). Of course, sheer quantity of parental speech is not all that matters. Parents can foster word learning by naming objects that are the focus of a child's attention (Dunham, Dunham, & Curwin, 1993). Parents can name different products on store shelves as they point to them. During a walk, parents can label the objects—birds, plants, vehicles—that the child sees.

Parents can also help children learn words by reading books with them. Reading together is fun for parents and children alike, and provides opportunities for children to learn new words. However, the way that parents read makes a difference. When parents carefully describe pictures as they read, preschoolers' vocabularies increase (Reese & Cox, 1999). Asking children questions also helps. In a study of 4-year-olds (Sénéchal, Thomas, & Monker, 1995), some parents simply read the story and children listened. Other parents read the story but stopped periodically to ask a "what" or "where" question that the child could answer with the target word. Later, the researchers tested children's abilities to recognize the target words and produce them. The graph shows that children who answered questions comprehended more target words than children who only listened. Children who answered questions were also much more likely to produce the target words.

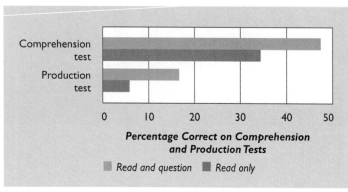

FIG 9–3

Why is questioning effective? When an adult reads a sentence (e.g., "Arthur is angling"), then asks a question (e.g., "What is Arthur doing?"), a child must match the new word (*angling*) with the pictured activity (*fishing*) and say the word aloud. When parents read without questioning, children can ignore words they don't understand. Questioning forces children to identify meanings of new words and practice saying them.

Viewing television can also help word learning under some circumstances. For example, preschool children who regularly watch *Sesame Street* usually have larger vocabularies by the time they enter kindergarten than preschoolers who watch *Sesame Street* only occasionally (Rice et al., 1990). Other television programs, notably cartoons, do not have this positive influence. What accounts for the difference? *Sesame Street* involves children in language activities that help them learn words (in the photo, words with *E*). Cartoons, however, require no interaction at all.

For school-age children, reading is one of the best ways to learn new words. Written material—books, magazines, textbooks—almost always contains more unfamiliar words than conversational language, so reading is rich in opportunities to expand vocabulary (Hayes, 1988). Not surprisingly, children who read a lot tend to have larger vocabularies than children who read less often (Allen, Cipielewski, & Stanovich, 1992).

Research on reading, along with research on television and parents' influence, points to a simple but powerful conclusion: Children are most likely to learn new words when they participate in activities that force them to understand the meanings of new words and use those new words. Is learning new words (and other aspects of language) more difficult for children learning two languages? The "Cultural Influences" feature has the answer.

CULTURAL INFLUENCES

### Growing Up Bilingual

About 6 million American schoolchildren come from homes where English is not the primary language. In some states, 25 percent or more of the children are bilingual, and the percentages are even higher in some urban areas (U.S. Bureau of the Census, 1995). These youngsters usually speak English and another language, such as Spanish or, like the children in the photo, Chinese.

Is learning two languages easier or harder than learning just one language? For much of the 20th century, the general view was that bilingualism harmed children's development. One child psychology text published in 1952 surveyed the research and concluded, "There can be no doubt that the child reared in a bilingual environment is handicapped in his language growth" (Thompson, 1952, p. 367). Today, we know that this conclusion is wrong because it was based on studies of poor, immigrant children's scores on intelligence tests. In retrospect, immigrant children's test scores had more to do with their poverty and unfamiliarity with a new culture than with their bilingualism.

In fact, modern studies lead to a different picture. When 1- and 2-year-olds learn two languages simultaneously, they often progress somewhat slowly at first because they mix words from the two languages. By age 3 or 4, however, children separate the languages; and by the time they begin elementary school, most are as proficient as monolinguals in both languages (Baker, 1993; Lanza, 1992).

Furthermore, bilingual children actually *surpass* monolingual children in some language skills. Bilingual preschoolers are more likely to understand that the printed form of a word is unrelated to the meaning of the word (Bialystok, 1997). For example, bilingual preschoolers are less likely to believe that words denoting large objects (e.g., *bus*) are longer than words denoting small objects (e.g., *bug*).

Bilingual children also better understand that words are simply arbitrary symbols. Bilingual youngsters, for instance, are more likely than monolingual children to understand that, as long as all English speakers agreed, *dog* could refer to cats and *cat* could refer to dogs (Bialystok, 1988; Campbell & Sais, 1995).

The benefits of being bilingual may extend beyond language: In one study (Bialystock, 1999), bilingual preschool children were more successful than monolingual children in learning complicated nonverbal rules.

Of course, many children in America can't speak English at the time when they should begin school. How to teach these children has prompted much national debate. One view is that all Americans should speak English and so all teaching should be in English. Another view is that children learn more effectively in their native tongue and so all teaching should be done in that language.

Much of the debate over the proper language of instruction is political, reflecting people's desire for a society with a universal cultural heritage and language rather than a society with pluralistic heritages and languages. Ignoring the political aspects, research shows that the best method uses the child's native language *and* English (Padilla et al., 1991; Wong-Fillmore et al., 1985). Initially,

> Bilingual children learn language as rapidly as monolingual children, and they better understand the symbolic nature of words.

children receive basic English-language teaching while they are taught other subjects in their native language. Gradually, more instruction is in English, in step with children's growing proficiency in the second language. When instruction is in children's native language and English, they are most likely to master academic content and English, outcomes that are less likely when instruction is solely in the native language or English. ●

## Check Your Learning

1. Children begin to _____ at about the same age that they begin to talk, and both apparently reflect children's growing understanding of symbols.

2. Children with a(n) _____ style of language learning typically have many social phrases (e.g., *go away*) in their vocabularies.

3. When children have a referential style of language learning, they tend to use language primarily as a(n) _____ tool.

4. Many strategies help children learn words, including joint attention, constraints on word learning, and _____.

5. When young children hear an unfamiliar word in the presence of a novel object, they _____.

6. Sometimes children define a word too broadly, an error known as _____.

7. Young children are most likely to learn new words when parents _____, when they regularly watch TV programs like *Sesame Street,* and when parents ask questions while reading to them.

 **How might Piaget, Vygotsky, and an information-processing theorist explain how children learn words?**

**Answers:** (1) gesture, (2) expressive, (3) intellectual, (4) sentence cues, (5) infer that the word denotes the novel object, (6) overextension, (7) label objects

# 9.3

— **From Two-Word Speech to Complex Sentences**

— **How Children Acquire Grammar**

## Speaking in Sentences

### Learning Objectives

● How do children progress from speaking single words to complicated sentences?

● How do children acquire the grammar of their native language?

*Jaime's daughter, Luisa, is a curious 2½-year-old who bombards her father with questions. Jaime enjoys Luisa's questioning, but he is bothered by the way she phrases her questions. Luisa will say, "What you are doing?" and "Why not she sleep?" Obviously, Jaime doesn't talk this way, so he wonders where Luisa learned to ask questions like this. Is it normal, or is it a symptom of some type of language disorder?*

Not long after children begin to talk, they start combining words to form simple sentences. These simple sentences are the first step in a new area of language learning, mastering syntax—a language's rules for combining words to create sentences. We'll begin this module by tracing the stages in children's acquisition of syntax and, along the way, see that Luisa's way of asking questions is quite normal for youngsters learning English. Then we'll examine different factors that influence children's mastery of syntax.

## From Two-Word Speech to Complex Sentences

At about 1½ years, children begin to combine individual words to create two-word sentences, like *more juice, gimme cookie, truck go, my truck, Daddy go, Daddy bike.* **Researchers call this kind of talk *telegraphic speech* because, like telegrams of days gone by, it consists of only words directly relevant to meaning.** Before phones and e-mail, people sent urgent messages by telegraph, and the charge was based on the number of words. Consequently, telegrams were brief and to the point, containing only the important nouns, verbs, adjectives, and adverbs, much like children's two-word speech.

In their two-word speech, children follow rules to express different meanings. For example, the sentences *truck go* and *Daddy eat* are both about agents—people or objects that do something and the actions they perform. Here the rule is "agent + action." In contrast, *my truck* is about a possessor and a possession; the rule for creating these sentences is "possessor + possession."

When children are in the two-word stage, they use several basic rules to express meaning (Brown, 1973). These are listed in the table.

### Rules Used to Express Meaning During the Two-Word Stage

| Rule | Example |
| --- | --- |
| agent + action | "Daddy eat" |
| possessor + possession | "my truck" |
| action + object | "gimme cookie" |
| agent + object | "boy car" (meaning the boy is pushing the car) |
| action + location | "put chair" (meaning put the object on the chair) |
| entity + location | "truck chair" (meaning the truck is on the chair) |
| attribute + entity | "big car" |
| demonstrative + entity | "that cup" |

Based on Brown, 1973

TABLE 9–1

Of course, not all children use all eight rules, but most do. And this is true of children around the world (Tager-Flusberg, 1993). Regardless of the language they learn, children's two-word sentences follow a common set of rules that are very useful in describing ideas concerning people and objects, their actions, and their properties.

When children move beyond two-word sentences, they quickly begin to use much longer sentences. For example, at 1½ years, my daughter Laura would say, "gimme juice" or "bye-bye Mom." As a 2½-year-old, she had progressed to "When I finish my ice cream, I'll take a shower, okay?" and "Don't turn the light out—I can't see better!" Her improvement was characteristic of most children.

Beginning at about the second birthday, children move to three-word and even longer sentences. **Their longer sentences are filled with *grammatical morphemes*, words or endings of words (such as -ing, -ed, or -s) that make a sentence grammatical.** To illustrate, a

Children around the world use a common set of rules to create two-word sentences that describe people, objects, actions, and properties.

1½-year-old might say, "kick ball," but a 3-year-old would be more likely to say, "I am kicking the ball." Compared to the 1½-year-old's telegraphic speech, the 3-year-old has added several elements, including a pronoun, *I*, to serve as the subject of the sentence, the auxiliary verb *am*, *-ing* to the verb *kick*, and an article, *the*, before *ball*. Each of these grammatical morphemes makes the older child's sentence slightly more meaningful and much more grammatical.

How do children learn all of these subtle nuances of grammar? Conceivably, a child might learn that *kicking* describes kicking that is ongoing and that *kicked* describes kicking that occurred in the past. Later, the child might learn that *raining* describes current weather and *rained* describes past weather. But learning different tenses for individual verbs—one by one—would be remarkably slow going. More effective would be to learn the general rules that "verb + *-ing*" denotes an ongoing activity and "verb + *-ed*" denotes a past activity. In fact, this is what children do: They learn general rules about grammatical morphemes.

Jean Berko (1958) conducted one of the first studies showing that children's use of grammatical morphemes is based on their growing knowledge of grammatical rules, not simply memory for individual words. She showed preschoolers pictures of nonsense objects like the one in the diagram. The experimenter labeled it, saying, "This is a wug." Then youngsters were shown pictures of two of the objects while the experimenter said, "Now there is another one. There are two of them. There are two . . ." Most children spontaneously said, "Wugs." Because *wug* is a novel word, children could answer correctly only by applying the rule of adding *-s* to indicate plural.

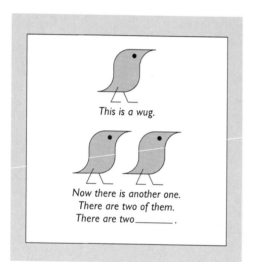

This is a wug.

Now there is another one. There are two of them. There are two_____ .

FIG 9–4

Sometimes, of course, applying the general rule can lead to very creative communication. As a 3-year-old, my daughter would say, "unvelcro it," meaning detach the Velcro. She had never heard *unvelcro*, but she created this word from the rule that "*un-* + verb" means to reverse or stop the action of a verb. Creating such novel words is, in fact, evidence that children learn grammar by applying rules, not learning individual words.

**Additional evidence that children master grammar by learning rules comes from preschoolers'** *overregularization*, **applying rules to words that are exceptions to the rule.** Youngsters learning English may incorrectly add an *s* instead of using an irregular plural—*two mans* instead of *two men* or *two foots* instead of *two feet*. With the past tense, children may add *ed* instead of using an irregular past tense—*I goed* instead of *I went* or *she runned* instead of *she ran* (Marcus et al., 1992). Children apparently know the general rule but not all the words that are exceptions.

The rules governing grammatical morphemes range from fairly simple to very complex. The rule for plurals—add *-s*—is simple to apply, and, as you might expect, it's one of the first grammatical morphemes that children master. Adding *-ing* to denote ongoing action is also simple, and it too is mastered early. More complex forms, such as the various forms of the verb *to be*, are mastered later; but, remarkably, by the end of the preschool years, children typically have mastered most of the rules that govern grammatical morphemes.

At the same time that preschoolers are mastering grammatical morphemes, they extend their speech beyond the subject-verb-object construction that is basic in English. You can see these changes in the way children ask questions. Children's questions during two-word speech are marked by intonation alone. Soon after a child can declare, "My ball," he can also ask "My ball?" Children quickly discover *wh* words (*who, what, when, where, why*), but they don't use them correctly. Like Luisa, the 2½-year-old in the module-opening vignette, many youngsters merely attach the *wh* word to the beginning of a sentence without changing the rest of the sentence: *What he eating? What we see?* But by 3 or 3½ years, youngsters insert the required auxiliary verb before the subject, creating *What is he eating?* or *What will we see?* (deVilliers & deVilliers, 1985).

Between ages 3 and 6 years, children also learn to use negation ("That isn't a butterfly") and embedded sentences ("Jennifer thinks that Bill took the book"). They begin to comprehend passive voice ("The ball was kicked by the girl") as opposed to the active voice ("The girl kicked the ball"), although full understanding of this form continues into the elementary-school years (Tager-Flusberg, 1993). In short, by the time most children enter kindergarten, they use most of the grammatical forms of their native language with great skill.

Ponder these accomplishments for a moment, particularly in light of what else you know about 5-year-old children. Most can neither read nor do arithmetic, and some don't know the letters of the alphabet, but virtually all have mastered the grammar of their native tongue. How do they do it? Some answers to this question are in the next section.

> As children move beyond two-word speech, they begin to master questions, negation, and other more complex sentences.

## How Children Acquire Grammar

If you were asked to explain how children master grammar, where would you begin? You might propose that children learn to speak grammatically by listening to and then copying adult sentences. In much the same way that Richard, the English-speaking baby at the beginning of Module 9.1, imitated the French language sounds that he heard, children might simply copy the grammatical forms they hear. In fact, B. F. Skinner (1957) and other learning theorists once claimed that all aspects of language—sounds, words, grammar, and communication—were learned through imitation and reinforcement (Whitehurst & Vasta, 1975).

Critics were quick to point to some flaws in the learning explanation of grammar, however. One problem is that children produce many more sentences than they have ever heard. In fact, most of children's sentences are novel, which is difficult to explain in terms of simple imitation of adults' speech. For example, when children create questions by inserting a *wh* word at the beginning of a sentence ("What she doing?"), who are they imitating?

Also troublesome for the learning view is that, even when children imitate adult sentences, they do not imitate adult grammar. In simply trying to repeat "I am drawing a picture," young children will say "I draw picture." Furthermore, linguists, particularly Noam Chomsky (1957, 1995), argued that grammatical rules are far too complex for toddlers and preschoolers to infer them solely on the basis of speech that they hear.

If grammatical rules are not acquired through imitation and reinforcement, what is the answer? Perhaps children are born with mechanisms that simplify the task of learning grammar (Slobin, 1985). According to this view, children are born with neural circuits in the brain that allow them to infer the grammar of the language that they hear. That is, grammar itself is not built into the child's nervous system, but processes that guide the learning of grammar are.

This proposal that inborn mechanisms help children learn grammar might not be as intuitively appealing as imitation, but many findings indirectly support this view:

Broca's area

FIG 9–5

1. *Specific regions of the brain are known to be involved in language processing.* If children are born with a "grammar-learning processor," it should be possible to locate a specific region or regions of the brain that are involved in learning grammar. In fact, you may remember from Module 4.3 that for most people the left hemisphere of the brain plays a critical role in understanding language. Some functions of language have been located even more precisely. For example, the shaded area in the diagram is Broca's area: a region in the left frontal cortex that is necessary for combining words into meaningful sentences. The fact that specific areas in the brain, such as Broca's area, have well-defined functions for language makes it plausible that children have specialized neural circuits that help them learn grammar.

2. *Only humans learn grammar readily.* If grammar is learned solely through imitation and reinforcement, then it should be possible to teach rudimentary grammar to nonhumans. If, instead, learning grammar depends upon specialized neural mechanisms that are unique to humans, then efforts to teach grammar to nonhumans should fail. This prediction has been tested many times by trying to teach grammar to chimpanzees, the species closest to humans on the evolutionary ladder. Chimpanzees like the one in the photo have been taught to communicate using gestures taken from sign language or with plastic chips to stand for words. The result? Chimps master only simple grammatical rules governing two-word speech, but only with massive effort that is completely unlike the preschool child's learning of grammar (Savage-Rumbaugh et al., 1993; Seyfarth & Cheney, 1996). Since numerous efforts to teach grammar to chimps have failed, this suggests that children rely upon some type of inborn mechanism specific to humans to master grammar.

3. *There is a critical period for learning language.* You recall, from Module 1.2, that a critical period refers to a time in development when children master skills or behaviors readily. Apparently, the period from birth to about 12 years is critical to acquiring language generally and mastering grammar particularly. If children do not acquire language in this period, they will never truly master language later. Evidence of a critical period for language comes from studies of isolated children. In one tragic instance, a baby girl named Genie was restrained by a harness during the day and a straightjacket-like device at night. No one was permitted to talk to Genie, and she was beaten when she made any noise. When Genie was discovered, at age 13, her language was very primitive. After several years of language training, her mastery of grammar remains limited, resembling the telegraphic speech of a 2-year-old (Curtiss, 1989; Rymer, 1993).

Further evidence for a critical period for language comes from studies of individuals learning second languages. Individuals master the grammar of a foreign language at the level of a native speaker only if they are exposed to the language prior to adolescence (Newport, 1991). Why is it that one period of time can be so much more influential for language than others? Why can't missed language experiences be made up after age 12? A critical period for language answers these questions. That is, just as females ovulate for only a limited portion of the life span, the neural mechanisms involved in learning grammar may function only during infancy and childhood.

The evidence in favor of an inborn grammar-learning device is impressive but only indirect. As yet, there is no definitive finding that makes an airtight case for the existence of a grammar-learning device (Maratsos, 1998). Consequently, scientists have continued to look for other explanations.

Some theorists (e.g., Braine, 1992) believe that children learn grammar using the same cognitive skills that allow them to learn other rules and regularities in their environments. **According to the *semantic bootstrapping hypothesis,* children rely upon their knowledge of the meanings of words to discover grammatical rules (Bates & MacWhinney, 1987).** That is, children notice that some words (nouns) typically refer to objects, and others (verbs) to actions. They also notice that nouns and verbs have distinct functions in sentences. By detecting such regularities in speech, children gradually infer the grammatical rules that provide structure for their language.

Both the grammar-learning device and the bootstrapping hypothesis could be correct: Children may learn grammar using some mechanisms that are specific to language as well as some that are not (Maratsos, 1998). And both views agree that language experience is important because it provides the information from which grammatical rules are inferred. After all, children growing up in a home where Japanese is spoken master Japanese grammar, not Russian or English grammar.

For many children, parents' speech is the prime source of information about language. Parents fine-tune their speech so that it includes examples of the speech that their children are attempting to master (Hoff-Ginsberg, 1990). For example, when 2- and 3-year-olds begin to experiment with pronouns like *you, I, she,* and *he,* their parents provide many examples of how to use pronouns correctly. Similarly, as these children begin to use auxiliary verbs such as *have, has, was,* and *did,* parents use speech that is especially rich in these verbs (Sokolov, 1993). By providing extra instances of the parts of speech that children are mastering, parents make it easier for children to unearth new grammatical rules.

Parents also provide feedback to help children evaluate their tentative grammatical rules. Most of the feedback is indirect. When a child's speech is incorrect or incomplete, parents don't say, "That's wrong!" or "How ungrammatical!" Instead, they rephrase or elaborate the child's remark. For example, if a child were to say, "Sara eating cookie," a parent might reply, "Yes, Sara is eating a cookie." "Doggie go" might lead to "Yes, the doggie left." A parent's reply captures the meaning of the child's remark while demonstrating correct grammatical forms (Bohannon, MacWhinney, & Snow, 1990). At the same time, when a child's grammar is accurate, a parent will often simply repeat it or continue the conversation. Thus, when parents rephrase their children's speech, it means that some aspect of the remark was ungrammatical; if they continue the conversation, it means the remark was grammatical.

Parents don't provide feedback for all utterances; in fact, a majority of children's errors go uncorrected. However, the amount of feedback is sufficient for children to reject incorrect hypotheses about grammatical rules and retain correct ones (Bohannon et al., 1996).

> Some researchers believe that built-in neural circuits help children infer the grammar of their native language; other researchers believe children use cognitive skills to find regular patterns in speech they hear.

Which of these different ideas about how children learn grammar is correct? As yet, there is no single, comprehensive theory of how grammar is mastered. But there is general agreement that such a theory will include some mechanisms that are specific to learning grammar, children actively seeking to identify regularities in their environment, and an environment that is rich in language. All three factors keep children on the trail that leads to mastering grammar (MacWhinney, 1998).

The "Making Children's Lives Better" feature suggests some ways parents and other adults can help children master grammar and other aspects of language.

### MAKING CHILDREN'S LIVES BETTER

### Promoting Language Development

Adults eager to promote children's language development can follow a few guidelines:

1. Talk with children frequently and treat them as partners in conversation. That is, try talking with children interactively, not directively.

2. Use a child's speech to show new language forms. Expand a child's remark to introduce new vocabulary or new grammatical forms. Rephrase a child's ungrammatical remark to show the correct grammar.

3. Encourage children to go beyond minimal use of language. Have them answer questions in phrases and sentences, not single words. Have them replace vague words such as *stuff* or *somebody* with more descriptive ones.

4. Listen. This guideline has two parts. First, because children often talk slowly, it's tempting for adults to complete their sentences for them. Don't. Let children express themselves. Second, pay attention to what children are saying and respond appropriately. Let children learn that language works.

5. Make language fun. Use books, rhymes, songs, jokes, and foreign words to increase a child's interest in learning language. ●

Of course, as children's language improves during the preschool years, others can understand it more readily, which means that children become better at communicating. The emergence and growth of communication skills are the topic of the next module.

### Check Your Learning

1. Children's first sentences are referred to as telegraphic speech because _____.

2. Children's two-word sentences are based on a common set of rules that are useful in describing _____.

3. As children move beyond two-word sentences, _____ appear in their speech, beginning with those that follow simple rules.

4. Evidence that children learn grammatical rules comes from overregularization, in which children _____.

5. One flaw in the learning explanation of grammar is that children say many novel sentences; another is that _____.

6. Evidence that children are born with specialized neural circuits for learning grammar includes the facts that specific brain regions are associated with

language processing, _____, and there is a critical period for learning language.

**7.** According to the semantic bootstrapping hypothesis, children _____ to discover grammatical rules.

**8.** Parents help their children learn grammar by _____ and by providing them with feedback.

 **What role does experience play in learning the aspects of language that we have considered so far in this chapter—phonology, semantics, and grammar?**

**Answers:** (1) they include only words that are essential to meaning, (2) ideas about people and objects, their actions, and their properties, (3) grammatical morphemes, (4) apply grammatical rules to words that are exceptions to the rule, (5) young children who imitate adults' speech do not imitate adults' grammar, (6) only humans learn grammar, (7) use their knowledge of word meanings, (8) providing extra examples of the parts of speech that children are trying to master.

## Using Language to Communicate

### Learning Objectives

● **When and how do children learn to take turns in conversation?**

● **What are the skills required to be an effective speaker?**

● **What is involved in becoming a good listener?**

> *Marla and Kitty, both 8-year-olds, usually are good friends, but right now they're boiling mad at each other. Marla was going to the mall with her dad to buy some new markers. Kitty found out and gave Marla money to buy some markers for her, too. Marla returned with the markers, but they weren't the kind that Kitty liked, so she was angry. Marla was angry because she didn't think Kitty should be mad; after all, it was Kitty's fault for not telling her what kind to buy. Meanwhile, Marla's dad hopes they come to some understanding soon and cut out all the racket.*

Imagining these girls arguing is an excellent way to learn what is needed for effective communication. Both talk at the same time, their remarks are rambling and incoherent, and neither bothers to listen to the other. In other words, for effective oral communication, don't do what they do. Follow these guidelines instead:

• People should take turns, alternating as speaker and listener.

• A speaker's remarks should relate to the topic and be understandable to the listener.

• A listener should pay attention and let the speaker know if his or her remarks don't make sense.

Complete mastery of these pragmatic skills is a lifelong pursuit; after all, even adults often miscommunicate with one another because they don't observe one or more of these rules. However, youngsters grasp many of the basics of communication early in life.

## Taking Turns

Many parents begin to encourage turn taking long before infants say their first words (Field & Widmayer, 1982):

PARENT:                     Can you see the bird?
INFANT (COOING):            ooooh
PARENT:                     It is a pretty bird.
INFANT:                     ooooh
PARENT:                     You're right, it's a cardinal.

Soon after 1-year-olds begin to speak, parents like the father in the photo encourage their youngsters to participate in conversational turn taking. To help children along, parents often carry both sides of a conversation to demonstrate how the roles of speaker and listener alternate (Shatz, 1983):

PARENT (TO INFANT):                 What's Amy eating?
PARENT (ILLUSTRATING REPLY):  She's eating a cookie.

Parents and other caregivers seem to do whatever is necessary to allow infants and toddlers to "fit in" to a conversation. That is, caregivers scaffold youngsters' attempts to converse, making it more likely that children will succeed.

Such early "conversations" between caregivers and infants are not universal. In some nonwestern cultures, preverbal infants are not considered appropriate conversational partners, so adults don't talk to them. Only after infants are older do others begin to converse with them (Ochs, 1988).

By age 2, spontaneous turn taking is common in conversations between youngsters and adults (Barton & Tomasello, 1991). And by age 3, children have progressed to the point that if a listener fails to reply promptly, the child repeats his or her remark in order to elicit a response (Garvey & Berninger, 1981). A 3-year-old might say, "Hi, Paul" to an older sibling who's busy reading. If Paul doesn't answer in a few seconds, the 3-year-old might say, "Hi, Paul" again. When Paul remains unresponsive, the 3-year-old is likely to shout, "PAUL!"—showing that by this age children understand the norm that a comment deserves a response. Preschool children seem to interpret the lack of a response as, "I guess you didn't hear me, so I'll say it again, louder!"

## Speaking Effectively

When do children first try to initiate communications with others? Wanting to tell something to someone else is a deliberate act, and, based on Piaget's description of sensorimotor thinking (pages 153–155), we wouldn't expect much communcation until near the first birthday. In fact, what appear to be the first deliberate attempts to communicate typically emerge at 10 months (Bates et al., 1979; Golinkoff, 1993). Infants at this age may touch or point to an object while simultaneously looking at another person. They continue this behavior until the person acknowledges them. It's as if the child is saying, "This is a neat toy! I want you to see it, too."

Beginning at 10 months, an infant may point, touch, or make noises to get an adult to do something. An infant in a playpen like the one in the photo who wants a toy that is out of reach may make noises while pointing to the toy. The noises capture an adult's attention, and the pointing indicates what the baby wants (Blake, O'Rourke, & Borzellino, 1994). The communication may be a bit primitive by adult standards, but it works for babies!

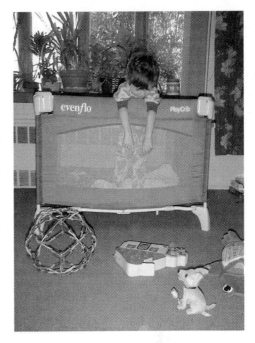

After the first birthday, children begin to use speech to communicate and often initiate conversations with adults (Bloom et al., 1996). Toddlers' first conversations are about themselves, but their conversational scope expands rapidly to include objects in the environment (e.g., toys, food). Later, conversations begin to include more abstract notions, such as hypothetical objects and past or future events (Foster, 1986).

Of course, young children are not always skilled conversational partners. At times their communications are confusing, leaving a listener to wonder, "What was that all about?" Every message—whether an informal conversation or a formal lecture—should have a clear meaning. But saying something clearly is often difficult because clarity can only be judged by considering the listener's age, experience, knowledge of the topic, and the context of the conversation. For example, think about the simple request "Please hand me the Phillips-head screwdriver." This message may be clear to older listeners familiar with different types of screwdrivers, but it won't mean much to younger listeners who think all screwdrivers are alike. And, if the tool box is filled with Phillips-head screwdrivers of assorted sizes, the message won't be clear even to a knowledgeable listener.

Constructing clear messages is a fine art, but, amazingly, by the preschool years, youngsters begin to adjust their messages to match the listener and the context. In a classic study, Marilyn Shatz and Rochel Gelman (1973) asked 4-year-olds to explain how a toy worked, once to a 2-year-old and once to an adult. Shatz and Gelman found that 4-year-olds talked more overall to adults than to 2-year-olds and used longer sentences with adult listeners than with 2-year-old listeners. Also, children used simpler grammar and more attention-getting words, such as *see, look, watch,* and *hey,* when speaking with 2-year-olds. Here, for example, is how one 4-year-old child explained the toy to her two different listeners (the toy is a garage with drivers and trucks that carry marbles to a dumping station):

> Young children adjust their messages based on a listener's age and knowledge.

> *Adult listener: You're supposed to put one of these persons in, see? Then one goes with the other little girl. And then the little boy. He's the little boy and he drives. And then they back up. . . . And then the little girl falls out and then it goes backwards.*

> *2-year-old listener: Watch, Perry. Watch this. He's back in here. Now he drives up. Look, Perry. Look here, Perry. Those are marbles, Perry. Put the men in here. Now I'll do it (Shatz & Gelman, 1973, p. 13).*

Shatz and Gelman's findings show that preschoolers are already sensitive to the importance of the audience in formulating a clear message. More recent findings also show that children consider the listener and setting in devising clear messages:

- Preschool children give more elaborate messages to listeners who are unfamiliar with a topic than to listeners who are familiar with it (O'Neill, 1996). For example, a child describing where to find a toy will give more detailed directions to a listener whose eyes were covered when the toy was hidden.

- School-age children speak differently to adults and peers. They are more likely to speak politely with adults and be more demanding with peers (Warren-Leubecker & Bohannon, 1989). A child might ask a parent, "May I have one of your cookies?" but say to a peer, "Give me one of your cookies."

- **Some African Americans speak** *Black English,* **a dialect of standard English that has slightly different grammatical rules.** For example, "He be tired" in Black English is synonymous with "He usually is tired" in standard English. Many African American children learn both Black English and standard English, and they switch dialects depending on the situation (Warren & McCloskey, 1993). They use standard English more often in school and when talking with European Americans but use Black English more often at home and when talking with African American peers.

All these findings show that school-age children (and sometimes preschoolers) are well on their way to understanding the factors that must be considered in creating clear messages. Even so, sometimes messages are not clear to listeners. Speakers need to pay attention to listeners; if they don't seem to understand the message, they need to try again. The "Focus on Research" feature shows that even young children have mastered this basic step toward effective communication.

**FOCUS ON RESEARCH**

### When Listeners Don't Understand, Preschoolers Try Again

*Who were the investigators, and what was the aim of the study?* A good general rule for effective communication is that speakers should monitor their listeners' comprehension. When listeners get puzzled expressions on their faces, this is usually a sign that the message was not crystal clear and the speaker should clarify. Do preschool children know this important communicative rule? Do they pay attention to a listener's comprehension? These were the questions that Helen Shwe and Ellen Markman (1997) wanted to answer.

*How did the investigators measure the topic of interest?* Shwe and Markman showed two objects (e.g., a toy car and a sock) to 2½-year-olds and asked which one they'd like to see. After the child had chosen, the experimenter said, "You asked for the _____. I think you want the _____. I'm going to give you the _____. Here's the _____." In one condition, the experimenter mentioned the chosen toy and actually gave the child the chosen toy. In three other conditions, the experimenter sometimes mentioned the wrong toy or gave the wrong toy or both. Then the experimenter recorded what the child did.

*Who were the children in the study?* Shwe and Markman tested 22 preschoolers with an average age of 31 months.

*What was the design of the study?* This study was experimental: There were two independent variables. One was whether the experimenter mentioned the correct toy in replying to the child's choice; the other was whether the experimenter gave the child the chosen toy. The dependent variable was the frequency with which children repeated their preference for the original toy, either by vocalizing, pointing, or gazing. The study was not developmental (only 2½-year-olds participated and they were tested just once), so it was neither cross-sectional nor longitudinal.

*Were there ethical concerns with the study?* No. The task—asking children to choose a toy—posed no danger to the children. Mothers were present during testing.

*What were the results?* The top of the graph shows what children did when they received the wrong toy. Not surprisingly, they were much more likely to repeat their preference spontaneously when they received the wrong toy than when they received the right one. (After all, when the child received the expected object, there was no reason for youngsters to repeat the request.) More interesting are the results in the bottom of the graph, which show what children did when the experimenter described the wrong toy. Children were much more likely to restate their preference when the experimenter *described* it incorrectly than when the experimenter described it correctly.

*What did the investigators conclude?* Even very young children seem to understand that, when listeners misunderstand, speakers need to do something. In the grander scheme of things, repeating what you've just said is not a very good strategy. But in this simple experimental setting, it was adequate to convey to the adult, "You think I wanted the sock but, no, I wanted the car." As Shwe and Markman (1997) phrased it, "Young children monitor their communicative partner's knowledge state and care about their listener's comprehension . . ." (p. 636). ●

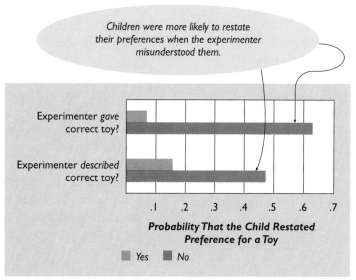

FIG 9–6

Thus, from a surprisingly young age, children express themselves to others and adjust their conversations to fit listeners. Are young children equally adept at listening? We'll find out in the next section.

## Listening Well

Listening well may seem easy but it's not. A skilled listener must continuously decide whether a speaker's remarks make sense. If they do, then a listener needs to make an appropriate reply, typically by extending the conversation with another remark that's on the topic.

Few toddlers master this fundamental conversation skill. Their replies are more likely to be unrelated to the topic than related to it (Bloom, Rocissano, & Hood, 1976). Asked "Where's the sock?" a 1½-year-old may say something like "I'm hungry!" By 3 years, children are more adept at continuing conversations by making remarks that relate to the topic being discussed.

If a message is vague or confusing, the listener should ask the speaker to clarify the message. This seems obvious enough, but young children do not always realize when a message is ambiguous. Told to find "the red toy," they may promptly select the red ball from a pile that includes a red toy car, a red block, and a red toy hammer. Instead of asking the speaker which *specific* red toy, young listeners often assume that they know which toy the speaker had in mind (Beal & Belgrad, 1990). Only when messages almost defy comprehension—they are too soft to be heard or give obviously ambiguous or even conflicting information— do youngsters detect a problem.

Because young children's remarks often contain ambiguities and because, as listeners, they often do not detect ambiguities, young children often miscommunicate, just like Marla and Kitty in the opening vignette. Kitty probably didn't communicate exactly what kind of markers she wanted, and Marla didn't understand that the directions were unclear. Throughout the elementary-school years, youngsters gradually master the many skills involved in determining if a message is consistent and clear (Ackerman, 1993).

Sometimes messages are confusing because they conflict with what a listener thinks is true. For example, suppose a child is told that the family cat, which always stays indoors, has run away. Even preschoolers are more likely to believe such a message when told by a parent than by a classmate because they know the parent is better informed about this particular topic (Robinson, Champion, & Mitchell, 1999).

Sometimes listeners must go beyond the words to understand the real meaning of a message. Metaphor is one example. When parents tell their teenagers, "Your bedroom is a junk yard," you (and they) know that this remark is not to be taken literally. Instead, the metaphor highlights the fact that the bedroom is a mess and filled with things that could be thrown away.

As you might expect, understanding nonliteral meanings of messages develops slowly (e.g., Dews et al., 1996). In the case of metaphor, young children easily

> Young children often ignore ambiguities in messages and sometimes interpret metaphor and sarcasm literally.

understand simple metaphors in which the nonliteral meaning is based on references to concrete objects and their properties. For example, a parent might say to a 5-year-old, "You're a fish," referring to how well the child swims and enjoys the water, and the child will likely understand.

More complex metaphors require that children make connections based upon abstract relations. For example, in Shakespeare's *Romeo and Juliet,* Romeo proclaims that "Juliet is the sun." You might interpret this line to mean that Juliet is the center of Romeo's universe or that without Juliet Romeo will die. The first interpretation depends upon your knowledge of astronomy; the second, on your knowledge of biology. Younger children lack this sort of knowledge to comprehend metaphors, so they try to interpret them literally. Only when children gain the necessary knowledge and formal operational abstract reasoning do they understand metaphors based on abstract relations (Winner, 1988).

Sarcasm is another form of communication that is not to be interpreted literally. When a soccer player misses the ball entirely and a teammate says, "Nice kick," the literal meaning of the remark is the opposite of the intended meaning. An understanding of sarcasm develops in much the same way as an understanding of metaphor. When people emphasize their sarcasm by speaking in mocking or overly enthusiastic tones, school-age children can detect their meaning. However, if sarcasm must be detected solely from the context—by realizing that the comment is the opposite of what would be expected—only adolescents and adults are likely to understand the real meaning of the remark (Capelli, Nakagawa, & Madden, 1990).

This discussion of listening skills completes our catalog of the important accomplishments that take place in communication during childhood. As children enter kindergarten, they have mastered many of the fundamental rules of communication, and as they grow older, they acquire even greater proficiency.

## Check Your Learning

**1.** In some nonwestern cultures, preverbal infants are not seen as _____.

**2.** If a listener doesn't respond promptly, a 3-year-old speaker will _____.

**3.** Before they can talk, infants often try to communicate by making noises or by

_____.

**4.** One example of the way that children adjust their speech to consider listeners is that many African American children _____.

**5.** When listeners do not understand them, toddlers will sometimes _____.

**6.** When toddlers respond to a remark, their comment is often _____.

**7.** Young children often ignore ambiguities in messages because _____.

According to Piaget's theory, preschool children are egocentric. How do you think this egocentrism influences their communication skill? Are the findings described in this module consistent with Piaget's view?

**Answers:** (1) appropriate conversational partners, (2) repeat the remark in an effort to elicit a reply, (3) touching or pointing at an object, (4) use Black English more often at home than in school, (5) repeat their remark, (6) not relevant to the speaker's topic, (7) they assume that they know what the speaker means.

# Language and Communication

## IN PERSPECTIVE

Helen Keller, an American lecturer and writer who was blind and deaf from a childhood illness, once described language development as a "vast distance between our first stammered syllable and the sweep of thought in a line of Shakespeare." The distance is indeed vast, yet children cover it with remarkable speed. We saw, in Module 9.1, that infants hear language sounds from very early in life but take much longer to produce language sounds correctly. In Module 9.2, we discovered that babies' first words at about age 1 reflect their ability to use symbols. We also learned that although children use different language learning styles, they all use rules to help them learn word meanings, and they learn words best from activities that make them think about the meanings of new words. In Module 9.3, we saw that although children's sentences become more complex during the preschool years, children always follow simple rules to organize words into sentences. Mastery of grammar probably involves a combination of built-in mechanisms and language experience. Finally, in Module 9.4, we found that, as speakers, young children often communicate unclearly and, as listeners, they don't recognize lack of clarity in others' messages.

This chapter is an appropriate occasion to stress the theme that _development in different domains is connected_: Language has important connections to biological, cognitive, and social development. A link to biological development would be children's mastery of grammar: In ways that we don't yet fully understand, children seem to be endowed with a mechanism that smooths the path to mastering grammar. A link to cognitive development would be children's first words: Speaking words reflects the cognitive insight that speech sounds are symbols. A link to social development would be the communication skills that enable children to interact with peers and adults.

## See for Yourself

Berko's (1958) "wugs" task is fun to try with preschool children. Photocopy the drawing on page 256 and show it to a preschooler, repeating the instructions that appear on that page. You should find that the child quite predictably says, "two wugs." Create some pictures of your own to examine other grammatical morphemes, such as adding *-ing* to denote ongoing activity or adding *-ed* to indicate past tense. See for yourself!

## Resources

*For more information about . . .*

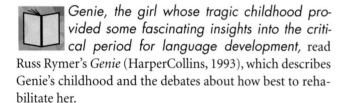 *Genie, the girl whose tragic childhood provided some fascinating insights into the critical period for language development,* read Russ Rymer's *Genie* (HarperCollins, 1993), which describes Genie's childhood and the debates about how best to rehabilitate her.

 *American Sign Language (ASL),* visit the Animated American Sign Language Dictionary Web site,

**http://www.bconnex.net/~randys/index_nf.html**

## Key Terms

**babbling** 245
**Black English** 264
**cooing** 245
**expressive style** 248
**fast mapping** 249
**grammar** 242
**grammatical morphemes** 255
**infant-directed speech** 244

**intonation** 245
**language** 242
**naming explosion** 249
**overextension** 251
**overregularization** 256
**phonemes** 243
**phonology** 242
**pragmatics** 242

**referential style** 248
**semantic bootstrapping
  hypothesis** 259
**semantics** 242
**syntax** 242
**telegraphic speech** 255
**underextension** 251

# SUMMARY 9

## 9.1 The Road to Speech

### Elements of Language

Language includes four distinct elements: phonology (sounds), semantics (word meaning), grammar (rules for language structure), and pragmatics (rules for communication). Syntax, which is part of grammar, describes how words are ordered in sentences.

### Perceiving Speech

Phonemes are the basic units of sound that make up words. Infants can hear phonemes soon after birth. They can even hear phonemes that are not used in their native language, but this ability is lost by the first birthday. Before they speak, infants can recognize words, apparently by noticing stress and syllables that go together. Infants prefer infant-directed speech—adults' speech to infants that is slower and has greater variation in pitch—because it provides them additional language clues.

### Public Speaking in a Few Easy Steps

Newborns are limited to crying, but at about 3 months, babies coo. Babbling soon follows, consisting of a single syllable; over several months, infants' babbling includes longer syllables and intonation. Deaf children babble later than children with normal hearing, but if adults use sign language with them they can learn to make partial signs that are thought to be analogous to babbling.

## 9.2 Learning the Meanings of Words

### Understanding Words as Symbols

Children's first words represent a cognitive accomplishment that is not specific to language. Instead, the onset of language is due to a child's ability to interpret and use symbols. Consistent with this view, there are parallel developments in the use of gestures.

### Styles of Learning Language

Some youngsters use a referential style in learning words that emphasizes words as names and views language as an intellectual tool. Other children use an expressive style that emphasizes phrases and views language as a social tool.

### Fast Mapping Meanings to Words

Most children learn the meanings of words too rapidly for them to consider all plausible meanings systematically. Instead, children use a number of fast-mapping rules to determine probable meanings of new words. Joint attention, constraints, and sentence cues all help children learn words. The rules do not always lead to the correct meaning. An underextension denotes a child's meaning that is nar-

rower than an adult's meaning; an overextension denotes a child's meaning that is broader.

### Encouraging Word Learning

Children's word learning is fostered by experience, including being read to, watching television, and, for school-age children, reading to themselves. The key ingredient is making children think about the meanings of new words.

## 9.3 Speaking in Sentences

### From Two-Word Speech to Complex Sentences

Not long after their first birthday, children produce two-word sentences that are based on simple rules for expressing ideas or needs. These sentences are sometimes called telegraphic because they use the fewest possible words to convey meaning. Moving from two-word to more complex sentences involves adding grammatical morphemes. Children first master grammatical morphemes that express simple relations, then those that denote complex relations.

As children acquire grammatical morphemes, they also extend their speech to other sentence forms, such as questions, and later to more complex constructions, such as passive sentences.

### How Children Acquire Grammar

Some researchers claim that grammar is too complex for children to learn solely from their experience; instead, the brain must be prewired to simplify the task. Findings consistent with this argument are specialized regions in the brain for processing language, the inability of chimpanzees to master grammar, and critical periods in language acquisition. Other researchers believe that children use general cognitive skills to infer grammatical rules from regularities in the speech that they hear.

Language experience is important for learning grammar. Parents provide examples of the rules of speech that their children are trying to master, and they provide children with feedback concerning grammatical rules.

## 9.4 Using Language to Communicate

### Taking Turns

Parents encourage turn taking even before infants talk and later demonstrate both the speaker and listener roles for their children. By age 3, children spontaneously take turns and prompt one another to speak.

### Speaking Effectively

Before they can speak, infants use gestures and noises to communicate. During the preschool years, children gradually become more skilled at constructing clear messages, in part by adjusting their speech to fit their listeners' needs. They also begin to monitor their listeners' comprehension, repeating messages if necessary.

### Listening Well

Toddlers are not good conversationalists because their remarks don't relate to the topic. Preschoolers are unlikely to identify ambiguities in another's speech. Also, they sometimes have difficulty understanding messages that are not to be taken literally, such as metaphor and sarcasm.

# 10

f you're a fan of *Star Trek,* you know that Mr. Spock feels little emotion because he's half Vulcan and people from the planet Vulcan don't have emotions. Would you like to live an emotionless life like Mr. Spock? Probably not. For most of us, feelings enrich our lives. As partial testimony to their importance, the English language has more than 500 words that refer to emotions (Averill, 1980). Joy, happiness, satisfaction, and yes, anger, guilt, and humiliation are just a few of the feelings that give life meaning.

In this chapter, we'll see how emotions emerge and how they affect development. In Module 10.1, we'll discuss when children first express different emotions and recognize emotions in others. Next, in Module 10.2, we'll see that children have different behavioral styles and that these styles are rooted, in part, in emotions. Finally, in Module 10.3, we'll examine the infant's first emotional relationship, the one that develops with the primary caregiver.

# Emotional Development

10.1  **Emerging Emotions**

10.2  **Temperament**

10.3  **Attachment**

# 10.1

# Emerging Emotions

## Learning Objectives

● At what ages do children begin to express basic emotions?

● What are complex emotions, and when do they develop?

● When do children begin to understand other people's emotions? How do they use this information to guide their own behavior?

● When do children show evidence of regulating emotion, and why is this an important skill?

> *Nicole was ecstatic that she was finally going to see her 7-month-old nephew, Claude. She rushed into the house and, seeing Claude playing on the floor with blocks, swept him up in a big hug. After a brief, puzzled look, Claude burst into angry tears and began thrashing around, as if saying to Nicole, "Who are you? What do you want? Put me down! Now!" Nicole quickly handed Claude to his mother, who was surprised by her baby's outburst and even more surprised that he continued to sob while she rocked him.*

Nicole's initial happiness, Claude's anger, and his mother's surprise illustrate three basic human emotions. Happiness, anger, and surprise, along with fear, disgust, and sadness, are considered basic emotions because people worldwide experience them and because each consists of three elements: a subjective feeling, a physiological change, and an overt behavior (Izard, 1991). For example, suppose you wake to the sound of a thunderstorm and then discover your roommate has left for class with your umbrella. Subjectively, you might feel ready to explode with anger; physiologically, your heart would beat faster; and behaviorally, you would probably be scowling.

*Facial expressions probably reflect an infant's emotions because expressions are associated with specific physiological changes, they are similar around the world, and they change predictably in response to infants' experiences.*

In addition to basic emotions, people feel complex emotions such as pride, guilt, and embarrassment. Unlike basic emotions, complex emotions have an evaluative component to them. For example, a 2-year-old who has spilled juice all over the floor may hang his head in shame; another 2-year-old who has, for the first time, finished a difficult puzzle by herself will smile in a way that radiates pride. Also, in contrast to basic emotions, complex emotions are not experienced the same way in all cultures.

In this module, we look at when children first express basic and complex emotions, how children come to understand emotions in others, and, finally, how children regulate their emotions.

## Basic Emotions

Is there a time when infants are like Mr. Spock—relatively free of emotion? No; emotions are with us from the first few months of life. To see for yourself, look at the photos of young babies at the top of page 273. Which one is angry? Which are the sad and happy babies? The facial expressions are so revealing that I'm sure you guessed that the babies are, in order, sad, happy, and angry. But do these distinctive facial expressions mean the infants are actually experiencing these emotions? Not necessarily. Remember that facial expressions are only one component of emotion—the behavioral manifestation. Emotion also involves physiological responses and subjective feelings. Of course, infants can't express their feelings to us verbally, so we don't know much about their subjective experiences. We're on firmer ground with the physiological element. At least some of the physiological responses that accompany facial expressions are the same in infants and adults. For example, when infants and adults smile—which suggests they're happy—the left frontal cortex of the brain tends to have more electrical activity than the right frontal cortex (Fox, Kimmerly, & Schafer, 1991).

Many scientists use this and similar findings to argue that facial expressions are reliable clues to an infant's emotional state. For example, research also shows that infants and adults worldwide express basic emotions in much the same way (Izard, 1991). The child in the photo shows the universal signs of fear. Her eyes are open wide, her eyebrows are raised, and her mouth is relaxed but slightly open. The universality of emotional expression suggests that humans are biologically programmed to express emotions in a specific way; it's simply in our genes to smile when we're happy and scowl when we're unhappy.

Another finding linking infants' facial expressions to emotions is that, by 5 to 6 months, infants' facial expressions change predictably and meaningfully in response to events. When a happy mother greets her baby, the baby usually smiles in return; when a tired, distracted mother picks up her baby roughly, the baby usually frowns at her. These findings suggest that by the middle of the first year (and maybe earlier) facial expressions are fairly reliable indicators of an infant's emotional state (Izard et al., 1995; Weinberg & Tronick, 1994).

If facial expressions provide a window on a baby's emotions, what do they tell us about the early phases of emotional development? Let's start with happiness. During the first few weeks after birth, infants begin to smile, but this seems to be related to internal physiological states. An infant may smile after feeding or while asleep, for example. **At about 2 months, *social smiles* first appear: Infants smile when they see another human face.** Sometimes social smiling is accompanied by cooing, the early form of vocalization described in Module 9.1 (Sroufe & Waters, 1976). Smiling and cooing seem to be the infant's way of expressing pleasure at seeing another person.

At about 4 months, smiling is joined by laughter, which usually occurs when a baby experiences vigorous physical stimulation (Sroufe & Wunsch, 1972). Tickling

4-month-olds or bouncing them on your knee is a good way to prompt a laugh. Toward the end of the first year, infants often laugh when familiar events take a novel turn. For example, a 1-year-old will laugh when her mother pretends to drink from a baby bottle or her father drapes a diaper around his waist. Laughter is now a response to psychological stimulation as well as physical stimulation.

The early stages of positive feelings, like happiness, are fairly clear: An infant's experience of happiness is first linked primarily to physical states, such as feeling full after a meal or being tickled. Later, feelings of happiness reflect psychological states, such as the pleasure of seeing another person or an unusual event.

We know much less about the development of negative emotions such as fear, anger, and sadness. Certainly, newborns express distress, but specific negative emotions are hard to verify. Anger emerges gradually, with distinct displays appearing between 4 and 6 months. Infants will become angry, for example, if a favorite food or toy is taken away (Sternberg & Campos, 1990). Reflecting their growing understanding of goal-directed behavior (see Module 6.2), infants also become angry when their attempts to achieve a goal are frustrated. For example, if a parent restrains an infant trying to pick up a toy, the guaranteed result is a very angry baby.

Like anger, fear seems to be rare in newborns and young infants. **The first distinct signs of fear emerge at about 6 months when infants become wary in the presence of an unfamiliar adult, a reaction known as *stranger wariness*.** When a stranger approaches, a 6-month-old typically looks away and begins to fuss (Mangelsdorf, Shapiro, & Marzolf, 1995). The baby in the photo is showing the signs of stranger wariness. The grandmother has picked him up without giving him a chance to warm up to her, and the outcome is as predictable as it was with Claude, the baby boy in the vignette who was frightened by his aunt: He cries, looks frightened, and reaches with arms outstretched in the direction of someone familiar.

How wary an infant feels around strangers depends on a number of factors (Thompson & Limber, 1991). First, infants tend to be less fearful of strangers when the environment is familiar and more fearful when it is not. Many parents know this firsthand from traveling with their infants: Enter a friend's house for the first time and the baby clings tightly to its mother. Second, the amount of anxiety depends on the stranger's behavior. Instead of rushing to greet or pick up the baby, as Nicole did in the vignette, a stranger should talk with other adults and, in a while, perhaps offer the baby a toy (Mangelsdorf, 1992). Handled this way, many infants will soon be curious about the stranger instead of afraid.

Wariness of strangers is adaptive because it emerges at the same time that children begin to master creeping and crawling (described in Module 4.4). Like Curious George, the monkey in a famous series of children's books, babies are inquisitive and want to use their new locomotor skills to explore their worlds. Being wary of strangers provides a natural restraint against the tendency to wander away from familiar caregivers.

*An infant is more likely to fear strangers in an unfamiliar environment and when strangers don't give the infant ample time to warm up to them.*

Wariness of strangers gradually declines as infants learn to interpret facial expressions and recognize when a stranger is friendly and not hostile, but then other fears develop. Many preschoolers are afraid of the dark and of imaginary creatures. These fears typically diminish during the elementary-school years as children grow cognitively and better understand the difference between appearance and reality (see Module 6.2). Replacing these fears are concerns about school, health, and personal harm (Silverman, La Greca, & Wasserstein, 1995). Such worries are common and are not cause for concern in most children. In some youngsters, however, they become so extreme they overwhelm the child (Chorpita & Barlow, 1998; Rutter & Garmezy, 1983). For example, a 7-year-old's worries about school would not be unusual unless her concern grew to the point that she refused to go to school at all. In the "Making Children's Lives Better" feature, we'll look at this form of excessive fear and how it can be treated.

### "But I Don't Want to Go to School!"

Many youngsters plead, argue, and fight with their parents daily over going to school. **An overwhelming fear of going to school and active resistance to attending school constitutes** *school phobia.* For example, every school day, 9-year-old Keegan would cling to his mother and start to sob as soon as he finished his breakfast. When it was time to leave the house to catch the bus, he would drop to the floor and start kicking.

Children may develop school phobia because they are overanxious generally and school is full of situations that can cause anxiety, such as reading aloud, taking tests, or learning new activities with competitive classmates. **School-phobic children can be helped with** *systematic desensitization,* **a technique that associates deep relaxation with progressively more anxiety-provoking situations.** First the therapist asks the child to generate a list of school-related situations, from pleasant ("I got the highest grade on my math test") to neutral ("We say the pledge of allegiance every morning") to very anxiety-provoking ("I got home and realized that I'd left my assignments in my locker"). Setting the list aside, the therapist then teaches the child how to reduce tension by relaxing different muscle groups. When the child masters the relaxation techniques, the therapist asks the child to relax and imagine the pleasant school-related situations. Over several sessions, the child imagines progressively more anxiety-provoking situations while relaxed, so that the anxiety the child used to feel is replaced by feelings of calm relaxation. Children taught this technique report feeling much less anxious, and their school attendance improves (Kearney & Silverman, 1995). ●

Although children worldwide express basic emotions, there are cultural differences in the frequency of emotional expression. In one study (Camras et al., 1998), European American 11-month-olds cried and smiled more often than Chinese 11-month-olds. In another study (Zahn-Waxler et al., 1996), U.S. preschoolers were more likely than Japanese preschoolers to express anger in interpersonal conflicts. Thus, even though basic emotions are rooted in biology, the way they are expressed is influenced by culture.

## Complex Emotions

Basic emotions emerge early in infancy, but complex emotions such as feelings of guilt, embarrassment, and pride don't surface until 18 to 24 months of age (Lewis, 1992). Complex emotions depend on the child having some understanding of the self, which typically occurs between 15 and 18 months (see Module 11.1). Children feel guilty or embarrassed, for example, when they've done something they know they shouldn't have done: A child who breaks a toy is thinking, "You told me to be careful. But I wasn't!" Similarly, children feel pride when they've done something that was challenging: A little girl catching a ball for the first time thinks, "This was

*(In the left margin, rotated:)* MAKING CHILDREN'S LIVES BETTER

hard, but I did it, all by myself!" For children to experience complex emotions, they need to be more advanced cognitively, which explains why complex emotions don't appear until the very end of infancy (Lewis, Alessandri, & Sullivan, 1992).

Cognitive growth also means that as youngsters progress through middle childhood and adolescence, they experience shame and guilt in situations where they would not have when they were younger (Reimer, 1996). For example, suppose a child is wrongly accused of theft. A school-age child who neglects to defend the classmate might feel shame but a preschool child probably wouldn't.

Complex emotions also depend upon the cultural setting: Situations that evoke pride in one culture may evoke embarrassment or shame in another. For example, American elementary-school children often show pride at personal achievement, such as getting the highest grade on a test or, as shown in the photo, coming in first place in a county fair. In contrast, Asian elementary-school children are embarrassed by a public display of individual achievement but show great pride when their entire class is honored for an achievement (Stevenson & Stigler, 1992). Thus, the conditions that trigger complex emotions such as pride, envy, and shame depend upon the culture, so children have to learn when these emotions are appropriate.

In sum, complex emotions like guilt and pride require more sophisticated understanding and are more culturally specific than basic emotions like happiness and fear, which are more biologically based and culturally universal. By age 2, however, children express both basic and complex emotions. Of course, expressing emotions is only part of the developmental story. Children must also learn to recognize others' emotions, which is our next topic.

## Recognizing and Using Others' Emotions

Imagine you are broke (only temporarily, of course) and plan to borrow $20 from your roommate when she returns from class. Shortly, she storms into your apartment, slams the door, and throws her backpack on the floor. Immediately, you change your plans, realizing that now is hardly a good time to ask for a loan. This example reminds us that we often need to recognize others' emotions and sometimes change our behavior as a consequence.

When can infants first identify emotions in others? By 6 or 7 months, infants begin to distinguish facial expressions associated with different emotions. A 6-month-old can, for example, distinguish a happy, smiling face from a sad, frowning face (Ludemann, 1991; Ludemann & Nelson, 1988). Strictly speaking, these studies tell us only that infants can discriminate facial expressions, not emotions per se. Other research, however, indicates that 6-month-olds have indeed begun to recognize the emotions themselves. The best evidence is that infants often match their own emotions to other people's emotions. When happy mothers smile and talk in a pleasant voice, infants express happiness themselves. If mothers are angry or sad, infants become distressed, too (Haviland & Lelwica, 1987).

Also like adults, infants use others' emotions to direct their behavior. **Infants in an unfamiliar or ambiguous environment often look at their mother or father, as if searching for cues to help them interpret the situation, a phenomenon known as** *social referencing.* For example, in a study by Hirshberg and Svejda (1990), 12-month-olds were shown novel toys that made sounds, such as a stuffed alligator that hissed. For some toys, parents were told to look happy; for others, parents were to look afraid. When parents looked afraid, their infants, too, appeared distressed and moved away from the toys.

In other studies of social referencing, infants watch an adult express happiness when looking inside one box but disgust when looking inside another. Infants are more likely to explore the box that elicited happiness (Repacholi, 1998). Furthermore, facial expressions or vocal expressions alone provide infants with enough information to decide if they want to explore an unfamiliar object (Mumme, Fernald, & Herrera, 1996). Thus, social referencing shows that infants rely on their parents' emotions to help them regulate their own behavior.

> By the first birthday, infants can recognize others' emotions and use these emotions to direct their own behavior.

As their cognitive skills grow, children begin to understand why people feel as they do. By kindergarten, for example, children know that undesirable or unpleasant events often make a person feel angry or sad (Levine, 1995). Children even know that they more often feel sad when they think about the undesirable event itself (e.g., a broken toy or a friend who moves away) but feel angry when they think about the person who caused the undesirable event (e.g., the person who broke the toy or the friend's parents who wanted to live in another city). Kindergarten children also understand that remembering past sad events can make a person unhappy again (Lagattuta, Wellman, & Flavell, 1997).

During the elementary-school years, children begin to comprehend that people sometimes experience "mixed feelings." Wintre and Vallance (1994) read sentences describing emotionally evocative situations to 4- through 8-year-olds and asked them how happy, angry, sad, scared, or loving they would feel in each situation. A sentence describing a fear-provoking situation was "You are home all alone," and one describing a sad situation was "Your best friend moves away." You can see in the results, shown in the figure, that by about 8 years of age children realize how people can feel good and bad at the same time. The increased ability to see multiple, differing emotions coincides with the decentered thinking that characterizes the concrete operational stage (Module 6.2).

**Stages in the Development of Children's Understanding That People Can Experience Multiple Emotions Simultaneously**

| Stage | Age | Understanding | Example |
|---|---|---|---|
| 1 | 5 years | A situation can cause a person to experience two different emotions. | A child could be sad and angry that a best friend is moving away. |
| 2 | 6 1/2 years | A situation can cause a person to experience two different emotions that differ in intensity. | A child could be very sad and a little angry that a best friend is moving away. |
| 3 | 8 years | A situation can cause a person to feel positively and negatively at the same time. | A child could be happy and scared about staying home alone. |

FIG 10–1

Based on Wintre and Vallance, 1994.

As children develop, they also begin to learn *display rules,* culturally specific standards for appropriate expressions of emotion in a particular setting or with a particular person or persons. Adults know, for example, that expressing sadness is appropriate at funerals but expressing joy is not. Similarly, expressing sadness is appropriate with relatives and close friends but less so with strangers. Preschool children's understanding of display rules is shown by the fact that they control their anger more when provoked by peers they like than when provoked by peers they don't like (Fabes et al., 1996). Also, school-age children and adolescents are more willing to express anger than sadness and, like the child in the photo, more willing to express both anger and sadness to parents than to peers (Zeman & Garber, 1996; Zeman & Shipman, 1997).

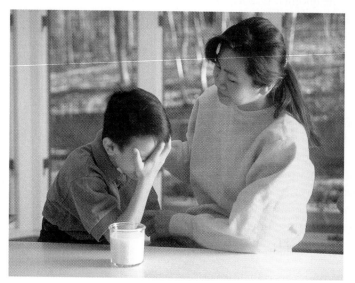

What experiences contribute to children's understanding of emotions? Not surprisingly, children learn about emotions when parents talk about feelings, explaining how they differ and the situations that elicit them (Brown & Dunn, 1996; Cervantes & Callanan, 1998). Also, a positive, rewarding relationship with parents and siblings is related to children's understanding of emotions (Brown & Dunn, 1996; Laible & Thompson, 1998). The nature of this connection is still a mystery. One possibility is that within positive parent-child and sibling relationships, people express a fuller range of emotions (and do so more often) and are more willing to talk about why they feel as they do, providing children more opportunities to learn about emotions.

Children's growing understanding of emotions in others contributes in turn to a growing ability to help others. They are more likely to recognize the emotions that signal a person's need. Better understanding of emotions in others also contributes to children's growing ability to play easily with peers because they can see the impact of their behavior on others. We'll cover empathy and social interaction in detail later in the book; for now, the important point is that recognizing emotions in others is an important prerequisite for successful, satisfying interactions. Another element of successful interactions is regulating emotions, our next topic.

## Regulating Emotions

Think back to a time when you were *really* angry at a good friend. Did you shout at the friend? Did you try to discuss matters camly? Or did you simply ignore the situation altogether? Shouting is a direct expression of anger, but calm conversation and overlooking a situation are purposeful attempts to regulate emotion. People often regulate emotions; for example, we routinely try to suppress fear (because we know there's no real need to be afraid of the dark), anger (because we don't want to let a friend know just how upset we are), and joy (because we don't want to seem like we're gloating over our good fortune).

Child development researchers have studied two aspects of emotion regulation: its origins and its links to social competence. Emotion regulation clearly begins in infancy. By 4 to 6 months, infants use simple strategies to regulate their emotions

(Buss & Goldsmith, 1998; Mangelsdorf, Shapiro, & Marzolf, 1995). When something frightens or confuses an infant—for example, a stranger or a mother who suddenly stops responding—he or she often looks away (just as older children and even adults often turn away or close their eyes to block out disturbing stimuli). Frightened infants also move closer to a parent, another effective way of helping to control their fear (Parritz, 1996).

Older children and adolescents encounter a wider range of emotional situations, so it's fortunate they develop many new ways to regulate emotion. School-age children and adolescents more often regulate emotions cognitively—they tell themselves to think about a positive aspect of an unpleasant situation or remind themselves to ignore something that upsets them. At the same time, they are less likely to release pent-up feelings publicly through crying or aggressing (Losoya, Eisenberg, & Fabes, 1998).

Children who don't regulate their emotions well tend to have problems interacting with peers. When children can't control their anger, worry, or sadness, they often have difficulty resolving the conflicts that inevitably surface in peer relationships (Eisenberg et al., 1997; Fabes et al., 1999). For example, faced with a dispute over what game to play or what movie to watch, children's unregulated anger interferes with finding a mutually satisfying solution. Thus, ineffective regulation of emotions leads to more frequent conflicts with peers, and, consequently, less satisfying interactions and relationships with them.

## Check Your Learning

1. Basic emotions include a subjective feeling, a physiological change, and _____.

2. During infancy, happiness is first linked to physical states and later to _____.

3. The first detectable form of fear is _____, which emerges at about 6 months.

4. Wariness of strangers is adaptive because it emerges at about the same time that _____.

5. Complex emotions, such as guilt and shame, emerge later than basic emotions because _____.

6. In social referencing, infants use a parent's facial expression _____.

7. School-age children and adolescents express anger and sadness more often with _____ than with peers.

8. When children cannot regulate their emotions well, they tend to have problems in _____.

The approaches to cognitive development described in Chapters 6 and 7 (Piaget's theory, Vygotsky's theory, information processing) don't explicitly consider emotion. How might emotion affect thinking? How could these approaches include emotion?

**Answers:** (1) an overt behavior, (2) psychological states, (3) wariness of strangers, (4) infants master creeping and crawling, (5) complex emotions require more advanced cognitive skills, (6) to direct their own behavior (for example, deciding if an unfamiliar situation is safe or frightening), (7) parents, (8) interacting with peers, especially when conflicts arise

# 10.2

# Temperament

## Learning Objectives

● What are the different features of temperament?

● How do heredity and environment influence temperament?

● How stable is a child's temperament across childhood?

● What are the consequences of different temperaments?

*Soon after Yoshimi arrived in the United States from Japan to begin graduate studies, she enrolled her 5-month-old son in day care. She was struck by the fact that, compared to her son, the European American babies in the day-care center were "wimps" (slang she had learned from American television). The other babies cried often and with minimal provocation. Yoshimi wondered whether her son was unusually "tough" or whether he was just a typical Japanese baby.*

When you've observed young babies—perhaps as part of "See for Yourself" in Chapter 3—were some babies like Yoshimi's, quiet most of the time, while others cried often and impatiently? Maybe you saw some infants who responded warmly to strangers and others who seemed very shy. **An infant's consistent mood and style of behavior is referred to as** *temperament.* Temperament does not refer so much to what babies do as to *how* they do what they do. For example, all babies become upset occasionally and cry. However, some, like Yoshimi's son, recover quickly while others are very hard to console. These differences in emotion and style of behavior are evident in the first few weeks after birth and are important throughout life.

Let's start this module by looking at different ways that scientists define temperament.

## What Is Temperament?

Alexander Thomas and Stella Chess (Chess & Thomas, 1986; Thomas, Chess, & Birch, 1968) pioneered the study of temperament. In 1956, they began the New York Longitudinal Study, which traced the lives of 141 individuals from infancy through adulthood. Thomas and Chess gathered their initial data by interviewing the babies' parents and asking individuals unfamiliar with the children to observe them at home. Based on these interviews and observations, Thomas and Chess evaluated the behavior of the 141 infants along the nine temperamental dimensions listed in the table at the top of page 281.

Using these nine dimensions, Thomas and Chess could place most infants into one of three groups. About 40 percent of the babies were categorized as "easy" babies. These infants were usually happy and cheerful, tended to adjust well to new situations, and had regular routines for eating, sleeping, and toileting. About 10 percent of the babies were categorized as "difficult." As you might imagine, in many respects they were the opposite of the easy babies: Difficult babies were often unhappy, did not adjust well to new situations, and had irregular routines for eating and sleeping. In addition, difficult babies tended to withdraw from novel experiences and to respond intensely to novel stimulation. About 15 percent of

> Thomas and Chess discovered that about two-thirds of the infants in their New York Longitudinal Study could be placed in one of three temperamental groups: easy, difficult, and slow to warm up.

| Dimensions of Temperament in the New York Longitudinal Study | |
|---|---|
| **Dimension** | **Description** |
| Activity level | Amount of physical and motor activity in daily situations |
| Rhythmicity | Regularity in eating, sleeping, toileting |
| Approach/withdrawal | Response to a novel object (accepting vs. rejecting) |
| Distractibility | Ease with which ongoing activity is disrupted by competing stimuli |
| Adaptability | Ease with which the child adjusts to changes in the environment |
| Intensity of reaction | Energy level of the child's responses |
| Mood | Balance between happy and unhappy behavior |
| Threshold | Level of stimulation needed for the child to respond |
| Attention span and persistence | Amount of time devoted to an activity, particularly with obstacles or distractions present |

TABLE 10–1

the babies were categorized as "slow to warm up." Like difficult babies, slow-to-warm-up babies tended to be unhappy and did not adjust well when placed in new situations. But unlike difficult babies, slow-to-warm-up babies did not respond intensely, and they tended to be relatively inactive. The remaining babies—roughly one-third—did not fit any of the groups; in general, they were average on most of the nine dimensions.

Although the New York Longitudinal Study launched the modern study of infant temperament, not all investigators agree with Thomas and Chess's nine dimensions and three groups. For example, Arnold Buss and Robert Plomin (1975, 1984) propose that temperament involves three primary dimensions—emotionality, activity, and sociability. **Emotionality refers to the strength of the infant's emotional response to a situation, the ease with which that response is triggered, and the ease with which the infant can be returned to a nonemotional state.** At one extreme are infants whose emotional responses are strong, easily triggered, and not easily calmed; at the other are infants whose responses are subdued, relatively difficult to elicit, and readily soothed. **Activity refers to the tempo and vigor of a child's movements.** Active infants are always busy, like to explore their environment, and enjoy vigorous play. Inactive infants have a more controlled behavioral tempo and are more likely to enjoy quiet play. **Sociability refers to a preference for being with other people.** Some infants relish contact with others, seek their attention, and prefer play that involves other people. Other infants, like the girl in the photo, enjoy solitude and are quite content to play alone with toys.

If you compare these three dimensions with the nine listed in the table above, you'll see a great deal of overlap. For example, Buss and Plomin's emotionality dimension combines the intensity and threshold dimensions of the New York Longitudinal Study. In fact, the major theories of temperament include most of the same elements (Shiner, 1998); what is still undecided is the best way to assemble these elements into a cohesive theory of temperament.

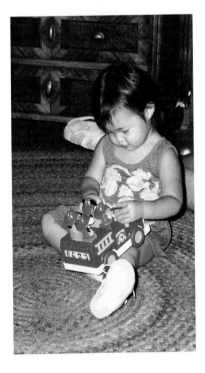

## Hereditary and Environmental Contributions to Temperament

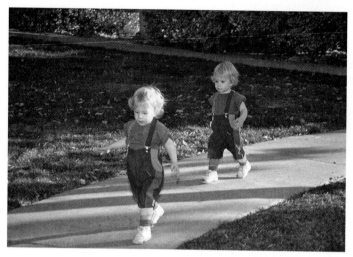

Most theories agree that temperament reflects both heredity and experience. The influence of heredity is shown in twin studies: Identical twins are more alike in most aspects of temperament than fraternal twins. For example, Goldsmith, Buss, and Lemery (1997) found that the correlation for identical twins' activity level was .72 but the correlation for fraternal twins was only .38. In other words, like the youngsters in the photo, if one identical twin is temperamentally active, the other usually is, too. Goldsmith et al. (1997) also found that identical twins were more alike than fraternal twins on social fearfulness (shyness), persistence, and proneness to anger.

Recently, scientists looking for links between genes and temperament came up with a surprising finding: Infants and toddlers who are upset by novel stimulation (and who often become shy preschoolers) have narrower faces than youngsters who respond calmly to novel stimulation (Arcus & Kagan, 1995). This observation is provocative because the brain and the facial skeleton originate in the same set of cells in prenatal development. Thus, one fascinating hypothesis is that genes influence levels of hormones that affect both facial growth and temperament.

The environment also contributes to children's temperament. Positive emotionality—youngsters who laugh often, seem to be generally happy, and often express pleasure—seems to reflect environmental influences (Goldsmith et al., 1997). Conversely, infants more often develop intense, difficult temperaments when mothers are abrupt in dealing with them and lack confidence (Belsky, Fish, & Isabella, 1991).

Heredity and experience may also explain why Yoshimi, the Japanese mother in the vignette, has such a hardy son. The "Cultural Influences" feature tells the story.

**CULTURAL INFLUENCES**

### Why Is Yoshimi's Son So Tough?

If you've ever watched an infant getting a shot, you know the inevitable response. After the syringe is removed, the infant's eyes open wide and then the baby begins to cry, as if saying, "Wow, that hurt!" Infants differ in how intensely they cry and in how readily they are soothed, reflecting differences in the emotionality dimension of temperament, but virtually all European American babies cry. It's easy to suppose that crying is a universal response to the pain from the inoculation, but it's not.

In stressful situations like getting a shot, Japanese and Chinese infants are less likely to become upset (Kagan et al., 1994). Lewis, Ramsay, and Kawakami (1993) found that most European American 4-month-olds cried loudly within 5 seconds of an injection, but only half the Japanese babies in their study cried. Furthermore, when Japanese and Chinese babies become upset, they are soothed more readily than European American babies. Lewis and his colleagues found that about three-fourths of the Japanese babies were no longer crying 90 seconds after the injection compared to fewer than half of the European American babies. The conclusion seems clear: Yoshimi's son appears to be a typical Japanese baby in crying less often and less intensely than the European American babies at his day-care center.

Why are Asian infants less emotional than their European American counterparts? Heredity may be involved. Perhaps the genes that contribute to emotionality are less common among Asians than among European Americans. But we can't overlook experience. Compared to European American mothers, Japanese mothers spend more time in close physical contact with their babies, constantly and gently soothing them; this may reduce the tendency to respond emotionally. ●

There's no question that heredity and experience cause babies' temperaments to differ, but how stable is temperament across childhood and adolescence? We'll find out in the next section.

## Stability of Temperament

Do calm, easygoing babies grow up to be calm, easygoing children, adolescents, and adults? Are difficult, irritable infants destined to grow up to be cranky, whiny children? The first answers to these questions came from the Fels longitudinal project, a study of many aspects of physical and psychological development from infancy. Although not a study of temperament per se, Jerome Kagan and his collaborators (Kagan, 1989; Kagan & Moss, 1962) found that fearful preschoolers in the Fels project tended to be inhibited as older children and adolescents.

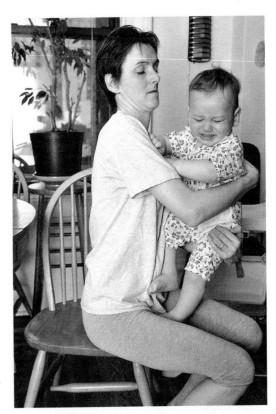

Spurred by findings like this one, later investigators attempted to learn more about the stability of temperament. Their research shows that temperament is somewhat stable early in development. An active fetus is more likely to be an active infant, and is also more likely to be a difficult, unadaptive infant (DiPietro et al., 1996). Newborns who cry under moderate stress tend, as 5-month-olds, to cry when they are placed in stressful situations like the one in the photo, in which the mother is not allowing her baby to move its body (Stifter & Fox, 1990). And, as I mentioned before, infants who are frightened or upset by novel stimulation tend to be inhibited and less sociable as preschoolers (Kagan, Snidman, & Arcus, 1998)

Thus, evidence suggests that temperament is at least somewhat stable throughout infancy and the preschool years (Bates, 1987). Of course, the links are not perfect. For example, some fearful infants became sociable preschoolers, and some infants who responded calmly to novel stimulation were inhibited as preschoolers.

Does temperament remain stable beyond infancy and the preschool years? Are emotional preschoolers likely to be emotional adults? Here, too, the evidence suggests moderate consistency. Most investigators report that measures of temperament obtained during the preschool years are related to measures obtained later in childhood and adolescence, but the correlations are not very strong. Exactly this pattern is described in the "Focus on Research" feature.

Temperament is somewhat stable in infancy: Active or emotional infants tend to become active or emotional preschoolers.

FOCUS ON RESEARCH

### Once a Difficult Child, Always a Difficult Child?

*Who were the investigators, and what was the aim of the study?* The overall aim of the Dunedin Multidisciplinary Health and Development Study is to trace health and behavior of children in New Zealand through infancy, childhood, and adolescence. Every two years, individuals participating in the ongoing study are assessed on medical, psychological, and sociological measures. In one part of the study, Avshalom Caspi and his colleagues, Bill Henry, Rob McGee, Terrie Moffitt, and Phil Silva (1995), examined the stability of children's temperament between ages 3 and 9.

*How did the investigators measure the topic of interest?* An observer watched as children performed several cognitive and motor tasks. The observer rated 22 specific behaviors, such as fear, self-confidence, impulsivity, restlessness, and self-criticism. These measures were then combined to determine children's scores on four dimensions of temperament:

- *Irritability:* Children with high scores on this dimension were unstable emotionally, often overreactive, impulsive, and very aggressive.

- *Distractibility:* Children with high scores on this dimension were unable to concentrate on tasks and often refused to continue when tasks became difficult.

- *Sluggishness:* Children with high scores on this dimension tended to be placid, shy, apprehensive, and emotionally flat.

- *Approach:* Children with high scores on this dimension adjusted readily to new situations and were friendly and self-confident.

*Who were the children in the study?* The Dunedin Study involved children born in Dunedin, New Zealand, within 12 months during 1972 and 1973. The study began with 1,037 three-year-olds. Of these, 991 were tested as 5-year-olds, 954 as 7-year-olds, and 955 as 9-year-olds.

*What was the design of the study?* This study was correlational because Caspi and his colleagues were interested in the relation that existed naturally between measures of temperament early and later in development. The study was longitudinal because children were tested many times, at ages 3, 5, 7, and 9 years.

*Were there ethical concerns with the study?* No. The cognitive and motor tasks that children performed were similar to tasks that they might do in school.

*What were the results?* Caspi and his colleagues reported correlations for all pairs of years between 3 and 9. For simplicity, the graph shows some typical correlations between scores at 5 and 9 years. The most remarkable aspect of the Dunedin data is that the correlations are not very large, which suggests that temperament is only moderately stable. This is true for both boys and girls. Irritability, an element of difficult temperament, is the most stable dimension overall.

*What did the investigators conclude?* There is continuity in temperament: A young child's temperament

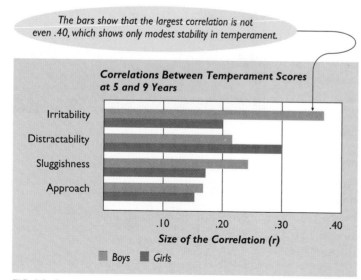

The bars show that the largest correlation is not even .40, which shows only modest stability in temperament.

**Correlations Between Temperament Scores at 5 and 9 Years**

Irritability
Distractibility
Sluggishness
Approach

.10    .20    .30    .40
*Size of the Correlation (r)*

■ Boys  ■ Girls

FIG 10–2

does give clues to that child's temperament later in childhood. However, early temperament predicts later temperament only roughly, not precisely. To put this concretely, we can contrast two hypothetical children. John, a difficult 5-year-old, has high scores on irritability and distractibility but a low score on the approach dimension. Jerry, an easy 5-year-old, has low scores on irritability and distractibility but a high score on the approach dimension. What does the future hold for these boys? John is certainly more likely than Jerry to become a difficult 9-year-old, but it is far from certain that John will remain difficult. ●

Though temperament is only moderately consistent over the years, it can still shape development in important ways. For example, an infant's temperament may determine the experiences that parents provide. Parents may read more to quiet babies but, like the parent in the photo, play more physical games with their active babies. These different experiences, driven by the infants' temperaments, contribute to each infant's development, despite the fact that the infants' temperaments may change over the years. In the next section, we'll see some of the connections between temperament and other aspects of development.

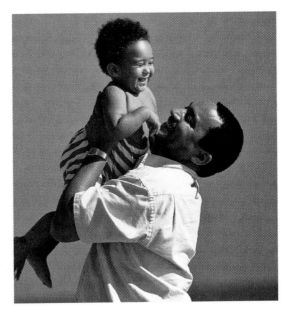

## Temperament and Other Aspects of Development

One of the goals of Thomas and Chess's New York Longitudinal Study was to discover temperamental features of infants that would predict later psychological adjustment. In fact, Thomas and Chess discovered that about two-thirds of the preschoolers with difficult temperaments had developed behavioral problems by the time they entered school. In contrast, fewer than one-fifth of the children with easy temperaments had behavioral problems (Thomas et al., 1968).

Other scientists have followed the lead of the New York Longitudinal Study in looking for links between temperament and outcomes of development, and they've found that temperament is an important influence on development. Here are some illustrative examples:

- Persistent children are likely to succeed in school whereas active and distractible children are less likely to succeed (Martin, Olejnik, & Gaddis, 1994).

- Shy, inhibited children often have difficulty interacting with their peers and often do not cope effectively with problems (Eisenberg et al., 1998; Kochanska & Radke-Yarrow, 1992).

- Anxious, fearful children are more likely to comply with a parent's rules and requests, even when the parent is not present (Kochanska, 1995).

- Children who are frequently angry or fearful are more prone to depression (Lengua, West, & Sandler, 1998).

Even more impressive are the findings from longitudinal studies showing that children's temperament predicts important

Temperament is linked to school success, good peer relations, and compliance with parental wishes as well as to mental health and behavioral problems.

aspects of adults' lives. In a study conducted in Sweden (Kerr, Lambert, & Bem, 1996), shy boys and girls married later than nonshy children. In addition, shy boys became fathers later than nonshy boys, and shy girls were less educated than nonshy girls.

More evidence for the impact of children's temperament on adults' lives comes from the Dunedin study described in the "Focus on Research" feature on page 284. Newman and her colleagues (1997) found that when undercontrolled 3-year-olds were adults, they tended to be poorly adjusted. For example, they found work and love unsatisfying and reported few friends to turn to. In addition, they had more interpersonal conflicts at home, work, and with friends.

Although these findings underscore that temperament is an important force in children's development, temperament rarely acts alone. Instead, the influence of temperament often depends on the environment in which children develop. To illustrate, let's consider the link between temperament and behavior problems. Infants and toddlers who temperamentally resist control—they are difficult to manage, often unresponsive, and sometimes impulsive—tend to be prone to behavior problems, particularly aggression, when they are older. However, more careful analysis shows that resistant temperament leads to behavior problems primarily when mothers do not exert much control over their children. Among mothers who do exert control—they prohibit, warn, and scold their children when necessary—resistant temperament is not linked to behavior problems (Bates et al., 1998).

Similarly, children who are anxious and fearful tend to be more compliant. But again, careful analysis shows this is true only when parents encourage compliance with discipline that elicits mild distress (Kochanska, 1997). When parents seek compliance by encouraging their children to cooperate, anxious temperament is no longer linked to compliance. (I discuss this research in more detail in Module 12.1, under "Temperamental Influences on Self-Control.")

Research on compliance and temperament illustrates a consistent theme in this module—emotion is an important aspect of temperament. In the next module, we'll look at emotion from yet another perspective, that of the emotional relationship formed between an infant and its primary caregiver.

## Check Your Learning

1. In their New York Longitudinal Study, Thomas and Chess identified infants with easy, difficult, and _____ temperaments.

2. Buss and Plomin's theory has three temperamental dimensions, including emotionality, _____, and sociability.

3. Compared to European American infants, Asian infants are calmer and _____.

4. An active fetus is more likely to be an active infant, and is also more likely to be a _____.

5. Research on the stability of temperament from the preschool years to adolescence and beyond typically finds that _____.

6. Thomas and Chess found that by the time difficult babies had entered school, many had _____.

7. Although temperament is an important developmental force, the influence of temperament often depends on _____.

Buss and Plomin's emotionality dimension of temperament includes the New York Longitudinal Study's intensity and threshold dimensions (see page 281). Which dimensions of the New York Longitudinal Study are comparable to Buss and Plomin's activity and sociability dimensions of temperament?

(7) the environment in which children develop

**Answers:** (1) slow to warm up, (2) activity, (3) are soothed more readily when upset, (4) difficult, unadaptive infant, (5) temperament is only moderately stable, (6) developed behavioral problems,

## Attachment

### Learning Objectives

- How does an attachment relationship develop between an infant and primary caregiver?

- What different types of attachment relationships are there? What are the consequences of different types of relationships?

*Ever since Samantha was a newborn, Karen and Dick looked forward to going to their favorite restaurant on Friday night. Karen enjoyed the break from child-care responsibilities and Dick liked being able to talk to Karen without interruptions. But recently they've had a problem. When they leave her with a sitter, 8-month-old "Sam" gets a frightened look on her face and usually begins to cry hysterically. Karen and Dick wonder if Sam's behavior is normal and if their Friday night dinners might be coming to an end.*

The social-emotional relationship that develops between an infant and a parent (usually, but not necessarily, the mother) is special. This is a baby's first social-emotional relationship, so scientists and parents alike believe it should be satisfying and trouble-free to set the stage for later relationships. In this module, we'll look at the steps involved in creating the baby's first emotional relationship. Along the way, we'll see why 8-month-old Sam has begun to cry when Karen and Dick leave her with a sitter.

### The Growth of Attachment

Sigmund Freud was the first modern theorist to emphasize the importance of emotional ties to the mother for psychological development. Today, the dominant view of early human relationships comes from John Bowlby (1969, 1991). His work originated in ethology, a branch of biology (described in Module 1.2) concerned with adaptive behaviors of different species. **According to Bowlby, children who form an *attachment* to an adult—that is, an enduring social-emotional relationship—are more likely to survive.** This person is usually the mother but need not be; the key is a strong emotional relationship with a responsive, caring person. Attachments can form with fathers, grandparents, or someone else.

Bowlby (1969) argued that evolutionary pressure favored behaviors likely to elicit caregiving from an adult, such as clinging, sucking, crying, and smiling. That is, over the course of human evolution, these behaviors have become a standard part of the human

Bowlby theorizes that many infant behaviors, such as clinging, crying, and smiling, are designed to elicit caregiving from adults and thus promote the development of an emotional bond between infant and parent.

infant's biological heritage, and the responses they evoke in adults create an interactive system that leads to the formation of attachment relationships.

The attachment relationship develops gradually over the first several months after birth, reflecting the baby's growing perceptual and cognitive skills described in Chapters 5 and 6. The first step is for the infant to learn the difference between people and other objects. Typically, in the first few months, babies begin to respond differently to people and to objects—for example, smiling more and vocalizing more to people—suggesting that they have begun to identify members of the social world.

During these months, mother and infant begin to synchronize their interactions. Remember from Module 3.4 that young babies' behaviors go through cycles. Infants move between states of alertness and attentiveness to states of distress and inattentiveness. Caregivers begin to recognize these states of behavior and adjust their own behavior accordingly. A mother who notices that her baby is awake and alert will begin to smile at and talk to her baby. These interactions often continue until the baby's state changes, which prompts the mother to stop. In fact, by 3 months of age, if a mother does not interact with her alert baby (but instead stares silently), babies become at least moderately distressed, looking away from her and sometimes crying (Toda & Fogel, 1993).

Thus, mothers and infants gradually calibrate their behaviors so that they are both "on" at the same time (Gable & Isabella, 1992). These interactions provide the foundation for more sophisticated communication and foster the infant's trust that the mother will respond predictably and reassuringly.

By approximately 7 or 8 months, most infants have singled out the attachment figure—usually the mother—as a special individual. An infant will smile at the mother and cling to her more than to other people. The attachment figure is now

the infant's stable social-emotional base. For example, a 7-month-old like the one in the photo will explore a novel environment but periodically look toward his mother, as if seeking reassurance that all is well. The behavior suggests the infant trusts his mother and indicates the attachment relationship has been established. In addition, this behavior reflects important cognitive growth: It means that the infant has a mental representation of the mother, an understanding that she will be there to meet the infant's needs (Lewis et al., 1997).

The formation of the attachment bond also explains why 8-month-old Sam cries whenever Karen and Dick try to leave her with a sitter. Sam is attached to Karen, expects her to be nearby, and is upset when separated from her.

Attachment typically first develops between infants and their mothers because mothers are usually the primary caregivers of American infants. Most babies soon become attached to their fathers, too, but they interact differently with fathers. Fathers typically spend much more time playing with their babies than taking care of them. In countries around the world—Australia, India, Israel, Italy, Japan, and the United States—"playmate" is the customary role for fathers (Roopnarine, 1992). Fathers even play with infants differently than mothers. Physical play is the norm for fathers, particularly with sons, whereas mothers spend more time reading and talking to babies, showing them toys, and playing games like patty-cake (Parke, 1990). Given the opportunity to play with mothers or fathers, infants more often choose their fathers. However, when infants are distressed, mothers are preferred (Field, 1990). Thus, although most infants become attached to both parents, mothers and fathers typically have distinctive roles in their children's early social development.

## Quality of Attachment

Attachment between infant and mother usually occurs by 8 or 9 months of age, but the attachment can take on different forms. Mary Ainsworth (1978, 1993) pioneered the study of attachment relationships using a procedure that has come to be known as the Strange Situation. You can see in the diagram that the Strange Situation involves a series of episodes, each about 3 minutes long. The mother and infant enter an unfamiliar room filled with interesting toys. The mother leaves briefly, then mother and baby are reunited. Meanwhile, the experimenter observes the baby, recording its response to both events.

1. Observer shows the experimental room to mother and infant, then leaves the room.

2. Infant is allowed to explore the playroom for 3 minutes; mother watches but does not participate.

3. A stranger enters the room and remains silent for 1 minute, then talks to the baby for a minute, and then approaches the baby. Mother leaves unobtrusively.

4. The stranger does not play with the baby but attempts to comfort it if necessary.

5. After 3 minutes, the mother returns, greets, and consoles the baby.

6. When the baby has returned to play, the mother leaves again, this time saying "bye-bye" as she leaves.

7. Stranger attempts to calm and play with the baby.

8. After 3 minutes, the mother returns and the stranger leaves.

FIG 10–3

Based on how the infant reacts to separation from the mother and then reunion, Ainsworth (1993) and other researchers (Main & Cassidy, 1988) have identified four primary types of attachment relationships. One is a secure attachment and three are insecure attachments (avoidant, resistant, disorganized):

- *Secure attachment:* **The baby may or may not cry when the mother leaves, but when she returns, the baby wants to be with her and if the baby is crying, it stops.** Babies in this group seem to be saying, "I missed you terribly, but now that you're back, I'm okay." Approximately 60 to 65 percent of American babies have secure attachment relationships.

- *Avoidant attachment:* **The baby is not upset when the mother leaves and, when she returns, may ignore her by looking or turning away.** Infants with an avoidant attachment look as if they're saying, "You left me again. I always have to take care of myself!" About 20 percent of American infants

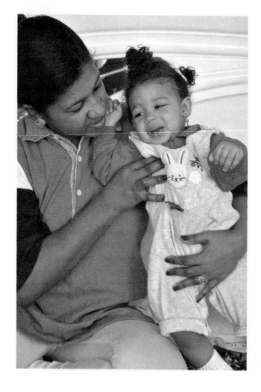

have avoidant attachment relationships, which is one of the three forms of insecure attachment.

- *Resistant attachment:* **The baby is upset when the mother leaves and remains upset or even angry when she returns, and is difficult to console.** Like the baby in the photo, these babies seem to be telling the mother, "Why do you do this? I need you desperately and yet you just leave me without warning. I get so angry when you're like this." About 10 to 15 percent of American babies have this resistant attachment relationship, which is another form of insecure attachment.

- *Disorganized (disoriented) attachment:* **The baby seems confused when the mother leaves and, when she returns, seems as if it doesn't really understand what's happening.** The baby often has a dazed look on its face as if wondering, "What's going on here? I want you to be here, but you left and now you're back. I don't know whether to laugh or cry!" About 5 to 10 percent of American babies have this disorganized attachment relationship, the last of the three kinds of insecure attachment.

Secure attachments and the different forms of insecure attachments are observed worldwide. As you can see in the graph, secure attachments are the most common throughout the world (van IJzendoorn & Kroonenberg, 1988). This is fortunate because, as we'll see, a secure attachment provides a solid base for later social development.

Infants typically form the same type of attachment relationships with both parents (Fox, Kimmerly, & Schafer, 1991). An infant who is securely attached to its mother is usually securely attached to its father, too. In addition, siblings usually have the same type of attachment relationships with their parents (Rosen & Burke, 1999).

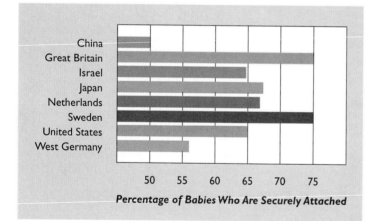

**Percentage of Babies Who Are Securely Attached**

FIG 10–4

## Consequences of Quality of Attachment.

Erikson, Bowlby, and other theorists (Sroufe & Fleeson, 1986) believe that attachment, as the first social relationship, lays the foundation for all of an infant's later social relationships. In this view, infants who experience the trust and compassion of a secure attachment should develop into preschool children who interact confidently and successfully with their peers. In contrast, infants who do not experience a successful, satisfying first relationship should be more prone to problems in their social interactions as preschoolers.

Both of these predictions are supported by research, as the following findings demonstrate:

- Children with secure attachment relationships have higher-quality friendships and fewer conflicts in their friendships than children with insecure attachment relationships (Lieberman, Doyle, & Markiewicz, 1999).

- School-age children are less likely to have behavior problems if they have secure attachment relationships and more likely if they have insecure attachment relationships (Carlson, 1998; Moss et al., 1998).

- At a summer camp, 11-year-olds who had secure attachment relationships as infants interacted more skillfully with their peers and had more close friends than 11-year-olds who had insecure attachment relationships (Elicker, Englund, & Sroufe, 1992).

The conclusion seems inescapable: As infants who have secure attachment relationships develop, their social interactions tend to be more satisfying. Why? Secure attachment evidently promotes trust and confidence in other humans, which leads to more skilled social interactions later in childhood. Of course, attachment is only one step along the long road of social development. Infants with insecure attachments are not doomed, but this initial misstep can interfere with their social development.

### Factors Determining Quality of Attachment.

Because secure attachment is so important to a child's later development, researchers have tried to identify the factors involved. Undoubtedly the most important is the interaction between parents and their babies (De Wolff & van IJzendoorn, 1997). A secure attachment is most likely when parents respond to infants predictably and appropriately. For example,

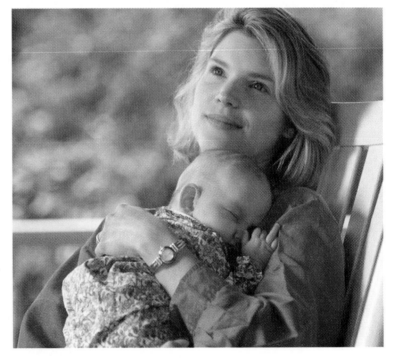

the mother in the photo has promptly responded to her baby's crying and is trying to reassure the baby. The mother's behavior evidently conveys that social interactions are predictable and satisfying, and apparently this behavior instills in infants the trust and confidence that are the hallmark of secure attachment.

Why does predictable and responsive parenting promote secure attachment relationships? To answer this question, think about your own friendships and romantic relationships. These relationships are usually most satisfying when we believe we can trust the other people and depend on them in times of need. The same formula seems to hold for infants. **Infants develop an *internal working model*, a set of expectations about parents' availability and responsivity, generally and in times of stress.** When parents are dependable and caring, babies come to trust them, knowing they can be relied upon for comfort. That is, babies develop an internal working model in which they believe their parents are concerned about their needs and will try to meet them (Bretherton, 1992).

Many research findings attest to the importance of a caregiver's sensitivity for developing secure attachment:

- In a longitudinal study, infants were more likely to have a secure attachment relationship at 12 months when their parents were sensitive and responded quickly and appropriately to their infant at 3 months (Cox et al., 1992).

- In a study conducted in Israel, infants were less likely to develop secure attachment when they slept in dormitories with other children under 12, where they received inconsistent (if any) attention when they became upset overnight (Sagi et al., 1994).

- In a study conducted in the Netherlands, infants were more likely to form a secure attachment when their mother had 3 months of training that emphasized monitoring an infant's signals and responding appropriately and promptly (van den Boom, 1994; 1995).

> A secure attachment relationship is most likely to develop between infant and parent when the parent responds to the infant's needs reliably and sensitively.

Thus, secure attachment is most likely when parents are sensitive and responsive. Of course, not all caregivers react to babies in a reliable and reassuring manner. Some respond intermittently or only after the infant has cried long and hard. And when these caregivers finally respond, they are sometimes annoyed by the infant's demands and may misinterpret the infant's intent. Over time, these babies tend to see social relationships as inconsistent and often frustrating, conditions that do little to foster trust and confidence.

Why are some parents more responsive (and thus more likely to foster secure attachment) than others? In modern attachment theory (e.g., Cassidy, 1994), parents have internal working models of the attachment relationship with their own parents, and these working models guide interactions with their own infants. When questioned about attachment relationships with the Adult Attachment Interview (George, Kaplan, & Main, 1985), adults can be classified into one of three groups:

- *Autonomous adults* describe childhood experiences objectively and mention both positive and negative aspects of their parents.
- *Dismissive adults* describe childhood experiences in very general terms and often idealize their parents.
- *Preoccupied adults* describe childhood experiences emotionally and often express anger or confusion regarding relationships with their parents.

According to attachment theory, only parents with autonomous attachment representations are likely to provide the sensitive caregiving that promotes secure attachment relationships. In fact, many studies show that parents' autonomous attachment representations are associated with sensitive caregiving, and, in turn, with secure attachment in their infants (van IJzendoorn, 1995; Pederson et al., 1998). Furthermore, longitudinal research (Beckwith, Cohen, & Hamilton, 1999) shows that infants with secure attachment relations tend to become adults with autonomous attachment representations, completing the circle.

The sensitive and responsive caregiving that is essential for secure attachments is often taxing, particularly for babies with difficult temperaments. That is, babies who fuss often and are difficult to console are more prone to insecure attachment (Goldsmith & Harman, 1994; Seifer et al., 1996). Insecure attachment may also be more likely when a difficult, emotional infant has a mother whose personality is rigid and traditional than when the mother is accepting and flexible (Mangelsdorf et al., 1990). Rigid mothers do not adjust well to the often erratic demands of their difficult babies; instead, they want the baby to adjust to them. This means that rigid mothers less often provide the responsive, sensitive care that leads to secure attachment.

Fortunately, even brief training for mothers of newborns can help them respond to their babies more effectively (Wendland-Carro, Piccinini, & Millar, 1999). Mothers can be taught how to interact more sensitively, affectionately, and responsively, paving the way for secure attachment and the lifelong benefits associated with a positive internal working model of interpersonal relationships.

## Check Your Learning

1. By approximately _____ months of age, most infants have identified a special individual—typically, but not always, the mother—as the attachment figure.

2. Around the world, _____ is the customary role for fathers.

3. Joan, a 12-month-old, was separated from her mother for about 15 minutes. When they were reunited, Joan would not let her mother pick her up. When her mother approached, Joan looked the other way and toddled to another part of the room. This behavior suggests that Joan has a(n) _____ attachment relationship.

4. _____ is the most common form of attachment worldwide.

5. The single most important factor in fostering a secure attachment relationship is

   _____.

6. Adults with _____ representations of the attachment relationships with their own parents are most likely to have secure attachments with their own children.

 **Cognitive development helps infants form an attachment bond with parents. According to Piaget's theory and the information-processing perspective, what specific cognitive changes might be crucial?**

**Answers:** (1) 7 or 8, (2) playmate, (3) avoidant, (4) Secure attachment, (5) responsive parenting that fosters an infant's trust and confidence, (6) autonomous

# Emotional Development
## IN PERSPECTIVE

Most of us would find life on Mr. Spock's emotionless home planet very unsatisfying because emotions are so central to our daily lives. In this chapter, we've seen that emotions take center stage very early in development. In Module 10.1, we learned that children express basic emotions like happiness before age 1 and complex emotions like guilt before age 2. Infants use others' emotions to guide their behavior, and this skill improves as children grow cognitively. As early as 4 to 6 months, infants begin to regulate emotion, another important social skill. In Module 10.2, we discovered that emotion is a defining characteristic of temperament, a consistent mood and style of behavior that is moderately stable as children develop. Both heredity and environment influence temperament. In Module 10.3, we traced the development of the emotion-filled attachment relationship between infant and parents. We saw that secure attachment reflects the infant's trust in the parent, which is rooted in responsive caregiving.

Temperament is one of the best examples in the entire book of the theme that *children help determine their own development.* Temperament helps determine how parents, peers, and other adults respond to children. Parents and peers, for example, usually respond positively to temperamentally easy children. Parents find it more straightforward to establish a secure attachment with an easy child than with a difficult child. Peers get along better with easy children than with shy, inhibited children. Children's temperament does not alone dictate the direction of their development, but it makes some directions much easier to follow than others.

## See for Yourself

Arrange to visit a local day-care center where you can unobtrusively observe preschoolers for several days. As you watch the children, see if you can detect the temperamental differences that are described in Module 10.2. Can you identify an emotional child, an active child, and a social child? Also, notice how adults respond to the children. See if the same behaviors lead to different responses from adults, depending on the child's temperament. See for yourself!

## Resources

*For more information about . . .*

 *the development of the attachment relationship,* read T. Berry Brazelton and Bertrand Cramer's *The Earliest Relationship* (Addison-Wesley, 1990), which illustrates the drama of attachment through lively case studies.

 *temperament,* visit the Web site of a publisher of questionnaires and software used to measure temperament:
**http://www.temperament.com**

## Key Terms

activity 281
attachment 287
autonomous attachment representation 292
avoidant attachment 289
dismissive attachment representation
   292
disorganized (disoriented)
   attachment 290

display rules 278
emotionality 281
internal working model 291
preoccupied attachment
   representation 292
resistant attachment 290
school phobia 275
secure attachment 289
sociability 281

social referencing 276
social smiles 273
stranger wariness 274
systematic desensitization 275
temperament 280

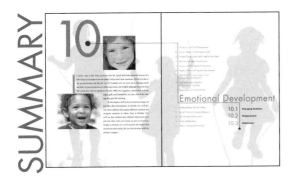

# SUMMARY

# 10.1 Emerging Emotions

## Basic Emotions

Scientists often use infants' facial expressions to judge when different emotional states emerge in development. The earliest indicator of happiness is the social smile, which emerges at about 2 months. Laughter appears at 4 months. Anger and fear are both evident by about 6 months of age. Fear first appears in infancy as stranger wariness; fears of specific objects develop later in childhood.

## Complex Emotions

Complex emotions have an evaluative component and include guilt, embarrassment, and pride. They appear between 18 and 24 months and require more sophisticated cognitive skills than basic emotions like happiness and fear.

## Recognizing and Using Others' Emotions

By 6 months, infants have begun to recognize the emotions associated with different facial expressions. They use this information to help them evaluate unfamiliar situations. Beyond infancy, children understand the causes and consequences of different emotions, that people can feel multiple emotions simultaneously, and the rules for displaying emotions appropriately.

## Regulating Emotions

Infants use simple strategies to regulate emotions such as fear. As children grow, they become better skilled at regulating their emotions. Children who do not regulate emotions well tend to have problems interacting with others.

# 10.2 Temperament

## What Is Temperament?

Temperament refers to stable patterns of behavior that are evident soon after birth. The New York Longitudinal Study suggests three temperamental patterns: easy, difficult, and slow to warm up; other research suggests that the dimensions of temperament are emotionality, activity, and sociability. The major theories of temperament include many of the same elements, organized differently.

## Hereditary and Environmental Contributions to Temperament

The major theories agree that both heredity and environment contribute to temperament. For many dimensions of temperament, identical twins are more alike than fraternal twins. Positive emotionality reflects environmental influences, and difficult temperment is linked to abrupt parenting.

## Stability of Temperament

Temperament is somewhat stable from infancy to the preschool years and moderately stable into childhood and adolescence. The correlations are not very strong, which means that, for many children, temperament does change as they develop.

## Temperament and Other Aspects of Development

Many investigators have shown that temperament is related to other aspects of development. Difficult babies are more likely to have behavioral problems by the time they are old enough to attend school. Persistent children are more successful in school, shy children sometimes have problems with peers, anxious children are more compliant with parents, and angry or fearful children are prone to depression. However, the impact of temperament always depends on the environment in which children develop.

# 10.3 Attachment

## The Growth of Attachment

Attachment is an enduring social-emotional relationship between infant and parent. Many of the behaviors that contribute to the formation of attachment are biologically programmed. Attachment develops gradually over the first year of life; by about 7 or 8 months, infants have identified an attachment figure, typically the mother. In the ensuing months, infants often become attached to other family members, including fathers, whose usual role is playmate.

## Quality of Attachment

Research with the Strange Situation, in which infant and mother are separated briefly, reveals four primary forms of attachment. Most common is a secure attachment, in which infants have complete trust in the mother. Less common are three types of insecure attachment relationships that lack this trust. In avoidant relationships, infants deal with the lack of trust by ignoring the mother; in resistant relationships, infants often seem angry with her; in disorganized (disoriented) relationships, infants seem to not understand the mother's absence.

Children who have had secure attachment relationships during infancy often interact with their peers more readily and more skillfully. Secure attachment is most likely to occur when mothers respond sensitively and consistently to their infants' needs. Adults who have autonomous representations of attachment to their own parents are most likely to use the sensitive caregiving that promotes secure attachments with their own infants.

N

early 100 years ago, G. Stanley Hall, an influential American developmental psychologist, wrote that adolescence was "strewn with wreckage of mind, body, and morals" (1904, p. xiv). Judging by today's movies and media, Hall's analysis would seem to have stood the test of time: When teens aren't presented as runaways, drug addicts, and shoplifters, they're moody and withdrawn or manic. But how accurate is this picture? What does current research show about adolescence and the process of developing independence and identity?

In Module 11.1, we'll look at the mechanisms that give rise to a person's identity, and we'll see if storm and stress are a necessary step in achieving an identity. Of course, people are often happier with some aspects of themselves than with others. These evaluative aspects of identity are the focus of Module 11.2. Finally, in Module 11.3, we'll look at how we develop an understanding of others, because as we learn more about ourselves, we learn more about other people, too.

# Understanding Self and Others

# 11.1

- Origins of Self-Recognition
- The Evolving Self-Concept
- The Search for Identity

# Who Am I? Self-Concept

## Learning Objectives

● When do infants first acquire a sense of self?

● How does self-concept become more elaborate as children grow?

● How do adolescents achieve an identity?

> *Dea was born in Seoul of Korean parents but was adopted by a Dutch couple in Michigan when she was 3 months old. Growing up, she considered herself a red-blooded American. In high school, however, Dea realized that others saw her as an Asian American, an identity about which she had never given much thought. She began to wonder, who am I really? American? Dutch American? Asian American?*

Like Dea, do you sometimes wonder who you are? **Answers to "Who am I?" reflect a person's *self-concept*, which refers to the attitudes, behaviors, and values that a person believes make him or her a unique individual.** Part of one teenage girl's self-concept is evident in her answer to "Who am I?"

> *I'm sensitive, friendly, outgoing, popular, and tolerant, though I can also be shy, self-conscious, and even obnoxious! I'd like to be friendly and tolerant all of the time. That's the kind of person I want to be, and I'm disappointed when I'm not. I'm responsible, even studious now and then, but on the other hand, I'm a goof-off, too, because if you're too studious, you won't be popular (Harter, 1990, p. 352).*

As an adult, your answer is probably even more complex because, after all, most people are complex creatures. But how did you acquire this complex self-concept? We'll answer that question in this module, beginning with the origins of an infant's sense of self.

## Origins of Self-Recognition

What is the starting point for self-concept? Following the lead of the 19th-century philosopher and psychologist William James, modern researchers believe that the foundation of self-concept is the child's awareness that he or she exists. At some point early in life, children must realize that they exist independently of other people and objects in the environment and that their existence continues over time.

Measuring the onset of this awareness is not easy. Obviously, we can't simply ask a 3-year-old, "So, tell me, when did you first realize that you existed and that you weren't simply part of the furniture?" A less direct approach is needed, and the photo shows one route that many investigators have taken. Like many babies his age, the 9-month-old in the photo is smiling at the face he sees in the mirror. Babies at this age sometimes touch the face in the mirror or wave at it, but none of their behaviors indicates that they recognize themselves in the mirror. Instead, babies act as if the face in the mirror is simply a very interesting stimulus.

How would we know that infants recognize themselves in a mirror? One clever approach is to have the mother place a red mark on her infant's nose; she does this surreptitiously, while wiping the baby's face. Then the infant is returned to the mirror. Many 1-year-olds touch the red mark on the mirror, showing that they notice the mark on the face in the mirror. By 15 months, however, an important change occurs: Babies see the red mark in the mirror, then reach up and touch *their own* noses. By age 2, virtually all children do this (Bullock & Lütkenhaus, 1990; Lewis & Brooks-Gunn, 1979). When these older toddlers notice the red mark in the mirror, they understand that the funny-looking nose in the mirror is their own.

Do you doubt that the mirror task shows an infant's emerging sense of self? Perhaps you think it tells more about an infant's growing understanding of mirrors than the baby's self-awareness. One way to examine this possibility would be to test infants who have never seen mirrors previously. Priel and deSchonen (1986) took this approach, testing infants from Israeli desert communities. These babies had never seen mirrors or, for that matter, virtually any reflective surfaces because they lived in tents. Nevertheless, the same developmental trend appeared in the desert infants as in a comparison group of infants living in a nearby city. No 6- to 12-month-olds in either group touched their noses after they saw the mark, a few 13- to 19-month-olds did, and nearly all the 20- to 26-month-olds did.

We don't need to rely solely on the mirror task to know that self-awareness emerges between 18 and 24 months. During this same period, toddlers look more at photographs of themselves than at photos of other children. They also refer to themselves by name or with a personal pronoun, such as *I* or *me,* and sometimes they know their age and their gender. These changes suggest that self-awareness is well established in most children by age 2 (Lewis, 1987).

As you might imagine, toddlers' self-awareness is quite fragile initially. To illustrate, in one study (Povinelli & Simon, 1998), 3-year-olds were videotaped playing a game during which an experimenter surreptitiously placed a sticker on the child's head. A few minutes later children watched a videotape of themselves playing the game. Although almost all children recognized themselves in the videotape, fewer than half reached up to take the sticker off their head. (In contrast, virtually all 4-year-olds reached.) The results suggest that toddlers' self-awareness is not strongly linked across time but is instead focused largely on the present. Young children seemingly don't make the connection between the current self ("I am watching a videotape") and previous selves ("just a few minutes ago, there was a sticker on my head").

Youngsters' growing self-recognition probably reflects cognitive development. For example, when children with Down syndrome achieve a mental age of approximately 18 months, they typically recognize themselves in the mirror task (Loveland, 1987a, b). Apparently, self-recognition requires cognitive skills that usually emerge sometime in the middle of the second year.

Once self-awareness is established, children begin to acquire a self-concept. That is, once children fully understand that they exist and that they have a unique mental life, they begin to wonder who they are. They want to define themselves. In the next section, we'll see how this self-concept becomes more complex as children develop.

Most children are self-aware by age 2 because they recognize themselves in mirrors and photos, and refer to themselves by name or with *I* and *me.*

## The Evolving Self-Concept

Before you go any further, return to the quotation on page 298 from the teenager. In describing herself, this girl relies heavily on psychological traits. The first sentence alone includes eight adjectives referring to psychological traits: *sensitive, friendly, outgoing, popular, tolerant, shy, self-conscious,* and *obnoxious.*

How do children develop such a complex view of themselves? Some important insights into this question come from Laura Levine (1983), who studied 20- to 28-month-olds. This is the period when children are just beginning to become self-aware. Children were tested on several measures of self-awareness, including the mirror recognition task. They were also observed as they interacted with an unfamiliar peer in a playroom filled with toys. The key finding was that children who were self-aware were much more likely to say, "Mine!" while playing with toys than children who were not yet self-aware.

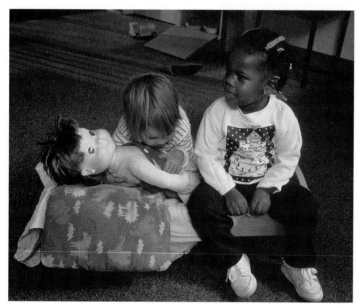

Maybe you think these self-aware children were being confrontational in saying, "Mine," as in "This car is mine and don't even think about taking it." But they weren't. Actually, self-aware children were more likely to say positive things during their interactions with peers. Levine argued that "claiming toys was not simply a negative or aggressive behavior, but appeared to be an important part of the child's definition of herself within her social world" (p. 547). In other words, the girl in the photo saying, "Mine!" is not trying to deny the doll to the other girl; she is simply saying that playing with dolls is part of who she is.

Throughout the preschool years, possessions continue to be one of the ways that children define themselves. Preschoolers are also likely to mention physical characteristics ("I have blue eyes"), their preferences ("I like spaghetti"), and their competencies ("I can count to 50"). What these features have in common is a focus on a child's characteristics that are observable and concrete (Damon & Hart, 1988).

Sometime between 6 and 8 years of age, children's self-descriptions begin to change (Harter, 1994; 1999). Children are more likely to mention emotions ("Sometimes I get angry"). They are also more likely to mention the social groups to which they belong ("I'm on the lacrosse team"). Finally, in contrast to preschool children, who simply mention their competencies, elementary-school children describe their level of skill in relation to their peers ("I'm the best speller in my whole class").

*A preschooler's self-concept is linked to the concrete and real, but an adolescent's self-concept is more abstract and more psychological.*

Self-concepts change again as children enter adolescence (Harter & Monsour, 1992). They now include attitudes ("I love algebra") and personality traits ("I'm usually a very happy person"). Adolescents also begin to make religious and political beliefs part of their self-concept ("I'm a Catholic" or "I'm a conservative Republican"). Another change is that adolescents' self-concepts often vary with the setting. A teenager might say, "I'm really shy around people that I don't know, but I let loose when I'm with my friends and family."

Yet another change is that adolescents' self-concepts are often future oriented: Adolescents often describe themselves in terms of what they will be when they reach adulthood (Harter, 1990; 1999). These descriptions may include occupational goals ("I'm going to be an English teacher"), educational plans ("I plan to go to a community college to learn about computers"), or social roles ("I want to get married as soon as I finish high school").

The gradual elaboration of self-concept from the preschool years to adolescence is summarized in the diagram. Two general changes are evident in the diagram. First, self-concept becomes richer as children grow; adolescents simply know much more about themselves than preschoolers. Second, the type of knowledge that children have of themselves changes. Preschoolers' understanding is linked to the concrete, the real, and the here and now. Adolescents' understanding, in contrast, is more abstract and more psychological, and sees the self as evolving over time. The change in children's knowledge of themselves should not surprise you because it's exactly the type of change that Piaget described. Concrete operational children's focus on the real and tangible extends to their thoughts about themselves, just as formal operational adolescents' focus on the abstract and hypothetical applies to their thoughts about themselves.

**Developmental Change in Self-Concept**

| **Preschoolers** | **School-Age Children** | **Adolescents** |
| --- | --- | --- |
| Possessions | Emotions | Attitudes |
| Physical characteristics | Social groups | Personality traits |
| Preferences | Comparisons with peers | Beliefs vary with the setting |
| Competencies | | Future oriented |

*I like cars and trucks.*

*I'm the best goalie in my class.*

*I'm quiet and shy at school.*

FIG 11-1

Adolescence is also a time of increasing self-reflection. Adolescents look for an identity to integrate the many different and sometimes conflicting elements of the self (Marcia, 1991). We'll look at this search for identity in detail in the next section.

## The Search for Identity

Erik Erikson (1968) believed that adolescents struggle to achieve an identity that will allow them to participate in the adult world. How exactly do they accomplish this? Adolescents use the hypothetical reasoning skills of the formal operational stage to experiment with different selves to learn more about possible identities (Nurmi, Poole, & Kalakoski, 1996). Adolescents' advanced cognitive skills allow them to imagine themselves in different roles.

Much of the testing and experimentation is career oriented. Some adolescents, like the ones shown in the photo, may envision themselves as rock stars; others may imagine being a professional athlete, a Peace Corps worker, or a best-selling novelist. Other testing is romantically oriented. Teens may fall in love and imagine living with the loved one. Still other exploration involves religious and political beliefs (King, Elder, & Whitbeck, 1997; Yates & Youniss, 1996). Teens give different identities a trial run just as you might test drive different cars before selecting one. By fantasizing about their future, adolescents begin to discover who they will be.

**The self-absorption that marks the teenage search for identity is referred to as *adolescent egocentrism*** (Elkind, 1978). Unlike preschoolers, adolescents know that others have different perspectives on the world. At the same time, many adolescents believe, wrongly, that they are the focus of others' thinking.

A teen like the one in the photo who spills food on herself may imagine that all her friends are thinking only about the stain on her blouse and how sloppy she is. **Many adolescents feel that they are, in effect, actors whose performance is being watched constantly by their peers, a phenomenon known as the *imaginary audience*.**

**Adolescent self-absorption is also demonstrated by the *personal fable*, teenagers' tendency to believe that their experiences and feelings are unique, that no one has ever felt or thought as they do.** Whether it is the excitement of first love, the despair of a broken relationship, or the confusion of planning for the future, adolescents often believe they are the first to experience these feelings and that no one else could possibly understand the power of their emotions (Elkind & Bowen, 1979). **Adolescents' belief in their uniqueness also contributes to an *illusion of invulnerability*—the belief that misfortune only happens to others.** They think they can have sex without becoming pregnant or drive recklessly without being in an auto accident. Those misfortunes only happen to others.

Adolescent egocentrism, imaginary audiences, personal fables, and the illusion of invulnerability become less common as adolescents make progress toward achieving an identity. What exactly is involved in achieving an identity? Most adolescents progress through different phases or statuses, though not necessarily in strict sequence (Marcia, 1980, 1991):

- *Diffusion:* **Individuals in this status are confused or overwhelmed by the task of achieving an identity and are doing little to achieve one.**
- *Foreclosure:* **Individuals in this status have an identity determined largely by adults, rather than from personal exploration of alternatives.**
- *Moratorium:* **Individuals in this status are still examining different alternatives and have yet to find a satisfactory identity.**
- *Achievement:* **Individuals in this status have explored alternatives and have deliberately chosen a specific identity.**

Unlike Piaget's stages, these four phases do not necessarily occur in sequence. Most young adolescents are in a state of diffusion or foreclosure. The common element in these phases is that teens are not exploring alternative identities. They are avoiding the crisis altogether or have resolved it by taking on an identity suggested by parents or other adults. However, as individuals move beyond adolescence and into young adulthood and have more opportunity to explore alternative identities, diffusion and foreclosure become less common, and, as the pie charts at the top of page 303 show, achievement and moratorium become more common (Meilman, 1979).

Typically, young people do not reach the achievement status for all aspects of identity at the same time (Dellas & Jernigan, 1990; Kroger & Green, 1996). Some adolescents may reach the achievement status for occupations before achieving it for religion and politics. Others reach the achievement status for religion before other domains. Evidently, few youth achieve a sense of identity all at once; instead, the crisis of identity is first resolved in some areas and then in others.

In achieving an identity, adolescents often begin in the diffusion status and end in the achievement status, sometimes passing through the moratorium and diffusion statuses en route.

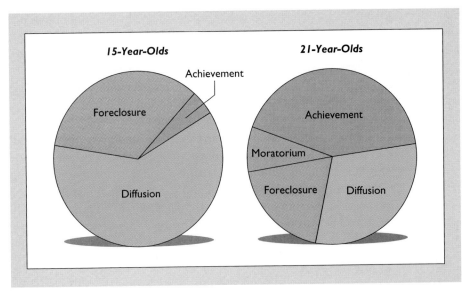

FIG 11–2

**Choosing a Career.**   One element of identity that has been examined in some detail is career development. According to a theory proposed by Donald Super (1976; 1980), identity is a primary force in an adolescent's choice of a career. **At about age 13 or 14, adolescents use their emerging identities as a source of ideas about careers, a process called *crystallization.*** Teenagers use their ideas about their own talents and interests to limit potential career prospects. A teenager who is extroverted and sociable may decide that working with people would be the career for him. Another who excels in math and science may decide she'd like to teach math. Decisions are provisional, and adolescents experiment with hypothetical careers, trying to envision what each might be like. Rarely, however, are careers as hypothetical as the one imagined by the teenager in the cartoon!

"Your son has made a career choice, Mildred. He's going to win the lottery and travel a lot."

By permission of Bunny Hoest, Wm. Hoest Enterprises, Inc.

At about age 18, adolescents extend the activities associated with crystallization and enter a new phase. **During *specification,* individuals further limit their career possibilities by learning more about specific lines of work and starting to obtain the training required for a specific job.** Our extroverted teenager who wants to work with people may decide that a career in sales would be a good match for his abilities and interests. The teen who likes math may have learned more about careers and decided she'd like to be an accountant. Some teens, like the young man in the photo, may begin an apprenticeship as a way to learn a trade.

The end of the teenage years or the early 20s mark the beginning of the third phase. **During *implementation,* individuals enter the work force and learn firsthand about jobs.** This is a time of learning about responsibility and productivity, of learning to get along with coworkers, and of altering one's lifestyle to accommodate work. This period is often unstable; individuals may change jobs frequently as they adjust to the reality of life in the workplace.

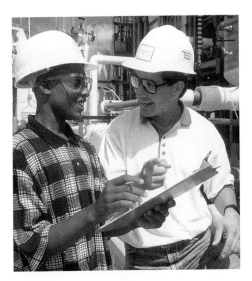

In each of Super's three phases of career development, there is continuous give and take between an individual's identity and career choice. A person's self-concept makes some careers more attractive than others; occupational experiences, in turn, refine and shape a person's identity.

What circumstances help adolescents decide on a career and achieve identity? Parents are influential (Marcia, 1980). When parents encourage discussion and recognize their children's autonomy, their children are more likely to reach the achievement status. Apparently these youth feel encouraged to undertake the personal experimentation that leads to identity. In contrast, when parents set rules with little justification and enforce them without explanation, children are more likely to remain in the foreclosure status. These teens are discouraged from experimenting personally; instead, their parents simply tell them what identity to adopt. Overall, adolescents are most likely to establish a well-defined identity in a family atmosphere where parents encourage children to explore alternatives on their own but do not pressure or provide explicit direction (Harter, 1990; 1999).

### Ethnic Identity.

For many adolescents growing up in North America today, achieving an identity is even more challenging because they are members of ethnic minority groups. The "Cultural Influences" feature describes one example.

**CULTURAL INFLUENCES**

### Dea's Ethnic Identity

Dea, the adolescent in the opening vignette, belongs to the one-third of adolescents and young adults living in the United States who are members of ethnic minority groups. They include African Americans, Asian Americans, Hispanic Americans, and Native Americans. **These individuals typically develop an *ethnic identity*: They feel a part of their ethnic group and learn the special customs and traditions of their group's culture and heritage** (Phinney, 1996).

An ethnic identity seems to be achieved in three phases. Initially, adolescents have not examined their ethnic roots. A teenage African American girl in this phase remarked, "Why do I need to learn about who was the first Black woman to do this or that? I'm just not too interested" (Phinney, 1989, p. 44). For this girl, ethnic identity is not yet an important personal issue.

In the second phase, adolescents begin to explore the personal impact of their ethnic heritage. The curiosity and questioning that are characteristic of this stage are captured in the comments of a teenage Mexican American girl who said, "I want to know what we do and how our culture is different from others. Going to festivals and cultural events helps me to learn more about my own culture and about myself" (Phinney, 1989, p. 44). Part of this phase involves learning cultural traditions; for example, like the girl in the photo, many adolescents learn to prepare ethnic food.

In the third phase, individuals achieve a distinct ethnic self-concept. One Asian American adolescent explained his ethnic identification like this: "I have been born Filipino and am born to be Filipino. . . . I'm here in America, and people of many different cultures are here, too. So I don't consider myself only Filipino, but also American" (Phinney, 1989, p. 44).

To see if you understand the differences between these stages of ethnic identity, reread the vignette on page 298 about Dea and decide which stage applies to her. The answer appears on page 307, just before "Check Your Learning." ●

Older adolescents are more likely than younger ones to have achieved an ethnic identity because they are more likely to have had opportunities to explore their cultural heritage (Phinney & Chavira, 1992). Also, as with overall identity, adolescents are most likely to achieve an ethnic self-concept when their parents encourage them to explore alternatives instead of pressuring them to adopt a particular ethnic identity (Rosenthal & Feldman, 1992).

Do adolescents benefit from a strong ethnic identity? Yes. Adolescents who have achieved an ethnic identity tend to have higher self-esteem and find their interactions with family and friends more satisfying (Phinney, Cantu, & Kurtz, 1997). In addition, many investigators have found that adolescents with a strong ethnic identity do better in school than adolescents whose ethnic identities are weaker (Stalikas & Gavaki, 1995; Taylor et al., 1994).

Some individuals achieve a well-defined ethnic self-concept and, at the same time, identify strongly with the mainstream culture. In the United States, for example, many Chinese Americans embrace both Chinese and American culture; in England, many Indians identify with both Indian and British cultures. For other individuals, the cost of strong ethnic identification is a weakened tie to mainstream culture. Some investigators report that, for Hispanic Americans, strong identification with American culture is associated with a weaker ethnic self-concept (Phinney, 1990).

> Adolescents who have achieved an ethnic identity have higher self-esteem, get more satisfaction from interactions with others and do better in school.

We shouldn't be too surprised that identifying with mainstream culture weakens ethnic identity in some groups but not others (Berry, 1993). Racial and ethnic groups living in the United States are diverse. African American, Asian American, Hispanic American, and Native American cultures and heritages differ, and so we should expect that the nature and consequences of a strong ethnic self-concept will differ across these and other ethnic groups.

Even within any particular group, the nature and consequences of ethnic identity may change over successive generations (Cuellar et al., 1997). As successive generations become more acculturated to mainstream culture, they may identify less strongly with ethnic culture. Thus, parents may maintain strong feelings of ethnic identity that their children don't share.

Ethnic identity is a particularly salient issue for children like Dea, who are members of minority groups and are adopted by European American parents. The "Focus on Research" feature shows how identity develops in these children.

### Identity in Children of Transracial Adoptions

*Who were the investigators, and what was the aim of the study?* For many years, the policy of many adoption agencies was that children could be adopted only by adults of their own race. However, in the 1960s, transracial adoption became more common. Why was this? Children from minority groups needing adoption far outnumbered the adults from minority groups who wanted to adopt, yet many European American adults were eager to adopt these children. When African American children are reared by European American parents, what racial identity do the children acquire? How does this identity affect their development? Kimberly DeBerry, Sandra Scarr, and Richard Weinberg (1996) wanted to answer these questions.

*How did the investigators measure the topic of interest?* The investigators created a structured interview that included 83 different items. Some items measured the children's orientation toward African Americans, including the number of African American friends they had, their knowledge of people of African descent, and whether they referred to themselves as African American. Other, comparable items measured children's orientation toward European Americans. Finally, general psychological adjustment was measured with questions addressing behavioral, emotional, interpersonal, and academic problems. Children and parents were interviewed separately.

*Who were the children in the study?* Scarr and Weinberg began the Minnesota Transracial Adoption Project in the 1970s. Their original sample included 131 families with 176 adopted children and 145 biological children. DeBerry and her colleagues focused on a subsample that included 88 African American children, 29 boys and 59 girls.

*What was the design of the study?* This study was correlational because DeBerry and her colleagues were interested in the relations that existed naturally between children's identity as African or European Americans and their adjustment. The study was longitudinal because testing took place when the children were approximately 4, 7, and 17 years old. However, I am describing only the results that were obtained when the children were 17.

*Were there ethical concerns with the study?* No. The investigators obtained permission from the parents for the children to participate.

*What were the results?* Parents' and children's responses to the interview were similar, so I'll just describe children's responses. Two results are key. First, most of the children in this sample identified more strongly as European Americans than as African Americans. Second, having a strong cultural identity was associated with better psychological adjustment. The correlation with adjustment was .45 for identifying with African Americans and .50 for identifying with European Americans. In other words, adolescents who identified strongly with *either* African or European Americans tended to be better adjusted than adolescents who identified with neither African nor European Americans.

*What did the investigators conclude?* The investigators caution that their results, which are based on African American children reared by European Americans in Minnesota, may not apply to all transracial adoptions. Nevertheless, the results underscore the importance of being able to identify with a cultural group. Being able to think of oneself as a member of some larger, recognized cultural group is an important part of being psychologically healthy. Adolescents who do not feel a part of any group are at risk for psychological problems. ●

Storm and Stress.   According to American novelists and filmmakers, the search for identity that I've described in the past few pages is inherently a struggle, a time of storm and stress for adolescents. Although this view may make for best-selling novels and hit movies, in reality the rebellious teen is largely a myth. Think about the following conclusions derived from research findings (Steinberg, 1990). Most adolescents

- admire and love their parents,
- rely upon their parents for advice,
- embrace many of their parents' values, and
- feel loved by their parents.

Not exactly the image of the rebel, is it? Cross-cultural research provides further evidence that adolescence is not necessarily a time of turmoil and conflict. Offer and his colleagues

(1988) interviewed adolescents from 10 different countries: the United States, Australia, Germany, Italy, Israel, Hungary, Turkey, Japan, Taiwan, and Bangladesh. These investigators found most adolescents moving confidently and happily toward adulthood. As the graphs show, most adolescents around the world reported that they were usually happy, and few avoided their homes.

Of course, parent-child relations do change during adolescence. As teens become more independent, their relationships with their parents become more egalitarian. Parents must adjust to their children's growing sense of autonomy by treating them more like equals (Laursen & Collins, 1994). This growing independence means that teens spend less time with their parents, are less affectionate toward them, and argue more often with them about matters of style, taste, and freedom. Teenagers are also more moody and more likely to enjoy spending some time alone (Larson, 1997; Wolfson & Carskadon, 1998).

None of these changes represents storm and stress, however. They are natural byproducts of an evolving parent-child relationship in which the "child" is nearly a fully independent young adult (Steinberg, 1990). Adolescence is an interesting and challenging time for youth and their parents, but not inherently tempestuous as the myth would lead us to believe.

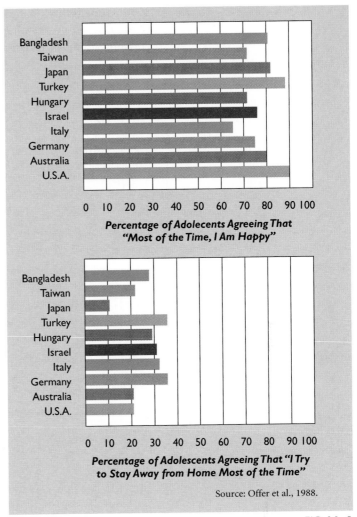

Source: Offer et al., 1988.

FIG 11–3

*Response to question on page 305 about Dea's ethnic identity:* Dea, the Dutch Asian American college student, doesn't know how to integrate the Korean heritage of her biological parents with the Dutch American culture in which she was reared. This would put her in the second phase of acquiring an ethnic identity. On the one hand, she is examining her ethnic roots, which means she's progressed beyond the initial stages. On the other hand, she has not yet integrated her Asian and European roots, and so has not reached the third and final phase.

## Check Your Learning

1. Apparently children become self-aware by age 2 because at this age they recognize themselves in a mirror and in photographs and they _____.

2. During _____, children's self-concepts begin to include emotions, membership in social groups, and comparisons with peers.

3. A focus on attitudes, personality traits, and the future characterizes self-concept during _____.

4. _____ refers to the fact that adolescents sometimes believe that their lives are a performance, with their peers watching them constantly.

5. The _____ status would describe an adolescent who has attained an identity based almost entirely on her parents' advice and urging.

6. A person who has simply put off searching for an identity because it seems too confusing and too overwhelming is in the _____ status.

**7.** In Super's theory of career development, at about 18 years individuals enter the _____ phase; at this time they limit career possibilities by learning more about specific lines of work or start training.

**8.** When individuals have a strong ethnic identity, their identification with mainstream culture _____.

**9.** Children's relations with their parents change in adolescence, reflecting adolescents' growing independence and a _____ parent-child relationship.

 **Although Piaget's theory was not concerned with identity formation, how might his theory explain why identity is a central issue in adolescence?**

**Answers:** (1) refer to themselves by name or with the pronouns *I* and *me*, (2) the elementary-school years, (3) adolescence, (4) Imaginary audience, (5) foreclosure, (6) diffusion, (7) specification, (8) is sometimes strong and sometimes weak, depending on specific circumstances, (9) more egalitarian

# 11.2

- **Measuring Self-Esteem**
- **Change and Stability in Self-Esteem**
- **Sources of Self-Esteem**
- **Consequences of Low Self-Esteem**

## Self-Esteem

### Learning Objectives

● **What is self-esteem? How is it measured?**

● **How does self-esteem change as children develop?**

● **What factors influence the development of self-esteem?**

● **How is children's development affected by low self-esteem?**

*Darnel, age 10, loves school and for good reason: Every year, he is always one of the best students in his class. Darnel's mother, Karen, wants to enroll him in a program for gifted children, where she believes the pace will be more appropriate for her talented son. Darnel's dad, Jon, doesn't think this is such a great idea. He's afraid that if Darnel doesn't do well against all those other bright kids, his son will begin to doubt his academic ability.*

**Jon is concerned about Darnel's *self-esteem*, which refers to a person's judgment and feelings about his or her own worth.** Children with high self-esteem judge themselves favorably and feel positive about themselves. In contrast, children with low self-esteem judge themselves negatively, are unhappy with themselves, and often would rather be someone else. In this module, we'll see how self-esteem is measured, how it changes as children develop, and what forces shape it.

### Measuring Self-Esteem

Think about your own self-esteem. Do you think you have high self-esteem or low self-esteem? To help you answer this question, read each of these sentences and decide how well each applies to you:

I'm very good at schoolwork.

I find it very easy to make friends.

I do very well at all kinds of different sports.

I'm happy with the way I look.

If you agreed strongly with each of these statements, you definitely have high self-esteem. Usually, however, people agree with some of these statements more strongly than others. This tells us that, in addition to an overall sense of self-worth, people evaluate themselves in different areas. That is, people have multiple self-esteems, each linked to a specific content area. This phenomenon should seem familiar because it's like intelligence: In Module 8.1, we saw that hierarchical theories of intelligence begin with a general intelligence that is divided into more specific abilities, such as verbal ability and spatial ability.

How can we measure different aspects of self-esteem? The method depends upon the age of the child. With 4- to 7-year-olds, one popular approach devised by Harter and Pike (1984) uses pairs of pictures. The sample pictures show a girl either solving a puzzle easily or having difficulty. During testing, children are first asked to point to the pictured child who is most like them. Then they point to the larger circle if they believe that they are "a lot" like the child in that picture or the smaller one if they believe they are "a little" like the child in that picture. Harter and Pike used 24 pairs of pictures like these to measure children's self-worth in four areas: cognitive competence, physical competence, acceptance by peers, and acceptance by mother.

FIG 11–4

Another productive approach with young children uses puppets (Ablow & Measelle, 1993; Measelle et al., 1998). One puppet describes itself to the child: "I like pizza." A second puppet then describes itself in opposite terms—"I don't like pizza"—and then motions to the child, "How about you?" Children can respond verbally ("I like pizza, too!"), by nodding their heads in agreement or disagreement, or by pointing to one of the puppets. Children are presented pairs of statements measuring academic competence ("I learn/don't learn things well"), achievement motivation ("I try/don't try my best at school"), social competence ("It's hard/not hard for me to make new friends"), and peer acceptance ("Kids are/are not nice to me").

Self-esteem in older children and adolescents can be measured with a questionnaire. The child reads statements like the ones at the beginning of this section. The most widely used self-esteem questionnaire of this sort is the *Self-Perception Profile for Children* (SPPC) devised by Susan Harter (1985; 1988). The SPPC is designed to evaluate self-worth in children age 8 and older in five domains (Harter, 1988, p. 62):

- *Scholastic competence:* How competent or smart the child feels in doing schoolwork
- *Athletic competence:* How competent the child feels at sports and games requiring physical skill or athletic ability
- *Social acceptance:* How popular or accepted the child feels in social interactions with peers
- *Behavioral conduct:* How adequate the child feels about behaving the way one is supposed to

• *Physical appearance:* How good-looking the child feels and how much the child likes his or her physical characteristics, such as height, weight, face, and hair

The *Self-Perception Profile for Children* measures children's overall self-worth and their self-worth in five areas: scholastic and athletic competence, social acceptance, behavioral conduct, and physical appearance.

The SPPC includes six statements for each domain. For example, the figure lists two of the statements used to evaluate scholastic competence, shown as they actually appear on the SPPC. In both statements, the child has checked the response that indicates the highest level of self-esteem. A child's answers to all six statements are used to create an average level of self-esteem in that domain. The averages for each of the five domains are then used to generate a self-perception profile for each child. Two profiles are illustrated in the figure. Allison's self-esteem is high across all five domains; Colleen's self-esteem is much more varied. She feels positive about her social acceptance and physical appearance and, to a lesser extent, about her conduct. However, she feels negative about her scholastic and athletic competence.

Source: Harter, 1985.

FIG 11–5

Notice that each profile ends with a bar graph depicting the child's overall self-worth. Overall self-worth is measured on the SPPC with six more items, such as "Some kids like the way they are leading their life" and "Some kids like the kind of person they are." Children's responses to these statements are then averaged to create a measure of overall self-worth.

Are you surprised that overall self-worth is measured separately? Why not simply average children's ratings on the five dimensions? The reason is that children's overall self-worth is usually not simply the average of their self-worth in specific domains. You can see that this is true in the profiles for Allison and Colleen. Both girls feel very positive about themselves overall. This isn't surprising for Allison based on her ratings in the individual domains. But it is hardly what we would expect for Colleen if overall self-worth were simply the sum of self-worth in specific domains. Evidently, overall feelings of self-worth somehow transcend feelings of self-worth in specific domains.

The SPPC is intended for use with children and young adolescents. For assessing self-esteem in older adolescents and young adults, Harter (1990) created a more extensive scale. This scale includes the five domains in the SPPC, along with job competence, close friendships, and romantic appeal. These additional domains were included because self-esteem becomes more differentiated during adolescence.

In the next section, we'll see that greater differentiation is only one of several important developmental changes in self-esteem.

## Change and Stability in Self-Esteem

At what age is self-esteem greatest? The answer may surprise you—it's during the preschool years. Most preschool children have very positive views of themselves across many different domains. For example, when Harter and Pike (1984) used the pictures shown on page 309 to estimate kindergarten children's cognitive competence, the average score was 3.6 out of a possible 4. In other words, virtually all the children said they were either a little or a lot like the competent child.

As children progress through the elementary-school years, self-esteem usually drops somewhat. Why? Unlike in Garrison Keillor's mythical Lake Wobegon, all children are not above average. During the elementary-school years, children begin to compare themselves with peers (Ruble et al., 1980). When they do, they discover that they are not necessarily the best reader or the fastest runner. They may realize, instead, that they are only an average reader. Or, like the girl in the background of the photo, they come to understand that they are one of the slowest runners in the class. This realization often produces a modest drop in those dimensions of self-esteem in which the child compares less favorably to peers.

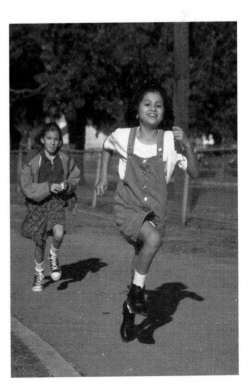

By the time most children enter adolescence, their self-esteem has usually stabilized (Harter, Whitesell, & Kowalski, 1992). That is, during the late elementary-school years, children's self-esteem neither increases nor decreases. Evidently, children learn their place in the "pecking order" of different domains and adjust their self-esteem accordingly.

Some studies indicate that self-esteem drops when children move from elementary school to middle school or junior high (Seidman et al., 1994). Apparently, when students from different elementary schools enter the same middle school or junior high, they know where they stand compared to their old elementary-school classmates but not compared to students from other elementary schools. Thus, peer comparisons begin anew, and self-esteem often suffers.

The drop in self-esteem associated with the transition to junior high is usually temporary. As children enter middle and late adolescence, self-esteem frequently increases (Savin-Williams & Demo, 1984). New schools become familiar and students gradually adjust to the new pecking order. In addition, adolescents begin to acquire more and more adult skills, such having a job or driving a car. Also, they see themselves acquiring many of the signs of adult status, such as greater independence and greater responsibility for their decisions. These changes foster self-esteem.

The overall pattern, then, is for self-esteem to start out very high during the preschool years, to decline during the elementary-school years, to level off during adolescence, and to increase toward the end of adolescence. These changes in overall level of self-esteem are accompanied by the change that I mentioned earlier: Self-esteem becomes more differentiated as children become older (Boivin, Vitaro, & Gagnon, 1992). Children are able to evaluate themselves in more domains as they develop, and their evaluations in each domain are increasingly independent. That is, younger children's ratings of self-esteem are often like Allison's (on page 310): The ratings are consistent across the different dimensions. In contrast, older children's and adolescents' ratings more often resemble Colleen's, with self-esteem varying from one domain to another.

> Self-esteem often declines as children enter middle school or junior high school because children don't know where they stand compared to their new classmates.

During the school years, children's academic self-concepts become particularly well defined (Byrne & Gavin, 1996; Marsh & Yeung, 1997). As children accumulate successes and failures in school, they form beliefs about their ability in different content areas (e.g., English, math, science), and these beliefs contribute to their overall academic self-concept. A child who believes that she is skilled at English and math but not so skilled in science will probably have a positive academic self-concept overall. But a child who believes he is untalented in most academic areas will have a negative academic self-concept.

Not only do self-esteem and self-concept vary with age, but they vary across settings. To show this variation, Harter and her colleagues (1998) modified SPPC items dealing with overall self-worth so they could assess self-worth in the context of specific relationships. For example, the item "some kids like the kind of person they are" was changed to "some kids like the kind of person they are when they are around _____" and the blank was filled with either *parents, teachers, male classmates,* or *female classmates.* In this manner, adolescents were asked to describe their self-worth in the context of different relationships. The important finding was that most adolescents clearly distinguish self-worth across these settings. Adolescents who judge themselves positively in the context of adults, for example, might value themselves less positively in the context of classmates. Or adolescents who feel negative about themselves at home may feel positive about themselves in relationships outside the home.

Sadly, at all ages and in all settings, many individuals do not view themselves very positively. Some children are ambivalent about who they are; others actually feel negative about themselves. The graph shows that roughly 25 percent of 9- and 10-year-olds in one study (Cole, 1991) had negative self-esteem on

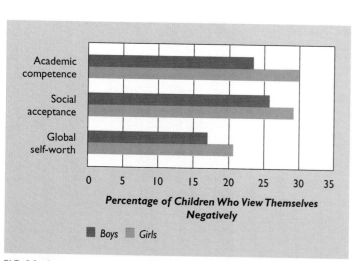

Percentage of Children Who View Themselves Negatively

■ Boys  ■ Girls

FIG 11–6

three scales of the SPPC. Why do these children have so little self-worth compared to their peers? We'll answer this question in the next section.

## Sources of Self-Esteem

Think back to Allison and Colleen, the two girls whose self-perceptions are graphed on page 310. Both girls evaluated their overall self-worth very positively. In general, they were happy with themselves and with their lives. Why do these girls feel so positive while some children feel so negative about themselves? You won't be surprised to learn that parenting plays a key role.

Children are more likely to view themselves positively when their parents are affectionate toward them and involved with them (Lord, Eccles, & McCarthy, 1994). Around the world, children have higher self-esteem when families live in harmony and parents nurture their children (Scott, Scott, & McCabe, 1991). A father who routinely hugs his daughter and gladly takes her to piano lessons is saying to her, "You are important to me." When children hear this regularly from parents, they evidently internalize the message and come to see themselves positively.

Parents' discipline also is related to self-esteem. Children with high self-esteem generally have parents who aren't afraid to set rules but are also willing to discuss rules and discipline with their children (Coopersmith, 1967). Parents who fail to set rules are, in effect, telling their children that they don't care—they don't value them enough to go to the trouble of creating rules and enforcing them. In much the same way, parents who refuse to discuss discipline with their children are saying, "Your opinions don't matter to me." Not surprisingly, when children internalize these messages, the result is lower overall self-worth.

Allison's and Colleen's positive self-worth can therefore be credited, at least in part, to their parents for being warm and involved, for establishing rules, and for discussing these rules with them. But how can we account for the fact that Allison views herself positively in all domains whereas Colleen's self-perceptions are more varied? As I've suggested before, social comparisons are important (Butler, 1992). Both girls have many opportunities during each day to compare themselves with peers. Allison is almost always the first to finish assignments, usually gets one of the highest grades in the class on exams, and is often asked by her teacher to help classmates on math and science problems. Meanwhile, Colleen is usually among the last to finish assignments, typically gets low grades on tests, and is one of the students Allison helps with math and science. Daily classroom routines give every student ample opportunities to discover everyone's academic standing within the room. Soon, everyone knows that Allison is one of the most capable students and Colleen is one of the least capable. Allison understands that her classmates see her as talented academically, so her academic self-esteem is quite high. Like the boy in the photo, Colleen knows that her classmates see her as not very talented academically, so her academic self-esteem is low.

The basic idea, then, is that children's self-esteem is based, in part, on how they are viewed by those around them. Children's self-esteem is high when others view them positively and low when others view them negatively (Hoge, Smit, & Hanson, 1990). This explanation has implications for academically talented youngsters, like Darnel in the opening vignette, who might be placed in classes for gifted children. We'll look at these implications in the "Making Children's Lives Better" feature.

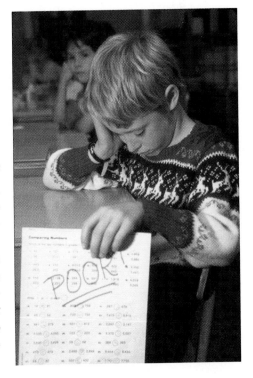

### Self-Esteem in Gifted Classes

In a traditional classroom of students with a wide range of ability, talented youngsters compare themselves with other students and develop positive academic self-esteem. But in classes for gifted students, many talented youngsters are only average and some are below average. The resulting social comparisons cause these children's academic self-esteem to drop (Marsh et al., 1995).

There is a clear lesson here for parents and teachers: When parents like Karen and Jon (from the module-opening vignette) think about enrolling their child in classes for gifted children, they should understand that accelerated academic progress often comes at a price: Children's academic self-esteem often declines somewhat, even though their actual skills are improving.

What can parents do? First, they should look honestly at their child and decide whether he or she values learning per se versus being at the top of the class. Students who value being at the top of the class will be more affected by social comparisons in a gifted class than students who are more intent on mastering challenging academic material. Second, parents should find out whether common assignments and comparative evaluations are made, as in typical classrooms, or whether the gifted class emphasizes individualized work. The latter is more conducive to self-esteem. Carefully considering these factors can help parents decide if a gifted program is likely to lower their child's self-esteem, a very unwelcome side effect. ●

> Children have greater self-esteem when they work hard in school, get along with peers, avoid disciplinary problems, participate in extracurricular activities, and feel that teachers care about them.

In examining sources of self-esteem—not just for children in gifted classes, but for all children—several characteristics of teachers and schools should also be taken into account (Hoge et al., 1990). In general, self-esteem is greater when students work hard in school, get along with their peers, and avoid disciplinary problems. In addition, self-esteem is greater when students participate in extracurricular activities, such as music, student council, sports, and clubs. Finally, students' self-esteem is enhanced when the overall climate of the school is nurturing—when students believe that teachers care about them and listen to them. Grades matter, too, but good grades affect students' self-esteem in specific disciplines—in math or English—not their overall self-esteem (Hoge et al., 1990; Marsh & Yeung, 1997).

By encouraging students to work to the best of their ability and by being genuinely interested in their progress, teachers can enhance the self-esteem of all students, regardless of their talent. Parents can do the same and, by encouraging their children to participate in extracurricular activities that match their talents, further promote self-esteem.

## Consequences of Low Self-Esteem

t is important that parents and teachers make an effort to enhance children's self-esteem because children with low self-esteem are at risk for many developmental problems. Children with low self-esteem are

- more likely to have problems with peers (Hymel et al., 1990),
- more prone to psychological disorders such as depression (Button et al., 1996; Garber, Robinson, & Valentiner, 1997),

- more likely to be involved in antisocial behavior (Dubow, Edwards, & Ippolito, 1997), and

- more likely to do poorly in school (Marsh & Yeung, 1997).

In looking at these outcomes, we need to be cautious about stating that each is "caused" by low self-esteem. In fact, in many cases, low self-esteem contributes to the outcome but is itself also caused by the outcome. Poor school performance is a case in point: Over time, children who are unskilled academically do not keep up in school, which causes a drop in their academic self-esteem, making them less confident and probably less successful in future school learning (Marsh & Yeung, 1997). Much the same vicious circle probably applies to the poor peer relationships seen in children with low self-esteem. Poor social skills lead to peer rejection, reducing self-esteem in the peer context and disrupting future peer interactions.

Understanding this complex cause-effect-cause pattern is important in deciding how to help children with low self-esteem. Some children benefit directly from therapy that increases their low self-esteem. Others, however, need additional treatment, such as improving their social skills (a topic that I discuss again in Modules 12.4 and 15.1). And, we need to remember that all children have some talents that can be nurtured. Taking the time to recognize each child creates the feelings of "being special" that promote self-esteem.

## Check Your Learning

1. One way to measure self-esteem in young children is to show pictures of children succeeding or failing in different domains; another is to _____.

2. Harter's *Self-Perception Profile for Children* (SPPC) is used to assess a child's self-esteem in five domains (scholastic competence, athletic competence, social acceptance, behavioral conduct, physical appearance) and the child's _____.

3. Self-esteem is usually at its peak during the _____ years.

4. Self-esteem often drops when children leave elementary school for middle school because _____.

5. As children develop, levels of self-esteem change and self-esteem becomes _____.

6. Children are more likely to have positive self-worth when parents are affectionate and involved with them and when parents _____.

7. A gifted child's self-esteem will not be harmed by a gifted class if the child values learning for its own sake or if the gifted class emphasizes _____.

8. Children with low self-esteem are more likely to have poor peer relations, _____, be involved in antisocial activities, and do poorly in school.

 **When gifted children are put in special classes, their intellectual development can be accelerated but sometimes at the expense of their self-esteem. Do you believe the intellectual gain is worth the potential drop in self-esteem? Why or why not?**

**Answers:** (1) have puppets describe themselves, then ask children which puppet is more like them, (2) overall self-worth, (3) preschool, (4) peer comparisons begin anew when children enter middle school, (5) more differentiated, (6) set rules and discuss discipline with their children, (7) individualized work, (8) be prone to psychological disorders such as depression

# 11.3

## Understanding Others

### Learning Objectives

● As children develop, how do they describe others differently?

● How does understanding of others' thinking change as children develop?

● When do children develop prejudice toward others?

> *When 12-year-old Ian agreed to baby-sit for his 5-year-old brother, Kyle, his mother reminded him to keep Kyle out of the basement because Kyle's birthday presents were there, unwrapped. But as soon as their mother left, Kyle wanted to go to the basement to ride his tricycle. When Ian told him no, Kyle burst into angry tears and shouted, "I'm gonna tell Mom that you were mean to me!" Ian wished he could explain to Kyle, but he knew that would just cause more trouble!*

We know from Modules 11.1 and 11.2 that Ian, as a young adolescent, has a growing understanding of himself. This vignette suggests that his understanding of other people is also growing. He understands why Kyle is angry, and he also knows that if he gives in to Kyle, his mother will be angry when she returns. Children's growing understanding of others is the focus of this module. We'll begin by looking at how children describe others, then examine their understanding of how others think. We'll also see how children's recognition of different social groups can lead to prejudices.

### Describing Others

As children develop, their self-descriptions become richer, more abstract, and more psychological. These same changes occur in children's descriptions of others. Children begin by describing other people in terms of concrete features, such as behavior and appearance, and progress to describing them in terms of abstract traits (Barenboim, 1981; Livesley & Bromley, 1973). The "Real Children" feature shows this progression in one child.

**REAL CHILDREN**

### Tell Me About a Girl You Like

Every few years, Tamsen was asked to describe a girl that she liked a lot. Each time, she described a different girl. More importantly, the contents of her descriptions changed, focusing less on behavior and emphasizing psychological properties. Let's start with the description she gave as a 7-year-old:

*Vanessa is short. She has black hair and brown eyes. She uses a wheelchair because she can't walk. She's in my class. She has dolls just like mine. She likes to sing and read.*

Tamsen's description of Vanessa is probably not too different from the way she would have described herself: The emphasis is on concrete characteristics, such as Vanessa's appearance, possessions, and preferences. Contrast this with the following description, which Tamsen gave as a 10-year-old:

*Kate lives in my apartment building. She is a very good reader and is also good at math and science. She's nice to everyone in our class. And she's very funny. Sometimes her jokes make me laugh so-o-o hard! She takes piano lessons and likes to play soccer.*

Tamsen's account still includes concrete features, such as where Kate lives and what she likes to do. However, psychological traits are also evident: Tamsen describes Kate as nice and funny. By age 10, children move beyond the purely concrete and observable in describing others. During adolescence, descriptions become even more complex, as you can see in the following, from Tamsen as a 16-year-old:

*Jeannie is very understanding. Whenever someone is upset, she's there to give a helping hand. Yet, in private, Jeannie can be so sarcastic. She can say some really nasty things about people. But I know she'd never say that stuff if she thought people would hear it because she wouldn't want to hurt their feelings.*

This description is more abstract: Tamsen now focuses on psychological traits like understanding and concern for others' feelings. It's also more integrated: Tamsen tries to explain how Jeannie can be both understanding and sarcastic. ●

Each of Tamsen's three descriptions is very typical. As a 7-year-old, she emphasized concrete characteristics; as a 10-year-old, she began to include psychological traits; and as a 16-year-old, she tried to integrate traits to form a cohesive picture.

The progression in how children perceive others was illustrated vividly in a classic study by Livesley and Bromley (1973). They interviewed 320 7- to 15-year-olds attending school in Merseyside, England (near Liverpool, home of the Beatles). All participants were asked to describe eight people that they knew: two boys, two girls, two men, and two women. The examiner told the participants, "I want you to describe what sort of person they are. I want you to tell me what you think about them and what they are like" (p. 97).

The participants at different ages typically produced descriptions much like Tamsen's at different ages. Livesley and Bromley then categorized the contents of the descriptions. Some of their results appear in the graph. Descriptions referring to appearances or possessions become less common as children grow older, as do descriptions giving general information, such as the person's age, gender, religion, or school. In contrast, descriptions of personality traits (for example, "friendly" or "conceited") increase between ages 8 and 14 years. This pattern of changes in children's descriptions of others resembles children's changing understanding of the self, which I explained on pages 300–301 of Module 11.1.

By age 5, children use the information in their descriptions to predict others' future behavior (Heyman & Gelman, 1999; Yuill & Pearson, 1998). To illustrate, suppose kindergarten children are told that Alissa did something nice (e.g., helped another child finish a difficult puzzle), but Celeste did something mean (e.g.,

**Children's descriptions of others first focus on concrete characteristics, then on psychological traits, then on integrating different characteristics.**

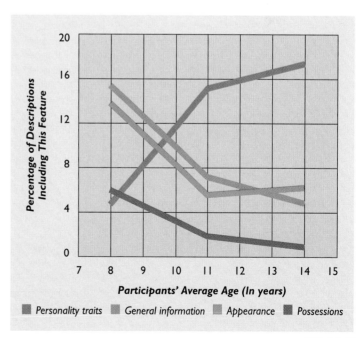

FIG 11–7

scribbled in another child's favorite book). Kindergarten children will judge that, in the future, Alissa is more likely than Celeste to help a child who is hurt, to give money to a needy child, and to hope that an elaborate art project turns out well for the child who created it. Thus, descriptions of others are useful, even for young children, because they allow children to predict how others will behave in the future.

## Understanding What Others Think

One trademark of the preschool child's thinking is difficulty in seeing the world from another's point of view. Piaget's term for this was *egocentrism,* and it was a defining characteristic of his preoperational stage of development (see Module 6.2). In much the same way, preschool children's communication is often ineffective because they don't consider the listener's perspective when they talk (see Module 9.4). As children move beyond the preschool years, though, they realize that others see the world differently, both literally and figuratively. For example, in the module-opening vignette, 12-year-old Ian knows why his little brother, Kyle, is angry: Kyle thinks that Ian is being bossy and mean. Ian understands that Kyle doesn't know there is a good reason why he can't go to the basement.

Sophisticated understanding of how others think is achieved gradually throughout childhood and adolescence. Robert Selman (1980, 1981) has proposed a theory of how understanding others' thinking—or perspective taking—occurs. Selman's theory is based on two of Piaget's key assumptions, namely, that understanding of others occurs in stages and that movement from one stage to the next is based on cognitive development. The table shows Selman's five stages of perspective taking.

## Selman's Stages of Perspective Taking

| Stage | Approximate Ages | Description |
|---|---|---|
| Undifferentiated | 3–6 years | Children know that self and others can have different thoughts and feelings, but often confuse the two. |
| Social-informational | 4–9 years | Children know that perspectives differ because people have access to different information. |
| Self-reflective | 7–12 years | Children can step into another's shoes and view themselves as others do; they know that others can do the same. |
| Third-person | 10–15 years | Children can step outside the immediate situation to see how they and another person are viewed by a third person. |
| Societal | 14 years to adult | Adolescents realize that a third person's perspective is influenced by broader personal, social, and cultural contexts. |

TABLE 11–1

A good way to appreciate the progression from stage to stage is to look at one of the social dilemmas that Selman used to explore children's perspective taking.

*Holly is an 8-year-old girl who likes to climb trees. She is the best tree climber in the neighborhood. One day while climbing down from a tall tree she falls off the bottom branch but does not hurt herself. Her father sees her fall. He is upset and asks her to promise not to climb trees anymore. Holly promises.*

*Later that day, Holly and her friends meet Sean. Sean's kitten is caught up in a tree and cannot get down. Something has to be done right away or the kitten may fall. Holly is the only one who climbs well enough to reach the kitten and get it down, but she remembers her promise to her father (Selman & Byrne, 1974, p. 805).*

This dilemma is typical in that it includes people who don't share the same knowledge about the events taking place. After hearing the story, children are asked questions to investigate their ability to take on each character's view and predict what Holly does.

As children grow, their answers reflect ever more sophisticated understanding of who is thinking what and why in these dilemmas (Selman, 1980; 1981; Selman & Byrne, 1974). The youngest children, those in the undifferentiated stage, might reply, "Holly's father will be happy if she gets the kitten because he likes kittens." This answer confuses the child's own feelings with the father's and ignores Holly's promise. Children in the social-informational stage might say, "If Holly's father knew why she climbed the tree, he probably wouldn't be angry." This answer indicates that the child thinks the father's response depends upon whether or not he knows the reason for Holly's behavior.

In the self-reflective stage, a child might say, "Holly's father would understand that she thought saving the kitten's life was really important, so he wouldn't be mad. He'd probably be proud." This comment shows Holly's father stepping into Holly's shoes, the defining characteristic of the self-reflective stage.

> In Selman's theory, young children confuse their own and others' views, but adolescents can see their own and another's views from a third person's perspective.

At the next level, the third-person stage, a child might respond, "Holly remembers the promise, but she doesn't think her father will be angry when she explains that she wouldn't have climbed the tree except to save the kitten's life. Her father might wish that Holly had asked an adult for help, but he'd also understand why it was important to Holly to save the kitten." This child simultaneously considers both Holly's and her father's perspectives on the dilemma. In answering, the child has stepped outside the immediate situation to take the perspective of a neutral third party who can look at both Holly's and her father's views.

At the most advanced level, the societal stage, an adolescent might reply, "Holly and her father both know that she almost always obeys him. So, they'd both know that if she disobeyed him to climb the tree, there would have to be an awfully good reason. So, they'd talk about it." This child's answer, like the previous one, considers Holly's and her father's perspectives simultaneously. The difference is that this comment puts the issue in the broader context of the history of their father-daughter relationship.

As predicted by Selman's theory, research shows that, as children develop, their reasoning moves through each stage, in sequence. In addition, regardless of age, children at more advanced cognitive levels tend to be at more advanced stages in perspective taking (Gurucharri & Selman, 1982; Krebs & Gillmore, 1982).

Additional support for Selman's theory comes from studies on perspective taking and social behavior. In the photo, the children with the soccer ball apparently recognize that the girl on the sideline wants to play, so they're inviting her to join the game. Children who can anticipate what others are thinking should get along better with their peers, and research indicates that they do. For example, children with good perspective-taking skills are typically well liked by their peers (LeMare & Rubin, 1987). Of course, mere understanding does not guarantee good social behavior; sometimes children who understand what another child is thinking take advantage of that child. But, in general, greater understanding of others seems to promote positive interactions, a topic that we'll discuss further in Chapter 12 on moral understanding and behavior.

## Prejudice

As children learn more about others, they discover that people belong to different social groups, based on variables such as gender, ethnicity, and social class. By the preschool years, most children can distinguish males from females and can identify people from different ethnic groups (Aboud, 1993). Once children learn their membership in a specific group—"I'm a Vietnamese American boy"—they typically show prejudice.

*Prejudice* **is a negative view of others based on their membership in a specific group.** At the same time, children view their own group more favorably. Preschool and kindergarten children more often attribute positive traits (being friendly and smart) to their own group and negative traits (being mean and fighting a lot) to other groups (Bigler, Jones, & Lobliner, 1997; Black-Gutman & Hickson, 1996).

As children move into the elementary-school years, prejudice usually declines somewhat (Powlishta et al., 1994). Cognitive development explains the decline. Preschool and kindergarten children usually view people in social groups as much more homogeneous than they really are. People from other groups are seen as all alike and, typically, not as good as people from the child's own group. Older children understand that people in social groups are heterogeneous—they know that individual European Americans, girls, and obese children, for example, are not all alike. And they have learned that people from different groups may be more alike than people from the same group. Gary, an African American whose passion is computers, finds that he enjoys being with Vic, an Italian American who shares his love of computers, but not Curtis, another African American whose passion is music. As children realize that social groups consist of all kinds of different people, prejudice lessens.

Prejudice may be less pronounced in older children, but it does not vanish. Older children and adolescents remain biased positively toward their own group and negatively toward others (Powlishta et al., 1994). Of course, many adults have these same biases, and children and adolescents simply reflect the attitudes of those around them.

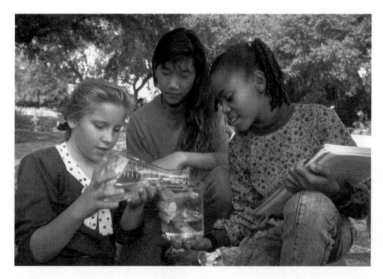

What can parents, teachers, and other adults do to rid children of prejudice? One way is to encourage friendly and constructive contacts between children from different groups (Ramsey, 1995). Adults can create situations in which children from different groups work together toward common goals. In class, this might be a class project, as shown in the photo. In sports, it might be mastering a new skill. By working together, Gary starts to realize that Vic acts, thinks, and feels as he does simply because he's Vic, not because he's an Italian American.

Another useful approach is to ask children to play different roles (Davidson & Davidson, 1994). They can be asked to imagine that, because of their race, ethnic background, or gender, they have been insulted verbally or not allowed to participate in special activities. A child might be asked to imagine that she can't go to a private swimming club because she's African American or that she wasn't invited to a party because she's Hispanic. Afterwards, children reflect on how they felt when prejudice and discrimination were directed at them. And they're asked to think about what would be fair—what should be done in situations like these?

From such experiences, children and adolescents discover for themselves that a person's membership in a social group tells us very little about that person. They learn, instead, that all children are different, each a unique mix of experiences, skills, and values.

## Check Your Learning

**1.** Children's descriptions of others begin with concrete characteristics (e.g., appearance, possessions) and next begin to include _____.

**2.** When adolescents describe others, they usually _____.

**3.** Selman's theory of perspective taking is based on Piaget's assumption that understanding of others consists of stages and that _____.

**4.** In Selman's theory, at the most advanced stage of perspective taking, adolescents _____.

**5.** Prejudice declines somewhat as children get older because _____.

**6.** One way to reduce prejudice is to encourage friendly and constructive contacts between people from different groups; another is to _____.

 **How might an information-processing theorist describe the stages of Selman's theory of perspective taking?**

**Answers:** (1) psychological traits, (2) try to provide a cohesive, integrated picture, (3) movement from one stage to the next reflects cognitive development, (4) take a third person's perspective and recognize the influence of context on this perspective, (5) with cognitive development, children realize that social groups are not homogeneous, (6) have children play roles that let them experience discrimination and prejudice

# Understanding Self and Others
## IN PERSPECTIVE

# 11.1

The cognitive growth that we examined in Chapters 6 and 7 allows children to understand themselves and other people with greater breadth and depth as they develop. In Module 11.1, we saw that 15-month-olds typically recognize themselves in a mirror, one of the first signs of the complex process of self-definition that reaches its peak in adolescence, when individuals achieve an identity. In Module 11.2, we discovered how children's self-esteem is measured and learned that self-esteem is highest during the preschool years, then declines until adolescence, when it begins to increase again. We also saw that children's self-esteem is greatest when parents and teachers support and encourage them. In Module 11.3, we learned that children's descriptions of others parallel their descriptions of themselves and that children's understanding of others becomes more complex with age. We also learned that prejudice declines with age, but positive steps can be taken to rid children of any lingering bias toward other social groups.

This chapter is a good occasion to feature the theme that *development is always jointly influenced by heredity and environment*. The emergence of self-awareness between 15 and 24 months is primarily due to biological forces. Regardless of circumstances, children become self-aware between ages 1 and 2. However, elaborating self-awareness into a specific self-concept depends largely upon a child's experiences at home and in school. The specific direction that children take in establishing an identity is strongly influenced by those around them, particularly their parents and teachers.

## See for Yourself

The mirror recognition task, described on pages 298–299, is great fun to do, and you'll be astonished by the rapid change in children's responses between 1 and 2 years. For this task, you simply need a mirror, some tissue, rouge, and a few cooperative parents of 12- to 18-month-olds. Have the parents play with their toddler near the mirror and, in the process, wipe the toddler's nose with a tissue that has rouge on it. Then see how the toddler responds to the now red nose. Some 12-month-olds will do nothing; others will touch the red nose in the mirror. When the 15- or 18-month-olds see themselves, though, they should stop, get a curious expression on their faces, and then reach up to touch their nose. See for yourself!

## Resources

*For more information about . . .*

*adolescent search for identity,* read Erik Erikson's *Gandhi* (Norton, 1969), a Pulitzer Prize–winning book in which Erikson shows how the adolescent search for identity influenced the development of this great leader of India.

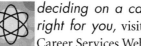 *deciding on a career or finding a job that's right for you,* visit the Northwestern University Career Services Web site: **http://www.stuaff.nwu.edu/ucs/**

## Key Terms

achievement status 302
adolescent egocentrism 301
crystallization 303
diffusion status 302
ethnic identity 304

foreclosure status 302
illusion of invulnerability 302
imaginary audience 302
implementation 303
moratorium status 302

personal fable 302
prejudice 320
self-concept 298
self-esteem 308
specification 303

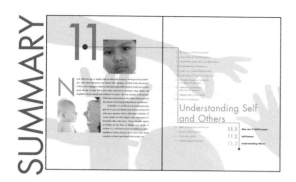

# SUMMARY

## 11.1 Who Am I? Self-Concept

### Origins of Self-Recognition

At about 15 months, infants begin to recognize themselves in the mirror, one of the first signs of self-recognition. They also begin to prefer to look at pictures of themselves, to refer to themselves by name and with personal pronouns, and sometimes to know their age and gender. Evidently, by 2 years, most children have the rudiments of self-awareness, but this early understanding is fragile.

### The Evolving Self-Concept

Preschoolers often define themselves in terms of observable characteristics, such as possessions, physical characteristics, preferences, and competencies. During the elementary-school years, self-concept begins to include emotions, a child's membership in social groups, and comparisons with peers. During adolescence, self-concept includes attitudes, personality traits, beliefs, and future plans. In general, adolescents' self-concepts are more abstract, more psychological, and more future oriented than self-concepts in younger children.

### The Search for Identity

The search for identity typically involves four statuses. Diffusion and foreclosure are more common in early adolescence; moratorium and achievement are more common in late adolescence and young adulthood. Adolescents are most likely to achieve an identity when parents encourage discussion and recognize their autonomy; they are least likely to achieve an identity when parents set rules and enforce them without explanation.

According to Super's theory, an adolescent's developing identity is a primary influence on his or her career aspirations. Super proposes three phases of vocational development during adolescence and young adulthood: crystallization, when basic ideas about careers are identified, based on the person's identity; specification, when lines of work associated with interests are identified; and implementation, which marks entry into the work force.

Adolescents from ethnic groups often progress through three phases in acquiring an ethnic identity: initial disinterest, exploration, and identity achievement. Achieving an ethnic identity usually results in higher self-esteem but is not consistently related to the strength of one's identification with mainstream culture.

Contrary to myth, adolescence is not usually a period of storm and stress. Most adolescents love their parents, feel loved by them, rely on them for advice, and adopt their values. The parent-child relationship becomes more egalitarian during the adolescent years, reflecting adolescents' growing independence.

## 11.2 Self-Esteem

### Measuring Self-Esteem

Most tasks assess self-esteem in different areas. One of the most common measures is Harter's *Self-Perception Profile for Children* (SPPC), which is designed for children as young as 8 years. It assesses self-esteem in five areas: scholastic competence, athletic competence, social acceptance, behavioral conduct, and physical appearance. It also measures overall self-worth. For measuring self-esteem in older adolescents, job competence, close friendships, and romantic appeal are added.

### Change and Stability in Self-Esteem

Self-esteem is very high during the preschool years but declines somewhat during the elementary-school years as children compare themselves to peers. Self-esteem begins to rise in adolescence as teenagers see themselves acquiring more adult skills and responsibilities. Self-esteem becomes more differentiated in older children and adolescents as they evaluate themselves on more aspects of self-esteem, including different types of academic skills.

### Sources of Self-Esteem

Children's self-esteem is greater when parents are affectionate and involved with them and when parents set rules and discuss disciplinary action. Self-esteem also depends on peer comparisons. Self-esteem is usually greater when children know that others view them positively.

### Consequences of Low Self-Esteem

When children have low self-esteem, they are more likely to have poor peer relations, suffer psychological disorders such as depression, be involved in antisocial activities, and do poorly in school. Therapy and improved skills can enhance children's self-esteem.

## 11.3 Understanding Others

### Describing Others

Children's descriptions of others change in much the same way that their descriptions of themselves change. During the early elementary-school years, descriptions emphasize concrete characteristics. In the late elementary-school years, they emphasize personality traits. In adolescence, they emphasize an integrated picture of a person. Children use their descriptions to predict others' behaviors.

### Understanding What Others Think

According to Selman's perspective-taking theory, children's understanding of how others think progresses through five stages. In the first, the undifferentiated stage, children often confuse their own and another's view. In the last, the societal stage, adolescents take a third person's perspective and understand that this perspective is influenced by context.

### Prejudice

Prejudice emerges in the preschool years, soon after children recognize different social groups. Prejudice declines during childhood, as children's cognitive growth helps them understand that social groups are heterogenous, not homogeneous. However, older children and adolescents still show prejudice, which is best reduced by additional exposure to individuals from other social groups and through role play that allows children to experience prejudice and discrimination.

# 12

onsider the following hypothetical situation. You enter a nursery filled with 2-day-olds. The babies look like babies in any nursery—some are asleep, some are crying, others are simply lying quietly. However, the nurse tells you that the newborns include Mother Teresa, Adolf Hitler, Mohandas Gandhi, and Martin Luther King Jr. Although seemingly identical now, three of the newborns will rank among the 20th century's greatest figures and one will be guilty of unspeakable horrors. Why? What determines whether children act morally or immorally? Whether they care about others or take from others? Whether they become Samaritans or follow a path of evil? The four modules in this chapter provide some answers to these questions. In Module 12.1, we'll see how children learn to control their behavior. In Module 12.2, we'll look at how children and adolescents reason about moral issues, and in Module 12.3, we'll look at factors that encourage children to be kind to others. Finally, in Module 12.4, we'll see why children act aggressively toward others.

# Moral Understanding and Behavior

12.1  **Self-Control**

12.2  **Reasoning About Moral Issues**

12.3  **Helping Others**

12.4  **Aggression**

# 12.1

## Self-Control

### Learning Objectives

● **When does self-control begin, and how does it change as children develop?**

● **What factors influence children's ability to maintain self-control?**

● **What strategies can children use to improve their self-control?**

> *Shirley returned from a long day at work tired but eager to celebrate her son Ryan's second birthday. Her excitement quickly turned to dismay when she discovered that Ryan had taken a huge bite of icing from the birthday cake while the baby sitter fixed lunch. Before she had left for work that morning, Shirley had explicitly told Ryan not to touch the cake. Why couldn't Ryan wait? Why did he give in to temptation? What could she do to help Ryan control himself better in the future?*

**In this vignette, Shirley wishes that Ryan had greater *self-control*, the ability to rise above immediate pressures and not give in to impulse.** A child who saves her allowance to buy a much-desired object instead of spending it immediately on candy is showing self-control, as is an adolescent who studies for an exam instead of going to the mall with his friends, knowing that tomorrow he can enjoy the mall and a good grade on his exam.

Self-control is one of the first steps toward moral behavior because children must learn that they cannot constantly do whatever tempts them at the moment. Instead, society has rules for behavior in certain situations, and children must learn to restrain themselves.

In this module, we'll first see how self-control emerges during the preschool years. Then we'll learn some of the factors that determine how well children control themselves. Finally, we'll look at strategies that children use to improve their self-control.

### Beginnings of Self-Control

n this cartoon, Calvin shows little self-control. Is he typical for his age? Thankfully, no. Self-control begins during infancy and the preschool years. Claire Kopp (1982, 1987) believes that self-control develops in three phases:

- At approximately the first birthday, infants become aware that people impose demands on them and they must react accordingly. They learn that they are not entirely free to behave as they wish; instead, others set limits on what they can do. These limits reflect both concern for their safety ("Don't touch! It's hot") as well as early socialization efforts ("Don't grab Ravisha's toy").

- At about 2 years, toddlers have internalized some of the controls imposed by others and are capable of some self-control in parents' absence. For example, although the boy on the left in the photo certainly looks as if he wants to play with the toy that the other toddler has, so far he has inhibited his desire to grab the toy, perhaps because he remembers that his parents have told him not to take things from others.

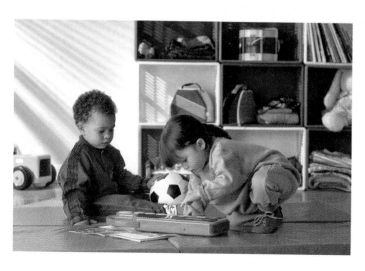

- At about 3 years, children become capable of self-regulation, which "involves flexible and adaptive control processes that can meet quickly changing situational demands" (Kopp, 1987, p. 38). Children can devise ways to regulate their own behavior. To return to the example of a playmate's interesting toy, children might tell themselves that they really don't want to play with it, or they might turn to another activity that removes the temptation to grab it.

> By age 3, children are capable of self-regulation, largely because they can formulate simple plans for dealing with the demands of different situations.

Of course, preschoolers have much to learn about regulating impulsive behavior, and control is achieved only gradually throughout the elementary-school years. For example, in a study by Rotenberg and Mayer (1990), after children had completed a task, they were offered the choice of a relatively small reward immediately or a much larger reward if they waited one day. The graph depicts a definite shift in responding as children grow. Only about one-third of the 6- to 8-year-olds and about half the 9- to 11-year-olds opted to wait for the larger reward. But by 12 to 15 years, nearly everyone waited a day to obtain the larger reward. Thus, although self-control may be evident in toddlers, mastery occurs gradually throughout childhood.

At any age, individuals differ tremendously in their self-control. Think of your peers and how they spend their money. You probably have some friends who spend money as fast as they earn it. Others steadily save their dollars for some long-range goal. Individual differences are evident in research that examines consistency in self-control. Vaughn, Kopp, and Krakow (1984), for example, examined preschoolers' self-control on three different tasks. On one task, the child was told to not touch a novel telephone while the experimenter left the room; on a second task, the child was asked to wait

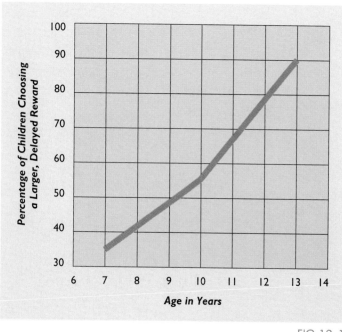

FIG 12–1

for a signal before beginning to search for hidden food; on a third, the experimenter said that an attractively wrapped package was a gift for the child, who was not to touch it until the experimenter and mother had finished some paperwork.

The correlations between children's performance on the different tasks ranged from .29 to .47. These correlations mean that, although children were far from perfectly consistent, in general a child who had good self-control on one task tended to have good control on other tasks, too.

Perhaps you wonder about the validity of these tasks. That is, are these tasks measuring important aspects of self-control in children's natural environments? Mothers' reports of their youngsters' self-control represent one source of evidence for the validity of these tasks. Children who are less likely to touch prohibited toys are, according to their mothers' reports, more likely to spontaneously confess to misdeeds at home and more likely to do as asked at home, without parental supervision (Kochanska et al., 1994).

> Preschoolers who are better able to resist temptation often grow up to be adolescents who have better self-control, are more planful, and have higher SAT scores.

Even more remarkable are the results from longitudinal studies on the long-term consistency of self-control. Shoda, Mischel, and Peake (1990) tracked down nearly 200 15- to 18-year-olds who had participated in self-control experiments as 4-year-olds. In the original experiments, 4-year-olds were told that if they waited alone in a room until the experimenter returned, they would receive a big prize. If they rang a bell to signal the experimenter to return, they would receive a much smaller prize. Then the researchers simply recorded the length of time children waited until the experimenter returned.

You may be surprised to learn that the length of time that 4-year-olds waited was related to a host of characteristics some 11 to 14 years later. The table shows some of the significant correlations between the 4-year-olds' ability to delay gratification and their coping skills, personality characteristics, and SAT scores as adolescents. In general, 4-year-olds who waited the longest before calling the experimenter were still, as

## Correlations Between Preschoolers' Delayed Gratification and Measures of Coping, Personality, and Academic Achievement in Adolescence

| Measure | r |
| --- | --- |
| *Coping* | |
| Is likely to yield to temptation | −.50 |
| Distractibility when trying to concentrate | −.41 |
| *Personality* | |
| Is planful, thinks ahead | .36 |
| Tends to go to pieces under stress, becomes rattled and disorganized | −.34 |
| *SAT scores* | |
| Verbal scale | .42 |
| Quantitative scale | .57 |
| Source: Shoda, Mischel, and Peake, 1990 | |

TABLE 12–1

15- to 18-year-olds, better able to exert self-control and more attentive and able to plan, and they had higher SAT scores.

Obviously, individuals differ in their ability to resist temptation, and this characteristic is remarkably stable over time. But why are some children and adults better able than others to exert self-control? As you'll see in the next section of this module, parents play an important role in determining children's self-control.

## Parental Influences

In the neighorhood where I grew up, there were next door neighbors where both husbands had similar jobs with an engineering company, and both wives were full-time homemakers. Nevertheless, their lifestyles had little in common. One family always seemed to be the first on the block to own new "toys": the first stereo record player, the first color TV, the first Ford Mustang in 1964, and so on. The other family was as frugal as the first family was free-spending: Occasional trips to the repair shop kept the black-and-white TV working, children wore hand-me-down clothes, and the dad rode a bus to work.

Obviously, the children growing up in these two families were exposed to very different models of self-control. Adults in the first family preferred immediate gratification, but those in the second family preferred to save their money for deferred goals. Is children's self-control influenced by their exposure to such models? Can self-control be changed by exposure to a model with less (or more) self-control?

Some of the first answers to these questions came from a classic study by Albert Bandura and Walter Mischel (1965). In the first phase of the study, fourth and fifth graders made several choices between a small immediate reward and a larger delayed outcome (for example, a small candy bar immediately or a larger one in a week). Children who most preferred immediate reward and the ones who most preferred delayed reward then went on to a second phase. Now they watched an adult choose between a less valuable item that could be obtained immediately and a more valuable item that required delay. For children who preferred waiting for a larger reward, the adult always chose the immediate reward. For children who had preferred immediate but small rewards, the adult always chose the delayed reward item. In both cases, the adult also briefly explained his behavior. For example, when the choice was between getting a plastic chess set immediately and a more expensive wooden set in two weeks, the adult commented, "Chess figures are chess figures. I can get much use out of the plastic ones right away" (p. 701).

Immediately after watching the model, children had the opportunity to choose between immediate but small rewards or delayed but larger rewards. What happened? Most children imitated the adult's behavior. Children exposed to a model who delayed gratification also delayed their choices. Similarly, most children exposed to models who showed little self-control were easily swayed and abandoned their own self-control. Apparently, children can show self-restraint or be incredibly impulsive, simply depending upon how they observe others behave in similar situations.

Are you skeptical of Bandura and Mischel's (1965) results, maybe because the setting seems artificial? Perhaps children's self-control can't be so easily influenced outside of the laboratory, in a normal home setting? In fact, correlational studies show that parents' behavior is related to their children's self-control, but not in a way that you may expect. Self-control is *lower* in children whose parents are very strict with them (Feldman & Wentzel, 1990).

One interpretation of this finding is that strict parents "overcontrol" their children: By constantly directing them to do one thing but not another, parents do not give their children either the opportunity or the incentive to internalize control. Consistent with this argument is the finding that children have greater self-control when parents encourage them to be independent and make their own decisions (Silverman & Ragusa, 1990).

So far, the story seems reasonably straightforward: For children to gain self-control, parents must relinquish control. By gradually giving children more opportunities to regulate their own behavior and see the consequences of their choices, parents foster self-control. For example, instead of insisting that elementary-school children follow a set after-dinner routine, parents can allow children to decide how to balance entertainment, homework, and household chores.

But more recent research shows that the story is not so simple after all. Remember from Module 10.2 that temperament affects children's responses to parents' efforts to promote self-control. We'll look at this research in the next section.

## Temperamental Influences on Self-Control

Children's temperament helps determine their level of self-control. Emotional toddlers and preschoolers are less able to control themselves (Stifter, Spinrad, & Braungart-Rieker, 1999). That is, youngsters who have difficulty regulating their emotions usually have difficulty regulating their behavior.

Temperament also influences how children respond to parents' efforts to teach self-control. The aspect of temperament that's most important for self-control is children's anxiety and fearfulness (Kochanska, 1991; 1993). Some anxious and fearful children become nervous at the prospect of potential wrongdoing. When told not to eat a cookie until after dinner, fearful children may leave the room because they're afraid that otherwise they might give in to temptation. With these children, a simple parental reminder usually guarantees compliance because they are so anxious about not following instructions, getting caught, or having to confess to a misdeed.

> Parents foster children's self-control by using gentle discipline with temperamentally fearful children and by using appeals to cooperate with temperamentally fearless children

For children who are not naturally fearful at the thought of misdeeds, other approaches are necessary. More effective with these children are positive appeals to the child to cooperate, appeals that build on the strong attachment relationship between parent and child. Fearless children comply with parental requests out of positive feelings for a loved one, not out of distress caused by fear of misdeeds.

The "Focus on Research" feature describes a study that links temperament to different methods for fostering self-control in children.

FOCUS ON RESEARCH

### Temperament, Parental Influence, and Self-Control

*Who was the investigator, and what was the aim of the study?* Grazyna Kochanska (1997a) wanted to evaluate proposed links between children's temperament, parents' influence, and children's self-control. In particular, she believed that temperamentally fearful children would have better self-control when parents used gentle discipline that elicited mild distress and that temperamentally fearless children would have better self-control when parents appealed to their strong mutual attachment.

*How did the investigator measure the topic of interest?* Kochanska's study included four key variables: children's fearful temperament, parents' use of gentle discipline, strength of parent-child attchment, and children's self-control and compliance. Temperament was measured by having mothers complete questionnaires and by recording children's anxiety as they were asked to do different novel acts (e.g., put a hand inside a large box, jump on a trampoline). Use of gentle discipline was measured by observing mothers interacting with their children and coding for the presence of guiding, gentle requests to comply (as opposed to threats or angry demands). Parent-child attachment was measured by having mothers complete questionnaires that assessed attachment security as described in Module 10.2. Finally, children's self-control and compliance were tested in two ways: with games that posed a strong temptation to cheat (because the games were impossible to win following the rules) and with stories that allowed children to support (or condemn) a story character who took desirable toys from another story character.

*Who were the children in the study?* Kochanska tested 103 2½- to 3-year-olds on the temperamental measures. At this time, mothers completed the attachment questionnaire and interacted with their children while experimenters observed their disciplinary styles. Kochanska retested 99 of these children as 4-year-olds and 90 of them as 5-year-olds. During these sessions, she administered the measures of self-control and compliance. (For simplicity, I'm only going to describe the results from the first two test sessions.)

*What was the design of the study?* This study was correlational because Kochanska was interested in relations that existed naturally between children's temperament, parental behaviors, and children's self-control and compliance. The study was longitudinal because children were tested three times, at approximately 2½, 4, and 5 years of age.

*Were there ethical concerns with the study?* No. Most of the tasks that children performed were fun. The tasks to assess fearfulness—for example, putting a hand inside a large box—were designed to elicit concern, not fear.

*What were the results?* Kochanska used the measures of temperament obtained from the 2½- to 3-year-olds to divide the sample into fearful and fearless toddlers. Next, she examined links between gentle discipline, attachment, and children's self-control. The correlations are shown in the graph and correspond to Kochanska's predictions. For fearful children, self-control was associated more strongly with a mother's gentle discipline than with attachment security. In contrast, for fearless children, self-control was associated more strongly with attachment security than with gentle discipline.

*What did the investigator conclude?* Parents do influence their children's ability to maintain self-control, but the nature of that influence depends on children's temperament. Fearful children respond to gentle reminders to comply, apparently because such reminders elicit mild distress. Fearless children respond to requests to cooperate because they appeal to the strong attachment relationship. ●

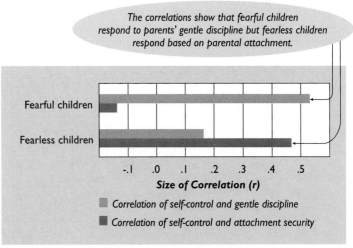

*The correlations show that fearful children respond to parents' gentle discipline but fearless children respond based on parental attachment.*

Fearful children

Fearless children

-.1   .0   .1   .2   .3   .4   .5
***Size of Correlation (r)***

■ *Correlation of self-control and gentle discipline*
■ *Correlation of self-control and attachment security*

FIG 12–2

Of course, regardless of their temperament, children are not perfectly consistent in their self-control. Children who are able to resist temptation on one occasion may give in the next time. Why do children show self-control on some tasks but not on others? As we'll see in the next section, the answer lies in children's plans for resisting temptation.

## Improving Self-Control

I magine it's one of the first nice days of spring. You have two major exams that you should study for, but it's so-o-o-o tempting to spend the entire day with your friends, sitting in the sun. What do you do to resist this temptation and stick to studying? You might remind yourself that these exams are very important. You might also move to a windowless room to keep your mind off the tempting weather. Stated more generally, effective ways to resist temptation include (a) reminding yourself of the importance of long-term goals over short-term temptations and (b) reducing the attraction of the tempting event.

During the preschool years, some youngsters begin to use both of these methods spontaneously. In an experiment by Mischel and Ebbesen (1970), 3- to 5-year-olds were asked to sit alone in a room for 15 minutes. If they waited the entire time, they would receive a desirable reward. Children could call the experimenter back to the room at any time by a prearranged signal; in this case, they would receive a much less desirable reward.

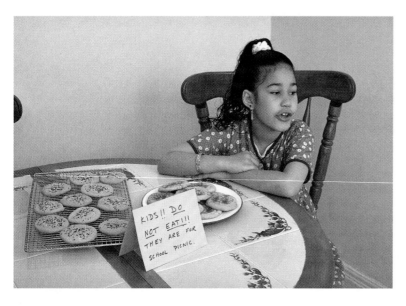

Some children, of course, were better able than others to wait the full 15 minutes. How did they do it? Some children talked to themselves: "I've gotta wait to get the best prize!" As Vygotsky described (Module 6.4), these youngsters were using private speech to control their own behavior. Others, like the child in the photograph, sang. Still others invented games. All were effective techniques for enduring 15 boring minutes to receive a desired prize.

Later studies show that children who have a concrete way of handling the situation are far better able to resist temptation (Mischel, Shoda, & Rodriguez, 1989). Effective plans include (a) reminders to avoid looking at the tempting object, (b) reminders of rules against touching a tempting object, and (c) activities designed to divert attention from the tempting object, such as playing with other objects. For example, in the vignette, Shirley could have helped Ryan make a plan to resist temptation. She might have told him, "When you feel like you want to eat some cake, tell yourself, 'No cake until Mom gets home' and go play in your bedroom."

Overall, then, how children think about tempting objects or outcomes makes all the difference. Even preschoolers can achieve self-control by making plans that include appropriate self-instruction. As children learn to regulate their own behavior, they also begin to learn about moral rules—cultural rights and wrongs—which are described in the next module.

## Check Your Learning

**1.** At approximately age _____, children first learn that other people make demands of them.

**2.** Fifteen- to 18-year-olds who were better able to resist temptation as preschoolers still have better self-control, are more attentive and planful, and have _____.

3. Bandura and Mischel's classic study of adults' influence on children's self-control revealed that, after viewing adults who showed little self-control, children _____.

4. When parents are very controlling, their children tend to _____.

5. With fearful children, parents can foster self-control by using gentle discipline; with fearless children, parents can foster self-control by _____.

6. Children can maintain self-control more effectively when they remind themselves to resist temptation and _____.

Compare and contrast the view of self-control presented in this module with Vygotsky's ideas of self-control, which appeared in Module 6.3

**Answers:** (1) 1, (2) higher SAT scores, (3) imitated the adults' poor self-control, (4) have poor self-control, (5) asking them to cooperate, which appeals to their strong attachment relationship, (6) they divert their attention from the tempting object or event

# Reasoning About Moral Issues

## 12.2

Piaget's Views ┐
Kohlberg's Theory ┤
Beyond Kohlberg's Theory ┘
●

## Learning Objectives

● How does reasoning about moral issues change during childhood and adolescence?

● How do concern for justice and caring for other people contribute to moral reasoning?

● What factors help promote more sophisticated reasoning about moral issues?

*Howard, the least popular boy in the entire fourth grade, had been wrongly accused of throwing food at lunch. Min-shen, another fourth grader, knew that Howard was innocent but said nothing to the lunchroom supervisor for fear of what his friends would say about siding with Howard. A few days later, when Min-shen's father heard about the incident, he was upset that his son apparently had so little "moral fiber." Why hadn't Min-shen acted in the face of an injustice?*

On one of the days when I was writing this module, my local paper had two articles about youth from the area. One article was about a 14-year-girl who was badly burned while saving her younger brothers from a fire in their apartment. Her mother said she wasn't surprised by her daughter's actions because she had always been an extraordinarily caring person. The other article was about two 17-year-old boys who had beaten an elderly man to death. They had only planned to steal his wallet, but when he insulted them and tried to punch them, they became enraged.

Reading articles like these, you can't help but question why some people act in ways that earn our deepest respect and admiration, whereas others earn our utter contempt as well as our pity. And, at a more mundane level, we wonder why Min-shen didn't tell the truth about the food fight to the lunchroom supervisor. In this module, we'll begin our exploration of moral understanding and behavior by looking at children's thinking about moral issues: How do children judge what is "good" and what is "bad"? Let's start by looking at Jean Piaget's ideas about the development of moral reasoning.

### Piaget's Views

Once, when my son Matt was about 6, we were playing Chutes and Ladders®. This is a board game in which you can advance rapidly when you land on a space that has a ladder but must go backward if you land on a chute. To speed up the game, I suggested to Matt that we be allowed to advance if we landed on a chute as well as a ladder. I reminded him that he liked to climb up slides at playgrounds, so my suggestion had some logic to it. Matt would have none of this. He told me, "It's a rule that you have to go backward when you land on a chute. You can't go forward. The people who made Chutes and Ladders® say so. Just read the instructions, Daddy." I tried again to persuade him (because, in my humble opinion, Chutes and Ladders® gives new meaning to "bored" games), but he was adamant.

Matt's inflexibility, which is typical of 6-year-olds, can be explained by Piaget's stage theory of moral development. Based on children's play and their responses to stories about children who misbehave, Piaget proposed one of the first theories of moral development. In the first stage of moral development, which lasts from age 2 years to about 4, children have no well-defined ideas about morality. **But, beginning at about 5 years and continuing through age 7, children are in a stage of *moral realism;* they believe that rules are created by wise adults and therefore must be followed and cannot be changed. Another characteristic of the stage of moral realism is that children believe in *immanent justice,* the idea that breaking a rule always leads to punishment.** Suppose I had forced Matt to use my new rules for Chutes and Ladders® and that, the next day, he had tripped on his way to school, scraping his knee. Believing in immanent justice, he would have seen the scraped knee as the inevitable consequence of breaking the rule the previous day.

**At about age 8, children progress to the stage of *moral relativism,* the understanding that rules are created by people to help them get along.** Children progress to this more advanced level of moral reasoning in part because advances in cognitive development allow them to understand the reasons for rules. Furthermore, from interactions with their peers, children come to understand the need for rules and how they are created. For example, as the boys in the photograph decide where to ride their skateboards, they might follow a rule that everybody can suggest some place and then they'll vote. The boys understand that this rule isn't absolute; they follow it because it's reasonably fair and, by using this rule, they spend more time skating and less time arguing.

Children in the stage of moral relativism also understand that because people agree to set rules in the first place, they can also change them if they see the need. If the skateboarding boys decided another rule would be fairer and would help them get along better, they could adopt the new rule.

Some of Piaget's ideas about moral reasoning have stood the test of time better than others. For example, later research showed that children's early moral reasoning does not consider adult authority final and absolute. Instead, preschool children believe adults' authority is limited. Preschoolers believe that pushing a child or damaging another child's possession is wrong even when an adult

In Piaget's view, from 5 to 7 years children are moral realists who believe that rules are absolute; by age 8, children understand that rules are relative and created by people to help them get along.

says that it's okay (Tisak, 1993). A lasting contribution of Piaget's work, however, is the idea that moral reasoning progresses through a sequence of stages, driven by cognitive development and interactions with peers. One modern theory that builds on Piaget's stage approach comes from Lawrence Kohlberg; it is the focus of the next section.

## Kohlberg's Theory

To begin, I'd like to tell you a story about Heidi, a star player on a soccer team that I coached. Heidi was terribly upset because our team was undefeated and scheduled to play in a weekend tournament to determine the league champion. But on Sunday of this same weekend, a Habitat-for-Humanity house was to be dedicated to her grandfather, who had died a few months previously. If Heidi skipped the tournament game, her friends on the team would be upset; if she skipped the dedication, her family would be disappointed. Heidi couldn't do both and didn't know what to do.

Kohlberg created stories like this one to study how people reason about moral dilemmas. He made it very difficult to reach a decision in his stories because every alternative involved some undesirable consequences. In fact, there is no "correct" answer—that's why the stories are referred to as moral "dilemmas." For Heidi, pleasing her friends means disappointing her family; pleasing her family means letting down her teammates. Kohlberg was more interested in the reasoning used to justify a decision—Why should Heidi go to the tournament? Why should she go to the dedication?—not the decision itself.*

Kohlberg's best-known moral dilemma is about Heinz, whose wife is dying:

> *In Europe, a woman was near death from cancer. One drug might save her, a form of radium that a druggist in the same town had recently discovered. The druggist was charging $2,000, ten times what the drug cost him to make. The sick woman's husband, Heinz, went to everyone he knew to borrow the money, but he could only get together about half of what it cost. He told the druggist that his wife was dying and asked him to sell it cheaper or let him pay later. But the druggist said, "No." The husband got desperate and broke into the man's store to steal the drug for his wife (Kohlberg, 1969, p. 379).*

Although more hangs in the balance for Heinz than for Heidi, both are moral dilemmas in that the alternative courses of action have desirable and undesirable features.

Kohlberg analyzed children's, adolescents', and adults' responses to a large number of dilemmas and identified three levels of moral reasoning, each divided into two stages. Across the six stages, the basis for moral reasoning shifts. In the earliest stages, moral reasoning is based on external forces, such as the promise of reward or the threat of punishment. At the most advanced levels, moral reasoning is based on a personal, internal moral code and is unaffected by others' views or society's expectations. You can clearly see this gradual shift in the three levels:

- *Preconventional level:* **For most children, many adolescents, and some adults, moral reasoning is controlled almost solely by obedience to authority and by rewards and punishments.**

---

*As is turned out, Heidi didn't have to wrestle with the moral dilemma. We lost our game on Saturday, so she went to the dedication on Sunday.

*Stage 1: Obedience orientation.* People believe that adults know what is right and wrong. Consequently, a person should do what adults say is right to avoid being punished. A person at this stage would argue that Heinz should not steal the drug because it is against the law (which was set by adults).

*Stage 2: Instrumental orientation.* People look out for their own needs. They often are nice to others because they expect the favor to be returned in the future. A person at this stage would say it was all right for Heinz to steal the drug because his wife might do something nice for him in return (that is, she might reward him).

- *Conventional level:* **For most adolescents and most adults, moral decision making is based on social norms—what is expected by others.**

*Stage 3: Interpersonal norms.* Adolescents and adults believe that they should act according to others' expectations. The aim is to win the approval of others by behaving like "good boys" and "good girls." An adolescent or adult at this stage would argue that Heinz should not steal the drug because then others would see him as an honest citizen who obeys the law.

In Kohlberg's theory, moral reasoning is first based on external forces such as reward and punishment, but ultimately is based on a personal moral code.

*Stage 4: Social system morality.* Adolescents and adults believe that social roles, expectations, and laws exist to maintain order within society and to promote the good of all people. An adolescent or adult in this stage would reason that Heinz should steal the drug because a husband is obligated to do all that he possibly can to save his wife's life. Or a person in this stage would reason that Heinz should not steal the drug because stealing is against the law and society must prohibit theft.

- *Postconventional level:* **For some adults, typically those older than 25, moral decisions are based on personal, moral principles.**

*Stage 5: Social contract orientation.* Adults agree that members of cultural groups adhere to a "social contract" because a common set of expectations and laws benefits all group members. However, if these expectations and laws no longer promote the welfare of individuals, they become invalid. Consequently, an adult in this stage would reason that Heinz should steal the drug because social rules about property rights are no longer benefiting individuals' welfare.

*Stage 6: Universal ethical principles.* Abstract principles like justice, compassion, and equality form the basis of a personal moral code that may sometimes conflict with society's expectations and laws. An adult at this stage would argue that Heinz should steal the drug because life is paramount and preserving life takes precedence over all other rights.

The table at the top of page 337 puts all the stages together, providing a quick summary of Kohlberg's theory.

## Support for Kohlberg's Theory.

Kohlberg proposed that his stages form an invariant sequence. That is, individuals move through the six stages in the order listed and in only that order. If his stage theory is right, then level of moral reasoning should be strongly associated with age and level of cognitive development: Older and more advanced thinkers should, on the average, be more advanced in their moral development, and indeed they usually are (Stewart & Pascual-Leone, 1992).

## Stages in Kohlberg's Theory

**Preconventional Level: Punishment and Reward**

Stage 1: Obedience to authority

Stage 2: Nice behavior in exchange for future favors

**Conventional Level: Social Norms**

Stage 3: Live up to others' expectations

Stage 4: Follow rules to maintain social order

**Postconventional level: Moral codes**

Stage 5: Adhere to a social contract when it is valid

Stage 6: Personal morality based on abstract principles

TABLE 12–2

For example, the graph shows developmental change in the percentage of individuals who reason at Kohlberg's different stages. Stages 1 and 2 are common among children and young adolescents but not older adolescents and adults. Stages 3 and 4 are common among older adolescents and adults. The graph also shows that most individuals do not progress to the final stages. Most adults' moral reasoning is at Stages 3 and 4.

Support for Kohlberg's invariant sequence of stages also comes from longitudinal studies measuring individuals' level of reasoning over several years. Individuals do progress through each stage in sequence, and virtually no individuals skip any stages (Colby et al., 1983). Longitudinal studies also show that, over time, individuals become more advanced in their level of moral reasoning or remain at the same level. They do not regress to a lower level (Walker & Taylor, 1991).

Additional support for Kohlberg's theory comes from research on the link between moral reasoning and moral behavior. In general, level of moral reasoning should be linked to moral behavior. Remember that less advanced moral reasoning reflects the influence of external forces such as rewards and social norms, whereas more advanced reasoning is based on a personal moral code. Therefore, individuals at the preconventional and conventional levels would act morally when external forces demand, but otherwise they might not. In contrast, individuals at the postconventional level, where reasoning is based on personal principles, should be compelled to moral action even when external forces may not favor it.

Let's consider a hypothetical example. Suppose you're one of the most popular students in the ninth grade. You learn that one of the least popular students has been wrongly accused of spray-painting graffiti on a school wall; you know that some friends in your group are actually responsible. What would you do? Speaking out on behalf of the unpopular student is unlikely to lead to reward. Furthermore, there are strong social norms against "squealing" on friends. So if you are in the preconventional or conventional level of moral reasoning like Min-shen, the boy in the

FIG 12–3

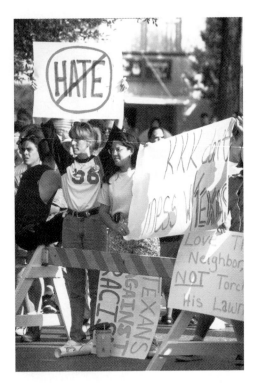

vignette at the beginning of the module, you would probably let the unpopular student be punished unfairly. But if you are at the postconventional level and see the situation in terms of principles of justice and fairness, you would be more likely to identify the real perpetrators, despite the price to be paid in rejection by the group.

Many researchers report findings that support the hypothesized link between moral reasoning and moral action. In one study (Gibbs et al., 1986), high-school teachers were asked to judge whether their students would defend their principles in difficult situations or if they would act morally only when it was fashionable or handy. High-school students who were judged by their teachers to have greater moral courage tended to be more advanced in Kohlberg's stages than students who were judged less courageous. That is, students like those in the photograph who protest social conditions tend to have higher moral reasoning scores. The converse is also true: Delinquent adolescents, whose actions are more likely to be morally offensive, tend to have lower moral reasoning scores than nondelinquent adolescents (Chandler & Moran, 1990). That is, delinquent adolescents are more likely to emphasize punishment and reward in their moral reasoning, not social norms and personal moral codes.

On another point of Kohlberg's theory, support is mixed. Kohlberg claimed that his sequence of stages is universal: All people in all cultures should progress through the six-stage sequence. Some research shows that children and adolescents in cultures worldwide reason about moral dilemmas at Stages 2 or 3, just like North American children and adolescents. But, as we'll see in the "Cultural Influences" feature, beyond the earliest stages, moral reasoning in other cultures is often not described well by Kohlberg's theory (Snarey, 1985).

## CULTURAL INFLUENCES

### Moral Reasoning in India

Many critics note that Kohlberg's emphasis on individual rights and justice reflects traditional American culture and Judeo-Christian theology. Not all cultures and religions share this emphasis; consequently, moral reasoning might be based on different values in other cultures (Carlo et al., 1996; Keller et al., 1998).

The Hindu religion, for example, emphasizes duty and responsibility to others, not individual rights and justice (Simpson, 1974). Accordingly, children and adults reared with traditional Hindu beliefs might emphasize caring for others in their moral reasoning more than individuals brought up in the Judeo-Christian tradition.

Miller and Bersoff (1992) tested the hypothesis that cultural differences affect moral reasoning by constructing dilemmas with both justice- and care-based solutions. For example:

*Ben planned to travel to San Francisco in order to attend the wedding of his best friend. He needed to catch the very next train if he was to be on time for the ceremony, as he had to deliver the wedding rings. However, Ben's wallet was stolen in the train station. He lost all of his money as well as his ticket to San Francisco.*

*Ben approached several officials as well as passengers . . . and asked them to loan him money to buy a new ticket. But, because he was a stranger, no one was willing to lend him the money he needed.*

*While Ben . . . was trying to decide what to do next, a well-dressed man sitting next to him walked away. . . . Ben noticed that the man had left his coat unattended. Sticking out of the man's coat pocket was a train ticket to San Francisco. . . . He also saw that the man had more than enough money in his coat pocket to buy another train ticket (p. 545).*

One solution emphasized individual rights and justice:

*Ben should not take the ticket from the man's coat pocket even though it means not getting to San Francisco in time to deliver the wedding rings to his best friend (p. 545).*

The other solution placed a priority on caring for others:

*Ben should go to San Francisco to deliver the wedding rings to his best friend even if it means taking the train ticket from the other man's coat pocket (p. 545).*

When children and adults living in the United States responded to dilemmas like this one about Ben, a slight majority selected the justice-based alternative. In contrast, when Hindu children and adults living in India, like the mother and son in the photo, responded to the same dilemmas, the overwhelming majority selected the care-based alternative.

Clearly, moral reasoning reflects the culture in which a person is reared. Consistent with Kohlberg's theory, judgments by American children and adults reflect their culture's emphasis on individual rights and justice. But judgments by Indian children and adults reflect their culture's emphasis on caring for other people. The bases of moral reasoning are not universal as Kohlberg claimed; instead, they reflect cultural values. ●

## Beyond Kohlberg's Theory

Kohlberg's theory obviously is not the final word on moral development. Much about his theory seems valid, but investigators have addressed its shortcomings. The next few pages describe some work that helps complete our picture of the development of moral thinking.

### Gilligan's Ethic of Caring.
Findings like those described in the "Cultural Influences" feature indicate that Kohlberg's theory is not universal but applies primarily to cultures with Western philosophical and religious traditions. But researcher Carol Gilligan (1982; Gilligan & Attanucci, 1988) questions how applicable Kohlberg's theory is even within the Western tradition. Gilligan argues that Kohlberg's emphasis on justice applies more to men than to women, whose reasoning about moral issues is often rooted in concern for others. Gilligan writes, "The moral imperative that emerges repeatedly in interviews with women is an injunction to care, a responsibility to discern and alleviate the real and recognizable trouble of this world" (1982, p. 100).

Gilligan proposes a developmental progression in which individuals gain greater understanding of caring and responsibility. In the first stage, children are preoccupied with their own needs. In the second stage, people care for others, particularly those who are less able to care for themselves, like infants and the aged. The third stage unites caring for others and for oneself by emphasizing caring in all human relationships.

Like Kohlberg, Gilligan also believes that moral reasoning becomes qualitatively more sophisticated as individuals develop, progressing through a number of distinct stages. However, Gilligan emphasizes care (helping people in need) instead of justice (treating people fairly).

Gilligan proposed that moral reasoning is sometimes based on concern for others, not solely on justice and individual rights as Kohlberg claimed.

What does research tell us about the importance of justice and care in moral reasoning? Gilligan's claim that females and males differ in the bases of their moral reasoning is not supported. Girls and boys as well as men and women reason about moral issues similarly (Walker, 1995). Both females and males often think about moral issues in terms of care and interpersonal relationships. Justice and care both serve as the basis for moral reasoning. It is the nature of the moral problem that largely determines whether justice, care, or both will be the basis for moral reasoning (Smetana, Killen, & Turiel, 1991).

### Origins of Moral Thinking.

Neither Piaget nor Kohlberg nor Gilligan had much to say about moral reasoning during the preschool years. For example, according to Piaget, children have no real understanding of moral issues until they enter the stage of moral realism at about age 5. In fact, research shows that the foundation of moral thinking is set in the preschool years. For example, understanding of the special status of moral rules emerges during the preschool years. Moral rules, such as prohibitions against theft and murder, are designed to protect people. **In contrast, *social conventions* are arbitrary standards of behavior agreed to by a cultural group to facilitate interactions within the group.** Thus social convention says that we can eat French fries but not green beans with our fingers and that children can address peers but not teachers by their first names.

By age 3, most children distinguish moral rules from social conventions. They judge that hurting other people and taking their possessions are more serious transgressions than eating ice cream with one's fingers and not paying attention to a story (Nucci & Weber, 1995; Smetana & Braeges, 1990).

Other research shows that preschoolers know the difference between lies and mistakes (Siegal & Peterson, 1998). And, when led to believe that they have damaged an object, preschoolers often show traditional signs of guilt, such as distress, apologizing, and trying to right their wrong (Kochanska, Casey, & Fukumoto, 1995). Collectively, these findings tell us that, although preschoolers lack the sophisticated thinking about moral issues associated with older children and adolescents, they have begun to understand the fundamental distinctions in the moral domain.

### Eisenberg's Levels of Prosocial Reasoning.

Nancy Eisenberg (1982; Eisenberg et al., 1995) argues that Kohlberg's theory is flawed because the dilemmas are unrealistic. They involve breaking a law or disobeying a person in authority. In real life, says Eisenberg, most children's moral dilemmas involve choosing between self-interest and helping others. For example, in one of Eisenberg's moral dilemmas, a child walking to a party comes upon a child injured from a fall. The first child must decide whether to continue to the party or help the second child and miss the party.

Like Kohlberg, Eisenberg focuses on how children explain their choices. **Most preschool and many elementary-school children have a *hedonistic orientation*: They pursue their own pleasure.** These children do not help the injured child because they would miss the party. Or they might help because they expect that the injured child would return the favor in the future. In either case, self-interest is the basis of their decision.

**Some preschool and many elementary-school children have a *needs-oriented orientation*: They are concerned about others' needs and want to help.** Children at this stage have learned a simple rule, to help others. They often explain their desire to help as a straightforward, "He needs my help." Their desire to help is not based on imagining how the injured child feels or on a personal moral code.

Many elementary-school children and adolescents have a *stereo-typed, approval-focused orientation,* behaving as they think society expects "good people" to behave. The helpful teen in the photo would explain her behavior by saying that the person she's helping will like her more because she's helping.

Finally, some children and many adolescents develop an *empathic orientation;* they consider the injured child's perspective and how their own actions will make them feel. An adolescent with this orientation might say, "He'd be in pain, so I'd feel bad if I didn't help."

The same kinds of evidence that support Kohlberg's theory support Eisenberg's. For example, longitudinal studies indicate that children in many countries move through Eisenberg's different orientations in sequence (Eisenberg, 1986; Eisenberg et al., 1995). Moreover, children who reason at more advanced levels are more likely to actually help others than children who reason at less advanced levels (Miller et al., 1996).

Eisenberg's theory is like Kohlberg's in emphasizing that moral development involves a developmental shift away from self-centered thinking to social norms and moral principles. Her theory is like Gilligan's in emphasizing that caring for others is an important element in everyday moral reasoning.

The net result of Eisenberg's studies, Gilligan's work, and research on the origins of moral thinking is a broader view of moral reasoning. As Kohlberg claimed, moral reasoning becomes progressively more sophisticated as children develop. However, contrary to Kohlberg's original claims, moral reasoning is not always based on justice and rights. Concern for others is sometimes the basis. And, although Kohlberg had little to say about the preschool years, this is when children begin to understand that moral rules are more important than social conventions.

Eisenberg argues that prosocial reasoning develops in stages, beginning with a hedonistic orientation and ending with an empathic orientation.

MAKING CHILDREN'S LIVES BETTER

### Promoting More Advanced Moral Reasoning

How do individuals develop more mature forms of moral reasoning? Kohlberg's answer to this question is based on an idea from Piaget. Kohlberg proposed that change occurs when people notice that their current level of moral reasoning is inadequate; either it leads to contradictions or it does not always lead to a clear course of action. Seeing that their thinking is inadequate, they abandon it in favor of a more advanced form.

Sometimes, too, simply being exposed to more advanced moral reasoning is sufficient to promote developmental change (Walker, 1980). A child may notice, for example, that older friends do not wait to be rewarded to help others. An adolescent may notice that respected peers take courageous positions regardless of the social consequences. Such experiences apparently cause youngsters to reevaluate their reasoning on moral issues and propel them toward more sophisticated thinking.

Discussion can be particularly effective in revealing shortcomings in moral reasoning. When people, like the adolescents in the photo, reason about moral issues with others whose reasoning is at a higher level, the usual result is that individuals who reason at lower levels improve (Berkowitz & Gibbs, 1985). Imagine, for example, two 9-year-olds discussing the Heinz dilemma. Suppose one takes the position that Heinz should not steal the drug because he might get caught—reasoning at the preconventional level. The other argues that Heinz should steal the drug because a husband should do anything to save his wife's life—reasoning at the conventional level. During conversations of this sort, 9- and 10-year-old children at the preconventional level usually adopt the logic of the children arguing at the higher conventional level.

**To foster discussion and expose students to more advanced moral thinking, Kohlberg and his colleagues set up** *Just Communities,* **special groups of students and teachers within public high schools** (Higgins, 1991; Power, Higgins, & Kohlberg, 1989). Teachers and students met weekly to plan school activities and to discuss school policies. Decisions were reached democratically, with teachers and students alike each having one vote. However, during discussions, teachers acted as facilitators, encouraging students to consider the moral consequences of different courses of action. Students who participated in Just Communities tended to be more advanced in their moral thinking (Higgins, 1991; Power, Higgins, & Kohlberg, 1989).

Research findings such as these send an important message to parents: Discussion is probably the best way for parents to help their children think about moral issues in more mature terms (Walker & Taylor, 1991). Research consistently shows that mature moral reasoning comes about when children are free to express their opinions on moral issues to their parents, who are, in turn, expressing their own opinions and, consequently, exposing their children to more mature moral reasoning (Hoffman, 1988; 1994).

Discussion and modeling, then, help children become more advanced in their moral reasoning. More advanced moral reasoning should then lead to moral behavior—an "other" rather than "self" orientation. We'll look at the development of other-oriented, helpful behavior in the next module. ●

## Check Your Learning

1. Children in Piaget's stage of moral realism believe that rules are created by _____.

2. Kohlberg's theory includes the preconventional, conventional, and _____ stages of moral reasoning.

3. For children in the preconventional level, moral reasoning is strongly influenced by _____.

4. Gilligan's views of morality emphasize _____ instead of justice.

5. Preschoolers' early moral thinking is revealed in their ability to distinguish moral rules from social conventions, in their ability to distinguish lies from mistakes, and _____.

6. When boys' and girls' moral reasoning is compared, the typical result is that _____.

7. In Just Communities, teachers encouraged students to _____.

8. If parents wish to foster their children's moral development, they should _____ with them.

How similar are Piaget's concrete operational thinking (see Module 6.2) and Kohlberg's preconventional level of moral reasoning? How similar are formal operational thinking and conventional moral reasoning?

**Answers:** (1) wise adults and therefore cannot be changed, (2) postconventional, (3) reward or punishment, (4) caring for others, (5) in showing signs of guilt for misdeeds, (6) they do not differ, (7) consider the moral consequences of their decisions, (8) discuss moral issues.

# Helping Others

# 12.3

## Learning Objectives

- At what age do children begin to act prosocially? How does prosocial behavior change with age?

- What skills do children need to behave prosocially?

- What situations influence children's prosocial behavior?

- How can parents foster prosocial behavior in their children?

**Development of Prosocial Behavior**

**Skills Underlying Prosocial Behavior**

**Situational Influences**

**Socializing Prosocial Behavior**

> *Six-year-old Juan got his finger trapped in the VCR when he tried to remove a tape. While he cried and cried, his 3-year-old brother, Antonio, and his 2-year-old sister, Carla, watched but did not help. Later, when their mother had soothed Juan and decided that his finger was not injured, she worried about her younger children's reactions. In the face of their brother's obvious distress, why had Antonio and Carla done nothing?*

Most parents, most teachers, and most religions try to teach children to act in cooperative, helping, giving ways—at least most of the time and in most situations. **Actions that benefit others are known as *prosocial behavior.*** Of course, cooperation often "works" because individuals gain more than they would by not cooperating. ***Altruism* is a particular kind of prosocial behavior; it is behavior that helps another with no direct benefit to the individual.** Altruism is driven by feelings of responsibility for other people. Two youngsters pooling their funds to buy a candy bar to share demonstrates cooperative behavior. One youngster giving half her lunch to a friend who forgot his demonstrates altruism.

But, as the story of Juan and his siblings shows, children (and adults, for that matter) are not always helpful or cooperative. In this module, you'll learn how prosocial behavior changes with age and some of the factors that promote prosocial behavior.

## Development of Prosocial Behavior

Simple acts of altruism can be seen by 18 months. When toddlers and preschoolers see other people who are obviously hurt or upset, they appear concerned, like the child in the photo. They try to comfort the person by hugging him or patting him, and they try to determine why the person is upset (Zahn-Waxler et al., 1992). Apparently, at this early age, children recognize signs of distress.

During the preschool years, children gradually begin to understand others' needs and learn appropriate altruistic responses (Farver & Branstetter,

1994). Their early attempts at altruistic behavior are limited because their knowledge of what they can do to help is modest. As youngsters acquire more strategies to help others, their preferred strategies become more adult-like (Strayer & Schroeder, 1989).

Thus, as a general rule, intentions to act prosocially increase with age, as do children's strategies for helping. Of course, not all children respond to the needs of others, either in toddlerhood or at later ages. Some children attach greater priority to looking out for their own interests. What makes some children more likely than others to help? We'll answer this question in the next section.

## Skills Underlying Prosocial Behavior

Think back to an occasion when you helped someone. How did you know that the person needed help? Why did you decide to help? Although you didn't realize it at the time, your decision to help was probably based on several skills:

- *Perspective taking.* In Module 6.2, you learned about Piaget's concept of egocentrism, the preoperational youngster's inability to see things from another's point of view. Egocentrism limits children's ability to share or help because they simply do not realize the need for prosocial behavior. They have only one perspective—their own. For example, young children might not help someone carrying many packages because they cannot envision that carrying lots of bulky things is a burden. Older children, however, can take the perspective of others, so they recognize the burden and are more inclined to help. In general, the better children understand the thoughts and feelings of other people, the more willing they are to share and help others (Eisenberg, 1988).

- *Empathy.* **The ability to experience another person's emotions is *empathy.*** Children who deeply feel another person's fear, disappointment, sorrow, or loneliness are more inclined to help that person than children who do not feel these emotions (Kochanska, Padavich, & Koenig, 1996; Roberts & Strayer, 1996). In other words, youngsters like the one in the photo, who is obviously distressed by what he is seeing, are most likely to help others.

- *Moral reasoning.* In Module 12.2, you learned that reward and punishment influence young children's moral reasoning, whereas a concern for moral principles characterizes adolescents' and adults' moral decision making. Therefore, as you would expect, prosocial behavior in young children is usually determined by the chance of reward or punishment. It also follows that, as children mature and begin to make moral decisions on the basis of fairness and justice, they become more prosocial, which is what the research shows (Eisenberg & Shell, 1986).

In sum, children who help others tend to be better able to take another's view, to feel another's emotions, and to act on the basis of principles, not rewards, punishments, or social norms. For example, a 15-year-old who spontaneously loans his favorite video game to a friend sees that the friend would like to play the game, feels the friend's disappointment at not owning the game, and believes that friends should share with others.

Of course, perspective taking, empathy, and moral reasoning skills do not guarantee that children always act altruistically. Even though children have the skills needed to act altruistically, they may not because of the particular situation, as we'll see in the next section.

## Situational Influences

Kind children occasionally disappoint us by being cruel, and children who are usually stingy sometimes surprise us by their generosity. Why? The setting helps determine whether children act altruistically or not.

- *Feelings of responsibility.* Children act altruistically when they feel responsible to the person in need. They are more likely to help siblings and friends than strangers, simply because they feel a direct responsibility to people that they know well (Costin & Jones, 1992).

- *Feelings of competence.* Children act altruistically when they feel that they have the skills necessary to help the person in need. Suppose, for example, that a preschooler is growing more and more upset because she can't figure out how to work a computer game. A classmate who knows little about computer games is not likely to help because he doesn't know what to do to help. By helping, he could end up looking foolish (Peterson, 1983).

- *Mood.* Children act altruistically when they are happy or feeling successful but not when they are sad or feeling as if they have failed. In other words, a preschooler who has just spent an exciting morning as the "leader" in nursery school is more inclined to share treats with siblings than a preschooler who was punished by the teacher (Moore, Underwood, & Rosenhan, 1973).

- *Cost of altruism.* Children act altruistically when it entails few or modest sacrifices. A preschooler who has received a snack that she doesn't particularly like is more inclined to share it than a child who has received her very favorite snack (Eisenberg & Shell, 1986).

When, then, are children most likely to help? When they feel responsible to the person in need, have the skills that are needed, are happy, and do not think they have to give up a lot by helping. When are children least likely to help? When they feel neither responsible nor capable of helping, are in a bad mood, and believe that helping will entail a large personal sacrifice.

Using these guidelines, how do you explain why Antonio and Carla, the children in the vignette, watched idly as their older brother cried? Hint: The last two factors—mood and cost—are not likely to be involved. However, the first two factors may explain Antonio and Carla's failure to help their older brother. My explanation appears on page 347, just before "Check Your Learning."

So far, we've seen that altruistic behavior is determined by children's skills (such as perspective taking) and by characteristics of situations (such as whether children feel competent to help in a particular situation). Whether children are altruistic is also determined by socialization, the topic of the next section.

> Children are most likely to help when they feel responsible, have the needed skills, are happy, and believe that they will lose little by helping.

## Socializing Prosocial Behavior

Dr. Martin Luther King Jr. said that his pursuit of civil rights for African Americans was particularly influenced by three people: Henry David Thoreau (a 19th-century American philosopher), Mohandas Gandhi (the leader of the Indian movement for independence from England), and his father, Dr. Martin Luther King, Sr. As is true of many humanitarians, Dr. King's prosocial behavior started in childhood, at home. But how do parents foster altruism in their children? The key factors are reasoning, modeling, and praise.

Parents whose favored disciplinary strategy is reasoning tend to have children who behave prosocially (Hoffman, 1988, 1994). The "Real Children" feature shows this approach in action.

REAL CHILDREN

### Using Reasoning to Promote Prosocial Behavior

Jim's 4-year-old daughter, Annie, was playing with a friend, Maurice. Annie asked Maurice if she could borrow his crayons. When Maurice refused, Annie pushed him aside and grabbed the crayons, which caused Maurice to cry. At this point, Jim returned the crayons to Maurice and had the following conversation with Annie:

JIM: Why did you take the crayons away from Maurice?
ANNIE: Because I wanted them.
JIM: How do you think he felt? Happy or sad?
ANNIE: I dunno.
JIM: I think that you know.
ANNIE: Okay. He was sad.
JIM: Would you like it if I took the crayons away from you? How would you feel?
ANNIE: I'd be mad. And sad, too.
JIM: Well, that's how Maurice felt, and that's why you shouldn't just grab things away from people. It makes them angry and unhappy. Ask first, and if they say "no," then you mustn't take them.

Jim's approach to discipline is to reason with Annie to help her see how her actions affect others. He emphasizes the rights and needs of others as well as the impact of one child's misbehavior on others. Repeated exposure to reasoning during discipline seems to promote children's ability to take the perspective of others (Hoffman, 1988). ●

Reasoning is one way that parents can influence prosocial behavior; modeling is another. Children imitate others' behavior, including prosocial behavior. In laboratory studies, children imitate their peers' altruism (Wilson, Piazza, & Nagle, 1990). For example, children are more likely to donate toys to hospitalized children or to help older adults with household chores when they see other children doing so.

Of course, parents are the models to whom children are most continuously exposed, so they exert a powerful influence. For example, parents who report frequent feelings of warmth and concern for others tend to have children who experience stronger feelings of empathy (Eisenberg et al., 1991). When a mother is helpful and responsive, her children often imitate her by being cooperative, helpful, sharing, and less critical of others (Bryant & Crockenberg, 1980).

Perhaps the most obvious way to foster sharing and other altruistic behavior in children is to reward them directly for acts of generosity. Many parents reward prosocial acts with praise. **Particularly effective is *dispositional praise,* which links the child's altruistic behavior to an underlying altruistic disposition.** In other words, a parent might say, "Thanks for helping me make breakfast; I knew I could count on you because you are such a helpful person." When children like the one in the photo repeatedly hear remarks like this, their self-concept apparently changes to include these characteristics. Children begin to believe that they really are helpful (or nice or friendly). Consequently, when they encounter a situation in which prosocial behavior is appropriate, their self-concept prompts them to act prosocially (Mills & Grusec, 1989).

One last, surprising way that parents can promote prosocial behavior is by having adolescents routinely help with household tasks, such as setting and clearing the table, helping to prepare meals, and helping with laundry. Adolescents (but not children) who perform these chores regularly are more helpful spontaneously. One interpretation of this finding is that helping with household tasks that benefit the entire family sensitizes adolescents to the welfare of others (Grusec, Goodnow, & Cohen, 1996).

Thus, parents can foster altruism in their youngsters by using reasoning to discipline them, by behaving altruistically themselves, by requiring them to complete family chores, and by praising their youngsters' altruistic acts. Remember, too, that altruism requires skills like perspective taking, empathy, and advanced moral reasoning and that the setting influences when children behave altruistically. Combining all these ingredients, we can describe the development of children's altruistic behavior this way: As children get older, their perspective taking and empathic skills develop, which enables them to see and feel another's needs. Nonetheless, children are never invariably altruistic (or, fortunately, invariably nonaltruistic) because properties of situations dictate altruistic behavior, too.

> Parents can foster altruism by using reasoning to discipline their children, by behaving altruistically themselves, by having children help with chores, and by praising children's altruism.

As parents and other adults try to encourage children's prosocial behavior, one of the biggest obstacles is aggressive behavior, which is common throughout childhood and adolescence. In the next module, we'll look at some of the forces that contribute to children's aggression.

*Answer to question on page 345 about why Antonio and Carla didn't help:* Here are two explanations: First, neither Antonio nor Carla may have felt sufficiently responsible to help because (a) with two children who could help, each child's feeling of individual responsibility is reduced, and (b) younger children are less likely to feel responsible for an older brother. Second, it's my guess that neither child has had many opportunities to use the VCR. In fact, it's likely they both have been strongly discouraged from venturing near it! Consequently, they don't feel competent to help because they don't know how it works or what they should do to help Juan remove his finger.

### Check Your Learning

**1.** Simple acts of altruism, such as hugging an unhappy peer, emerge at age _____.

**2.** Preschool children who want to act prosocially may not because _____.

**3.** The factors that contribute to prosocial behavior are prosocial skills, _____, and socialization.

**4.** The skills that help children behave prosocially include _____, empathy, and moral reasoning.

**5.** Children are more likely to behave prosocially when they feel responsible, competent, and happy and when _____.

**6.** Parents can encourage prosocial behavior by using reasoning when they discipline their children, _____, having children do household chores that benefit the entire family, and praising children for behaving prosocially.

**7.** In _____, parents link a child's altruistic behavior to an underlying altruistic disposition.

Suppose kindergarten children want to raise money for a gift for one of their classmates who is in the hospital. Based on what you know about the factors that influence children to be altruistic, how would you help the kindergartners plan their fund-raising?

**Answers:** (1) 18 months, (2) their knowledge of appropriate prosocial behaviors is limited, (3) situational influences, (4) perspective taking, (5) the costs of prosocial behavior are minimal, (6) modeling prosocial behavior, (7) dispositional praise

# 12.4

- Change and Stability
- Roots of Aggressive Behavior
- Victims of Aggression

## Aggression

### Learning Objectives

● When does aggressive behavior first emerge? How stable is aggression across childhood, adolescence, and adulthood?

● How do families, television, and the child's own thoughts contribute to aggression?

● Why are some children victims of aggression?

*Every day, 7-year-old Reza follows the same routine when he gets home from school: He watches one action-adventure cartoon on TV after another until it's time for dinner. Reza's mother is disturbed by her son's constant TV viewing, particularly because of the amount of violence in the shows that he likes. Her husband tells her to stop worrying: "Let him watch what he wants to. It won't hurt him and, besides, it keeps him out of your hair."*

If you think back to your years in elementary school, you can probably remember a class "bully"—a child who was always teasing classmates and picking fights. **Such acts typify** *aggression,* **behavior meant to harm others.** Aggressiveness is not the same as assertiveness, even though laypeople often use these words interchangeably. You've probably heard praise for an "aggressive businessperson" or a ballplayer who was "aggressive at running the bases." Psychologists and other behavioral scientists, however, would call these behaviors assertive. Assertive behaviors are goal-directed actions to further the legitimate interests of individuals or the groups they represent, while respecting the rights of other persons. In contrast, aggressive behavior, which may be physical or verbal, is intended to harm, damage, or injure and is carried out without regard for the rights of others.

In this module, we will examine aggressive behavior in children and see how it changes with age. Then we'll examine some causes of children's aggression and, in the process, learn more about the impact of Reza's TV watching on his behavior.

## Change and Stability

By the time youngsters are old enough to play with one another, they show aggression. When 1- and 2-year-olds play, conflicts frequently arise over contested playthings, and youngsters often use aggression to resolve their conflicts (Cummings, Iannotti, & Zahn-Waxler, 1989). Among toddlers and preschoolers, common aggressive behaviors include hitting, kicking, pushing, or biting the other child or, as shown in the photo, trying to grab a toy from another child.

By the end of the preschool years, different forms of aggression are evident (Coie et al., 1991). **The most common form of aggression is *bullying,* in which the aggression is unprovoked and seems to have as its sole goal to intimidate, harass, or humiliate another child.** Bullying is illustrated by a child who spontaneously says, "You're stupid!" and then kicks the child.

Two other forms of aggression are less common than bullying but still occur fairly often. **In *instrumental aggression,* a child uses aggression to achieve an explicit goal.** Instrumental aggression would include shoving a child to get at the head of a lunch line or grabbing a toy away from another child. **In *reactive aggression,* one child's behavior leads to another child's aggression.** Reactive aggressive would include a child who loses a game and then punches the child who won or a child not chosen for the starring role in a play kicking the child who was.

By the end of the preschool years, bullying and instrumental and reactive aggression are common.

Bullying and instrumental and reactive aggression are most likely to be expressed physically in younger children. As children get older, they more often use language to express their aggression. **A particularly common form of verbal aggression is *relational aggression,* in which children try to hurt others by undermining their social relationships.** In relational aggression, which is more typical of girls than boys, children try to hurt others by telling friends to avoid a particular classmate, by spreading malicious gossip, or by making remarks meant to hurt others, such as "You're the dumbest, ugliest kid in third grade and everyone hates you!" (Crick & Werner, 1998; Galen & Underwood, 1997).

Although verbal aggression occurs more often as children grow, physical aggression still occurs during childhood and early adolescence, particularly among boys. In one study, fourth- and seventh-grade boys reported that nearly 50 percent of their conflicts with other boys involved physical aggression (Cairns et al., 1989).

Although forms of aggression change with development, individual children's tendencies to behave aggressively are moderately stable, especially among boys. Kupersmidt and Coie (1990) measured aggressiveness in a group of 11-year-olds by having children list the names of classmates who frequently started fights. Seven years later, more than half the aggressive children had police records, compared to less than 10 percent of the nonaggressive children.

In another study, conducted in Sweden by Stattin and Magnusson (1989), teachers rated the aggressive behavior of more than one thousand 10-year-olds. Their results, shown in the graph, indicate that teachers' ratings accurately predicted subsequent criminal activity. Boys in the least aggressive group committed relatively few criminal offenses of any sort, whereas two-thirds of the most aggressive boys had committed offenses, and nearly half had committed major offenses such as assault, theft, or robbery. Overall, girls committed far fewer offenses, but teachers' ratings of aggressive behavior still predicted which girls were more likely to have criminal records.

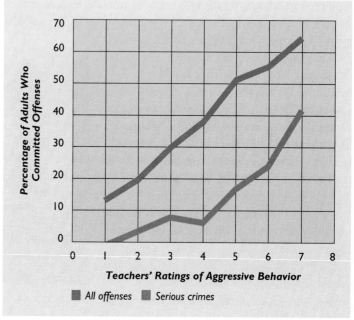

FIG 12–4

Findings from these and similar studies show that aggression is not simply a case of playful pushing and shoving that most children outgrow. To the contrary, a small minority of children who are highly aggressive develop into young adults who create havoc in society. What causes children to behave aggressively? Let's look at some of the roots of aggressive behavior.

## Roots of Aggressive Behavior

For many years, psychologists believed that aggression was caused by frustration. The idea was that when children or adults were blocked from achieving a goal, they became frustrated and they aggressed, often against the interfering person or object. Although frustration can lead to aggression (Berkowitz, 1989), researchers no longer believe that it's the sole cause of aggression, and therefore investigators have looked to other causes, including the family, television, and the child's own thoughts.

### Impact of the Family.
Early family experiences are a prime training ground for learning patterns of aggression. The pioneering work in this area was conducted by Gerald Patterson (1984), whose findings were based almost entirely on careful,

systematic observation of aggressive children in their home environments. One fact that comes through clearly in Patterson's work is that parents and siblings play an enormous role in cultivating aggressive behavior in children, and in ways that are subtle as well as obvious. Many parents and older siblings, for example, use physical punishment or threats to stop aggressive behavior. Although the immediate effect may be to suppress aggression, physical punishment also serves as a model, vividly demonstrating that physical force "works" as a means of controlling others. A parent like the one in the photo is saying, in effect, "You were right. The best way to get people to do what you want, or to stop them from doing what you don't want, is to hit them hard enough."

Not surprisingly, parents' use of harsh physical punishment is associated with aggressive behavior in children. Dodge, Bates, and Pettit (1990) studied children who were so harshly punished physically that they were bruised or needed medical treatment. These children were rated twice as aggressive by both teachers and peers as children who had not experienced such harsh punishment. But strong or aggressive parental responses are not essential in making a child aggressive. When parents are coercive, unresponsive, and emotionally uninvested, their children are more likely to be aggressive (Hart et al., 1998; Rubin, Berkowski, & Parker, 1998).

In many families with aggressive children, a vicious circle seems to develop. Compared to families with nonaggressive children, both aggressive children and their parents are more likely to respond to neutral behavior with aggression. Furthermore, once an aggressive exchange has begun, both parents and children are likely to escalate the exchange, rather than break it off. And once a child has been labeled aggressive by parents and others, that child is more likely to be accused of aggression and to be singled out for punishment, even when the child has been behaving entirely appropriately on the occasion in question (Patterson, 1984). The "aggressive child" will be accused of all things that go wrong—from missing cookies to broken appliances—and other children's misbehaviors will be ignored.

Patterson's work emphasizes the point that hitting a child for aggression does not usually inhibit aggression for very long. What is the best response to a child's aggression? Discourage it either by ignoring it or punishing it while encouraging and rewarding other forms of nonaggressive social behavior. An older brother who simply grabs the remote control from a younger sister should be punished ("No TV for 3 days!"), and then shown a better way to resolve the conflict ("Wait until your sister finishes her program, then ask if you can change the channel. If she says, 'no,' come see me."). Later, the child should be praised for cooperating rather than aggressing ("Thanks for asking your sister instead of just grabbing the remote control.").

Parents are not the only family members who influence children's aggression—siblings matter, too. Among aggressive children, those who have good relationships with their siblings tend to be less aggressive and better adjusted than aggressive children who have conflicted relationships with their siblings (Stormshak et al., 1996). Good sibling relationships may provide aggressive children with opportunities to improve their social skills, or they may provide emotional support for aggressive youngsters.

In families with aggressive children, a vicious circle often develops in which parents and children respond to neutral behavior aggressively and escalate aggressive exchanges.

Finally, it's important to remember that children may elicit some of the very parental behaviors that foster their aggression. That is, Module 2.3 described evocative gene-environment interactions, in which children inherit characteristics that make some experiences more likely than others. In the case of aggression, adoption and twin studies point to hereditary components in aggression (Deater-Deckard & Plomin, 1999; Rowe, Almeida, & Jacobson, 1999). Some children inherit a tendency to be impulsive, to have an angry temperament, or to regulate their own behavior poorly. These characteristics often lead parents to discipline these children more harshly, which then makes them more aggressive (Ge et al., 1996). Thus, parents and child can both contribute to a vicious circle of escalating aggression.

### Impact of Television.

Most children today watch television regularly by the time they're 3 years old, and by the time they turn 15, they have spent more time watching television than going to school. In fact, throughout childhood they will have spent more time watching television than in any other activity except sleep (Liebert & Sprafkin, 1988).

What do children see when they watch all this television? The answer varies somewhat from child to child, but most American children spend considerable time watching action-adventure programs that contain a heavy dose of modeled aggression. Heroes and "good guys" on these shows almost invariably end up in a fight with the "bad guys." The good guys always win, of course, and are typically rewarded with praise, admiration, and sometimes more tangible rewards (such as a vacation in the sun).

What are the effects of watching all these rewarded aggressive models for so long? This question first attracted attention in the mid-1950s. At that time, only about half the households in the United States had television sets, yet the public was already aware of the frequent portrayal of violence in TV programs and worried about its effects on viewers, especially young ones. Anecdotal evidence suggested a link. One 6-year-old fan of Hopalong Cassidy (a TV cowboy of the 1950s) asked his father for real bullets for his toy gun because his toy bullets didn't kill people the way Hopalong's did (Schramm, Lyle, & Parker, 1961).

More than 40 years later, we are still concerned about violence on TV, with good reason. Children's cartoons like the one shown in the photo typically show one violent act every 3 minutes (*violence* meaning use of physical force against another person). And the average American youngster will see several thousand murders on TV before reaching adolescence (Waters, 1993). (If you find these numbers hard to believe, try the activities described in "See for Yourself" at the end of the chapter.)

Both experimental and correlational studies link children's viewing of television violence to increased aggression.

What does research tell us about this steady diet of televised mayhem and violence? According to Bandura's (1986) social cognitive theory, children learn by observing others; so if they watch violent behavior (either real or televised), they will act violently. In fact, laboratory studies conducted in the 1960s by Bandura, Ross, and Ross (1963) made just this point. Children watched specially created TV programs showing an adult kicking and hitting a plastic "Bobo" doll. When children were given the opportunity to play with the doll, those who had seen the TV program were much more likely to behave aggressively toward the doll than children who had not seen the program.

Critics thought the laboratory setting of this and other early studies affected the results, and they doubted that viewing TV violence in more realistic settings would have such pronounced effects on children (Klapper, 1968). Today, however, we know that viewing TV violence "hardens" children, making them more accepting of interpersonal violence. Suppose, for example, a teen is baby-sitting two youngsters who begin to argue and then fight. Baby sitters who are frequent viewers of TV violence are more inclined to let them "slug it out" because they see this as a normal, acceptable way of resolving conflicts (Drabman & Thomas, 1976).

Is this increased tolerance for aggression reflected in children's behavior? Will Reza, the avid cartoon watcher in the vignette at the beginning of the module, become more aggressive? Or, as his father believes, is his TV watching simply "fun"? The answer from research is clear: Reza's father is wrong. Frequent exposure to TV violence makes children more aggressive.

One of the most compelling studies examined the impact of children's TV viewing at age 8 on criminal activity at age 30 (Huesmann, 1986). The graph shows that 8-year-old boys who watched large doses of TV violence had the most extensive criminal records as 30-year-olds. This was true for both males and females, even though females' overall level of criminal activity was much lower.

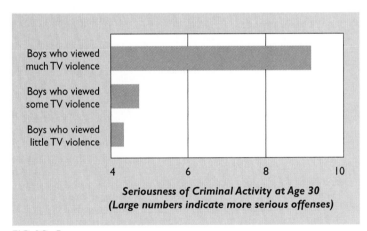

FIG 12–5

These findings are correlational and thus complicate conclusions about cause and effect. But experimental studies demonstrate that viewing televised violence breeds aggression, so it is reasonable to conclude that children who regularly view TV violence resort to aggression in interacting with others. For some, their aggression eventually puts them behind bars. Of course, TV violence is not the sole cause of aggression in children. But it is an important factor in a highly complex process to which parents and peers also contribute.

Cognitive Processes.   The perceptual and cognitive skills described in Chapters 5 through 7 also play a role in aggression. Dodge, Bates, and Pettit (1990) were the first to explore the cognitive aspects of aggression. They discovered that aggressive boys often respond aggressively because they are not skilled at interpreting other people's intentions and, without a clear interpretation in mind, they respond aggressively by default. That is, aggressive boys far too often think, "I don't know what you're up to, and, when in doubt, attack."

From findings like these, Crick and Dodge (1994; Dodge & Crick, 1990) formulated the information-processing model of children's thinking shown in the diagram. According to the model, responding to a social stimulus involves several steps. First, children selectively attend to certain features of the social stimulus but not others, in the manner described on pages 141–143 of Module 5.3. Second, children try to interpret the features that they have processed; that is, they try to give meaning to the social stimulus. Third, children evaluate their goals for the situation. Fourth, children retrieve from memory a behavioral response that is associated with the interpretation and goals of the situation. Fifth, children evaluate this response to determine if it is appropriate. Finally, the child proceeds with the behavior.

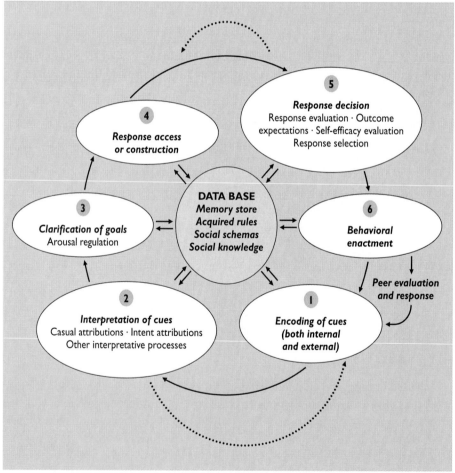

FIG 12–6                                                                          Source: Crick & Dodge, 1994.

Several investigators have shown that aggressive children's processing is biased and restricted in many of these steps, and that this flawed information processing is associated with increased aggression (Crick & Werner, 1998; Egan, Monson, & Perry, 1998). For example, aggressive children are less likely to attend to features that would signal nonhostile motives (Crick & Dodge, 1994). A surprised, chagrined look suggesting that a negative event was an accident is often not processed by aggressive children. And, based on a personal history of being rejected and ridiculed by peers, many aggressive children believe that unfamiliar peers are unfriendly and uncaring (Burks et al., 1999; MacKinnon-Lewis, Rabiner, & Starnes, 1999).

If aggressive children are unskilled at interpreting and responding to others' actions, would training in these skills improve their social behavior? The answer seems to be "yes" (Dodge & Crick, 1990). One approach is to teach aggressive children that aggression is painful and does not solve problems, that intentions can be understood by attending to relevant cues, and that there are more effective, prosocial ways to solve interpersonal disputes. In a study by Guerra and Slaby (1990), adolescents incarcerated for committing violent acts received training designed to increase their understanding of social situations. For example, they were taught to pay attention to nonhostile cues in a social situation, to think of alternative ways of responding to social problems, and to evaluate responses in terms of their consequences. Supervisors at the correctional facility judged that the adolescents were better adjusted following training than before. They were less aggressive, less impulsive, and more flexible in their solutions. Thus, training in social skills can reduce aggressive behavior and increase positive interactions with peers.

To sum up, the vicious cycle of aggression usually begins early. Once youngsters are labeled aggressive, environmental factors may lead them quite unwittingly along an aggressive path. The punishments that parents and teachers dole out may increase the child's hostility and serve as evidence that aggression "works." The child may then choose aggressive companions who further encourage aggressive behavior.

Of course, families are not the sole causes of aggression and violence. Poverty, unemployment, racism, and terrorism create a culture of aggression and violence (Coie & Dodge, 1998). But individual parents can be careful to not set the cycle of aggression in motion. Parents can respond to misbehavior with reasoning instead of physical punishment. And children prone to aggression can be taught equally effective but more prosocial ways to deal with conflict.

## Victims of Aggression

Every aggressive act is directed at someone. Most schoolchildren are the targets of an occasional aggressive act—a shove or kick to gain a desired toy, or a stinging insult by someone trying to save face. However, a small percentage of children are chronic targets of bullying. In both Europe and the United States, about 10 percent of elementary-school children and adolescents are chronic victims of aggression (Kochenderfer & Ladd, 1996; Olweus, 1994). Dorothy Allison provides a frightening glimpse of this victimization in her novel *Bastard Out of Carolina*. As Shannon got on the school bus, she walked

> *past a dozen hooting boys and another dozen flushed and whispering girls. As she made her way up the aisle, I watched each boy slide to the end of his seat to block her sitting with him and every girl flinch away as if whatever Shannon had might be catching. In the seat ahead of us Danny Yarboro leaned far over into the aisle and began making retching noises. "Cootie train! Cootie train" somebody yelled as the bus lurched into motion and Shannon still hadn't found a seat (pp. 153–154).*

In this episode, Shannon is the victim of verbal bullying. But victimization by physical force also occurs frequently: Think of a child who is beat up daily on the playground.

As you can imagine, being tormented daily by their peers is hard on children. Research consistently shows that children who are chronic victims of aggression are often lonely, anxious, and, depressed; they dislike school; and they have low self-esteem (Graham & Juvonen, 1998; Ladd & Ladd, 1998).

Why do some children suffer the sad fate of being victims? A first step in answering this question is to look at victimized children more carefully. A small percentage of victims are actually aggressive themselves (Olweus, 1978; Schwartz et al., 1997). These youngsters often overreact, are restless, and are easily irritated. Their aggressive peers soon learn that these children are easily baited. A group of children will, for example, insult or ridicule them, knowing that they will probably start a fight even though they are outnumbered.

*Some children who are chronic victims of aggression overreact when provoked; others withdraw and submit to aggression.*

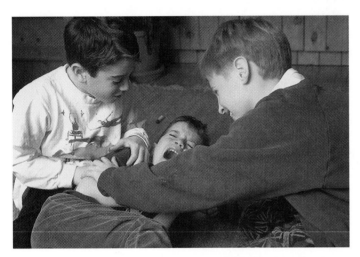

The vast majority of children victimized by aggression are not overreactive, restless, or irritable. Instead, these victims tend to be withdrawn and submissive. They are unwilling or unable to defend themselves from their peers' aggression, and so they are usually referred to as passive victims (Ladd & Ladd, 1998; Olweus, 1978). When attacked, like the child in the photo, they show obvious signs of distress and usually give in to their attackers, thereby rewarding the aggressive behavior.

How do children end up as victims? Family history and parenting help decide. To understand these forces, we need to distinguish victims who overreact from those who respond passively, and within the latter group, distinguish boys from girls. Victims who overreact often come from hostile, punitive, or even abusive family environments (Schwartz et al., 1997). Among passive victims, boys tend to have mothers who are overprotective or emotionally overinvolved with them; in contrast, girls who are passive victims tend to have mothers who are controlling and unresponsive (Ladd & Ladd, 1998).

Victimization is always pathetic and sometimes tragic, but these children can be helped. They can be taught ways of dealing with aggression that are more effective than either overreacting or withdrawing passively (e.g., don't lash out when you're insulted; don't show that you're afraid when you're threatened). In addition, increasing their self-esteem can help. When attacked, children with low self-esteem may think, "I'm a loser and have to put up with this because I have no choice." Increasing children's self-esteem makes them less tolerant of personal attacks (Egan & Perry, 1998). Finally, one of the easiest ways to help victims is to foster their friendships with peers. When children have friends, they're not as likely to be victimized (Hodges, Malone, & Perry, 1997).

### Check Your Learning

1. During the elementary-school years, physical aggression becomes less common but _____ becomes more common, especially among girls.

2. After the preschool years, bullying is the most common form of aggression, but instrumental and _____ aggression also occur often.

3. As adults, highly aggressive children are more likely to _____.

4. Aggressive behavior in children is linked to parents' use of _____ punishment.

**5.** Family influences on children's aggression include parental behavior (including punishment), _____, and inherited tendencies that may evoke harsh parenting.

**6.** Children who regularly watch televised violence are more likely to behave aggressively, and they also _____.

**7.** Aggressive children often interpret neutral stimuli in _____ terms.

**8.** Some chronic victims of aggression tend to overreact when provoked, whereas other chronic victims tend to _____.

 **Crick and Dodge's model of decision making draws upon the information-processing approach to cognitive development presented in Chapter 7. Use that approach to suggest other possible causes of and remedies for children's aggressive behavior.**

**Answers:** (1) verbal aggression, (2) reactive, (3) engage in criminal activity, (4) harsh physical, (5) the quality of children's relationships with siblings, (6) become hardened to violence, (7) hostile or aggressive, (8) withdraw or submit.

# Moral Understanding and Behavior

## IN PERSPECTIVE

12·2

Think back to the nursery filled with the newborn Mother Teresa, Adolf Hitler, Mohandas Gandhi, and Martin Luther King Jr. The material in this chapter doesn't tell us exactly why those newborns developed as they did, following paths of good or evil, but it does help us understand some of the general features involved in the development of moral reasoning and behavior. In Module 12.1, we saw that self-control emerges gradually between 1 and 3 years and is enhanced when parents don't over-control their children but give them opportunities to regulate their own behavior. In Module 12.2, we learned that moral reasoning progresses through stages and includes children's developing understanding of justice, social conventions, and caring for others. In Module 12.3, we saw that prosocial behavior depends upon specific skills, characteristics of the situation, and parenting practices. Finally, in Module 12.4, we found that aggression takes on different forms as children develop, and it can be fostered by parents, television viewing, and children's cognitive processes.

This chapter has some nice illustrations of the theme that *early development is related to later development but not perfectly*. For example, look at the table on page 328, which shows correlations between preschoolers' delayed gratification and several measures in adolescence. Preschoolers who were best able to delay gratification were, as adolescents, less likely to yield to temptation and to be distractible. Yet the correlations were far from 1, which shows that many preschoolers who quickly gave into temptation became adolescents who were not distractible.

The same conclusion is evident in the results in the graph on page 350. Among children who were rated by their teachers as the most aggressive, about 40 percent had committed serious crimes by age 30, yet 60 percent had not. Among the children who were rated least aggressive, more than 90 percent were crime-free as adults, but 5 percent had committed serious crimes. Behaving aggressively in childhood definitely increases the odds of adult criminal activity, but it does not guarantee it.

## See for Yourself

This assignment may seem like a dream come true—you are being required to watch TV. Pick an evening when you can watch network television programming from 8 until 10 p.m. (prime time). Your job is to count each instance of (a) physical force by one person against another and (b) threats of harm to compel another to act against his or her will. Select one network randomly and watch the program for 10 minutes. Then turn to another network and watch that program for 10 minutes. Continue changing the channels every 10 minutes until the 2 hours are over. Of course, it won't be easy to follow the plots of all these programs, but you will end up with a wider sample of programming this way. Repeat this procedure on a Saturday morning when you can watch 2 hours of children's cartoons (not *South Park!*).

Now simply divide the total number of aggressive acts by 4 to estimate the amount of aggression per hour. Then multiply this figure by 11,688 to estimate the number of aggressive acts seen by an average adolescent by age 19. (Why 11,688? Two hours of daily TV viewing—a very conservative number—multiplied by 365¼ days and 16 years.) Then ponder the possible results of that very large number. If your parents told you, nearly 12,000 times, that stealing was okay, would you be more likely to steal? Probably. Then what are the consequences of massive exposure to the televised message, "Solve conflicts with aggression"? See for yourself!

## Resources

*For more information about . . .*

people who have devoted their lives to helping others, read Anne Colby and William Damon's *Some Who Do Care: Contemporary Lives of Moral Commitment* (The Free Press, 1992). The authors, developmental psychologists interested in moral development, use biographies of humanitarians to identify the forces that make some people commit their lives to helping others.

 *the impact of media violence on children,* visit the Web site of the University of Oregon's Media Literacy On-Line Project, **http://interact.uoregon.edu/MediaLit/HomePage**

## Key Terms

# SUMMARY

Moral Understanding and Behavior

12.1 Self-Control
12.2 Reasoning About Moral Issues
12.3 Helping Others
12.4 Aggression

## 12.1 Self-Control

### Beginnings of Self-Control

At 1 year, infants are first aware that others impose demands on them; by 3 years, youngsters can devise plans to regulate their behavior. During the school-age years, children become better able to control their behavior.

Children differ in their self-control, but individuals are fairly consistent across tasks and over time: Preschoolers who have good self-control tend to become adolescents with good self-control.

### Parental Influences

When children observe adults who delay gratification, they are more likely to delay gratification themselves. Similarly, when children observe adults who show little self-control, they are likely to show little self-control themselves. Children who have the best self-control tend to have parents who do not use harsh punishment and who encourage their children to be independent and make their own decisions.

### Temperamental Influences on Self-Control

Temperament helps determine how parents influence their children's self-control. With temperamentally fearful children, gentle reminders are effective; with fearless children, parents should appeal to the attachment relationship.

### Improving Self-Control

Children are better able to regulate their own behavior when they have plans to help them remember the importance of the goal and something to distract them from tempting objects.

## 12.2 Reasoning About Moral Issues

### Piaget's Views

Piaget theorized that 5- to 7-year-olds are in a stage of moral realism. They believe that rules are created by wise adults; therefore, rules must be followed and cannot be changed. At about 8 years, children enter a stage of moral relativism, believing that rules are created by people to help them get along.

### Kohlberg's Theory

Kohlberg proposed that moral reasoning includes preconventional, conventional, and postconventional levels. Moral reasoning is first based on rewards and punishments, and, later, on personal moral codes. As predicted by Kohlberg's theory, people progress through the stages in sequence and do not regress, and morally advanced reasoning is associated with more frequent moral behavior. However, few people attain the most advanced levels, and cultures differ in the bases for moral reasoning.

### Beyond Kohlberg's Theory

Gilligan proposed that females' moral reasoning is based on caring and responsibility for others, not justice. Research does not support consistent sex differences, but has found that males and females both consider caring as well as justice in their moral judgments, depending upon the situation.

The roots of moral reasoning emerge in the preschool years, when children distinguish moral rules from social conventions, distinguish lies from mistakes, and show signs of guilt. According to Eisenberg, children's reasoning about prosocial dilemmas shifts from a self-interested, hedonistic orientation to concern for others based on empathy.

## 12.3 Helping Others

### Development of Prosocial Behavior

Even toddlers know when others are upset, and they try to offer comfort. As children grow older, they more often see the need to act prosocially and are more likely to have the skills to do so.

### Skills Underlying Prosocial Behavior

Children are more likely to behave prosocially when they are able to take others' perspectives, are empathic, and have more advanced moral reasoning.

### Situational Influences

Children's prosocial behavior is often influenced by situational characteristics. Children more often behave prosocially when they feel that they should and can help, when they are in a good mood, and when they believe that they have little to lose by helping.

### Socializing Prosocial Behavior

Parenting approaches that promote prosocial behavior include using reasoning in discipline, modeling prosocial behavior, praising children for prosocial behavior, and having adolescents do family-oriented chores.

## 12.4 Aggression

### Change and Stability

As children grow older, physical aggression decreases and verbal aggression becomes more common. Typical forms of aggression include bullying and instrumental and reactive aggression. Overall levels of aggression are fairly stable, which means that very aggressive young children often become involved in criminal activities as adolescents and adults.

### Roots of Aggressive Behavior

Children's aggressive behavior has been linked to their parents' use of harsh physical punishment. Other factors that contribute to children's aggression are excessive viewing of televised violence and lack of skill at interpreting others' actions and intentions.

### Victims of Aggression

Children who are chronic targets of aggression are often lonely and anxious. Some victims of aggression tend to overreact when provoked; others tend to withdraw and submit. Victimization can be overcome by increasing children's social skills, their self-esteem, and their number of friends.

**13**

**Y**ou barely have the phone to your ear before your brother-in-law shouts, "Jeannie had the baby!" "That's great," you say. "A boy or a girl?" Why is this always the first question people ask new parents? Why are people so interested in a baby's sex? The answer is that being a *boy* or *girl* is not simply a biological distinction. Instead, these terms are associated with distinct social roles. **Like a role in a play, a *social role* is a set of cultural guidelines for how a person should behave.** The social roles associated with gender are among the first that children learn. **Starting in infancy, children learn about *gender roles*—the culturally prescribed behaviors that are considered appropriate for males and females.** As youngsters learn the behaviors assigned to males and females, they begin to identify with one of these groups. **Children forge a *gender identity,* the perception of oneself as either male or female.**

In this chapter, we will see how children acquire a gender role and a gender identity. We'll begin, in Module 13.1, by considering cultural stereotypes of males and females. In Module 13.2, we will examine actual psychological differences between boys and girls. In Module 13.3, we'll focus on how children come to identify with one sex. Finally, in Module 13.4, we'll discuss recent changes in gender roles. Throughout this chapter, I'll use *sex* to refer to aspects of males and females that are clearly biological (such as differences in anatomy) and *gender* to refer all other characteristics that relate to maleness and femaleness.

# Gender and Development

**13.1**    **Gender Stereotypes**

**13.2**    **Differences Related to Gender**

**13.3**    **Gender Identity**

**13.4**    **Gender Roles in Transition**

# 13.1

- How Do We View Men and Women?
- Learning Gender Stereotypes

## Gender Stereotypes

### Learning Objectives

- What are gender stereotypes, and how do they differ for males and females?
- How do gender stereotypes influence behavior?
- When do children learn their culture's stereotypes for males and females?

*When Nancy was 7 months pregnant, her 11-year-old son Clark announced that he really wanted a brother, not a sister. Clark explained, "A sister would drive me crazy. Girls never make up their minds about stuff, and they get all worked up over nothin'." "Where did Clark get these ideas?" Nancy wondered. "Is this typical for 11-year-olds?"*

All cultures have *gender stereotypes*—beliefs about how males and females differ in personality traits, interests, and behaviors. Of course, because stereotypes are beliefs, they may or may not be true. In this module, we'll look at the features associated with gender stereotypes and discover when children like Clark learn about gender stereotypes.

### How Do We View Men and Women?

"Terry is active, independent, competitive, and aggressive." As you were reading this sentence, you probably assumed that Terry was a male. Why? Although Terry is a common name for both males and females, the adjectives used to describe Terry are more commonly associated with men than with women. The table lists traits that college students typically associate with males and females.

| Features Judged by College Students to Be Characteristically Male or Female ||
| --- | --- |
| **Male** | **Female** |
| Independent | Emotional |
| Aggressive | Home-oriented |
| Not excitable | Kind |
| Skilled in business | Cries easily |
| Mechanical aptitude | Creative |
| Outspoken | Considerate |
| Acts as a leader | Devotes self to others |
| Self-confident | Needs approval |
| Ambitious | Gentle |
| Not easily influenced | Aware of others' feelings |
| Dominant | Excitable |
| Based on T. L. Ruble, 1983 ||

TABLE 13–1

**The traits associated with males are called *instrumental* because they describe individuals who act on the world and influence it. In contrast, the traits associated with females are called *expressive*, because they describe emotional functioning and individuals who value interpersonal relationships.**

American men and women both believe that instrumental traits typify males whereas expressive traits typify females (Lutz & Ruble, 1995; Ruble, 1983; Williams & Best, 1990). But are these views shared by adults worldwide? The "Cultural Influences" feature has the answer.

### Around the World with Four Gender Stereotypes

Are men seen as aggressive and independent worldwide? And are women seen as emotional and gentle worldwide? Or are these stereotypes of men and women unique to the United States? John Williams and Deborah Best (1990) addressed these questions in an ambitious project involving 300 different traits and participants in 30 countries. The graphs present the results for just 4 traits and 7 countries. You can see that each trait shows considerable cultural variation. For example, virtually all American participants consider men aggressive, but only a slight majority of Nigerian participants do. Thus, American views of men and women are not shared worldwide. In fact, what's notable about the research results is that Americans' gender stereotypes are more extreme than are those in any other country listed. Keep this in mind as you think about what men and women can and cannot do and what they should and should not do. Your ideas about gender are shaped by your culture's beliefs, which are *not* held universally. ●

Compared to people in other countries, American adults have more extreme stereotypes of men and women.

FIG 13–1

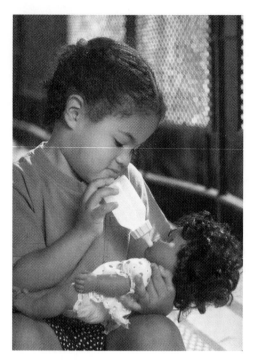

It's important to understand our tendency to stereotype gender behavior because stereotypes are very limiting. If we have stereotyped views, we expect males to act in particular ways and females to act in other ways, and we respond to males and females solely on the basis of gender, not as individuals. For example, do you assume the youngster in the photo is a girl based on her taste in toys? Assuming the child is a girl would, in turn, probably lead you to think she plays more quietly and is more easily frightened than if you assume the child is a boy (Stern & Karraker, 1989). Making stereotyped assumptions about gender leads to a whole host of inferences about behavior and personality that may not be true.

When do children begin to learn their culture's stereotypes for males and females? We'll answer this question in the next section.

### Learning Gender Stereotypes

By the time children enter elementary school, they are well on their way to forming gender stereotypes; and by the time they complete elementary school, their ideas of gender stereotypes are virtually as well formed as adults'. Children's growing understanding of gender stereotypes was demonstrated in a study by Deborah Best and her colleagues (1977). Children were asked if 16 stereotypically masculine and 16 stereotypically feminine traits were more typical of boys or girls. At age 5, boys and girls judged one-third of the traits the way adults would; by age 11, they judged about 90 percent of the traits according to adult stereotypes. The table at the top of page 365 shows the traits that children judged stereotypically at ages 5 and 11. A check means that boys and girls agreed with the listed stereotype.

Obviously, by 11 years, children have adultlike knowledge of gender stereotypes; in this regard, Clark's view of girls in the opening vignette is quite typical for his age. Children understand gender stereotypes by the time they enter kindergarten, and their understanding grows throughout the elementary-school years (Etaugh & Liss, 1992).

As children develop, they also begin to understand that gender stereotypes do not always apply; older children are more willing than younger children to ignore stereotypes when judging other children. In one study (Martin, 1989), 4- and 8-year-olds were told about hypothetical children, some of whom had same-sex friends and gender-role-appropriate interests. Others had other-sex friends and gender-role-inappropriate interests: "Tommy is a 5-year-old boy whose best friend is a girl. Tommy likes to iron with an ironing board." Children were asked how much the hypothetical child would like to play with masculine and feminine toys.

*By the end of elementary school, children are very familiar with adults' stereotypes of males and females and they understand that these stereotypes are not binding on individuals.*

The key finding was that 4-year-olds based their judgments solely on the hypothetical child's sex: The hypothetical boys would like masculine toys, the hypothetical girls, the feminine ones. Even though Tommy likes to play with a girl and pretend to iron, 4-year-olds thought he would want to play with masculine toys. The 8-year-olds, however, considered the hypothetical child's stated interests. They believed, for example, that a boy whose interests were not stereotypic would be more interested in feminine toys. They believed Tommy would want to play with a doll because he likes to iron clothes.

Thus, although older children are more familiar with gender stereotypes, they see these stereotypes as general guidelines for behavior that are not necessarily binding

## Children's Stereotypes of Boys and Girls

| Boys are . . . | | | Girls are . . . | | |
|---|---|---|---|---|---|
| | *5-year-olds* | *11-year-olds* | | *5-year-olds* | *11-year-olds* |
| strong | ✓ | ✓ | emotional | ✓ | ✓ |
| aggressive | ✓ | ✓ | gentle | ✓ | ✓ |
| disorderly | ✓ | ✓ | soft-hearted | ✓ | ✓ |
| cruel | ✓ | ✓ | affectionate | ✓ | ✓ |
| coarse | ✓ | ✓ | weak | ✓ | ✓ |
| ambitious | ✓ | ✓ | appreciative | | ✓ |
| dominant | ✓ | ✓ | excitable | | ✓ |
| adventurous | | ✓ | sophisticated | | ✓ |
| independent | | ✓ | fickle | | ✓ |
| loud | | ✓ | meek | | ✓ |
| boastful | | ✓ | submissive | | ✓ |
| jolly | | ✓ | whiny | | ✓ |
| steady | | ✓ | talkative | | ✓ |
| confident | | ✓ | frivolous | | ✓ |

Based on Best et al., 1977

TABLE 13–2

for all boys and girls (Signorella, Bigler, & Liben, 1993; Taylor, 1996). In fact, older children consider gender stereotypes less binding than many social conventions and moral rules (Levy, Taylor, & Gelman, 1995; Serbin, Powlishta, & Gulko, 1993).

Increased age is not the only factor leading to more flexible views of stereotypes. Social class also contributes. Adolescents and young adults (but not children) from middle-class homes tend to have more flexible ideas about gender than individuals from lower-class homes (e.g., Serbin et al., 1993). This difference may be due to education: Better educated middle-class parents may impart less rigid views of gender to their children.

Ethnicity is another factor associated with flexible views of gender. Some studies find that African American youngsters have more flexible ideas about gender than their European American peers (e.g., Bardwell, Cochran, & Walker, 1986). Compared to European American mothers, African American mothers are more frequently employed outside the home, and this may contribute to their children's more open attitudes.

At this point, perhaps you're wondering whether there's any truth to gender stereotypes. For example, are boys really more dominant than girls? Are girls really more excitable than boys? For answers to these questions, let's go to Module 13.2.

## Check Your Learning

**1.** Male gender stereotypes include instrumental traits, while female gender stereotypes emphasize _____ traits.

**2.** Compared to adults from other countries, Americans' view on gender are _____ .

3. Gender stereotypes are harmful because they lead people to make inferences about a child's behavior or personality based solely on the child's _____, not on individual characteristics.

4. Compared to younger children, older children know more of the contents of gender stereotypes and they know that _____.

5. _____-class adolescents and adults tend to have more flexible views of gender roles, as do African American children.

 **Examine the traits listed in the table on page 365. How might Piaget have explained the differences between 5- and 11-year-olds' responses?**

**Answers:** (1) expressive, (2) more stereotyped, (3) sex, (4) gender stereotypes are not binding on all boys and girls, (5) Middle

# 13.2

- Differences in Physical Development and Behavior
- Differences in Intellectual Abilities and Achievement
- Differences in Personality and Social Behavior
- Frank Talk About Gender Differences

# Differences Related to Gender

## Learning Objectives

- How do boys and girls differ in physical development, intellectual abilities, and social behavior?

- What factors are responsible for these gender differences?

- What are the implications of these gender differences for boys' and girls' development?

*All through elementary and middle school, Darlene was one of the best students. When she moved into high school, she was particularly proud that she always got the highest grades in her math classes. But she noticed that, as each year went by, even though she got the best grades in math, the boys got higher scores on the standardized tests given every spring.*

Is Darlene's experience typical? Do girls usually get higher grades than boys in math class but lower scores on standardized tests? Some of the first answers to these questions came in *The Psychology of Sex Differences,* a book by Eleanor Maccoby and Carol Jacklin published in 1974. Maccoby and Jacklin did no new research; rather, they summarized results from approximately 1,500 research studies that had been done over the years on gender differences. According to Maccoby and Jacklin,

*physical differences between the sexes are obvious and universal. The psychological differences are not. The folklore that has grown up about them is often vague and inconsistent. We believe there is a great deal of myth in the popular view about sex differences. There is also some substance. . . . we hope to be able to identify the generalizations that may be relied upon with some confidence (p. 3).*

Maccoby and Jacklin's methodology was quite simple: First they searched psychological journals for studies on gender differences. Then they categorized the studies according to the behaviors that were studied and the ages of the children. Finally, they examined the results for gender differences. For example, girls are thought to be more sensitive to touch, but Maccoby and Jacklin found that, in 6 studies of touch sensitivity, infant boys and girls were equally sensitive. In 3 other studies, girls were more sensitive. In 11 studies of older children and adults, 9 found no differences and 2 found that females were more sensitive. Maccoby and Jacklin concluded that "if a sex difference exists in touch sensitivity . . . our survey has revealed only hints of it" (1974, p. 23).

Maccoby and Jacklin examined many studies of cognition and social behavior, and concluded that gender differences had been established in only four areas: Girls have greater verbal ability whereas boys have greater mathematical and visual-spatial ability, and boys are more aggressive than girls. Just as important, Maccoby and Jacklin did *not* find evidence to support popular ideas that girls are more social and suggestible than boys, have lower self-esteem, are less analytic in thinking, and lack achievement motivation.

Some critics challenged Maccoby and Jacklin on the grounds that they had included some weak studies and defined behaviors in ways that other researchers might not (Block, 1976). Others questioned outright findings about some specific behaviors. The debate stimulated more research; some of this research applied new statistical techniques that allowed for finer analysis (Eagly, 1995). Many developmentalists now believe that gender differences are more extensive than Maccoby and Jacklin suggested, but their book remains a classic because its comprehensiveness provided an excellent starting point for further research.

In the remainder of this module, we'll see what we've discovered about gender differences since Maccoby and Jacklin did their analysis. We'll focus on differences in physical development, cognitive processes, and social behavior.

> Maccoby and Jacklin concluded that girls have greater verbal ability than boys, but that boys have greater mathematical and spatial abilities and are more aggressive.

### Differences in Physical Development and Behavior

Of course, differences in the reproductive system are what differentiate boys and girls, along with differences in secondary sex characteristics such as lower voices and facial hair in boys and breast development and wider hips in girls. Boys are usually larger and stronger than girls, which means that they often physically outperform girls. You can see the difference at high school track meets: Boys usually run faster, jump higher, and throw objects farther and more accurately. Outside of sports, on tasks that involve fine-motor coordination, such as tracing and drawing, girls do better than boys (Thomas & French, 1985).

As infants, boys are more active than girls, and this difference increases during childhood (Eaton & Enns, 1986). For example, in a classroom, boys are more likely than girls to have a hard time sitting still. On a playground like the one in the photos, boys more often play vigorously and girls, quietly. And, recall from Module 5.3 that boys are three times more likely than girls to be diagnosed with attention deficit hyperactivity disorder.

Girls tend to be healthier than boys. Female embryos are more likely than male embryos to survive prenatal development. This trend continues after birth. Infant boys are more prone to birth complications, and throughout life boys are more prone to many diseases and dysfunctions (Jacklin, 1989). Finally, adolescent boys and young men are more likely to engage in unhealthy, risk-taking behaviors, including drinking, reckless driving, and sexual activity (Byrnes, Miller, & Schafer, 1999).

To summarize, boys tend to be bigger, stronger, and more active; girls tend to have better fine-motor coordination and to be healthier. In the next section, which concerns intellectual skills, you'll again see that gender differences vary from one skill to the next.

## Differences in Intellectual Abilities and Achievement

Of the four gender-based differences discovered by Maccoby and Jacklin (1974), three concern intellectual skills: Girls tend to have greater verbal skill but boys tend to have greater mathematical and visual-spatial skill. Since Maccoby and Jacklin's work, we've learned much about the nature of gender differences in these areas.

Verbal Ability.  When Janet Hyde and Marcia Linn (1988) updated Maccoby and Jacklin's summary of research, they found that females had greater verbal ability in 75 percent of the 165 studies that they analyzed. Usually the difference was small. But it was larger for general measures of verbal ability, unscrambling scrambled words, and quality of speech production. Girls also read, write, and spell better than boys (Feingold, 1993; Hedges & Nowell, 1995), and more boys have reading and other language-related problems such as stuttering (Halpern, 1986).

Why are girls more talented verbally than boys? Part of the explanation may lie in biology. The left hemisphere of the brain, which is central to language (see Module 4.3), may mature more rapidly in girls than in boys (Diamond et al., 1983). But experience also contributes. Reading, for instance, is often stereotyped as an activity for girls (Huston, 1983). Consequently, girls are more willing than boys to invest time and effort in mastering verbal skills like reading.

Spatial Ability.   In Module 8.1, you saw that spatial ability is a component of most models of intelligence. **One aspect of spatial ability is *mental rotation*, the ability to imagine how an object will look after it has been moved in space.** The items in the figure below test mental rotation: The task is to determine which of the figures labeled

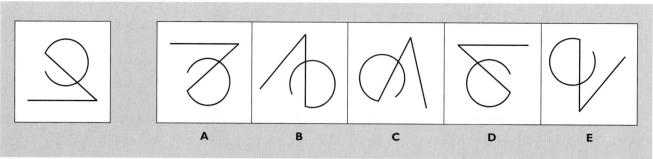

FIG 13–2

Source: Pellegrino & Kail, 1982.

A through E are rotated versions of the figure in the box on the left. From childhood on, boys tend to have better mental rotation skill than girls (Vederhus & Krekling, 1996; Voyer, Voyer, & Bryden, 1995). (The correct answers are C and D.)

Spatial ability also involves determining relations between objects in space while ignoring distracting information. For example, which of the tilted bottles of water in the figure has the waterline drawn correctly? In an upright bottle, the waterline is at right angles to the sides of the bottle, but selecting the correct answer for the tilted bottle (A, in this case) requires that you ignore the conflicting perceptual information provided by the sides of the bottle. From adolescence on, boys are more accurate than girls on these kinds of spatial tasks (Voyer, Voyer, & Bryden, 1995).

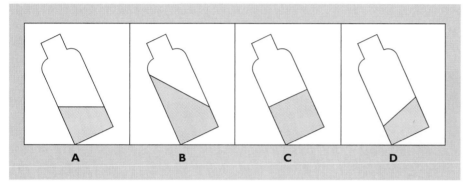

FIG 13–3

Explanations for gender differences in spatial ability abound:

- A recessive gene on the X chromosome may promote spatial ability (Thomas & Kail, 1991). In this type of inheritance, males only have to inherit a recessive gene from their mother to score high in spatial ability, but females must inherit the recessive gene from both parents.

- The right hemisphere of the brain may be more specialized for spatial processing in males than in females, perhaps because boys mature more slowly than girls (Waber, 1977).

- Boys are more likely than girls to participate in activities that foster spatial skill, such as estimating the trajectory of an object moving through space (e.g., a baseball), using two-dimensional plans to assemble an object such as a scale model (Baenninger & Newcombe, 1995), or, like the boys in the photo, playing video games that involve visual-perceptual skills (Okagaki & Frensch, 1994).

Each of these possible explanations of gender differences in spatial ability is supported by some studies but not by others. And, of course, the explanations are not necessarily mutually exclusive. Biological and experiential forces may both contribute to gender differences in spatial ability, just as both contribute to gender differences in verbal ability. Thus, parents and others can foster verbal and spatial abilities in boys and girls because each is influenced considerably by experience.

**Mathematics.**    Gender differences in math skill are complex. Let's start with performance on standardized math achievement tests. Standardized tests emphasize computational skills during the elementary- and middle-school years, and girls usually score higher than boys. Solving problems and applying math concepts are emphasized in high school and college; here boys often score higher than girls. Thus, initially girls excel in math computation, but later boys excel in math problem solving (Hyde, Fennema, & Lamon, 1990). The gender difference remains even when boys and girls take an equal number of math courses (Kimball, 1989).

The gender difference in performance on math achievement tests is not restricted to the United States. Beller and Gafni (1996) analyzed math scores from the International Assessment of Educational Progress. For 9-year-olds, gender differences were inconsistent; for 13-year-olds, boys' scores exceeded girls' scores in 17 of the 20 countries studied, including Brazil, China, Ireland, and Israel.

Paradoxically, the results are different for grades in math courses. Often no differences are detected in boys' and girls' grades, but when a difference occurs, it invariably favors girls. This is even true for courses in high school and college—when males are getting higher scores on achievement tests (Kimball, 1989). Darlene's experience,

described in the module-opening vignette, is common: Girls get better grades in math courses but lower scores on standardized tests of math achievement.

Why should females get lower scores on tests of math achievement but higher grades in math courses? One idea is that girls are confident when dealing with relatively familiar math problems on classroom tests. However, when girls like the ones in the photo take standardized achievement tests that have many novel problems, they are less confident and don't do as well. Boys are confident in their math skills and like the challenge of novel problems on standardized tests (Kimball, 1989). Because math is stereotyped as a masculine pursuit, girls tend to lack confidence in their math skills and are less likely to succeed in math (Casey, Nuttall, & Pezaris, 1997; Crawford, Chaffin, & Fitton, 1995).

This argument probably sounds familiar to you because the explanation is basically the same one used to explain gender differences in verbal skill: Boys succeed in math and girls succeed in language because children in each group are encouraged to pursue activities consistent with gender stereotypes.

Because of findings like these, educators have worked hard to reduce gender stereotypes associated with math (Secada, Fennema, & Adajian, 1995). Unfortunately, gender differences in math continue. Hedges and Nowell (1995) evaluated data from the National Assessment of Educational Progress (NAEP), which administers standardized tests in several areas to approximately 70,000 to 100,000 American students in grades 3, 7, and 11. The researchers found that the gender difference in math achievement has been remarkably constant since the NAEP test was first administered in 1978.

What does it mean that gender differences were just as large in the 1990s as they were in the 1970s? Perhaps stereotypes for language and math have not changed. Maybe math was still "a guy thing" in the 1990s, despite decades of efforts to show girls that math is just as appropriate and interesting a subject for them and that girls can be just as successful in math as boys.

Another possibility is that biological factors contribute to the gender difference in math. In particular, spatial ability, which we just discussed, may play a role. Some aspects of math are easier to

Girls often get higher grades than boys in math courses, but boys typically get higher scores on standardized tests of math achievement.

understand if they can be visualized mentally. For example, being able to imagine a three-dimensional space where lines and planes intersect simplifies learning geometry. Boys may be more successful in some areas of math because they more often have the spatial skills that promote understanding (Casey et al., 1997).

Most likely, the gender difference in math is due to multiple factors. Some have roots in biology (e.g., spatial skill) but others have roots in experience (e.g., stereotypes concerning math). As you'll see in the next section, nature and nurture also contribute to gender differences in personality and social behavior.

## Differences in Personality and Social Behavior

Maccoby and Jacklin (1974) found convincing evidence of only one gender difference in personality and social behavior: Boys were more aggressive than girls. In this section, we'll see what research in the 25-plus years since has found.

### Aggressive Behavior.
No one doubts Maccoby and Jacklin's conclusion that boys are more aggressive physically than girls. As mentioned in Module 12.4 and as you can see in the photos, the gender difference in physical aggression is readily observed. No matter how you slice it, boys *are* more aggressive than girls (Collaer & Hines, 1995; Knight, Fabes, & Higgins, 1996). Of course, some qualifications apply. Boys are not always aggressive. They are, for example, more likely to be physically aggressive toward other boys than toward girls (Maccoby & Jacklin, 1980): Boys may try to beat up other boys, but, as a general rule, they don't try to beat up girls. And, when they're provoked, girls can be physically aggressive, too (Bettencourt & Miller, 1996).

Because boys and men are more aggressive in virtually all cultures and because males in nonhuman species are also more aggressive, scientists are convinced that biology contributes heavily to this gender difference. **Aggressive behavior has been linked to *androgens*, hormones secreted by the testes.** Androgens do not lead to aggression directly. Instead, androgens make it more likely that boys will be aggressive by making boys more excited or angry and by making boys stronger (e.g., Marcus et al., 1985).

Just because hormones are involved, though, we can't ignore experience. The media are filled with aggressive male models—from John Wayne to Jedi Knights—

*Boys are physically more aggressive than girls, who more often aggress by trying to damage other children's relationships with peers.*

who are rewarded for their behavior. Furthermore, parents are more likely to use physical punishment with sons than with daughters and are more tolerant of aggressive behavior in sons than in daughters (Block, 1978; Condry & Ross, 1985). As we saw in Module 12.4, these are just the sort of experiences that precipitate a vicious cycle of increasing aggression, and this cycle is much more common for boys than girls. Although androgens may make boys more prone to aggression, experience encourages boys rather than girls to express their aggression physically.

Although boys' aggression may be more obvious because of its physical nature, girls can be aggressive, too, resorting to nonphysical forms such as spreading rumors or malicious gossip (Cairns et al., 1989). The "Focus on Research" feature describes a study that shows how boys and girls differ in their aggressive behavior.

**FOCUS ON RESEARCH**

### Aggression Appears in Boys and Girls Differently

*Who were the investigators, and what was the aim of the study?* Through the early 1990s, most research on children's aggression focused on physical aggression. Yet children do not have to hit, kick, or push others to harm them. In relational aggression, children try to hurt others by damaging their relationships with peers. They may call children names, make fun of them, spread rumors about them, or—just as bad—pointedly ignore them. Nicki Crick and Jennifer Grotpeter (1995) conducted a study to test the hypothesis that, although physical aggression may be more common among boys, relational aggression is more common among girls.

*How did the investigators measure the topic of interest?* Crick and Grotpeter asked children to complete questionnaires nominating peers who fit different descriptions. To measure physical aggression, children nominated peers who fit descriptions such as "hits, pushes" and "starts fights." For relational aggression, they nominated peers who fit descriptions such as "when mad at a person, ignores them or stops talking to them" and "when mad, gets even by keeping the person from being in their group of friends." Children also completed other questionnaires that measured anxiety, depression, and peer relationships.

*Who were the children in the study?* The researchers tested 491 children in grades 3 to 6 in public schools in the Midwest United States. The sample included 60 percent European American children and 37 percent African American children.

*What was the design of the study?* This study was correlational because Crick and Grotpeter were interested in the relation that existed naturally between two variables—children's gender and form of aggression. Although the study included children of different ages, Crick and Grotpeter did not examine age differences in aggression. Thus, the study was neither cross-sectional nor longitudinal.

*Were there ethical concerns with the study?* No. The questionnaires were completed anonymously, so children did not know if peers had nominated them for undesirable characteristics. Crick and Grotpeter obtained permission from the parents for the children to participate.

*What were the results?* Based on how often boys and girls were nominated for different descriptions, Crick and Grotpeter placed each child in one of four categories: not aggressive, physically aggressive, relationally aggressive, or physically *and* relationally aggressive. The graph shows the percentage of children in each category. Thankfully, most children were not aggressive. The top pair of bars shows that nearly three-fourths of the boys and girls in the study were in this category. Unfortunately, the bottom bars show that a small percentage of children have mastered both physical and relational aggression.

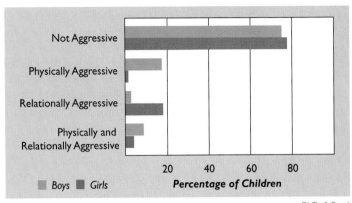

FIG 13–4

It is the other two categories, however, that are critical to Crick and Grotpeter's hypothesis. They expected to find a greater percentage of boys who were physically aggressive and a greater percentage of girls who were relationally aggressive, and the two middle pairs of bars show exactly this pattern. Many boys but few girls relied solely upon physical aggression; in contrast, many girls but few boys relied solely upon relational aggression.

*What did the investigators conclude?* Boys and girls are both aggressive; the genders simply differ in their preferred methods of aggression. When they want to harm peers, boys try to hurt them physically but girls try to damage their relationships with peers. Crick and Grotpeter suggest that previous research underestimated girls' aggressiveness because relational aggression is not as obvious to observers as physical aggression. ●

Emotional Sensitivity.   According to the stereotypes listed on page 365, girls are better able to express their emotions and interpret others' emotions. In fact, this is a gender difference supported by research (Hall & Halberstadt, 1981; Weinberg et al., 1999). But does greater emotional sensitivity mean that girls are more empathic? Are they better able to experience another person's emotions? Girls are more willing to admit to feelings, but generally boys and girls are equally able to feel what others are feeling (Zahn-Waxler et al., 1992), just as both boys and girls in the photo are concerned by the distressed child.

Most developmentalists believe that the gender difference in emotional sensitivity is largely due to experience. Parents are more "feeling-oriented" with daughters than with sons. They are more likely to talk about emotions with daughters than with sons and to emphasize the importance of considering others' feelings (Kuebli, Butler, & Fivush, 1995; Zahn-Waxler, Cole, & Barrett, 1991).

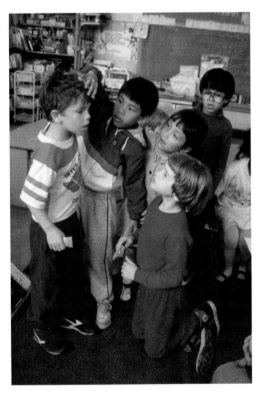

Social Influence.   Another gender stereotype is that females are more easily influenced by others, more persuadable. In fact, young girls are more likely than young boys to comply with an adult's request, and they are more likely to seek an adult's help (Jacklin & Maccoby, 1978). Girls and women are also influenced more than boys and men by persuasive messages and others' behavior, especially when they are under group pressure (Becker, 1986; Eagly, Karau, & Makhijani, 1995). However, these gender differences may stem from the fact that females value group harmony more than boys and thus *seem* to give in to others (Miller, Danaher, & Forbes, 1986). For instance, at a meeting to plan a school function, girls are just as likely as boys to recognize the flaws in a bad idea, but girls are more willing to go along simply because they don't want the group to start arguing.

## Frank Talk About Gender Differences

et's review the gender differences we've discussed in this module. Research conducted in the quarter century since Maccoby and Jacklin's (1974) landmark work indicates that boys are bigger, stronger, and more active but that girls are healthier; girls excel in verbal ability but boys excel in spatial ability and math; boys are more aggressive physically but girls are more aggressive relationally, understand emotions better, and are more readily influenced by others. What should we make of these differences? What do they tell us about the experience of growing up male versus growing up female?

First, remember that the gender differences described in this module represent differences in the *averages* for boys and girls. These differences are all relatively small and are illustrated in the figure. You can see that small differences in group averages mean that boys' and girls' abilities overlap substantially. For example, many girls have greater spatial skill than boys; many boys are more susceptible to social influence than girls. A boy who wants to become a writer or a girl who wants to become a mathematician should not be deterred because of small differences in average scores for boys and girls.

FIG 13–5

At the same time, even small differences in group averages produce substantial differences at the extremes of ability, at the ends of distributions like those shown in the diagram. Thus, for example, even though the average gender difference in verbal ability is small, there are many more boys with very low ability, which explains why boys are far more likely to have reading or language disabilities.

Second, think about the huge number of abilities, behaviors, and traits that do not appear in this module. Boys and girls do not differ in many, many aspects of cognition, personality, and social behavior, a point that is easily lost when focusing on gender differences. In reality, a list of ways that boys and girls are similar is much longer than a list of differences. In cognitive processing, memory, and understanding people—to name just a few areas—boys and girls are much more alike than different. If development is a journey, both boys and girls have many choices as they travel; few if any routes have signs that say "for girls only" or "for boys only."

## Check Your Learning

1. Maccoby and Jacklin found that girls had greater verbal skill, that boys excelled in math and visual-spatial ability, and that boys _____.

2. In physical development and behavior, boys are bigger, stronger, and _____.

3. Girls may excel in verbal ability because of gender differences in brain development and because _____.

4. Explanations for the gender difference in spatial ability include a recessive gene, brain specialization, and _____.

5. In math, girls get better grades but boys _____.

6. Boys specialize in physical aggression; girls specialize in _____.

7. When working in groups, girls may be more influenced by other group members than boys because _____.

8. A small average gender difference can still produce large differences in _____.

 According to Hedges and Nowell's (1995) results (described on page 370), gender differences in math have not become smaller in the past quarter century. One interpretation of this finding is that gender stereotypes of math have not changed much over this period of time. What could be done to encourage girls toward more math?

**Answers:** (1) were more aggressive, (2) more active, (3) verbal activities such as reading are stereotyped as "for girls," (4) differences in experiences that promote spatial skill, (5) get higher scores on standardized tests, (6) relational aggression, (7) girls put greater emphasis on maintaining group harmony, (8) the number of boys and girls at the ends of distributions

## Gender Identity

### Learning Objectives

- How do parents, peers, and the media influence children's learning of gender roles?

- How do cognitive theories explain children's learning of gender roles?

- How does biology influence children's learning of gender roles?

> *Taryn, who has just turned 4, knows that she's a girl but is convinced that she'll grow up to be a man. Taryn plays almost exclusively with boys and her favorite toys are trucks and cars. Taryn tells her parents that when she's bigger, she'll grow a beard and will be a daddy. Taryn's father is confident that his daughter's ideas are a natural part of a preschooler's limited understanding of gender, but her mother wonders if they've neglected some important aspect of Taryn's upbringing.*

According to the old saying, "Boys will be boys and girls will be girls," but how, in fact, do boys become boys and girls become girls when it comes to gender roles? That is, how do children acquire their culture's roles for males and females? And how do

**13.3**

The Socializing Influences of People and the Media

Cognitive Theories of Gender Identity

Biological Influences

children develop a sense of identity as a male or female? We'll answer these questions in this module and, as we do, learn whether Taryn's wish to grow up to be a man is typical for youngsters her age.

## The Socializing Influences of People and the Media

Folklore holds that parents and other adults—teachers and television characters, for example—directly shape children's behavior toward the roles associated with their sex. Boys are rewarded for boyish behavior and punished for girlish behavior.

The folklore even has a theoretical basis: According to social learning theorists like Albert Bandura (1977, 1986) and Walter Mischel (1970), children learn gender roles in much the same way that they learn other social behaviors: through reinforcement and observational learning. Parents and others thus shape appropriate gender roles in children, and children learn what their culture considers appropriate behavior for males and females by simply watching how adults and peers act. How well does research support social learning theory? Let's look first at research done with parents.

> Parents treat sons and daughters similarly, except for gender-related behavior.

**Parents.** An extensive analysis of 172 studies involving 27,836 children (Lytton & Romney, 1991) found that parents tend to treat sons and daughters similarly except when it comes to gender-related behavior. That is, parents interact equally with sons and daughters, are equally warm to both, and encourage both sons and daughters to achieve and be independent. But in behavior related to gender roles, parents respond differently to sons and daughters. Activities such as playing with dolls, dressing up, or helping an adult are more often encouraged in daughters than in sons; rough-and-tumble play and playing with blocks are more encouraged in sons than in daughters. Parents also assign sons and daughters different household chores. Daughters tend to be assigned stereotypically female chores such as washing dishes or housecleaning, whereas sons are assigned stereotypically male chores such as taking out the garbage or mowing the lawn (McHale et al., 1990).

Fathers are more likely than mothers to treat sons and daughters differently. More than mothers, fathers like the one in the photo often encourage gender-related play. Fathers also push their sons more but accept dependence in their daughters (Snow, Jacklin, & Maccoby, 1983). A father, for example, may urge his frightened young son to jump off the diving board ("Be a man!") but not be so insistent with his daughter ("That's okay, honey"). Apparently mothers are more likely to respond based on their knowledge of the individual child's needs, but fathers respond based on gender stereotypes. A mother responds to her son knowing that he's smart but unsure of himself; a father may respond because of what he thinks boys should be like.

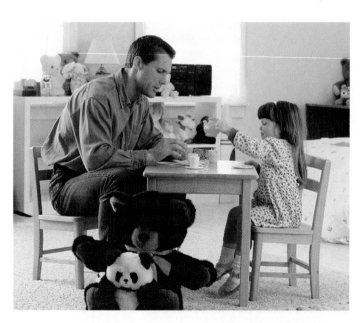

**Teachers.** After parents, teachers may be the most influential adults in children's lives. Yet we know surprisingly little about how exactly teachers influence children's learning of gender roles. Two facts do stand out. First, most teachers favor behaviors that are considered feminine—being task oriented, nondisruptive, and perhaps dependent—believing that they contribute to a classroom atmosphere that is more conducive to effective teaching and learning. Teachers encourage both boys and girls to be obedient rather than assertive (Minuchin & Shapiro, 1983). Second, teachers spend more time interacting with boys than girls. Teachers praise boys more for their schoolwork and spend more time scolding them for disruptive classroom behavior (Block, 1983). Teachers' emphasis on obedience and their spending more time with boys may promote gender role learning, but researchers have not yet determined how this happens.

**Peers.**  By 3 years, most children's play shows the impact of gender stereotypes—boys prefer blocks and trucks whereas girls prefer tea sets and dolls—and youngsters are critical of peers who engage in cross-gender play (Langlois & Downs, 1980). This is particularly true of boys who like feminine toys or who play at feminine activities. A boy who plays with dolls and a girl like the one in the photo who plays with trucks will both be ignored, teased, or ridiculed by their peers, but the boy more harshly than the girl (Levy, Taylor, & Gelman, 1995). Once children learn rules about gender-typical play, they often harshly punish peers who violate those rules.

Peers influence gender roles in another way, too. Between 2 and 3 years of age, children begin to prefer playing with same-sex peers. Little boys play together with cars, and little girls play together with dolls. This preference increases during childhood, reaching a peak in preadolescence. Then the tide begins to turn, but even in adulthood, time spent at work and at leisure is, quite commonly, segregated by gender (Hartup, 1983). Men play sports or cards together; women shop or have lunch together. This tendency for boys to play with boys and girls with girls has several distinctive features (Maccoby, 1990):

- In some cultures, adults select playmates for children. However, in cultures where children choose playmates, boys select boys as playmates and girls select girls.
- Children spontaneously select same-sex playmates. Adult pressure ("James, why don't you play with John, not Amy") is not necessary.
- Children resist parents' efforts to get them to play with members of the opposite sex. Girls are often unhappy when parents encourage them to play with boys, and boys are unhappy when parents urge them to play with girls.
- Children's reluctance to play with members of the opposite sex is not restricted to gender-typed games, such as playing house or playing with cars. Boys and girls prefer same-sex playmates even in gender-neutral activities such as playing tag or doing puzzles.

Why do boys and girls seem so attracted to same-sex play partners? Eleanor Maccoby (1988; 1990) believes that two factors are critical. First, boys specifically prefer rough-and-tumble play and generally are more competitive and dominating in their interactions. Girls' play is not as rough and is less competitive, so Maccoby argues that boys' style of play may be aversive to girls.

Second, when girls and boys play together, girls do not readily influence boys. **Girls' interactions with one another are typically *enabling*—their actions and**

Boys and girls don't play together often because girls don't like boys' style of play and because girls find that their enabling interaction style is ineffective with boys.

remarks tend to support others and sustain the interaction. In contrast, boy's interactions are often *constricting*—one partner tries to emerge as the victor by threatening or contradicting the other, by exaggerating, and so on. When these styles are brought together, girls find that their enabling style is ineffective with boys. The same subtle overtures that work with other girls have no impact on boys. Boys ignore girls' polite suggestions about what to do and ignore girls' efforts to resolve conflicts with discussion.

Regardless of the exact cause, early segregation of playmates by style of play means that boys learn primarily from boys and girls from girls. This helps solidify a youngster's emerging sense of membership in a particular gender group and sharpens the contrast between genders.

Television.  Another source of influence on gender-role learning is television, which often portrays males and females in stereotyped ways. Women on television tend to be cast in romantic, marital, or family roles; they are depicted as emotional, passive, and weak. Men are more often cast in leadership or professional roles and are depicted as rational, active, and strong (Huston et al., 1992).

What is the impact of these stereotyped portrayals? As you can imagine, children who watch a lot of TV end up with more stereotyped views of males and females. For example, Kimball (1986) studied gender-role stereotypes in a small Canadian town that was located in a valley and could not receive TV programs until a transmitter was installed in 1974. Children's views of personality traits, behaviors, occupations, and peer relations were measured before and after TV was introduced.

Boys' views became more stereotyped on all four dimensions. For example, in their more stereotyped views of occupations, boys now believed that girls could be teachers and cooks whereas boys could be physicians and judges. Girls' views became more stereotyped only for traits and peer relations. After TV was introduced, girls believed that boasting and swearing were characteristic of boys and sharing and helping were characteristic of girls. Findings like these indicate that TV viewing causes children to adopt many of the stereotypes that dominate television programming (Signorielli & Lears, 1992).

Let's now return to our original question: How well does research support the social learning explanation of gender roles? Studies of parents, teachers, and peers show that children learn much about gender roles simply by observing males and females. But simple observation of real-life models or television characters cannot be the entire explanation. After all, young boys traditionally have far more opportunities to observe their mother's behavior than their father's, but are more likely to imitate their father (for example, by using hammer and saw) than their mother (for example, by cooking). Thus, an important element in learning about gender is identifying with one gender and then actively seeking out activities that are typical for that gender. This aspect of gender role learning is the focus of cognitive theories, which we'll examine in the next section.

## Cognitive Theories of Gender Identity

According to Lawrence Kohlberg (1966; Kohlberg & Ullian, 1974), full understanding of gender develops gradually and involves three elements:

- *Gender labeling:* **By age 2 or 3, children understand that they are either boys or girls and label themselves accordingly.**

- *Gender stability:* **During the preschool years, children begin to understand that gender is stable: Boys become men and girls become women.** However, children in this stage believe that a girl who wears her hair like a boy will become a boy and that a boy who plays with dolls will become a girl (Fagot, 1985).

- *Gender consistency:* **Between 4 and 7 years, most children understand that maleness and femaleness do not change over situations or according to personal wishes.** They understand that a child's sex is unaffected by the clothing that a child wears or the toys that a child likes.

Taryn, the 4-year-old in the opening vignette, is in the first stage—she knows that she's a girl. However, she has yet to develop a sense of gender stability or gender consistency. **When children understand labels, stability, and consistency, they have mastered *gender constancy.***

According to Kohlberg's theory, only children who understand gender constancy should have extensive knowledge of sex-stereotyped activities (Newman, Cooper, & Ruble, 1995). That is, not until children understand that gender is constant do they begin to learn what is appropriate and possible for their gender and what is not, as you'll see in the "Real Children" feature.

REAL CHILDREN

### Laura Trades Her Penis for Pom-poms

When my daughter Laura was 2½, she knew that she was a girl but she also insisted that she would grow up to be a daddy. She also claimed that she had a penis, which she would show by pulling her labia away from her body until they were extended about an inch. I have no idea why she did these things, but they clearly document her limited understanding of gender! At about the same time, my son Ben was on a school wrestling team. Laura often went with me to watch Ben wrestle. Afterwards, she thought it was great fun to wrestle on the living room floor, slapping her hand down on the carpet when she pinned me. Never did she comment on the fact that all the wrestlers were boys; evidently this was irrelevant.

By the time she turned 4, Laura's understanding of gender was much better. She knew that she would become a woman and that she did not have a penis. At this age, I remember vividly taking her to watch Ben play football. I wondered if she would become so bored and restless that we'd need to leave. Wrong. Laura immediately discovered the cheerleaders (all girls) and insisted we sit right in front of them. Throughout the game (and the rest of the season), Laura's eyes were riveted to the cheerleaders' every move, and when we'd get home, she'd imitate their routines. According to Kohlberg's theory, 4-year-old Laura knew that cheerleading was for girls and that because she was a girl, cheerleading was for her. ●

Laura's interest in gender-typical behavior emerged only after she understood gender constancy. You can see this same pattern in findings from research (Szkrybalo & Ruble, 1999). For example, Martin and Little (1990) measured preschool children's understanding of gender and their knowledge of gender-stereotyped activities (for example, that girls play with dolls and that boys play with airplanes). The youngest

According to cognitive theories, after children understand that gender is constant, they try to learn more about activities and behaviors typically associated with their gender.

children in their study—3½- to 4-year-olds—did not understand gender constancy and knew little of gender-stereotyped activities. By age 4, children understood gender constancy but still knew little of gender-stereotyped activities. By 4½ years, many children understood gender constancy *and* knew gender-typical and gender-atypical activities. Importantly, there were no children who lacked gender constancy but knew about gender-stereotyped activities, a combination that is impossible according to Kohlberg's theory.

Kohlberg's theory specifies *when* children begin learning about gender-appropriate behavior and activities (once they understand gender constancy) but not *how* such learning takes place. A theory proposed by Martin and Halverson (1987), illustrated in the diagram, addresses how children

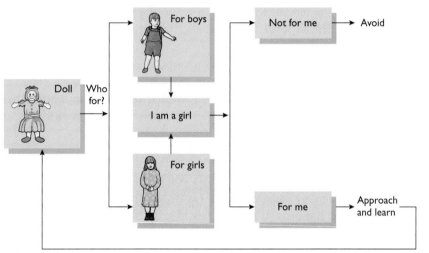

FIG 13–6                                                        Source: Martin & Halvarson, 1981.

learn about gender. **In *gender-schema theory,* children first decide if an object, activity, or behavior is female or male, then use this information to decide whether or not they should learn more about the object, activity, or behavior.** That is, once children know their gender, they pay attention primarily to experiences and events that are gender-appropriate (Martin & Halverson, 1987). According to gender-schema theory, a preschool boy watching a group of girls playing in sand will decide that playing in sand is for girls and that, because he is a boy, playing in sand is not for him. Seeing a group of older boys playing football, he will decide that football is for boys, and because he is a boy, football is acceptable and he should learn more about it.

According to gender-schema theory, after children understand gender, it's as if they see the world through special glasses that allow only gender-typical activities to be in focus (Liben & Signorella, 1993). After children understand gender, their tastes in TV programs begin to shift along gender-specific lines (Luecke-Aleksa et al., 1995). In addition, they begin to use gender labels to evaluate toys and activities. Shown an unfamiliar toy and told that children of a specific gender *really* like this toy, children like the toy much more if others of their gender do, too (Martin, Eisenbud, & Rose, 1995).

This selective viewing of the world explains a great deal about children's learning of gender roles, but as we'll see in the next section, there is one final important element that needs to be considered.

## Biological Influences

A fertilized human egg has 23 pairs of chromosomes. If the 23rd pair includes an X and a Y chromosome, then testes develop about 6 weeks after conception; if the 23rd pair includes two X chromosomes, then ovaries appear about 10 weeks after conception. During prenatal development, the testes and ovaries secrete hormones that regulate the formation of male and female genitals and some features of the central nervous system. This raises an obvious question: Do these hormones also contribute to gender differences in behavior and, in turn, social roles? As you can imagine, this question is not easy to answer because scientists cannot experiment directly with hormones as they are secreted during prenatal development. We do know that hormones are a factor in gender differences in aggressive behavior; however, their role in other gender-based differences in behavior is less clear.

Let's look at some evidence that supports a role for biological influence:

- On questionnaires that measure instrumental traits associated with males (such as being independent, self-confident, aggressive) and expressive traits associated with females (such as being emotional, creative, considerate), identical twins' answers are more similar than fraternal twins' answers (Mitchell, Baker, & Jacklin, 1989). This result suggests that how expressive or instrumental a child is depends, in part, on heredity.

- During prenatal development the adrenal glands sometimes malfunction and, as a result, some females are inadvertently exposed to unusually large amounts of male hormones, such as androgen. In growing up, some of these girls prefer masculine activities (such as playing with cars instead of dolls) and male playmates to a much greater extent than girls not exposed to these amounts of androgen (Berenbaum & Snyder, 1995; Collaer & Hines, 1995), which suggests that androgen influences the development of masculine traits.

Neither of these findings provides ironclad evidence that biology promotes children's learning of gender roles. The studies of twins, at best, suggest hereditary influence but don't tell how biology promotes learning of gender roles. The studies of prenatal exposure to androgen are not completely convincing because the levels of hormone are so much greater than normal that it's risky to make judgments about normal hormone levels.

Perhaps the most accurate conclusion to draw is that biology, the socializing influence of people and media, and the child's own efforts to understand gender-typical behavior all contribute to gender roles and differences. Recognizing the interactive nature of these influences on gender learning also enables us to better understand how gender roles are changing today, which is the focus of the next module.

## Check Your Learning

**1.** Parents treat sons and daughters similarly except when it comes to _____.

**2.** When children engage in cross-gender play, their peers _____.

**3.** Same-sex play is common because most girls don't enjoy boys' rough-and tumble play and because _____.

**4.** When it comes to gender stereotypes, children who watch TV often _____.

**5.** In Kohlberg's theory, during the preschool years, children master _____; that is, they understand that boys become men and girls become women.

**6.** According to cognitive theories, children want to learn about gender-typical activities only after _____.

**7.** Some girls exposed to large amounts of male hormones during prenatal development _____.

 Television depicts men and women in stereotyped roles that do not accurately reflect the real range of roles that men and women fill in American society. What could you do to help children understand that television's portrayal of men and women is distorted?

**Answers:** (1) gender-related behavior, (2) criticize, tease, or punish them, (3) girls find that their enabling style of interaction is ineffective with boys, (4) have more stereotyped views of gender than children who watch TV less often, (5) gender stability, (6) they have learned that gender is constant, (7) prefer masculine activities and male playmates.

# 13.4

- **Emerging Gender Roles**
- **Beyond Traditional Gender Roles**

# Gender Roles in Transition

## Learning Objectives

● **What is androgyny, and how is it related to traditional conceptions of masculinity and femininity?**

● **Can parents rear gender-neutral children?**

*Meda and Perry want their 6-year-old daughter, Hope, to pick activities, friends, and ultimately a career based on her interests and abilities, not on her gender. They have done their best to encourage gender-neutral values and behavior. Both are therefore astonished that Hope seems to be totally indistinguishable from other 6-year-olds reared by conventional parents. Hope's close friends are all girls. When Hope is with her friends, they play house or play with dolls. What seems to be going wrong with Meda and Perry's plans for a gender-neutral girl?*

Gender roles are not etched in stone; they change with the times. In the United States, the range of acceptable roles for girls and boys and women and men has never been greater than today. For example, fathers like the man in the photo stay home to be the primary caregivers for children, and some women work full time as sole support for the family. What is the impact of these changes on children? In this module, we'll answer this question by looking at new gender roles and at efforts by parents like Meda and Perry to rear gender-neutral children.

## Emerging Gender Roles

Traditionally, masculinity and femininity were seen as ends of a continuum: Children possessing many traits associated with males were considered highly masculine, and youngsters possessing many traits associated with females were considered highly feminine. A newer view of gender roles is based on the independent dimensions of instrumentality and expressiveness that were described in Module 13.1 (Bem, 1984). In this view, traditional males are rated high on instrumentality but low on expressiveness, whereas traditional females are low on instrumentality but high on expressiveness. In other words, this approach recognizes that other combinations of traits are possible. **Androgynous persons are rated high on both the instrumental and expressive dimensions.** (The term *androgyny* originated from the Greek words for male, *andro,* and female, *gyn.*) That is, androgynous individuals combine many of the traits listed in the table on page 365: They can be both independent and emotional, self-confident and considerate, ambitious and creative.

Many theorists (e.g., Bem, 1984) argue that the ability to react with both instrumental and expressive behaviors is psychologically healthier than reacting primarily with one or the other. In fact, androgynous children often have higher self-esteem than children whose gender roles are highly stereotyped (Markstrom-Adams, 1989). But the benefits of androgyny are greater for girls than for boys. Androgynous girls have higher self-esteem than expressive girls and are more likely to express their thoughts and feelings publicly (Harter et al., 1998) For example, a girl like the one in the photo, who is independent and ambitious as well as considerate and creative, is more likely to feel positive about herself than a girl who embodies only the expressive traits traditionally associated with females. However, highly instrumental boys have nearly as high self-esteem as androgynous boys (Lau, 1989).

Evidently, a balance of expressiveness and instrumentality may be especially adaptive across life's many tasks. Being independent and confident has benefits at home and work but so does being kind and considerate. Teaching children to adopt nontraditional views of gender is no simple task, however, as we'll see in the next section.

## Beyond Traditional Gender Roles

Many researchers (e.g., Bem, 1989; Eagly, 1995) believe gender is overemphasized to children. They argue that adults often group children by gender unnecessarily. Examples include a minister who rewards perfect church attendance with blue pencils for boys and pink pencils for girls or an elementary-school teacher who has boys and girls form separate lines for lunch. In both cases, children's gender is irrelevant, yet distinguishing boys and girls makes gender seem important and increases children's gender stereotypes (Bigler, 1995).

Many developmentalists believe that gender should be linked strictly to reproductive function instead of, as now, to traits, behaviors, and abilities. Is this possible? Children can certainly learn less stereotyped views of gender, at least in the short run. In one study (Bigler & Liben, 1990), some 6- to 11-year-olds were taught how to decide if a person can perform a particular job or occupation. They were told that the person's gender was not relevant; instead, they should decide if the person would like to do at least some of the activities that are part of the job and if the person has some of the skills necessary for the job. For example, to be a construction worker, a person should like to build things and should know how to drive heavy machinery.

When tested later on their attitudes toward household activities and occupations, these children had significantly fewer stereotyped responses than children who had not been taught to think of occupations in terms of interests and skills. That is, children who have this type of training are more likely to think it perfectly natural for women to be construction workers or men to be nurses.

Short-term interventions like the one just described show that more balanced attitudes and behaviors are possible (Gash & Morgan, 1993). But accomplishing

Children can be taught to have fewer stereotypes about males and females, but it's more difficult to change boys' and girls' style of play and their preference for same-sex playmates.

change over the long term in a natural setting may be more complicated, based on some results of the Family Lifestyles Project (Weisner & Wilson-Mitchell, 1990). This research examined families whose adults were members of the 1960s and 1970s counterculture and deeply committed to rearing their children without traditional gender stereotypes. In these families, men and women shared the household, financial, and child-care tasks.

The Family Lifestyle Project indicates that parents like Meda and Perry in the opening vignette can influence some aspects of gender stereotyping more readily than others. The children studied in the Family Lifestyles Project had few stereotypes about occupations: They agreed that girls could be president of the United States and drive trucks and that boys could be nurses and secretaries. They also had fewer stereotyped attitudes about the use of objects: Boys and girls were equally likely to use an iron, a shovel, hammer and nails, and needle and thread. Nevertheless, children in these families tended to have same-sex friends, and they liked gender-stereotyped activities: The boys enjoyed physical play and the girls enjoyed drawing and reading.

It should not surprise you that some features of gender roles and identities are more readily influenced by experience than others. For 250,000 years, homo sapiens have existed in small groups of families, hunting animals and gathering vegetation. Because women have borne the children and cared for them, it has been adaptive for women to be caring and nurturing. As we saw in Module 10.3, a nurturing caregiver increases the odds of a secure attachment and, ultimately, the survival of the infant. Men's responsibilities included hunting and protecting the family unit from predators, roles for which physical strength and aggressiveness were crucial.

Circumstances of life at the beginning of the 21st century are, of course, substantially different. Nevertheless, the cultural changes of the past few decades cannot erase hundreds of thousands of years of evolutionary history (Kenrick, 1987). We should not be surprised that boys and girls play differently, that girls tend to be more supportive in their interactions with others, and that boys are usually more aggressive.

The "Making Children's Lives Better" feature suggests ways children can be helped to go beyond traditional gender roles and learn the best from both roles.

MAKING CHILDREN'S LIVES BETTER

### Encouraging Valuable Traits, Not Gender Traits

Parents and other adults can encourage children to learn the best from both of the traditional gender roles. Being independent, confident, caring, and considerate are valuable traits for all people, not just for boys or girls. Here are some guidelines to help achieve these aims:

1. Since children learn gender roles from those around them, parents should be sure that they themselves are not gender-bound. Mothers and fathers can mow lawns, make repairs, and work outside the home. Mothers and fathers can prepare meals, do laundry, and care for the young. This *does* make a difference: I've always done most of the laundry in our house, and my daughter, at 5, was astonished when I told her that in most homes mothers do the wash.

2. Don't base decisions about children's toys, activities, and chores on the child's sex. Decide if a toy, activity, or chore is appropriate for the child as an individual (based on age, abilities, and interests), not because the child is a boy or girl.

3. Forces outside the home, such as media and teachers, often work against parents who want their children to go beyond traditional gender roles. It's neither feasible nor wise to shelter children from these influences, but you can encourage them to think critically about others' gender-based decisions. When teachers have boys and girls form separate lines to go to lunch, ask children why this segregation by gender makes sense. When a TV program shows a man coming to aid the stereo-typic damsel in distress, ask the child why the woman simply didn't get herself out of her predicament. ●

### Check Your Learning

**1.** Androgynous children tend to have higher self-esteem than children with highly stereotyped gender roles, but this difference is found primarily among _____ .

**2.** When children learn that skills and interests are the most important factors in determining whether a person can perform a job, their gender stereotypes of occupations _____ .

**3.** In the Family Lifestyles Project, parents' efforts to rear gender-neutral children have been most successful when it comes to _____ .

 The women's liberation movement became a powerful social force in America during the 1960s. Describe how you might do research to determine whether the movement has changed the gender roles that children learn.

**Answers:** (1) girls, (2) become smaller, (3) children's views of occupations and objects

# 13

## Gender and Development
### IN PERSPECTIVE

People play many roles in their lives, but few are cast as early or are as significant as gender. We saw, in Module 13.1, that Americans have well-defined stereotypes for males and females and that children learn these stereotypes early. Yet, we discovered in Module 13.2 that, in terms of cognition, personality, and social behavior, boys and girls are generally more alike than different. In Module 13.3, we found that children learn gender roles through a combination of social forces (parents, for example), self-study, and biology. Finally, in Module 13.4, we found that efforts to rear children without traditional gender roles have been moderately successful.

Research on gender illustrates the theme that *development in different domains is connected.* Think about how children learn gender roles. According to conventional wisdom, children acquire masculine or feminine traits and behaviors through social-ization by parents and other knowledgeable persons in the child's culture. This process is important, but we saw that learning gender roles is not simply a social phenomenon: Cognitive processes are essential. Kohlberg's theory shows that children don't really begin to learn about gender until they understand that they will remain a boy or girl for life. Once they understand gender constancy, gender-schema theory shows how children use this information to decide which experiences are relevant to them.

Biology apparently contributes, too, although we still don't really understand how. Biology, cognition, and social forces all shape the unique gender role that individual boys or girls play.

## See for Yourself

To see that older children know more about gender stereotypes and understand that stereotypes are not binding, you'll need to create some simple stories that illustrate stereotyped traits. You could create stories for any of the traits listed in the tables on pages 362 and 365, but I suggest that you use "independent," "confident," "appreciative," and "gentle." Each story should include two to three sentences that describe a child. Be sure that your stories contain no other clues that would hint that the child in the story is a boy or a girl. For example, this story illustrates "independent":

> *I know a child who likes to do things without help from adults. This child likes to do homework without help and enjoys traveling alone to visit cousins who live in another city.*

Read your stories to some 11- and 12-year-olds. After you've read each story, ask, "Is this child a boy, a girl, or could it be either?" Record the reply, and then ask, "Would most people think that the child is a boy or would most think that the child is a girl?"

In the first question, you're measuring children's understanding that gender stereotypes are flexible. You should find that children answer with "either one" about half of the time, indicating that they believe in some, but not total, flexibility in gender stereotypes. In the second question, you're measuring children's awareness of gender stereotypes. You should find that most children always answer the second question stereotypically: that people would identify the independent and confident children as boys and the appreciative and gentle children as girls. See for yourself!

## Resources

*For more information about . . .*

*gender stereotypes and gender differences,* try Carol Tavris's *The Mismeasure of Women* (Simon and Schuster, 1992), in which the author argues that women are constantly being measured according to standards developed for men.

*ways to encourage girls and young women to pursue interests in science, math, and technology,* visit the Web site of the Advocates for Women in Science, Engineering, and Mathematics: **http://www.awsem.com**

## Key Terms

**androgens** 371
**androgynous** 383
**constricting** 378
**enabling** 377
**expressive traits** 363
**gender consistency** 379

**gender constancy** 379
**gender identity** 360
**gender labeling** 379
**gender role** 360
**gender-schema theory** 380
**gender stability** 379

**gender stereotypes** 362
**instrumental traits** 363
**mental rotation** 368
**social role** 360

# **13.1** Gender Stereotypes

### **How Do We View Men and Women?**
Instrumental traits describe individuals who are acting on the world and are usually associated with males. Expressive traits describe individuals who value interpersonal relationships and are usually associated with females.

### **Learning Gender Stereotypes**
By age 5, children have begun to learn some of the traits typically associated with males and females; by 11 years, children's knowledge of these traits is very similar to adults' knowledge. Older children also understand that stereotypes are not necessarily binding.

# **13.2** Differences Related to Gender

In *The Psychology of Sex Differences,* published in 1974, Eleanor Maccoby and Carol Jacklin concluded that males and females differed in only four areas—verbal ability, spatial ability, math achievement, and aggression. Subsequent investigators have used their work as the starting point for analyzing gender differences.

### **Differences in Physical Development and Behavior**
Boys tend to be bigger, stronger, and more active than girls, who tend to have better fine-motor coordination and to be healthier.

### **Differences in Intellectual Abilities and Achievement**
Girls excel in verbal skills whereas boys excel in spatial ability. Girls get better grades in math; boys get better scores on math achievement tests. This difference in math skill has remained the same over the past few decades. Differences in intellectual abilities reflect some combination of hereditary and environmental factors.

### **Differences in Personality and Social Behavior**
Boys are more aggressive physically than girls, and biology probably contributes heavily to this difference. Girls usually express their aggression by trying to damage other children's relations with peers. Girls are more sensitive to others' feelings and are more influenced by others; both differences are probably due to experience.

### **Frank Talk About Gender Differences**
Most gender differences are fairly small, which means that abilities for boys and girls overlap considerably. Nevertheless, small differences in average performance can mean fairly large differences at the extremes of ability. Also, despite the emphasis on gender differences, boys and girls are quite similar in many aspects of cognition, personality, and social behavior.

# **13.3** Gender Identity

### **The Socializing Influences of People and the Media**
Parents treat sons and daughters similarly, except in gender-related behavior. Fathers may be particularly important in teaching about gender because they are more likely to treat sons and daughters differently. Teachers value feminine behaviors but devote more time to boys.

By the preschool years, peers discourage cross-gender play by ridiculing peers who do it. Peers also influence gender roles because children play almost exclusively with same-sex peers.

Television depicts men and women in stereotyped fashion, and children who watch a lot of television are likely to have very stereotyped views of men and women.

### **Cognitive Theories of Gender Identity**
According to Kohlberg's theory, children gradually learn that gender is constant over time and cannot be changed according to personal wishes. After children understand gender constancy, they begin to learn gender-typical behavior. According to gender-schema theory, children learn about gender by paying attention to behaviors of members of their own sex and ignoring behaviors of members of the other sex.

### **Biological Influences**
The idea that biology influences some aspects of gender roles is supported by twin studies and by research on females exposed to male hormones during prenatal development.

# **13.4** Gender Roles in Transition

### **Emerging Gender Roles**
Androgynous persons embody both instrumental and expressive traits. Androgynous girls have higher self-esteem than traditional girls and are more likely to express themselves publicly; androgynous boys have about the same level of self-esteem as traditional boys.

### **Beyond Traditional Gender Roles**
Training studies show that children can learn less stereotyped views of gender, but studies of parents trying to rear gender-neutral children suggest that many stereotyped behaviors are resistant to change.

# 14.

*F*amily. The term is as sacred to most Americans as baseball, apple pie, and Chevrolet. But what comes to mind when you think of family? Television gives us one answer—from *Leave It to Beaver* to *Family Ties* to *Married with Children,* the American family is portrayed as a mother, father, and 2 or 3 children. In reality, of course, American families are as diverse as the people in them. Some families consist of a single parent and an only child. Others include two parents, many children, and grandparents or other relatives.

All of these family configurations, however, have a common goal: nurturing children and helping them become full-fledged adult members of their culture. To learn how families achieve these goals, we'll begin, in Module 14.1, by looking at relationships between parents and children. Next, in Module 14.2, we'll look at relationships between siblings. Then, in Module 14.3, we'll consider how children are influenced by divorce and remarriage. Finally, in Module 14.4, we'll examine the forces that can cause parents to abuse their children.

# Family Relationships

14.1  **Parenting**

14.2  **Brothers and Sisters**

14.3  **Divorce and Remarriage**

14.4  **Parent-Child Relationships Gone Awry**

# 14.1

# Parenting

## Learning Objectives

● **What is a systems view of family dynamics?**

● **What are the primary dimensions of parenting?**

● **What parental behaviors affect children's development?**

● **How do children help determine how parents rear them?**

● **What role do culture and family configuration play in children's development?**

*Tanya and Sheila, both sixth graders, wanted to go to a Smashing Pumpkins concert with two boys from their school. When Tanya asked if she could go, her mom said, "No way!" Tanya responded defiantly, "Why not?" In return, her mother exploded, "Because I say so. That's why. Stop pestering me." Sheila wasn't allowed to go either. When she asked why, her mom said, "I just think you're still too young to be dating. I don't mind your going to the concert. If you want to go just with Tanya, that would be fine. What do you think of that?"*

The vignette illustrates what we all know well from personal experience—parents go about child rearing in many different ways. In this module, you'll learn about different approaches that parents take to raising children. But let's begin thinking about parents as an important element in the family system.

## The Family as a System

A simple-minded view of child-rearing is that parents' actions are all that really matter. That is, through their behavior, parents directly and indirectly determine their children's development. This view of parents as "all powerful" was part of early psychological theories (e.g., Watson, 1925) and is held even today by some first-time parents. But most theorists now view families from an ecological perspective (described in Module 1.2). That is, families form a system of interacting elements—parents and children influence one another (Parke & Buriel, 1998).

In the systems view, parents still influence their children, both directly—for example, by encouraging them to study hard—and indirectly—for example, by being generous and kind to others. However, the influence is no longer exclusively from parent to children but is mutual: Children influence their parents, too. By their behaviors, attitudes, and interests, children affect how their parents behave toward them. When, for example, children resist discipline, parents may become less willing to reason and more inclined to use force.

Even more subtle influences become apparent when families are viewed as systems of interacting elements. For example, fathers' behaviors can affect mother-child relationships. A demanding husband may leave his wife with little time, energy, or interest in helping her daughter with her homework. Or, when siblings argue constantly, parents may become preoccupied with avoiding problems rather than encouraging their children's development.

These many examples show that narrowly focusing on parents' impact on children misses the complexities of family life. But there is even more to the systems view. The family itself is embedded in other social systems, such as neighborhoods and religious institutions (Parke & Buriel, 1998). These other institutions can affect family dynamics. Sometimes they simplify child-rearing, as when neighbors are trusted friends and can help care for each other's children. Sometimes, however, they complicate child-rearing. Grandparents who live nearby can create friction within the family. At times, the impact of the larger systems is indirect, as when work schedules cause a parent to be away from home or when schools must eliminate programs that benefit children.

The diagram summarizes the numerous interactive influences that exist in a systems view of families. In the remainder of this module, we'll describe parents' influences on children and then how children affect their parents' behavior. Finally, we'll consider how parent-child influences vary with culture and family configuration.

## Dimensions and Styles

Parenting can be described in terms of general dimensions that are like personality traits in that they represent stable aspects of parental behavior—aspects that hold across different situations (Holden & Miller, 1999). Research consistently reveals two general dimension of parental behavior. One is the degree of warmth and responsiveness that parents show their children. Another is the amount of control parents exert over their children.

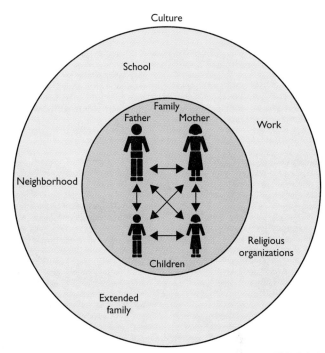

FIG 14–1

Let's look first at warmth and responsiveness. At one end of the spectrum are parents who are openly warm and affectionate with their children. They are involved with them, respond to their emotional needs, and spend considerable time with them. At the other end of the spectrum are parents who are relatively uninvolved with their children and sometimes even hostile toward them. These parents often seem more focused on their own needs and interests than their children's. Warm parents enjoy hearing their children describe the day's activities; uninvolved or hostile parents aren't interested, considering it a waste of their time. Warm parents see when their children are upset and try to comfort them; uninvolved or hostile parents pay little attention to their children's emotional states and invest little effort comforting them when they're upset.

As you might expect, children benefit from warm and responsive parenting (Pettit, Bates, & Dodge, 1997). When parents are warm toward them, children typically feel secure and happy, and they're better behaved. In contrast, when parents are uninvolved or hostile, their children are often anxious and less controlled. And, as we saw in Module 11.2, children often have low self-esteem when their parents are uninvolved (Rothbaum & Weisz, 1994).

A second general dimension of parental behavior concerns the control that parents exercise over their children's behavior. At one end of this spectrum are controlling, demanding parents. These parents virtually run their children's lives. Overcontrol is shown by parents who always want to know where their teenagers are and what they are doing. At the other end of the spectrum are parents who make few demands and rarely exert control. Their children are free to do almost anything without fear of parental reproach. Parents who undercontrol don't care where their teenagers are or what they are doing.

Children benefit from warm, responsive parenting and from a moderate amount of parental control.

Neither of these extremes is desirable. Overcontrol deprives children of the opportunity to meet behavioral standards on their own, which is the ultimate goal of socialization. Teenagers who constantly "report in" never learn to make decisions for themselves (e.g., "Should I go to this party with people that I don't know really well?"). Undercontrol fails children because it doesn't teach them cultural standards for behavior. Teenagers who never "report in" don't believe they are accountable for their behavior, which is definitely not true in the long run.

Parents need to strike a balance, maintaining adequate control while still allowing children freedom to make some decisions for themselves. This is often easier said than done, but a good starting point is setting standards that are appropriate for the child's age, then showing the child how to meet them, and, finally, rewarding the child for complying (Powers & Roberts, 1995; Rotto & Kratochwill, 1994). Suppose a mother wants her preschooler to fold and put away her socks. This is a reasonable request because the child is physically capable of this simple task and she knows where the socks should be stored. Like the mother in the photo, she should show her daughter how to complete the task, and then praise her when she does.

Once standards are set, they should be enforced consistently. Time and time again, research has shown that children and adolescents are more compliant when parents enforce rules regularly. For example, the mother should insist that her daughter always fold and put away her socks, not just occasionally. When parents enforce rules erratically, children come to see rules as optional instead of obligatory, and they try to avoid complying with them (Conger, Patterson, & Ge, 1995).

Effective control is also based on good communication. Parents should explain why they've set standards and why they reward or punish as they do. If a mother wants her son to clean his room, she should explain that a messy room is unsafe, makes it difficult to find toys that he wants, and makes it difficult for her to clean. Parents can also encourage children to ask questions if they don't understand or disagree with standards. If the son feels that his mother's standards for orderliness are so high that it's impossible to play in his room, he should feel free to raise the issue with his mother without fear of making her angry.

A balanced approach to control—based on age-appropriate standards, consistency, and communication—avoids the problems associated with overcontrol because the expectations more likely reflect the child's level of maturity and they are open to discussion. A balanced approach also avoids the problems of undercontrol because standards are set and parents expect children to meet those standards consistently.

**Parenting Styles.** Combining the dimensions of warmth and control produces four prototypic styles of parenting, as shown in the diagram (Baumrind, 1975; 1991).

• **Authoritarian parenting combines high control with little warmth.** These parents lay down the rules and expect them to be followed without discussion. Hard work, respect, and obedience are what authoritarian parents wish to cultivate in their children. There is little

|  | **Parental Control** | |
|---|---|---|
|  | High | Low |
| High | Authoritative | Indulgent-Permissive |
| Low | Authoritarian | Indifferent-Uninvolved |

*Parental Involvement*

FIG 14-2

give-and-take between parent and child because authoritarian parents do not consider children's needs or wishes. This style is illustrated by Tanya's mother in the opening vignette, who feels no obligation whatsoever to explain her decisions.

- *Authoritative parenting* **combines a fair degree of parental control with being warm and responsive to children.** Authoritative parents explain rules and encourage discussion. This style is exemplified by Sheila's mother in the opening vignette. She explained why she did not want Sheila going to the concert and encouraged her daughter to discuss the issue with her.

- *Indulgent-permissive parenting* **offers warmth and caring but little parental control.** These parents generally accept their children's behavior and punish them infrequently. An indulgent-permissive parent would readily agree to Tanya or Sheila's request to go to the concert, simply because it is something the child wants to do.

- *Indifferent-uninvolved parenting* **provides neither warmth nor control.** Indifferent-uninvolved parents provide for their children's basic physical and emotional needs but little else. They try to minimize the amount of time spent with their children and avoid becoming emotionally involved with them. If Tanya or Sheila had parents with this style, she might have simply gone to the concert without asking, knowing that her parents wouldn't care and would rather not be bothered.

Parenting style is fairly stable over time. Parents who are authoritative with their school-age children tend to be authoritative when their children are adolescents (McNally, Eisenberg, & Harris, 1991). Given this stability, you shouldn't be surprised to learn that parenting style influences children's development (Baumrind, 1991; Maccoby & Martin, 1983):

- Children with authoritarian parents typically have lower grades in school, lower self-esteem, and are less skilled socially.

- Children with authoritative parents tend to have higher grades and be responsible, self-reliant, and friendly.

- Children with indulgent-permissive parents have lower grades and are often impulsive and easily frustrated.

- Children with indifferent-uninvolved parents have low self-esteem and are impulsive, aggressive, and moody.

> Authoritative parenting fosters achievement in school, self-reliance, and good conduct; other parenting styles are often linked to lower self-esteem and less social skill.

Many of these outcomes are illustrated in a study by Lamborn and her colleagues (1991). The researchers examined the influence of parenting style on high-school students' psychosocial development and school performance. The graphs at the top of page 394 show very consistent patterns: Adolescents with authoritative parents have the best scores on all measures. They are the most self-reliant, have the best grades, and misbehave the least in school. Adolescents with indifferent-uninvolved parents tend to be at the other extreme. They are lower in self-reliance, have the lowest grades, and are the most likely to be involved in school misconduct.

Adolescents with either authoritarian or indulgent-permissive parents are in between the other groups on most measures. Adolescents with authoritarian parents are the least self-reliant of all four groups; but in grades and school misconduct, they rank behind adolescents with authoritative parents. Adolescents with indulgent-permissive parents are nearly as self-reliant as children of authoritative parents, but their grades are lower and they are more likely to misbehave in school.

FIG 14–3

The benefits of authoritative parenting are not restricted to European American children. They apply as well to children and parents from several different ethnic groups in the United States, including people of African, Asian, and Hispanic descent (Brody & Flor, 1998; Steinberg et al., 1992). However, some researchers find that authoritarian parenting can benefit children growing up in poverty (Furstenberg, 1993).Why? When youngsters grow up in neighborhoods with a lot of violence and crime, strict obedience to parents can protect children (Kelley, Power, & Wimbush, 1992).

To sum up, a parental style that combines control, warmth, and affection is usually best for children. However, other factors, such as a dangerous neighborhood, may make an authoritarian parenting style more appropriate for some children.

As important as these different dimensions and styles are for understanding parenting, there is more to effective child-rearing, as we'll see in the next section.

### Parental Behavior

Dimensions and styles are general characterizations of how parents typically behave. If, for example, I describe a parent as warm or controlling, you immediately have a sense of that parent's usual style in dealing with his or her children. Nevertheless, the price for such a broad description is that it tells us little about how parents behave in specific situations and how these parental behaviors influence children's development. Put another way, what specific behaviors can parents use to influence their children? Researchers who study parents name three: direct instruction, modeling, and feedback.

**Parents can influence children through direct instruction, by acting as models, and by providing feedback.**

Direct Instruction.    Parents often tell their children what to do. But simply playing the role of drill sergeant in ordering children around—"Clean your room!" "Turn off the TV!"—is not very effective. **A better approach is *direct instruction,* telling a child what to do, when, and why.** Instead of just shouting "Share your candy with your brother!" a parent should explain when and why it's important to share with a sibling.

In addition, just as coaches help athletes master sports skills, parents can help their youngsters master social and emotional skills. Parents can explain links between emotions and behavior—"Catlin is sad because you broke her crayon" (Gottman, Katz, & Hooven, 1996). They can also teach how to deal with difficult social situations—"When you ask Lindsey if she can sleep over, do it privately so you won't hurt Kaycee's or Hannah's feelings" (Mize & Pettit, 1997). In general, children who get this sort of parental "coaching" tend to be more socially skilled and, not surprisingly, get along better with their peers. (I'll have more to say about this in Module 15.1.)

Direct instruction and coaching are particularly powerful when paired with modeling. Urging children to act in a particular way, such as sharing with others, is more compelling when children also see others sharing. In the next section, we'll see how children learn by observing others.

Learning by Observing.   Children learn a great deal from parents simply by watching them. For example, in Module 12.4 we saw that youngsters often learn how to interact with others by watching how their parents interact. The parents' modeling and the youngsters' observational learning thus lead to imitation, so children's behavior resembles the behavior they observe. **Observational learning can also produce *counterimitation,* learning what should not be done.** If an older sibling kicks a friend and parents punish the older sibling, the younger child may learn not to kick others.

**Sometimes observational learning leads to *disinhibition,* an increase in all behaviors like those observed.** Children who watch their parents shouting angrily, for example, are more likely to yell at or push a younger sibling. In other words, observation can lead to a general increase in aggression, or put still another way, aggressive responses become disinhibited. **The opposite effect, in which an entire class of behaviors is made less likely, is known as *inhibition.*** When a child like the one in the photo sees parents punish a sibling, the child is less likely to behave in the ways that led the sibling to be punished.

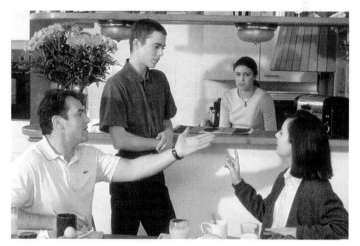

So far, we've seen that parents influence their children's development by direct instruction and by acting as models that children can observe. In the next section, we'll see how parents use feedback to affect children's behavior.

Feedback.   By giving feedback to their children, parents indicate whether a behavior is appropriate and should continue or is inappropriate and should stop. Feedback comes in two general forms. ***Reinforcement* is any action that increases the likelihood of the response that it follows.** Parents may use praise to reinforce a child's studying or give a reward for completing household chores. ***Punishment* is any action that discourages the reoccurrence of the response that it follows.** Parents may forbid children to watch television when they get poor grades in school or make children go to bed early for neglecting household chores.

Of course, parents have been rewarding and punishing their children for centuries, so what do psychologists know that parents don't know already? In fact, researchers have made some surprising discoveries concerning the nature of reward and punishment. **Parents often unwittingly reinforce the very behaviors they want to discourage, a situation called the *negative reinforcement trap*** (Patterson, 1980). The negative reinforcement trap occurs in three steps, most often between a mother and her son. In the first step, the mother tells her son to do something he doesn't want to do. She might tell him to clean up his room, to come inside while he's outdoors playing with friends, or to study instead of watching television. In the next step, the son responds with some behavior that most parents find intolerable: He

Many forms of punishment have limited effectiveness because they only suppress behavior temporarily and have undesirable side effects.

argues, complains, or whines—not just briefly, but for an extended period of time. In the last step, the mother gives in—saying that the son needn't do as she told him initially—simply to get the son to stop the behavior that is so intolerable.

The feedback to the son is that arguing (or complaining or whining) works; the mother rewards that behavior by withdrawing the request that the son did not like. That is, although we usually think a behavior is strengthened when it is followed by the presentation of something that is valued, behavior is also strengthened when it is followed by removing something that is disliked.

As for punishment, research (Parke, 1977) shows that punishment works best when

- administered directly after the undesired behavior occurs, not hours later.
- an undesired behavior *always* leads to punishment, not usually or occasionally.
- accompanied by an explanation of why the child was punished and how punishment can be avoided in the future.
- the child has a warm, affectionate relationship with the person administering the punishment.

At the same time, research reveals some serious drawbacks to punishment. One is that punishment is primarily suppressive: Punished responses are stopped, but only temporarily if children do not learn new behaviors to replace those that were punished. For example, denying TV to brothers who are fighting stops the undesirable behavior, but fighting is likely to recur unless the boys learn new ways of solving their disputes.

A second drawback is that punishment can have undesirable side effects. Children become upset as they are being punished, which makes it unlikely that they will understand the feedback that punishment is meant to convey. A child denied TV for misbehaving may become angry over the punishment itself and ignore why he's being punished. Furthermore, as we saw in Module 12.4, when children are punished physically, they often imitate this behavior with peers and younger siblings (Whitehurst & Vasta, 1977). Children who are spanked often use aggression to resolve their disputes with others.

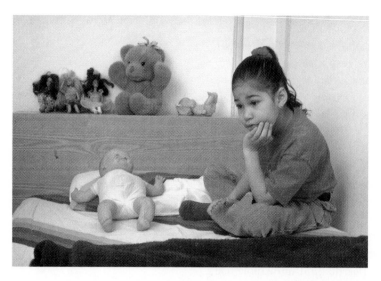

One method combines the best features of punishment while avoiding its shortcomings. **In time-out, a child who misbehaves must briefly sit alone in a quiet, unstimulating location.** Some parents have children sit alone in a bathroom; others have children sit alone in a room, as shown in the photo. Time-out is punishing because it interrupts the child's ongoing activity and isolates the child from other family members, toys, books, and, generally, all forms of rewarding stimulation.

The period is sufficiently brief—usually just a few minutes—for a parent to use the method consistently. During time-out, both parent and child typically calm down. Then, when time-out is over, a parent can talk with the child and explain why the punished behavior is objectionable and what the child should do instead. "Reasoning" like this—even with preschool children—is effective because it emphasizes why a parent punished initially and how punishment can be avoided in the future.

Thus, parents can influence children by direct instruction, by modeling behavior that they value and not modeling what they don't want their children to learn, by giving feedback, and through the parenting styles that we examined in the first section of this module. In the next section, we'll switch perspectives and see how children affect their parents' behavior.

## Children's Contributions

I emphasized earlier that the family is a dynamic, interactive system with parents and children influencing each other. In fact, children begin at birth to influence the way their parents treat them.

One way to see the influence of children on parents is by looking at how parenting changes as children grow. The same parenting that is marvelously effective with infants and toddlers is inappropriate for adolescents. Let's look again at the two basic dimensions of parental behavior—warmth and control. Warmth is beneficial throughout development—toddlers and teens alike enjoy knowing that others care about them. But the manifestation of parental affection changes, becoming more reserved as children develop. The enthusiastic hugging and kissing that delights toddlers embarrasses adolescents.

Parental control also changes gradually as children develop (Maccoby, 1984). As children develop cognitively and are better able to make their own decisions, parents gradually relinquish control and expect children to be responsible for themselves. For instance, parents of elementary-school children often keep track of their children's progress on school assignments, but parents of adolescents don't, expecting their children to do this themselves.

Not only do parents change their expressions of warmth and control as children develop, but parents behave differently depending upon a child's specific behavior (Kochanska, 1993). To illustrate the reciprocal influence of parents and children, imagine two children with different temperaments as they respond to a parent's authoritative style. The first child has an "easy" temperament and readily complies with parental requests and responds well to family discussions about parental expectations. These parent-child relations are a textbook example of successful authoritative parenting. But suppose, like the child in the photo, the second child has a "difficult temperament" and complies reluctantly and sometimes not at all. Over time, the parent becomes more controlling and less affectionate. The child in turn complies even less in the future, leading the parent to adopt an authoritarian parenting style (Bates et al., 1998).

As this example illustrates, parenting behaviors and styles often evolve as a consequence of the child's behavior. With a young child who is eager to please adults and less active, a parent may discover that a modest amount of control is adequate. But for a child who is not as eager to please and very active, a parent may need to be more controlling and directive (Dumas, LaFreniere, & Serketich, 1995; Hastings & Rubin, 1999). Influence is reciprocal: Children's behavior helps determine how parents treat them and the resulting parental behavior influences children's behavior, which in turn causes parents to again change their behavior (Stice & Barrera, 1995).

A study by Rueter and Conger (1998) shows reciprocal influence in action in early adolescence. Once a year these investigators videotaped parents and their young adolescents as they discussed current family conflicts dealing with issues such as household chores, homework, and transportation. When parents were angry, hostile, and bullying during the discussions, their adolescents became disruptive or refused to participate in the discussion. In turn, these behaviors increased parents' anger, hostility, and bullying.

As time goes by, these reciprocal influences lead many families to adopt routine ways of interacting with each other. Some families end up functioning smoothly: Parents and children cooperate, anticipate each other's needs, and are generally happy. Unfortunately, other families end up troubled: Disagreements are common, parents spend much time trying unsuccessfully to control their defiant children, and everyone is often angry and upset (Belsky, Woodworth, & Crnic, 1996; Kochanska, 1997).

Over the long term, such troubled families do not fare well, so it's important that these negative reciprocal influences are nipped in the bud (Carrere & Gottman, 1999; Christensen & Heavey, 1999).

## Cultural Influences and Family Configuration

The general aim of child-rearing—helping children become contributing members of their cultures—is much the same worldwide (Whiting & Child, 1953). However, cultures have different ideas of the best ways to achieve this goal. And, within cultures, families do not always consist of a mother, father, and their children; different family configurations can affect family dynamics. We'll look at some of these variations in values and practices in this section.

### Cultural Differences in Warmth and Control.

Warmth and control are universal aspects of parents' behavior, but views about the "proper" amount of warmth and the "proper" amount of control vary with particular cultures. European Americans want their children to be happy and self-reliant individuals, and they believe these goals can best be achieved when parents are warm and exert moderate control (Goodnow, 1992; Spence, 1985). In many Asian and Latin American countries, however, individualism is less important than cooperation and collaboration (Okagaki & Sternberg, 1993). In China, for example, Confucian principles dictate that parents are always right and that emotional restraint is the key to family harmony (Chao, 1994).

*Chinese parents tend to be more controlling and less affectionate than American parents.*

Accordingly, we would expect to find that Chinese parents are not as warm toward their children and are more controlling than their American counterparts. Lin and Fu (1990) found exactly this pattern, as shown in the graphs on page 399. Compared to mothers and fathers in the United States, mothers and fathers in China are more likely to emphasize parental control and less likely to express affection.

Also shown in the graphs are the results for a third group studied by Lin and Fu—Chinese parents who emigrated from Taiwan to live in the United States, where their children were born. The findings for this group were between the other groups: Immigrant Chinese parents were less controlling than Taiwanese parents but more controlling than U.S. parents. They were also warmer toward their children than Taiwanese parents but not as warm as U.S. parents. Both results suggest that the immigrant group was gradually becoming assimilated into U.S. culture.

Lin and Fu's study shows that Chinese parents' behavior reflects the Confucian principles at the center of traditional Chinese culture, and European American parents'

Chinese
Immigrant Chinese
U.S.

2   3   4   5

*Parents' Emphasis on Controlling Their Children*
*(5 = greatest emphasis)*

2   3   4   5

*Parents' Emphasis on Expressing Affection*
*(5 = greatest emphasis)*

FIG 14–4

behavior reflects long-standing American beliefs in the importance of individualism and self-reliance. Cultural values help specify appropriate ways for parents to interact with their offspring.

### The Role of Grandparents.

In many cultures around the world, grandparents play important roles in children's lives. One influential analysis suggested five specific styles of grandparenting (Neugarten & Weinstein, 1964):

- *Formal grandparents* express strong interest in the grandchild but maintain a hands-off attitude toward child rearing.
- *Fun-seeking grandparents* see themselves as a primary source of fun for their grandchildren but avoid more serious interactions.
- *Distant grandparents* have little contact with children, except as part of holidays or other family celebrations.
- *Dispensing-family-wisdom grandparents* provide information and advice to parents and child alike.
- *Surrogate-parent grandparents* assume many of the normal roles and responsibilities of a parent.

Of these different styles, we know the most about the surrogate-parent style because it is particularly common in African American families. The "Cultural Influences" feature describes the important role of grandmothers in African American family life.

CULTURAL INFLUENCES

### Grandmothers in African American Families

Approximately 1 in 8 African American children lives with a grandmother, compared to only 1 in 25 European American children (U.S. Bureau of the Census, 1994). Why is this? A quarter of all African American children grow up in chronic poverty, and living with relatives is one way of sharing—and thereby reducing—the costs associated with housing and child care.

African American grandmothers who live with their daughters and their children frequently become involved in rearing their grandchildren, adopting the surrogate-parent style (Pearson et al., 1990). When the daughter is a teenage mother, the grandmother may be the child's primary caregiver, an arrangement that benefits both the adolescent mother and the child. Freed from the obligations of child-rearing, the adolescent mother is able to improve her situation by, for

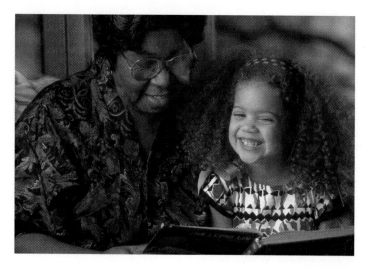

example, finishing school. The child benefits because grandmothers are often more effective mothers than teenage mothers: Grandmothers are less punitive and, like the grandmother in the photo, very responsive to their grandchildren (Chase-Lansdale, Brooks-Gunn, & Zamsky, 1994; Wilson, 1989).

This family arrangement works well for children. In terms of achievement and adjustment, children living with their mothers and grandmothers resemble children living in two-parent families, and they tend to be better off than children in single-parent families (Wilson, 1989). Even when grandmothers are not living in the house, children benefit when their mothers receive social and emotional support from grandmothers and other relatives: Children are more self-reliant and less likely to become involved in delinquent activities such as drug use and vandalism (Taylor & Roberts, 1995).

Thus, grandmothers and other relatives can ease the burden of child-rearing in African American families living in poverty, and, not surprisingly, children benefit from the added warmth, support, and guidance of an extended family. ●

### Children of Gay and Lesbian Parents.

More than a million youngsters in the United States have a gay or lesbian parent. In most of these situations, children were born in a heterosexual marriage that ended in divorce when one parent revealed his or her homosexuality. Less frequent, but becoming more common, are children born to single lesbians or to lesbian couples.

Research on gay and lesbian parents and their children is scarce, and most has involved children who were born to a heterosexual marriage that ended in divorce when the mother came out as a lesbian. Most of these lesbian mothers are European American and well-educated.

As parents, gay and lesbian couples are more similar to heterosexual couples than different. There is no indication that gay and lesbian parents are less effective than heterosexual parents. In fact, some evidence suggests that gay men may be especially responsive to children's needs, perhaps because their self-concepts include emotional sensitivity that is traditionally associated with the female gender role (Bigner & Jacobsen, 1989).

*In many areas—including gender roles, self-concept, and social skill—children of gay and lesbian parents resemble children of heterosexual parents.*

Children reared by gay and lesbian parents seem to develop much like children reared by heterosexual couples (Patterson, 1992). Preschool boys and girls apparently identify with their own gender and acquire the usual accompaniment of gender-based preferences, interests, activities, and friends. As adolescents and young adults, the vast majority are heterosexual (Bailey et al., 1995). In other respects—such as self-concept, social skill, moral reasoning, and intelligence—children of lesbian mothers resemble children of heterosexual parents. For example, in one study of 80 families—55 headed by a lesbian and 25 headed by a heterosexual—the children were comparable in social competence and behavioral adjustment (Chan, Raboy, & Patterson, 1998).

Research on children reared by gay and lesbian couples, along with findings concerning African American grandmothers and warmth and control in Asian parents, remind us that "good parenting" takes on somewhat different meanings in different cultures. These research results also challenge the conventional wisdom that a two-parent family with mother and father both present necessarily provides the best circumstances for development. Multiple adults *are* important (a fact that will become even clearer in Module 14.3 on divorce), but *who* the adults are seems to matter less than what they do. Children benefit from good parenting skills, whether it's a mother and father or grandparents or two women or two men doing the parenting.

## Check Your Learning

**1.** According to the systems approach, the family consists of interacting elements who influence each other and the family itself is _____.

**2.** Children who have low self-esteem and are impulsive, aggressive, and moody often have parents with an _____ style of parenting.

**3.** In a _____, parents unwittingly reinforce undesirable behaviors.

**4.** Parental behaviors that influence children include direct instruction, modeling (learning through observation), and _____.

**5.** The effectiveness of punishment depends on timing, consistency, the presence of an accompanying explanation, and _____.

**6.** Compared to American parents, Chinese parents tend to be more controlling and less _____.

**7.** _____ grandparents are very interested in their grandchildren but avoid becoming involved in child-rearing.

**Suppose you heard the host of a radio talk show say, "What's wrong with American youth today is that parents don't discipline the way they used to. 'Spare the rod and spoil the child' made sense before and still makes sense today." If you called in, what would you say in response to the host's remarks?**

**Answers:** (1) embedded in other social systems, such as neighborhoods, (2) indifferent-uninvolved, (3) negative reinforcement trap, (4) feedback (reward and punishment), (5) the child's relationship with the person who is punishing, (6) affectionate, (7) Formal

# 14.2

Firstborn, Laterborn, and Only Children

Qualities of Sibling Relationships

## Brothers and Sisters

### Learning Objectives

● **How do firstborn, laterborn, and only children differ?**

● **How do sibling relationships change as children grow? What determines how well siblings get along?**

*Bob and Alice adored their 2-year-old son, Robbie, who was friendly, playful, and always eager to learn new things. In fact, Bob thought Robbie was nearly perfect and saw no reason to tempt fate by having another child. However, Alice had heard stories that only children were conceited, spoiled, and unfriendly. Alice was sure that Robbie would grow up like this unless she and Bob had another child. What to do?*

For most of a year, all firstborn children are only children like Robbie. Some children remain "onlies" forever, but most get brothers and sisters. Some firstborns are joined by many siblings in rapid succession; others are simply joined by a single brother or sister. As the family acquires these new members, parent-child relationships become more complex. Parents can no longer focus on a single child but must adjust to the needs of multiple children. Just as important, siblings influence each other's development, not just during childhood but, as the cartoon reminds us, throughout life. To understand sibling influence, let's look at differences between firstborns, laterborns, and only children.

PEANUTS © 1993. Reprinted with permission of United Feature Syndicate.

## Firstborn, Laterborn, and Only Children

Firstborn children are often "guinea pigs" for most parents, who have lots of enthusiasm but little practical experience rearing children. Parents typically have high expectations for their firstborns and are both more affectionate and more punitive with them. As more children arrive, parents become more adept at their roles, having learned "the tricks of the parent trade" with earlier children. With laterborn children, parents have more realistic expectations and are more relaxed in their discipline (e.g., Baskett, 1985).

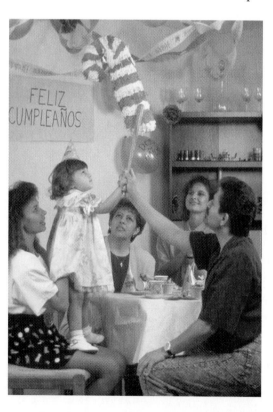

The different approaches that parents take with their firstborns and laterborns help explain differences that are commonly observed between these children. Firstborn children generally have higher scores on intelligence tests and are more likely to go to college. They are also more willing to conform to parents' and adults' requests. Laterborn children, perhaps because they are less concerned about pleasing parents and adults but need to get along with older siblings, are more popular with their peers and more innovative (Eaton, Chipperfield, & Singbeil, 1989).

And what about only children? Alice, the mother in the opening vignette, was well acquainted with the conventional wisdom which says that parents like the ones in the photo dote on "onlies," with the result that they are selfish and egotistical. Is the folklore correct? From a comprehensive analysis of more than 100 studies, the answer is "no." In fact, only children were found more likely to succeed in school than other children and to have higher levels of intelligence, leadership, autonomy, and maturity (Falbo & Polit, 1986).

This general pattern is not limited to only children growing up in the United States and Canada. In China, only children are the norm because the government limits population growth. There, too, comparisons between only and non-only children often find no differences; when differences are found, the advantage usually goes to the only child (Jiao, Ji, & Jing, 1996; Yang et al., 1995). Thus, contrary to the popular stereotype, only children are not "spoiled brats" (or, in China, "little emperors") who boss around parents, peers, and teachers. Instead, only children are, for the most part, much like children who grow up with siblings. Alice and Bob needn't have another child just to guarantee that Robbie will grow up to be generous and sensitive to others instead of selfish and egotistical.

In discussing firstborn, laterborn, and only children, we have ignored relationships that exist between siblings. These can be powerful forces on development, as we'll see in the next section.

## Qualities of Sibling Relationships

From the very beginning, sibling relationships are complicated. On the one hand, most expectant parents are excited by the prospect of another child, and their enthusiasm is contagious: Their children, too, eagerly await the arrival of the newest family member. On the other hand, the birth of a sibling is often distressing for older children, who may become withdrawn or return to more childish behavior because of the changes that occur in their lives, particularly the need to share parental attention and affection (Gottlieb & Mendelson, 1990). However, distress can be avoided if parents remain responsive to their older children's needs (Howe & Ross, 1990). In fact, one of the benefits of a sibling's birth is that fathers become more involved with their older children (Stewart et al., 1987).

Many older siblings enjoy helping their parents take care of newborns (Wagner, Schubert, & Schubert, 1985). Like the sibling in the photo, older children play with the baby, console it, feed it, or change its diapers. As the infant grows, interactions between siblings become more frequent and more complicated. For example, toddlers tend to talk more to parents than to older siblings. But, by the time the younger sibling is 4 years old, the situation is reversed: Now young siblings talk more to older siblings than to their mother (Brown & Dunn, 1992). Older siblings become a source of care and comfort for younger siblings when they are distressed or upset (Garner, Jones, & Palmer, 1994).

As time goes by, some siblings grow close, becoming best friends in ways that nonsiblings can never be. Other siblings constantly argue, compete, and simply do not get along with each other. The basic pattern of sibling interaction seems to be established early in development and remains fairly stable. Dunn, Slomkowski, and Beardsall (1994), for example, interviewed mothers twice about their children's interaction, first when the children were 3- and 5-year-olds and again 7 years later, when the children were 10- and 12-year-olds. Dunn and her colleagues found that siblings who got along as preschoolers often continued to get along as young adolescents, whereas siblings who quarreled as preschoolers often quarreled as young adolescents.

To reduce the stress associated with a sibling's birth, parents should remain responsive to their older children's needs.

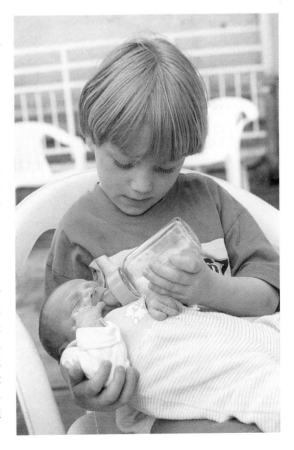

The "Real Children" feature presents two sibling relationships that, although very different in quality, reveal the stability that Dunn and her colleagues (1994) discovered.

REAL CHILDREN

### A Tale of Two Sibling Relationships

When Calvin, age 4, learned that his mother was going to have a baby, he cried uncontrollably and refused to talk to his mother for the rest of the day. After Hope was born, Calvin tried to ignore her, which was impossible because he wanted to be near his mother, and Hope, of course, was there, too. He couldn't see why his mother liked this new baby so much and seemed to have so little time for him. As Hope grew older, Calvin argued with her over just about everything and continued to compete with her for their parents' attention. When Hope entered adolescence and boyfriends entered the scene, Calvin teased her and hassled them. Over the years, Hope was too nice to give Calvin the treatment he deserved, but she was glad when he left for college and only came home for vacations.

In contrast, Hillary and Elizabeth were always close. Beginning in the preschool years, the two girls played together constantly. When Elizabeth was upset, Hillary was quick to console her. When Hillary had special activities—a piano recital or a soccer match—Elizabeth always wanted to be there, and she was very proud of her sister's accomplishments. When Hillary and Elizabeth were both in high school, they remained as close as ever, sharing clothes and secrets about their teen romances. Hillary still played soccer and Elizabeth remained her biggest fan. Elizabeth had become the family's pianist and was quite talented; she won several state competitions, and Hillary never missed a performance.

Calvin and Hope's relationship is remarkable for Calvin's jealousy and hostility; Hillary and Elizabeth's relationship is remarkable for its enduring intimacy, love, and mutual respect. What the relationships have in common is stability: The quality of relationship that was established early in childhood was maintained. ●

Why was Hillary and Elizabeth's relationship so filled with love and respect, whereas Calvin and Hope's was dominated by jealousy and resentment? Put more simply, what factors contribute to the quality of sibling relationships? First, children's sex and temperament matter. Sibling relations are more likely to be warm and harmonious between siblings of the same sex than between siblings of the opposite sex (Dunn & Kendrick, 1981) and when neither sibling is temperamentally emotional (Brody, Stoneman, & McCoy, 1994). Age is also important: Sibling relationships generally improve as the younger child approaches adolescence because siblings begin to perceive one another as equals (Buhrmester & Furman, 1990).

> When parents fight, they no longer treat their children similarly, which increases conflicts between siblings.

Parents contribute to the quality of sibling relationships, both directly and indirectly (Brody, 1998). The direct influence stems from parents' treatment. Siblings more often get along when they believe that parents have no "favorites" but treat all siblings fairly (Kowal & Kramer, 1997). When parents lavishly praise one child's accomplishments while ignoring another's, children notice the difference and their sibling relationship suffers.

This doesn't mean that parents must treat all their children the same. Children understand that parents should treat their kids differently—based on their age or personal needs. Only when differential treatment is not justified do sibling relationships deteriorate (Kowal & Kramer, 1997).

The indirect influence of parents on sibling relationships stems from the quality of the parents' relationship with each other: A warm, harmonious relationship between parents fosters positive sibling relationships; conflict between parents is associated with conflict between siblings (Erel, Margolin, & John, 1998; Volling & Belsky, 1992). When parents don't get along, they no longer treat their children the same, leading to conflict among siblings (Brody et al., 1994).

One practical implication of these findings is that in their pursuit of family harmony (otherwise known as peace and quiet), parents can influence some of the factors affecting sibling relationships but not others. Parents can help reduce friction between siblings by being equally affectionate, responsive, and caring with all of their children and by caring for one another. At the same time, some dissension is natural in families, especially those with young boys and girls: Children's different interests lead to arguments, like the one in the photo. Faced with common simple conflicts—Who decides which TV show to watch? Who gets to eat the last cookie? Who gets to hold the new puppy?—a 3-year-old brother and a 5-year-old sister *will* argue because they lack the social and cognitive skills that allow them to find mutually satisfying compromises.

When siblings do fight—particularly young children—parents should intervene. By helping their children settle differences, parents show children more sophisticated ways to negotiate; later, children often try to use these techniques themselves instead of fighting (Pearlman & Ross, 1997).

Regardless of the quality of their sibling relationships, American children are more likely than children in other countries to have their family relationships disrupted by divorce. What is the impact of divorce on children and adolescents? Module 14.3 has some answers.

## Check Your Learning

1. Compared to firstborn children, laterborn children are more innovative and more _____.

2. When compared to children who have siblings, only children are, for the most part, _____.

3. Siblings are more likely to get along when they are of the same sex, not temperamentally emotional, and when the younger child _____.

4. Sibling relationships are harmed when parents treat their children differently if _____.

5. Parents can influence sibling relationships directly by treating children fairly and indirectly by _____.

 **Most research on sibling relationships is based on families with two children because these families are easier to find than families with three or more children and because there's only one sibling relationship to consider. Think how the conclusions about sibling relationships described in this module might need to be modified to apply to larger families.**

**Answers:** (1) popular, (2) similar, not different, (3) enters adolescence, (4) the differential treatment is not justified, (5) getting along with each other

# 14.3

# Divorce and Remarriage

## Learning Objectives

● How does family life change for children following divorce?

● What are some of the effects of divorce on children?

● How do children adjust to a parent's remarriage?

*Jack has lived with his dad for the 4 years since his parents' divorce; he visits his mother every other weekend. Although Jack was confused and depressed when his parents divorced, he has come to terms with the new situation. He's excelling in school, where he is well liked by peers and teachers. One of Jack's friends is Troy. Troy's parents are married but bicker constantly since his dad lost his job. His parents are unable to agree on anything; the pettiest event or remark triggers an argument. Troy's grades have fallen, and whereas he was once a leader among the boys in his class, now he prefers to be alone.*

Like Jack, many American youngsters' parents divorce. In fact, the following statistics show that divorce has become a common part of childhood in America (Burns & Scott, 1994; Goodman, Emery, & Haugaard, 1998; Hernandez, 1997; Stevenson & Black, 1995):

- The divorce rate in the United States tripled between 1960 and 1980 but has remained fairly stable since 1980.
- The United States has by far the highest divorce rate in the entire world.
- Roughly one American child in three will, before age 18, see his or her parents divorce.
- Annually, approximately one million American children have parents who divorce.

According to all theories of child development, divorce is distressing for children because it involves conflict between parents and usually separation from one of them. But what aspects of children's development are most affected by divorce? Are these effects long-lasting, or are at least some of them temporary (as seems to be true for Jack)? To begin to answer these questions, let's start with a profile of life after divorce.

## Family Life After Divorce

After divorce, children usually live with their mothers, though fathers are more likely to get custody today than in previous generations. About 15 percent of children live with their fathers after divorce (Meyer & Garasky, 1993). Not much is known about family life in homes headed by single fathers, so the description on the next few pages is based entirely on research done on children living with their mothers.

The best portrait of family life after divorce comes from the Virginia Longitudinal Study of Divorce and Remarriage conducted by Mavis Hetherington (1988; 1989; 1999; Hetherington, Cox, & Cox, 1982). The Virginia Study traced the lives of families for several years after divorce along with a comparison sample of families with parents who did not divorce.

In the first few months after divorce, many mothers were less affectionate toward their children. They also accepted less mature behavior from their children than they would have before the divorce and had a harder time controlling their children. The overall picture shows both mothers and children suffering the distress of a major change in life circumstances: Children regressed to less mature forms of behavior, and mothers were less able to parent effectively. Fathers, too, were less able to control their children, but this was probably because most were extremely indulgent.

Two years after the divorce, mother-child relationships had improved, particularly for daughters. Mothers were more affectionate. They were more likely to expect age-appropriate behavior from their children and discipline their children effectively. Fathers also demanded more mature behavior of their children, but many had become relatively uninvolved with their children.

> When children living with their divorced mothers enter adolescence, mothers and daughters are often quite close, but mothers and sons fight.

Six years after divorce, the children in the study were entering adolescence. Family life continued to improve for mothers with daughters; many mothers and daughters grew extremely close over the years following divorce. Unfortunately, family life was problematic for mothers with sons. These mothers often complained about their sons, who resisted discipline. Many mothers fell into the negative reinforcement trap described in Module 14.1. Mothers and sons were frequently in conflict, and neither was very happy with the other or with the general quality of family life. Of course, conflict between mothers and adolescent sons is common when parents are married, but it was more intense with single moms, perhaps because adolescent sons are more willing to confront their single mothers concerning standards for their behavior.

Results like these from the Virginia Study underscore that divorce changes family life for parents and children alike. In the next section, we'll look at the effects of these changes on children's development.

## Impact of Divorce on Children

Do the disruptions, conflict, and stress associated with divorce affect children? Of course they do. Having answered this easy question, however, a host of more difficult questions remain: Are all aspects of children's lives affected equally by divorce? Are there factors that make divorce more stressful for some children than others? Finally, *how* does divorce influence development? Some of the first steps toward answering these questions came from the study that is the subject of the "Focus on Research" feature.

FOCUS ON RESEARCH

### Impact of a Father's Absence on Daughters' Development

*Who was the investigator, and what was the aim of the study?* Divorce rates in the United States began to skyrocket in the late 1960s and early 1970s. By that time, research had already established that a father's absence was harmful to sons. Mavis Hetherington (1972) decided to study the impact of a father's absence on daughters. Because she was primarily interested in the impact of father absence—not divorce per se—she studied daughters whose fathers had died as well as daughters whose fathers were absent due to divorce.

*How did the investigator measure the topic of interest?* Hetherington was interested in daughters' attitudes and behaviors toward males, particular toward their father and toward boys their own age. She measured this in two ways: by creating an interview that included questions about girls' attitudes toward gender roles and by observing the girls during a dance at a local recreation center.

*Who were the children in the study?* Hetherington studied 13- to 17-year-old girls, 24 from families with the fathers present, 24 girls' fathers had died, and 24 girls' fathers were absent due to divorce. For the latter 48 girls, there were no males (siblings or adults) living at home.

*What was the design of the study?* This study was correlational because Hetherington was interested in the relation that existed naturally between the presence or absence of a father (and the reasons for his absence) and different aspects of daughters' attitudes and behaviors. Adolescents were tested only once, so the study was neither longitudinal nor cross-sectional.

*Were there ethical concerns with the study?* No. The questions in the interview were not threatening, and, of course, most of the girls enjoyed attending the dance.

*What were the results?* Hetherington found no differences whatsoever among the three groups of girls in terms of gender roles. That is, they all had friendships with other girls, feelings of warmth toward their mothers, and comparable interest in gender-typical activity. However, striking differences were found on the questions dealing with men. As the first two sets of bars in the graph show, daughters from intact families felt much more secure around males than daughters of widows or divorced mothers.

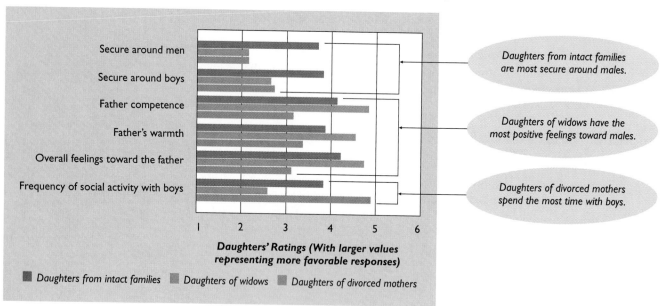

FIG 14–5

The next three sets of bars in the graph concern attitudes toward the father. In each case, daughters of widows had the most positive views of the father, followed by daughters from intact families, and then daughters of divorced mothers.

Perhaps the most intriguing finding is shown by the last set of bars: Daughters of divorced mothers—despite feeling relatively less secure around males and having the most negative views of their fathers—reported spending the most time with boys.

Hetherington confirmed this last result during her observations of the girls at the dance: Daughters of divorced mothers were more likely to seek the attention of the male chaperones, more likely to initiate contact with boys, and more likely to spend time in the boys' areas of the recreation center.

*What did the investigator conclude?* When a father is absent—either because of death or divorce—girls have no trouble acquiring feminine interests and a feminine identity. However, when the father is absent, "the lack of opportunity for constructive interaction with a loving, attentive father [results] in apprehension and inadequate skills in relating to males" (p. 324). This explains why father-absent girls may differ from girls whose fathers are present, but it doesn't explain why divorce and death seem to affect girls in such different ways. Here, attitudes of the mother are important. Hetherington interviewed all the girls' mothers and found that, although the divorced mothers described their relationship with their daughter positively, they were negative about their former husbands and about life in general. Widows, too, reported strong relationships with their daughters but, unlike the divorced mothers, had fond views of their husband and generally positive views about life.

Thus, differences in mothers' attitudes explain why divorce affects girls differently than a father's death. Daughters of divorced women undoubtedly see some of their mother's hostility toward their father, which explains their own negative views toward men and fathers. But then why do daughters of divorced women seek the company of males so aggressively? Perhaps they see their mother's unhappiness and believe that a male's company is essential to happiness. Perhaps they find life with an unhappy mother difficult and believe that a relationship with a boy is a way out of the house. In contrast, widows are relatively happy with life in general, so their daughters have less reason to seek males, either as an apparent source of happiness or as a means of avoiding a mother's unhappiness. ●

Hetherington's (1972) study shows that divorce affects children through multiple routes. Some effects of divorce are linked directly to the father's absence. When a father is absent, girls have fewer opportunities to learn how to interact with males. But other effects of divorce depend upon the mother's attitudes and feelings. Many of the divorced mothers in Hetherington's study were unhappy and bitter (in part because divorce was less common and less accepted in the early 1970s), and the mothers' unhappiness and bitterness affected their daughters.

By 1990, nearly 20 years after Hetherington's (1972) pioneering study, almost 100 studies involving more than 13,000 preschool-through college-age children had been conducted. Amato and Keith (1991) integrated the results of these studies. In all areas they reviewed, including school achievement, conduct, adjustment, self-concept, and parent-child relations, children whose parents had divorced fared poorly compared to children from intact families. However, the effects of divorce were greater in the 1960s and 1970s than in later years when divorce became more frequent (and thus more familiar). School achievement, conduct, adjustment, and the like are still affected by divorce but not as much as before the 1980s.

> Compared to children from intact families, children from divorced families fare poorly in school achievement, conduct, adjustment, self-concept, and parent-child relations.

When children of divorced parents become adults, the effects of divorce persist. As adults, children of divorce are more likely to become teenage parents and to become divorced themselves. Also, they report less satisfaction with life and are more likely to become depressed (Furstenberg & Teitler, 1994; Kiernan, 1992). For example, in one study (Chase-Lansdale, Cherlin, & Kiernan, 1995), 11 percent of children of divorce had serious emotional problems as adults compared to 8 percent of children from intact families. The difference is small—11 percent versus 8 percent—but divorce does increase the risk of emotional disorders in adulthood.

Some children are more affected by divorce than others. Amato and Keith's (1991) analysis, for example, showed that although the overall impact of divorce is the same for boys and girls, divorce is more harmful when it occurs during childhood and adolescence than during the preschool or college years. Also, children who are temperamentally more emotional tend to be more affected by divorce (Lengua et al., 1999).

Some children suffer more from divorce because of their tendency to interpret events negatively. We know, from Module 12.4, that two children often have differing interpretations of exactly the same social event. Suppose, for example, that a father forgets to take a child on a promised outing. One child might believe that an emergency prevented the father from taking the child. A second child might believe that the father hadn't really wanted to spend time with the child in the first place and will never make similar plans again. Children who—like the second child—tend to interpret life events negatively are more likely to have behavioral problems following divorce (Mazur et al., 1999).

*How* exactly does divorce influence development? Researchers have identified several aspects of a child's life that change (Amato & Keith, 1991). First, the absence of one parent means that children lose a role model, a source of parental help and emotional support, and a supervisor. For instance, a single parent may have to choose between helping one child complete an important paper or watching another child perform in a school play. She can't do both, and one child will miss out.

Second, single-parent families experience economic hardship, which creates stress and often means that activities once taken for granted are no longer available (Goodman et al., 1998). A family may no longer be able to afford books for pleasure reading, music lessons, or other activities that promote child development. Moreover, when a single parent worries about having enough money for food and rent, she has less energy and effort to devote to parenting.

Third, conflict between parents is extremely distressing to children and adolescents (Fincham, 1998), particularly for children who are emotionally insecure (Davies & Cummings, 1998). In fact, many of the problems that are ascribed to divorce are really caused by marital conflict occurring before the divorce (Erel & Burman, 1995; Shaw, Winslow, & Flanagan, 1999). Children like Troy, the boy in the opening vignette whose parents are married but fight constantly, often show many of the same effects associated with divorce.

Life for children after divorce is *not* all gloom and doom. Children adjust to their new circumstances (Chase-Lansdale & Hetherington, 1990). However, certain factors can ease the transition. Children adjust to divorce more readily if their divorced parents cooperate with each other, especially on disciplinary matters (Hetherington, 1989). **In *joint custody*, both parents retain legal custody of the children.** Children benefit from joint custody if their parents get along (Maccoby et al., 1993).

Of course, many parents do not get along after a divorce, which eliminates joint custody as an option. Traditionally, mothers have been awarded custody; but in recent years fathers more often have been given custody, especially of sons. This practice coincides with findings that children like Jack, the other boy in the opening vignette, often adjust better when they live with same-sex parents: Boys often fare better with fathers and girls fare better with mothers (Goodman et al., 1998). One reason boys are often better off with their fathers is that boys are likely to become involved in negative reinforcement traps (described in Module 14.1) with their mothers. Another explanation is that both boys and girls may forge stronger emotional relationships with same-sex parents than with other-sex parents (Zimiles & Lee, 1991).

The "Making Children's Lives Better" feature tells how parents can make divorce easier on their children, regardless of the child's sex and the living arrangements.

### Helping Children Adjust After Divorce

Divorce causes major changes in children's lives that are very stressful. Here are some ways parents can reduce stress and help children adjust to their new life circumstances. Parents should

- explain together to children why they are divorcing and what their children can expect to happen to them.
- reassure children that they will always love them and always be their parents; parents must back up these words with actions by remaining involved in their children's lives, despite the increased difficulty of doing so.
- expect that their children will sometimes be angry or sad about the divorce, and they should encourage children to discuss these feelings with them.

Parents should not

- compete with each other for their children's love and attention; children adjust to divorce best when they maintain good relationships with both parents.
- take out their anger with each other on their children.
- criticize their ex-spouse in front of the children.
- ask children to mediate disputes; parents should work out problems without putting the children in the middle.

Following all these rules all the time is not easy. After all, divorce is stressful and painful for adults, too. But parents owe it to their children to try to follow most of these rules most of the time in order to minimize the disruptive effects of their divorce on their children's development. ●

## Blended Families

Following divorce, most children live in a single-parent household for about 5 years. However, like the adults in the photo, more than two-thirds of men and women eventually remarry (Glick, 1989; Glick & Lin, 1986). **The resulting unit, consisting of a biological parent, stepparent, and children is known as a *blended family*.** Because mothers are more often granted custody of children, the most common form of blended family is a mother, her children, and a stepfather. Preadolescent boys typically benefit from the presence of a stepfather, particularly when he is warm and involved. Preadolescent girls, however, do not adjust readily to their mother's remarriage, apparently because it disrupts the intimate relationship they have established with her. Nevertheless, as boys and girls enter adolescence, both benefit from the presence of a caring stepfather (Hetherington, 1993).

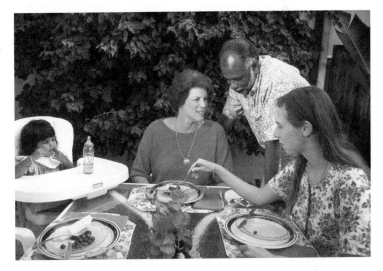

The best strategy for stepfathers is to be interested in their new stepchildren but avoid encroaching on established relationships. Newly remarried mothers must be careful that their enthusiasm for their new spouse does not come at the expense of time and affection for their children. And both parents and children need to have realistic expectations. The blended family can be successful, but it takes effort because of the complicated relationships, conflicting loyalties, and jealousies that usually exist (Anderson et al., 1999).

Much less is known about blended families consisting of a father, his children, and a stepmother, though several factors make a father's remarriage difficult for his children (Brand, Clingempeel, & Bowen-Woodward, 1988). First, fathers are often awarded custody when judges believe that children are unruly and will profit from a father's "firm hand." Consequently, many children living with their fathers do not adjust well to many of life's challenges, which certainly includes a father's remarriage. Second, fathers are sometimes granted custody because they have a particularly close relationship with their children, especially their sons. When this is the case, children sometimes fear that their father's remarriage will disturb this relationship. Finally, noncustodial mothers are more likely than noncustodial fathers to maintain close and frequent contact with their children (Maccoby et al., 1993). The constant presence of the noncustodial mother may interfere with a stepmother's efforts to establish close relationships with her stepchildren, particularly with her stepdaughters.

> Children in blended families often fear that remarriage will disrupt the close relationship they have with their biological parent.

Over time, children adjust to the blended family. If the marriage is happy, most children profit from the presence of two caring adults. Unfortunately, second marriages are slightly more likely than first marriages to end in divorce, so many children relive the trauma. As you can imagine, another divorce—and possibly another remarriage—severely disrupts children's development, accentuating the problems that followed the initial divorce (Capaldi & Patterson, 1991).

Regrettably, divorce is not the only way that parents can disturb their children's development. As we'll see in the next module, some parents harm their children more directly, by abusing them.

## Check Your Learning

1. In the first few months after divorce, mothers do not parent effectively and children often _____.

2. As children approach adolescence, mother-_____ relationships after a divorce remain positive.

3. The impact of divorce on children became _____ in the 1980s.

4. Divorce affects children's development by depriving them of a role model and source of help, _____, and because the conflict associated with divorce is very distressing for children.

5. Children are most likely to be affected by divorce during the _____ years.

6. Fathers are often awarded custody when _____ or when they have a particularly close relationship with their children.

7. One difficulty for custodial fathers and stepmothers is that the children's biological mother _____.

 **Suppose you were asked to prepare a brochure for mothers who have recently divorced and will have custody of their children. What advice would you give them about what to expect as a single parent?**

# Parent-Child Relationships Gone Awry

## Learning Objectives

- What are the consequences of child maltreatment?

- What factors cause parents to mistreat their children?

- How can maltreatment be prevented?

# 14.4

Consequences of ⌐
Maltreatment

Causes of Maltreatment ⌐

Preventing Maltreatment ⌐

*The first time 7-year-old Max came to school with bruises on his face, he said he'd fallen down the basement steps. When Max had similar bruises a few weeks later, his teacher spoke with the school principal, who contacted local authorities. They discovered that Max's mother hit him with a paddle for even minor misconduct; for serious transgressions, she beat Max and made him sleep alone in an unheated, unlighted basement.*

Unfortunately, cases like Max's occur far too often in modern America. Maltreatment comes in many forms (Goodman et al., 1998). The two that often first come to mind are physical abuse involving assault that leads to injuries and sexual abuse involving fondling, intercourse, or other sexual behaviors. Another form of maltreatment is neglect, not giving children adequate food, clothing, or medical care. And, as the poster reminds us, children can also be harmed by psychological abuse—ridicule, rejection, and humiliation.

The frequency of these various forms of child maltreatment is difficult to estimate because so many cases go unreported. According to the National Center on Child Abuse and Neglect (1997), approximately 1 million children annually suffer maltreatment or neglect. About 50 percent are neglected, about 25 percent are abused physically, and about 15 percent are abused sexually (National Center on Child Abuse and Neglect, 1997).

We'll begin this module by looking at the consequences of maltreatment, then look at some causes, and, finally, examine ways to prevent maltreatment.

## Consequences of Maltreatment

You probably aren't surprised to learn that the prognosis for youngsters like Max is not very good. Some, of course, suffer permanent physical damage. Even when there is no lasting physical damage, the children's social and emotional development is often disrupted. They tend to have poor relationships with peers, often because they are too aggressive (Bolger, Patterson, & Kupersmidt, 1998; Parker & Herrera, 1996). Their cognitive development and academic performance are also disturbed. Abused youngsters tend to get lower grades in school, score lower on standardized achievement tests, and be retained in a grade rather than promoted. Also, school-related behavior problems are common, such as being disruptive in class (Goodman et al., 1998; Trickett & McBride-Chang, 1995).

Adults who were abused as children often experience emotional problems such as depression or anxiety, are more

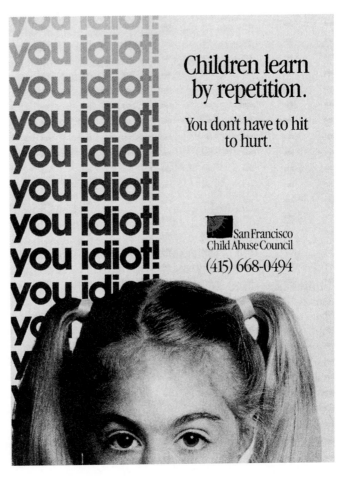

prone to think about or attempt suicide, and are more likely to abuse spouses and their own children (Malinosky-Rummell & Hansen, 1993). In short, when children are maltreated, virtually all aspects of their development are affected and these effects do not vanish with time.

## Causes of Maltreatment

Why would a parent abuse a child? Maybe you think parents would have to be severely disturbed or deranged to harm their own flesh and blood. Not really. Today, we know that the vast majority of abusing parents cannot be distinguished from nonabusing parents in terms of standard psychiatric criteria (Wolfe, 1985). That is, adults who mistreat their children are not suffering from any specific mental or psychological disorder, and they have no distinctive personality profile.

Modern accounts of child abuse no longer look to a single or even a small number of causes. Instead, a host of factors put some children at risk for abuse and protect others; the number and combination of factors determine if the child is a likely target for abuse (Belsky, 1993). Let's look at three of the most important factors: cultural context, the parents, and the children themselves.

The most general category of contributing factors has to do with cultural values and the social conditions in which parents rear their children. For example, a culture's view of physical punishment contributes to child maltreatment. Many countries in Europe and Asia have strong cultural prohibitions against physical punishment. It simply isn't done and would be viewed in much the same way we would view an American parent who punished by not feeding the child for a few days. In Sweden, for example, spanking is against the law. But the scene in the photo, a mother spanking her child, is common in the United States. Countries that do not condone physical punishment tend to have lower rates of child maltreatment than the United States (Zigler & Hall, 1989).

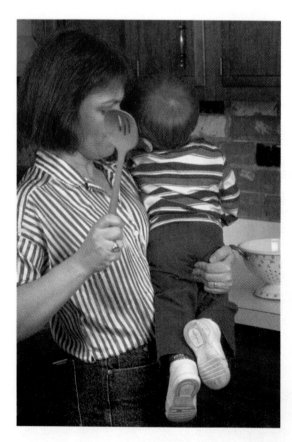

What social conditions seem to foster maltreatment? Poverty is one: Maltreatment is more common in families living in poverty, in part because lack of money increases the stress of daily life (Goodman et al., 1998). When parents are worrying if they can buy groceries or pay the rent, they are more likely to punish their children physically instead of making the extra effort to reason with them.

Social isolation is a second force. Abuse is more likely when families are socially isolated from other relatives or neighbors. When a family lives in relative isolation, it deprives the children of adults who could protect them and deprives parents of social support that would help them cope with life stresses (Garbarino & Kostelny, 1992; Korbin, 1987).

Work by Claudia Coulton and her colleagues (1995) shows the influence of poverty and isolation on child maltreatment. They obtained data from 177 U.S. census tracts in Cleveland, Ohio. (A typical census tract includes about 2,000 residents.) Child maltreatment was more common in census tracts that were poorer, as indicated by more people living in poverty, higher unemployment, more vacant housing, and greater population loss. In addition, maltreatment was more common in census tracts that had fewer elderly residents, a greater ratio of children to adults, and fewer males. Thus, maltreatment is more common in neighborhoods that are poor and that have few other adults to help with child rearing. Apparently, maltreatment often occurs when parents are unable to cope with the financial and psychological burdens that child-rearing entails.

Social factors like those studied by Coulton and her colleagues (1995) clearly contribute to child abuse, but they are only part of the puzzle. Although maltreatment is more common among families living in poverty, it does not occur in a majority of these families and it does occur in middle-class families, too. Consequently, we need to look for additional factors to explain why abuse occurs in some families but not others.

Today, we know that parents who abuse their children

- were, as children, sometimes maltreated themselves (Simons et al., 1991).
- have high expectations for their children but do little to help them achieve these goals (Trickett et al., 1991).
- rely upon physical punishment to control their children (Trickett & Kuczynski, 1986).

Overall, then, the typical abusing parent often had an unhappy childhood and has limited understanding of effective parenting techniques.

To place the last few pieces in the puzzle, we must look at the abused children themselves. The discussion in Module 14.1 of reciprocal influence between parents and children should remind you that children may inadvertently, through their behavior, bring on their own abuse. In fact, infants and preschoolers are more often abused than older ones. Why? They are easier targets of abuse and they are less able to regulate aversive behaviors that elicit abuse (Belsky, 1993). You've probably heard stories about a parent who shakes a baby to death because the baby won't stop crying. Because younger children are more likely to cry or whine excessively—behaviors that irritate all parents sooner or later—they are more likely to be the targets of abuse.

For much the same reason, children who are frequently ill are more often abused. When children are sick, they're more likely to cry and whine, annoying their parents. Also, when children are sick, they need medical care, which means additional expense, and they can't go to school, which means that parents must arrange alternate child care. By increasing the level of stress in a family, sick children can inadvertently become the targets of abuse (Sherrod et al., 1984).

Stepchildren form another group at risk for abuse (Daly & Wilson, 1996). Just as Cinderella's stepmother doted on her biological children but abused Cinderella, so stepchildren are more prone to abuse and neglect than biological children. Adults are less invested emotionally in their stepchildren, and this lack of emotional investment leaves stepchildren more vulnerable.

Obviously the children are not at fault and do not deserve the abuse. Nevertheless, normal infant or child behavior can provoke anger and maltreatment from some parents.

Thus, cultural, parental, and child factors all contribute to child maltreatment. Any single factor will usually not result in abuse. For instance, a sick infant who cries constantly would not be maltreated in countries where physical punishment is not

> Children are most likely to be abused when their culture condones physical punishment, their parents lack effective child-rearing skills, and their own behavior is often aversive.

tolerated. Maltreatment is likely only when cultures condone physical punishment, parents lack effective skills for dealing with children, and a child's behavior is frequently aversive.

## Preventing Maltreatment

The complexity of child abuse dashes any hopes for a simple solution. Because maltreatment is more apt to occur when several contributing factors are present, eradicating child maltreatment would entail a massive effort.

American attitudes toward "acceptable" levels of punishment and poverty would have to change. American children will be abused as long as physical punishment is considered acceptable and effective and as long as poverty-stricken families live in chronic stress from simply trying to provide food and shelter. Parents also need counseling and training in parenting skills. Abuse will continue as long as parents remain ignorant of effective methods of parenting and discipline.

It would be naive to expect all of these changes to occur overnight. However, by focusing on some of the more manageable factors, the risk of maltreatment can be reduced, if not eliminated entirely. For example, families can be taught more effective ways of coping with situations that might otherwise trigger abuse (Wicks-Nelson & Israel, 1991). Parents can learn the benefits of authoritative parenting and effective ways of using feedback and modeling (described in Module 14.1) to regulate children's behavior. In role-playing sessions that recreate problems from home, child development professionals can demonstrate more effective means of solving problems, and then parents can practice these themselves.

Social supports also help. When parents know that they can turn to other helpful adults for advice and reassurance, they better manage the stresses of child-rearing that might otherwise lead to abuse. Finally, we need to remember that most parents who have mistreated their children deserve compassion, not censure. In most cases, parents and children are attached to each other; maltreatment is a consequence of ignorance and burden, not malice.

## Check Your Learning

1. Maltreatment includes physical abuse, sexual abuse, psychological abuse, and _____.

2. Adults who were abused as children are more likely to have emotional problems, to be suicide-prone, and to _____.

3. Children who are maltreated frequently have poor peer relationships, sometimes because they are _____.

4. Social factors that contribute to child maltreatment include cultural views toward physical punishment, poverty, and _____.

5. Children who are at special risk for maltreatment include infants and toddlers, children who are ill frequently, and _____.

6. Programs for preventing maltreatment often try to help families learn _____.

 **A sociologist claims that child maltreatment would vanish if poverty were eliminated. Do you agree? Why or why not?**

**Answers:** (1) neglect, (2) abuse spouses and children, (3) too aggressive, (4) social isolation, (5) stepchildren, (6) new ways of coping with situations that might trigger maltreatment

# Family Relationships
## IN PERSPECTIVE

The basic goal of all families is to nurture children until they achieve adulthood, but we've seen in this chapter that families pursue this goal in many different ways and with varying degrees of success. In Module 14.1, we saw that families are systems of interacting elements: Parents affect children through styles differing in warmth and control, and children influence the type of parenting they receive. In Module 14.2, we learned that a child's position in the birth order can affect development and that how well siblings get along with each other depends on the parents and the children's temperament, sex, and age. In Module 14.3, we discovered that the effects of divorce on children are broad and last for years, and that children and parents in blended families face special challenges. Finally, in Module 14.4, we found that child maltreatment, which affects virtually all aspects of children's development, is caused by cultural, parental, and child factors.

In this chapter, I want to emphasize the theme that children *help determine their own development.* This may seem to be an unusual chapter to emphasize this theme because, after all, we usually think of how parents influence their children. But several times in this chapter we've seen that parenting is determined, in part, by children themselves. We saw that parents change their behavior as their children grow older. Parents also adjust their behavior depending upon how their children respond to previous efforts to discipline. And, in discussing causes of child maltreatment, we discovered that younger and sick children often unwittingly place themselves at risk for abuse because of their behavior. Constant whining and crying is trying for all parents and prompts a small few to harm their children.

Of course, parents do influence their children's development in many important ways. But effective parenting recognizes that there is no all-purpose formula that works for all children or, for that matter, for all children in one family. Instead, parents must tailor their child-rearing behavior to each child, recognizing his or her unique needs, strengths, and weaknesses.

## See for Yourself

Many students find it hard to believe that parents actually use the different styles described in Module 14.1. To observe how parents differ in their warmth and control, visit a place where parents and children interact together. Shopping malls and fast-food restaurants are two good examples. Observe parents and children, then judge their warmth (responsive to the child's needs versus uninterested) and degree of control (relatively controlling versus uncontrolling). As you observe, decide if parents are using feedback and modeling effectively or not. You should observe an astonishing variety of parental behavior, some effective and some not. See for yourself!

## Resources

*For more information about . . .*

*ways to help children deal with divorce,* try Neil Kalter's *Growing Up with Divorce* (Free Press, 1990), which describes practical ways for parents to help their children deal with the stresses of divorce.

 *how to deal with all of the different problems—large and small—that come up in rearing children,* visit the Today's Parent Web site, **http://www.todaysparent.com**

## Key Terms

authoritarian parenting 392
authoritative parenting 393
blended family 411
counterimitation 395
direct instruction 394
disinhibition 395
dispensing-family-wisdom
  grandparents 399

distant grandparents 399
formal grandparents 399
fun-seeking grandparents 399
indifferent-uninvolved
  parenting 393
indulgent-permissive parenting 393
inhibition 395
joint custody 410

negative reinforcement trap 395
punishment 395
reinforcement 395
surrogate-parent grandparents 399
time-out 396

# 14.1 Parenting

### The Family as a System
According to the systems approach, the family consists of interacting elements—parents and children influence each other. The family itself is influenced by other social systems, such as neighborhoods and religious organizations.

### Dimensions and Styles
One dimension of parenting is the degree of parental warmth: Children clearly benefit from warm, caring parents. Another dimension is control. Effective parental control involves setting appropriate standards and enforcing them consistently.

Combining warmth and control yields four parental styles: (a) authoritarian parents are controlling but uninvolved, (b) authoritative parents are controlling but responsive to their children, (c) indulgent-permissive parents are loving but exert little control, and (d) indifferent-uninvolved parents are neither warm nor controlling. Authoritative parenting is usually best for children.

### Parental Behavior
Parents influence development by direct instruction and coaching. In addition, parents serve as models for their children, who sometimes imitate parents' behavior directly; sometimes children behave in ways that are similar to what they have seen (disinhibition), and sometimes in ways that are the opposite of what they've seen (counterimitation).

Parents also use feedback to influence children's behavior. Sometimes parents fall into the negative reinforcement trap, inadvertently reinforcing behaviors that they want to discourage. Punishment is effective when it is prompt, consistent, accompanied by an explanation, and delivered by a person with whom the child has a warm relationship. Punishment has limited value because it suppresses behaviors but does not eliminate them, and it often has side effects. Time-out is one useful form of punishment.

### Children's Contributions
Parenting is influenced by characteristics of children themselves. As children grow, parents display affection more discretely and are less controlling. Over time, families develop routine ways of interacting, which can be harmful if based largely on negative mutual influences.

### Cultural Influences and Family Configuration
Child-rearing is influenced by culture and family configuration. Compared to American parents, Chinese parents are more controlling and less affectionate. In African American families, grandmothers often live with their daughters, an arrangement that eases the cost burden of housing and child care and benefits children because grandmothers can play an active role in child-rearing.

Research on gay and lesbian parents suggests that they are more similar to heterosexual parents than different and that their children develop much like children reared by heterosexual couples.

# 14.2 Brothers and Sisters

### Firstborn, Laterborn, and Only Children
Firstborn children often are more intelligent and more likely to go to college, but laterborn children are more popular and more innovative. Only children are comparable to children with siblings on most dimensions and better off on some, such as achievement and autonomy.

### Qualities of Sibling Relationships
The birth of a sibling can be stressful for older children, particularly when parents ignore their older child's needs. Siblings get along better when they are of the same sex, believe that parents treat them fairly, enter adolescence, and have parents who get along well.

# 14.3 Divorce and Remarriage

### Family Life After Divorce
In the months after a divorce, a mother's parenting is often less effective and her children behave immaturely. By 2 years after the divorce, family life is much improved. At 6 years after the divorce, mother-daughter relationships are often very positive but mother-son relationships are often conflict-filled.

### Impact of Divorce on Children
A divorce can harm children in many ways, ranging from school achievement to adjustment. The impact of divorce stems from less supervision of children, economic hardship, and conflict between parents. Children often benefit when parents have joint custody following divorce or when they live with the same-sex parent.

### Blended Families
When a mother remarries, daughters sometimes have difficulty adjusting because the new stepfather encroaches on an intimate mother-daughter relationship. A father's remarriage can cause problems because children fear that the stepmother will disturb intimate father-child relationships and because of tension between the stepmother and the noncustodial mother.

# 14.4 Parent-Child Relationships Gone Awry

### Consequences of Maltreatment
Children who are maltreated sometimes suffer permanent physical damage. Their peer relationships are often poor, and they tend to lag in cognitive development and academic performance.

### Causes of Maltreatment
A culture's views on violence, poverty, and social isolation can foster child maltreatment. Parents who abuse their children are often unhappy, socially unskilled individuals. Younger, unhealthy children are more likely to be targets of maltreatment, as are stepchildren.

### Preventing Maltreatment
Prevention should target each of the factors that contribute to child maltreatment. In reality, prevention programs often focus on providing families with new ways of coping with problems and providing parents with resources to help them cope with stress.

# 15

f you stand outside a kindergarten classroom on the first day of school, you'll probably see some children in tears, fearful of facing a novel environment on their own. What may surprise you is that many parents, too, are struggling to hold back their tears. Why? Parents realize that when their children begin school, they are taking an important step toward independence. Other forces now become influential in children's lives, sometimes challenging parents' influence. Among these forces are children's agemates (their peers), the media, and school itself. In this chapter, we'll examine these forces and see how they affect children. We'll look at peer influence in Module 15.1. Next, in Module 15.2, we'll see how electronic media—particularly television and computers—affect children's development. Finally, Module 15.3 examines the influences on children's development of other cultural institutions, including day care, schools, and the workplace.

# Influences Beyond the Family

15.1   **Peers**

15.2   **Electronic Media**

15.3   **Institutional Influences**

# 15.1

- **Development of Peer Interactions**
- **Friendship**
- **Groups**
- **Popularity and Rejection**

## Peers

### Learning Objectives

● When do youngsters first begin to interact with each other, and how do these interactions change during infancy, childhood, and adolescence?

● Why do children become friends, and what are the benefits of friendship?

● What are the important features of groups in childhood and adolescence? How do groups influence individuals?

● Why are some children more popular than others? What are the causes and consequences of being rejected?

> Only 36 hours had passed since campers arrived at Crab Orchard Summer Camp. Nevertheless, groups had already formed spontaneously, based on the campers' main interests: arts and crafts, hiking, and swimming. And, within each group, leaders and followers had already emerged. This happened every year, but the staff was always astonished at how quickly a "social network" emerged.

Many of the major developmental theorists—including, Freud, Erikson, Piaget, and Vygotsky—believed that children's development is strongly shaped by their participation in social groups. Whether the group consists of fellow campers, classmates, teammates, or a small circle of friends, an individual child's interactions with agemates are important developmental events.

In this module, we'll trace the development of peer interactions. Then we'll look at friendship and groups like those that form at summer camps. Finally, we'll consider children's social status within peer groups.

### Development of Peer Interactions

Peer interactions begin surprisingly early in infancy. Two 6-month-olds together will look, smile, and point at one another. Over the next few months, infants laugh and babble when with other infants (Hartup, 1983; Rubin, Bukowski, & Parker, 1998).

Beginning at about the first birthday and continuing through the preschool years, peer relations rapidly become more complex. **In a classic early study, Parten (1932) identified a developmental sequence that began with** *nonsocial play*—**children playing alone or watching others play but not playing themselves.** Later, children progressed to more elaborate forms of play with each child having a well-defined role. Today, researchers no longer share Parten's view that children move through each stage of play in a rigid sequence, but the different forms of play that she distinguished are useful nonetheless.

**The first type of social play to appear—soon after the first birthday—is** *parallel play:* **youngsters play alone but maintain a keen interest in what other children are doing.** For example, each boy in the photo has his own toy but is watching the other play, too. During parallel play, exchanges between youngsters begin to occur. When one talks or smiles, the other usually responds (Howes, Unger, & Seidner, 1990).

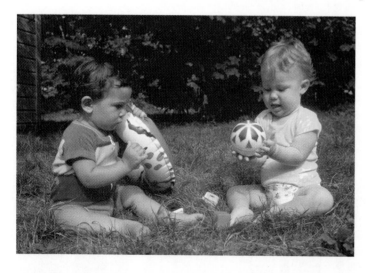

Beginning at roughly 15 to 18 months, toddlers no longer just watch one another at play. **In *simple social play,* youngsters engage in similar activities, talk or smile at one another, and offer each other toys.** Play is now truly interactive (Howes & Matheson, 1992). An example of simple social play would be two 20-month-olds pushing toy cars along the floor, making "car sounds," and periodically trading cars.

**Toward the second birthday, *cooperative play* begins: Now children organize their play around a distinct theme and take on special roles based on the theme.** For example, children may play "hide-and-seek" and alternate roles of hider and finder, or they may have a tea party and alternate being the host and guest.

The pie charts show how the nature of young children's play changes dramatically in a few years. These charts are based on observing 1- to 5-year-olds interacting with their peers at a day-care center (Howes & Matheson, 1992). The 1½-year-olds spend the vast majority of their time in parallel play; other forms of play are relatively rare. By the time children are 3½ to 4 years old, parallel play is much less common and cooperative play is the norm. Cooperative play typically involves peers of the same gender, a preference that increases until, by age 6, youngsters choose same-sex playmates about two-thirds of the time (LaFreniere, Strayer, & Gauthier, 1984).

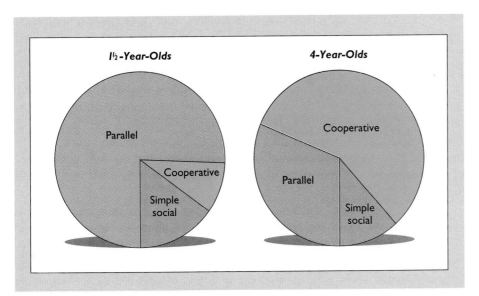

FIG 15–1

**Make-Believe.**   During the preschool years, cooperative play often takes the form of make-believe. Preschoolers have telephone conversations with imaginary partners or pretend to drink imaginary juice. In early phases of make-believe, children rely on realistic props to support their play. While pretending to drink, younger preschoolers use a real cup; while pretending to drive a car, they use a toy steering wheel.

In later phrases of make-believe, children no longer need realistic props; instead, they can imagine that a block is the cup, or, like the boys in the photo, that a paper plate is the steering wheel. Of course, this gradual movement toward more abstract make-believe is possible because of cognitive growth that occurs during the preschool years (Harris & Kavanaugh, 1993).

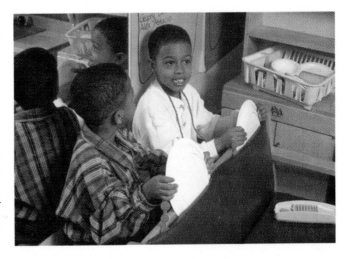

As you might suspect, make-believe reflects the values important in a child's culture (Bornstein et al., 1999). For example, Farver and Shin (1997) studied make-believe play of European American preschoolers and Korean American preschoolers. The Korean American children came from recently immigrated families, so they still held traditional Korean values, such as an emphasis on the family and on harmony over conflict. The two groups of children differed in the themes of their make-believe play. Adventure and fantasy were favorite themes for European American youngsters, but family roles and everyday activities were favorites of the Korean American children.

In addition, the groups differed in their style of play during make-believe. European American children were more assertive in their make-believe and more likely to disagree with their play partner's ideas about pretending ("*I* want to be the the king; *you* be the mom!"). Korean American children were more polite and more likely to strive for harmony ("Could I *please* be king?"). Thus, cultural values influence both the content and the content form of make-believe.

> Make-believe play promotes cognitive development and lets children explore emotional topics that frighten them.

Make-believe play is not only entertaining for children; it seems to promote cognitive development (Berk, 1994). Children who spend much time in make-believe play tend to be more advanced in language, memory, and reasoning. They also tend to have a more sophisticated understanding of other people's thoughts, beliefs, and feelings (Howe, Petrakos, & Rinaldi, 1998; Youngblade & Dunn, 1995).

Yet another benefit of make-believe is that it allows children to explore topics that frighten them. Children who are afraid of the dark may reassure a doll who is also afraid of the dark. By explaining to the doll why she shouldn't be afraid, children come to understand and regulate their own fear of darkness. Or children may pretend that a doll has misbehaved and must be punished, which allows them to experience the parent's anger and the doll's guilt. Make-believe allows children to explore other emotions, too, including joy and affection (Gottman, 1986).

For many preschool children, make-believe play involves imaginary companions. Children can usually describe their imaginary playmates in some detail, mentioning sex and age as well as the color of their hair and eyes. Imaginary companions were once thought to be fairly rare and a sign of possible developmental problems. But more recent research shows that nearly two-thirds of all preschoolers report imaginary companions (Taylor, Cartwright, & Carlson, 1993).

Moreover, an imaginary companion is associated with many positive social characteristics: Preschoolers with imaginary friends tend to be more sociable and have more real friends than other preschoolers. Furthermore, vivid fantasy play with imaginary companions does not mean that the distinction between fantasy and reality is blurred: Children with imaginary companions can distinguish fantasy from reality just as accurately as youngsters without imaginary companions (Taylor et al., 1993).

Solitary Play.  At times throughout the preschool years, many children prefer to play alone. Should parents be worried? Usually, no. Solitary play comes in many forms and most are normal—even healthy. Spending free play time alone coloring, solving puzzles, or assembling Legos® is not a sign of maladjustment. Many youngsters enjoy solitary activities and, at other times, choose very social play.

However, some forms of solitary play *are* signs that children are uneasy interacting with others (Coplan et al., 1994; Harrist et al., 1997). One type of unhealthy solitary play is wandering aimlessly. Sometimes children go from one preschool activity center to the next, as if trying to to decide what to do. But really they just keep wandering, never settling into play with others or into constructive solitary play. Another unhealthy type of solitary play is hovering: A child stands nearby peers who are playing, watching them play but not participating. Over time, these behaviors do not bode well for youngsters (as we'll see on pages 433–435), so it's best for these youngsters to see a professional who can help them overcome their reticence in social situations (Ladd, 1998).

### Parental Influence.

Parents get involved in their preschool children's play in several ways. Sometimes they take the role of playmate (and many parents deserve an Oscar for their performances). They use the opportunity to scaffold their children's play (see Module 6.4), often raising it to more sophisticated levels (Tamis-LeMonda & Bornstein, 1996). For example, if a toddler is stacking toy plates, a parent might help the child stack the plates (play at the same level) or might pretend to wash each plate (play at a more advanced level). When parents demonstrate more advanced forms of play, their children often play at the more advanced levels later (Bornstein et al., 1996).

Another parental role during preschoolers' play is mediator. Preschoolers often disagree, argue, and sometimes fight. As shown in the photo, children play more cooperatively and longer when parents are present to help iron out conflicts (Mize, Pettit, & Brown, 1995; Parke & Bhavnagri, 1989). When young children can't agree on what to play, a parent can negotiate a mutually acceptable activity. When both youngsters want to play with the same toy, a parent can arrange for them to share. Here, too, parents scaffold their preschoolers' play, smoothing the interaction by providing some of the social skills that preschoolers lack.

Yet another parental role is coach. Preschool children often encounter social problems that, although minor from an adult's perspective, seem overwhelming to the child. For example, a child might be coloring when another child approaches and demands the crayon the child is using. Parents can help their preschoolers understand and handle such problems. When parents coach—and when their advice is constructive—their children tend to be skilled socially and less aggressive (Mize & Pettit, 1997).

Parents also influence the success of their children's peer interactions in a much less direct manner. Recall from Module 10.3 that children's relationships with peers are most successful when, as infants, they had a secure attachment relationship with their mother (Ladd & LeSieur, 1995; Lieberman, Doyle, & Markiewicz, 1999).

Why does quality of attachment predict the success of children's peer relationships? One view is that a child's relationship with his or her parents is the internal working model for all future social relationships. When the parent-child relationship is high quality and emotionally satisfying, children are encouraged to form relationships with other people. Another possibility is that a secure attachment relationship with the mother makes an infant feel more confident about exploring the environment, which, in turn, provides more opportunities to interact with peers. These two views are not mutually exclusive; both may contribute to the relative ease with which securely attached children interact with their peers (Hartup, 1992b).

Peer Relations After Preschool.   When children attend elementary school, the context of peer relations changes dramatically. Not only does the sheer number of peers increase dramatically, but children are often exposed to a far more diverse set of peers than before. In addition, children find themselves interacting with peers in situations that range from reasonably structured with much adult supervision (e.g., a classroom) to largely unstructured with minimal adult supervision (e.g., a playground during recess).

An obvious change in children's peer relations during the elementary-school years is that children get along better than when they were younger. When conflicts arise, elementary-school children are better able to resolve them because of their greater cognitive and social skills. They are able to to take another's perspective and be empathic (see Module 12.3), characteristics that help smoothe the bumps encountered in all social interactions.

What do school-age children do when they're together? In one study (Zarbatany, Hartmann, & Rankin, 1990), investigators asked Canadian students in grades 5 and 6 how they spent their time with peers. The students in the study indicated how often they participated with peers in each of 29 different activities. The results, shown in the graph, are not too surprising, eh? The most common activities with peers are simple—just being together and talking.

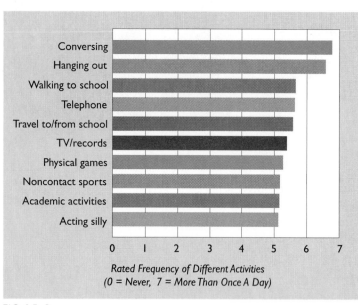

FIG 15–2

*Rated Frequency of Different Activities*
*(0 = Never,  7 = More Than Once A Day)*

The graph also highlights another important feature of peer relations during the elementary-school years. Children reported that they played physical games a few times each week, which reflects, in part, the emergence of a special type of play in school-age children. **In *rough-and-tumble play,* children playfully chase, punch, kick, shove, fight, and wrestle with peers.** Notice "playfully" in this definition: Unlike aggression, where the intention is to do harm, rough-and-tumble play is for fun. When children are involved in rough-and-tumble play, they are usually smiling and sometimes laughing (Pellegrini & Smith, 1998). When parents or teachers intervene, the youngsters usually explain that there's no problem, they're just playing. Rough-and-tumble play is more common among boys than girls, and girls' rough-and-tumble play tends to emphasize running and chasing over wrestling and fighting.

As children move into adolescence, two features of their peer relationships loom large: Friendships become more intimate and groups take on greater significance. These changes are so important that we'll consider each one separately. First we'll look at friendship.

## Friendship

Over time, even young children develop special relationships with certain peers. ***Friendship* is a voluntary relationship between two people involving mutual liking.** By age 4 or 5 years, most children claim to have a "best friend." If you ask them how they can tell a child is their best friend, their response will probably resemble 5-year-old Katelyn's:

INTERVIEWER: Why is Heidi your best friend?

KATELYN:  Because she plays with me. And she's nice to me.

INTERVIEWER: Are there any other reasons?

KATELYN:  Yeah, Heidi lets me play with her dolls.

Of course, older children and adolescents also have best friends, but they describe them differently. Here is a typical 13-year-old's response:

INTERVIEWER: Why is Heather your best friend?

ANNA:  She helps me. And we think alike. My mom says we're like twins!

INTERVIEWER: What else tells you that Heather's your best friend?

ANNA:  Because I can tell her stuff—special stuff, like secrets—and I know that she won't tell anybody else.

INTERVIEWER: Anything else?

ANNA:  Yeah. If we fight, later we always tell each other that we're sorry.

For both Katelyn and Anna, best friends have common interests and like each other. However, Anna's friendship with Heather has other features as well. Older children and adolescents believe that loyalty, trust, and intimacy are important ingredients of friendship. Also, adolescents, much more so than children, believe that friends should defend one another. They also strongly believe that friends should not deceive or abandon one another (Newcomb & Bagwell, 1995).

The emphasis on loyalty in adolescent friendships apparently goes hand in hand with the emphasis on intimacy: If a friend is disloyal, adolescents are afraid that they may be humiliated because their intimate thoughts and feelings will become known to a much broader circle of people (Berndt & Perry, 1990).

Intimacy is more common in friendships among girls, who are more likely than boys to have one exclusive "best friend." Because intimacy is at the core of their friendships, girls are also more likely to be concerned about the faithfulness of their friends and worry about being rejected (Buhrmester & Furman, 1987). And when one friend makes another mad, girls' anger tends to be more intense and last longer (Whitesell & Harter, 1996).

The emergence of intimacy in adolescent friendships means that friends also come to be seen as sources of social and emotional support. Levitt, Guacci-Franco, and Levitt (1993) asked African American, European American, and Hispanic American 7-, 10-, and 14-year-olds to whom they would turn if they needed help or were bothered by something. For all ethnic groups, 7- and 10-year-olds relied upon close family members—parents, siblings, and grandparents—as primary sources of support, but not friends. However, 14-year-olds relied upon close family members less often and said they would turn to friends instead. Because adolescent friends share intimate thoughts and feelings, they can provide support during emotional or stressful periods.

Friendships in childhood and adolescence are both based on common interests and mutual liking, but only in adolescence is intimacy important, particularly for girls' friendships.

### Who Become Friends?

Like the friends shown in the photo, most friends are alike in age, gender, and race (Hartup, 1992a). Because friends are supposed to treat each other as equals, friendships are rare between an older, more experienced child and a younger, less experienced child. Because children typically play with same-sex peers (see Module 13.3), boys and girls rarely become friends.

Friendships are more common between children from the same race or ethnic group than between children from different groups, reflecting racial segregation in American society. Friendships among children of different groups are more common in schools where classes are smaller (Hallinan & Teixeira, 1987). Evidently, when classes are large, children select friends from the large number of available same-race peers. When fewer same-race peers are available in smaller classes, children more often become friends with other-race children. Interracial friendships are usually confined to school, unless children come from integrated neighborhoods. That is, when children live in different, segregated neighborhoods, their friendship does not extend to out-of-school settings (DuBois & Hirsch, 1990).

Of course, not only are friends usually alike in age, sex, and race. Children and adolescents are also drawn together because they have similar attitudes toward school, recreation, and the future (Newcomb & Bagwell, 1995). Tom, who enjoys school, likes to read, and plans to go to Harvard, will probably not befriend Barry, who thinks that school is stupid, listens to his disc player constantly, and plans to quit high school to become a rock star (Haselager et al., 1998). As time passes, friends become more similar in their attitudes and values (Kandel, 1978).

Although children's friendships are overwhelmingly with members of their own sex, a few children have friendships with opposite-sex children. Who are these children, and why do they have opposite-sex friendships? Boys and girls are equally likely to have opposite-sex friendships. The important factor in understanding these children is whether they have same- *and* opposite-sex friends or *only* opposite-sex friends. Children with same- and opposite-sex friendships tend to be very well adjusted, whereas children with only opposite-sex friendships tend to be unpopular and less competent academically and socially, and to have lower self-esteem. Apparently, children with both same- and opposite-sex friends are so socially skilled and popular that both boys and girls are eager to be their friends. In contrast, children with only opposite-sex friendships are socially unskilled, unpopular youngsters who are rejected by their same-sex peers and form friendships with opposite-sex children as a last resort (Kovacs, Parker, & Hoffman, 1996).

### Quality and Consequences of Friendship.

If you think back to your childhood friendships, you probably remember some that were long-lasting and satisfying as well as others that rapidly wore thin and soon dissolved. What accounts for these differences in the quality and longevity of friendships? Sometimes friendships are brief because children have the skills to create friendships—they know funny stories, they kid around, they know good gossip—but lack the skills to sustain them—they can't keep secrets, or they're too bossy (Jiao, 1999; Parker & Seal, 1996). Sometimes friendships end because, when conflicts arise, children are more concerned about their own interests and are unwilling to compromise or negotiate (Fonzi et al., 1997; Rose & Asher, 1999). And sometimes friendships end when children discover that their needs and interests aren't as similar as they thought initially (Gavin & Furman, 1996).

Considering that friendships disintegrate for many reasons, you're probably reminded that truly good friends are to be treasured. In fact, researchers consistently find that children benefit from having good friends. Compared to children who lack friends, children with good friends have higher self-esteem, are less likely to be lonely and depressed, and more often act prosocially—sharing and cooperating with others (Hartup & Stevens, 1999; Ladd, 1998). Children with good friends cope better with life stresses, such as the transition

When children have good friends, they are more likely to behave prosocially and are better adjusted.

from elementary school to middle school or junior high (Berndt & Keefe, 1995), and they're less likely to be victimized by peers (Hodges et al., 1999). The benefits of friendship are also long-lasting: Children who have friends have greater self-worth as young adults (Bagwell, Newcomb, & Bukowski, 1998).

Thus, friends are not simply special playmates and companions; they are important resources. Children learn from their friends and turn to them for support in times of stress. Friendships are one important way peers influence development. Peers also influence development through groups, the topic of the next section.

## Groups

As was the case at the summer camp in the opening vignette, whenever strangers are brought together, they form groups. Psychologist Muzafer Sherif and his colleagues (1961) used this phenomenon to conduct a landmark study of children's groups at the Robbers Cave State Park in Oklahoma. The boys in this study did not know one another before coming to camp. They were put in two groups that were comparable in the boys' size, their athletic ability, and previous camping experience. For the first week, the two groups were kept apart and spent their time in traditional camp activities that required considerable cooperation, such as transporting camping equipment and organizing hikes.

After just a few days, leaders emerged within each group. Boys acquired nicknames and the groups themselves acquired names, Rattlers and Eagles. Each group established norms to regulate behavior within the group. For example, boys who complained about minor injuries or being homesick were teased for not being "tough."

At the end of the first week, it was arranged that the groups discover each other. Each immediately insisted that the other had intruded on its "turf," which helped solidify the emerging feelings of group membership. Each group challenged the other in baseball, so a game was planned, along with other competitions (such as tent pitching and cleaning the cabins). Prizes were announced for the winners.

Preparing for these events further solidified group loyalties, and activities that had once been avoided—cleaning the cabins, for example—were now pursued vigorously because they contributed to the goal of establishing the group's superiority. In this phase, boys became antagonistic to members of the other group. During the competitions, boys heckled and cursed the other group. After losing to the Rattlers in the first baseball game, the Eagles burned the Rattlers' flag and hung the remnants for the Rattlers to find. One Eagle said, "You can tell those guys *I* did it if they say anything. I'll fight 'em!"

Relations deteriorated so rapidly between the groups that in just a few days the boys abandoned displays of good sportsmanship and refused to eat together in the same mess hall. And stereotypes formed. Rattlers were convinced that Eagles were unfriendly and sneaky. Of course, Eagles felt the same way about Rattlers.

After two weeks, the final phase of the study began: Now the aim was to reduce hostility between the groups. First, researchers arranged for the two groups to participate in enjoyable, noncompetitive events, such as watching a movie or shooting firecrackers together. This approach failed completely, and the antagonism continued.

The second approach involved creating common goals for the two groups that required cooperation. When the boys wanted to see a popular movie, the staff said that the camp could not afford the rental. After some debate, the two groups agreed to contribute equally to the cost of the movie. A few days later, a truck that was to pick up supplies would not start. A Rattler suggested they use a rope to pull the truck to start it. As the photo shows, all group members joined in and, after a few tries, started the truck (which was in working condition all along). The boys congratulated one another, and the groups intermingled.

These and other situations involving common goals eliminated the hostility between groups just as rapidly as the competition had elicited it. By the end of the week, Rattlers and Eagles were sitting together in the mess hall. When camp was over, the Rattlers and Eagles asked to travel home on the same bus.

The Robbers Cave study tells us a great deal about group formation and group functioning. Three conclusions are particularly worth remembering. First, when groups of children are brought together, a structure emerges rapidly with individuals having specific roles, for example, as a leader. Second, when groups compete for scarce resources (for example, prizes), individuals identify with and support their own group more strongly. At the same time, they develop negative stereotypes of members of other groups and feel antagonistic toward them. Third, when common goals require that groups cooperate, group boundaries become less pronounced and hostility between groups ceases.

Though it's been nearly 50 years since Sherif's study at Robbers Cave, the findings are still important to understanding the social landscape of late childhood and adolescence. Two types of groups are particularly common as children enter adolescence. **A *clique* consists of four to six individuals who are good friends and, consequently, tend to be similar in age, sex, race, and interests.** Members of a clique spend time together and often dress, talk, and act alike. Cliques are often part of a larger group, too. **A *crowd* is a larger group of older children or adolescents who have similar values and attitudes and are known by a common label.** Maybe you remember some of the different crowds from your own youth? Jocks, preppies, burnouts, nerds, and brains—adolescents use these or similar terms to refer to crowds of older children or adolescents (Brown et al., 1993; Cairns et al., 1995).

Some crowds have more status than others. For example, students in many junior and senior high schools claim that the "jocks" are the most prestigious crowd whereas the "burnouts" are among the least prestigious. Self-esteem in older children and adolescents often reflects the status of their crowd. During the school years, youth from high-status crowds tend to have greater self-esteem than those from low-status crowds (Brown & Lohr, 1987).

Why do some students become nerds while others join the burnouts? Parenting style (discussed in Module 14.1) is part of the answer. A study by Brown and his colleagues (1993) examined the impact of three parental practices on students' membership in particular crowds. The investigators measured the extent to which parents emphasized academic achievement, monitored their children's out-of-school activities, and involved their children in joint decision making. When parents emphasized achievement, their children were more likely to be in the popular, jock, and normal crowds and less likely to be in the druggie crowd. When parents monitored out-of-school behavior, their children were more likely to be in the brain crowd and less likely to be in the druggie crowd. Finally, when parents included their children in joint decision making, their children were more likely to be in the brain and normal crowds and less likely to be in the druggie crowd. These findings were true for African American, Asian American, European American, and Hispanic American children and their parents.

What seems to happen is that when parents practice authoritative parenting— they are warm but controlling—their children become involved with crowds that endorse adult standards of behavior (for example, normals, jocks, brains). But, when parents' style is neglecting or permissive, their children are less likely to identify with adult standards of behavior and, instead, join crowds like druggies that disavow adult standards.

Group Structure.    Groups—whether in school, at a summer camp, or anyplace else—typically have a well-defined structure. **Most groups have a *dominance hierarchy* consisting of a leader to whom all other members of the group defer.** Other members know their position in the hierarchy. They yield to members who are above them in the hierarchy and assert themselves over members who are below them. A dominance hierarchy is useful in reducing conflict within groups because every member knows his or her place.

What determines where members stand in the hierarchy? With children, especially boys, physical power is often the basis for the dominance hierarchy. The leader is usually the the most physically intimidating child (Pettit et al., 1990). Among girls and older boys, hierarchies are often based on individual traits that relate to the group's main function. At Crab Orchard Summer Camp, for example, the leaders most often are the children with the greatest camping experience. Among Girl Scouts, girls chosen to be patrol leaders tend to be bright and goal oriented and to have new ideas (Edwards, 1994). These characteristics are appropriate because the primary function of patrols is to help plan activities for the entire troop of Girl Scouts. Thus, leadership based on key skills is effective because it gives the greatest influence to those with the skills most important to group functioning (Hartup, 1983).

> Groups have a dominance hierarchy in which group members defer to a leader, who usually has the skills important to the group's function.

Peer Pressure.    Groups establish norms—standards of behavior that apply to all group members—and groups may pressure members to conform to these norms. Such "peer pressure" is often characterized as an irresistible, harmful force. The stereotype is that teenagers exert enormous pressure on each other to behave antisocially. In reality, peer pressure is neither all-powerful nor always evil. For example, most junior and senior high students resist peer pressure to behave in ways that are clearly antisocial, such as stealing (Brown, Lohr, & McClenahan, 1986). Peer pressure can be positive, too; peers often urge one another to participate in school activities, such as trying out for a play or working on the yearbook, or become involved in community action projects, such as Habitat for Humanity.

Peer pressure is most powerful when the standards for appropriate behavior are not clear-cut. Taste in music and clothing, for example, is completely subjective, so youths conform to peer group guidelines, as you can see in the all-too-familiar sight shown in the photo at the top of page 432—girls all wearing "in" clothing.

Similarly, standards on smoking, drinking, and using drugs are often fuzzy. Drinking is a good case in point. Parents and groups like SADD (Students Against Driving Drunk) may discourage teens from drinking, yet American culture is filled with youthful models who drink, seem to enjoy it, and suffer no apparent ill effects.

To the contrary, they seem to enjoy life even more. With such contradictory messages, it is not surprising that youth look to their peers for answers (Urberg, Değirmencioğlu, & Pilgrim, 1997). Consequently, some youth drink (or smoke, use drugs, or have sex) to conform to their group's norms, while others abstain, again reflecting their group's norms.

## Popularity and Rejection

Eileen is definitely the most popular child in her class. Other youngsters always want to play with her and sit near her at lunch or on the school bus. In contrast, Jay is the least popular child in the class. When he tries to join a game of four-square, the others quit. Students in the class dislike Jay as much as they like Eileen.

Popular and rejected children like Eileen and Jay can be found in every classroom and neighborhood. In fact, studies of popularity (Newcomb, Bukowski, & Pattee, 1993) reveal that most children can be placed in one of five categories:

- *Popular children* are liked by many classmates.
- *Rejected children* are disliked by many classmates.
- *Controversial children* are both liked and disliked by classmates.
- *Average children* are liked and disliked by some classmates but without the intensity found for popular, rejected, or controversial children.
- *Neglected children* are ignored by classmates.

What determines who's hot and who's not? Why is a child popular, rejected, controversial, average, or neglected? Smarter and physically attractive children are more often popular (Johnstone, Frame, & Bouman, 1992). However, the most important ingredient in popularity is social skill. Popular children are better at initiating social interactions with other children. They are more skillful at communicating and better at integrating themselves into an ongoing conversation or play session.

Popular children also seem relatively gifted in assessing and monitoring their own social impact in various situations and in tailoring their responses to the requirements of new social situations (Ladd, 1998; Wentzel & Asher, 1995). In one study, popular youngsters were more likely than unpopular children to share, cooperate, and help and less likely to start fights and break rules (Wentzel & Erdley, 1993). In another study, popular children were more likely to take turns and less likely to interrupt others (Black & Logan, 1995).

Why do some children fail in their efforts to be popular and end up in one of the other categories—rejected, controversial, average, or neglected? We know the most about rejected children. Rejected children tend to be socially unskilled (Stormshak et al., 1999). Many rejected children are aggressive, attacking their peers without provocation (Dodge, Bates, & Pettit, 1990). Other rejected youngsters have poor self-control and are often disruptive in school (French, 1988; 1990). When conflicts arise, rejected children often become angry and retaliate (Bryant, 1992).

Being well liked seems straightforward: Be pleasant and friendly, not obnoxious. Share, cooperate, and help instead of being disruptive. Are these rules specific to American children, or do they apply more generally? The "Cultural Influences" feature has the answer.

### Keys to Popularity

In America, popular children seem to know how to get along with others. These results don't apply just to American children; they hold for children in many cultures around the world, including Canada, European countries, Israel, and China (e.g., Casiglia, Coco, & Zappulla, 1998). Sometimes, however, popular children have other characteristics that are unique to their cultural setting. In Israel, for example, popular children are more likely to be direct and assertive than in other countries (Krispin, Sternberg, & Lamb, 1992). In China, popular children are more likely to be shy than in other countries (Chen, Rubin, & Li, 1995). Evidently, good social skills are at the core of popularity in most countries, but other features may also be important, reflecting culturally specific values. ●

**Consequences of Rejection.**   No one enjoys being rejected. In fact, repeated peer rejection in childhood can have serious long-term consequences (DeRosier, Kupersmidt, & Patterson, 1995; Downey et al., 1998; Ladd, 1998). Rejected youngsters are more likely than youngsters in the other categories to drop out of school, commit juvenile offenses, and suffer from psychopathology. The "Focus on Research" feature describes one study that showed some of the long-term effects of popularity and rejection.

### Long-Term Consequences of Popularity and Rejection

*Who were the investigators, and what was the aim of the study?* Patricia Morison and Ann Masten (1991) set out to determine if the outcome of development is similar for popular and unpopular children. That is, they wanted to know if popular and rejected children take the same or different developmental paths.

*How did the investigators measure the topic of interest?* Morison and Masten identified popular and rejected children by asking children in grades 3 to 6 to nominate classmates for roles in an imaginary class play. Popular children were defined as those who were frequently nominated for roles like "a good leader," "everyone likes to be with," and "has many friends." Rejected children were those frequently nominated for roles like "picks on other kids," "too bossy," and "teases other children too much." Seven years later, the children and their parents completed questionnaires measuring academic achievement, social skill, and self-worth.

*Who were the children in the study?* Initially, 207 children in grades 3 to 6 were tested, and 183 of them completed the questionnaires 7 years later.

*What was the design of the study?* This study was correlational because Morison and Masten were interested in the relation that existed naturally between two sets of variables: popularity and rejection at the first testing and academic achievement, social skill, and self-worth at the second. The study was longitudinal because children were tested twice, once in grades 3 to 6 and again 7 years later.

> When children are rejected, they usually do less well in school, have lower self-esteem, and are more likely to have behavioral problems.

*Were there ethical concerns with the study?* No. The general purpose of the study was explained and then parents and children consented to participate.

*What were the results?* The table shows the correlations between popularity and rejection in grades 3 to 6 and academic achievement, social skill, and self-worth measured 7 years later. Children who were popular in grades 3 to 6 were doing well in school, were socially skilled, and had high self-esteem. In contrast, children who were rejected in grades 3 to 6 were not doing well in school and had low self-esteem.

| Correlations Between Children's Popularity and Rejection in Grades 3 to 6 and Academic Achievement, Social Skill, and Self-Worth | | |
| --- | --- | --- |
| **Outcome** | **Popularity in grades 3–6** | **Rejection in grades 3–6** |
| Academic achievement | .27 | −.25 |
| Social Skill | .24 | .03 |
| Self-Worth | .24 | −.22 |

TABLE 15–1

*What did the investigators conclude?* Popular children fit in with groups instead of trying to make groups adjust to them. When conflicts arise with peers, popular children try to understand the problem and provide useful solutions. Over time, popular children's prosocial skill pays long-term dividends; unfortunately, rejected children's lack of prosocial skill has a price as well. ●

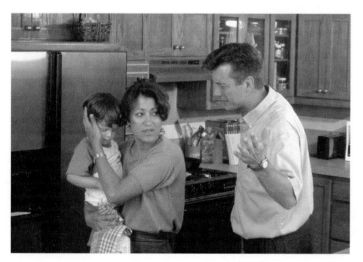

**Causes of Rejection.** Peer rejection can be traced, at least in part, to parental influence (Ladd, 1998). Children see how their parents respond to different social situations and often imitate these responses later. Parents who are friendly and cooperative with others demonstrate effective social skills. Parents who are belligerent and combative demonstrate much less effective social skills. In particular, when parents typically respond to interpersonal conflict like the couple in the photo—with intimidation or aggression—their children may imitate them; this hampers their development of social skills and makes them less popular in the long run (Keane, Brown, & Crenshaw, 1990).

Parents' disciplinary practices also affect their children's social skill and popularity. Inconsistent discipline—punishing a child for misbehaving one day and ignoring the same behavior the next—is associated with antisocial and aggressive behavior, paving the way to rejection (Dishion, 1990). Consistent punishment that is tied to parental love and affection is more likely to promote social skill and, in the process, popularity (Dekovic & Janssens, 1992).

In sum, parenting can lead to an aggressive interpersonal style in a child, which in turn leads to peer rejection. The implication, then, is that by teaching youngsters (and their parents) more effective ways of interacting with others, we can make rejection less likely. With improved social skills, rejected children would not need to resort to antisocial behaviors. Rejected children (and other types of unpopular children) can be taught how to initiate interaction, communicate clearly, and be friendly. They can also be discouraged from behaviors that peers dislike, such as whining and fighting. This training is very similar to the training given aggressive adolescents, who are typically unpopular (see Module 12.4). Training of this sort does work. Rejected children can learn skills that lead to peer acceptance and thereby avoid the long-term harm associated with being rejected (LaGreca, 1993; Mize & Ladd, 1990).

## Check Your Learning

1. Toddlers often engage in _____ play, which consists of playing separately but looking at one another and sometimes communicating verbally.

2. _____ play promotes cognitive development and helps children explore topics that frighten them.

3. Solitary play is worrisome when children wander aimlessly or _____.

4. Parents influence play in their roles as playmate, _____, and coach.

5. Beginning in adolescence, friendships include an emphasis on loyalty, trust, and _____.

6. Friends are usually alike in age, sex, race, and _____.

7. As groups form, a _____ typically emerges, with the leader at the top.

8. Peer pressure is most powerful when _____.

9. Compared to unpopular children, popular children are usually _____.

How might developmental change in the nature of friendship be explained by Piaget's stages of cognitive development, described in Module 6.2?

**Answers:** (1) parallel, (2) Make-believe, (3) hover around other children who are playing, (4) negotiator, (5) intimacy, (6) interests, (7) dominance hierarchy, (8) standards for appropriate behavior are vague, (9) more skilled socially

# Electronic Media

15.2

## Learning Objectives

Television
Computers

● How does watching television affect children's attitudes and behavior?

● How does TV viewing influence children's cognitive development?

● How are computers used in school, and what are their effects on instruction?

● How do computer and video games affect children?

*Whenever Bill visits his granddaughter, Harmony, he is struck by the amount of time Harmony spends watching television. Many of the programs she watches are worthwhile. Nevertheless, Bill wonders if such a steady diet of TV watching might somehow be harmful. Images pop on and off the screen so rapidly that Bill wonders how Harmony will ever learn to pay attention. And he worries that she won't be as attentive in other settings that aren't as rich in video stimulation.*

Think about some of the technological developments that today's children take for granted that were completely foreign to youngsters growing up just a few decades ago. Your list would probably include VCRs, cable TV, CD players, video game players, personal computers, cell phones, pagers, and the World Wide Web. More forces than ever before can potentially influence children's development. In generations past, children learned their culture's values from parents, teachers, religious leaders, and print media. These sources of cultural knowledge are still with us, but they coexist with new technologies that do not always portray parents' values. Two of these technologies—television and computers—are the focus of this module. As we look at their influence, we'll see if Bill's concern for his granddaughter is well founded.

## Television

"MRS. HORTON, COULD YOU STOP BY SCHOOL TODAY?"
© 1995 Martha F. Campbell.
Reprinted with permission.

The cartoon exaggerates TV's impact on American children, but only somewhat. After all, think about how much time you spent in front of a TV while you were growing up. If you were a typical U.S. child and adolescent, you spent much more time watching TV than interacting with your parents or in school. The numbers tell an incredible story. School-age children spend about 25 hours each week watching TV (Nielson, 1990). Extrapolated through adolescence, the typical American high-school graduate has watched 20,000 hours of TV—the equivalent of 2 full years of watching TV 24 hours daily! No wonder social scientists and laypeople alike think TV plays an important role in socializing American children.

For most youngsters, viewing time increases gradually during the preschool and elementary-school years, reaching a peak just before adolescence. Boys watch more TV than girls. Also, children with lower IQs watch more than those with higher IQs; children from lower-income families watch more TV than children from higher-income families (Huston & Wright, 1998).

It is hard to imagine that all this TV viewing would not affect children's behavior. For this reason, scientists have been studying the impact of TV since the 1950s. Much of the research has addressed the impact of the medium per se; other research has examined the impact of the contents of TV programs (Huston & Wright, 1998). In this section, we'll look at the results of both types of research.

### The Medium Is the Message . . . Or Is It?

When TV first became popular, critics argued that the medium itself—independent of the contents of programs—has several harmful effects on viewers, particularly children (Huston & Wright, 1998). Among the criticisms were these:

- Because TV programs consist of many brief segments presented in rapid succession, children who watch a lot of TV develop short attention spans and have difficulty concentrating in school.
- Because TV provides ready-made, simple-to-interpret images, children who watch a lot of TV become passive, lazy thinkers and become less creative.
- Children who spend a lot of time watching TV spend less time in more productive and valuable activities, such as reading, participating in sports, and playing with friends.

In fact, as stated, *none* of these criticisms is consistently supported by research (Huston & Wright, 1998). The first criticism—TV watching reduces attention—is the easiest to dismiss. Research repeatedly shows that increased TV viewing does not lead to reduced attention, greater impulsivity, reduced task persistence, or increased activity levels. The contents of TV programs can influence these dimensions of children's behavior—children who watch impulsive models behave more impulsively themselves (see Module 12.1)—but TV per se does not harm children's ability to pay attention. Bill, the grandfather in the opening vignette, need not worry that his granddaughter's TV viewing will limit her ability to pay attention later in life.

As for the criticism that TV viewing fosters lazy thinking and stifles creativity, the evidence is mixed. Many studies find no link between amount of TV viewing and creativity. Some find a negative relation: As children watch more TV, they tend to be less creative on tests of divergent thinking like those described in Module 8.3 (Valkenburg & van der Voort, 1994; 1995). Child development researchers don't know why the negative effects aren't found more consistently, although one idea is that the effects depend on what programs children watch, not simply the amount of TV watched.

Finally, according to the last criticism, TV viewing replaces other socially desirable activities: The simple-minded view is that every hour of TV viewing replaces an hour of some more valuable activity, such as reading or doing homework. To illustrate the problems with this view, let's look at reading. The correlation between time spent watching TV and time spent reading *is* negative—heavy TV viewers read less (Huston & Wright, 1998). But we need to be cautious in interpreting this correlation (see Figure 1-3 on page 26). The easy interpretation is that watching much TV *causes* children to read less. However, other evidence suggests an alternate interpretation is more plausible: Children who are poor readers (and thus are unlikely to spend much time reading) end up watching a lot of TV. For youngsters who read poorly, an hour spent watching TV replaces some activity, but not an hour that would have been spent reading.

The research on each of these criticisms points to one conclusion: To understand the impact of TV on children, we need to move past the medium per se and consider other variables, including the contents of TV programs. Scientists who have done this have discovered that TV does, indeed, substantially affect children's development, as you'll see in the next three sections.

### Influence on Attitudes and Social Behavior.

Children are definitely influenced by what they see on TV. Module 12.4, for example, described how some children become more aggressive after viewing violence on television, and Module 13.3 discussed how children adopt gender stereotypes from TV.

Television can definitely have negative effects, but can TV be put to prosocial goals? Can TV viewing help children learn to be more generous and cooperative and have greater self-control? Yes, according to early laboratory studies. In these experiments, children were more likely to act prosocially after they watched brief films showing a peer acting prosocially (Liebert & Sprafkin, 1988). For example, children were more likely to share or more likely to resist the temptation to take from others after they watched other children sharing or resisting temptation.

In one of the early laboratory studies on the impact of TV viewing on prosocial behavior, Bryan and Walbek (1970) gave third- and fourth-grade children a prize for playing a game. Then the children watched a film about another child who had received the same prize and was asked to donate some of the prize to charity. In one version of the film, the child agreed, but in another version the child did not. The children in the study were then given the opportunity to donate a portion of their winnings to the same charity shown in the film. Children were much more likely to donate when they saw the film about the generous child than when they saw the film about the greedy one. Thus, from watching others who were generous, children learned to be generous themselves.

*Children can learn prosocial behavior from television—they are more likely to be cooperative and generous after having seen TV characters act this way.*

Research with actual TV programs leads to the same conclusion. Youngsters who watch TV shows that emphasize prosocial behavior, such as *Mister Rogers' Neighborhood*, are more likely to behave prosocially (Huston & Wright, 1998). In fact, a comprehensive analysis revealed that the impact of viewing prosocial TV programs is much greater than the impact of viewing televised violence (Hearold, 1986). Boys, in particular, benefit from viewing prosocial TV, perhaps because they usually are much less skilled prosocially than girls.

Although research indicates that prosocial behavior can be influenced by TV watching, two important factors restrict the actual prosocial impact of TV viewing. First, prosocial behaviors are portrayed far less frequently than aggressive behaviors, so opportunities to learn prosocial behaviors from television are limited. Second, the relatively small number of prosocial programs compete with other kinds of television programs and other non-TV activities for children's time, so children simply may not watch the few prosocial programs that are televised. Consequently, we are far from harnessing the power of television for prosocial uses.

**Influence on Consumer Behavior.** Sugary cereals, hamburgers and french fries, snack foods, toys, jeans, and athletic shoes . . . A phenomenal number of TV advertisements for these products are directed toward children and adolescents. A typical youth may see more than 50 commercials a day! Children as young

as 3 years can distinguish commercials from programs, though preschoolers believe commercials are simply a different form of entertainment—one designed to inform viewers. Not until age 8 or 9 do most children understand the persuasive intent of commercials. At the same time, children also begin to realize that commercials are not always truthful (Liebert & Sprafkin, 1988). They understand that a toy rocket will not really fly or that a doll will not really talk, contrary to how they're shown in commercials.

Even though children gradually understand the real intent of commercials, commercials are still effective sales tools (Donkin, Neale, & Tilston, 1993). Children grow to like many of the products advertised on TV and, like the youngster in the photograph, urge parents to buy products they've seen on television. In one study (Greenberg, Fazel, & Weber, 1986), for example, more than 75 percent of the children reported that they had asked their parents to buy a product they had seen advertised on TV. And more often than not, parents had purchased the product for them!

This selling power of TV has long concerned advocates for children because so many commercials are for foods that have little nutritional value and can lead to obesity and tooth decay. The U.S. government once regulated the amount and type of advertising on children's TV programs (Huston et al., 1989), but today the responsibility falls largely to parents.

**Influence on Cognition.** The year 1969 was a watershed in the history of children's television. That year marked the appearance of a program designed to use the power of video and animation to foster preschool skills, including recognizing letters and numbers, counting, and building vocabulary. The program achieved its goals. Preschoolers who watched the show regularly were more proficient at the targeted academic skills than preschoolers who watched infrequently. Regular viewers also adjusted to school more readily, according to teachers' ratings (Bogatz & Ball, 1972).

By now, of course, you know that I'm talking about Big Bird, Bert, Ernie, and other members of the cast of *Sesame Street,* shown in the photo. Since appearing in 1969, *Sesame Street,* produced by Children's Television Workshop, has helped educate generations of preschoolers. Today, mothers and fathers who watched *Sesame Street* as preschoolers are watching with their own youngsters.

More recent studies confirm that *Sesame Street* remains effective. Rice and her colleagues (1990), for example, found that children who had watched *Sesame Street* frequently at age 3 had larger vocabularies as 5-year-olds than children who had watched infrequently.

Building on the success of *Sesame Street,* Children's Television Workshop has developed a number of other successful programs. *Electric Company* teaches reading skills, *3-2-1 Contact* focuses on science and technology, and *Square One TV* teaches mathematics (Fisch & McCann, 1993). Other public television programs include *Reading Rainbow*, which introduces children's books; *Where in Time Is Carmen Sandiego?*, which teaches history; and *Bill Nye the Science Guy,* which makes science lessons fun and exciting. Programs like these leave little doubt that children can learn academic skills and useful social skills from TV, particularly by following the guidelines in the "Making Children's Lives Better" feature.

Children who watch *Sesame Street* often learn academic skills and adjust to school easily.

MAKING CHILDREN'S LIVES BETTER

### Get the Kids Off the Couch!

If you know a child who sits glued to the TV screen from after school until bedtime, has his or her own remote control, and reads the contents of *TV Guide* from cover to cover, it's time to take action. Here are some suggestions:

1. Children need absolute rules concerning the amount of TV and the types of programs that they can watch. These rules must be enforced consistently.

2. Children shouldn't fall into the trap of "I'm bored, so I'll watch TV." Children should be encouraged to know what they want to watch before they turn on the TV set.

3. Adults should watch TV with children and discuss the programs. Parents can, for example, express their disapproval of a character's use of aggression and suggest other means of resolving conflicts. Parents can also point to the stereotypes that are depicted. The aim is for children to learn that TV's account of the world is often inaccurate and that TV should be watched critically.

4. Parents need to be good TV viewers themselves. The first two tips listed here apply to viewers of all ages. When a child is present, parents shouldn't watch violent programs or others that are inappropriate for the young. And parents should throw away the remote control so that they, too, watch TV deliberately and selectively, instead of simply mindlessly flipping between channels. ●

TV can be beneficial if parents monitor their youngsters' viewing and if they insist that the television industry improves the quality and variety of programs available for children and adolescents. In the next section, we'll see that both guidelines apply as well to computers. Like television, computers can influence children positively or negatively, depending upon how they are used.

## Computers

How has new computer technology influenced children? Are computers just expensive toys? Yes, say some, pointing to the proliferation of video games. Others, however, cite the benefits of computers in schools. In this section, we'll look at both uses.

### Video Games.

According to one recent survey of U.S. adolescents, about two-thirds of girls and nearly 90 percent of boys play video games at least 1 to 2 hours each week (Funk, 1993). Nevertheless, we know relatively little about the impact of video games on children. Many of the popular games, such Mortal Kombat, Doom, and Quake, are violent, with players killing game characters in extraordinarily gruesome ways (Funk, 1993). Just as exposure to televised violence can make children behave more aggressively, playing violent video games can make children more aggressive (Irwin & Gross, 1995).

Some parents fear that video games consume too much of their children's time and divert their attention from schoolwork, other activities, and peers. Although a relatively small number of children develop an overwhelming need to play video games (termed by researchers "video-game addiction"), the more common pattern is a period of intense play after a new game or system is purchased, followed soon by a return to other activities (Fisher, 1994; Funk, 1992). In general, how often children play video games does not seem to influence their peer relationships or their grades. One exception is that boys who frequent video arcades often have lower grades. This may reflect a third variable, however—lack of parental supervision. Parents who allow their sons to spend hours "hanging out" at video arcades may also not be overly concerned about their sons' progress in school (Funk, 1992; Sakamato, 1994).

We're far from fully understanding the impact of video games on children, but it seems fair to say that video games are relatively benign, as long as parents monitor the content of the games and the amount of time that children spend playing them.

### Computers in the Classroom.

New technologies—whether TV, videotape, or pocket calculator—soon find themselves in the classroom. Personal computers are no exception; virtually all American public schools now use personal computers to aid instruction. As one computer advocate put it, "We are moving rapidly toward a future when computers will comprise the dominant delivery system in education. . . . Not since the invention of the printing press has a technological device borne such implications for the learning process" (Bork, 1985, p. 1).

Computers are used in schools as tutors, for experiential learning, and to help children accomplish traditional academic goals more simply.

A primary function of computers in the schools is as a tutor (Lepper & Gurtner, 1989). Children use computers to learn reading, spelling, arithmetic, science, and social studies. Computers allow instruction to be individualized and interactive. Students proceed at their own pace, receiving feedback and help when necessary.

Computers are also a valuable medium for experiential learning (Lepper & Gurtner, 1989). Simulation programs allow students to explore the world in ways that would be impossible or dangerous otherwise. Students can change the law of gravity or see what happens to a city when no taxes are imposed.

Finally, the computer is a multipurpose tool that can help students achieve traditional academic goals (Steelman, 1994). A graphics program can allow artistically untalented students to produce beautiful illustrations. A word-processing program can relieve much of the drudgery associated with revising, thereby encouraging better writing. The "Real Children" feature shows how one youngster was helped this way.

### REAL CHILDREN

### A Word Processor Saves Robert's Writing

Throughout elementary school, Robert had hated to write. From a two-paragraph essay to a two-page report, he dreaded them all. The reasons were simple. First, Robert's penmanship was awful: Teachers always complained that they simply could not read his scribbles. Second, Robert was a lousy speller: His completed assignments always contained many misspelled words. Teachers often liked the ideas that Robert expressed in his writing, but his grades on written assignments were always low because of his penmanship and poor spelling.

All this changed in seventh grade. Robert's English class attended a weekly writing lab where all students used computers with word-processing software. Robert's typing was painfully slow, but it was worth the effort because the laser printer made his assignments look spectacular. And the spell checker meant that Robert could eliminate many of his misspelled words. When the spell checker flagged a word and presented alternate spellings, Robert would use the dictionary to determine which one he needed. (Of course, this wasn't foolproof; once he wrote that "Alexander the Great was seriously ignored in battle.") Robert's grades now began to reflect his excellent ideas, and he began to write more and more. When Robert went to high school, he began to write for the school newspaper and, in his senior year, became the editor: a success story possible because the computer helped Robert focus on the creative aspects of writing, not the tedious aspects. ●

Despite success stories like Robert's, some critics fear that computers eliminate an important human element in learning. To some, "a classroom in which children spend the day plugged into their own individual desktop computers seems a chilling spectacle" (Lepper & Gurtner, 1989, p. 172). Many worry that computers isolate students from each other and from the teacher and that learning becomes a solitary activity. In reality, though, students interact with each other more when computers are introduced into the classroom, not less (Pozzi, Healy, & Hoyles, 1993). As the photo shows, students often cluster around one student as he or she works, and they often consult the class "expert" on a particular program. Teachers, freed from many of the drill-type tasks that occupy the school day, can turn their attention to more creative aspects of instruction.

### Check Your Learning

**1.** Preschool children believe that commercials _____.

**2.** Youngsters who are frequent viewers of *Sesame Street* typically improve their academic skills and, according to their teachers, _____.

**3.** When children play violent video games, they _____.

**4.** Computers are used in schools as tutors, _____, and to help students accomplish traditional academic tasks more simply.

**Answers:** (1) represent a different, informative type of program but do not understand their intent to persuade, (2) adjust to school more readily, (3) become more aggressive, (4) as a medium for experiential learning

# 15.3

- **Day Care**
- **School**
- **Part-Time Employment**

# Institutional Influences

## Learning Objectives

● **How are children affected by nonparental child care?**

● **What are the hallmarks of effective schools and effective teachers?**

● **What is the impact of part-time employment on children's development?**

> *When 15-year-old Aaron announced that he wanted an after-school job at the local supermarket, his mother was delighted, believing that he would learn much from the experience. Five months later, she had her doubts. Aaron had lost interest in school, and they argued constantly about how he spent his money.*

So far in this chapter, we've seen the potent influences of peers and media on children's development. Yet there are other noteworthy influences on children and their development—cultural institutions where children spend much of their lives. In this module, we'll look at three such institutions: day care, school, and the workplace. As we do, we'll see whether part-time jobs like Aaron's help or harm youth.

## Day Care

Each day, approximately 10 million U. S. children age 5 and under are cared for by someone other than their mother, a phenomenon linked to more dual-earner couples and to more single-parent households in the United States in the 1990s. Who is caring for America's children? About one-third of America's infants and preschoolers are cared for in their home, typically by the father or a grandparent (U. S. Bureau of the Census, 1995) . Another third receive care in the provider's home. The provider is often but not always a relative. Finally, another third attend day-care or nursery-school programs. The patterns are very similar for European American, African American and Hispanic American youngsters (Singer et al., 1998).

Many parents, particularly mothers, have misgivings about their children spending so much time in the care of others. Should parents worry? Does nonmaternal care harm the parent-child relationship? Before turning to research for answers to these questions, let's put them in historical and cross-cultural perspective. Although nonparental care of children is often portrayed as unnatural—and therefore potentially harmful—the truth is that for most of history and in most cultures, a majority of children have been cared for by nonparents at least some of the time (Lamb, 1999). When viewed from the larger perspective of history, there is nothing "natural" or "traditional" about mothers having nearly exclusive responsibility for child care.

Nevertheless, in the United States (and many other industrialized countries) since World War II, the cultural ideal has been that children are better off when cared for at home by their mothers. Does research support the cultural ideal? In answering this question, most researchers have focused on the impact child care has on mother-infant attachment (see pages 287–293). Their results suggest that, although secure attachments were the norm for both working and nonworking parents, odds of secure attachments were somewhat less for infants placed in full-time day care before their first birthday (Clarke-Stewart, 1989).

To provide definitive answers on the broader question of how child care affects children's development, the National Institute of Child Health and Human Development began a comprehensive study of early child care in 1991. Researchers recruited 1,364 mothers and their newborns from 12 U.S. cities. Both mothers and children have been tested repeatedly (and the testing continues, since the study is ongoing).

One of the first reports from this project concerned the impact of early child care on 15-month-olds' attachment to their mothers (NICHD Early Child Care Research Network, 1997). The results indicated no overall effects of child-care experience on mother-infant attachment, which was measured with the Strange Situation (described on pages 289–290). A secure mother-infant attachment was just as likely, regardless of the quality of child care, the amount of time the child spent in care, the age when the child began care, how frequently the parents changed child-care arrangements, and the type of child care (e.g., child-care center, in the home with a nonrelative).

However, when the effects of child care were considered along with characteristics of mothers, an important trend emerged: When mothers who were less sensitive and less responsive placed their infants in low-quality child care, insecure attachments were more common. As the investigators put it "poor quality, unstable, or more than minimal amounts of child care apparently added to the risks already inherent in poor mothering, so that the combined effects were worse than those of low maternal sensitivity and responsiveness alone" (p. 877).

Of course, the effects of day care need not be limited to attachment; other aspects of children's development might be affected, too. A second report from this project looked at links between early child care and behavior problems at ages 2 and 3 years (NICHD Early Child Care Research Network, 1998). The research showed that children who had started child care at an early age were *not* more likely to have behavioral problems than children who had limited experience in child care. Here, too, quality of care was a factor—children who had poor-quality child care were slightly more likely to have behavior problems.

> Parents can enroll their children in high-quality day care without fear of harmful consequences.

In general, working parents can enroll their infants and preschoolers in high-quality day-care programs with no fear of harmful consequences. What should parents look for in a day-care center? A first-rate program should have (a) a low ratio of children to caregivers, (b) a well-trained, experienced staff, (c) low staff turnover, (d) ample opportunities for educational and social stimulation, and (e) effective communication between parents and day-care workers concerning the general aims and routine functioning of the day-care program (Lamb, 1998; Rosenthal & Vandell, 1996).

Collectively, these variables do *not* guarantee that a child will receive high-quality care. Sensitive, responsive caregiving—the same behavior that promotes secure attachment relationships—is the real key to high-quality child care. Centers that have well-trained, experienced staff caring for a relatively small number of children are more likely to provide good care, but the only way to know the quality of care with certainty is to see for yourself (Lamb, 1998).

When children enter elementary school, child care becomes easier for working parents. However, many children still need care before or after school. Formal programs for before- and after-school care have been studied much less than day care for infants and toddlers (Lamb, 1998). Nevertheless, the limited research that has been done suggests that many of the same variables associated with high-quality day care are associated with high-quality before- and after-school care. Children benefit from well-trained, encouraging teachers; from low child-to-teacher ratios; and from a flexible, age-appropriate curriculum (Rosenthal & Vandell, 1996).

Many school-age children—approximately 10 percent of all 5- to 13-year-olds in the United States—receive no formal care after school; they are left alone to care for themselves (Galambos & Maggs, 1991). **Children who care for themselves are sometimes called *latchkey children*, a term that originated more than 200 years ago to describe children who raised a door latch to enter their own homes.** Some latchkey children, like the child in photo, stay at home alone (sometimes with parental supervision in absentia via the telephone). Others may stay at friends' homes where adults are sometimes present, or they may be unsupervised in public places such as shopping malls.

The popular perception is that latchkey children are a frightened, endangered lot. But research provides little support for this view. To the contrary, most older children and adolescents who care for themselves at home after school fare as well as children in the care of parents or other adults (Lamb, 1998). In one study, third, fourth, and fifth graders who cared for themselves at home were no more anxious, headstrong, or dependent than children cared for by their mothers (Vandell & Ramanan, 1991).

Research does reveal one group that is at risk—children and adolescents who spend their after-school hours away from home, unsupervised. These individuals are more prone to antisocial influences of peers and more prone to engage in problem behavior (Galambos & Maggs, 1991; Pettit et al., 1999).

This generally rosy picture does not mean that parents should begin self-care without careful planning. Robinson, Rowland, and Coleman (1986) suggest that parents contemplating self-care for their children should ask themselves several basic questions:

- Is the child old enough and emotionally mature enough, regardless of age, to assume the responsibility of self-care? For example, does the child stay home for short time periods?
- Does the child live in a safe neighborhood where crime is low and community cohesion is high and where neighbors and community facilities can be depended upon as support systems?
- Does the child's self-care arrangement provide for some type of adult supervision, such as a telephone or pager?

Children can care for themselves after school if they are mature enough, live in a safe neighborhood, and are supervised by an adult.

If each of these questions can be answered "yes," then self-care will probably work. The next step is to prepare the child for self-care. Children need to know after-school routines (for example, acceptable ways of getting home from school and how to check in with a parent), rules for their own behavior after school (for example, acceptable and unacceptable activities), and guidelines on how to handle emergencies (Peterson, 1989). Posting procedures and emergency phone numbers in a conspicuous location is often enough reassurance for children.

Fortunately, employers have begun to realize that convenient, high-quality child care makes for a better employee. In Flint, Michigan, for example, child care was part of the contract negotiated between the United Auto Workers and General Motors. Many cities have modified their zoning codes so that new shopping complexes and office buildings must include child-care facilities, like those in the photograph. Businesses are realizing that the availability of excellent child care helps attract and retain a skilled labor force. With effort, organization, and help from the community and business, full-time employment and high-quality caregiving *can* be compatible.

## School

At age 5 or 6, most American children head off to kindergarten, starting an educational journey that lasts 13 years for most and more than 16 years for some. How do schools influence children's development? Answering this question is difficult because American education is a smorgasbord, reflecting local control by communities throughout the United States. Schools differ on many dimensions, including their emphasis on academic goals and parent involvement. Teachers, too, differ in many ways, such as how they run their classrooms and how they teach. These and other variables affect how much students learn, as you'll see in the next few pages. Let's begin with school-based influences.

### School-Based Influences on Student Achievement.

Roosevelt High School, in the center of Detroit, has an enrollment of 3,500 students in grades 9 to 12. Opened in 1936, the building shows its age. The rooms are drafty, the desks are decorated with generations of graffiti, and new technology means an overhead projector. Nevertheless, attendance at Roosevelt is good. Most students graduate, and many continue their education at community colleges and state universities. Southport High School, in Boston, has about the same enrollment as Roosevelt High and the building is about the same age. Yet truancy is commonplace at Southport, where fewer than half the students graduate and almost none go to college.

These schools are hypothetical, but accurately portray American education. Some schools are much more successful than others, whether success is defined in terms of the percentage of students who are literate, graduate, or go to college. Why are some schools successful and not others? Researchers (Good & Brophy, 1994; Stevenson & Stigler, 1992; Walberg, 1995) have identified a number of factors:

- *Staff and students alike understand that academic excellence is the primary goal of the school and of every student in the school.* The school day emphasizes instruction, and students are recognized publicly for their academic accomplishments.

- *The school climate is safe and nurturant.* Students know that they can devote their energy to learning (instead of worrying about being harmed in school), and they know the staff truly wants to see them succeed.

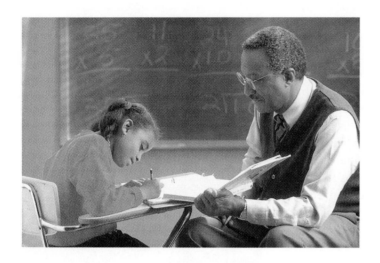

- *Parents are involved.* In some cases, this may be through formal arrangements, such as parent-teacher organizations. Or it may be informal. Parents may spend some time each week in school grading papers or, like the dad in the photo, tutoring a child. Such involvement signals both teachers and students that parents are committed to students' success.

- *Progress of students, teachers, and programs is monitored.* The only way to know if schools are succeeding is by measuring performance. Students, teachers, and programs need to be evaluated regularly, using objective measures that reflect academic goals.

In schools that follow these guidelines, students usually succeed. In schools where the guidelines are ignored, students more often fail.

Of course, on a daily basis, individual teachers have the most potential for impact. Let's see how teachers can influence their students' achievement.

### Teacher-Based Influences.

Take a moment to recall your teachers in elementary school, junior high, and high school. Some you probably remember fondly, because they were enthusiastic and innovative and they made learning fun. You may remember others with bitterness. They seemed to have lost their love of teaching and children, making class a living hell. Your experience tells you that some teachers are better than others, but what exactly makes a good teacher? Personality and enthusiasm are *not* the key elements. Although you may enjoy warm and eager teachers, research (Good & Brophy, 1994; Stevenson & Stigler, 1992; Walberg, 1995) shows several other factors are critical when it comes to students' achievement. Students tend to learn the most when teachers

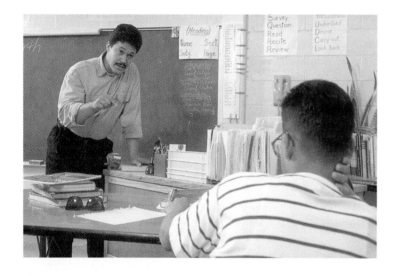

- *manage the classroom effectively so they can devote most of their time to instruction.* When teachers like the man in the photo spend a lot of time disciplining students, or when students do not move smoothly from one class activity to the next, instructional time is wasted, and students are apt to learn less.

- *believe they are responsible for their students' learning and that their students will learn when taught well.* When students don't understand a new topic, these teachers repeat the original instruction (in case the student missed something) or create new instruction (in case the student heard everything but just didn't "get it"). These teachers keep plugging away because they feel at fault if students don't learn.

- *emphasize mastery of topics.* Teachers should introduce a topic, then give students many opportunities to understand, practice, and apply the topic.

Just as you'd find it hard to go directly from driver's ed to driving a race car, students more often achieve when they grasp a new topic thoroughly, then gradually move on to other, more advanced topics.

- *teach actively.* They don't just talk or give students an endless stream of worksheets. Instead, they demonstrate topics concretely or have hands-on demonstrations for students. They also have students participate in class activities and encourage students to interact, generating ideas and solving problems together.

- *pay careful attention to pacing.* They present material slowly enough that students can understand a new concept, but not so slowly that students get bored.

- *value tutoring.* They work with students individually or in small groups, so they can gear their instruction to each student's level and check each student's understanding. They also encourage peer tutoring, in which more capable students tutor less capable students. Children who are tutored by peers *do* learn, and so do the tutors, evidently because teaching helps tutors organize their knowledge.

- *teach children techniques for monitoring and managing their own learning.* Students are more likely to achieve when they are taught how to recognize the aims of school tasks and know effective strategies for achieving those aims (like those described on pages 189–190).

When teachers teach according to these guidelines, most of their students learn the material and enjoy school. When teachers don't observe these guidelines, their students often fail or, at the very least, find learning difficult and school tedious (Good & Brophy, 1994; Stevenson & Stigler, 1992; Walberg, 1995).

## Part-Time Employment

The teen in the photo is engaged in an American adolescent ritual—the part-time job. Today, a substantial majority of high-school seniors work part-time. Out of every five adolescent part-time workers, one works at a fast-food restaurant like McDonald's or Burger King, and another works in a retail store as a cashier or salesperson. Boys are more likely to be manual laborers, busboys, or newspaper carriers. Girls are more often baby sitters, housekeepers, or restaurant workers, and they are usually paid less than boys (Call, 1996; Mortimer, 1991).

Most adults praise teens for working, believing that early exposure to the workplace teaches self-discipline, self-confidence, and important job skills (Snedeker, 1982). For most adolescents, however, the reality is very different. Part-time work can actually be harmful, for several reasons:

1. *School performance suffers.* When students work more than approximately 15 hours per week, they devote less time to homework and are more apt to cut classes.

Not surprisingly, their grades are lower than those of their peers who work less or not at all (Steinberg, Fegley, & Dornbusch, 1993). Why should 15 hours of work be so detrimental to school performance? A 15-hour work schedule usually means four 3-hour shifts after school and another 3-hour shift on the weekend. This would seem to leave ample opportunity to study, but only if students use their time effectively. In fact, many high-school students apparently do not have the foresight and discipline necessary to consistently meet the combined demands of work and school. Like the boy in the photo, many teens have great difficulty balancing work, study, and sleep.

2. *There are mental health and behavioral problems.* Adolescents who work long hours—more than 15 or 20 hours a week—are more likely to experience anxiety and depression, and their self-esteem often suffers. Many adolescents find themselves in jobs that are repetitive and boring but stressful, and such conditions undermine self-esteem and breed anxiety.

Extensive part-time work frequently leads to substance abuse, including cigarettes, alcohol, marijuana, and cocaine (Bachman & Schulenberg, 1993; Mortimer et al., 1996). Extensive work is also associated with more frequent problem behavior, including violence toward others, trouble with police, and arguments with parents (Bachman & Schulenberg, 1993).

Why employment is associated with all of these problems is not clear. Perhaps employed adolescents turn to drugs to help them cope with the anxiety and depression brought on by work. Arguments with parents may become more common because anxious, depressed adolescents are more prone to argue or because wage-earning adolescents may believe that their freedom should match their income. Whatever the exact mechanism, extensive part-time work is clearly detrimental to the mental health of most adolescents.

3. *Affluence is misleading.* Adults sometimes argue that work is good for teenagers because it teaches them "the value of a dollar." Here, too, reality is at odds with the adage. The typical teenage pattern is to "earn and spend." Working adolescents spend most of their earnings on themselves—to buy clothing, snack food, or cosmetics and to pay for entertainment. Few working teens set aside much of their income for future goals, such as a college education, or use it to contribute to their family's expenses (Shanahan et al., 1996a; 1996b). Because parents customarily pay for many of the essential expenses associated with truly independent living—rent, utilities, and groceries, for example—working adolescents often have a vastly higher percentage of their income available for discretionary spending than working adults. Thus, for many teens, the part-time work experience provides unrealistic expectations about how income can be allocated (Bachman, 1983).

The message that emerges repeatedly from research on part-time employment is hardly encouraging. Like Aaron, the teenage boy in the vignette, adolescents who work long hours at part-time jobs do not benefit from the experience. To the contrary, they do worse in school, are more likely to have behavioral problems, and learn how to spend money rather than how to manage it. These effects are similar for adolescents from different ethnic groups (Steinberg & Dornbusch, 1991) and are comparable for boys and girls (Bachman & Schulenberg, 1993).

Does this mean that teenagers who are still in school should never work part-time? Not necessarily. Part-time employment can be a good experience, depending on the circumstances. One key is the number of hours of work. Although the exact number of hours varies, of course, from one student to the next, most students could easily work 5 hours weekly without harm, and many could work 10 hours weekly. Another key is the type of job (Barling, Rogers, & Kelloway, 1995). When adolescents have jobs that allow them to use their skills (for example, bookkeeping, computing, or typing) and acquire new ones, self-esteem is enhanced, and they learn from their work experience. Yet another factor is how teens spend their earnings. When they save their money or use it to pay for clothes and school expenses, their parent-child relationships often improve (Shanahan et al., 1996a; 1996b).

> When adolescents work many hours in part-time jobs, they do worse in school, often have behavioral problems, and experience misleading affluence.

By these criteria, who is likely to show the harmful effects of part-time work? A teen who spends 30 hours a week bagging groceries and spends most of it on CDs or videos. And who is likely to benefit from part-time work? A teen who likes to tinker with cars, who spends Saturdays working in a repair shop, and who sets aside some of his earnings for college.

Finally, summer jobs typically do not involve conflict between work and school. Consequently, many of the harmful effects associated with part-time employment during the school year do not hold for summer employment. In fact, such employment sometimes enhances adolescents' self-esteem, especially when they save part of their income for future plans (Marsh, 1991).

## Check Your Learning

1. An insecure attachment is likely when an infant receives poor-quality child care and _____.

2. Older children and adolescents who care for themselves after school get along well as long as _____.

3. In successful schools, academic excellence is a priority, the school is safe and nurturant, progress of students and teachers is monitored, and _____.

4. Effective teachers manage classrooms well, believe they are responsible for their students' learning, _____, teach actively, pay attention to pacing, value tutoring, and show children how to monitor their own learning.

5. Adolescents who work extensively at part-time jobs during the school year often get lower grades, have behavior problems, and _____.

6. Part-time employment during the school year can be beneficial if adolescents limit the number of hours that they work and _____.

💡 Imagine your best friend is the mother of a 3-month-old. Your friend is about to return to her job as a social worker, but she's afraid that she'll harm her baby by going back to work. What could you say to reassure her?

**Answers:** (1) insensitive, unresponsive mothering, (2) they are at home rather than unsupervised and away from home (e.g., at a mall), (3) parents are involved, (4) emphasize mastery of subjects, (5) mistakenly think they are affluent, (6) hold jobs that allow them to use and develop skills

# 15 Influences Beyond the Family
## IN PERSPECTIVE

Maybe now you better understand parents who shed tears as their children go off to kindergarten. Tearful parents know that peers, media, and schools are indeed influential forces in children's development. In Module 15.1, we saw the emergence of play during the toddler and preschool years and the emergence of friendship. We also learned how groups influence children and why some youngsters are popular and others aren't. In Module 15.2, we discovered that television and computers can benefit children but often don't. In Module 15.3, we learned that many factors beyond the family influence children's development, including their experiences in day care, in schools, and at part-time work.

In this last chapter of the book, I want to remind you that *early development is related to later development but not perfectly.* Children who are rejected by their peers are, over time, more likely to do poorly in school, have lower self-esteem, and have behavioral problems. Of course, not all rejected children suffer this fate. Some do well in school, have high self-esteem, and avoid behavioral problems. Positive outcomes are more likely to occur when children learn effective skills for interacting with others. As we've seen many times in previous chapters, early experiences often point children toward a particular developmental path, but later experiences can cause them to change course.

## See for Yourself

The best way to understand the differences between good and bad teaching is to visit some actual school classrooms. Try to visit three or four classes in at least two different schools. (You can usually arrange this by speaking with the school's principal.) Take along the principles of good teaching that are listed on pages 446–447. Start by watching how the teachers and children interact. Then, decide how much the teacher relies upon each of the principles. You'll probably see that most teachers use some but not all of these principles. And you'll also see that, in today's classroom, consistently following all the principles is very challenging. See for yourself!

## Resources

*For more information about . . .*

*what makes some schools more effective than others,* read Edward Fiske's *Smart Schools, Smart Kids* (Simon and Schuster, 1991), which examines some exceptional U.S. schools to discover the key ingredients to a successful school.

 *use of computers and other technology in schools,* visit the Web site of Twenty-First Century Teachers, a nationwide volunteer initiative to encourage teachers to use technology in their teaching, **http://www.21ct.org/**

## Key Terms

clique 430
cooperative play 423
crowd 430
dominance hierarchy 431

friendship 426
latchkey children 444
nonsocial play 422

parallel play 422
rough-and-tumble play 426
simple social play 423

Influences Beyond
the Family

15.1 Peers
15.2 Electronic Media
15.3 Institutional Influences

# 15.1 Peers

### Development of Peer Interactions

Children's first real social interactions, at about 12 to 15 months, take the form of parallel play, in which infants play alone while watching each other. A few months later, simple social play emerges, in which toddlers engage in similar activities and interact with one another. At about 2 years, cooperative play organized around a theme becomes common.

Make-believe play is also common and, in addition to being fun, promotes cognitive development and lets children examine frightening topics in a nonthreatening way. Most forms of solitary play are harmless. Parents foster children's play by acting as skilled playmates, mediating disputes, and coaching social skills.

Beyond preschool, peer relations improve and emphasize talking and being together, as well as rough-and-tumble play.

### Friendship

Friendships among preschoolers are based on common interests and getting along well. As children grow, loyalty, trust, and intimacy become more important features in their friendships. Friends are usually similar in age, sex, race, and attitudes. Children with friends are more skilled socially and better adjusted.

### Groups

Older children and adolescents often form cliques—small groups of like-minded individuals that become part of a crowd. Some crowds have higher status than others, and members of higher-status crowds often have higher self-esteem than members of lower-status crowds.

Most groups have a dominance hierarchy, a well-defined structure with a leader at the top. Physical power often determines the dominance hierarchy, particularly among younger boys. With older children and adolescents, dominance hierarchies are more often based on skills that are important to group functioning.

Peers are particularly influential when standards of behavior are unclear, such as for taste in music or clothing, or concerning drinking, using drugs, and sex.

### Popularity and Rejection

Popular children are socially skilled. They generally share, cooperate, and help others; they are unlikely to behave antisocially (fight or whine). Some children are rejected by their peers because they are too aggressive. These children are often unsuccessful in school and have behavioral problems. Their aggressive style of interacting can often be traced to parents who are belligerent or inconsistent in their discipline.

# 15.2 Electronic Media

### Television

Many popular criticisms about TV as a medium (e.g., it shortens children's attention span) are not supported by research. However, the content of TV programs can affect children's attitudes and social behavior, their consumer behavior, and their cognitive development. Youngsters who frequently watch prosocial TV become more skilled socially, and preschoolers who watch *Sesame Street* improve their academic skills and adjust more readily to school.

### Computers

Most children play video games, but we still know relatively little about their impact. Children are more aggressive after playing violent video games. Computers are used in school as tutors, to provide experiential learning, and as a multipurpose tool to achieve traditional academic goals.

# 15.3 Institutional Influences

### Day Care

Many U.S. children are cared for at home by a father or other relative, in a day-care provider's home, or in a day-care center. Infants and young children are not harmed by such arrangements as long as the care is high quality and parents remain responsive to their children. Children can care for themselves after school if they are mature enough, live in a safe neighborhood, and are supervised by an adult.

### School

Schools influence students' achievement in many ways. Students are most likely to achieve when their school emphasizes academic excellence, has a safe and nurturing environment, monitors pupils' and teachers' progress, and encourages parents to be involved.

Students achieve at higher levels when their teachers manage classrooms effectively, take responsibility for their students' learning, teach mastery of material, pace material well, value tutoring, and show children how to monitor their own learning.

### Part-Time Employment

Most adolescents in the United States have part-time jobs. Adolescents who are employed more than 15 hours per week during the school year typically do poorly in school, often have lowered self-esteem and increased anxiety, and have problems interacting with others. Employed adolescents save relatively little of their income. Instead, they spend most of it on clothing, food, and entertainment for themselves, which can give misleading expectations about how to allocate income.

Part-time employment can be beneficial if adolescents work relatively few hours, if the work allows them to use existing skills or acquire new ones, and if teens save some of their earnings. Summer employment, because it does not conflict with the demands of school, can also be beneficial.

## A

**accommodation** According to Piaget, changing existing knowledge based on new knowledge.

**achievement status** The identity status in Marcia's theory in which adolescents have explored alternative identities and are now secure in their chosen identities.

**active gene-environment relation** The phenomenon in which individuals actively seek environments related to their genetic makeup.

**active-passive child issue** The issue of whether children are simply at the mercy of the environment (passive child) or actively influence their own development through their own unique individual characteristics (active child).

**activity** The dimension of temperament defined by the tempo and vigor of a child's movement during play.

**adolescent egocentrism** The self-absorption that is characteristic of teenagers as they search for identity.

**age of viability** The age at which a fetus can survive because most of its bodily systems function adequately, typically at 7 months after conception.

**aggression** Behavior meant to harm others.

**allele** A variation of a specific gene.

**altruism** Prosocial behavior, such as helping and sharing, in which the individual does not benefit directly from his or her behavior.

**amniocentesis** A prenatal diagnostic technique that involves withdrawing a sample of amniotic fluid through the abdomen using a syringe.

**amnion** An inner sac in which the developing child will rest.

**amniotic fluid** Fluid in the amnion that cushions the embryo and maintains a constant temperature.

**androgens** Hormones secreted by the testes that influence aggressive behavior.

**androgynous** Having a combination of gender-role traits that includes both instrumental and expressive behaviors.

**animism** Crediting inanimate objects with life and lifelike properties such as feelings.

**anorexia nervosa** A persistent refusal to eat, accompanied by an irrational fear of being overweight.

**anoxia** Lack of oxygen during delivery, typically because the umbilical cord becomes pinched or tangled during delivery.

**Apgar score** A measure to evaluate the newborn's condition, based on breathing, heart rate, muscle tone, presence of reflexes, and skin tone.

**assimilation** According to Piaget, taking in information that is compatible with what one already knows.

**attachment** The affectionate, reciprocal relationship that is formed at about 6 or 7 months between an infant and his or her primary caregiver, usually the mother.

**attention** Processes that determine which information will be processed further by an individual.

**auditory threshold** The quietest sound that a person can hear.

**authoritarian parenting** A style of parenting that combines high levels of control and low levels of warmth toward children.

**authoritative parenting** A style of parenting that combines a moderate degree of control with being warm and responsive toward children.

**autobiographical memory** People's memory of the significant events and experiences of their own lives.

**automatic processes** Cognitive activities that require virtually no effort.

**autonomous attachment representation** A representation of parent-child relations in which adults describe childhood experiences objectively and mention both positive and negative aspects of their parents.

**autosomes** The first 22 pairs of chromosomes.

**avoidant attachment** A relationship in which infants turn away from their mothers when they are reunited following a brief separation.

**axon** A tubelike structure that emerges from the cell body and transmits information to other neurons.

## B

**babbling** Speechlike sounds that consist of vowel-consonant combinations.

**basal metabolic rate** The speed with which the body consumes calories.

**basic cry** A cry that starts softly and gradually becomes more intense; often heard when babies are hungry or tired.

**behavioral genetics** The branch of genetics that deals with inheritance of behavioral and psychological traits.

**Black English** A dialect of standard English spoken by some African Americans that has slightly different grammatical rules than standard English.

**blended family** A family consisting of a biological parent, a stepparent, and children.

**breech presentation** A birth in which the feet or bottom are delivered first, before the head.

**bulimia nervosa** An eating disorder in which individuals alternate between binging (when they eat uncontrollably) and purging through self-induced vomiting or with laxatives.

**bullying** Aggression that is unprovoked and seems to have as its sole goal to intimidate, harass, or humiliate another child; the most common form of aggression.

## C

**cardinality principle** The counting principle that the last number name denotes the number of objects being counted.

**cell body** The center of the neuron that keeps the neuron alive.

**centration** Narrowly focused thought characteristic of Piaget's preoperational stage.

**cephalocaudal principle** The principle that growth occurs from the head first and then down the spine.

**cerebral cortex** The wrinkled surface of the brain that regulates many functions that are distinctly human.

**cesarean section (C-section)** A surgical procedure in which an incision is made in the abdomen to remove the baby from the uterus.

**chorionic villus sampling (CVS)** A prenatal diagnostic technique that involves taking a sample of tissue from the chorion.

**chromosomes** Threadlike structures in the nucleus of the cell that contain genetic material.

**clique**   Small groups of friends who are similar in age, sex, race, and interests.

**cognitive approach**   An approach to perception in which sensory experience influences perception and understanding also influences sensory and perceptual processing.

**cohort effects**   A potential problem in cross-sectional studies in which differences between age groups (cohorts) may result from environmental events, not developmental processes.

**componential subtheory**   In Sternberg's triarchic theory, the idea that intelligence depends on basic cognitive processes.

**components**   Fundamental cognitive processes that, in Sternberg's componential subtheory, are the basis of intelligence.

**comprehension**   The process of extracting meaning from a sequence of words.

**concrete operational stage**   The third of Piaget's stages, from 7 to 11 years, in which children first use mental operations to solve problems and to reason.

**cones**   Specialized neurons in the back of the eye that detect wavelength and, therefore, color.

**constricting**   An interaction style, common among boys, in which one child tries to emerge as the victor by threatening or contradicting the others, by exaggerating, and so on.

**contextual subtheory**   In Sternberg's triarchic theory, the idea that intelligent behavior involves adapting to an environment to achieve one's goals.

**continuity-discontinuity issue**   An issue concerned with whether a developmental phenomenon follows a smooth progression throughout the life span or a series of abrupt shifts.

**conventional level**   The second level of reasoning in Kohlberg's theory, where moral reasoning is based on society's norms.

**convergent thinking**   Using information to arrive at one standard, correct answer.

**cooing**   Early vowel-like sounds that babies produce.

**cooperative play**   Play that is organized around a theme, with each child taking on a different role; begins at about 2 years of age.

**corpus callosum**   A thick bundle of neurons that connects the two cerebral hemispheres.

**correlation coefficient**   A statistic that reveals the strength and direction of the relation between two variables.

**correlational study**   A research design in which investigators look at relations between variables as they exist naturally in the world.

**counterimitation**   A type of observational learning in which the child observes and learns what should not be done.

**critical period**   A time in development when a specific type of learning can take place; before or after the critical period, the same learning is difficult or even impossible.

**cross-sectional study**   A research design in which people of different ages are compared at the same point in time.

**crowd**   A large group that includes many cliques with similar attitudes and values.

**crowning**   The appearance of the top of the baby's head during labor.

**crystallization**   The first phase in Super's theory of career development, in which adolescents use their emerging identities for ideas about careers.

**culture**   The knowledge, attitudes, and behavior associated with a group of people.

**culture-fair intelligence tests**   Tests designed to reduce the impact of different experiences by including items based on experiences common to many cultures.

# D

**deductive reasoning**   Drawing conclusions from facts; characteristic of formal operational thought.

**dendrite**   The end of the neuron that receives information; it looks like a tree with many branches.

**deoxyribonucleic acid (DNA)**   A molecule composed of four nucleotide bases that is the biochemical basis of heredity.

**dependent variable**   The behavior that is observed after other variables are manipulated.

**depression**   A disorder characterized by pervasive feelings of sadness, irritability, and low self-esteem.

**differentiation**   Distinguishing and mastering individual motions.

**differentiation theory**   A theory of perceptual development formulated by Gibson in which perception reflects children's growing ability to identify the features that distinguish complex patterns.

**diffusion status**   The identity status in Marcia's theory in which adolescents do not have an identity and are doing nothing to achieve one.

**direct instruction**   A parental behavior in which adults try to influence their children's behavior by telling them what to do, when, and why.

**disinhibition**   A type of observational learning in which all behaviors like those observed are more likely after observation.

**dismissive attachment representation**   A representation of parent-child relations in which adults describe childhood experiences in very general terms and often idealize their parents.

**disorganized (disoriented) attachment**   A relationship in which infants don't seem to understand what's happening when they are separated and later reunited with their mothers.

**dispensing-family-wisdom grandparents**   Grandparents who assume an authoritarian position and dispense information and advice to parents and child alike.

**display rules**   Culturally specific standards for appropriate expressions of emotion in a particular setting or with a particular person or persons.

**dispositional praise**   Praise that links a child's altruistic behavior to an underlying altruistic disposition.

**distant grandparents**   Grandparents who have little contact except on holidays, birthdays, or other family celebrations.

**divergent thinking**   Thinking in novel and unusual directions.

**dizygotic (fraternal) twins**   Twins that are the result of the fertilization of two separate eggs by two sperm.

**dominance hierarchy**   An ordering of individuals within a group in which group members with lower status defer to those with greater status.

**dominant**   The form of an allele whose chemical instructions are followed.

**Down syndrome**   A disorder, caused by an extra chromosome, in which individuals are mentally retarded and have a distinctive appearance.

**dynamic systems theory**   A theory that views motor development as involving many distinct skills that are organized and reorganized over time to meet demands of specific tasks.

**dynamic testing**   An approach to intelligence testing that measures a child's learning potential by having the child learn something new in the presence of the examiner and with the examiner's help.

## E

**ectoderm**   The outer layer of the embryo, which will become the hair, outer layer of skin, and nervous system.

**edges**   Lines that mark the boundaries of objects.

**ego**   According to Freud, the rational component of the personality; develops during the first few years of life.

**egocentrism**   Difficulty in seeing the world from another's point of view; typical of children in Piaget's preoperational stage.

**electroencephalogram (EEG)**   A pattern of brain waves recorded from electrodes that are placed on the scalp.

**embryo**   The name given to the developing baby once the zygote is completely embedded in the uterine wall.

**emotionality**   The aspect of temperament that refers to the strength of the infant's emotional response to a situation, the ease with which that response is triggered, and the ease with which the infant can be returned to a nonemotional state.

**empathic orientation**   According to Eisenberg, a level of prosocial reasoning common in some children and many adolescents in which their thinking considers the injured child's perspective and how their own actions would make the child feel.

**empathy**   Experiencing another person's feelings.

**empirical approach**   An approach to perception in which sensory experience is the building block of all perception and, ultimately, all knowledge.

**enabling**   An interaction style, common among girls, in which children's actions and remarks tend to support others and to sustain the interaction.

**endoderm**   The inner layer of the embryo, which will become the lungs and the digestive system.

**epiphyses**   Ends of bone tissue, which are formed first before the center is formed.

**equilibration**   According to Piaget, the process by which children reorganize their schemes and, in the process, move to the next developmental stage.

**ethnic identity**   The feeling that one is part of an ethnic group and the understanding of special customs and traditions of the group's culture and heritage.

**ethological theory**   A theory in which development is seen from an evolutionary perspective and behaviors are examined for their survival value.

**evocative gene-environment relation**   The phenomenon in which different genotypes evoke different responses from the environment.

**exosystem**   According to Bronfenbrenner, social settings that influence one's development even though one does not experience them firsthand.

**experiential subtheory**   In Sternberg's triarchic theory, the idea that intelligence is revealed on both novel and familiar tasks.

**experiment**   A systematic way of manipulating factors that a researcher thinks cause a particular behavior.

**expressive style**   A style of language learning that describes children whose vocabularies include many social phrases that are used like one word.

**expressive traits**   Psychological characteristics that describe a person who is focused on emotions and interpersonal relationships.

## F

**familial mental retardation**   A form of mental retardation that does not involve biological damage but represents the low end of the normal distribution of intelligence.

**fast mapping**   The fact that children make connections between new words and referents so quickly that they can't be considering all possible meanings.

**fetal alcohol syndrome (FAS)**   A disorder affecting babies whose mothers consumed large amounts of alcohol while they were pregnant.

**fetal medicine**   The branch of medicine that deals with treating prenatal problems before birth.

**fine-motor skills**   Motor skills associated with grasping, holding, and manipulating objects.

**foreclosure status**   The identity status in Marcia's theory in which adolescents have an identity that was chosen based on advice from adults, rather than one that was a result of personal exploration of alternatives.

**formal grandparents**   Grandparents who see their role in traditional terms, expressing a strong interest in the grandchild but maintaining a hands-off attitude toward child-rearing.

**formal operational stage**   The fourth of Piaget's stages, from roughly age 11 into adulthood, in which children and adolescents can apply mental operations to abstract entities, allowing them to think hypothetically and reason deductively.

**friendship**   A voluntary relationship between two people involving mutual liking.

**frontal cortex**   A brain region that regulates personality and goal-directed behavior.

**functional magnetic resonance imaging (F-MRI)**   A technique for measuring brain activity that uses magnetic fields to track the flow of blood in the brain.

**fun-seeking grandparents**   Grandparents who see themselves as a primary source of fun for their grandchildren and who avoid more serious interactions.

## G

**gender consistency**   The understanding, usually acquired between ages 4 and 7 years, that maleness and femaleness do not change over situations or according to personal wishes.

**gender constancy**   A stage in which children have mastered gender labels, gender stability, and gender consistency.

**gender identity**   The perception of oneself as either male or female.

**gender labeling**   Children's understanding, by 2 or 3 years, that they are either boys or girls, and their use of these words to label themselves.

**gender role**   Culturally prescribed behaviors considered appropriate for males and females.

**gender-schema theory**   A theory that children learn gender roles by first deciding if an object, activity, or behavior is female or male, then using this information to decide whether they should learn more about the object, activity, or behavior.

**gender stability**   Children's understanding, during the preschool years, that gender does not change: Boys become men and girls become women.

**gender stereotypes**   Beliefs and images about males and females that are not necessarily true.

**gene**   A group of nucleotide bases that provide a specific set of biochemical instructions.

**genotype**   A person's hereditary makeup.

**germ disc**   A small cluster of cells near the center of the zygote that develops into the baby.

**gifted**   Traditionally, individuals with intelligence test scores of at least 130.

**grammar**   A language's rules for combining words to create sentences.

**grammatical morphemes**   Words or endings of words that make a sentence grammatical.

## H

**habituation**   Becoming unresponsive to a stimulus that is presented repeatedly.

**hedonistic orientation**   According to Eisenberg, a level of prosocial reasoning common in preschool and elementary-school children in which they emphasize pursuing their own pleasure.

**hemispheres**   The right and left halves of the cortex.

**heterozygous**   When the genes for any hereditary characteristic differ from each other.

**homozygous**   When the genes for any hereditary characteristic are the same.

**hormones**   Chemicals released by glands throughout the body that travel in the bloodstream to act on other body parts.

**Huntington's disease**   A type of dementia.

## I

**id**   According to Freud, the element of personality that wants immediate gratification of bodily wants and needs; present at birth.

**illusion of invulnerability**   The belief, common among adolescents, that misfortune only happens to others.

**imaginary audience**   Adolescents' feeling that their behavior is constantly being watched by their peers.

**imitation (observational learning)**   Learning that takes place simply by observing others.

**immanent justice**   A characteristic of the stage of moral realism in which children believe that breaking a rule always leads to punishment.

**implantation**   The process in which the zygote burrows into the uterine wall and establishes connections with a woman's blood vessels.

**implementation**   The third phase in Super's theory of career development, in which individuals enter the work force.

**imprinting**   Learning that occurs during a critical period soon after birth or hatching, as demonstrated by chicks creating an emotional bond with the first moving object they see.

**in vitro fertilization**   The technique of fertilizing eggs with sperm in a petri dish and then transferring several of the fertilized eggs to the mother's uterus, where they might implant in the lining of the uterine wall.

**incomplete dominance**   The situation in which one allele does not dominate another completely.

**independent variable**   The factor that is manipulated by the researcher in an experiment.

**indifferent-uninvolved parenting**   A style of parenting that provides neither warmth nor control and that minimizes the amount of time parents spend with children.

**indulgent-permissive parenting**   A style of parenting that offers warmth and caring but little parental control over children.

**infant-directed speech**   Speech that adults use with babies that is slow and loud and has exaggerated changes in pitch.

**infant mortality**   The number of infants out of 1,000 births who die before their first birthday.

**infantile amnesia**   The inability to remember events from early in one's life.

**information-processing theory**   A view that human cognition consists of mental hardware and software.

**inhibition**   A type of observational learning in which all behaviors like those observed are less likely after observation.

**inhibitory processes**   Processes that prevent task-irrelevant information from entering working memory.

**inner speech**   Vygotsky's term for thought.

**instrumental traits**   Psychological characteristics that describe a person who acts on and influences the world.

**instrumental aggression**   Aggression used to achieve an explicit goal.

**integration**   Linking individual motions into a coherent, coordinated whole.

**intelligence quotient (IQ)**   A ratio of mental age to chronological age, multiplied by 100.

**internal working model**   An infant's understanding of how responsive and dependable the mother is; thought to influence close relationships throughout the child's life.

**interposition**   A perceptual cue to depth based on the fact that nearby objects partially obscure more distant objects.

**intonation**   A pattern of rising and falling pitch in speech or babbling that often indicates whether the utterance is a statement, question, or command.

## J

**joint custody**   When both parents retain legal custody of their children following a divorce.

**Just Communities**   Special groups of students and teachers within public high schools created by Kohlberg to foster discussion and expose students to more advanced moral thinking.

## K

**knowledge-telling strategy**   A strategy for writing, often used by younger writers, in which information is written in sequence as it is retrieved from memory.

**knowledge-transforming strategy**   A strategy for writing, often used by older writers, in which they decide what information to include and how best to organize it for the point they wish to convey to their reader.

# L

**language**   Any rule-based system for expressing ideas.

**latchkey children**   Children who care for themselves after school.

**learning disability**   When a child with normal intelligence has difficulty mastering at least one academic subject.

**locomotion**   The ability to move around in the world.

**long-term memory**   A permanent storehouse for memories that has unlimited capacity.

**longitudinal study**   A research design in which a single cohort is studied over multiple times of measurement.

# M

**macrosystem**   According to Bronfenbrenner, the cultural and subcultural settings in which the microsystems, mesosystems, and exosystems are embedded.

**mad cry**   A more intense version of a basic cry.

**malnourished**   Being small for one's age because of inadequate nutrition.

**maturational theory**   The view that child development reflects a specific and prearranged scheme or plan within the body.

**memory strategies**   Activities that improve remembering.

**menarche**   The onset of menstruation.

**mental age (MA)**   In intelligence testing, a measure of children's performance corresponding to the chronological age of those whose performance equals the child's.

**mental operations**   Cognitive actions that can be performed on objects or ideas.

**mental retardation**   A disorder in which, before 18 years of age, individuals have substantially below-average intelligence and problems adapting to an environment.

**mental rotation**   One aspect of spatial ability involving the ability to imagine how an object will look after it has been moved in space.

**mesoderm**   The middle layer of the embryo, which will become the muscles, bones, and circulatory system.

**mesosystem**   According to Bronfenbrenner, the interrelations between different microsystems.

**microsystem**   According to Bronfenbrenner, the people and objects that are present in one's immediate environment.

**monozygotic (identical) twins**   Twins that result when a single fertilized egg splits to form two new individuals.

**moral realism**   A stage described by Piaget that begins at about 5 years and continues through age 7, in which children believe that rules are created by wise adults and therefore must be followed and cannot be changed.

**moral relativism**   A stage described by Piaget that begins at about age 8, in which children understand that rules are created by people to help them get along.

**moratorium status**   The identity status in Marcia's theory in which adolescents are still examining different alternatives and have yet to find a satisfactory identity.

**motor skills**   Coordinated movements of the muscles and limbs.

**Müller-Lyer illusion**   The tendency to see a line with inward-facing arrows as longer than the same line with outward-facing arrows.

**myelin**   A fatty sheath that surrounds neurons in the central nervous system and allows them to transmit information more rapidly.

# N

**naming explosion**   A period, beginning at about age 18 months, in which children learn new words very rapidly.

**naturalistic observation**   A method of observation in which children are observed as they behave spontaneously in a real-life situation.

**nature-nurture issue**   An issue concerning the manner in which genetic and environmental factors influence development.

**needs-oriented orientation**   According to Eisenberg, a level of prosocial reasoning common in some preschool and many elementary-school children in which they are concerned about others' needs and want to help.

**negative reinforcement trap**   A situation in which parents often unwittingly reinforce the very behaviors they want to discourage; particularly likely between mothers and sons.

**neo-Piagetian theories**   Theories that share Piaget's basic assumptions about cognitive development.

**neural plate**   A flat group of cells present in prenatal development that becomes the brain and spinal cord.

**neuron**   A cell that is the basic unit of the brain and nervous system; specializes in receiving and transmitting information.

**neurotransmitters**   Chemicals released by terminal buttons that carry information to nearby neurons.

**niche-picking**   The process of deliberately seeking environments that are compatible with one's genetic makeup.

**non-REM (regular) sleep**   Sleep in which heart rate, breathing, and brain activity are steady.

**nonshared environmental influences**   Forces within a family that make children different from one another.

**nonsocial play**   An early form of play, identified by Parton (1932), in which children play alone or watch others play but do not play themselves.

# O

**one-to-one principle**   The counting principle that states that there must be one and only one number name for each object counted.

**operant conditioning**   A view of learning, proposed by Skinner, that emphasizes reward and punishment.

**organic mental retardation**   Mental retardation that can be traced to a specific biological or physical problem.

**orienting response**   The response to an unfamiliar or unusual stimulus in which a person startles, fixates the eyes on the stimulus, and shows changes in heart rate and brain-wave patterns.

**overextension**   When children define words more broadly than adults do.

**overregularization**   Children's application of rules to words that are exceptions to the rule; used as evidence that children master grammar by learning rules.

# P

**pain cry**   A cry that begins with a sudden, long burst, followed by a long pause and gasping.

**parallel play** When children play alone but are aware of and interested in what another child is doing; occurs soon after the first birthday.

**passive gene-environment relation** The phenomenon in which parents pass on genotypes to their children and provide much of the early environment for their young children.

**period of the fetus** The longest period of prenatal development, extending from the ninth week after conception until birth.

**personal fable** The feeling of many adolescents that their feelings and experiences are unique and have never been experienced by anyone else before.

**phenotype** The physical, behavioral, and psychological features that are the result of the interaction between one's genes and the environment.

**phenylketonuria (PKU)** An inherited disorder in which babies are born lacking a liver enzyme.

**phonemes** Unique speech sounds that can be used to create words.

**phonological awareness** The ability to hear the distinctive sounds associated with specific letters.

**phonology** The sounds of a language.

**placenta** The structure through which nutrients and wastes are exchanged between the mother and the developing child.

**placental abruption** A condition in which the placenta becomes detached from the wall of the uterus, severing the connection to the mother's blood supply; can lead to anoxia.

**plasticity** In the context of neural development, the extent to which brain organization is flexible.

**polygenic inheritance** When phenotypes are the result of the combined activity of many separate genes.

**population** A broad group of children that are the usual focus of research in child development.

**positron emission tomography (PET-scan)** A procedure that shows the amount of activity in various regions of the brain by monitoring levels of radioactive glucose.

**postconventional level** The third level of reasoning in Kohlberg's theory, in which morality is based on a personal moral code.

**postpartum depression** A condition affecting 10 to 15 percent of new mothers in which irritability continues for months and is often accompanied by feelings of low self-worth, disturbed sleep, poor appetite, and apathy.

**pragmatics** How people use language to communicate effectively.

**preconventional level** The first level of reasoning in Kohlberg's theory, where moral reasoning is based on external forces.

**prejudice** A view of other people, usually negative, that is based on their membership in a specific group.

**premature infant** A baby born before the 38th week after conception.

**prenatal development** The many changes that turn a fertilized egg into a newborn human.

**preoccupied attachment representation** A representation of parent-child relations in which adults describe childhood experiences emotionally and often express anger or confusion regarding relationships with their parents.

**preoperational stage** The second of Piaget's stages, from 2 to 7 years, in which children first use symbols to represent objects and events.

**primary circular reaction** According to Piaget, when infants accidentally produce pleasant events that are centered on the body and then try to recreate the events.

**private speech** Comments that are not intended for others but that help children regulate their own behavior.

**propositions** Ideas created during reading by combining words.

**prosocial behavior** Any behavior that benefits another person.

**proximodistal principle** The principle that growth occurs first from the center of the body and then moves out to the extremities.

**psychodynamic theory** A view first formulated by Sigmund Freud in which development is largely determined by how well people resolve conflicts they face at different ages.

**psychometricians** Psychologists who specialize in the measurement of psychological characteristics such as intelligence and personality.

**psychosocial theory** A theory proposed by Erik Erikson in which personality development is the result of the interaction of maturation and societal demands.

**puberty** A collection of physical changes that marks the onset of adolescence, such as the growth spurt and the growth of breasts or testes.

**punishment** Applying an aversive stimulus (e.g., a spanking) or removing an attractive stimulus (e.g., TV viewing); an action that discourages the reoccurrence of the response that it follows.

# R

**rapid-eye-movement (REM) sleep (irregular sleep)** Irregular sleep in which an infant's eyes dart rapidly beneath the eyelids, while the body is quite active.

**reaction range** The phenomenon that a particular genotype can interact with various environments to produce a range of phenotypes.

**reactive aggression** Aggression prompted by another child's behavior.

**recessive** An allele whose instructions are ignored when it is combined with a dominant allele.

**referential style** A style of language learning that describes children whose vocabularies are dominated by names of objects, persons, or actions.

**reflexes** Unlearned responses that are triggered by specific stimulation.

**reinforcement** A consequence that increases the likelihood that a behavior will be repeated in the future.

**relational aggression** A form of verbal aggression in which children try to hurt others by undermining their social relationships.

**relative size** A perceptual cue to depth based on the fact that nearby objects look substantially larger than objects in the distance.

**reliability** As applied to tests, how consistent test scores are from one testing time to another.

**resistant attachment** A relationship in which, after a brief separation, infants want to be held but are difficult to console.

**retinal disparity** A perceptual cue to depth based on the fact that, when a person views an object, the retinal images in the left and right eyes differ.

**rough-and-tumble play** A form of play common during the elementary-school years in which children playfully chase, punch, kick, shove, fight, and wrestle with peers.

# S

**sample** A group of children drawn from a population that participates in research.

**savants** Individuals with mental retardation who are quite talented in one domain.

**scaffolding** A teaching style in which adults adjust the amount of assistance that they offer, based on the learner's needs.

**scheme** According to Piaget, a mental structure that organizes information and regulates behavior.

**schizophrenia** A psychological disorder in which individuals hallucinate, have confused language and thought, and often behave bizarrely.

**school phobia** An overwhelming fear of going to school and active resistance to attending school.

**script** The means by which people remember common events consisting of sequences of activities.

**secondary circular reaction** According to Piaget, when infants accidentally produce interesting events with objects and then try to repeat those events.

**secular growth trends** Changes in physical development from one generation to the next; for example, the fact that people in industrialized societies are larger and are maturing earlier than in previous generations.

**secure attachment** A relationship in which infants have come to trust and depend on their mothers.

**self-concept** Attitudes, behaviors, and values that a person believes make him or her a unique individual.

**self-control** The ability to rise above immediate pressures and not give in to impulse.

**self-efficacy** The belief that one is capable of performing a certain task.

**self-esteem** A person's judgment and feelings about his or her own worth.

**self reports** Children's answers to questions about specific topics.

**semantic bootstrapping hypothesis** A view that children rely on their knowledge of word meanings to discover grammatical rules.

**semantics** The study of words and their meaning.

**sensorimotor stage** The first of Piaget's four stages of cognitive development, which lasts from birth to approximately 2 years, in which infants progress from responding reflexively to using symbols.

**sensory and perceptual processes** The means by which the nervous system receives, selects, modifies, and organizes stimulation from the world.

**sensory memory** A type of memory in which information is held in raw, unanalyzed form very briefly (no longer than a few seconds).

**sequential processing** A scale on the K-ABC intelligence test that assesses how well a child integrates information over time.

**severe malnourishment** A state in which children weigh less than 60 percent of the average body weight for their age.

**sex chromosomes** The 23rd pair of chromosomes; these determine the sex of the child.

**short-term storage space** In Case's neo-Piagetian theory, a memory used to store schemes; its capacity increases with age.

**sickle cell trait** A disorder in which individuals show signs of mild anemia only when they are seriously deprived of oxygen; occurs in individuals who have one dominant allele for normal blood cells and one recessive sickle cell allele.

**simple social play** Play that begins at about 15 to 18 months; toddlers engage in similar activities as well as talk and smile at each other and offer each other toys.

**simultaneous processing** A scale on the K-ABC intelligence test that measures how well a child integrates different information at the same time.

**size constancy** The realization that an object's actual size remains the same despite changes in the size of its retinal image.

**small-for-date infants** Newborns who are substantially smaller than would be expected based on the length of time since conception.

**sociability** The dimension of temperament defined by preference for being with other people.

**social-cognitive flexibility** A person's skill in solving social problems with relevant social knowledge; an aspect of interpersonal intelligence.

**social cognitive theory** A theory developed by Albert Bandura in which children use reward, punishment, and imitation to try to understand what goes on in their world.

**social conventions** Arbitrary standards of behavior agreed to by a cultural group to help coordinate interactions of individuals within the group.

**social referencing** A phenomenon in which infants in an unfamiliar or ambiguous environment look at their mother or father, as if searching for cues to help them interpret the situation.

**social role** A set of cultural guidelines about how one should behave, especially with other people.

**social smiles** Smiles that first appear at about 2 months of age, when infants see another human face.

**specification** The second phase in Super's theory of career development, in which adolescents learn more about specific lines of work and begin training.

**spina bifida** A disorder in which the embryo's neural tube does not close properly during the first month of pregnancy.

**stable-order principle** The counting principle that states that number names must always be counted in the same order.

**stereotyped, approval-focused orientation** According to Eisenberg, a level of prosocial reasoning common in many elementary-school children and adolescents in which they behave as they think society would expect "good people" to behave.

**stranger wariness** An infant's apparent concern or anxiety in the presence of an unfamiliar adult, typically observed at about 6 months of age.

**stress** A person's physical and psychological responses to threatening or challenging situations.

**structured observation** Observation taken in a setting created by the researcher so that it will elicit the behavior of interest.

**sudden infant death syndrome (SIDS)** A disorder in which a healthy baby dies suddenly, for no apparent reason, typically occurring between 2 and 4 months of age.

**superego** According to Freud, the moral component of the personality that has incorporated adult standards of right and wrong.

**surrogate-parent grandparents** Grandparents who assume many of the normal roles of parents.

**synapse** The gap between one neuron and the next.

**synaptic pruning** Gradual loss of unused synapses, beginning in infancy and continuing into early adolescence.

**syntax**   Rules that specify how words are combined to form sentences.

**systematic desensitization**   A therapeutic technique that associates deep relaxation with progressively more anxiety-provoking situations.

**systematic observation**   A method of observation in which investigators watch children and carefully record what they do or say.

# T

**telegraphic speech**   A style of speaking common in 1-year-olds that includes only words directly relevant to meaning.

**temperament**   A consistent style or pattern of behavior.

**teratogen**   An agent that causes abnormal prenatal development.

**terminal buttons**   Small knobs at the end of an axon that release neurotransmitters.

**tertiary circular reaction**   According to Piaget, repeating old schemes with new objects.

**texture gradient**   A perceptual cue to depth based on the fact that the texture of objects changes from coarse but distinct for nearby objects to finer and less distinct for distant objects.

**theoretical perspective**   A group of theories that share ideas and assumptions about children and their development but differ in their details.

**theory**   An organized set of ideas that is designed to explain development.

**theory of mind**   An intuitive understanding of the connections between thoughts, beliefs, intentions, and behavior; develops rapidly in the preschool years.

**thyroxine**   A hormone essential for the development of nerve cells.

**time-out**   Punishment that involves removing a child who is misbehaving to a quiet, unstimulating environment.

**toddlers**   Young children who have just learned to walk.

**triarchic theory**   A theory of intelligence proposed by Sternberg that includes componential, experiential, and contextual subtheories.

# U

**ultrasound**   A prenatal diagnostic technique that involves bouncing sound waves off the fetus to generate an image of the fetus.

**umbilical cord**   A structure containing veins and arteries that connects the developing child to the placenta.

**underextension**   When children define words more narrowly than adults do.

# V

**validity**   As applied to tests, the extent to which the test measures what it is supposed to measure.

**vernix**   A thick, greasy substance that covers the fetus and protects it during prenatal development.

**visual acuity**   The smallest pattern that one can distinguish reliably.

**visual cliff**   A glass-covered platform that appears to have a "shallow" side and "deep" side; used to study infants' depth perception.

# W

**word recognition**   The process of identifying a unique pattern of letters.

**working memory**   A type of memory in which a small number of items can be stored briefly.

# Z

**zone of proximal development**   The difference between what children can do with assistance and what they can do alone.

**zygote**   The fertilized egg.

# REFERENCES

Ablow, J. C., & Measelle, J. R. (1993). *Berkeley puppet interview: Administration and scoring system manuals.* Berkeley: University of California.

Aboud, F. E. (1993). The developmental psychology of racial prejudice. *Transcultural Psychiatric Research Review, 30,* 229–242.

Ackerman, B. P. (1993). Children's understanding of the speaker's meaning in referential communication. *Journal of Experimental Child Psychology, 55,* 56–86.

Adams, M. J., Treiman, R., & Pressley, M. (1998). Reading, writing, and literacy. In W. Damon (Ed.), *Handbook of child psychology* (Vol. 4). New York: Wiley.

Adams, R. J., & Courage, M. L. (1995). Development of chromatic discrimination in early infancy. *Behavioural Brain Research, 67,* 99–101.

Adler, N. (1994). *Adolescent sexual behavior looks irrational—But looks are deceiving.* Washington, DC: Federation of Behavioral, Psychological, and Cognitive Sciences.

Adolph, K. E. (1997). Learning in the development of infant locomotion. *Monographs of the Society for Research in Child Development, 62,* 1–140.

Adolph, K. E., Eppler, M. A., & Gibson, E. J. (1993). Crawling versus walking infants' perception of affordances for locomotion over sloping surfaces. *Child Development, 64,* 1158–1174.

Adolph, K. E., Vereijken, B., & Denny, M. A. (1998). Learning to crawl. *Child Development, 69,* 1299–1312.

Ainsworth, M. D. S. (1978). The development of infant-mother attachment. In B. M. Caldwell & H. N. Ricciuti (Eds.), *Review of child development research* (Vol. 3). Chicago: The University of Chicago Press.

Ainsworth, M. S. (1993). Attachment as related to mother-infant interaction. *Advances in Infancy Research, 8,* 1–50.

Ales, K. L., Druzin, M. L., & Santini, D. L. (1990). Impact of maternal age on the outcome of pregnancy. *Surgery, Gynecology & Obstetrics, 171,* 209–216.

Alibali, M. W. (1999). How children change their minds: Strategy change can be gradual or abrupt. *Developmental Psychology, 35,* 127–145.

Allen, L., Cipielewski, J., & Stanovich, K. E. (1992). Multiple indicators of children's reading habits and attitudes: Construct validity and cognitive correlates. *Journal of Educational Psychology, 84,* 489–503.

Aman, C. J., Roberts, R. J., & Pennington, B. F. (1998). A neuropsychological examination of the underlying deficit in attention deficit hyperactivity disorder: Frontal lobe versus right parietal lobe theories. *Developmental Psychology, 34,* 956–969.

Amato, P. R., & Keith, B. (1991). Parental divorce and the well-being of children: A meta-analysis. *Psychological Bulletin, 110,* 26–46.

American Psychiatric Association. (1987). *Diagnostic and statistical manual of mental disorders* (3rd ed., revised). Washington, DC: Author.

Ames, G. J., & Murray, F. B. (1982). When two wrongs make a right: Promoting cognitive change by social conflict. *Developmental Psychology, 18,* 894–897.

Anand, K. J., & Hickey, P. R. (1987). Pain and its effect in the human neonate and fetus. *New England Journal of Medicine, 31,* 1321–1329.

Anastasi, A. (1988). *Psychological testing* (6th ed.) New York: Macmillan.

Anastopoulos, A. D., Shelton, T. L., DuPaul, G. J., & Guevremont, D. C. (1993). Parent training for attention-deficit hyperactivity disorder: Its impact on parent functioning. *Journal of Abnormal Child Psychology, 21,* 581–596.

Anderson, E. R., Greene, S. M., Hetherington, E. M., & Clingempeel, W. G. (1999). The dynamics of parental remarriage: Adolescent, parent, and sibling. In E. M. Hetherington (Ed), *Coping with divorce, single parenting, and remarriage: A risk and resiliency perspective.* Mahwah, NJ: Erlbaum.

Anglin, J. M. (1993). Vocabulary development: A morphological analysis. *Monographs of the Society for Research in Child Development, 58*(10, Serial No. 238).

Antonarakis, S. E., & the Down Syndrome Collaborative Group. (1991). Parental origin of the extra chromosome in trisomy 21 as indicated by analysis of DNA polymorphisms. *New England Journal of Medicine, 324,* 872–876.

Apgar, V. (1953). A proposal for a new method of evaluation of the newborn infant. *Current Researches in Anesthesia and Analgesia, 32,* 260–267.

Arcus, D., & Kagan, J. (1995). Temperament and craniofacial variation in the first two years. *Child Development, 66,* 1529–1540.

Ashcraft, M. H. (1982). The development of mental arithmetic: A chronometric approach. *Developmental Review, 2,* 212–236.

Aslin, R. N. (1987). Visual and auditory discrimination in infancy. In J. D. Osofsky (Ed.), *Handbook of infant development* (2nd ed.). New York: Wiley.

Aslin, R. N., Jusczyk, P. W., & Pisoni, D. B. (1998). Speech and auditory processing during infancy: Constraints on and precursors to language. In W. Damon (Ed.), *Handbook of child psychology* (Vol. 2). New York: Wiley.

Aslin, R. N., Saffran, J. R., & Newport, W. L. (1998). Computation of conditional probability statistics by 8-month-old infants. *Psychological Science, 9,* 321–324.

Attie, I., Brooks-Gunn, J., & Petersen, A. C. (1990). A developmental perspective on eating disorders and eating problems. In M. Lewis & S. M. Miller (Eds.), *Handbook of developmental psychopathology.* New York: Plenum.

Au, T. K. (1994). Developing an intuitive understanding of substance kinds. *Cognitive Psychology, 27,* 71–111.

Au, T. K., & Glusman, M. (1990). The principle of mutual exclusivity in word learning: To honor or not to honor? *Child Development, 61,* 1474–1490.

Averill, J. A. (1980). A constructivist view of emotion. In R. Plutchik & H. Kellerman (Eds.), *Emotion: Theory, research, and experience* (Vol. 1): *Theories of emotion.* New York: Academic Press.

Bachman, J. (1983, Summer). Premature affluence: Do high school students earn too much? *Economic Outlook USA,* 64–67.

Bachman, J.G., & Schulenberg, J. (1993). How part-time work intensity relates to drug use, problem behavior, time use, and satisfaction among high school seniors: Are these consequences or merely correlates? *Developmental Psychology, 29,* 229–230.

Backscheider, A., G., Shatz, M., & Gelman, S. A. (1993). Preschoolers' ability to distinguish living kinds as a function of regrowth. *Child Development, 64,* 1242–1257.

Baddeley, A. (1996). Exploring the central executive. *Quarterly Journal of Experimental Psychology: Human Experimental Psychology, 49,* 5–28.

Baenninger, M., & Newcombe, N. (1995). Environmental input to the development of sex-related differences in spatial and mathematical ability. *Learning & Individual Differences, 7,* 363–379.

Baer, D. M., & Wolf, M. M. (1968). The reinforcement contingency in preschool and remedial education. In R. D. Hess & R. M Baer (Eds.), *Early education.* Chicago: Aldine.

Bagwell, C. L., Newcomb, A. F., & Bukowski, W. M. (1998). Preadolescent friendship and peer rejection as predictors of adult adjustment. *Child Development, 69,* 140–153.

Bahrick, L. E., Netto, D., & Hernandez-Reif, M. (1998). Intermodal perception of adult and child faces and voices by infants. *Child Development, 69,* 1263–1275.

Bailey, J. M., Bobrow, D., Wolfe, M., & Mikach, S. (1995). Sexual orientation of adult sons of gay fathers. *Developmental Psychology, 31,* 124–129.

Baillargeon, R. (1987). Object permanence in $3\frac{1}{2}$- and $4\frac{1}{2}$-month-old infants. *Developmental Psychology, 23,* 655–664.

Baillargeon, R. (1994). How do infants learn about the physical world? *Current Directions in Psychological Science, 3,* 133–140.

Baillargeon, R. (1998). Infants' understanding of the physical world. *Advances in Psychological Science, 2,* 503–529.

Baker, C. (1993). *Foundations of bilingual education and bilingualism.* Clevedon, England: Multilingual Matters.

Baker, L. (1994). Fostering metacognitive development. In H. W. Reese (Ed.), *Advances in child development and behavior* (Vol. 25). San Diego: Academic Press.

Baker, L., & Brown, A. L. (1984). Metacognitive skills and reading. In P. D. Pearson (Ed.), *Handbook of Reading Research, Part 2.* New York: Longman.

Baldwin, D. A., Markman, E. M, Bill, B., Desjardins, R. N., & Irwin, J. M. (1996). Infants' reliance on a social criterion for establishing word-object relations. *Child Development, 67,* 3135–3153.

Bancroft, J., Axworthy, D., & Ratcliffe, S. (1982). The personality and psycho-sexual development of boys with 47-XXY chromosome constitution. *Journal of Child Psychology and Psychiatry, 23,* 169–180.

Bandura, A. (1977). *Social learning theory.* Englewood Cliffs, NJ: Prentice-Hall.

Bandura, A. (1986). *Social foundations of thought and action: A social-cognitive theory.* Englewood Cliffs, NJ: Prentice-Hall.

Bandura, A., & Mischel, W. (1965). Modification of self-imposed delay of reward through exposure to live and symbolic models. *Journal of Personality and Social Psychology, 2,* 698–705.

Bandura, A., Ross, D., & Ross, S. A. (1963). Imitation of film-mediated aggressive models. *Journal of Abnormal and Social Psychology, 66,* 3–11.

Bardwell, J. R., Cochran, S. W., & Walker, S. (1986). Relationship of parental education, race, and gender to sex role stereotyping in five-year-old kindergartners. *Sex Roles, 15,* 275–281.

Barenboim, C. (1981). The development of person perception in childhood and adolescence: From behavioral comparisons to psychological constructs to psychological comparisons. *Child Development, 52,* 129–144.

Barinaga, M. (1997). Researchers find signals that guide young brain neurons. *Science, 278,* 385–386.

Barkley, R. A. (1990). Attention deficit disorders: History, definition, and diagnosis. In M. Lewis & S. M. Miller (Eds.), *Handbook of developmental psychopathology.* New York: Plenum.

Barkley, R. A. (1994). Impaired delayed responding: A unified theory of attention-deficit hyperactivity disorder. In R. A. Barkley (Ed.), *Disruptive behavior disorders in childhood.* New York: Plenum.

Barkley, R. A. (1996). Attention-deficit hyperactivity disorder. In E. J. Mash & R. A. Barkley (Eds.), *Child psychopathology.* New York: Guilford.

Barling, J., Rogers, K., & Kelloway, E. K. (1995). Some effects of teenagers' part-time employment: The quantity and quality of work make the difference. *Journal of Organizational Behavior, 16,* 143–154.

Barton, M. E., & Tomasello, M. (1991). Joint attention and conversation in mother-infant-sibling triads. *Child Development, 62,* 517–529.

Bartsch, K., & Wellman, H. M. (1995). *Children talk about the mind.* New York: Oxford University Press.

Baskett, L. M. (1985). Sibling status effects: Adult expectations. *Developmental Psychology, 21,* 441–445.

Bates, E., Benigni, L., Bretherton, I., Camaioni, L., & Volterra, V. (1979). *The emergence of symbols: Cognition and communication in infancy.* New York: Academic Press.

Bates, E., Bretherton, I., & Snyder, L. (1988). *From first words to grammar: Individual differences and dissociable mechanisms.* New York: Cambridge University Press.

Bates, E., & MacWhinney, B. (1987). Competition, variation, and language learning. In B. MacWhinney (Ed.), *Mechanisms of language acquisition* (pp. 157–193). Hillsdale, NJ: Erlbaum.

Bates, J. E. (1987). Temperament in infancy. In J. D. Osofsky (Ed.), *Handbook of infant development* (2nd ed.). New York: Wiley.

Bates, J. E., Pettie, G. S., Dodge, K. A., & Ridge, B. (1998). Interaction of temperamental resistance to control and restrictive parenting in the development of externalizing behavior. *Developmental Psychology, 34,* 982–995.

Baumeister, A. A., & Baumeister, A. A. (1995). Mental retardation. In M. Hersen & R. T. Ammerman (Eds.), *Advanced abnormal child psychology.* Hillsdale, NJ: Erlbaum.

Baumrind, D. (1975). *Early socialization and the discipline controversy.* Morristown, NJ: General Learning Press.

Baumrind, D. (1991). Parenting styles and adolescent development. In R. M. Lerner, A. C. Petersen, & J. Brooks-Gunn (Eds.), *Encyclopedia of adolescence.* New York: Garland.

Bayley, N. (1970). Development of mental abilities. In P. H. Mussen (Ed.), *Carmichael's manual of child psychology.* New York: John Wiley.

Bayley, N. (1993). *Bayley scales of infant development: Birth to two years* (2nd ed.). San Antonio, TX: Psychological Corporation.

Beal, C. R. (1996). The role of comprehension monitoring in children's revision. *Educational Psychology Review, 8,* 219–238.

Beal, C. R., & Belgrad, S. L. (1990). The development of message evaluation skills in young children. *Child Development, 61,* 705–712.

Beck, M. (1994). How far should we push Mother Nature? *Newsweek* (January 16), 54–57.

Becker, B. J. (1986). Influence again: An examination of reviews and studies of gender differences in social influence. In J. S. Hyde & M. C. Linn (Eds.), *The psychology of gender differences. Advances through meta-analysis.* Baltimore, MD: Johns Hopkins University Press.

Beckwith, L., Cohen, S. E., & Hamilton, C. E. (1999). Maternal sensitivity during infancy and subsequent life events relate to attachment representation at early adulthood. *Developmental Psychology, 35,* 693–700.

Behnke, M., & Eyler, F. D. (1993). The consequences of prenatal substance use for the developing fetus, newborn, and young child. *International Journal of the Addictions, 28,* 1341–1391.

Bell, A.P., Weinberg, M.S., & Hammersmith, S.K. (1981). *Sexual preference: Its development in men and women.* New York: Simon & Schuster.

Beller, M., & Gafni, N. (1996). The 1991 international assessment of educational progress in mathematics and sciences: The gender differences perspective. *Journal of Educational Psychology, 88,* 365–377.

Bellinger, D., Leviton, A., Waternaux, C., Needleman, H., & Rabinowitz, M. (1987). Longitudinal analyses of prenatal and postnatal lead exposure and early cognitive development. *New England Journal of Medicine, 316,* 1037–1043.

Belsky, J. (1993). Etiology of child maltreatment: A developmental-ecological analysis. *Psychological Bulletin, 114,* 413–434.

Belsky, J., Fish, M., & Isabella, R. A. (1991). Continuity and discontinuity in infant negative and positive emotionality: Family antecedents and attachment consequences. *Developmental Psychology, 27,* 421–431.

Belsky, J., Steinberg, L., & Draper, P. (1991). Childhood experience, interpersonal development, and reproductive strategy: An evolutionary theory of socialization. *Child Development, 62,* 647–670.

Belsky, J., Woodworth, S., & Crnic, K. (1996). Trouble in the second year: Three questions about family interaction. *Child Development, 67,* 556–578.

Bem, D. J. (1996). Exotic becomes erotic: A developmental theory of sexual orientation. *Psychological Review, 103,* 320–335.

Bem, S. L. (1984). Androgyny and gender schema theory: A conceptual and empirical integration. In T. B. Sonderegger (Ed.), *Nebraska symposium on motivation: Psychology and gender.* Lincoln, NE: University of Nebraska Press.

Bem, S. L. (1989). Genital knowledge and gender constancy in preschool children. *Child Development, 60,* 649–662.

Benton, S. L., Corkill, A. J., Sharp, J. M., Downey, R. G., et al. (1995). Knowledge, interest, and narrative writing. *Journal of Educational Psychology, 87,* 66–79.

Bereiter, C., & Scardamalia, M. (1987). *The psychology of written composition.* Hillsdale NJ: Erlbaum.

Berenbaum, S. A., & Snyder, E. (1995). Early hormonal influences on childhood sex-typed activity and playmate preferences: Implications for the development of sexual orientation. *Developmental Psychology, 31,* 31–42.

Berk, L. E. (1992). Children's private speech: An overview of theory and the status of research. In R. M. Diaz & L. E. Berk (Eds.), *Private speech: From social interaction to self-regulation*. Hillsdale, NJ: Erlbaum.

Berk, L. E. (1994). Vygotsky's theory: The importance of make believe play. *Young Children, 50,* 30–38.

Berko, J. (1958). The child's learning of English morphology. *Word, 14,* 150–177.

Berkowitz, L. (1989). Frustration-aggression hypothesis: Examination and reformulation. *Psychological Bulletin, 106,* 59–73.

Berkowitz, M. W., & Gibbs, J. C. (1985). The process of moral conflict resolution and moral development. In M. W. Berkowitz (Ed.), *Peer conflict and psychological growth* (pp. 71–84). San Francisco: Jossey-Bass.

Berndt, T. J., & Keefe, K. (1995). Friends' influence on adolescents' adjustment to school. *Child Development, 66,* 1312–1329.

Berndt, T. J., & Perry, T. B. (1990). Distinctive features and effects of adolescent friendships. In R. Montemeyer, G. R. Adams, & T. P. Gullotta (Eds.), *From childhood to adolescence: A transition period?* London: Sage.

Bernier, J. C., & Siegel, D. H. (1994). Attention-deficit hyperactivity disorder: A family ecological systems perspective. *Families in Society, 75,* 142–150.

Berry, J. W. (1993). Ethnic identities in plural societies. In M. E. Bernal & G. P. Knight (Eds.), *Ethnic identity: Formation and transmission among Hispanics and other minorities*. New York: State University of New York Press.

Bertenthal, B. H., & Clifton, R. K. (1998). Perception and action. In W. Damon (Ed.), *Handbook of child psychology* (Vol. 2). New York: Wiley.

Bertenthal, B. I., Campos, J. J., & Kermoian, R. (1994). An epigenetic perspective on the development of self-produced locomotion and its consequences. *Current Directions in Psychological Science, 3,* 140–145.

Berthier, N. E. (1996). Learning to reach: A mathematical model. *Developmental Psychology, 32,* 811–823.

Besharov, D. J., & Gardiner, K. N. (1997). Trends in teen sexual behavior. *Children and Youth Services Review, 19,* 341–367.

Best, C. T. (1995). Learning to perceive the sound pattern of English. In C. Rovee-Collier (Ed.), *Advances in infancy research*. Norwood, NJ: Ablex.

Best, D. L., Williams, J. E., Cloud, J. M., Davis, S. W., Robertson, L. S., Edwards, J. R., Giles, H., & Fowles, J. (1977). Development of sex-trait stereotypes among young children in the United States, England, and Ireland. *Child Development, 48,* 1375–1384.

Bettencourt, B. A., & Miller, N. (1996). Gender differences in aggression as a function of provocation: A meta-analysis. *Psychological Bulletin, 119,* 422–447.

Bialystok, E. (1988). Levels of bilingualism and levels of linguistic awareness. *Developmental Psychology, 24,* 560–567.

Bialystok, E. (1997). Effects of bilingualism and biliteracy on children's emerging concepts of print. *Developmental Psychology, 33,* 429–440.

Bialystok, E. (1999). Cognitive complexity and attentional control in the bilingual mind. *Child Development, 70,* 636–644.

Bigler, R. S. (1995). The role of classification skill in moderating environmental influences on children's gender stereotyping: A study of the functional use of gender in the classroom. *Child Development, 66,* 1072–1087.

Bigler, R. S., Jones, L. C., & Lobliner, D. B. (1997). Social categorization and the formation of intergroup attitudes in children. *Child Development, 68,* 530–543.

Bigler, R. S., & Liben L. S. (1990). The role of attitudes and interventions in gender-schematic processing. *Child Development, 61,* 1440–1452.

Bigner, J. J., & Jacobsen, R. B. (1989). Parenting behavior of homosexual and heterosexual fathers. *Journal of Homosexuality, 18,* 173–186.

Birch, L. L. (1991). Obesity and eating disorders: A developmental perspective. *Bulletin of the Psychonomic Society, 29,* 265–272.

Birch, L. L., & Fisher, J. A. (1995). Appetite and eating behavior in children. *Pediatric Clinics of North America, 42,* 931–953.

Birnholz, J. C., & Benacerraf, B. R. (1983). The development of human fetal hearing. *Science, 222,* 516–518.

Bisanz, G. L., Das, J. P., Varnhagen, C. K., & Henderson, H. R. (1992). Structural components of reading time and recall for sentences in narratives: Exploring changes with age and reading ability. *Journal of Educational Psychology, 84,* 103–114.

Black, B., & Logan, A. (1995). Links between communication patterns in mother-child, father-child, and child-peer interactions and children's social status. *Child Development, 66,* 255–271.

Black-Gutman, D., & Hickson, F. (1996). The relationship between racial attitudes and social-cognitive development in children: An Australian study. *Developmental Psychology, 32,* 448–456.

Blake, J., O'Rourke, P., & Borzellino, G. (1994). Form and function in the development of pointing and reaching gestures. *Infant Behavior & Development, 17,* 195–203.

Block, J. (1976). Debatable conclusions about sex differences. *Contemporary Psychology, 21,* 517–522.

Block, J. H. (1978). Another look at sex differentiation in the socialization behaviors of mothers and fathers. In J. Sherman & F. L. Denmark (Eds.), *Psychology of women: Future directions for research* (pp. 29–87). New York: Psychological Dimensions.

Block, J. H. (1983). Differential premises arising from differential socialization of the sexes: Some conjectures. *Child Development, 54,* 1335–1354.

Bloom, L., Margulis, C., Tinker, E., & Fujita, N. (1996). Early conversations and word learning: Contributions from child and adult. *Child Development, 67,* 3154–3175.

Bloom, L., Rocissano, L., & Hood, L. (1976). Adult-child discourse: Developmental interaction between information processing and linguistic knowledge. *Cognitive Psychology, 8,* 521–552.

Bogatz, G. A., & Ball, S. (1972). *The second year of "Sesame Street": A continuing evaluation*. Princeton, NJ: Educational Testing Service.

Bohannon, J. N., MacWhinney, B., & Snow, C. (1990). No negative evidence revisited: Beyond learnability or who has to prove what to whom. *Developmental Psychology, 26,* 221–226.

Bohannon, J. N., Padgett, R. J., Nelson, K. E., & Mark, M. (1996). Useful evidence on negative evidence. *Developmental Psychology, 32,* 551–555.

Boivin, M., Vitaro, F., & Gagnon, C. (1992). A reassessment of the self-perception profile for children: Factor structure, reliability, and convergent validity of a French version among second through sixth grade children. *International Journal of Behavioral Development, 15,* 275–290.

Bogler, K. E., Patterson, C. J., & Kupersmidt, J. B. (1998). Peer relationships and self-esteem among children who have been maltreated. *Child Development, 69,* 1171–1197.

Bolger, K. E., Patterson, C. J., Thompson, W. W., & Kupersmidt, J. B. (1995). Psychosocial adjustment among children experiencing persistent and intermittent family economic hardship. *Child Development, 66,* 1107–1129.

Bork, A. (1985). *Personal computers for education*. New York: Harper & Row.

Bornstein, M. H. (1981). Psychological studies of color perception in human infants: Habituation, discrimination and categorization, recognition, and conceptualization. *Advances in Infancy Research, 1,* 1–40.

Bornstein, M. H. (1997). Stability in mental development from early life: Methods, measures, models, meanings, and myths. In G. E. Butterworth & F. Simion (Eds.), *The development of sensory, motor, and cognitive capacities in early infancy: From sensation to perception*. Hove, England: Psychology Press.

Bornstein, M. H., Haynes, O. M., Pascual, L., Painter, K. M., & Galperin, C. (1999). Play in two societies: Pervasiveness of process, specificity of structure. *Child Development, 70,* 317–331.

Bornstein, M. H., Haynes, O. M., O'Reilly, A. W., & Painter, K. M. (1996). Solitary and collaborative pretense play in early childhood: Sources of individual variation in the development of representational competence. *Child Development, 67,* 2910–2929.

Bowlby, J. (1969). *Attachment and loss* (Vol. 1). New York: Basic Books.

Bowlby, J. (1991). Ethological light on psychoanalytical problems. In P. Bateson et al. (Ed.), *The development and integration of behaviour: Essays in honour of Robert Hinde.* Cambridge, England: Cambridge University Press.

Boyer, C. B., & Hein, K. (1991). AIDS and HIV infection in adolescents: The role of education and antibody testing. In R. M. Lerner, A. C. Petersen, & J. Brooks-Gunn (Eds.), *Encyclopedia of adolescence* (Vol. 1). New York: Garland.

Bradley, L., & Bryant, P. E. (1983). Categorising sounds and learning to read—a causal connection. *Nature, 301,* 419–421.

Bradley, R. H., Caldwell, B. M., & Rock, S. L. (1988). Home environment and school performance: A ten-year follow-up and examination of three models of environmental action. *Child Development, 59,* 852–867.

Bradley, R. H., Caldwell, B. M., Rock, S. L., Casey, P. M., & Nelson, J. (1987). The early development of low-birthweight infants: Relationship to health, family status, family context, family processes, and parenting. *International Journal of Behavioral Development, 10,* 301–318.

Bradley, R. H., Caldwell, B. M., Rock, S. L., Ramey, C. T., Barnard, K. E., Gray, C., Hammond, M. A., Mitchell, S., Gottfried, A. W., Siegel, L., & Johnson, D. L. (1989). Home environment and cognitive development in the first 3 years of life: A collaborative study involving six sites and three ethnic groups in North America. *Developmental Psychology, 25,* 217–235.

Braet, C., Mervielde, I., & Vandereycken, W. (1997). Psychological aspects of childhood obesity: A controlled study in a clinical and nonclinical sample. *Journal of Pediatric Psychology, 22,* 59–71.

Braine, M. D. S. (1992). What sort of innate structure is needed to "bootstrap" into syntax? *Cognition, 45,* 77–100.

Brainerd, C. J. (1996). Piaget: A centennial celebration. *Psychological Science, 7,* 191–203.

Brand, E., Clingempeel, W. G., & Bowen-Woodward, D. (1988). Family relationships and children's psychological adjustment in stepmother and stepfather families. In E. M. Hetherington & J. D. Arasten (Eds.), *Impact of divorce, single parenting and step parenting on children* (pp. 299–324). Hillsdale, NJ: Erlbaum.

Braungart, J. M., Plomin, R., DeFries, J. C., & Fulker, D. W. (1992). Genetic influence on tester-rated infant temperament as assessed by Bayley's Infant Behavior Record: Nonadoptive and adoptive siblings and twins. *Developmental Psychology, 28,* 40–47.

Brazelton, T. B. (1984). *Brazelton Behavior Assessment Scale* (rev. ed.). Philadelphia: Lippincott.

Brazelton, T. B., Nugent, J. K., & Lester, B. M. (1987). Neonatal behavioral assessment scale. In J. D. Osofsky (Ed.), *Handbook of infant development* (2nd ed.). New York: Wiley.

Bretherton, I. (1992). The origins of attachment theory: John Bowlby and Mary Ainsworth. *Developmental Psychology, 28,* 759–775.

Brigham, J. C., & Spier, S. A. (1992). Opinions held by professionals who work with child witnesses. In H. Dent & R. Flin (Eds.), *Children as witnesses.* New York: J. Wiley & Sons.

Brockington, I. (1996). *Motherhood and mental health.* Oxford, England: Oxford University Press.

Brody, G. H. (1998). Sibling relationship quality: Its causes and consequences. *Annual Review of Psychology, 49,* 1–24.

Brody, G. H., & Flor, D. L. (1998). Maternal resources, parenting practices, and child competence in rural, single-parent African American families. *Child Development, 69,* 803–816.

Brody, G. H., Stoneman, A., & McCoy, J. K. (1994). Forecasting sibling relationships in early adolescence from child temperaments and family processes in middle childhood. *Child Development, 65,* 771–784.

Brody, N. (1992). *Intelligence* (2nd ed.). San Diego: Academic Press.

Bronfenbrenner, U. (1979). *The ecology of human development.* Cambridge: Harvard University Press.

Bronfenbrenner, U. (1989). Ecological systems theory. In R. Vasta (Ed.), *Annals of child development* (Vol. 6). Greenwich, CT: JAI Press.

Bronfenbrenner, U. (1995). Developmental ecology through space and time: A future perspective. In P. Moen, G. H. Elder, Jr., & K. Luscher (Eds.), *Examining lives in context: Perspectives on the ecology of human development.* Washington, DC: American Psychological Association.

Bronfenbrenner, U. (1999). Environments in developmental perspective: Theoretical and operational models. In S. L. Friedman & T. D. Wachs (Eds.), *Measuring environments across the life span: Emerging methods and concepts.* Washington, DC: American Psychological Association.

Brooks-Gunn, J., Klebanov, P. K., & Duncan, G. J. (1996). Ethnic differences in children's intelligence test scores: Role of economic deprivation, home environment, and maternal characteristics. *Child Development, 67,* 396–408.

Brown, B. B., & Lohr, M. J. (1987). Peer-group affiliation and adolescent self-esteem: An integration of ego-identity and symbolic-interaction theories. *Journal of Personality and Social Psychology, 52,* 47–55.

Brown, B. B., Lohr, M. J., & McClenahan, E. L. (1986). Early adolescents' perceptions of peer pressure. *Journal of Early Adolescence, 6,* 139–154.

Brown, B. B., Mounts, N., Lamborn, S. D., & Steinberg, L. (1993). Parenting practices and peer group affiliation in adolescence. *Developmental Psychology, 64,* 467–482.

Brown, J. R., & Dunn, J. (1992). Talk with your mother or your sibling? Developmental changes in early family conversations about feelings. *Child Development, 63,* 336–349.

Brown, J. R., & Dunn, J. (1996). Continuities in emotion understanding from three to six years. *Child Development, 67,* 789–802.

Brown, R. (1973). *A first language: The early stages.* Cambridge, MA: Harvard University Press.

Brown, R., Pressley, M., Van Meter, P., & Schuder, T. (1996). A quasi-experimental validation of transactional strategies instruction with low-achieving second-grade readers. *Journal of Educational Psychology, 88,* 18–37.

Bryan, J. H., & Walbek, N. B. (1970). Preaching and practicing generosity: Children's actions and reactions. *Child Development, 41,* 329–353.

Bryant, B. K., (1992). Conflict resolution strategies in relation to children's peer relations. *Journal of Applied Developmental Psychology, 13,* 35–50.

Bryant, B. K., & Crockenberg, S. B. (1980). Correlates and dimensions of prosocial behavior: A study of female siblings with their mothers. *Child Development, 51,* 529–554.

Buchholz, M., Karl, H. W., Pomietto, M., & Lynn, A. (1998). Pain scores in infants: A modified infant pain scale versus visual analogue. *Journal of Pain & Symptom Management, 15,* 117–124.

Buhrmester, D., & Furman, W. (1987). The development of companionship and intimacy. *Child Development, 58,* 1101–1113.

Buhrmester, D., & Furman, W. (1990). Perceptions of sibling relationships during middle childhood and adolescence. *Child Development, 61,* 1387–1398.

Bullock, M., & Lütkenhaus, P. (1990). Who am I? The development of self-understanding in toddlers. *Merrill-Palmer Quarterly, 36,* 217–238.

Burks, V. S., Dodge, K. A., Price, J. M., & Laird, R. D. (1999). Internal representational models of peers: Implications for the development of problematic behavior. *Developmental Psychology, 35,* 802–810.

Burns, A., & Scott, C. (1994). *Mother-headed families and why they have increased.* Hillsdale, NJ: Erlbaum.

Buss, A. H., & Plomin, R. (1975). *A temperamental theory of personality development.* New York: Wiley-Interscience.

Buss, A. H., & Plomin, R. (1984). *Temperament: Early developing personality traits.* Hillsdale, NJ: Erlbaum.

Buss, K. A., & Goldsmith, H. H. (1998). Fear and anger regulation in infancy: Effects on the temporal dynamics of affective expression. *Child Development, 69,* 359–374.

Butler, R. (1992). What young people want to know when: The effects of mastery and ability on social information seeking. *Journal of Personality and Social Psychology, 62,* 934–943.

Button, E. J., Sonuga-Burke, E. J. S., Davis, J., & Thompson, M. (1996). A prospective study of self-esteem in the prediction of eating problems in schoolgirls: Questionnaire findings. *British Journal of Clinical Psychology, 35,* 193–203.

Byrne, B. M., & Gavin, D. A. W. (1996). The Shavelson model revisited: Testing for the structure of academic self-concept across pre-, early, and late adolescents. *Journal of Educational Psychology, 88,* 215–228.

Byrnes, J. P., Miller, D. C., & Schafer, W. D. (1999). Gender differences in risk taking: A meta-analysis. *Psychological Bulletin, 125,* 367–383.

Cairns, R. B., Cairns, B. D., Neckerman, H. J., Ferguson, L. L., & Gariépy, J-L. (1989). Growth and aggression: 1. Childhood to early adolescence. *Developmental Psychology, 25,* 320–330.

Cairns, R. B., Leung, M. C., Buchannan, L., & Cairns, B. D. (1995). Friendships and social networks in childhood and adolescence: Fluidity, reliability, and interrelations. *Child Development, 66,* 1330–1345.

Caldwell, B. M., & Bradley, R. H. (1994). Environmental issues in developmental follow-up research. In S. L. Friedman & H. C. Haywood (Eds.), *Developmental follow-up.* San Diego: Academic Press.

Calkins, S. D., Fox, N. A., & Marshall, T. R. (1996). Behavioral and physiological antecedents of inhibited and uninhibited behavior. *Child Development, 67,* 523–540.

Call, K. T. (1996). Adolescent work as an "arena of comfort" under conditions of family discomfort. In J. T. Mortimer & M. D. Finch (Eds.), *Adolescents, work, and family: An intergenerational developmental analysis.* Thousand Oaks, CA: Sage.

Cameron, C. A., Edmunds, G., Wigmore, B., Hunt, A. K., & Linton, M. J. (1997). Children's revision of textual flaws. *International Journal of Behavioral Development, 20,* 667–680.

Campbell, F. A., & Ramey, C. T. (1994). Effects of early intervention on intellectual and academic achievement: A follow-up study of children from low-income families. *Child Development, 65,* 684–698.

Campbell, R., & Sais, E. (1995). Accelerated metalinguistic (phonological) awareness in bilingual children. *British Journal of Developmental Psychology, 13,* 61–68.

Campbell, S.B., Cohn, J.F., Flanagan, C., Popper, S., & Meyers, T. (1992). Course and correlates of postpartum depression during the transition to parenthood. *Development and Psychopathology, 4,* 29–47.

Campos, J. J., Hiatt, S., Ramsay, D., Henderson, C., & Svejda, M. (1978). The emergence of fear on the visual cliff. In M. Lewis & L. Rosenblum (Eds.), *The origins of affect.* New York: Plenum.

Camras, L. A., Oster, H., Campos, J., Campos, R., Ujiie, T., Miyake, K., Wang, L., & Meng. Z. (1998). Production of emotional facial expressions in European, American, Japanese, and Chinese infants. *Developmental Psychology, 34,* 616–628.

Canfield, R. L., & Smith, E. G. (1996). Number-based expectations and sequential enumeration by 5-month-old infants. *Developmental Psychology, 32,* 269–279.

Capaldi, D. M., Crosby, L., & Stoolmiller, M. (1996). Predicting the timing of first sexual intercourse for at-risk adolescent males. *Child Development, 67,* 344–359.

Capaldi, D. M., & Patterson, G. R. (1991). Relation of parental transitions to boys' adjustment problems: I. A linear hypothesis. II. Mothers at risk for transitions and unskilled parenting. *Developmental Psychology, 27,* 489–504.

Capelli, C. A., Nakagawa, N., & Madden, C. M. (1990). How children understand sarcasm: The role of context and intonation. *Child Development, 61,* 1824–1841.

Carey, S. (1978). The child as a word learner. In M. Halle, J. Bresnan, & G. Miller (Eds.), *Linguistic theory and psychological reality.* Cambridge, MA: MIT Press.

Carey, S. (1992). Becoming a face expert. In V. Bruce, A. Cowey, A. W. Ellis, & D. I. Perrett (Eds.), *Processing the facial image.* Oxford: Clarendon Press.

Carlo, G., Koller, S. H., Eisenberg, N., Da Silva, M. S., & Frohlich, C. B. (1996). A cross-national study on the relations among prosocial moral reasoning, gender role orientations, and prosocial behaviors. *Developmental Psychology, 32,* 231–240.

Carlson, C. L., Pelham, W. E., Milich, R., & Dixon, J. (1992). Single and combined effects of methylphenidate and behavior therapy on the classroom performance of children with attention-deficit hyperactivity disorder. *Journal of Abnormal Child Psychology, 20,* 213–232.

Carlson, E. A. (1998). A prospective longitudinal study of attachment disorganization/disorientation. *Child Development, 69,* 1107–1128.

Carpenter, P. A., & Daneman, M. (1981). Lexical retrieval and error recovery in reading: A model based on eye fixations. *Journal of Verbal Learning and Verbal Behavior, 20,* 137–160.

Carrere, S., & Gottman, J. M. (1999). Predicting the future of marriages. In E. M. Hetherington (Ed.), *Coping with divorce, single parenting, and remarriage: A risk and resiliency perspective.* Mahwah, NJ: Erlbaum.

Carroll, J. B. (1993). *Human cognitive abilities: A survey of factor-analytic studies.* New York: Cambridge University Press.

Carroll, J. L., & Loughlin, G. M. (1994). Sudden infant death syndrome. In F. A. Oski, C. D. DeAngelis, R. D. Feigin, J. A. McMillan, & J. B. Warshaw (Eds.), *Principles and practice of pediatrics.* Philadelphia: Lippincott.

Casaer, P. (1993). Old and new facts about perinatal brain development. *Journal of Child Psychology and Psychiatry, 34,* 101–109.

Case, R. (1985). *Intellectual development: Birth to adulthood.* Orlando, FL: Academic Press.

Case, R. (1992). *The mind's staircase: Exploring the conceptual underpinnings of children's thought and knowledge.* Hillsdale, NJ: Erlbaum.

Case, R. (1998). The development of conceptual structures. In W. Damon (Ed.), *Handbook of child psychology* (Vol. 2). New York: Wiley.

Casey, B. J., Trainor, R. J., Orendi, J. L., Schubert, A. B., Nystrom, L. E., Giedd, J. N., Castellanos, F. X., Haxby, J. V., Noll, Douglas C., Cohen, J. D., Forman, S. D., Dahl, R. E., & Rapoport, J. L. (1997). A developmental functional MRI study of prefrontal activation during performance of a Go-No-Go task. *Journal of Cognitive Neuroscience, 9,* 835–847.

Casey, M. B., Nuttall, R. L., & Pezaris, E. (1997). Mediators of gender differences in mathematics college entrance test scores: A comparison of spatial skills with internalized beliefs and anxieties. *Developmental Psychology, 33,* 669–680.

Casiglia, A. C., Coco, A. L., & Zappulla, C. (1998). Aspects of social reputation and peer relationships in Italian children: A cross-cultural perspective. *Developmental Psychology, 34,* 723–730.

Caspi, A., Henry, B., McGee, R. O., Moffitt, T. E., & Silva, P. A. (1995). Temperamental origins of child and adolescent behavior problems: From age three to age fifteen. *Child Development, 66,* 55–68.

Cassidy, J. (1994). Emotion regulation: Influences of attachment relationships. *Monographs of the Society for Research in Child Development, 59,* 228–283.

Cattell, R. B. (1965). *The scientific analysis of personality.* Baltimore: Penguin.

Ceci, S.J., & Bruck, M. (1995). *Jeopardy in the courtroom: A scientific analysis of children's testimony.* Washington, DC: American Psychological Association.

Ceci, S. J., & Bruck, M. (1998). Children's testimony: Applied and basic issues. In W. Damon (Ed.), *Handbook of child psychology* (Vol. 4). New York: Wiley.

Cerella, J., & Hale, S. (1994). The rise and fall in information-processing rates over the life span. *Acta Psychologica, 86,* 109–197.

Cervantes, C. A., & Callanan, M. A. (1998). Labels and explanations in mother-child emotion talk: Age and gender differentiation. *Developmental Psychology, 34,* 88–98.

Chan, R. W., Raboy, B., & Patterson, C. J. (1998). Psychosocial adjustment among children conceived via donor insemination by lesbian and heterosexual mothers. *Child Development, 69,* 443–457.

Chandler, M., & Moran, T. (1990). Psychopathy and moral development: A comparative study of delinquent and nondelinquent youth. *Development and Psychopathology, 2,* 227–246.

Chao, R. K. (1994). Beyond parental control and authoritarian parenting style: Understanding Chinese parenting through the cultural notion of training. *Child Development, 65,* 1111–1119.

Chapman, P. D. (1988). *Schools as sorters: Lewis M. Terman, applied psychology, and the intelligence testing movement, 1890–1930.* New York: New York University Press.

Chase-Lansdale, P. L., Brooks-Gunn, J., & Zamsky, E. S. (1994). Young African-American multigenerational families in poverty: Quality of mothering and grandmothering. *Child Development, 65,* 373–393.

Chase-Lansdale, P. L., Cherlin, A. J., & Kiernan, K. E. (1995). The long-term effects of parental divorce on the mental health of young adults: A developmental perspective. *Child Development, 66,* 1614–1634.

Chase-Lansdale, P. L., & Hetherington, E. M. (1990). The impact of divorce on life-span development: Short and long term effects. In P. B. Baltes, B. L. Featherman, & R. M. Lerner (Eds.), *Life-span development and behavior* (Vol. 10). Hillsdale, NJ: Erlbaum.

Chen, X., Rubin, K. H., & Li, Z. (1995). Social functioning and adjustment in Chinese children. *Developmental Psychology, 31,* 531–539.

Chess, S., & Thomas, A. (1986). *Temperament in clinical practice.* New York: Guilford.

Chi, M. T. H. (1978). Knowledge structures and memory development. In R. Siegler (Ed.), *Children's thinking: What develops?* Hillsdale, NJ: Erlbaum.

Children's Defense Fund. (1996). *The state of America's children yearbook, 1996.* Washington, DC: Author.

Chilman, C. S. (1983). *Adolescent sexuality in a changing American society* (2nd ed.). New York: Wiley.

Chisholm, J. S. (1983). *Navajo infancy: An ethological study of child development.* New York: Aldine.

Chomitz, V. R., Cheung, L. W. Y., & Lieberman, E. (1995). The role of lifestyle in preventing low birth weight. *The Future of Children, 5,* 121–138.

Chomsky, N. (1957). *Syntactic structures.* The Hague: Mouton.

Chomsky, N. (1995). *The minimalist program.* Cambridge: MIT Press.

Chorpita, B. F., & Barlow, D. H. (1998). The development of anxiety: The role of control in the early environment. *Psychological Bulletin, 124,* 3–21.

Christensen, A., & Heavey, C. L. (1999). Intervention for couples. *Annual Review of Psychology, 50,* 165–190.

Chugani, H. T., & Phelps, M. E. (1986). Maturational changes in cerebral function in infants determined by 18FDG positron emission tomography. *Science, 231,* 840–843.

Cipani, E. (1991). Educational classification and placement. In J. L. Matson & J. A. Mulick (Eds.), *Handbook of mental retardation* (2nd ed.). New York: Pergamon.

Clarke, A. M., & Clarke, A. D. (1989). The later cognitive effects of early intervention. *Intelligence, 13,* 289–297.

Clarke-Stewart, K. A. (1989). Infant day care: Maligned or malignant? *American Psychologist, 44,* 266–273.

Clifton, R., Perris, E., & Bullinger, A. (1991). Infants' perception of auditory space. *Developmental Psychology, 27,* 187–197.

Cohen, S., & Williamson, G. M. (1991). Stress and infectious disease in humans. *Psychological Bulletin, 109,* 5–24.

Coie, J. D., Dodge, K. A., Terry, R., & Wright, V. (1991). The role of aggression in peer relations: An analysis of aggression episodes in boys' play groups. *Child Development, 62,* 812–826.

Coie, J. D., & Dodge, K. A. (1998). Aggression and antisocial behavior. In W. Damon (Ed.), *Handbook of child psychology* (Vol. 3). New York: Wiley.

Colby, A., Kohlberg, L., Gibbs, J. C., & Lieberman, M. (1983). A longitudinal study of moral development. *Monographs of the Society for Research in Child Development, 48* (Whole #200).

Cole, D. A. (1991). Preliminary support for a competency-based model of depression in children. *Journal of Abnormal Psychology, 100,* 181–190.

Collaer, M. L., & Hines, M. (1995). Human behavioral sex differences: A role for gonadal hormones during early development? *Psychological Bulletin, 118,* 55–107.

Coltheart, M., Curtis, B., Atkins, P., & Haller, M. (1993). Models of reading aloud: Dual-route and parallel-distributed-processing approaches. *Psychological Review, 100,* 589–608.

Committee on Genetics. (1996). Newborn screening fact sheet. *Pediatrics, 98,* 473–501.

Condry, J. C., & Ross, D. F. (1985). Sex and aggression: The influence of gender label on the perception of aggression in children. *Child Development, 56,* 225–233.

Conger, R. D., Patterson, G. R., & Ge, X. (1995). It takes two to replicate: A mediational model for the impact of parents' stress on adolescent adjustment. *Child Development, 66,* 80–97.

Cooper, R.L., Goldenberg, R.L., Creasey, R.K., DuBard, M.B., Davis, R.O., Entman, S.S., Iams, J.D., & Cliver, S.P. (1993). A multicenter study of preterm birth weight and gestational age-specific neonatal mortality. *American Journal of Obstetrics and Gynecology, 168,* 78–84.

Coopersmith, S. (1967). *The antecedents of self-esteem.* San Francisco: W. H. Freeman.

Coplan, R. J., Rubin, K. H., Fox, N. A., Calkins, S. D., et al. (1994). Being alone, playing alone, and acting alone: Distinguishing among reticence and passive and active solitude in young children. *Child Development, 65,* 129–137.

Copper, R. L., Goldenberg, R. L., Das, A., Elder, N., et al. (1996). The preterm prediction study: Maternal stress is associated with spontaneous preterm birth at less than thirty-five weeks' gestation. National Institute of Child Health and Human Development Maternal-Fetal Medicine Units Network. *American Journal of Obstetrics & Gynecology, 175,* 1286–1292.

Corballis, M. C. (1997). The genetics and evolution of handedness. *Psychological Review, 104,* 714–727.

Cornelius, M. Taylor, P., Geva, D., & Day, N. (1995). Prenatal tobacco exposure and marijuana use among adolescents: Effects on offspring gestational age, growth, and morphology. *Pediatrics, 95,* 738–743.

Cornwell, K. S., Harris, L. J., & Fitzgerald, H. E. (1991). Task effects in the development of hand preference in 9-, 13-, and 20-month-old infant girls. *Developmental Neuropsychology, 7,* 19–34.

Costin, S. E., & Jones, D. C. (1992). Friendship as a facilitator of emotional responsiveness and prosocial interventions among young children. *Developmental Psychology, 28,* 941–947.

Coulton, C. J., Korbin, J. E., Su, M., & Chow, J. (1995). Community level factors and child maltreatment rates. *Child Development, 66,* 1262–1276.

Cox, M. J., Owen, M. T., Henderson, V. K., & Margand, N. A. (1992). Prediction of infant-father and infant-mother attachment. *Developmental Psychology, 28,* 474–483.

Craig, K. D., Whitfield, M. F., Grunau, R. V. E., Linton, J., & Hadjistavropoulos, H. D. (1993). Pain in the preterm neonate: Behavioural and physiological indices. *Pain, 52,* 238–299.

Crawford, M., Chaffin, R., & Fitton, L. (1995). Cognition in social context. *Learning & Individual Differences, 7,* 341–362.

Crick, N. R., & Dodge, K. A. (1994). A review and reformulation of social information-processing mechanisms in children's social adjustment. *Psychological Bulletin, 115,* 74–101.

Crick, N. R., & Grotpeter, J. K, (1995). Relational aggression, gender, and social-psychological adjustment. *Child Development, 66,* 710–722.

Crick, N. R., & Werner, N. E. (1998). Response decision processes in relational and overt aggression. *Child Development, 69,* 1630–1639.

Crowder, R. G., & Wagner, R. K. (1992). *The psychology of reading: An introduction* (2nd ed.). New York: Oxford University Press.

Crowley, K., & Siegler, R. S. (1999). Explanation and generalization in young children's strategy learning. *Child Development, 70,* 304–316.

Cuellar, I., Nyberg, B., Maldonado, R. E., & Roberts, R. E. (1997). Ethnic identity and acculturation in a young adult Mexican-origin population. *Journal of Community Psychology, 25,* 535–549.

Cummings, E. M., Iannotti, R. J., & Zahn-Waxler, C. (1989). Aggression between peers in early childhood: Individual continuity and developmental change. *Child Development, 60,* 887–895.

Cunningham, F. G., MacDonald, P. C., & Gant, N. F. (1989). *Williams obstetrics* (18th ed.) London: Appleton & Lange.

Curtiss, S. (1989). The independence and task-specificity of language. In M. H. Bornstein & J. S. Bruner (Eds.), *Interaction in human development* (pp. 105–137). Hillsdale, NJ: Erlbaum.

D'Augelli, A. R. (1996). Lesbian, gay, and bisexual development during adolescence and young adulthood. In R. P. Cabaj & T. S. Stein (Eds.), *Textbook of homosexuality and mental health.* Washington, DC: American Psychiatric Press.

Daly, M., & Wilson, M. (1996). Violence against stepchildren. *Current Directions in Psychological Science, 5,* 77–81.

Damon, W., & Hart, D. (1988). *Self-understanding in childhood and adolescence.* New York: Cambridge University Press.

Dannemiller, J. L. (1998). Color constancy and color vision during infancy: Methodological and empirical issues. In V. Walsh & J. Kulikowski (Eds.), *Perceptual constancy: Why things look as they do.* New York: Cambridge University Press.

Dannemiller, J. L., & Stephens, B. R. (1988). A critical test of infant pattern preference models. *Child Development, 59,* 210–216.

Davidson, F. H., & Davidson, M. M. (1994). *Changing childhood prejudice: The caring work of the schools.* Westport, CT: Bergin & Garvey/Greenwood.

Davidson, K. M., Richards, D. S., Schatz, D. A., & Fisher, D. A. (1991). Successful in utero treatment of fetal goiter and hypothyroidism. *New England Journal of Medicine, 324,* 543–546.

Davies, P. T., & Cummings, E. M. (1998). Exploring children's emotional security as a mediator of the link between marital relations and child adjustment. *Child Development, 69,* 124–139.

Day, J. D., Engelhardt, S. E., Maxwell, S. E., & Bolig, E. E. (1997). Comparison of static and dynamic assessment procedures and their relation to independent performance. *Journal of Educational Psychology, 89,* 358–368.

Deater-Deckard, K., & Plomin, R. (1999). An adoption study of the etiology of teacher and parent reports of externalizing behavior problems in middle childhood. *Child Development, 70,* 144–154.

DeBerry, K. M., Scarr, S., & Weinberg, R. (1996). Family racial socialization and ecological competence: Longitudinal assessments of African-American transracial adoptees. *Child Development, 67,* 2375–2399.

DeCasper, A. J., & Spence, M. J. (1986). Prenatal maternal speech influences newborn's perception of speech sounds. *Infant Behavior and Development, 9,* 133–150.

Dekovic, M., & Janssens, J. M. (1992). Parents' child-rearing style and child's sociometric status. *Developmental Psychology, 28,* 925–932.

Dellas, M., & Jernigan, L. P. (1990). Affective personality characteristics associated with undergraduate ego identity formation. *Journal of Adolescent Research, 5,* 306–324.

DeLoache, J. S. (1984). Oh where, oh where: Memory-based searching by very young children. In C. Sophian (Ed.), *Origins of cognitive skills.* Hillsdale, NJ: Erlbaum.

DeLoache, J. S. (1995). Early understanding and use of models: The model model. *Current Directions in Psychological Science, 4,* 109–113.

DeLoache, J. S., Miller, K. F., & Rosengren, K.S. (1997). The credible shrinking room: Very young children's performance with symbolic and nonsymbolic relations. *Psychological Science, 8,* 308–313.

Dempster, F. N. (1995). Interference and inhibition in cognition: An historical perspective. In F. N. Dempster & C. J. Brainerd (Eds.), *Interference and inhibition in cognition.* San Diego, CA: Academic Press.

Dennis, W., & Dennis, M. G. (1940). The effects of cradling practices upon the onset of walking in Hopi children. *Journal of Genetic Psychology, 56,* 77–86.

DeRosier, M. E., Kupersmidt, J. B., & Patterson, C. J. (1995). Children's academic and behavioral adjustment as a function of the chronicity and proximity of peer rejection. *Child Development, 65,* 1799–1813.

deVilliers, J. G., & deVilliers, P. A. (1985). The acquisition of English. In D. I. Slobin (Ed.), *The cross-linguistic study of language acquisition.* Hillsdale, NJ: Erlbaum.

DeWolff, M. S., & van IJzendoorn, M. H. (1997). Sensitivity and attachment: A meta-analysis on parental antecedents of infant attachment. *Child Development, 68,* 571–591.

Dews, S., Winner, E., Kaplan, J., Rosenblatt, E., Hunt, M., Lim, K., McGovern, A., Qualter, A. & Smarsh, B. (1996). Children's understanding of the meaning and functions of verbal irony. *Child Development, 67,* 3071–3085.

Diamond, A., Prevor, M. B., Callender, G., & Druin, D. P. (1997). Prefontal cortex deficits in children treated early and continuously for PKU. *Monographs of the Society for Research in Child Development, 62* (4, Serial No. 252).

Diamond, M., Johnson, R., Young, D., & Singh, S. (1983). Age-related morphologic differences in the rat cerebral cortex and hippocampus: Male-female; right-left. *Experimental Neurology, 81,* 1–13.

DiBlasio, F. A., & Benda, B. B. (1990). Adolescent sexual behavior: Multivariate analysis of a social learning model. *Journal of Adolescent Research, 5,* 449–466.

DiPietro, J. A., Hodgson, D. M., Costigan, K. A., & Hilton, S. C. (1996). Fetal neurobehavioral development. *Child Development, 67,* 2553–2567.

DiPietro, J. A., Hodgson, D. M., Costigan, K. A., & Johnson, T. R. B. (1996). Fetal antecedents of infant temperament. *Child Development, 67,* 2568–2583.

Dishion, T. J. (1990). The family ecology of boys' peer relations in middle childhood. *Child Development, 61,* 874–892.

Dockrell, J., & McShane, J. (1993). *Children's learning difficulties: A cognitive approach.* Cambridge: Blackwell Publishers.

Dodge, K. A., Bates, J. E., & Pettit, G. S. (1990). Mechanisms in the cycle of violence. *Science, 250,* 1678–1683.

Dodge, K. A., & Crick, N. R. (1990). Social information-processing bases of aggressive behavior in children. *Personality and Social Psychology Bulletin, 16,* 8–22.

Donkin, A. J. M., Neale, R. J., & Tilston, C. (1993). Children's food purchase requests. *Appetite, 21,* 291–294.

Downey, G., Lebolt, A., Rincon, C., & Freitas, A. L. (1998). Rejection sensitivity and children's interpersonal difficulties. *Child Development, 69,* 1074–1091.

Drabman, R. S., & Thomas, M. H. (1976). Does watching violence on television cause apathy? *Pediatrics, 52,* 329–331.

Dryfoos, J. G. (1990). *Adolescents at risk: Prevalence and prevention.* New York: Oxford University Press.

DuBois, D. L., & Hirsch, B. J. (1990). School and neighborhood friendship patterns of black and whites in early adolescence. *Child Development, 61,* 524–536.

Dubow, E. F., Edwards, S., & Ippolito, M. F. (1997). Life stressors, neighborhood disadvantage, and resources: A focus on inner-city children's adjustment. *Journal of Clinical Child Psychology, 26,* 130–144.

Dumas, J. E., LaFreniere, P. J., & Serketich, W. J. (1995). "Balance of power": A transactional analysis of control in mother-child dyads involving socially competent, aggressive, and anxious children. *Journal of Abnormal Psychology, 104,* 104–113.

Dunham, P. J., Dunham, F., & Curwin, A. (1993). Joint-attentional states and lexical acquisition at 18 months. *Developmental Psychology, 29,* 827–831.

Dunn, J., & Kendrick, C. (1981). Social behavior of young siblings in the family context: Differences between same-sex and different-sex dyads. *Child Development, 52,* 1265–1273.

Dunn, J., & Plomin, R. (1990). *Separate lives: Why siblings are so different.* New York: Basic Books.

Dunn, J., Slomkowski, C., & Beardsall, L. (1994). Sibling relationships from the preschool period through middle childhood and early adolescence. *Developmental Psychology, 30,* 315–324.

Eacott, M. J. (1999). Memory for the events of early childhood. *Current Directions in Psychological Science, 8,* 46–49.

Eagly, A. H. (1995). The science and politics of comparing women and men. *American Psychologist, 50,* 145–158.

Eagly, A. H., Karau, S. J., & Makhijani, M. G. (1995). Gender and the effectiveness of leaders: A meta-analysis. *Psychological Bulletin, 117,* 125–145.

Eaton, W. O., Chipperfield, J. G., & Singbeil, C. E. (1989). Birth order and activity level in children. *Developmental Psychology, 25,* 668–672.

Eaton, W. O., & Enns, L. R. (1986). Sex differences in human motor activity level. *Psychological Bulletin, 100,* 19–28.

Edelbrock, C., Rende, R., Plomin, R., & Thompson, L. A. (1995). A twin study of competence and problem behavior in childhood and early adolescence. *Journal of Child Psychology and Psychiatry, 36,* 775–785.

Edwards, C. A. (1994). Leadership in groups of school-age girls. *Developmental Psychology, 30,* 920–927.

Egan, S. K., Monson, T. C., & Perry, D. G. (1998). Social-cognitive influences on change in aggression over time. *Developmental Psychology, 34,* 996–1006.

Egan, S. K., & Perry, D. G. (1998). Does low self-regard invite victimization? *Developmental Psychology, 34,* 299–309.

Eisenberg, N. (1982). The development of reasoning regarding prosocial behavior. In N. Eisenberg (Ed.), *The development of prosocial behavior.* New York: Academic Press.

Eisenberg, N. (1986). *Altruistic emotion, cognition, and behavior.* Hillsdale, NJ: Erlbaum.

Eisenberg, N. (1988). The development of prosocial and aggressive behavior. In M. H. Bornstein & M. E. Lamb (Eds.), *Developmental psychology: An advanced textbook* (2nd ed.). Hillsdale, NJ: Erlbaum.

Eisenberg, N., Carlo, G., Murphy, B., & Van Court, P. (1995). Prosocial development in late adolescence: A longitudinal study. *Child Development, 66,* 1179–1197.

Eisenberg, N., Fabes, R. A., Schaller, M., Carlo, G., & Miller, P. A. (1991). The relations of parental characteristics and practices to children's vicarious emotional responding. *Child Development, 62,* 1393–1408.

Eisenberg, N., Fabes, R. A., Shepard, S. A., Murphy, B. C., Guthrie, I. K., Jones, S., Friedman, J., Poulin, R., & Maszk, P. (1997). Contemporaneous and longitudinal prediction of children's social functioning from regulation and emotionality. *Child Development, 68,* 642–664.

Eisenberg, N., Guthrie, I. K., Fabes, R. A., Reiser, M., Murphy, B. C., Hogren, R., Maszk, P., & Losoya, S. (1997). The relations of regulation and emotionality to resiliency and competent social functioning in elementary school children. *Child Development, 68,* 295–311.

Eisenberg, N., & Shell, R. (1986). Prosocial moral judgment and behavior in children: The mediating role of cost. *Personality and Social Psychology Bulletin, 12,* 426–433.

Eisenberg, N., Shepard, S. A., Fabes, R. A., Murphy, B. C., & Guthrie, I. K. (1998). Shyness and children's emotionality, regulation, and coping: Contemporaneous, longitudinal, and across-context relations. *Child Development, 69,* 767–790.

Eizenman, D. R., & Bertenthal, B. I. (1998). Infants' perception of object unity in translating and rotating displays. *Developmental Psychology, 34,* 426–434.

Elicker, J., Englund, M., & Sroufe, L. A. (1992). Predicting peer competence and peer relationships in childhood from early parent-child relationships. In R. D. Parke & G. W. Ladd (Eds.), *Family-peer relationships: Modes of linkage.* Hillsdale, NJ: Erlbaum.

Elkind, D. (1978). *The child's reality: Three developmental themes.* Hillsdale, NJ: Erlbaum.

Elkind, D., & Bowen, R. (1979). Imaginary audience behavior in children and adolescents. *Developmental Psychology, 15,* 38–44.

Ellis, W. K., & Rusch, F. R. (1991). Supported employment: Current practices and future directions. In J. L. Matson & J. A. Mulick (Eds.), *Handbook of mental retardation* (2nd ed.). New York: Pergamon.

Elmer-DeWitt, P. (1994). The genetic revolution. *Time* (January 17), 46–53.

Enns, J. T. (1990). Relations between components of visual attention. In J. T. Enns (Ed.), *The development of attention.* Amsterdam: North Holland.

Epstein, L. H., & Cluss, P. A. (1986). Behavioral genetics of childhood obesity. *Behavior Therapy, 17,* 324–334.

Epstein, L. H., Valoski, A. M., Vara, L. S., McCurley, J., et al. (1995). Effects of decreasing sedentary behavior and increasing activity on weight change in obese children. *Health Psychology, 14,* 109–108.

Erel, O., & Burman, B. (1995). Interrelatedness of marital relations and parent-child relations: A meta-analytic review. *Psychological Bulletin, 118,* 108–132.

Erel, O., Margolin, G., & John, R. S. (1998). Observed sibling interaction: Links with the marital and the mother-child relationship. *Developmental Psychology, 34,* 288–298.

Erikson, E. H. (1968). *Identity: Youth and crisis.* New York: Norton.

Etaugh, C., & Liss, M. B. (1992). Home, school, and playroom: Training grounds for adult gender roles. *Sex Roles, 26,* 129–147.

Fabes, R. A., Eisenberg, N., Jones, S., Smith, M., Guthrie, I., Poulin, R., Shepard, S., & Friedman, J. (1999). Regulation, emotionality, and preschoolers' socially competent peer interactions. *Child Development, 70,* 432–442.

Fabes, R. A., Eisenberg, N., Smith, M. C., & Murphy, B. C. (1996). Getting angry at peers: Associations with liking of the provocateur. *Child Development, 67,* 942–956.

Fagot, B. I. (1985). Changes in thinking about early sex role development. *Developmental Review, 5,* 83–98.

Falbo, T., & Polit, E. F. (1986). Quantitative review of the only child literature: Research evidence and theory development. *Psychological Bulletin, 100,* 176–186.

Farver, J. M., & Branstetter, W. H. (1994). Preschoolers' prosocial responses to their peers' distress. *Developmental Psychology, 30,* 334–341.

Farver, J. M., & Shin, Y. L. (1997). Social pretend play in Korean- and Anglo-American preschoolers. *Child Development, 68,* 544–556.

Feingold, A. (1993). Cognitive gender differences: A developmental perspective. *Sex Roles, 29,* 91–112.

Feldhusen, J. F. (1996). Motivating academically able youth with enriched and accelerated learning experiences. In C. P. Benbow & D. J. Lubinski (Eds.), *Intellectual talent: Psychometric and social issues*. Baltimore: Johns Hopkins Press.

Feldman, D. H., & Goldsmith, L. T. (1991). *Nature's gambit*. New York: Teachers College Press.

Feldman, S. S., & Wentzel, K. R. (1990). The relationship between parental styles, sons' selfrestraint, and peer relations in early adolescence. *Journal of Early Adolescence, 10*, 439–454.

Fenson, L., Dale, P. S., Reznick, J. S., Bates, E., et al. (1994). Variability in early communicative development. *Monographs of the Society for Research in Child Development, 59*, Whole No. 173.

Field, T. M. (1990). *Infancy*. Cambridge, MA: Harvard University Press.

Field, T. M., & Widmayer, S. M. (1982). Motherhood. In B. J. Wolman (Ed.), *Handbook of developmental psychology*. Englewood Cliffs, NJ: Prentice Hall.

Fincham, F. (1998). Child development and marital relations. *Child Development, 69*, 543–574.

Fisch, S., & McCann, S. K. (1993). Making broadcast television participative: Eliciting mathematical behavior through *Square One TV. Educational Technology Research and Development, 41*, 103–109.

Fischer, K.W., & Granott, N. (1995). Beyond one-dimensional change: Parallel, concurrent, socially distributed processes in learning and development. *Human Development, 38*, 302–314.

Fischer, M., Barkley, R. A., Fletcher, K. E., & Smallish, L. (1993). The adolescent outcome of hyperactive children: Predictors of psychiatric, academic, social, and emotional adjustment. *Journal of the American Academy of Child and Adolescent Psychiatry, 32*, 324–332.

Fisher, S. (1994). Identifying video game addiction in children and adolescents. *Addictive Behaviors, 19*, 545–553.

Fisher, C. (1996). Structural limits on verb mapping: The role of analogy in children's interpretations of sentences. *Cognitive Psychology, 31*, 41–81.

Fitzgerald, J. (1987). Research on revision in writing. *Review of Educational Research, 57*, 481–506.

Flavell, J. H. (1985). *Cognitive development* (2nd ed.). Englewood Cliffs, NJ: Prentice-Hall.

Flavell, J. H. (1996). Piaget's legacy. *Psychological Science, 7*, 200–203.

Fonzi, A., Schneider, B. H., Tani, F., & Tomada, G. (1997). Predicting children's friendship status from their dynamic interaction in structured situations of potential conflict. *Child Development, 68*, 496–506.

Foreyt, J. P., & Goodrick, G. K. (1995). Obesity. In R. T. Ammerman & M. Hersen (Eds.), *Handbook of child behavior therapy in the psychiatric setting*. New York: Wiley.

Foster, S. H. (1986). Learning discourse topic management in the preschool years. *Journal of Child Language, 13*, 231–250.

Fox, N. A. (1991). If it's not left, it's right. *American Psychologist, 46*, 863–872.

Fox, N. A., Kimmerly, N. L., & Schafer, W. D. (1991). Attachment to mother/attachment to father: A meta-analysis. *Child Development, 62*, 210–225.

Frankenburg, W. K., & Dobbs, J. B. (1969). The Denver Developmental Screening Test. *Journal of Pediatrics, 71*, 181–191.

French, D. C. (1988). Heterogeneity of peer-rejected boys: Aggressive and nonaggressive subtypes. *Child Development, 53*, 976–985.

French, D. C. (1990). Heterogeneity of peer-rejected girls. *Child Development, 61*, 2028–2031.

Fried, P. A., O'Connell, C. M., & Watkinson, B. (1992). 60- and 72-month follow-up of children prenatally exposed to marijuana, cigarettes, and alcohol: Cognitive and language assessment. *Journal of Developmental & Behavioral Pediatrics, 13*, 383–391.

Friedman, J. M., & Polifka, J. E. (1996). *The effects of drugs on the fetus and nursing infant : A handbook for health care professionals*. Baltimore: Johns Hopkins University Press.

Friend, M., & Davis, T. L. (1993). Appearance-reality distinction: Children's understanding of the physical and affective domains. *Developmental Psychology, 29*, 907–914.

Funk, J. B. (1992). Video games: Benign or malignant? *Journal of Developmental and Behavioral Pediatrics, 13*, 53–54.

Funk, J. B. (1993). Reevaluating the impact of video games. *Clinical Pediatrics, 32*, 86–90.

Frye, D. (1993). Causes and precursors of children's theories of mind. In D. F. Hay & A. Angold (Eds.), *Precursors and causes in development and psychopathology*. Chichester, England: Wiley.

Furstenberg, F. F. (1993). How families manage risk and opportunity in dangerous neighborhoods. In W. J. Wilson (Ed.), *Sociology and the public agenda*. Newbury Park, CA: Sage.

Furstenburg, F. F., Brooks-Gunn, J., & Morgan, S. P. (1987). *Adolescent mothers and their children in later life*. Cambridge: Cambridge University Press.

Furstenburg, F. F., & Teitler, J. O. (1994). Reconsidering the effects of marital disruption: What happens to children of divorce in early adulthood? *Journal of Family Issues, 15*, 173–190.

Gable, S., & Isabella, R. A. (1992). Maternal contributions to infant regulation of arousal. *Infant Behavior and Development, 15*, 95–107.

Galambos, N. L., & Maggs, J. L. (1991). Out-of-school care of young adolescents and self-reported behavior. *Developmental Psychology, 27*, 644–655.

Galen, B. R., & Underwood, M. K. (1997). A developmental investigation of social aggression among children. *Developmental Psychology, 33*, 589–600.

Galler, J. R., & Ramsey, F. (1989). A follow-up study of the influence of early malnutrition on development: Behavior at home and at school. *Journal of the American Academy of Child and Adolescent Psychiatry, 28*, 254–261.

Galler, J. R., Ramsey, F., & Forde, V. (1986). A follow-up study of the influence of early malnutrition on subsequent development: IV. Intellectual performance during adolescence. *Nutrition and Behavior, 3*, 211–222.

Garbarino, J., & Kostelny, K. (1992). Child maltreatment as a community problem. *Child Abuse and Neglect, 16*, 455–464.

Garber, J., Robinson, N. S., & Valentiner, D. (1997). The relation between parenting and adolescent depression: Self-worth as a mediator. *Journal of Adolescent Research, 12*, 12–33.

Gardner, H. (1983). *Frames of mind: The theory of multiple intelligences*. New York: Basic Books.

Gardner, H. (1993). *Multiple intelligences: The theory in practice*. New York: Basic Books.

Gardner, H. (1995). Reflections on multiple intelligences: Myths and messages. *Phi Delta Kappan, 77*, 200–203, 206–209.

Garner, P. W., Jones, D. C., & Palmer, D. J. (1994). Social cognitive correlates of preschool children's sibling caregiving behavior. *Developmental Psychology, 30*, 905–911.

Garvey, C., & Berninger, G. (1981). Timing and turn taking in children's conversations. *Discourse Processes, 4*, 27-59.

Gash, H., & Morgan, M. (1993). School-based modifications of children's gender-related beliefs. *Journal of Applied Developmental Psychology, 14*, 277–287.

Gavin, L. A., & Furman, W. (1996). Adolescent girls' relationships with mothers and best friends. *Child Development, 67*, 375–386.

Ge, X., Congr, R. D., Cadoret, R. J., Neiderhiser, J. M., et al. (1996). The developmental interface between nature and nurture: A mutual influence model of child antisocial behavior and parent behaviors. *Developmental Psychology, 32*, 574–589.

Ge, X., Conger, R. D., & Elder, G. H. (1996). Coming of age too early: Pubertal influences on girls' vulnerability to psychological distress. *Child Development, 67*, 3386–3400.

Geisel, T. (1960). *Green eggs and ham, by Dr. Seuss*. New York: Beginner.

Gelman, R. (1969). Conservation acquisition: A problem of learning to attend to relevant attributes. *Journal of Experimental Child Psychology, 7*, 167–187.

Gelman, R., & Meck, E. (1986). The notion of principle: The case of counting. In J. Hiebert

(Ed.), *Conceptual and procedural knowledge: The case of mathematics.* Hillside, NJ: Erlbaum.

Gelman, S. A., & Gottfried, G. M. (1996). Children's casual explanations of animate and inanimate motion. *Child Development, 67,* 1970–1987.

Gelman, S. A., & Markman, E. M. (1985). Implicit contrast in adjectives vs. nouns: Implications for word-learning in preschoolers. *Journal of Child Language, 12,* 125–143.

George, C., Kaplan, N., & Main, M. (1985). *The Adult Attachment Interview.* Unpublished manuscript, University of California, Department of Psychology, Berkeley.

Ghim, H. (1990). Evidence for perceptual organization in infants: Perception of subjective contours by young infants. *Infant Behavior and Development, 13,* 221–248.

Gibbs, J. C., Clark, P. M., Joseph, J. A., Green, J. L., Goodrick, T. S., & Makowski, D. (1986). Relations between moral judgment, moral courage, and field independence. *Child Development, 57,* 185–193.

Giberson, P. K., & Weinberg, J. (1992). Fetal alcohol syndrome and functioning of the immune system. *Alcohol Health and Research World, 16,* 29–38.

Gibson, E. J. (1969). *Principles of perceptual learning and development.* New York: Appleton-Century-Crofts.

Gibson, E. J., Riccio, G., Schmuckler, M. A., Stoffregen, T. A., Rosenberg, D., & Taormina, J. (1987). Detection of the traversability of surfaces by crawling and walking infants. *Journal of Experimental Psychology: Human Perception & Performance, 13,* 533–544.

Gibson, E. J., & Walk, R. D. (1960). The "visual cliff." *Scientific American, 202,* 64–71.

Gibson, E. J., & Walker, A. S. (1984). Development of knowledge of visual-tactual affordances of substance. *Child Development, 55,* 453–460.

Gilligan, C. (1982). *In a different voice: Psychological theory and women's development.* Cambridge, MA: Harvard University Press.

Gilligan, C., & Attanucci, J. (1988). Two moral orientations: Gender differences and similarities. *Merrill- Palmer Quarterly, 34,* 223–237.

Glick, P. C. (1989). The family life cycle and social change. *Family Relations, 38,* 123–129.

Glick, P. C., & Lin, S. (1986). Recent changes in divorce and remarriage. *Journal of Marriage and the Family, 48,* 737–747.

Goldenberg, R. L., & Klerman, L. V. (1995). Adolescent pregnancy—Another look. *New England Journal of Medicine, 332,* 1161–1162.

Goldman, S. R. (1989). Strategy instruction in mathematics. *Learning Disability Quarterly, 12,* 43–55.

Goldsmith, H. H., Buss, K. A., & Lemery, K. S. (1997). Toddler and childhood temperament:

Expanded content, stronger genetic evidence, new evidence for the importance of environment. *Developmental Psychology, 33,* 891–905.

Goldsmith, H. H., & Harman, C. (1994). Temperament and attachment: Individuals and relationships. *Current Directions in Psychological Science, 3,* 53–57.

Golinkoff, R. M. (1993). When is communication a "meeting of minds"? *Journal of Child Language, 20,* 199–207.

Golombok, S., & Tasker, F. (1996). Do parents influence the sexual orientation of their children? Findings from a longitudinal study of lesbian families. *Developmental Psychology, 32,* 3–11.

Good, T. L., & Brophy, J. E. (1994). *Looking in classrooms* (6th ed.). New York: HarperCollins.

Goodman, G. S., Emery, R. E., & Haugaard, J. J. (1998). Developmental psychology and law: Divorce, child maltreatment, foster care, and adoption. In W. Damon (Ed.), *Handbook of child psychology* (Vol. 4). New York: Wiley.

Goodnow, J. J. (1992). *Parental belief systems: The psychological consequences for children.* Hillsdale, NJ: Erlbaum.

Goodwyn, S. W., & Acredolo, L. P. (1993). Symbolic gesture versus work: Is there a modality advantage for onset of symbol use? *Child Development, 64,* 688–701.

Gordon, C. P. (1996). Adolescent decision making: A broadly based theory and its application to the prevention of early pregnancy. *Adolescence, 31,* 561–584.

Goswami, U., & Bryant, P. (1990). *Phonological skills and learning to read.* London: Erlbaum.

Gottesman, I. I. (1993). Origins of schizophrenia: Past as prologue. In R. Plomin & G. E. McClearn (Eds.), *Nature, nurture, and psychology.* Washington, DC: American Psychological Association.

Gottfredson, L. S. (1997). Why *g* matters: The complexity of everyday life. *Intelligence, 24,* 79–132.

Gottlieb, L. N., & Mendelson, M. J. (1990). Parental support and firstborn girls' adaptation to the birth of a sibling. *Journal of Applied Developmental Psychology, 11,* 29–48.

Gottman, J. M. (1986). The world of coordinated play: Same- and cross-sex friendships in children. In J. M. Gottman & J. G. Parker (Eds.), *Conversations of friends.* New York: Cambridge University Press.

Gottman, J. M., Katz, L. F., & Hooven, C. (1996). Parental meta-emotion philosophy and the emotional life of families: Theoretical models and preliminary data. *Journal of Family Psychology, 10,* 243–268.

Graber, J. A., Brooks-Gunn, J., Paikoff, R. L., & Warren, M. P. (1994). Prediction of eating problems: An 8-year study of adolescent girls. *Developmental Psychology, 30,* 823–834.

Graber, J. A., Brooks-Gunn, J., & Warren, W. P. (1995). The antecedents of menarcheal age: Heredity, family environment, and stressful life events. *Child Development, 66,* 346–359.

Graesser, A. C., Singer, M., & Trabasso, T. (1994). Constructing inferences during narrative text comprehension. *Psychological Review, 101,* 371–395.

Graham, S., Berninger, V. W., Abbott, R. D., Abbott, S. P., & Whitaker, D. (1997). Role of mechanics in composing of elementary school students: A new methodological approach. *Journal of Educational Psychology, 89,* 170–182.

Graham, S., & Juvonen, J. (1998). Self-blame and peer victimization in middle school: An attributional analysis. *Developmental Psychology, 34,* 587–599.

Granrud, C. E. (1986). Binocular vision and spatial perception in 4- and 5-month-old infants. *Journal of Experimental Psychology: Human Perception and Performance, 12,* 36–49.

Greenberg, B. S., Fazel, S., & Weber, M. (1986). *Children's view on advertising.* New York: Independent Broadcasting Authority Research Report.

Greenberg, M. T., & Crnic, K. A. (1988). Longitudinal predictors of developmental status and social interaction in premature and full-term infants at age two. *Child Development, 59,* 554–570.

Grigorenko, E. L., & Sternberg, R. J. (1998). Dynamic testing. *Psychological Bulletin, 124,* 75–111.

Groen, G. J., & Resnick, L. B. (1977). Can preschool children invent addition algorithms? *Journal of Educational Psychology, 69,* 645–652.

Grovak, M. (1999, February 4). Baby born after spina bifidia surgery seems fine. *Journal and Courier,* p. A1.

Grusec, J. E., Goodnow, J. J., & Cohen, L. (1996). Household work and the development of concern for others. *Developmental Psychology, 32,* 999–1007.

Guerra, N. G., & Slaby, R. G. (1990). Cognitive mediators of aggression in adolescent offenders: 2. Intervention. *Developmental Psychology, 26,* 269–277.

Guilford, J. P. (1967). *The nature of human intelligence.* New York: McGraw-Hill.

Guillemin, J. (1993). Cesarean birth: Social and political aspects. In B. K. Rothman (Ed.), *Encyclopedia of childbearing.* Phoenix, AZ: Oryx Press.

Gurucharri, C., & Selman, F. L. (1982). The development of interpersonal understanding during childhood, preadolescence, and adolescence: A longitudinal follow-up study. *Child Development, 53,* 924–927.

Guttmacher, A. F., & Kaiser, I. H. (1986). *Pregnancy, birth, and family planning.* New York: New American Library.

Hahn, W. (1987). Cerebral lateralization of function: From infancy through childhood. *Psychological Bulletin, 101,* 376–392.

Halford, G. S. (1988). A structure mapping approach to cognitive development. In A. Demetriou (Ed.), *The neo-Piagetian theories of cognitive development: Toward an integration.* Amsterdam: North Holland.

Halford, G. S. (1993). *Children's understanding: The development of mental models.* Hillsdale, NJ: Erlbaum.

Hall, D. G. (1996). Preschoolers' default assumptions about word meaning: Proper names designate unique individuals. *Developmental Psychology, 32,* 177–186.

Hall, D. G., & Graham. S. A. (1999). Lexical form class information guides word-to-object mapping in preschoolers. *Child Development, 70,* 78–91.

Hall, D. G., Waxman, S. R., & Hurwitz, W. R. (1993). How two- and four-year-old children interpret adjectives and count nouns. *Child Development, 64,* 1651–1664.

Hall, G. S. (1904). *Adolescence, I.* New York: Appleton.

Hall, J. A., & Halberstadt, A. G. (1981). Sex roles and nonverbal communication skills. *Sex Roles, 7,* 273–287.

Hallinan, M. T., & Teixeira, R. A. (1987). Opportunities and constraints: Black-white differences in the formation of interracial friendships. *Child Development, 58,* 1358–1371.

Halpern, C. T., Udry, J. R., Campbell, B., & Suchindran, C. (1999). Effects of body fat on weight concerns, dating, and sexual activity: A longitudinal analysis of black and white adolescent girls. *Developmental Psychology, 35,* 721–736.

Halpern, D. F. (1986). *Sex differences in cognitive abilities.* Hillsdale, NJ: Erlbaum.

Halpern, J. J., & Luria, Z. (1989). Labels of giftedness and gender-typicality: Effects on adults' judgments of children's traits. *Psychology in the Schools, 26,* 301–310.

Halpern, L. F., MacLean, W. E., & Baumeister, A. A. (1995). Infant sleep-wake characteristics: Relation to neurological status and the prediction of developmental outcome. *Developmental Review, 15,* 255–291.

Hamer, D. H., Hu, S., Magnuson, V. L., Hu, N., et al. (1993). A linkage between DNA markers on the X chromosome and male sexual orientation. *Science, 261,* 321–327.

Hammill, D. D. (1990). On defining learning disabilities: An emerging consensus. *Journal of Learning Disabilities, 23,* 74–84.

Harnishfeger, K. K. (1995). The development of cognitive inhibition: Theories, definitions, and research evidence. In F. N. Dempster & C. J. Brainerd (Eds.), *Interference and inhibition in cognition.* San Diego, CA: Academic Press.

Harris, B., Lovett, L., Newcombe, R.G., Read, G.F., Walker, R., & Riad-Fahmy, D. (1994). Maternity blues and major endocrine changes: Cardiff puerperal mood and hormone study II. *British Medical Journal, 308,* 949–953.

Harris, L. J. (1983). Laterality of function in the infant: Historical and contemporary trends in theory and research. In G. Young, S. J. Segalowitz, C. M. Corter, & S. E. Trehub (Eds.), *Manual specialization and the developing brain.* New York: Academic Press.

Harris, P. L., Brown, E., Marriot, C., Whithall, S., & Harmer, S. (1991). Monsters, ghosts, and witches: testing the limits of the fantasy-reality distinction in young children. *British Journal of Developmental Psychology, 9,* 105–123.

Harris, P. L., & Kavanaugh, R. D. (1993). Young children's understanding of pretense. *Monographs of the Society for Research in Child Development, 58,* Serial No. 231.

Harrist, A. W., Zaia, A. F., Bates, J. E., Dodge, K. A., & Pettit, G. S. (1997). Subtypes of social withdrawal in early childhood: Sociometric status and social-cognitive differences across four years. *Child Development, 68,* 278–294.

Hart, C. H., Nelson, D. A., Robinson, C. C., Olsen, S. F., & McNeilly-Choque, M. K. (1998). Overt and relational aggression in Russian nursery-school-age children: Parenting style and marital linkages. *Developmental Psychology, 34,* 687–697.

Harter, S. (1985). *Manual for the self-perception profile for children.* Denver, CO: University of Denver.

Harter, S. (1988). Developmental processes in the construction of the self. In T. D. Yawkey & J. E. Johnson (Eds.), *Integrative processes and socialization: Early to middle childhood.* Hillsdale, NJ: Erlbaum.

Harter, S. (1990). Self and identity development. In S. S. Feldman & G. R. Elliott (Eds.), *At the threshold: The developing adolescent.* Cambridge, MA: Harvard University Press.

Harter, S. (1994). Developmental changes in self-understanding across the 5 to 7 shift. In A. Sameroff & M. M. Haith (Eds.), *Reason and responsibility: The passage through childhood.* Chicago: University of Chicago Press.

Harter, S. (1999). *The construction of the self: A developmental perspective.* New York: Guilford.

Harter, S., & Monsour, A. (1992). Developmental analysis of conflict caused by opposing attributes in the adolescent self-portrait. *Developmental Psychology, 28,* 251–260.

Harter, S., & Pike, R. (1984). The pictorial scale of perceived competence and social acceptance for young children. *Child Development, 55,* 1969–1982.

Harter, S., Waters, P., & Whitesell, N. R. (1998). Relational self-worth: Differences in perceived worth as a person across interpersonal contexts among adolescents. *Child Development, 69,* 756–766.

Harter, S., Waters, P. L., Whitesell, N. R., & Kastelic, D. (1998). Level of voice among female and male high school students: Relational context, support, and gender orientation. *Developmental Psychology, 34,* 892–901.

Harter, S., Whitesell, N. R., & Kowalski, P. S. (1992). Individual differences in the effects of educational transitions on young adolescents' perceptions of competence and motivational orientation. *American Educational Research Journal, 29,* 777–807.

Hartup, W. W. (1983). Peer relations. In P. H. Mussen (Ed.), *Handbook of child psychology* (Vol. 4). New York: Wiley.

Hartup, W. W. (1992a). Peer relations in early and middle childhood. In V. B. Van Hasselt & M. Hersen (Eds.), *Handbook of social development: A lifespan perspective.* New York: Plenum.

Hartup, W. W. (1992b). Friendships and their developmental significance. In H. McGurk (Ed.), *Contemporary issues in childhood social development.* London: Routledge.

Hartup, W. W., & Stevens, N. (1999). Friendships and adaptation across the life span. *Current Directions in Psychological Science, 8,* 76–79.

Haselager, G. J. T., Hartup, W. W., van Lieshout, C. F. M., & Riksen-Walraven, J. M. A. (1998). Similarities between friends and nonfriends in middle childhood. *Child Development, 69,* 1198–1208.

Hastings, P. D., & Rubin, K. H. (1999). Predicting mothers' beliefs about preschool-aged children's social behavior: Evidence for maternal attitudes moderating child effects. *Child Development, 70,* 722–741.

Hatcher, P. J., & Hulme, C. (1999). Phonemes, rhymes, and intelligence as predictors of children's responsiveness to remedial reading instruction: Evidence from a longitudinal study. *Journal of Experimental Child Psychology, 72,* 130–153.

Haviland, J. M., & Lelwica, M. (1987). The induced affect response: 10-week-old infants' responses to three emotion expressions. *Developmental Psychology, 23,* 97–104.

Hayes, D. P. (1988). Speaking and writing: Distinct patterns of word choice. *Journal of Memory and Language, 27,* 572–585.

Hearold, S. (1986). A synthesis of 1,043 effects of television on social behavior. In G. Comstock (Ed.), *Public communications and behavior* (Vol. 1, pp. 65–133). New York: Academic Press.

Hedges, L. V., & Nowell, A. (1995). Sex differences in mental test scores, variability, and numbers of high-scoring individuals. *Science, 269,* 41–45.

Henshaw, S. K. (1993). Teenage abortion, birth and pregnancy statistics by state, 1988. *Family Planning Perspectives, 25*, 122–126.

Hernandez, D. J. (1997). Child development and the social demography of childhood. *Child Development, 68*, 149–169.

Herrnstein, R. J., & Murray, C. (1994). *The bell curve: Intelligence and class structure in American life*. New York: Free Press.

Hetherington, E. M. (1972). Effects of father absence on personality development in adolescent daughters. *Developmental Psychology, 7*, 313–326.

Hetherington, E. M. (1988). Family relations six years after divorce. In K. Pasley & M. Ihinger-Tallman (Eds.), *Remarriage and stepparenting: Current research and theory*. New York: Guilford Press.

Hetherington, E. M. (1989). Coping with family transitions: Winners, losers and survivors. *Child Development, 60*, 1–14.

Hetherington, E. M. (1993). An overview of the Virginia Longitudinal Study of Divorce and Remarriage with a focus on early adolescence. *Journal of Family Psychology, 7*, 39–56.

Hetherington, E. M. (1999). Social capital and the development of youth from nondivorced, divorced, and remarried families. In W. A. Collins & B. Laursen (Eds.), *Minnesota Symposia on Child Psychology*. Mahwah, NJ: Erlbaum.

Hetherington, E. M., Cox, M., & Cox, R. (1982). Effects of divorce on parents and children. In M. E. Lamb (Ed.), *Nontraditional families*. Hillsdale, NJ: Erlbaum.

Hetherington, S. E. (1990). A controlled study of the effect of prepared childbirth classes on obstetric outcomes. *Birth, 17*, 86–90.

Heyman, G. D., & Gelman, S. A. (1999). The use of trait labels in making psychological inferences. *Child Development, 70*, 604–619.

Higgins, A. (1991). The just community approach to moral education: Evolution of the idea and recent findings. In W.M. Kurtines & J.L. Gewirtz (Eds.), *Handbook of moral behavior and development* (Vol. 3). Hillsdale, NJ: Erlbaum.

Hirshberg, L. M., & Svejda, M. (1990). When infants look to their parents: I. Infants' social referencing of mothers compared to fathers. *Child Development, 61*, 1175–1186.

Ho, C. S., & Bryant, P. (1997). Phonological skills are important in learning to read Chinese. *Developmental Psychology, 33*, 946–951.

Hodges, E. V. E., Boivin, M., Vitaro, F., & Bukowski, W. M. (1999). The power of friendship: Protection against an escalating cycle of peer victimization. *Developmental Psychology, 35*, 94–101.

Hodges, E. V. E., Malone, M. J., & Perry, D. G. (1997). Individual risk and social risk as interacting determinants of victimization in the peer group. *Developmental Psychology, 33*, 1032–1039.

Hoff-Ginsberg, E. (1990). Maternal speech and the child's development of syntax: A further look. *Journal of Child Language, 17*, 85–99.

Hoffman, M. L. (1988). Moral development. In M. H. Bornstein & M. E. Lamb (Eds.), *Developmental psychology : An advanced textbook* (2nd ed.). Hillsdale, NJ: Erlbaum.

Hoffman, M. L. (1994). Discipline and internalization. *Developmental Psychology, 30*, 26–28.

Hoge, D. D., Smit, E. K., & Hanson, S. L. (1990). School experiences predicting changes in self-esteem of sixth- and seventh-grade students. *Journal of Educational Psychology, 82*, 117–127.

Hogge, W. A. (1990). Teratology. In I. R. Merkatz & J. E. Thompson (Eds.), *New perspectives on prenatal care*. New York: Elsevier.

Holden, G. W., & Miller, P. C. (1999). Enduring and different: A meta-analysis of the similarity in parents' child rearing. *Psychological Bulletin, 125*, 223–254.

Horowitz, F. D., & O'Brien, M. (1986). Gifted and talented children: State of knowledge and directions for research. *American Psychologist, 41*, 1147–1152.

Howard, M., & McCabe, J. B. (1990). Helping teenagers postpone sexual involvement. *Family Planning Perspectives, 22*, 21–26.

Howe, M. L., & Courage, M. L. (1997). The emergence and early development of autobiographical memory. *Psychological Review, 104*, 499–523.

Howe, N., Petrakos, H., & Rinaldi, C. M. (1998). "All the sheeps are dead. He murdered them": Sibling pretense, negotiation, internal state language, and relationship quality. *Child Development, 69*, 182–191.

Howe, N., & Ross, H. S. (1990). Socialization perspective taking and the sibling relationship. *Developmental Psychology, 26*, 160–165.

Howes, C., & Matheson, C. C. (1992). Sequences in the development of competent play with peers: Social and social pretend play. *Developmental Psychology, 28*, 961–974.

Howes, C., Unger, O., & Seidner, L. B. (1990). Social pretend play in toddlers: Parallels with social play and with solitary pretend. *Child Development, 60*, 77–84.

Hudson, J. (1988). Children's memory for atypical actions in script-based stories: Evidence for a disruption effect. *Journal of Experimental Child Psychology, 46*, 159–173.

Huesmann, L. R. (1986). Psychological processes promoting the relation between exposure to media violence and aggressive behavior by the viewer. *Journal of Social Issues, 42*, 125–139.

Huston, A. C. (1983). Sex typing. In P. H. Mussen (Ed.), *Handbook of child psychology* (Vol. 4). New York: Wiley.

Huston, A. C., Donnerstein, E., Fairchild, H., Feshbach, N. D., Katz, P. A., Murray, J. P., Rubinstein, E. A., Wilcox, B. L., & Zuckerman, D. (1992). *Big world, small screen: The role of television in American society*. Lincoln, NE: University of Nebraska Press.

Huston, A. C., Watkins, B. A., & Kunkel, D. (1989). Public policy and children's television. *American Psychologist, 44*, 424–433.

Huston, A. C., & Wright, J. C. (1998). Mass media and children's development. In W. Damon (Ed.), *Handbook of child psychology* (Vol. 4). New York: Wiley.

Hutchins, E. (1983). Understanding Micronesian navigation. In D. A. Gentner & A. Stevens (Eds.), *Mental models*. Hillsdale, NJ: Erlbaum.

Hyde, J. S., Fennema, E., & Lamon, S. J. (1990). Gender differences in mathematics performance: A meta-analysis. *Psychological Bulletin, 107*, 139–155.

Hyde, J. S., & Linn, M. C. (1988). Gender differences in verbal ability. *Psychological Bulletin, 104*, 53–69.

Hymel, S., Rubin, K. H., Rowden, L., & LeMare, L. (1990). Children's peer relationships: Longitudinal prediction of internalizing and externalizing problems from middle to late childhood. *Child Development, 61*, 2004–2021.

Inhelder, B., & Piaget, J. (1958). *The growth of logical thinking from childhood to adolescence*. New York: Basic Books.

Institute of Medicine. (1990). *Nutrition during pregnancy*. Washington, DC: National Academy Press.

Irwin, R. A., & Gross, A. M. (1995). Cognitive tempo, violent video games, and aggressive behavior in young boys. *Journal of Family Violence, 10*, 337–350.

Israel, A. C., Guile, C. A., Baker, J. E., & Silverman, W. K. (1994). An evaluation of enhanced self-regulation training in the treatment of childhood obesity. *Journal of Pediatric Psychology, 19*, 737–749.

Izard, C. E. (1991). *The psychology of emotions*. New York: Plenum.

Izard, C. E., Fantauzzo, C. A., Castle, J. M., Haynes, O. M., Rayias, M. F., & Putnam, P. H. (1995). The ontogeny and significance of infants' facial expressions in the first 9 months of life. *Developmental Psychology, 31*, 997–1013.

Jacklin, C. N. (1989). Female and male: Issues of gender. *American Psychologist, 44*, 127–133.

Jacklin, C. N., & Maccoby, E. E. (1978). Social behavior at thirty-three months in same-sex and mixed-sex dyads. *Child Development, 49*, 557–569.

Jackson, N. E., & Butterfield, E. C. (1986). A conception of giftedness designed to promote research. In R. J. Sternberg & J. E. Davidson (Eds.), *Conceptions of giftedness.* Cambridge: Cambridge University Press.

Jacobson, J. L., Jacobson, S. W., & Humphrey, H. E. B. (1990). Effects of in utero exposure to polychlorinated biphenyls and related contaminants on cognitive functioning in young children. *Journal of Pediatrics, 116,* 38–45.

Jakobsen, R. (1997). Stages of progression in noncoital sexual interactions among young adolescents: An application of the Mokken scale analysis. *International Journal of Behavioral Development, 21,* 537–553.

Jensen, M. D., Benson, R. C., & Bobak, I. M. (1981). *Maternity care.* St. Louis, MO: C. V. Mosby.

Jiao, S., Ji, G., & Jing, Q. (1996). Cognitive development of Chinese urban only children and children with siblings. *Child Development, 67,* 387–395.

Jiao, Z. (1999, April). Which students keep old friends and which become new friends across a school transition? Paper presented at the 1999 meeting of the Society for Research in Child Development, Albuquerque, New Mexico.

Johanson, R. B., Rice, C., Coyle, M., Arthur, J., Anyanwu, L., Ibrahim, J., Warwick, A., Redman, C. W. E., & O'Brien, P. M. S. (1993). A randomized prospective study comparing the new vacuum extractor policy with forceps delivery. *British Journal of Obstetrics and Gynecology, 100,* 524–530.

Johnson, M. H. (1998). The neural basis of cognitive development. In W. Damon (Ed.), *Handbook of child psychology* (Vol. 2). New York: Wiley.

Johnson, S. P., & Aslin, R. N. (1995). Perception of object unity in 2-month-old infants. *Developmental Psychology, 31,* 739–745.

Johnstone, B., Frame, C. L., & Bouman, D. (1992). Physical attractiveness and athletic and academic ability in controversial-aggressive and rejected-aggressive children. *Journal of Social and Clinical Psychology, 11,* 71–79.

Jones, D., & Christensen, C. A. (1999). Relationship between automaticity in handwriting and students' ability to generate written text. *Journal of Educational Psychology, 91,* 44–49.

Jones, K., & Day, J. D. (1997). Discrimination of two aspects of cognitive-social intelligence from academic intelligence. *Journal of Educational Psychology, 89,* 486–497.

Jusczyk, P. W. (1995). Language acquisition: Speech sounds and phonological development. In J. L. Miller & P. D. Eimas (Eds.), *Handbook of perception and cognition: Vol. 11. Speech, language, and communication.* Orlando, FL: Academic Press.

Jusczyk, P. W., & Aslin, R. N. (1995). Infants' detection of the sound patterns of words in fluent speech. *Cognitive Psychology, 29,* 1–23.

Kagan, J. (1989). Temperamental contributions to social behavior. *American Psychologist, 44,* 668–674.

Kagan, J., Arcus, D., Snidman, N., Feng, W. Y., Hendler, J., & Greene, S. (1994). Reactivity in infants: A cross-national comparison. *Developmental Psychology, 30,* 342–345.

Kagan, J., & Moss, H. A. (1962). *Birth to maturity: A study in psychological development.* New York: Wiley.

Kagan, J., Snidman, N., & Arcus, D. (1998). Childhood derivatives of high and low reactivity in infancy. *Child Development, 69,* 1483–1493.

Kaijura, H., Cowart B. J., & Beauchamp, G. K. (1992). Early developmental change in bitter taste responses in human infants. *Developmental Psychobiology, 25,* 375–386.

Kail, R. (1990). *The development of memory in children* (3rd ed.). New York: W. H. Freeman.

Kail, R. (1995). Processing speed, memory, and cognition. In F. E. Weinert & W. Schneider (Eds.), *Memory performance and competencies.* Mahway, NJ: Erlbaum.

Kail, R. (2000). Speed of information processing: Developmental change and links to intelligence. *Journal of School Psychology, 38,* 51–61.

Kail, R., & Bisanz, J. (1992). The information-processing perspective on cognitive development in childhood and adolescence. In R. J. Sternberg & C. A. Berg (Eds.), *Intellectual development.* New York: Cambridge University Press.

Kail, R., & Park, Y. (1990). Impact of practice on speed of mental rotation. *Journal of Experimental Child Psychology, 49,* 227–244.

Kamerman, S. B. (1993). International perspectives on child care policies and programs. *Pediatrics, 91,* 248–252.

Kandel, D. B. (1978). Homophily, selection, and socialization in adolescent friendships. *American Journal of Sociology, 84,* 427–436.

Kaplan, P. S., Goldstein, M. H., Huckeby, E. R., & Cooper, R. P. (1995). Habituation, sensitization, and infants' responses to motherese speech. *Developmental Psychobiology, 28,* 45–57.

Karniol, R. (1989). The role of manual manipulative states in the infant's acquisition of perceived control over objects. *Developmental Review, 9,* 205–233.

Kaufman, A. S. (1979). *Intelligent testing with the WISC-R.* New York: Wiley.

Kaufman, A. S., & Kaufman, N. L. (1983a). *K-ABC administration and scoring manual.* Circle Pines, MN: American Guidance Service.

Kaufman, A. S., & Kaufman, N. L. (1983b). *K-ABC interpretive manual.* Circle Pines, MN: American Guidance Service.

Keane, S. P., Brown, K. P., & Crenshaw, T. M. (1990). Children's intention-cue detection as a function of maternal social behavior: Pathways to social rejection. *Developmental Psychology, 26,* 1004–1009.

Kearney, C. A., & Silverman, W. K. (1995). Family environment of youngsters with school refusal behavior: A synopsis with implications for assessment and treatment. *American Journal of Family Therapy, 23,* 59–72.

Keller, M., Edelstein, W., Schmid, S., Fang, F., & Fang, G. (1998). Reasoning about responsibilities and obligations in close relationships: A comparison across two cultures. *Developmental Psychology, 34,* 731–741.

Kelley, M. L., Power, T.G., & Wimbush, D. D. (1992). Determinants of disciplinary practices in low-income Black mothers. *Child Development, 63,* 573–582.

Kellman, P. J., & Banks, M. S. (1998). Infant visual perception. In W. Damon (Ed.), *Handbook of child psychology* (Vol. 2). New York: Wiley.

Kenrick, D. T. (1987). Gender, genes, and the social environment. In P. C. Shaver & C. Hendrick (Eds.), *Review of Personality and Social Psychology, 8,* 14–43.

Kerr, M., Lambert, W. W., & Bem, D. J. (1996). Life course sequelae of childhood shyness in Sweden: Comparison with the United States. *Developmental Psychology, 32,* 1100–1105.

Kiernan, K. E. (1992). The impact of family disruption in childhood on transitions made in young adult life. *Population Studies, 46,* 213–234.

Kim, Y. H., & Goetz, E. T. (1994). Context effects on word recognition and reading comprehension of good and poor readers: A test of the interactive compensatory hypothesis. *Reading Research Quarterly, 29,* 178–188.

Kimball, M. M. (1986). Television and sex-role attitudes. In T. M. Williams (Ed.), *The impact of television* (pp. 265–301). New York: Academic Press.

Kimball, M. M. (1989). A new perspective on women's math achievement. *Psychological Bulletin, 105,* 198–214.

King, V., Elder, G. H., & Whitbeck, L. B. (1997). Religious involvement among rural youth: An ecological and life-course perspective. *Journal of Research on Adolescence, 7,* 431–456.

Kisilevsky, B. S., & Low, J. A. (1998). Human fetal behavior: 100 years of study. *Developmental Review, 18,* 1–29.

Klaczynski, P. A., & Narasimham, G. (1998). Development of scientific reasoning biases: Cognitive versus ego-protective explanations. *Developmental Psychology, 34,* 175–187.

Klahr, D. & MacWhinney, B. (1998). Information processing. In W. Damon (Ed.), *Handbook of child psychology* (Vol. 2). New York: Wiley.

Klapper, J. T. (1968). The impact of viewing "aggression": Studies and problems of extrapolation. In O. N. Larsen (Ed.), *Violence and the mass media.* New York: Harper & Row.

Klatzky, R. L. (1980). *Human memory* (2nd ed.). San Francisco: Freeman.

Knight, G. P., Fabes, R. A., & Higgins, D. A. (1996). Concerns about drawing causal inferences from meta-analyses: An example in the study of gender differences in aggression. *Psychological Bulletin, 119,* 410–421.

Kochanska, G. (1991). Socialization and temperament in the development of guilt and conscience. *Child Development, 62,* 1379–1392.

Kochanska, G. (1993). Toward a synthesis of parental socialization and child temperament in early development of conscience. *Child Development, 64,* 325–347.

Kochanska, G. (1995). Children's temperament, mothers' discipline, and security of attachment: Multiple pathways to emerging internalization. *Child Development, 66,* 597–615.

Kochanska, G. (1997a). Multiple pathways to conscience for children with different temperaments: From toddlerhood to age 5. *Developmental Psychology, 33,* 228–240.

Kochanska, G. (1997b). Mutually responsive orientation between mothers and their young children: Implications for early socialization. *Child Development, 68,* 94–112.

Kochanska, G., Casey, R. J., & Fukumoto, A. (1995). Toddlers' sensitivity to standard violations. *Child Development, 66,* 643–656.

Kochanska, G., DeVet, K., Goldman, M., Murray, K., et al. (1994). Maternal reports of conscience development and temperament in young children. *Child Development, 65,* 852–868.

Kochanska, G., Padavich, D. L., & Koenig, A. L. (1996). Children's narratives about hypothetical moral dilemmas and objective measures of their conscience: Mutual relations and socialization antecedents. *Child Development, 67,* 1420–1436.

Kochanska, G., & Radke-Yarrow, M. (1992). Inhibition in toddlerhood and the dynamics of the child's interaction with an unfamiliar peer at age five. *Child Development, 63,* 325–335.

Kochenderfer, B. J., & Ladd, G. W. (1996). Peer victimization: Cause or consequence of school maladjustment? *Child Development, 67,* 1305–1317.

Kogan, N. (1983). Stylistic variation in childhood and adolescence: Creativity, metaphor, and cognitive style. In P. H. Mussen (Ed.), *Handbook of child psychology* (Vol. 3). New York: Wiley.

Kohlberg, L. (1966). A cognitive-developmental analysis of children's sex-role concepts and attitudes. In. E. E. Maccoby (Ed.), *The development of sex differences.* Stanford: Stanford University Press.

Kohlberg, L. (1969). Stage and sequence: The cognitive-developmental approach to socialization. In D. Goslin (Ed.), *Handbook of socialization theory and research* (pp. 347–480). Chicago: Rand McNally.

Kohlberg, L., & Ullian, D. Z. (1974). Stages in the development of psychosexual concepts and attitudes. In R. C. Friedman, R. M. Richart, & R. L. Van Wiele (Eds.), *Sex differences in behavior.* New York: Wiley.

Kolb, B. (1989). Brain development, plasticity, and behavior. *American Psychologist, 44,* 1203–1212.

Kolb, B., & Whishaw, I. Q. (1998). Brain plasticity and behavior. *Annual Review of Psychology, 49,* 43–64.

Kopp, C. B. (1982). The antecedents of self-regulation. *Developmental Psychology, 18,* 199–214.

Kopp, C. B. (1987). The growth of self-regulation: Caregivers and children. In N. Eisenberg (Ed.), *Contemporary topics in developmental psychology.* New York: Wiley.

Kopp, C. B., & McCall, R. B. (1982). Predicting later mental performance for normal, at-risk, and handicapped infants. In P. B. Baltes & O. G. Brim (Eds.), *Life-span development and behavior* (Vol. 4). New York: Academic Press.

Korbin, J. E. (1987). Child abuse and neglect: The cultural context. In R. E. Helfer & R. S. Kempe (Eds.), *The battered child* (4th ed., pp. 23–41). Chicago: University of Chicago Press.

Kotovsky, L., & Baillargeon, R. (1998).The development of calibration-based reasoning about collision events in young infants. *Cognition, 67,* 311–351.

Kovacs, D. M., Parker, J. G., & Hoffman, L. W. (1996). Behavioral, affective, and social correlates of involvement in cross-sex friendship in elementary school. *Child Development, 67,* 2269–2286.

Kowal, A., & Kramer, L. (1997). Children's understanding of parental differential treatment. *Child Development, 68,* 113–126.

Krebs, D., & Gillmore, J. (1982). The relationship among the first stages of cognitive development, role-taking abilities, and moral development. *Child Development, 53,* 877–886.

Krispin, O., Sternberg, K. J., & Lamb, M. E. (1992). The dimensions of peer evaluation in Israel: A cross-cultural perspective. *International Journal of Behavioral Development, 15,* 299–314.

Kroger, J., & Green, K. E. (1996). Events associated with identity status change. *Journal of Adolescence, 19,* 477–490.

Kuebli, J., Butler, S., & Fivush, R. (1995). Mother-child talk about past emotions: Relations of maternal language and child gender over time. *Cognition & Emotion, 9,* 265–283.

Kuhl, P. K. (1993). Early linguistic experience and phonetic perception: Implications for theories of developmental speech perception. *Journal of Phonetics, 21,* 125–139.

Kunzig, R. (1998). Climbing through the brain. *Discover, 19,* 60–69.

Kupersmidt, J. B., & Coie, J. D. (1990). Preadolescent peer status, aggression, and school adjustment as predictors of externalizing problems in adolescence. *Child Development, 61,* 1350–1362.

Ladd, G. W. (1998). Peer relationships and social competence during early and middle childhood. *Annual Review of Psychology, 50,* 333–359.

Ladd, G. W., & Ladd, B. K. (1998). Parenting behaviors and parent-child relationships: Correlates of peer victimization in kindergarten? *Developmental Psychology, 34,* 1450–1458.

Ladd, G. W., & Le Sieur, K. D. (1995). Parents and children's peer relationships. In M. H. Bornstein (Ed.), *Handbook of parenting, Vol. 4. Applied and practical parenting* (pp. 377–410). Mahwah, NJ: Erlbaum.

LaFreniere, P., Strayer, F. F., & Gauthier, R. (1984). The emergence of same-sex affiliative preferences among preschool peers: A developmental/ethnological perspective. *Child Development, 55,* 1958–1965.

Lagattuta, K. H., Wellman, H. M., & Flavell, J. H. (1997). Preschoolers' understanding of the link between thinking and feeling: Cognitive cuing and emotional change. *Child Development, 68,* 1081–1104.

LaGreca, A. M. (1993). Social skills training with children: Where do we go from here? *Journal of Clinical Child Psychology, 22,* 288–298.

Laible, D. J., & Thompson, R. A. (1998). Attachment and emotional understanding in preschool children. *Developmental Psychology, 34,* 1038–1045.

Lamb, M. E. (1999). Nonparental child care. In M. E. Lamb (Ed.), *Parenting and child development in "nontraditional" families.* Mahwah, NJ: Erlbaum.

Lamborn, S. D., Mounts, N. S., Steinberg, L., & Dornbusch, S. M. (1991). Patterns of competence and adjustment among adolescents from authoritative, authoritarian, indulgent, and neglectful families. *Child Development, 62,* 1049–1065.

Lampinen, J. M., & Smith, V. L. (1995). The incredible (and sometimes incredulous) child witness: Child eyewitnesses' sensitivity to source credibility cues. *Journal of Applied Psychology, 80,* 621–627.

Langlois, J. H., & Downs, A. C. (1980). Mothers, fathers, and peers as socialization agents of sex-typed play behaviors in young children. *Child Development, 51,* 1237–1247.

Lanza, E. (1992). Can bilingual two-year-olds code-switch? *Journal of Child Language, 19,* 633–658.

Larson, R. W. (1997). The emergence of solitude as a constructive domain of experience in early adolescence. *Child Development, 68,* 80–93.

Lau, S. (1989). Sex role orientation and domains of self-esteem. *Sex Roles, 21,* 415–422.

Laursen, B., & Collins, W. A. (1994). Interpersonal conflict during adolescence. *Psychological Bulletin, 115,* 197–209.

Leichtman, M. D., & Ceci, S. L. (1995). The effects of stereotypes and suggestions on preschoolers' reports. *Developmental Psychology, 31,* 568–578.

LeMare, L. J., & Rubin, K. H. (1987). Perspective taking and peer interaction: Structural and developmental analyses. *Child Development, 58,* 306–315.

Lengua, L. J., Sandler, I. N., West, S. G., Wolchik, S. A., & Curran, P. J. (1999). Emotionality and self-regulation, threat appraisal, and coping in children of divorce. *Development & Psychopathology, 11,* 15–37.

Lengua, L. J., West, S. G., & Sandler, I. N. (1998). Temperament as a predictor of symptomatology in children: Addressing contamination of measures. *Child Development, 69,* 164–181.

Lepper, M. R., & Gurtner, J. (1989). Children and computers. *American Psychologist, 44,* 170–178.

Levine, L. E. (1983). *Mine*: Self-definition in 2-year-old boys. *Developmental Psychology, 19,* 544–549.

Levine, L. J. (1995). Young children's understanding of the causes of anger and sadness. *Child Development, 66,* 697–709.

Levitt, A. G., & Utman, J. A. (1992). From babbling towards the sound systems of English and French: A longitudinal two-case study. *Journal of Child Language, 19,* 19–49.

Levitt, M. J., Guacci-Franco, N., & Levitt, J. L. (1993). Convoys of social support in childhood and early adolescence: Structure and function. *Developmental Psychology, 29,* 811–818.

Levy, G. D., & Boston, M. B. (1994). Preschoolers' recall of own-sex and other-sex gender scripts. *Journal of Genetic Psychology, 155,* 367–371.

Levy, G. D., Taylor, M. G., & Gelman, S. A. (1995). Traditional and evaluative aspects of flexibility in gender roles, social conventions, moral rules, and physical laws. *Child Development, 66,* 515–531.

Levy, J. (1976). A review of evidence for a genetic component in the determination of handedness. *Behavior Genetics, 6,* 429–453.

Lewis, M. (1987). Social development in infancy and early childhood. In J. D. Osofsky (Ed.), *Handbook of infant development.* New York: Wiley.

Lewis, M. (1992). *Shame: The exposed self.* New York: Free Press.

Lewis, M., Alessandri, S. M., & Sullivan, M. W. (1992). Differences in shame and pride as a function of children's gender and task difficulty. *Child Development, 63,* 630–638.

Lewis, M., & Brooks-Gunn, J. (1979). *Social cognition and the acquisition of self.* New York: Plenum.

Lewis, M., Ramsay, D. S., & Kawakami, K. (1993). Differences between Japanese infants and Caucasian American infants in behavioral and cortisol response to inoculation. *Child Development, 64,* 1722–1731.

Lewis, M. D., Koroshegyi, C., Douglas, L., & Kampe, K. (1997). Age-specific associations between emotional responses to separation and cognitive performance in infancy. *Developmental Psychology, 33,* 32–42.

Liben, L. S., & Signorella, M. L. (1993). Gender-schematic processing in children: The role of initial interpretations of stimuli. *Developmental Psychology, 29,* 141–149.

Lieberman, M., Doyle, A., & Markiewicz, D. (1999). Developmental patterns in security of attachment to mother and father in late childhood and early adolescence: Associations with peer relations. *Child Development, 70,* 202–213.

Liebert, R. M., & Sprafkin, J. (1988). *The early window: Effects of television on children and youth.* New York: Pergamon.

Lillard, A. (1999). Developing a cultural theory of mind: The CIAO approach. *Current Directions in Psychological Science, 8,* 57–61.

Lin, C. C., & Fu, V. R. (1990). A comparison of childrearing practices among Chinese, immigrant Chinese, and Caucasian-American parents. *Child Development, 61,* 429–433.

Linden, M. G., Bender, B. G., Harmon, R. J., Mrazek, D. A., & Robinson, A. (1988). 47-XXX: What is the prognosis? *Pediatrics, 82,* 619–630.

Livesley, W. J., & Bromley, D. B. (1973). *Person perception in childhood and adolescence.* New York: Wiley.

Lord, S. E., Eccles, J. S., & McCarthy, K. A. (1994). Surviving the junior high transition: Family processes and self-perception as protective and risk factors. *Journal of Early Adolescence, 14,* 162–199.

Losoya, S., Eisenberg, N., & Fabes, R. (1998). Developmental issues in the study of coping. *International Journal of Behavioral Development, 22,* 287–313.

Loveland, K. A. (1987a). Behavior of young children with Down syndrome before the mirror: Exploration. *Child Development, 58,* 768–778.

Loveland, K. A. (1987b). Behavior of young children with Down syndrome before the mirror: Finding things reflected. *Child Development, 58,* 928–936.

Lovett, S. B., & Pillow, B. H. (1996). Development of the ability to distinguish between comprehension and memory: Evidence from goal-state evaluation tasks. *Journal of Educational Psychology, 88,* 546–562.

Ludemann, P. M. (1991). Generalized discrimination of positive facial expressions by seven- and ten-month-old infants. *Child Development, 62,* 55–67.

Ludemann, P. M., & Nelson, C. A. (1988). Categorical representation of facial expressions by 7-month-old infants. *Developmental Psychology, 24,* 492–501.

Luecke-Aleksa, D., Anderson, D. R., Collins, P. A., & Schmitt, K. L. (1995). Gender constancy and television viewing. *Developmental Psychology, 31,* 773–780.

Luthar, S. S., Zigler, E., & Goldstein, D. (1992). Psychosocial adjustment among intellectually gifted adolescents: The role of cognitive-developmental and experiential factors. *Journal of Child Psychology and Psychiatry and Allied Disciplines, 33,* 361–373.

Lutz, S. E., & Ruble, D. N. (1995). Children and gender prejudice: Context, motivation, and the development of gender conceptions. In R. Vasta (Ed.), *Annals of child development: A research annual* (Vol. 10). London, England: Jessica Kingsley.

Lyon, G. R. (1996). Learning disabilities. In E. J. Mash & R. A. Barkley (Eds.), *Child psychopathology.* New York: Guilford.

Lytton, H., & Romney, D. M. (1991). Parents' differential socialization of boys and girls: A meta-analysis. *Psychological Bulletin, 109,* 267–296.

Maccoby, E. E. (1984). Socialization and developmental change. *Child Development, 55,* 317–328.

Maccoby, E. E. (1988). Gender as a social category. *Developmental Psychology, 24,* 755–765.

Maccoby, E. E. (1990). Gender and relationships: A developmental account. *American Psychologist, 45,* 513–520.

Maccoby, E. E., Buchanon, C. M., Mnookin, R. H., & Dornbusch, S. M. (1993). Postdivorce roles of mothers and fathers in the lives of their children. *Journal of Family Psychology, 7,* 24–38.

Maccoby, E. E., & Jacklin, C. N. (1974). *The psychology of sex differences.* Stanford, CA: Stanford University Press.

Maccoby, E. E., & Jacklin, C. N. (1980). Sex differences in aggression: A rejoinder and reprise. *Child Development, 51,* 964–980.

Maccoby, E. E., & Martin, J. A. (1983). Socialization in the context of the family: Parent-child interaction. In P. H. Mussen (Ed.), *Handbook of child psychology* (Vol. 4). New York: Wiley.

MacKinnon-Lewis, C., Rabiner, D., & Starnes, R. (1999). Predicting boys' social acceptance and aggression: The role of mother-child interactions and boys' beliefs about peers. *Developmental Psychology, 35,* 632–639.

MacWhinney, B. (1998). Models of the emergence of language. *Annual Review of Psychology, 49,* 199–227.

Main, M., & Cassidy, J. (1988). Categories of response to reunion with the parent at age 6: Predictable from infant attachment classifications and stable over a 1-month-period. *Developmental Psychology, 24,* 415–426.

Malina, R. M. (1990). Physical growth and development during the transitional years (9–16). In R. Montemayor, G. R. Adams, & T. P. Gullotta (Eds.), *From childhood to adolescence: A transitional period* (pp. 41–62). Newbury Park, CA: Sage.

Malinosky-Rummell, R., & Hansen, D. J. (1993). Long-term consequences of childhood physical abuse. *Psychological Bulletin, 114,* 68–79.

Mandel, D. R., Jusczyk, P. W., & Pisoni, D. B. (1995). Infants' recognition of the sound patterns of their own names. *Psychological Science, 6,* 314–317.

Mandler, J. M., & McDonough, L. (1998). On developing a knowledge base in infancy. *Developmental Psychology, 34,* 1274–1288.

Mandler, J. M., & McDonough, L. (1998). Studies in inductive inference in infancy. *Cognitive Psychology, 37,* 60–96.

Mangelsdorf, S. C. (1992). Developmental changes in infant-stranger interaction. *Infant Behavior and Development, 15,* 191–208.

Mangelsdorf, S., Gunnar, M., Kestenbaum, R., Lang, S., & Andreas, D. (1990). Infant proneness-to-distress temperament, maternal personality, and mother-infant attachment: Associations and goodness of fit. *Child Development, 61,* 820–831.

Mangelsdorf, S. C., Shapiro, J. R., & Marzolf, D. (1995). Developmental and temperamental differences in emotional regulation in infancy. *Child Development, 66,* 1817–1828.

Maratsos, M. (1998). The acquisition of grammar. In W. Damon (Ed.), *Handbook of child psychology* (Vol 2). New York: Wiley.

Marcia, J. E. (1980). Identity in adolescence. In J. Adelson (Ed.), *Handbook of adolescent psychology.* New York: Wiley.

Marcia, J. E. (1991). Identity and self-development. In R. M. Lerner, A. C. Petersen, & J. Brooks-Gunn (Eds.), *Encyclopedia of adolescence* (Vol. 1). New York: Garland.

Marcus, G. F., Pinker, S., Ullman, M., Hollander, M., Rosen, T. J., & Xu, F. (1992). Overregularization in language acquisition. *Monographs of the Society for Research in Child Development, 58* (4, Serial No. 228).

Marcus, J., Maccoby, E. E., Jacklin, C. N., & Doering, C. H. (1985). Individual differences in mood in early childhood: Their relation to gender and neonatal sex steroids. *Developmental Psychobiology, 18,* 327–340.

Markovits, H., & Vachon, R. (1989). Reasoning with contrary-to-fact propositions. *Journal of Experimental Child Psychology, 47,* 398–412.

Markstrom-Adams, A. (1989). Androgyny and its relation to adolescent well-being: A review of the literature. *Sex Roles, 21,* 325–340.

Marsh, H. W. (1991). Employment during high school: Character building or a subversion of academic goals? *Sociology of Education, 64,* 172–189.

Marsh, H. W., Chessor, D., Craven, R., & Roche, L. (1995). The effects of gifted and talented programs on academic self-concept: The big fish strikes again. *American Educational Research Journal, 32,* 285–319.

Marsh, H. W., & Yeung, A. S. (1997). Causal effects of academic self-concept on academic achievement: Structural equation models of longitudinal data. *Journal of Educational Psychology, 89,* 41–54.

Marshall, E. (1995). Gene therapy's growing pains. *Science, 269,* 1050–1052.

Martin, C. L. (1989). Children's use of gender-related information in making social judgments. *Developmental Psychology, 25,* 80–88.

Martin, C. L., Eisenbud, L., & Rose, H. (1995). Children's gender-based reasoning about toys. *Child Development, 66,* 1453–1471.

Martin, C. L., & Halverson, C. F. (1987). The roles of cognition in sex roles and sex typing. In D. B. Carter (Ed.), *Current conceptions of sex roles and sex typing: Theory and research.* New York: Praeger.

Martin, C. L., & Little, J. K. (1990). The relation of gender understandings to children's sex-typed preferences and gender stereotypes. *Child Development, 61,* 1427–1439.

Martin, R. P., Olejnik, S., & Gaddis, L. (1994). Is temperament an important contributor to schooling outcomes in elementary school? Modeling effects of temperament and scholastic ability on academic achievement. In W. B. Casey & S. C. McDevitt (Eds.), *Prevention and early intervention.* New York: Brunner/Mazel.

Masur, E. F. (1995). Infants' early verbal imitation and their later lexical development. *Merrill-Palmer Quarterly, 41,* 286–306.

Mattys, S. L., Jusczyk, P. W., Luce, P. A., & Morgan, J. L. (1999). Phonotactic and prosodic effects on word segmentation in infants. *Cognitive Psychology, 38,* 465–494.

Mazur, E., Wolchik, S. A., Virdin, L., Sandler, I. N., & West, S. G. (1999). Cognitive moderators of children's adjustment to stressful divorce events: The role of negative cognitive errors and positive illusions. *Child Development, 70,* 231–245.

McCall, R. B. (1989). Commentary. *Human Development, 32,* 177–186.

McCall, R. B., Applebaum, M. I., & Hogarty, P. S. (1973). Developmental changes in mental performance. *Monographs of the Society for Research in Child Development, 38*(Whole No. 150).

McCarty, M. E., & Ashmead, D. H. (1999). Visual control of reaching and grasping in infants. *Developmental Psychology, 35,* 620–631.

McCutchen, D., Covill, A., Hoyne, S. H, & Mildes, K. (1994). Individual differences in writing: Implications of translating fluency. *Journal of Educational Psychology, 86,* 256–266.

McCutchen, D., Francis, M., & Kerr, S. (1997). Revising for meaning: Effects of knowledge and strategy. *Journal of Educational Psychology, 89,* 667–676.

McGee, R., Stanton, W. R., & Sears, M. R. (1993). Allergic disorders and attention deficit disorder in children. *Journal of Abnormal Child Psychology, 21,* 79–88.

McGee, R., Williams, S., & Feehan, M. (1992). Attention deficit disorder and age of onset of problem behaviors. *Journal of Abnormal Child Psychology, 20,* 487–502.

McGraw, M.B. (1935). *Growth: A study of Johnny and Jimmy.* East Norwalk, CT: Appleton-Century-Crofts.

McHale, S. M., Bartko, W. T., Crouter, A. C., & Perry-Jenkins, M. (1990). Children's housework and psychosocial functioning: The mediating effects of parents' sex-role behaviors and attitudes. *Child Development, 61,* 1413–1426.

McKusick, V. A. (1995). *Mendelian inheritance in man: Catalogs of autosomal dominant, autosomal recessive, and X-linked phenotypes* (10th ed.). Baltimore: Johns Hopkins University Press.

McManus, I. C., Sik, G., Cole, D. R., Kloss, J., Mellon, A. F., & Wong, J. (1988). The development of handedness in children. *British Journal of Developmental Psychology, 6,* 257–273.

McNally, S., Eisenberg, N., & Harris, J. D. (1991). Consistency and change in maternal child-rearing practices and values: A longitudinal study. *Child Development, 62,* 190–198.

McNaughton, S., & Leyland, J. (1990). The shifting focus of maternal tutoring across different difficulty levels on a problem solving task. *British Journal of Developmental Psychology, 8,* 147–155.

Measelle, J. R., Ablow, J. C., Cowan, P. A., & Cowan, C. P. (1998). Assessing young children's views of their academic, social, and emotional lives: An evaluation of the self-perception scales of the Berkeley puppet interview. *Child Development, 69,* 1556–1576.

Meilman, P. W. (1979). Cross-sectional age changes in ego identity status during adolescence. *Developmental Psychology, 15,* 230–231.

Mennella, J. A., & Beauchamp, G. K. (1996). The human infant's response to vanilla flavors in mother's milk and formula. *Infant Behavior and Development, 19,* 13–19.

Mennella, J., & Beauchamp, G. K. (1997). The ontogeny of human flavor perception. In G. K. Beauchamp & L. Bartoshuk (Eds.), *Tasting and smelling. Handbook of perception and cognition.* San Diego, CA: Academic Press.

Meyer, D. R., & Garasky, S. (1993). Custodial fathers: Myths, realities, and child support policy. *Journal of Marriage and the Family, 55,* 73–79.

Meyer-Bahlburg, H. F. L., Ehrhardt, A. A., Rosen, L. R., Gruen, R. S., et al. (1995). Prenatal estrogens and the development of homosexual orientation. *Developmental Psychology, 31,* 12–21.

Miller, B. C., Norton, M. C., Curtis, T., Hill, E. J., Schvaneveldt, P., & Young, M. H. (1997). The timing of sexual intercourse among adolescents: Family, peer, and other antecedents. *Youth and Society, 29,* 54–83.

Miller, J. G., & Bersoff, D. M. (1992). Culture and moral judgment: How are conflicts between justice and interpersonal responsibilities resolved? *Journal of Personality and Social Psychology, 62,* 541–554.

Miller, K. F., Smith, C. M., Zhu, J., & Zhang, H. (1995). Preschool origins of cross-national differences in mathematical competence: The role of number-naming systems. *Psychological Science, 6,* 56–60.

Miller, P. A., Eisenberg, N., Fabes, R. A., & Shell, R. (1996). Relations of moral reasoning and vicarious emotion to young children's prosocial behavior toward peers and adults. *Developmental Psychology, 32,* 210–219.

Miller, P. M., Danaher, D. L., & Forbes, D. (1986). Sex-related strategies of coping with interpersonal conflict in children aged five to seven. *Developmental Psychology, 22,* 543–548.

Miller, S. A., & Brownell, C. A. (1975). Peers, persuasion, and Piaget: Dyadic interaction between conservers and nonconservers. *Child Development, 46,* 992–997.

Mills, R. S. L., & Grusec, J. E. (1989). Cognitive, affective, and behavioral consequences of praising altruism. *Merrill-Palmer Quarterly, 35,* 299–326.

Minuchin, P. P., & Shapiro, E. K. (1983). The school as a context for social development. In E. M. Hetherington (Ed.), *Handbook of child psychology* (Vol. 4, 4th ed.). New York: Wiley.

Mischel, W. (1970). Sex-typing and socialization. In P. H. Mussen (Ed.) *Carmichaels' manual of child psychology* (Vol. 2). New York: Wiley.

Mischel, W., & Ebbesen, E. (1970). Attention in delay of gratification. *Journal of Personality and Social Psychology, 16,* 329–337.

Mischel, W., Shoda, Y., & Rodriguez, M. L. (1989). Delay of gratification in children. *Science, 244,* 933–938.

Mitchell, J. E., Baker, L. A., & Jacklin, C. N. (1989). Masculinity and femininity in twin children: Genetic and environmental factors. *Child Development, 60,* 1475–1485.

Miura, I. T., Kim, C. C., Chang, C. M., & Okamoto, Y. (1988). Effects of language characteristics on children's cognitive representation of number: Cross-national comparisons. *Child Development, 59,* 1445–1450.

Mize, J., & Ladd, G. W. (1990). A cognitive social-learning approach to social skill training with low-status preschool children. *Developmental Psychology, 26,* 388–397.

Mize, J., & Pettit, G. S. (1997). Mothers' social coaching, mother-child relationship style, and children's peer competence: Is the medium the message? *Child Development, 68,* 312–332.

Mize, J., Pettit, G. S., & Brown, E. G. (1995). Mothers' supervision of their children's peer play: Relations with beliefs, perceptions, and knowledge. *Developmental Psychology, 31,* 311–321.

Mizes, J., Scott, P., & Tonya, M. (1995). Eating disorders. In M. Hersen & R. T. Ammerman (Eds.), *Handbook of prevention and treatment with children and adolescents: Intervention in the real world context.* New York: Wiley.

Moats, L. C., & Lyon, G. R. (1993). Learning disabilities in the United States: Advocacy, science, and the future of the field. *Journal of Learning Disabilities, 26,* 282–294.

Moffitt, T. E., Caspi, A., Belsky, J., & Silva, P. A. (1992). Childhood experience and the onset of menarche: A test of a sociobiological model. *Child Development, 63,* 47–58.

Molfese, D. L., & Burger-Judisch, L. M. (1991). Dynamic temporal-spatial allocation of resources in the human brain: An alternative to the static view of hemisphere differences. In F. L. Ketterle (Ed.), *Cerebral laterality: Theory and research. The Toledo symposium.* Hillsdale, NJ: Erlbaum.

Moore, B. S., Underwood, B., & Rosenhan, D. L. (1973). Affect and altruism. *Developmental Psychology, 8,* 99–104.

Moore, C., Angelopoulos, M., & Bennet, P. (1999). Word learning in the context of referential and salience cues. *Developmental Psychology, 35,* 60–68.

Moore, K. L., & Persaud, T. V. N. (1993). *Before we are born* (4th ed.). Philadelphia: W. B. Saunders.

Morgan, B., & Gibson, K. R. (1991). Nutritional and environmental interactions in brain development. In K. R. Gibson & A. C. Peterson (Eds.), *Brain maturation and cognitive development: Comparative and crosscultural perspectives.* New York: Aldine De Gruyter.

Morgane, P. J., Austin-LaFrance, R., Bronzino, J. D., Tonkiss, J., Diaz-Cintra, S., Cintra, L., Kemper, T., & Galler, J. R. (1993). Prenatal malnutrition and development of the brain. *Neuroscience and Biobehavioral Reviews, 17,* 91–128.

Morison, R., & Masten, A. S. (1991). Peer reputation in middle childhood as a predictor of adaptation in adolescence: A seven-year follow-up. *Child Development, 62,* 991–1007.

Morris, R. K. (1994). Lexical and message-level sentence context effects on fixation times in reading. *Journal of Experimental Psychology: Learning, Memory, and Cognition, 20,* 92–103.

Mortimer, J.T. (1991). Employment. In R.M. Lerner, A.C. Petersen, & J. Brooks-Gunn (Eds.), *Encyclopedia of adolescence* (Vol. 1). New York: Garland.

Mortimer, J. T., Finch, M. D., Rye, S., Shanahan, M. J., & Call, K. T. (1996). The effects of work intensity on adolescent mental health, achievement, and behavioral adjustment: New evidence from a prospective study. *Child Development, 67,* 1243–1261.

Morton, J., & Johnson, M. H. (1991). CONSPEC and CONLERN: A two-process theory of infant face recognition. *Psychological Review, 98,* 164–181.

Moss, E., Rousseau, D., Parent, S., St-Laurent, D., & Saintonge, J. (1998). Correlates of attachment at school age: Maternal reported stress, mother-child interaction, and behavior problems. *Child Development, 69,* 1390–1405.

Mumme, D. L., Fernald, A., & Herrera, C. (1996). Infants' responses to facial and vocal emotional signals in a social referencing paradigm. *Child Development, 67,* 3219–3237.

Murray, L., Fiori-Cowley, A., Hooper, R., & Cooper, P. (1996). The impact of postnatal depression and associated adversity on early mother-infant interactions and later infant outcomes. *Child Development, 67,* 2512–2526.

Naigles, L. G., & Gelman, S. A. (1995). Overextensions in comprehension and production revisited: Preferential-looking in a study of dog, cat, and cow. *Journal of Child Language, 22,* 19–46.

Nation, K., Adams, J. W., Bowyer-Crane, C. A., & Snowling, M. J. (1999). Working memory deficits in poor comprehenders reflect underlying language impairments. *Journal of Experimental Child Psychology, 73,* 139–158.

National Center on Child Abuse and Neglect. (1997). *Child maltreatment 1995: Reports from the states to the National Center on Child Abuse and Neglect.* Washington, DC: Department of Health, Education, and Welfare. (OHDS 78-30137)

National Research Council. (1987). *Risking the future: Adolescent sexuality, pregnancy, and childbearing* (Vol. 1). Washington, DC: National Academy Press.

National Research Council. (1989). *Recommended dietary allowances* (10th edition). Washington, DC: National Academy Press.

Neisser, U., Boodoo, G., Bouchard, T. J., Boykin, A. W., Brody, N., Ceci, S. J., Halpern, D. F., Loehlin, J. C., Perloff, R., Sternberg, R. J., & Urbina, S. (1996). Intelligence: Knowns and unknowns. *American Psychologist, 51,* 77–101.

Nelson, C. A. (1999). Neural plasticity and human development. *Current Directions in Psychological Science, 8,* 42–45.

Nelson, K. (1973). Structure and strategy in learning to talk. *Monographs of the Society for Research in Child Development, 38* (No. 149).

Nelson, K. (1993). Explaining the emergence of autobiographical memory in early childhood. In A. F. Collins & S. E. Gathercole (Eds.), *Theories of memory.* Hove, England: Erlbaum.

Neugarten, B. L., & Weinstein, K. K. (1964). The changing American grandparent. *Journal of Marriage and the Family, 26,* 299–304.

Newcomb, A. F., & Bagwell, C. L. (1995). Children's friendship relations: A meta-analytic review. *Psychological Bulletin, 117,* 306–347.

Newcomb, A. F., Bukowski, W. M., & Pattee, L. (1993). Children's peer relations: A meta-analytic review of popular, rejected, neglected, controversial, and average sociometric status. *Psychological Bulletin, 113,* 99–123.

Newman, D.L., Caspi, A., Mofitt, T.E., & Silva, P.A. (1997). Antecedents of adult interpersonal functioning: Effects of individual differences in age 3 temperament. *Developmental Psychology, 33,* 206–217.

Newman, L. S., Cooper, J., & Ruble, D. N. (1995). Gender and computers: II. Interactive effects of knowledge and constancy on gender-stereotyped attitudes. *Sex Roles, 33,* 325–351.

Newport, E. L. (1991). Contrasting conceptions of the critical period for language. In S. Carey & R. Gelman (Eds.), *The epigenesis of mind: Essays on biology and cognition* (pp. 111–130). Hillsdale, NJ: Erlbaum.

NICHD Early Child Care Research Network. (1997). The effects of infant child care on infant-mother attachment security: Results of the NICHD Study of Early Child Care. *Child Development, 68,* 860–879.

NICHD Early Child Care Research Network. (1998). Early child care and self-control, compliance, and problem behavior at twenty-four and thirty-six months. *Child Development, 69,* 1145–1170.

Niebyl, J. R. (1991). Drugs in pregnancy and lactation. In S. G. Gabbe, J. R. Niebyl, & J. L. Simpson (Eds.), *Obstetrics: Normal and problem pregnancies* (2nd ed.). New York: Churchill Livingstone.

Nielson, A. C. (1990). *Annual Nielsen report on television: 1990.* New York: Nielson Media Research.

NIH. (1998). SIDS rate drops as more babies are placed to sleep on their backs or sides. *National Institute of Child Health and Human Development,* July.

Nucci, L., & Weber, E. K. (1995). Social interactions in the home and the development of young children's conceptions of the personal. *Child Development, 66,* 1438–1452.

Nurmi, J., Poole, M. E., & Kalakoski, V. (1996). Age differences in adolescent identity exploration and commitment in urban and rural environments. *Journal of Adolescence, 19,* 443–452.

O'Neill, D. K. (1996). Two-year-old children's sensitivity to a parent's knowledge state when making requests. *Child Development, 67,* 659–677.

Ochs, E. (1988). *Culture and language development.* Cambridge: Cambridge University Press.

Offer, D. Ostrov, E., Howard, K. I., & Atkinson, R. (1988). *The teenage world: Adolescents' self-image in ten countries.* New York: Plenum.

Ohlendorf-Moffat, P. (1991). Surgery before birth. *Discover* (February), 59–65.

Okagaki, L., & Frensch, P. A. (1994). Effects of video game playing on measures of spatial performance: Gender effects in late adolescence. *Journal of Applied Developmental Psychology, 15,* 33–58.

Okagaki, L., & Sternberg, R. J. (1993). Parental beliefs and children's school performance. *Child Development, 64,* 36–56.

Oliver, M. B., & Hyde, J. S. (1993). Gender differences in sexuality: A meta-analysis. *Psychological Bulletin, 114,* 29–51.

Oller, D. K. (1986). Metaphonology and infant vocalizations. In B. Lindblom & R. Zetterstrom (Eds.), *Precursors of early speech.* Basingstoke, Hampshire: Macmillan.

Oller, D. K., & Eilers, R. E. (1988). The role of audition in infant babbling. *Child Development, 59,* 441–449.

Oller, D. K., & Lynch, M. P. (1992). Infant vocalizations and innovations in infraphonology: Toward a broader theory of development and disorders. In C. A. Ferguson, L. Menn, & C. Stoel-Gammon (Eds.), *Phonological development: Models, research, and implications* (pp. 509–538). Timonium, MD: York Press.

Olweus, D. (1978). *Aggression in the schools: Bullies and whipping boys.* Washington, DC: Hemisphere.

Olweus, D. (1994). Bullying at school: Basic facts and effects of school based intervention program. *Journal of Child Psychology and Psychiatry, 35,* 1171–1190.

Paarlberg, K. M., Vingerhoets, A. J. J. M., Passchier, J., Dekker, G. A., et al. (1995). Psychosocial factors and pregnancy outcome: A review with emphasis on methodological issues. *Journal of Psychosomatic Research, 39,* 563–595.

Pacifici, C., & Bearison, D. J. (1991). Development of children's self-regulations in idealized and mother-child interactions. *Cognitive Development, 6,* 261–277.

Padilla, A. M., Lindholm, K. J., Chen, A., Duran, R., Hakuta, K., Lambert, W., & Tucker, G. R. (1991). The English-only movement. Myths, reality, and implications for psychology. *American Psychologist, 46,* 120–130.

Palca, J. (1991). Fetal brain signals time for birth. *Science, 253,* 1360.

Panksepp, J. (1998). Attention deficit hyperactivity disorders, psychostimulants, and intolerance of childhood playfulness: A tragedy in the making? *Current Directions in Psychological Science, 7,* 99–103.

Parazzini, F., Luchini, L., La Vecchia, C., & Crosignani, P.G. (1993). Video display terminal use during pregnancy and reproductive outcome—A meta-analysis. *Journal of Epidemiology and Community Health, 47,* 265–268.

Parke, R.D. (1977). Punishment in children: Effects, side effects and alternative strategies. In H.L. Hom, Jr., & A. Robinson (Eds.), *Psychological processes in early education.* New York: Academic.

Parke, R. D. (1990). In search of fathers: A narrative of an empirical journey. In I. Sigel & G. Brody (Eds.), *Methods of family research.* Hillsdale, NJ: Erlbaum.

Parke, R. D., & Bahvnagri, N. P. (1989). Parents as managers of children's peer relationships. In D. Belle (Ed.), *Children's social networks and social supports.* New York: Wiley.

Parke, R. D., & Buriel, R. (1998). Socialization in the family: Ethnic and ecological perspectives. In W. Damon (Ed.), *Handbook of child psychology* (Vol. 3). New York: Wiley.

Parker, J. G., & Herrera, C. (1996). Interpersonal processes in friendship: A comparison of abused and nonabused children's experiences. *Developmental Psychology, 32,* 1025–1038.

Parker, J. G., & Seal, J. (1996). Forming, losing, renewing, and replacing friendships: Applying temporal parameters to the assessment of children's friendship experiences. *Child Development, 67,* 2248–2268.

Parritz, R. H. (1996). A descriptive analysis of toddler coping in challenging circumstances. *Infant Behavior and Development, 19,* 171–180.

Parten, M. (1932). Social participation among preschool children. *Journal of Abnormal and Social Psychology, 27,* 243–269.

Pascual-Leone, J. (1970). A mathematical model for the transition rule in Piaget's developmental stages. *Acta Psychologica, 32,* 301–345.

Patterson, C. J. (1992). Children of lesbian and gay parents. *Child Development, 63,* 1025–1042.

Patterson, G. R. (1980). Mothers: The unacknowledged victims. *Monographs of the Society for Research in Child Development, 45* (5, Serial No. 186).

Patterson, G. R. (1984). Microsocial process: A view from the boundary. In J. C. Masters & K. Yarkin-Levin (Eds.), *Boundary areas in social and developmental psychology.* New York: Academic Press.

Pearlman, M., & Ross, H. S. (1997). The benefits of parent intervention in children's disputes: An examination of concurrent changes in children's fighting styles. *Child Development, 68,* 690–700.

Pearson, J. L., Hunter, A. G., Ensminger, M. E., & Kellam, S. G. (1990). Black grandmothers in multigenerational households: Diversity in family structure and parenting involvement in the Woodlawn community. *Child Development, 61,* 434–442.

Pederson, D. M., & Wheeler, J. (1983). The Müller-Lyer illusion among Navajos. *Journal of Social Psychology, 121,* 3–6.

Pederson, D. R., Gleason, K. E., Moran, G., & Bento, S. (1998). Maternal attachment representations, maternal sensitivity, and the infant-mother attachment relationship. *Developmental Psychology, 34,* 925–933.

Pellegrini, A. D., & Smith, P. K. (1998). Physical activity play: The nature and function of a neglected aspect of play. *Child Development, 69,* 577–598.

Pennington, B. F., Groisser, D., & Welsh, M. C. (1993). Contrasting cognitive deficits in attention deficit hyperactivity disorder versus reading disability. *Developmental Psychology, 29,* 511–523.

Perfetti, C. A., & Curtis, M. E. (1986). Reading. In R. F. Dillon & R. J. Sternberg (Eds.), *Cognition and instruction.* Orlando, FL: Academic Press.

Peterson, C., & Rideout, R. (1998). Memory for medical emergencies experienced by 1- and 2-year-olds. *Developmental Psychology, 34,* 1059–1072.

Peterson, L. (1983). Role of donor competence, donor age, and peer presence on helping in an emergency. *Developmental Psychology, 19,* 873–880.

Peterson, L. (1989). Latchkey children's preparation for self-care: Overestimated, under rehearsed and unsafe. *Journal of Child Clinical Psychology, 18,* 36–43.

Petrie, R. H. (1991). Intrapartum fetal evaluation. In S. G. Gabbe, J. R. Niebyl, & J. L. Simpson (Eds.), *Obstetrics: Normal & problem pregnancies* (2nd ed.). New York: Churchill Livingstone.

Pettit, G. S., Bakshi, A., Dodge, K. A., & Coie, J. D. (1990). The emergence of social dominance in young boys' play groups: Developmental differences and behavioral correlates. *Developmental Psychology, 26,* 1017–1025.

Pettit, G. S., Bates, J. E., & Dodge, K. A. (1997). Supportive parenting, ecological context, and children's adjustment: A seven-year longitudinal study. *Child Development, 68,* 908–923.

Pettit, G. S., Bates, J. E., Dodge, K. A., & Meece, D. W. (1999). The impact of after-school peer contact on early adolescent externalizing problems is moderated by parental monitoring, perceived neighborhood safety, and prior adjustment. *Child Development, 70,* 768–778.

Pettito, L. A., & Marentette, P. F. (1991). Babbling in the manual mode: Evidence for the ontogeny of language. *Science, 251,* 1493–1496.

Phinney, J. (1989). Stage of ethnic identity in minority group adolescents. *Journal of Early Adolescence, 9,* 34–49.

Phinney, J. (1990). Ethnic identity in adolescents and adults. *Psychological Bulletin, 108,* 499–514.

Phinney, J. S. (1996). When we talk about American ethnic groups, what do we mean? *American Psychologist, 51,* 918–927.

Phinney, J. S., & Chavira, V. (1992). Ethnic identity and self-esteem: An exploratory longitudinal study. *Journal of Adolescence, 15,* 271–281.

Phinney, J. S., Cantu, C. L., & Kurtz, D. A. (1997). Ethnic and American identity as predictors of self-esteem among African American, Latino, and White adolescents. *Journal of Youth and Adolescence, 26,* 165–185.

Piaget, J. (1929). *The child's conception of the world.* New York: Harcourt, Brace.

Piaget, J., & Albertini, B. von. (1950–1952). Recherches sur le développement des perceptions: XI. L'illusion de Müller-Lyer. *Arch. Psycholog., Genève, 33,* 1–48.

Piaget, J., & Inhelder, B. (1956). *The child's conception of space.* Boston: Routledge & Kegan Paul.

Plomin, R. (1990). *Nature and nurture.* Pacific Grove, CA: Brooks/Cole.

Plomin, R., Fulker, D. W., Corley, R., & DeFries, J. C. (1997). Nature, nurture, and cognitive development from 1 to 16 years: A parent-offspring adoption study. *Psychological Science, 8,* 442–447.

Plomin, R., & Petrill, S. A. (1997). Genetics and intelligence: What's new? *Intelligence, 24,* 53–77.

Plomin, R., & Rowe, D. C. (1979). Genetic and environmental etiology of social behavior in infancy. *Developmental Psychology, 15,* 62–72.

Plomin, R., & Rutter, M. (1998). Child development, molecular genetics, and what to do with genes once they are found. *Child Development, 69,* 1223–1242.

Plumert, J. M., & Nichols-Whitehead, P. (1996). Parental scaffolding of young children's spatial communication. *Developmental Psychology, 32,* 523–532.

Pollitt, E. (1994). Poverty and child development: Relevance of research in developing countries to the United States. *Child Development, 65,* 283–295.

Porter, R. H., Makin, J. W., Davis, L. B., & Christensen, K. M. (1991). An assessment of the salient olfactory environment of formula-fed infants. *Physiology and Behavior, 50,* 907–911.

Potter, M. C. (1966). On perceptual recognition. In J. S. Bruner et al. (Eds.), *Studies in cognitive growth.* New York: Wiley.

Potter, M. C., Moryada, A., Abrams, I., & Noel, A. (1993). Word perception and misperception in context. *Journal of Experimental Psychology: Learning, Memory, and Cognition, 19,* 3–22.

Poulin-Dubois, D., Serbin, L. A., Kenyon, B., & Derbyshire, A. (1994). Infants' intermodal knowledge about gender. *Developmental Psychology, 30,* 436–442.

Poulson, C. L., Kymissis, E., Reeve, K.F., Andreatos, M., & Reeve, L. (1991). Generalized vocal imitation in infants. *Journal of Experimental Child Psychology, 51,* 267–279.

Povinelli, D. J., & Simon, B. B. (1998). Young children's understanding of briefly versus extremely delayed images of the self: Emergence of the autobiographical stance. *Developmental Psychology, 34,* 188–194.

Power, F. C., Higgins, A., & Kohlberg, L. (1989). *Lawrence Kohlberg's approach to moral education.* New York: Columbia University Press.

Powers, S. W., & Roberts, M. W. (1995). Simulation training with parents of oppositional children: Preliminary findings. *Journal of Clinical Child Psychology, 24,* 89–97.

Powlishta, K., Serbin, L. A., Doyle, A., & White, D. R. (1994). Gender, ethnic, and body type biases: The generality of prejudice in childhood. *Developmental Psychology, 30,* 526–536.

Pozzi, S., Healy, L., & Hoyles, C. (1993). Learning and interaction in groups with computers: When do ability and gender matter? *Social Development, 2,* 222–241.

Priel, B., & deSchonen, S. (1986). Self-recognition: A study of a population without mirrors. *Journal of Experimental Child Psychology, 41,* 237–250.

Quas, J. A., Goodman, G. S., Bidrose, S., Pipe, M., Craw, S., & Ablin, D. S. (1999). Emotion and memory: Children's long-term remembering, forgetting, and suggestibility. *Journal of Experimental Child Psychology, 72,* 235–270.

Rakic, P. (1995). Corticogenesis in human and nonhuman primates. In M. S. Gazzaniga (Ed.), *The cognitive neurosciences.* Cambridge, MA: MIT Press.

Ramey, C. T., & Campbell, F. A. (1991). Poverty, early childhood education, and academic competence: The Abecedarian experiment. In A. Huston (Ed.), *Children reared in poverty.* New York: Cambridge University Press.

Ramey, C. T. & Ramey, S. L. (1990). Intensive educational intervention for children of poverty. *Intelligence, 14,* 1–9.

Ramsey, P. G. (1995). Growing up with the contradictions of race and class. *Young Children, 50,* 18–22.

Rapport, M. D. (1995). Attention-deficit hyperactivity disorder. In M. Hersen & R. T. Ammerman (Eds.), *Advanced abnormal child psychology.* Hillsdale, NJ: Erlbaum.

Rathunde, K. R., & Csikszentmihalyi, M. (1993). Undivided interest and the growth of talent: A longitudinal study of adolescents. *Journal of Youth and Adolescence, 22,* 385–405.

Reese, E., & Cox, A. (1999). Quality of adult book reading affects children's emergent literacy. *Developmental Psychology, 35,* 20–28.

Reich, P. A. (1986). *Language development.* Englewood Cliffs, NJ: Prentice-Hall.

Reid, D. H., Wilson, P. G., & Faw, G. D. (1991). Teaching self-help skills. In J. L. Matson & J. A. Mulick (Eds.), *Handbook of mental retardation* (2nd ed.). New York: Pergamon.

Reimer, M. S. (1996). "Sinking into the ground": The development and consequences of shame in adolescence. *Developmental Review, 16,* 321–363.

Reis, S. M., & Renzulli, J. S. (1995). Gifted and talented students. In M. C. Wang, M. C. Reynolds, & H. J. Walberg (Eds.), *Handbook of special and remedial education: Research and practice* (2nd ed.). Oxford, England:Elsevier, Science.

Repacholi, B. M. (1998). Infants' use of attentional cues to identify the referent of another person's emotional expression. *Developmental Psychology, 34,* 1017–1025.

Reubens, B., Harrison, J., & Kupp, K. (1981). *The youth labor force, 1945–1995: A cross-national analysis.* Totowa, NJ: Allanheld, Osmun.

Reynolds, A. J., & Temple, J. A. (1998). Extended early childhood intervention and school achievement: Age thirteen findings from the Chicago longitudinal study. *Child Development, 69,* 231–246.

Ricciuti, H. N. (1993). Nutrition and mental development. *Current Directions in Psychological Science, 2,* 43–46.

Rice, M. L., Huston, A. C., Truglio, R., & Wright, J. (1990). Words from "Sesame Street": Learning vocabulary while viewing. *Developmental Psychology, 26,* 421–428.

Richardson, G. A. (1998). Prenatal cocaine exposure. A longitudinal study of development. *Annals of the New York Academy of Sciences, 846,* 144–152.

Roberton, M. A., & Halverson, L. E. (1988). The development of locomotor coordination: Longitudinal change and invariance. *Journal of Motor Behavior, 20,* 197–241.

Roberts, J. E., Burchinal, M., & Durham, M. (1999). Parents' report of vocabulary and grammatical development of African American preschoolers: Child and environmental associations. *Child Development, 70,* 92–106.

Roberts, W., & Strayer, J. (1996). Empathy, emotional expressiveness, and prosocial behavior. *Child Development, 67,* 449–470.

Robinson, A., & Clinkenbeard, P. R. (1998). Giftedness: An exceptionality examined. *Annual Review of Psychology, 49,* 117–139.

Robinson, B. E., Rowland, B. H., & Coleman, M. (1986). *Latchkey kids: Unlocking doors for children and their families.* Lexington MA: Lexington Books, Heath.

Robinson, E. J., Champion, H., & Mitchell, P. (1999). Children's ability to infer utterance veracity from speaker informedness. *Developmental Psychology, 35,* 535–546.

Rodgers, J. L., & Rowe, D. C. (1993). Social contagion and adolescent sexual behavior: A developmental EMOSA model. *Psychological Review, 100,* 479–510.

Roffwarg, H. P., Muzio, J. N., & Dement, W. C. (1966). Ontogenetic development of the human sleep-dream cycle. *Science, 152,* 604–619.

Rogoff, B., Mistry, J., Goncu, A., & Mosier, C. (1993). Guided participation in cultural activity by toddlers and caregivers. *Monographs of the Society for Research in Child Development, 58* (Serial No. 236).

Rooks, J. P., Weatherby, N. L., Ernst, E. K. M., Stapleton, S., Rosen, D., & Rosenfield, A. (1989). Outcomes of care in birth centers: The national birth center study. *New England Journal of Medicine, 321,* 1804–1811.

Roopnarine, J. (1992). Father-child play in India. In K. MacDonald (Ed.), *Parent-child play.* Albany: State University of New York Press.

Rose, A. J., & Asher, S. R. (1999). Children's goals and strategies in response to conflicts within a friendship. *Developmental Psychology, 35,* 69–79.

Rose, S. A., Feldman, J. F., Futterweit, L. R., & Jankowski, J. J. (1997). Continuity in visual recognition memory: Infancy to 11 years. *Intelligence, 24,* 381–392.

Rosen, K. S., & Burke, P. B. (1999). Multiple attachment relationships within families: Mothers and fathers with two young children. *Developmental Psychology, 35,* 436–444.

Rosengren, K. S., Gelman, S. A., Kalish, C., & McCormick, M. (1991) As time goes by: Children's early understanding of growth in animals. *Child Development, 62,* 1302–1320.

Rosenthal, D. A., & Feldman, S. S. (1992). The relationship between parenting behaviour and ethnic identity in Chinese-American and Chinese-Australian adolescents. *International Journal of Psychology, 27,* 19–31.

Rosenthal, R., & Vandell, D. L. (1996). Quality of care at school-aged child-care programs: Regulatable features, observed experiences, child perspectives, and parent perspectives. *Child Development, 67,* 2434–2445.

Rostenstein, D., & Oster, H. (1997). Differential facial responses to four basic tastes in newborns. In P. Ekman & E. L. Rosenberg (Eds), *What the face reveals: Basic and applied studies of spontaneous expression using the Facial Action Coding System (FACS).* New York: Oxford University Press.

Rotenberg, K. J., & Mayer, E. V. (1990). Delay of gratification in native and white children: A cross-cultural comparison. *International Journal of Behavioral Development, 13,* 23–30.

Rothbaum, F., & Weisz, J. R. (1994). Parental caregiving and child externalizing behavior in nonclinical samples: A meta-analysis. *Psychological Bulletin, 116,* 55–74.

Rotto, P. C., & Kratochwill, T. R. (1994). Behavioral consultation with parents: Using competency-based training to modify child noncompliance. *School Psychology Review, 23,* 669–693.

Rovee-Collier, C. (1987). Learning and memory in infancy. In J. D. Osofsky (Ed.), *Handbook of infant development* (2nd ed.). New York: Wiley.

Rovee-Collier, C. (1997). Dissociations in infant memory: Rethinking the development of implicit and explicit memory. *Psychological Review, 104,* 467–498.

Rovee-Collier, C. (1999). The development of infant memory. *Current Directions in Psychological Science, 8,* 80–85.

Rowe, D. C. (1994). No more than skin deep. *American Psychologist, 49,* 215–216.

Rowe, D. C., Almeida, D. M., & Jacobson, K. C. (1999). School context and genetic influences on aggression in adolescence. *Psychological Science, 10,* 277–280.

Rubin, K. H., Bukowski, W., & Parker, J. G. (1998). Peer interactions, relationships, and groups. In W. Damon (Ed.), *Handbook of child psychology* (Vol. 3). New York: Wiley.

Ruble, D. N., Boggiano, A. D., Feldman, N. S., & Loebl, N. H. (1980). Developmental analysis of the role of social comparision in self-evaluation. *Developmental Psychology, 16,* 105–115.

Ruble, T. L. (1983). Sex stereotypes: Issues of changes in the 1970s. *Sex Roles, 9,* 397–402.

Rueter, M. A., & Conger, R. D. (1998). Reciprocal influences between parenting and adolescent problem-solving behavior. *Developmental Psychology, 34,* 1470–1482.

Ruff, H. A., Capozzoli, M., & Weissberg, R. (1998). Age, individuality, and context as factors in sustained visual attention during the preschool years. *Developmental Psychology, 34,* 454–464.

Rumelhart, D. E., & McClelland, J. L. (1981). Interactive processing through spreading activation. In A. M. Lesgold & C. A. Perfetti (Eds.), *Interactive processes in reading.* Hillsdale, NJ: Erlbaum.

Rutter, M., & Garmezy, N. (1983). Developmental psychopathology. In P. H. Mussen (Ed.), *Handbook of child psychology* (Vol. 4). New York: Wiley.

Rymer, R. (1993). *Genie.* New York: HarperCollins.

Saffran, J. R., Aslin, R. N., & Newport, E. L. (1996). Statistical learning by 8-month-old infants. *Science, 274,* 1926–1928.

Sagi, A., van IJzendoorn, M. H., Aviezer, O., Donnell, F., & Mayseless, O. (1994). Sleeping out of home in a kibbutz communal arrangement: It makes a difference for infant-mother attachment. *Child Development, 65,* 992–1004.

Sakamoto, A. (1994). Video game use and the development of sociocognitive abilities in children: Three surveys of elementary school students. *Journal of Applied Social Psychology, 24,* 21–42.

Savage-Rumbaugh, E. S., Murphy, J., Sevcik, R. A., Brakke, K. E., Williams, S. L., & Rumbaugh, D. M. (1993). Language comprehension in ape and child. *Monographs of the Society for Research in Child Development, 58* (3–4, Serial No. 233).

Savin-Williams, R. C., & Demo, D. H. (1984). Developmental change and stability in adolescent self-concept. *Developmental Psychology, 20,* 1100–1110.

Saxe, G. B. (1988). Candy selling and math learning. *Educational Researcher, 17,* 14–21.

Scarr, S. (1992). Developmental theories for the 1990s: Development and individual differences. *Child Development, 63,* 1–19.

Scarr, S., & McCartney, K. (1983). How people make their own environments: A theory of genotype environment effects. *Child Development, 54,* 424–435.

Schaal, B., Marlier, L., & Soussignan, R. (1998). Olfactory function in the human fetus: Evidence from selective neonatal responsiveness to the odor of amniotic fluid. *Behavioral Neuroscience, 112,* 1438–1449.

Schmidt, F. L., & Hunter, J. E. (1998). The validity and utility of selection methods in personnel psychology: Practical and theoretical implications of 85 years of research findings. *Psychological Bulletin, 124,* 262–274.

Schneider, M. L. (1992). The effect of mild stress during pregnancy on birthweight and neuromotor maturation in rhesus monkey infants

(*Macaca mulatta*). *Infant Behavior and Development, 15,* 389–403.

Schneider, W., & Bjorklund, D. F. (1998). Memory. In W. Damon (Ed.), *Handbook of child psychology* (Vol. 2). New York: Wiley.

Schnorr, T. M., Grajewski, B. A., Hornung, R. W., Thun, M. J., Egeland, G. M., Murray, W. E., Conover, D. L., & Halperin, W. E. (1991). Video display terminals and the risk of spontaneous abortion. *New England Journal of Medicine, 324,* 727–733.

Schramm, W., Lyle, J., & Parker, E. B. (1961). *Television in the lives of our children.* Stanford, CA: Stanford University Press.

Schwartz, D., Dodge, K. A., Pettit, G. S., & Bates, J. E. (1997). The early socialization of aggressive victims of bullying. *Child Development, 68,* 665–675.

Scott, W. A., Scott, R., & McCabe, M. (1991). Family relationships and children's personality: A cross-cultural, cross-source comparison. *British Journal of Social Psychology, 30,* 1–20.

Sears, R. R. (1975). Your ancients revisited: A history of child development. In E. M. Hetherington (Ed.), *Review of child development research* (Vol. 5). Chicago: University of Chicago Press.

Secada, W. G., Fennema, E., & Adajian, L. B. (Eds.). (1995). *New directions for equity in mathematics education.* New York: Cambridge University Press.

Segall, M. H., Dasen, P. R., Berry, J. W., & Poortinga, Y. (1990). *Human behavior in global perspective.* New York: Pergamon.

Seidenberg, M. S., & McClelland, J. L. (1989). A distributed, developmental model of word recognition and naming. *Psychological Review, 96,* 523–568.

Seidman, E., Allen, L., Aber, J. L., Mitchell, C., & Feinman, J. (1994). The impact of school transitions in early adolescence on the self-system and perceived social context of poor urban youth. *Child Development, 65,* 507–522.

Seifer, R., Schiller, M., Sameroff, A. J., Resnick, S., & Riordan, K. (1996). Attachment, maternal sensitivity, and infant temperament during the first year of life. *Developmental Psychology, 32,* 12–25.

Selman, R. L. (1980). *The growth of interpersonal understanding: Developmental and clinical analyses.* New York: Academic Press.

Selman, R. L. (1981). The child as a friendship philosopher: A case study in the growth of interpersonal understanding. In S. R. Asher & J. M. Gottman (Eds.), *The development of children's friendships.* Cambridge, England: Cambridge University Press.

Selman, R. L., & Byrne, D F. (1974). A structural-developmental analysis of levels of role-taking in middle childhood. *Child Development, 45,* 803–806.

Sénéchal, M., Thomas, E., & Monker, J. (1995). Individual differences in 4-year-old children's acquisition of vocabulary during storybook reading. *Journal of Educational Psychology, 87,* 218–229.

Serbin, L. A., Powlishta, K. K. & Gulko, J. (1993). The development of sex typing in middle childhood. *Monographs of the Society for Research in Child Development, 58* (Serial no. 232).

Serdula, M.K., Ivery, D., Coates, R.J., Freedman, D.S., Williamson, D.F., & Byers, T. (1993). Do obese children become obese adults? A review of the literature. *Preventive Medicine, 22,* 167–177.

Seyfarth, R., & Cheney, D. (1996). Inside the mind of a monkey. In M. Bekoff & D. Jamieson (Eds.), *Readings in animal cognition.* Cambridge, MA: MIT Press.

Shanahan, M. J., Elder, G. H., Burchinal, M., & Conger, R. D. (1996a). Adolescent earnings and relationships with parents: The work-family nexus in urban and rural ecologies. In J. T. Mortimer & M. D. Finch (Eds.), *Adolescents, work, and family: An intergenerational developmental analysis.* Thousand Oaks, CA: Sage.

Shanahan, M. J., Elder, G. H., Burchinal, M., & Conger, R. D. (1996b). Adolescent paid labor and relationships with parents: Early work-family linkages. *Child Development, 67,* 2183–2200.

Sharpe, R.M., & Skakkebaek, N.E. (1993). Are oestrogens involved in falling sperm counts and disorders of the male reproductive tract? *Lancet, 341,* 1392–1395.

Shatz, M. (1983). Communication. In P. H. Mussen (Ed.), *Handbook of child psychology* (Vol. 3). New York: Wiley.

Shatz, M., & Gelman, R. (1973). The development of communication skills: Modifications in the speech of young children as a function of listener. *Monographs of the Society for Research in Child Development, 38*(5, Serial No. 152).

Shaw, D. S., Winslow, E. B., & Flanagan, C. (1999). A prospective study of the effects of marital status and family relations on young children's adjustment among African American and European American families. *Child Development, 70,* 742–755.

Shaw, G. M., Schaffer, D., Velie, E. M., Morland, K., & Harris, J. A. (1995). Periconceptional vitamin use, dietary folate, and the occurrence of neural tube defects. *Epidemiology, 6,* 219–226.

Shelov, S. P. (1993). *Caring for your baby and young child: Birth to age 5.* New York: Bantam.

Sherif, M., Harvey, O. J., White, B. J., Hood, W. R., & Sherif, C. W. (1961). *Intergroup conflict and cooperation.* Norman, OK: The University Book Exchange.

Sherrod, K. B., O'Connor, S., Vietze, P. M., & Altemeier, W. A. III (1984). Child health and maltreatment. *Child Development, 55,* 1174–1183.

Shiner, R. L. (1998). How shall we speak of children's personalities in middle childhood? A preliminary taxonomy. *Psychological Bulletin, 124,* 308–332.

Shirley, M. M. (1931). The first two years: A study of twenty-five babies: Vol. 1. *Postural and locomotor development.* Westport, CT: Greenwood Press.

Shiwach, R. (1994). Psychopathology in Huntington's disease patients. *Acta Psychiatrica Scandinavica, 90,* 241–246.

Shoda, Y., Mischel, W., & Peake, P. K. (1990). Predicting adolescent cognitive and self-regulatory competencies from preschool delay of gratification: Identifying diagnostic conditions. *Developmental Psychology, 26,* 978–986.

Shrager, J., & Siegler, R. S. (1998). SCADS: A model of children's strategy choices and strategy discoveries. *Psychological Science, 9,* 405–410.

Shuter-Dyson, R. (1982). Musical ability. In D. Deutsch (Ed.), *The psychology of music.* New York: Academic Press.

Shwe, H. I., & Markman, E. M. (1997). Young children's appreciation of the mental impact of their communicative signals. *Developmental Psychology, 33,* 630–636.

Siddiqui, A. (1995). Object size as a determinant of grasping in infancy. *Journal of Genetic Psychology, 156,* 345–358.

Siegal, M., & Peterson, C. C. (1998). Preschoolers' understanding of lies and innocent and negligent mistakes. *Developmental Psychology, 34,* 332–341.

Siegel, L. S. (1994). Working memory and reading: A life-span perspective. *International Journal of Behavioral Development, 17,* 109–124.

Siegler, R. S. (1981). Developmental sequences within and between concepts. *Monographs of the Society for Research in Child Development, 46* (Serial No. 189).

Siegler, R. S. (1986). Unities in strategy choices across domains. In M. Perlmutter (Ed.), *Minnesota symposia on child development* (Vol. 19). Hillsdale, NJ: Erlbaum.

Siegler, R. S. (1988). Strategy choice procedures and the development of multiplication skill. *Journal of Experimental Psychology: General, 117,* 258–278.

Siegler, R. S. (1989). Mechanisms of cognitive development. *Annual Review of Psychology, 40,* 353–379.

Siegler, R. S. (1998). *Children's thinking* (3rd ed). Upper Saddle River, NJ: Prentice-Hall.

Siegler, R. S., & Jenkins, E. (1989). *How children discover new strategies.* Hillsdale, NJ: Erlbaum.

Siegler, R. S., & Robinson, M. (1982). The development of numerical understandings. In H. W. Reese & L. P. Lipsitt (Eds.), *Advances in child development and behavior* (Vol. 16). New York: Academic Press.

Siegler, R. S., & Shrager, J. (1984). Strategy choices in addition and subtraction: How do children know what to do? In C. Sophian (Ed.), *Origins of cognitive skills.* Hillsdale, NJ: Erlbaum.

Signorella, M. L., Bigler, R. S., & Liben, L. S. (1993). Developmental differences in children's gender schemata about others: A meta-analytic review. Early gender-role development. *Developmental Review, 13,* 147–183.

Signorielli, N., & Lears, M. (1992). Children, television, and conceptions about chores: Attitudes and behaviors. *Sex Roles, 27,* 157–170.

Silverman, I. W., & Ragusa, D. M. (1990). Child and maternal correlates of impulse control in 24-month-old children. *Genetic, Social, and General Psychology Monographs, 116,* 435–473.

Silverman, W. K., La Greca, A. M., & Wasserstein, S. (1995). What do children worry about? Worries and their relations to anxiety. *Child Development, 66,* 671–686.

Simmons, R., & Blyth, D. (1987). *Moving into adolescence.* New York: Aldine de Gruyter.

Simons, D. J., & Keil, F. C. (1995). An abstract to concrete shift in the development of biological thought: The insides story. *Cognition, 56,* 129–163.

Simons, R. L., Whitbeck, L. B., Conger, R. D., & Chyi-In, W. (1991). Intergenerational transmission of harsh parenting. *Developmental Psychology, 27,* 159–171.

Simpson, E. L. (1974). Moral development research: A case study of scientific cultural bias. *Human Development, 17,* 81–106.

Singer, J. D., Fuller, B., Keiley, M. K., & Wolf, A. (1998). Early child-care selection: Variation by geographic location, maternal characteristics, and family structure. *Developmental Psychology, 34,* 1129–1144.

Skinner, B. F. (1957). *Verbal behavior.* New York: Appleton-Century-Crofts.

Slate, J. R., Jones, C. H., & Dawson, P. (1993). Academic skills of high school students as a function of grade, gender, and academic track. *High School Journal, 76,* 245–251.

Slobin, D. I. (1985). Crosslinguistic evidence for the language-making capacity. In D. I. Slobin (Ed.), *The crosslinguistic study of language acquisition: Vol. 2: Theoretical issues.* Hillsdale, NJ: Erlbaum.

Smetana, J. G., & Braeges, J. L. (1990). The development of toddlers' moral and conventional judgments. *Merrill-Palmer Quarterly, 36,* 329–346.

Smetana, J. G., Killen, M., & Turiel, E. (1991). Children's reasoning about interpersonal and moral conflicts. *Child Development, 62,* 629–644.

Smith, L. B., Quittner, A. L, Osberger, M. J., & Miyamoto, R. (1998). Audition and visual attention: The developmental trajectory in deaf and hearing populations. *Developmental Psychology, 34,* 840–850.

Smith, L. B., Thelen, E., Titzer, R., & McLin, D. (1999). Knowing in the context of acting: The task dynamics of the A-not-B error. *Psychological Review, 106,* 235–260.

Snarey, J. R. (1985). Cross-cultural universality of social-moral development: A critical review of Kohlbergian research. *Psychological Bulletin, 97,* 202–232.

Snedeker, B. (1982). *Hard knocks: Preparing youth for work.* Baltimore, MD: Johns Hopkins University Press.

Snow, C. W. (1998). *Infant development* (2nd ed.). Upper Saddle River, NJ: Prentice Hall.

Snow, M. E., Jacklin, C. N., & Maccoby, E. E. (1983). Sex-of-child differences in father-child interaction at one year of age. *Child Development, 54,* 227–232.

Sokolov, J. L. (1993). A local contingency analysis of the fine-tuning hypothesis. *Developmental Psychology, 29,* 1008–1023.

Solley, C. M. (1966). Affective processes in perceptual development. In A. H. Kidd & J. L. Rivoire (Eds.), *Perceptual development in children.* New York: International Universities Press.

Solomon, G.E. A., Johnson, S.C., Zaitchik, D., & Carey, S. (1996). Like father, like son: Young children's understanding of how and why offspring resemble their parents. *Child Development, 67,* 151–171.

Sophian, C., & Wellman, H. M. (1987). The development of indirect search strategies. *British Journal of Developmental Psychology, 5,* 9–18.

Spearman, C. (1904). "General intelligence" objectively determined and measured. *American Journal of Psychology, 15,* 201–293.

Spelke, E. S. (1994). Initial knowledge: Six suggestions. *Cognition, 50,* 431–445.

Spence, J. T. (1985). Achievement American style: The rewards and costs of individualism. *American Psychologist, 40,* 1285–1295.

Sporkin, E., Wagner, J., & Tomashof, C. (1992, February). A terrible hunger. *People,* 92–98.

Springer, K., & Keil, F. C. (1991). Early differentiation of causal mechanisms appropriate to biological and nonbiological kinds. *Child Development, 62,* 767–781.

Springer, S. P., & Deutsch, G. (1998). *Left brain, right brain: Perspectives from cognitive neuroscience* (5th ed.). New York: Freeman.

Sroufe, L. A., & Fleeson, J. (1986). Attachment and the construction of relationships. In W. W. Hartup & Z. Rubin (Eds.), *Relationships and development.* Hillsdale, NJ: Erlbaum.

Sroufe, L. A., & Waters, E. (1976). The ontogenesis of smiling and laughter: A perspective on the organization of development in infancy. *Psychological Review, 83,* 173–189.

Sroufe, L. A., & Wunsch, J. P. (1972). The development of laughter in the first year of life. *Child Development, 43,* 1324–1344.

St. James-Roberts, I., & Plewis, I. (1996). Individual differences, daily fluctuations, and developmental changes in amounts of infant waking, fussing, crying, feeding, and sleeping. *Child Development, 67,* 2527–2450.

Stalikas, A., & Gavaki, E. (1995). The importance of ethnic identity: Self-esteem and academic achievement of second-generation Greeks in secondary school. *Canadian Journal of School Psychology, 11,* 1–9.

Stanovich, K. E. (1993). Dysrationalia: A new specific learning disability. *Journal of Learning Disabilities, 26,* 501–515.

Stattin, H., & Magnusson, D. (1989). The role of early aggressive behavior in the frequency, seriousness, and types of later crime. *Journal of Consulting and Clinical Psychology, 57,* 710–718.

Steelman, J. D. (1994). Revision strategies employed by middle level students using computers. *Journal of Educational Computing Research, 11,* 141–152.

Steinberg, L. (1990). Autonomy, conflict, and harmony in the family relationship. In S. S. Feldman & G. R. Elliott (Eds.), *At the threshold: The developing adolescent.* Cambridge, MA: Harvard University Press.

Steinberg, L., & Dornbusch, S. M. (1991). Negative correlates of part-time employment during adolescence: Replication and elaboration. *Developmental Psychology, 27,* 304–313.

Steinberg, L., Fegley, S., & Dornbusch, S. M. (1993). Negative impact of part-time work on adolescent adjustment: Evidence from a longitudinal study. *Developmental Psychology, 29,* 171–180.

Steinberg, L., Lamborn, S. D., Dornbusch, S. M., & Darling, N. (1992). Impact of parenting practices on adolescent achievement: Authoritative parenting, school involvement, and encouragement to succeed. *Child Development, 63,* 1266–1281.

Stern, M., & Karraker, K. H. (1989). Sex stereotyping of infants: A review of gender labeling studies. *Sex Roles, 20,* 501–522.

Sternberg, R. J. (1977). *Intelligence, information processing, and analogical reasoning.* Hillsdale, NJ: Erlbaum.

Sternberg, C. R., & Campos, J. (1990). The development of anger expressions in infancy. In N. Stein, B. Leventhal, & T. Trabasso (Eds.), *Psychological and biological approaches to emotion.* Hillsdale, NJ: Erlbaum.

Sternberg, R. J., & Kaufman, J. C., (1998). Human abilities. *Annual Review of Psychology, 49,* 479–502.

Sternberg, R. J. (1985). *Beyond IQ: A triarchic theory of human intelligence.* Cambridge: Cambridge University Press.

Stevenson, H. W., & Lee, S. (1990). Contexts of achievement. *Monographs of the Society for Research in Child Development, 55* (Serial No. 221).

Stevenson, H. W., Parker, T., Wilkinson, A., Hegion, A., & Fish, E. (1976). Longitudinal study of individual differences in cognitive development and scholastic achievement. *Journal of Educational Psychology, 68,* 377–400.

Stevenson, H. W., & Stigler, J. W. (1992). *The learning gap.* New York: Summit Books.

Stevenson, M. R., & Black, K. N. (1995). *How divorce affects offspring: A research approach.* Madison, WI: Brown & Benchmark.

Stewart, L., & Pascual-Leone, J. (1992). Mental capacity constraints and the development of moral reasoning. *Journal of Experimental Child Psychology, 54,* 251–287.

Stewart, R. B., Mobley, L. A., Van Tuyl, S. S., & Salvador, W. A. (1987). The firstborns' adjustment to the birth of a sibling: A longitudinal assessment. *Child Development, 58,* 341–355.

Stice, E., & Barrera, M., Jr. (1995). A longitudinal examination of the reciprocal relations between perceived parenting and adolescents' substance use and externalizing behaviors. *Developmental Psychology, 31,* 322–334.

Stifter, C. A., & Fox, N. A. (1990). Infant reactivity: Physiological correlates of newborn and 5-month temperament. *Developmental Psychology, 26,* 582–588.

Stifter, C. A., Spinrad, T. L., & Braungart-Rieker, J. M. (1999). Toward a developmental model of child compliance: The role of emotion regulation in infancy. *Child Development, 70,* 21–32.

Stiles, J. (1998). The effects of early focal brain injury on lateralization of cognitive function. *Current Directions in Psychological Science, 7,* 21–26.

Stiles, J., Trauner, D., Engel, M., & Nass, R. (1997). The development of drawing in children with congenital focal brain injury: Evidence for limited functional recovery. *Neuropsychologia, 35,* 299–312.

Stiles, J., Bates, E. A., Thal, D., Trauner, D., & Reilly, J. (in press). Linguistic, cognitive, and affective development in children with pre- and perinatal focal brain injury: A ten-year overview from the San Diego Longitudinal Project. In C. Rovee-Collier (Ed.), *Advances in infancy research.* Norwood, NJ: Ablex.

Stormshak, E. A., Bellanti, C. J., Bierman, K. L., & the Conduct Problems Prevention Research Group (1996). The quality of sibling relationships and the development of social competence and behavioral control in aggressive children. *Developmental Psychology, 32,* 79–89.

Stormshak, E. A., Bierman, K. L., Bruschi, C., Dodge, K. A., Coie, J. D., & the Conduct Problems Prevention Research Group. (1999). The relation between behavior problems and peer

preference in different classroom contexts. *Child Development, 70,* 169–182.

Strauss, M. S., & Curtis, L. E. (1984). Development of numerical concepts in infancy. In C. Sophian (Ed.), *Origins of cognitive skills.* Hillsdale, NJ: Erlbaum.

Strayer, J., & Schroeder, M. (1989). Children's helping strategies: Influences of emotion, empathy, and age. In N. Eisenberg (Ed.), *New directions for child development: Empathy and related emotional responses* (Vol. 44). San Francisco: Jossey-Bass.

Streissguth, A. P., Barr, H. M., Sampson, P.D., & Bookstein, F. L. (1994). Prenatal alcohol and offspring development: The first fourteen years. *Drugs & Alcohol Dependence, 36,* 89–99.

Strober, M. (1995). Family-genetic perspectives on anorexia nervosa and bulimia nervosa. In K. Brownell & C. G. Fairburn (Eds.), *Eating disorders and obesity: A comprehensive handbook.* New York: Guilford Press.

Stunkard, A. J., Sorensen, T. I. A., Hanis, C., Teasdale, T. W., Chakraborty, R., Schull, W. J., & Schulsinger, F. (1986). An adoption study of human obesity. *New England Journal of Medicine, 314,* 193–198.

Sullivan, L. W. (1987). The risks of the sickle-cell trait: Caution and common sense. *New England Journal of Medicine, 317,* 830–831.

Sullivan, S. A., & Birch, L. L. (1990). Pass the sugar, pass the salt: Experience dictates preference. *Developmental Psychology, 26,* 546–551.

Super, C. M. (1981). Cross-cultural research on infancy. In H. C. Triandis & A. Heron (Eds.), *Handbook of cross-cultural psychology, Vol. 4: Developmental psychology.* Boston: Allyn & Bacon.

Super, C. M., Herrera, M. G., & Mora, J. O. (1990). Long-term effects of food supplementation and psychosocial intervention on the physical growth of Colombian infants at risk of malnutrition. *Child Development, 61,* 29–49.

Super, D. E. (1980). A life span, life space approach to career development. *Journal of Vocational Behavior, 16,* 282–298.

Super, D. E. (1976). *Career education and the meanings of work.* Washington, DC: U. S. Offices of Education.

Swarr, A. E., & Richards, M. H. (1996). Longitudinal effects of adolescent girls' pubertal development, perceptions of pubertal timing, and parental relations in eating problems. *Developmental Psychology, 32,* 636–646.

Szkrybalo, J., & Ruble, D. N. (1999). "God made me a girl": Sex-category constancy judgments and explanations revisited. *Developmental Psychology, 35,* 392–402.

Tager-Flusberg, H. (1993). Putting words together: Morphology and syntax in the preschool years. In J. Berko Gleason (Ed.), *The development of language* (3rd ed.). New York: Macmillan.

Tamis-LeMonda, C. S., & Bornstein, M. H. (1996). Variation in children's exploratory, nonsymbolic, and symbolic play: An explanatory multidimensional framework. In C. Rovee-Collier & L. P. Lipsitt (Eds.), *Advances in infancy research* (Vol. 10). Norwood, NJ: Ablex.

Tanner, J. M. (1970). Physical growth. In P. H. Bussen (Ed.), *Carmichael's manual of child psychology* (3rd ed.). New York: Wiley.

Tanner, J. M. (1990). *Fetus into man: Physical growth from conception to maturity* (2nd ed.) Cambridge, MA: Harvard University Press.

Taylor, M. G. (1996). The development of children's beliefs about social and biological aspects of gender differences. *Child Development, 67,* 1555–1571.

Taylor, M., Cartwright, B. S., & Carlson, S. M. (1993). A developmental investigation of children's imaginary companions. *Developmental Review, 29,* 276–285.

Taylor, R., Casten, R., Flickinger, S. M., Roberts, D., & Fulmore, C. D. (1994). Explaining the school performance of African-American adolescents. *Journal of Research on Adolescence, 4,* 21–44.

Taylor, R. D., & Roberts, D. (1995). Kinship support and maternal and adolescent well-being in economically disadvantaged African-American families. *Child Development, 66,* 1585–1597.

Teller, D. Y., & Bornstein, M. H. (1987). Infant color vision and color perception. In P. Salapatek & L. Cohen (Eds.), *Handbook of infant perception* (Vol. 1.) Orlando, FL: Academic Press.

Thelen, E., & Smith, L. B. (1998). Dynamic systems theories. In W. Damon (Ed.), *Handbook of Child Psychology* (Vol. 1). New York: Wiley.

Thelen, E., & Ulrich, B. D. (1991). Hidden skills. *Monographs of the Society for Research in Child Development, 56* (Serial No. 223).

Thelen, E., Ulrich, B. D., & Jensen, J. L. (1989). The developmental origins of locomotion. In M. H. Woollacott & A. Shumway-Cook (Eds.), *Development of posture and gait across the life span.* Columbia, SC: University of South Carolina Press.

Thomas, A., Chess, S., & Birch, H. G. (1968). *Temperament and behavior disorders in children.* New York: New York University Press.

Thomas, H., & Kail, R. (1991). Sex differences in the speed of mental rotation and the X-linked genetic hypothesis. *Intelligence, 15,* 17–32.

Thomas, J. R., & French, K. E. (1985). Gender differences across age in motor performance: A meta-analysis. *Psychological Bulletin, 98,* 260–282.

Thompson, G. G. (1952). *Child psychology.* Boston: Houghton Mifflin.

Thompson, R. A., & Limber, S. (1991). "Social anxiety" in infancy: Stranger wariness and separation distress. In H. Leitenberg (Ed.), *Handbook of social and evaluation anxiety.* New York: Plenum.

Thurstone, L. L., & Thurstone, T. G. (1941). Factorial studies of intelligence. *Psychometric Monograph,* No. 2.

Tincoff, R., & Jusczyk, P. W. (1999). Some beginnings of word comprehension in 6-month-olds. *Psychological Science, 10,* 172–175.

Tisak, M. (1993). Preschool children's judgements of moral and personal events involving physical harm and property damage. *Merrill Palmer Quarterly, 39,* 375–390.

Toda, S., & Fogel, A. (1993). Infant response to the still-face situation at 3 and 6 months. *Developmental Psychology, 29,* 532–538.

Treboux, D., & Busch-Rossnagel, N. A. (1990). Social network influence on adolescent sexual attitudes and behaviors. *Journal of Adolescent Research, 5,* 175–189.

Trickett, P. K., & Kuczynski, L. (1986). Children's misbehaviors and parental discipline strategies in abusive and nonabusive families. *Developmental Psychology, 22,* 115–123.

Trickett, P. K., Aber, J. L., Carlson, V., & Cicchetti, D. (1991). Relationship of socioeconomic status to the etiology and developmental sequelae of physical child abuse. *Developmental Psychology, 27,* 148–158.

Trickett, P. K., & McBride-Chang, C. (1995). The developmental impact of different forms of child abuse and neglect. *Developmental Review, 15,* 311–337.

U. S. Bureau of the Census. (1994). *Marital status and living arrangements: March 1993.* Washington, DC: U. S. Government Printing Office.

U. S. Bureau of the Census. (1995). *Statistical abstract of the United States* (115th ed.). Washington, DC: U. S. Government Printing Office.

U. S. Department of Health and Human Services. (1995). *Vital statistics of the United States, 1992.* Washington, DC: U.S. Government Printing Office.

Urberg, K. A., Değirmencioğlu, S. M., & Pilgrim, C. (1997). Close friend and group influence on adolescent cigarette smoking and alcohol use. *Developmental Psychology, 33,* 834–844.

Valenzuela, M. (1997). Maternal sensitivity in a developing society: The context of urban poverty and infant chronic undernutrition. *Developmental Psychology, 33,* 845–855.

Valkenburg, P. M., & van der Voort, T. H. A. (1994). Influence of TV on daydreaming and creative imagination: A review of research. *Psychological Bulletin, 116,* 316–339.

Valkenburg, P. M., & van der Voort, T. H. A. (1995). The influence of television on children's daydreaming styles: A 1-year-panel study. *Communication Research, 22,* 267–287.

van den Boom, D. C. (1994). The influence of temperament and mothering on attachment and exploration: An experimental manipulation of sensitive responsiveness among lower-class mothers with irritable infants. *Child Development, 65,* 1457–1477.

van den Boom, D. C. (1995). Do first-year intervention effects endure? Follow-up during toddlerhood of a sample of Dutch irritable infants. *Child Development, 66,* 1798–1816.

van IJzendoorn, M. (1995). Adult attachment representations, parental responsiveness, and infant attachment: A meta-analysis on the predictive validity of the Adult Attachment Interview. *Psychological Bulletin, 117,* 387–403.

van IJzendoorn, M. H., & Kroonenberg, P. M. (1988). Cross-cultural patterns of attachment: A meta-analysis of the Strange Situation. *Child Development, 59,* 147–156.

Vandell, D. L., & Ramanan, J. (1991). Children of the National Longitudinal Survey of Youth: Choices in after-school care and child development. *Developmental Psychology, 27,* 637–643.

Vaughn, B. E., Kopp, C. B., & Krakow, J. B. (1984). The emergence and consolidation of self-control from eighteen to thirty months of age: Normative trends and individual differences. *Child Development, 55,* 990–1004.

Vederhus, L., & Krekling, S. (1996). Sex differences in visual spatial ability in 9-year-old children. *Intelligence, 23,* 33–43.

Ventura, S. J., Martin, J. A., Curtin, S. C., & Mathews, T. J. (1997). Report of final natality statistics, 1995. *Monthly Vital Statistics Report, 45,* June 1997.

Ventura, S. J., Martin, J. A., Hartin, A., Taffell, S. M., Mathews, T. J., & Clarke, S. C. (1994). Advance report of final natality statistics, 1992. *National Center for Health Statistics, Monthly Vital Statistics Report, 43.*

Verma, I. M. (1990). Gene therapy. *Scientific American, 263,* 68–84.

Volling, B. L., & Belsky, J. (1992). The contribution of mother-child and father-child relationships to the quality of sibling interaction: A longitudinal study. *Child Development, 63,* 1209–1222.

von Hofsten, C., Vishton, P., Spelke, E. S., Feng, Q., & Rosander, K. (1998). Predictive action in infancy: Tracking and reaching for moving objects. *Cognition, 67,* 255–285.

Vorhees, C. V., & Mollnow, E. (1987). Behavior teratogenesis: Long-term influences on behavior. In J. D. Osofsky (Ed.), *Handbook of infant development* (2nd ed.). New York: Wiley.

Voyer, D., Voyer, S., & Bryden, M. P. (1995). Magnitude of sex differences in spatial abilities: A meta-analysis and consideration of critical variables. *Psychological Bulletin, 117,* 250–270.

Vurpillot, E. (1968). The development of scanning strategies and their relation to visual differentiation. *Journal of Experimental Child Psychology, 6,* 632–650.

Vygotsky, L. S. (1978). *Mind in society: The development of higher psychological processes* (M. Cole,

V. John-Steiner, S. Scribner, & E. Soubermen, Eds.). Cambridge, MA: Harvard University Press.

Vygotsky, L. S. (1934/1986). *Thought and language* (A. Kozulin, Trans.). Cambridge, MA: MIT Press. (Original work published in 1934.)

Waber, D. P. (1977). Sex differences in mental abilities, hemispheric lateralization, and rate of physical growth at adolescence. *Developmental Psychology, 13*, 29–38.

Wachs, T. D. (1983). The use and abuse of environment in behavior-genetic research. *Child Development, 54*, 396–407.

Wagner, N. E., Schubert, H. J. P., & Schubert, D. S. P. (1985). Family size effects: A revision. *Journal of Genetic Psychology, 146*, 65–78.

Wagner, R. K., Torgesen, J. K., & Rashotte, C. A. (1994). Development of reading-related phonological processing abilities: New evidence of bidirectional causality from a latent variable longitudinal study. *Developmental Psychology, 30*, 73–87.

Wagner, R. K., Torgesen, J. K., Rashotte, C. A., Hecht, S. A., Barker, T. A., Burgess, S. R., Donahue, J., & Garon, T. (1999). Changing relations between phonological processing abilities and word-level reading as children develop from beginning to skilled readers: A 5-year longitudinal study. *Developmental Psychology, 33*, 468–479.

Walberg, H. J. (1995). General practices. In G. Cawelti (Ed.), *Handbook of research on improving student achievement*. Arlington, VA: Educational Research Service.

Walker, L. J. (1980). Cognitive and perspective-taking prerequisites for moral development. *Child Development, 51*, 131–139.

Walker, L. J. (1995). Sexism in Kohlberg's moral psychology? In W. M. Kurtines & J. L. Gewirtz (Eds.), *Moral development: An introduction*. Boston: Allyn & Bacon.

Walker, L. J., & Taylor, J. H. (1991). Family interactions and the development of moral reasoning. *Child Development, 62*, 264–283.

Ward, S. L., & Overton, W. F. (1990). Semantic familiarity, relevance, and the development of deductive reasoning. *Developmental Psychology, 26*, 288–493.

Warren, A. R., & McCloskey, L. A. (1993). Pragmatics: Language in social contexts. In J. Berko Gleason (Ed.), *The development of language* (3rd. ed., pp. 195–238). New York: Macmillan.

Warren-Leubecker, A., & Bohannon, J. N. (1989). Pragmatics: Language in social contexts. In J. Berko Gleason (Ed.), *The development of language* (2nd ed., pp. 327–368). Columbus, OH: Merrill.

Waters, H. F. (1993, July 12). Networks under the gun. *Newsweek*, 64–66.

Waters, H. S. (1980). "Class news": A single-subject longitudinal study of prose production

and schema formation during childhood. *Journal of Verbal Learning and Verbal Behavior, 19*, 152–167.

Watson, J.B. (1925). *Behaviorism*. New York: Norton.

Waxman, S. R., & Markow, D. B. (1995). Words as invitations to form categories: Evidence from 12- to 13-month-old infants. *Cognitive Psychology, 29*, 257–303.

Wechsler, D. (1991). *Manual for the Wechsler Intelligence Test for Children - III*. New York: The Psychological Corporation.

Wegman, M. E. (1994). Annual summary of vital statistics—1993. *Pediatrics, 95*, 792–803.

Weinberg, M. K., & Tronick, E. Z. (1994). Beyond the face: An empirical study of infant affective configurations of facial, vocal, gestural, and regulatory behaviors. *Child Development, 65*, 1503–1515.

Weinberg, M. K., Tronick, E. Z., Cohn, J. F., & Olson, K. L. (1999). Gender differences in emotional expressivity and self-regulation during early infancy. *Developmental Psychology, 35*, 175–188.

Weisner, T. S., & Wilson-Mitchell, J. E. (1990). Nonconventional family lifestyles and sex typing in six-year-olds. *Child Development, 61*, 1915–1933.

Weissman, M. D., & Kalish, C. W. (1999). The inheritance of desired characteristics: Children's view of the role of intention in parent-offspring resemblance. *Journal of Experimental Child Psychology, 73*, 245–265.

Wellman, H. M. (1992). *The child's theory of mind*. Cambridge, MA: MIT Press.

Wellman, H. M. (1993). Early understanding of mind: The normal case. In S. Baron-Cohen, H. Tager-Flusberg, & D. J. Cohen (Eds.), *Understanding other minds: Perspectives from autism*. Oxford, England: Oxford University Press.

Wellman, H. M., Cross, D., & Bartsch, K. (1986). Infant search and object permanence: A meta-analysis of the A not B error. *Monographs of the Society for Research in Child Development, 51* (Serial No. 214).

Wellman, H. M., & Gelman, S. A. (1998). Knowledge acquisition in foundational domains. In W. Damon (Ed.), *Handbook of child psychology* (Vol. 2). New York: Wiley.

Welsh, M. C., Pennington, B. F., & Groisser, D. B. (1991). A normative-developmental study of executive function: A window on prefrontal function in children. *Developmental Neuropsychology, 7*, 131–149.

Wendland-Carro, J., Piccinini, C. A., & Millar, W. S. (1999). The role of an early intervention on enhancing the quality of mother-infant interaction. *Child Development, 70*, 713–721.

Wentzel, K. R., & Asher, S. R. (1995). The academic lives of neglected, rejected, popular, and controversial children. *Child Development, 66*, 754–763.

Wentzel, K. R., & Erdley, C. A. (1993). Strategies for making friends: Relations to social behavior and peer acceptance. *Developmental Psychology, 29*, 819–826.

Werker, J. F., & Lalonde, C. E. (1988). Cross-language speech perception: Initial capabilities and developmental change. *Developmental Psychology, 24*, 672–683.

Werner, E. E. (1995). Resilience in development. *Current Directions in Psychological Science, 4*, 81–85.

Werner, H. (1948). *Comparative psychology of mental development*. Chicago: Follet.

Wertsch, J. V., & Tulviste, P. (1992). L. S. Vygotsky and contemporary developmental psychology. *Developmental Psychology, 28*, 548–557.

Whitehurst, G. J., & Vasta, R. (1975). Is language acquired through imitation? *Journal of Psycholinguistic Research, 4*, 37–59.

Whitehurst, G. J., & Vasta, R. (1977). *Child behavior*. Boston: Houghton Mifflin.

Whitesell, N. R., & Harter, S. (1996). The interpersonal context of emotion: Anger with close friends and classmates. *Child Development, 67*, 1345–1359.

Whiting, J. W. M., & Child, I. L. (1953). *Child training and personality: A cross-cultural study*. New Haven: Yale University Press.

Whitney, E. N., Cataldo, C. B., & Rolfes, S. R. (1987). *Understanding normal and clinical nutrition* (2nd ed.). St. Paul, MN: West.

Whitney, E. N., & Hamilton, E. M. N. (1987). *Understanding nutrition* (4th ed). St. Paul: West.

Wicks-Nelson, R., & Israel, A. C. (1991). *Behavior disorders of childhood* (2nd ed.). Englewood Cliffs, NJ: Prentice-Hall.

Wigfield, A., Eccles, J. S., Mac Iver, D., Reuman, D. A., & Midgley, C. (1991). Transitions during early adolescence: Changes in children's domain-specific self-perceptions and general self-esteem across the transition to junior high school. *Developmental Psychology, 27*, 552–564.

Williams, J. E., & Best, D. L. (1990). *Measuring sex stereotypes: A thirty-nation study* (rev. ed.). Newbury Park, CA: Sage.

Williams, J. M. (1997). *Style: Ten lessons in clarity and grace* (5th ed.). New York: Longman.

Willinger, M. (1995). Sleep position and sudden infant death syndrome. *Journal of the American Medical Association, 273*, 818–819.

Wilson, C. C., Piazza, C. C., & Nagle, R. (1990). Investigation of the effect of consistent and inconsistent behavioral example upon children's donation behavior. *Journal of Genetic Psychology, 151*, 361–376.

Wilson, G. T., Heffernan, K., & Black, C. M. D. (1996). Eating disorders. In E.J. Marsh & R.A. Barkley (Eds.), *Child psychopathology*. New York: Guilford.

Wilson, M. (1989). Child development in the context of the black extended family. *American Psychologist, 44,* 380–383.

Wilson, R.S. (1983). The Louisville Twin Study: Developmental synchronies in behavior. *Child Development, 54,* 298–316.

Wilson, R. S. (1986). Growth and development of human twins. In F. Falkner & J. M. Tanner (Eds.), *Human growth: A comprehensive treatise* (Vol. 3). New York: Plenum.

Windle, M., & Windle, R. C. (1996). Coping strategies, drinking motives, and stressful life events among middle adolescents: Associations with emotional and behavioral problems and with academic functioning. *Journal of Abnormal Psychology, 105,* 551–560.

Winer, G. A., Craig, R. K., & Weinbaum, E. (1992). Adults' failure on misleading weight-conservation tests: A developmental analysis. *Developmental Psychology, 28,* 109–120.

Winner, E. (1988). *The point of words.* Cambridge, MA: Harvard University Press.

Wintre, M. G., & Vallance, D. D. (1994). A developmental sequence in the comprehension of emotions: Intensity, multiple emotions, and valence. *Developmental Psychology, 30,* 509–514.

Wise, B. W., Ring, J., & Olson, R. K. (1999). Training phonological awareness with and without explicit attention to articulation. *Journal of Experimental Child Psychology, 72,* 271–304.

Witelson, S. F. (1987). Neurobiological aspects of language in children. *Child Development, 58,* 653–688.

Wolfe, D. A. (1985). Child-abusive parents: An empirical review and analysis. *Psychological Bulletin, 97,* 462–482.

Wolff, P. H. (1987). *The development of behavioral states and the expression of emotions in early infancy.* Chicago: University of Chicago Press.

Wolfson, A. R., & Carskadon, M. A. (1998). Sleep schedules and daytime functioning in adolescents. *Child Development, 69,* 875–887.

Wolraich, M. L., Lindgren, S. D., Stumbo, P. J., Stegink, L. D., Appelbaum, M. I., & Kiritsy, M. C. (1994). Effects of diets high in sucrose or aspartame on the behavior and cognitive performance of children. *New England Journal of Medicine, 330,* 301–307.

Wong-Fillmore, L., Ammon, P., McLaughlin, B., & Ammon, M. S. (1985). *Learning English through bilingual instruction.* Rosslyn, VA: National Clearinghouse for Bilingual Education.

Woodward, A. L., & Markman, E. M. (1998). Early word learning. In W. Damon (Ed.), *Handbook of child psychology* (Vol. 2). New York: Wiley.

Woollacott, M. H., Shumway-Cook, A., & Williams, H. (1989). The development of balance and locomotion in children. In M. H. Woollacott & A. Shumway-Cook (Eds.), *Development of posture and gait across the life span.* Columbia, SC: University of South Carolina Press.

World Health Organization. (1995). *First annual report on global health.* Geneva, Switzerland: Author.

Wynn, K. (1996). Infants' individuation and enumeration of actions. *Psychological Science, 7,* 164–169.

Yang, B., Ollendick, T. H., Dong, Q., Xia, Y., & Lin, L. (1995). Only children and children with siblings in the People's Republic of China: Levels of fear, anxiety, and depression. *Child Development, 66,* 1301–1311.

Yates, M., & Youniss, J. (1996). Community service and political-moral identity in adolescents. *Journal of Research on Adolescence, 6,* 271–284.

Yonas, A., & Owsley, C. (1987). Development of visual space perception. In P. Salapatek & L. Cohen (Eds.), *Handbook of infant perception* (Vol. 2). Orlando, FL: Academic Press.

Youngblade, L. M., & Dunn, J. (1995). Individual differences in young children's pretend play with mother and sibling: Links to relationships and understanding of other people's feelings and beliefs. *Child Development, 66,* 1472–1492.

Yuill, N., & Pearson, A. (1998). The development of bases for trait attribution: Children's understanding of traits as causal mechanisms based on desire. *Developmental Psychology, 34,* 574–586.

Zahn-Waxler, C., Cole, P. M., & Barrett, K. C. (1991). Guilt and empathy: Sex differences and implications for the development of depression. In J. Garber & K. Dodge (Eds.), *The development of emotion regulation and dysregulation* (pp. 243–272). Cambridge: Cambridge University Press.

Zahn-Waxler, C., Friedman, R. J., Cole, P. M., Mizuta, I., & Hiruma, N. (1996). Japanese and United States preschool children's responses to conflict and distress. *Child Development, 67,* 2462–2477.

Zahn-Waxler, C., Radke-Yarrow, M., Wagner, E., & Chapman, M. (1992). Development of concern for others. *Developmental Psychology, 28,* 126–136.

Zarbatany, L., Hartmann, D. P., & Rankin, D. B. (1990). The psychological functions of preadolescent peer activities. *Child Development, 61,* 1067–1080.

Zelazo, N. A., Zelazo, P. R., Cohen, K. M., & Zelazo, P. D. (1993). Specificity of practice effects on elementary neuromotor patterns. *Developmental Psychology, 29,* 686–691.

Zelazo, P. R. (1983). The development of walking: New findings and old assumptions. *Journal of Motor Behavior, 15,* 99–137.

Zelazo, P. R., Weiss, M. J., Papageorgiou, A. N., & Laplante, D. P. (1989). Recovery and dishabituation of sound localization among normal-, moderate-, and high-risk newborns: Discriminant validity. *Infant Behavior and Development, 12,* 321–340.

Zeman, J., & Garber, J. (1996). Display rules for anger, sadness, and pain: It depends on who is watching. *Child Development, 67,* 957–973.

Zeman, J., & Shipman, K. (1997). Social-contextual influences on expectancies for managing anger and sadness: The transition from middle childhood to adolescence. *Developmental Psychology, 33,* 917–924.

Zigler, E., & Finn-Stevenson, M. (1992). Applied developmental psychology. In M. H. Bornstein & M. E. Lamb (Eds.), *Developmental psychology: An advanced textbook.* Hillsdale, NJ: Erlbaum.

Zigler, E., & Hall, N. W. (1989). Physical child abuse in America: Past, present, and future. In D. Cicchetti & V. Carlson (Eds.), *Child maltreatment: Theory and research on the causes and consequences of child abuse and neglect.* New York: Cambridge University Press.

Zimiles, H., & Lee, V. E. (1991). Adolescent family structure and educational progress. *Developmental Psychology, 27,* 314–320.

# ACKNOWLEDGMENTS

## Photographs

**Cover** Courtesy of nonstøck and DigitalVision.

**About the Author** Page xxii, Courtesy of Robert V. Kail.

**Chapter 1** Pages 2–3 background image from Ad Windig. Page 12 (top) AP/Wide World Photos; (bottom) Nina Leen, Time Life Syndication. Page 13 (top) Corbis; (bottom) Jon Erikson, Courtesy of the Library of Congress. Page 15 (top) B.F. Skinner Foundation; (bottom) Bob Daemmrich, The Image Works. Page 16 (top) Courtesy of Albert Bandura; (bottom) Corbis. Page 18 (top) Dr. Michael Cole, Courtesy of A.R. Luria; (bottom) AP/Wide World Photos. Page 22 Owen Franken, Corbis. Page 23 William Tobin. Page 30 Will and Deni McIntyre/Science Source, Photo Researchers, Inc.

**Chapter 2** Pages 34–35 background image from Ad Windig. Page 34 (bottom) Shelley Rotner, Omni-Photo Communications, Inc. Page 36 (left) Dr. Gopal Murti/Science Photo Library, Custom Medical Stock Photo, Inc.; (right) Francis Leroy/Biocosmos/Science Photo Library, Photo Researchers, Inc.; (bottom) David Phillips, Photo Researchers, Inc. Page 37 (top) Alexander Tsiaras/Science Source, Photo Researchers, Inc.; (bottom) Biophoto Associates, Photo Researchers, Inc. Page 41 Corbis. Page 47 Laura Dwight, Peter Arnold, Inc. Page 51 Bob Daemmrich, Stock Boston.

**Chapter 3** Pages 56–57 background image from Ad Windig. Page 59 Photo Lennart Nilsson/Albert Bonniers Forlag AB. Page 60 (left) Photo Lennart Nilsson/Albert Bonniers Forlag AB; (right) Petit Format/Nestle/Science Source, Photo Researchers, Inc. Page 62 Photo Lennart Nilsson/Albert Bonniers Forlag AB. Page 65 Amy C. Etra, PhotoEdit. Page 66 Laura Dwight, Laura Dwight Photography. Page 68 Washington University School of Medicine. Page 73 Brownie Harris, The Stock Market. Page 77 Lawrence Migdale, Photo Researchers, Inc. Page 78 Margaret Miller, Photo Researchers, Inc. Page 80 Tom Stewart, The Stock Market. Page 82 Courtesy of Robert V. Kail. Page 84 Jennie Woodcock, Reflections Photolibrary, Corbis. Page 86 Courtesy of Robert V. Kail.

**Chapter 4** Pages 90–91 background image from Ad Windig. Page 97 Stock Boston. Page 98 Peter Byron, Monkmeyer Press. Page 100 Barbara Penoya, PhotoDisc, Inc. Page 101 David Woo, Stock Boston. Page 102 David Young-Wolff, PhotoEdit. Page 103 M. Douglas, The Image Works. Page 105 (top) PhotoDisc, Inc.; (middle) Ed Reschke; (bottom) D.W. Fawcett/Komuro/Science Source, Photo Researchers, Inc. Page 107 (top) Alexander Tsiaras, Stock Boston; (bottom) Dr. Michael E. Phelps, U.C.L.A. School of Medicine. Page 108 Peter Menzel, Stock Boston. Page 112 (right) Myrleen Ferguson, PhotoEdit; (left) Bill Tocker, International Stock Photography Ltd. Page 1114 Dexter Gormley. Page 116 (top) Felicia Martinez, PhotoEdit; (bottom) Erika Stone, Photo Researchers, Inc. Page 117 Rick Browne, Stock Boston. Page 118 Mitch Reardon, Photo Researchers, Inc.

**Chapter 5** Pages 122–123 background image from Ad Windig. Page 122 (bottom) Steve Mason, PhotoDisc, Inc. Page 127 Russell C. Hamilton, Cornell University Photography. Page 128, Elsa Peterson, Stock Boston. Page 130 (top) Dion Ogust, The Image Works; (bottom) Michael Tamborrino, Medichrome/The Stock Shop, Inc. Page 136 Michael Agliolo Productions, International Stock Photography Ltd. Page 139 (top) Innervisions; (bottom) Tadao Kimura, The Image Bank. Page 140 (top) Bob Daemmrich, Stock Boston; (bottom) John William Banagan, The Image Bank. Page 142 Laima Druskis, Pearson Education/PH College. Page 144 Coco McCoy, Rainbow.

**Chapter 6** Pages 148–149 background image from Ad Windig. Page 151 Laura Dwight, Laura Dwight Photography. Page 154 Laura Dwight, Laura Dwight Photography. Page 155 Gary Goodman, Index Stock Imagery, Inc. Page 156 Courtesy of Judy S. DeLoache. Page 158 Tony Freeman, PhotoEdit. Page 159 Tony Freeman, PhotoEdit. Page 162, Richard Hutchings, Photo Researchers, Inc. Page 168 Courtesy of Beaura Katherine Ringrose. Page 174 D. Young-Wolff, PhotoEdit. Page 175 Eric A. Wessman, Stock Boston.

**Chapter 7** Pages 181–182 background image from Ad Windig. Page 185 Bob Daemmrich, Stock Boston. Page 188 Courtesy of Carolyn Rovee-Collier. Page 190 Amy Etra, PhotoEdit. Page 192 Gale Zucker, Stock Boston. Page 193 Courtesy of Robert V. Kail. Page 194 Tony Freeman, PhotoEdit. Page 199 Tony Freeman, PhotoEdit. Page 200 Laura Dwight, Laura Dwight Photography. Page 203 Jennie Woodcock, Reflections Photolibrary, Corbis. Page 205 Elizabeth Zuckerman, PhotoEdit. Page 208 Gottlieb, Monkmeyer Press.

**Chapter 8** Pages 212–213 background image from Ad Windig. Page 216 Paul L. Merideth. Page 218 (top) Macduff Everton; (bottom) Anna E. Zuckerman, PhotoEdit. Page 222 Laura Dwight, Laura Dwight Photography. Page 228 Mark Wise, Stock Boston. Page 232 Okoniewski, Liaison Agency, Inc. Page 235 MacPherson, Monkmeyer Press. Page 236 SuperStock, Inc.

**Chapter 9** Pages 240–241 background image from Ad Windig. Page 244 Dreyfuss, Monkmeyer Press. Page 245 © Peter Southwick/ Stock Boston/PNI. Page 248 Laura Dwight, Laura Dwight Photography. Page 249 David Young-Wolff, PhotoEdit. Page 251 Jeff Persons, Stock Boston. Page 252 Tom Prettyman, PhotoEdit. Page 253 Elena Rooraid, PhotoEdit. Page 258 Susan Kuklin/Science Source, Photo Researchers, Inc. Page 262 Tony Freeman, PhotoEdit. Page 263 Courtesy of Beaura Katherine Ringrose.

**Chapter 10** Pages 270–271 background image from Ad Windig. Page 270 (bottom) David Young-Wolff, PhotoEdit. Page 273 (left) Laura Dwight, Laura Dwight Photography; (middle) Michael Newman, PhotoEdit; (right) Comstock; (bottom) Peter Southwick, Stock Boston. Page 274 Courtesy of Robert V. Kail. Page 276 Bob Daemmrich, Stock Boston. Page 278 SuperStock, Inc. Page 281 Courtesy of Robert V. Kail. Page 282 Myrleen Ferguson, PhotoEdit. Page 283 Innervisions. Page 285 Steve Starr, Stock Boston. Page 288 Mark Richards, PhotoEdit. Page 290 Laura Dwight, Laura Dwight Photography. Page 291 Frank Clarkson, Liaison Agency, Inc.

**Chapter 11** Pages 296–297 background image from Ad Windig. Page 296 (bottom) Penny Gentieu, Tony Stone Images. Page 298 PT Santana, Tony Stone Images. Page 300 Comstock. Page 301 Richard Hutchings, PhotoEdit. Page 302 Richard Hutchings. Page 303 Stock Boston. Page 304 Myrleen Ferguson, PhotoEdit. Page 311 Bob Daemmrich, Stock Boston. Page 313 D&I MacDonald, Index Stock Imagery, Inc. Page 319 Courtesy of Robert V. Kail. Page 320 Bob Daemmrich, Stock Boston.

**Chapter 12** Pages 324–325 background image from Ad Windig. Page 324 (bottom) Corbis Digital Stock. Page 327 Elizabeth Hathon, The Stock Market. Page 332 Laura Dwight, Laura Dwight Photography. Page 334 Tony Freeman, PhotoEdit. Page 338 John Boykin, Index Stock Imagery, Inc. Page 339 David R. Frazier, David R. Frazier Photolibrary, Inc. Page 341 (top) Michael Newman, PhotoEdit; (bottom) © Bob Daemmrich/Stock Boston/PNI. Page 343 Lawrence Migdale, Lawrence Midgale/Pix. Page 344 Martin Adler, Panos Pictures. Page 347 Amy Etra, PhotoEdit. Page 349 Laura Dwight, Laura Dwight Photography. Page 351 Mark M. Walker, Index Stock Imagery, Inc. Page 352 John Coletti, Index Stock Imagery, Inc. Page 356 Yale, Monkmeyer Press.

**Chapter 13** Pages 360–361 background image from Ad Windig. Page 364 David Young-Wolff, PhotoEdit. Page 367 (left) Mark Downey, Mark Downey/Lucid Images; (right) Bernard Wolf, Monkmeyer Press. Page 369 Kirk Anderson, International Stock Photography Ltd. Page 370 Stephen Collins, Photo Researchers, Inc. Page 371 (left) © Bob Daemmrich/Stock Boston/PNI; (right) © Bob Daemmrich/Stock Boston/PNI. Page 373 Elizabeth Crews, Elizabeth Crews Photography. Page 376 Corbis. Page 377 Goodwin, Monkmeyer Press. Page 382 Denise Marcotte, Stock Boston. Page 383 Nancy Sheehan, PhotoEdit.

**Chapter 14** Pages 388–389 background image from Ad Windig. Page 392 Jean Hangarter, Index Stock Imagery, Inc. Page 395 Photo Researchers, Inc. Page 396 Laura Dwight, Laura Dwight Photography. Page 397 Charles Thatcher, Tony Stone Images. Page 400 Pam Francis, Liaison Agency, Inc. Page 402 Bachmann, PhotoEdit. Page 403 Owen Franken, Corbis. Page 405 Cathlyn Melloan, Tony Stone Images. Page 411 Michael Newman, PhotoEdit. Page 413 Copyright by the San Francisco Child Abuse Council. Reprinted with permission. Page 414 Stephen Agricola, The Image Works.

**Chapter 15** Pages 420–421 background image from Ad Windig. Page 422 David M. Grossman. Page 423 Laura Dwight, Laura Dwight Photography. Page 425 © Rob Crandall/Stock Boston/PNI. Page 427 David Young-Wolff, PhotoEdit. Page 430 Courtesy of Robert V. Kail. Page 432 Richard Hutchings, Photo Researchers, Inc. Page 434 Bob Daemmrich, Stock Boston. Page 438 Tony Freeman, PhotoEdit. Page 439 R. Termine/CTW, Everett Collection, Inc. Page 441 David M. Grossman. Page 444 © Jeff Dunn/Stock Boston/PNI. Page 445 Boulton-Wilson, Jeroboam, Inc. Page 446 (top) Jose L. Pelaez, The Stock Market; (bottom) Blair Seitz, Photo Researchers, Inc. Page 447 David Young-Wolff, PhotoEdit. Page 448 Billy E. Barnes, Stock Boston.

## Cartoons, Figures, and Tables

**Chapter 1** Page 9 *Hi and Lois* © 1993. Reprinted with special permission of King Features Syndicate.

**Chapter 2** Fig. 2-5 From I. Gottesman (1963). Genetic aspects of intellectual behavior. In N.R. Ellis (Ed.), *Handbook of mental deficiency.* New York: McGraw-Hill. Reprinted with permission of Norman R. Ellis.

**Chapter 3** Figs. 3-4 and 3-6 From Moore & Persaud (1993). *Before we are born.* Philadelphia: W.B. Saunders. Reprinted with permission.

**Chapter 4** Fig. 4-5 From J.M. Tanner (1989). *Fetus into man.* Cambridge, MA: Harvard University Press. Reprinted by permission of the publishers. Copyright © 1978, 1989 by J.M. Tanner.

**Chapter 5** Fig. 5-11 From H. Ghim. Evidence for perceptual organization in infants. *Infant Behavior and Development, 13,* 221–248. Copyright © 1990, with permission from Elsevier Science. Fig. 5-15 from J. Morton & M.H. Johnson (191). CONSPEC and CONLERN: A two-process theory of infant face recognition. *Psychological Review, 98,* 164–181. Copyright © 1991 by the American Psychological Association. Reprinted with permission.

**Chapter 6** Fig. 6-7 From U. Frith (1989). *Autism: Explaining the enigma.* Oxford, UK: Blackwell Publishers. Copyright © Axel Scheffler, Illustrator. Reprinted with permission.

**Chapter 7** Fig. 7-7 From R. Kail (1990). *The development of memory in children,* 3rd ed. New York: Freeman. Reprinted with permission.

**Chapter 8** Fig. 8-1 From John B. Carroll (1993). *Human cognitive abilities.* New York: Cambridge University Press. Reprinted with the permission of Cambridge University Press. Fig. 8-3 Simulated items similar to those in the Wechsler Intelligence Scales for Adults and Children. Copyright © 1948, 1974, 1981, 1997 by The Psychological Corporation. Reproduced by permission. All rights reserved. Fig. 8-4 From B. Bloom (1974). *Stability and change in human characteristics.* New York: John Wiley & Sons. Copyright by Benjamin S. Bloom. Reprinted with permission. Fig. 8-6 From R. Plomin, D.W. Fulker, R. Corlev, & J.C. Defries (1997). Nature, nurture, and cognitive development from 1 to 16 years. *Psychological Science, 8,* 442–447. Reprinted with permission. Fig. 8-10 Copyright by Scholastic Testing Service, Inc., Bensonville, IL. Reprinted with permission. (Test completed by Laura Kail.)

**Chapter 9** Page 246 Reprinted by permission of Johnny Hart and Creators Syndicate, Inc.

**Chapter 11** Page 303 Reprinted by permission of Bunny Hoest, Wm. Hoest Enterprises, Inc. Fig. 11-4 Adapted from S. Harter & R. Pike (1984). The pictorial scale of perceived competence and social acceptance for young children. *Child Development, 55,* 1973. Copyright © Society for Research in Child Development, Inc. Reprinted with permission.

**Chapter 12** Page 326 *Calvin and Hobbes* © 1993 Watterson. Distributed by Universal Press Syndicate. Reprinted with permission. All rights reserved. Table 12-1 From Shoda et al. (1990). Predicting adolescent cognitive and self-regulatory competencies from preschool delay of gratification: Identifying diagnostic conditions. *Developmental Psychology, 26,* 978–986. Copyright © 1990 by the American Psychological Association. Reprinted with permission. Fig. 12-6 From N.R. Crick & K.A. Dodge (1994). A review and reformulation of social information-processing mechanisms in children's social adjustment. *Psychological Bulletin, 115,* 74–101. Copyright © 1994 by the American Psychological Association. Reprinted with permission.

**Chapter 13** Fig. 13-3 From J.W. Pellegrino & R. Kail (1982). Process analyses of spatial aptitude. In R. Sternberg (Ed.), *Advances in the psychology of human intelligence.* Vol. 1. Hillsdale, NJ: Lawrence Erlbaum Associates. Copyright by Lawrence Erlbaum Associates. Reprinted with permission. Fig. 13-7 Adapted from C.L. Martin & C.F. Halvorsen, Jr. (1981) A schematic processing model of sex typing and stereotyping in children. *Child Development, 52,* 1121. Copyright © Society for Research in Child Development, Inc. Reprinted with permission.

**Chapter 14** Page 402 *PEANUTS* © 1993 United Feature Syndicate. Reprinted by permission.

**Chapter 15** Table 15-1 Adapted from Morison & A.S. Masten (1991). Peer reputation in middle childhood as a predictor of adaptation in adolescence: A seven-year follow-up. *Child Development, 62,* 1001. Copyright © Society for Research in Child Development, Inc. Reprinted with permission. Page 436 Copyright by Martha F. Campbell. Reprinted with permission.

# SUBJECT INDEX

# CONNECTIONS

**9.1  The Road to Speech**
Perceiving Speech

**Learning to talk depends on the perceptual skills described in Module 5.2.**

**10.2  Temperament**
Hereditary and
Environmental
Contributions to
Temperament

**Temperament is partially inherited, through mechanisms explained in Module 2.1.**

**11.2  Self-Esteem**
Sources of
Self-Esteem

**Children's self-esteem is affected by the parenting practices that are described in Module 14.1.**

**12.1  Self-Control**
Beginnings of
Self-Control
and the Media

**Self-control has much in common with regulating emotions, discussed in Module 10.1.**

1   **The Science of
    Child Development**

2   **Genetic Bases of
    Child Development**

3   **Prenatal Development,
    Birth, and the Newborn**

4   **Physical and Motor
    Development**

5   **Sensory and Perceptual
    Development**

6   **Piaget's Theory of
    Cognitive Development**

7   **Information-Processing
    Approaches to
    Cognitive Development**

8   **Intelligence and Individual
    Differences in Cognition**

9   **Language and
    Communication**

10  **Emotional Development**

11  **Understanding Self
    and Others**

12  **Moral Understanding
    and Behavior**

13  **Gender and Development**

14  **Family Relationships**

15  **Influences Beyond
    the Family**